On Heroes,
Hero-Worship, & the Heroic
in History

THE NORMAN AND CHARLOTTE STROUSE EDITION OF THE WRITINGS OF

Thomas Carlyle

On Heroes, Hero-Worship, & the Heroic in History

Notes and Introduction by
Michael K. Goldberg

Text Established by
Michael K. Goldberg,
Joel J. Brattin, and Mark Engel

University of California Press

BERKELEY   LOS ANGELES   OXFORD

```
CENTER FOR EDITIONS OF
AMERICAN AUTHORS
AN APPROVED TEXT
MODERN LANGUAGE
ASSOCIATION OF AMERICA
```

University of California Press
Berkeley and Los Angeles, California

University of California Press, Ltd.
Oxford, England

© 1993 by
The Regents of the University of California

Library of Congress Cataloging-in-Publication Data

Carlyle, Thomas, 1795–1881.
    On heroes, hero-worship, & the heroic in history / notes and
introduction by Michael K. Goldberg ; text established by Michael
K. Goldberg, Joel J. Brattin, and Mark Engel.
        p.   cm. — (The Norman and Charlotte Strouse edition of
the writings of Thomas Carlyle)
    Includes bibliographical references and index.
    ISBN 0-520-07515-3
    1. Heroes. 2. Hero worship. I. Goldberg, Michael K. (Michael
Kenneth) II. Brattin, Joel J., 1956–   III. Engel, Mark. IV.
Title. V. Title: On heroes, hero-worship, and the heroic in history.
VI. Series: Carlyle, Thomas, 1795–1881. Works. 1991.
    PR4426.A2G65   1993
    824'.8—dc20   91-33937
                                                                   CIP

Printed in the United States of America

This book is a print-on-demand volume. It is manufactured using toner in place
of ink. Type and images may be less sharp than the same material seen in traditionally
printed University of California Press editions.

The paper used in this publication meets the minimum requirements of
ANSI/NISO Z39.48-1992 (R 1997) (Permanence of Paper).

CONTENTS

ILLUSTRATIONS

Following page ciii

PREFACE

ALTHOUGH Thomas Carlyle was acclaimed throughout the nineteenth century in both England and the United States as the "undoubted head of English letters,"[1] reliable editions of his work, providing both an accurate text based on modern bibliographical principles and full explanatory annotation, have not been readily available. Even the standard edition, the Centenary, originally published 1896–99, is unsatisfactory: it is without annotation and textually inaccurate.[2] This injustice, both to Carlyle and his readers, the editors of the Strouse Carlyle Edition seek to redress.

To establish an accurate text the editors have devised an integrated system for the computer-assisted production of the edition, based on the CASE (Computer Assistance to Scholarly Editing) programs.[3] The application of electronic technology in every stage of the editorial process, from the collection of evidence through the final typesetting of the text and apparatus, allows a high level of accuracy, while leaving all decisions requiring editorial judgment in the control of scholars. (A valuable byproduct of the use of computer technology throughout the project has been the creation of a machine-readable archive of Carlylean texts, textual apparatus, and annotation.) The text is preceded by a discussion of the evidence and editorial principles used to establish it, and a full textual apparatus is appended, including a list of all emendations of the copy-text and a complete collation of authoritative versions, keyed to the present text by page and line number. To facilitate reading, we present Carlyle's work as clear text, without added editorial or reference symbols.

The historical introduction is intended to elaborate the significance of the work for Carlyle's era and to suggest its importance for our own, as well as explaining its origin and biographical context. The works cited in the introductory essay may be taken as a selected bibliography of Carlylean commentary and criticism, a starting point for the student of Carlyle and his influence. By providing a full critical and explanatory annotation, the editors hope to assist the contemporary reader in negotiating Carlyle's densely referential prose. A tissue of quotation from varied and disparate sources intertwined with the

---

[1] "Literary Work of Thomas Carlyle," 92. (For complete citations, see the list of works cited, pp. 393–417.)

[2] See "Note on the Text," pp. c–ci below.

[3] For a description of the CASE programs, see Shillingsburg, *Scholarly Editing in the Computer Age*, 128–46.

historic events of Victorian life, Carlyle's art weaves together multifarious references and allusions, which we have sought, wherever possible, to identify, gloss, and translate. The editors hope that the explanatory annotation, like the critical text, will be a starting point for the work of reading and interpretation, a foundation on which readers of the present and future may build the often-changing structures of cultural analysis. We have resisted the temptation to impose our own readings, offering instead the essential materials for interpretation, hoping thereby to approximate Carlyle's own ideal book, in which the reader is "excited . . . to self-activity."[4]

The materials of the edition, both on paper and in electronic form, have been added to the Norman and Charlotte Strouse Collection of Thomas Carlyle, housed in Special Collections, University Library, at the University of California, Santa Cruz. In recovering the impact of the original Carlyle and making his work accessible to readers of the present and the future, the edition fulfills the central purposes of the Strouse Collection, which has been our inspiration, base of operations, and invaluable resource. In recognition of their inestimable service to Carlyle studies, the edition is dedicated to Norman and Charlotte Strouse.

This work would not have been possible without the assistance of many people and institutions. Their contributions can only imperfectly be acknowledged by a brief mention here.

Funding for the edition was provided by research grants from the University of California, Santa Cruz, for which we must thank Chancellors Robert Sinsheimer, Robert B. Stevens, and Karl S. Pister; Academic Vice Chancellors Kivie Moldave, Isebill V. Gruhn, and Michael Tanner; Deans Michael Cowan, Gary Lease, and Geoffrey Pullum; and the Committee on Research of the Academic Senate. Other University officers who have aided the project, providing facilities and administrative support, include Assistant Vice Chancellor Daniel G. Aldrich III; University Librarian Alan Dyson; Janice Crooks and Richard W. Jensen of the Academic Vice Chancellor's office; Robert E. Jorgensen, Cindi Smith, and Kathie Kenyon of the office of the Dean of Humanities; and Peggy M. Hathcock and Joan A. Houston of the Humanities Business Office.

Our funding was supplemented by generous contributions from private patrons including Lou and Isabell Bartfield, Donald and Emily Clark, Wendell B. Coon, Donald D. Cummins, Mrs. Fred C. Foy, Dr.

---

[4] *Sartor*, 1.4.21

James D. Hart, Frederick B. Henderson, Stephen G. Herrick, Alan and Judy Levin, Dean and Jane McHenry, Charles M. Merrill, Gurden Mooser, and of course Norman Strouse.

Michael Goldberg wishes to express his gratitude to the Social Sciences and Humanities Research Council of Canada for funding his research on this volume. In 1984–85 the Council awarded him a Leave Fellowship, and in 1988 further funding was provided under the Council's International Collaborative Research Programme. He also wishes to thank the Humanities and Social Sciences Grants Committee of the University of British Columbia for a research grant award in 1986, and the Work Study Programme of the Provincial Government.

Our work has been assisted by the genuine collaboration of the members of the Editorial Board and the Advisory Board, who are listed facing the title page of this volume. These scholars travelled to Santa Cruz for a series of organizational meetings, participated in the formulation of policies for the edition, and read and commented on various stages of the manuscript. We must mention in particular the assistance of K. J. Fielding of the University of Edinburgh, whose detailed comments on the introduction and annotation were most helpful, and who, together with his colleagues Ian M. Campbell of Edinburgh and Clyde de L. Ryals of Duke University, made available to us the essential resources of their ongoing project to publish the *Collected Letters of Thomas and Jane Welsh Carlyle.* Carlyle biographer Fred Kaplan of the City University of New York prepared the Chronology of Carlyle's Life that appears on pp. xv–xix, and Carlyle bibliographer Rodger L. Tarr of Illinois State University guided us in our collection of materials. Jerry D. James, UC Santa Cruz librarian and bibliographer, was a heroic detective in the underworld of footnote sources. Our textual advisor, David Nordloh of Indiana University, shared his experience and expertise and helped us to understand the range of issues involved in establishing the text.

We must also thank Robert Hirst, the general editor of the Mark Twain Project, who was appointed our inspector by the Committee for Scholarly Editions of the Modern Language Association, and who functioned in that capacity as our advisor as well as our judge. Other scholars who have assisted our work include Michael J. Warren, professor of English, UC Santa Cruz; Professor I. B. Cowan of the Department of Scottish History, University of Glasgow; Professor Scott Cook of the Department of Philosophy, San Jose State University; Professor Catherine Kerrigan of the University of Guelph; Michael

Wolfe of Santa Cruz, California; and at the University of British
Columbia Professors James Russell and Elizabeth Bongie of the
Department of Classics, Edward Mornin of the Department of Germanic Studies, Hanna E. Kassis of the Department of Religious Studies, and J. A. Lavin of the Department of English.

We have needed and received the help of many libraries and librar-
ians, above all University Archivist Rita B. Bottoms and her staff,
Carol Champion, Paul S. Stubbs, Irene Crawley Berry, and Paul Machlis
of Special Collections, University Library, UC Santa Cruz, the wor-
thy keepers of the Strouse Carlyle Collection, as well as the staff of
Interlibrary Loan headed by Betty Rentz and Judith A. Steen, and the
Reference staff including Margaret N. Gordon, Alan Ritch, and
Deborah Murphy. In addition, grateful use has been made of the rich
resources of institutions including the University Library of the
University of British Columbia, the University of Michigan Libraries,
the Bibliothèque Nationale du Québec, the National Trust, Carlyle
House, the British Museum, the National Portrait Gallery, the Uni-
versity Library Cambridge, and the Trinity College Cambridge Library. Permission to quote from unpublished correspondence or to
use illustrations from their collections was graciously granted by Paul
C. Allen of the Beinecke Library, Yale University; Michael Komanecky
of the Yale University Art Gallery; Don C. Skemer of the Princeton
University Libraries; R. C. Andrew of Sidney Sussex College, Cambridge; and Lorna MacEchern, private secretary to the Duke of
Buccleuch and Queensberry. For the loan of their Hinman Collator,
we must thank Donald Kunitz and John Skarstad of Special Collections, Shields Library, University of California, Davis.

Our use of computer technology in all stages of the project has of
course required the assistance of many programmers and consultants
who are to us as heroes in their arcane skills and technical compe-
tence. Professor Peter L. Shillingsburg of Mississippi State University
generously shared with us the CASE collation programs that were
developed under his supervision for the Thackeray Edition of which
he is the general editor. Rob Strand of the UC Santa Cruz Computer
Center modified the CASE programs so that they could be run on a
CMS-based IBM mainframe. Much of the pre- and post-collation
processing of the text and collation lists was done on the UC Santa
Cruz campuswide unix-based mainframe system, while typesetting
and layout was done on Macintosh personal computers in the edition
office. James Ganong, programmer extraordinaire, currently Unix
Systems Administrator for the College of Environmental Design at

UC Berkeley, designed our system and wrote magical filter programs that make it possible for us to move our complex text files freely among the CMS, unix, and Macintosh platforms. Noah Kaplan, besides assisting James Ganong with the unix programming, showed endless patience in carrying out the tedious experimentation needed to make everything work. In addition we must thank Jeff Berryman, Bruce Joliffe, and Mike Patterson of the University of British Columbia Computing Centre, and at UC Santa Cruz Daniel Wenger, computing director of the Division of Humanities, and the staff of Computer and Telecommunications Services, especially Assistant Vice Chancellor Alan Schlenger, User Services Manager Dennie Van Tassel, and Senior Data Analysis Consultant James P. Mulherin.

We have had the support throughout of our publishers, the University of California Press, and must mention in particular our sponsoring editors, Dr. Jack R. Miles and William J. McClung, design assistance from Czeslaw Jan Grycz, Jeanne Sugiyama, and Steve Renick, and editorial assistance from Marilyn Schwartz, Douglas Abrams, and our acute copy editor Nancy Evans. The index was prepared by Shirley J. Manley.

Among the many who have labored valiantly on this book are the typists of the UCSC Services to Academic Staff office, supervised by Happy H. Hunter and Cheryl Van De Veer, and Betsy G. Wootten of the Kresge College Services to Academic Staff office. Our own yeoman staff of clerical and research assistants has included Pam Dunn, Elizabeth Jones, Rosemarie Milazzo, Marc Moskowitz, Mary Kate St. Clair, Leslie Sweeney, Erik Trump, and Hesper Wilson.

The Strouse Carlyle Edition is administered by the Dickens Project, a multicampus research group of the University of California. Our special thanks go to its past and present staff including Dorene Blake, Tom Graves, and T. Lark Letchworth—and notably Linda M. Hooper, who gave us indispensable assistance with production and layout—and its director, Professor John O. Jordan, without whom our list of heroes would not be complete.

All of those mentioned here have made this volume better than it would have been without their help; none are responsible for any errors that may remain in it.

— Murray Baumgarten
Editor-in-Chief

CHRONOLOGY OF CARLYLE'S LIFE

1795 Thomas Carlyle born on December 4 in Ecclefechan, Scotland.

1801 Jane Baillie Welsh born in Haddington, near Edinburgh, on July 14.

1806 Carlyle enrolls as a day student at Annan Academy.

1809 Begins his education at the University of Edinburgh.

1813 Enrolls in Divinity Hall to fulfill his parents' expectation that he will become a minister.

1814 Leaves the university and returns to Annan Academy as mathematics tutor.

1816 Meets Edward Irving, a teacher and minister. Begins teaching in parish school in Kirkcaldy near Edinburgh.

1817 Tours the Highlands and western Scotland with Irving. Writes articles, letters to newspapers, and occasional poems on scientific and philosophic subjects.

1819 Moves to Edinburgh.

1820 Does translations from the French; writes a series of encyclopedia articles.

1821 Irving introduces him to Jane Welsh. Carlyle takes a well-paid position, arranged by Irving, as a private tutor to Charles and Arthur Buller.

1822 Has a conversion experience in Leith Walk, near Edinburgh, in which he commits himself to the primacy and importance of work, rather than belief or theology, as the essence of personal self-definition. With his brother John's help, he translates Legendre's *Elements of Geometry*.

1823 Translates Goethe's *Wilhelm Meister* (1824) and expands an article on Schiller into *The Life of Schiller* (1825).

1824 Beginning in June, makes an extended visit to London. A guest of the Buller family and the Irving circle, he is introduced to London literary society, including Coleridge and Charles Lamb.

1825   Translates various German authors, and falls strongly under the influence of Goethe.

1826   Marries Jane Baillie Welsh on October 17. Begins an autobiographical bildungsroman, the unfinished *Wotton Reinfred*.

1827   Francis Jeffrey, editor of the *Edinburgh Review*, becomes his patron and family friend. Jeffrey publishes a series of Carlyle's review-essays, mainly on German literature and culture, which initiate his Scottish and English reputation. *German Romance* published in four volumes.

1828   Unsuccessful efforts to find suitable employment. Carlyles move to Craigenputtoch, a remote farm near Dunscore.

1828–29 Publishes "Burns" and "Signs of the Times" in the *Edinburgh Review* and articles on German literature in the *Foreign Review*.

1830   "On History" published in *Fraser's Magazine*. Begins *Sartor Resartus*.

1831   In London for an extended visit, he renews contact with the Buller-Irving circle, begins a friendship with John Stuart Mill, and unsuccessfully tries to find a publisher for *Sartor Resartus*. "Characteristics" published in the *Edinburgh Review*.

1832   Death of his father, James Carlyle. Thomas writes a substantial memoir of him, later included in *Reminiscences* (1881). Carlyles return to Craigenputtoch.

1833   *Sartor Resartus* is published serially in *Fraser's Magazine* from November 1833 to August 1834. Encouraged by Mill, he begins to write about the French Revolution ("The Diamond Necklace"). In August, Emerson visits Carlyle at Craigenputtoch, the beginning of a lifelong friendship. Carlyle gives thought to emigrating to America.

1834   The Carlyles move to 24 Cheyne Row, London, their residence for the remainder of their lives. Edward Irving dies. In September, Carlyle begins to write *The French Revolution*.

1835   In March he is forced to begin *The French Revolution* again when the only copy of the manuscript (one-third completed) is accidentally destroyed while in the keeping of John Stuart Mill. Meets Southey and Wordsworth, and becomes friends with John Sterling. In the next five years his circle of London friends expands to include Leigh Hunt, Harriet Martineau, Erasmus Darwin, Monckton Milnes, John Forster, Dickens, Thackeray, Tennyson, FitzGerald, and Browning.

1836   *Sartor Resartus* first published in book form in Boston.

1837   Gives seven public lectures on German literature beginning in May. *The French Revolution* is published.

1838   Course of twelve lectures on European literature. *Sartor Resartus* is published in book form in London. With Emerson's help, *Critical and Miscellaneous Essays* is published in Boston.

1839   Six lectures on the revolutions of modern Europe. "On Chartism" published. Plays a formative role in the creation of the London Library.

1840   Delivers six lectures on heroes. Spends the summer in Scotland, henceforth an annual practice, and considers writing a biography of Cromwell.

1841   *On Heroes, Hero-Worship, and the Heroic in History* published.

1842   While visiting the Bury St. Edmunds area, he conceives the idea for *Past and Present*.

1843   *Past and Present* published.

1844   John Sterling dies.

1845   *Oliver Cromwell's Letters and Speeches* published.

1847   Emerson visits England and spends time with the Carlyles.

1848   Carlyle meets Sir Robert Peel, whom he admires and whose leading role in the repeal of the Corn Laws he has supported.

1849   Carlyle tours Ireland with his friend Gavan Duffy and finds English policies substantially responsible for the condition of Ireland. Writes his *Reminiscences of My Irish Journey*, published posthumously in 1882. Anger and despair about political and cultural conditions in Britain expressed in reviews and essays, including "Occasional Discourse on the Negro Question," published in *Fraser's Magazine;* contemplates a work on the negative effects of democracy, materialism, and sexual permissiveness.

1850   Publishes *Latter-Day Pamphlets,* a series of eight satirical essays on the condition of modern Britain. Ruskin visits Carlyle for the first time and soon becomes a disciple. Friendships with a younger generation of intellectuals and writers, including William Allingham and John Tyndall.

1851   *Life of John Sterling.* In the fall, he visits Paris, accompanied by Robert and Elizabeth Browning. Begins to consider Frederick the Great as a subject for a biography.

1852   In the late summer, travels to Germany for the first time, visiting sites associated with Luther, Goethe, and Frederick the Great.

1856   Completes the writing of the first two volumes of *Frederick the Great.*

1857–58 *Collected Works* (the Uniform Edition) published in sixteen volumes.

1858   First two volumes of *Frederick the Great* published. In late summer, makes a second visit to Germany to complete a survey of sites associated with Frederick.

1863   Jane Carlyle's health deteriorates. Volume 3 of *Frederick the Great* is published.

1864   Volume 4 of *Frederick the Great* is published.

1865   Completes *Frederick the Great;* volumes 5 and 6 are published. In November he is elected Lord Rector of Edinburgh University, an honorary position.

1866   On April 2, Carlyle delivers his "Inaugural Address" in Edinburgh. On April 21, Jane Carlyle dies of a stroke. Carlyle writes a biographical and autobiographical memoir of Jane and another of Edward Irving, both later included in *Reminiscences.* In the fall joins the Governor Eyre committee whose purpose is to defend Eyre against the charge that his suppression of the Jamaican slave revolt (1865) was too harsh.

1867   Writes brief memoirs of Southey, Wordsworth, and William Hamilton. In August, he publishes a satiric attack on the Reform Bill of 1867, "Shooting Niagara: And After?" The essay also attacks environmental pollution. Ruskin and Carlyle become estranged.

1868–69   Works sporadically at a selected edition of Jane's letters, then decides to postpone publication.

1869   A second edition of the *Collected Works* (the Library Edition, thirty volumes) begins publication. In March, he has an interview with Queen Victoria.

1870   Publishes a letter in the *Times* strongly supporting Germany in the Franco-Prussian War.

1871   Turns over to James Anthony Froude some personal papers and manuscripts, particularly Jane's letters, in effect appointing Froude his biographer and Jane's editor. In 1873 he gives Froude most of the remaining documents. His right hand becomes palsied, making it difficult for him to write.

1872   He dictates *Early Kings of Norway* (1875), but finds dictation an unsatisfactory way of writing.

1873   Carlyle's portrait is painted by Whistler.

1874–75   Enters the controversy about the authenticity of a portrait of John Knox and dictates an essay, "Portraits of John Knox" (1875).

1875   His eightieth birthday in December is the occasion for an international celebration, with gifts, honorary degrees, testimonial letters, and an engraved gold medallion. He declines Disraeli's offer of a title.

1875–76   Publishes two letters in the *Times* opposing Disraeli's policy of support for the Turks against the Russians.

1879   Visits Scotland. With the death of his favorite younger brother John, he has outlived most of his family and personal and professional friends.

1881   On February 5, Carlyle dies at Cheyne Row. He is buried on February 10 next to his parents in the churchyard at Ecclefechan.

INTRODUCTION

I. CARLYLE AS LECTURER

On Heroes, Hero-Worship, and the Heroic in History is Carlyle's literary reconstruction of a series of six public lectures, delivered between May 5 and 22, 1840, which were the culmination of his four-year experiment as a public lecturer. Considering his distrust of cant, his puritanically inspired phobia about the "swim gloat" of popularity which he feared and thought ruinous, and his deep-rooted suspicion of oratory as inherently insincere, it is perhaps surprising that he ventured onto the public platform at all. As a matter of fact, however, between 1837 and 1840 he made annual excursions to the public podium to lecture fashionable London society on literature, politics, and history.[1]

Carlyle's explanation was that he was "driven into that Lecture-room" by the "bayonets of Necessity."[2] In 1837, when he first began to lecture, he fully expected to have to quit a literary career, for, as he had informed his brother John, "with only Literature for shelter there is I think no continuance." Better, like Teufelsdröckh, to take a stick and roam Europe or emigrate to the backwoods of America in search of alternative employment.[3] Though his *French Revolution* was finished, no immediate financial return could be expected from it, and it was only by extraordinary thrift that the Carlyles were able to live off the proceeds of "Mirabeau" and "The Diamond Necklace," empty "in purse and in hope."[4] Finance then, rather than fame, was the spur that first prodded Carlyle onto the public platform, where he began to lecture "for subsistence,"[5] and it remained a keen incentive

---

[1] The four series were: in 1837 "German Literature," seven lectures, unpublished (but see Hill Shine's edition of *Carlyle's Unfinished History of German Literature* [1951]); in 1838 "The History of Literature," twelve lectures, published in two posthumous editions as *Lectures on the History of Literature* (New York, 1892, and Bombay, 1892; see p. 279 below); in 1839 "Revolutions of Modern Europe," six lectures, unpublished (but see Shepherd, *Memoirs of Carlyle* 1:197–214 for reports of them taken from the *Examiner*); in 1840 the six lectures on heroes on which the present work is based.

[2] *Letters* 10:52, TC to Ralph Waldo Emerson, March 16, 1838.

[3] *Letters* 9:78, TC to John A. Carlyle, October 20, 1836; see also Froude, *Life in London* 1:83; *Letters* 8:18, TC to Alexander Carlyle, January 28, 1835; *Letters* 9:311, TC to John A. Carlyle, September 21, 1837.

[4] Froude, *Life in London* 1:82.

[5] Wilson, *Carlyle on Cromwell*, 39.

the following year. "If dire famine drive me, I must . . . lecture, but not otherwise," he wrote to his brother John in July 1838.[6]

Financial considerations aside, Carlyle was fascinated as well as repelled by the idea of lecturing. "A mixture of prophecy and play-acting," it was something to be cultivated as a powerful instrument for the conveying of moral truths.[7] Though he found it difficult to "unite the characters of the prophet and the mountebank" as his wife is reported to have put it,[8] public speaking, he wrote, was "a thing I have always had some hankering after: it seems to me I could really *Swim* in that element, were I once thrown into it; that in fact it would develope several things in me, which struggle violently for developement."[9] With this in mind he was "inclined to experiment,"[10] and felt that, were he "once girded up for it," lecturing had a "far greater capability in it" than book writing.[11] Despite his determination, he felt "a kind of shudder" through his "whole heart" at the thought.[12] The feeling was proleptic, for on the evidence of his journals and letters, lecturing was always to be an ordeal and sometimes a martyrdom to him, which may account for the "sort of crucified Expression" Edward FitzGerald recalled him wearing during his lectures on heroes.[13] "However, it is a thing I have long wanted and meant to try,"[14] and so, in 1837, with a series of seven lectures on German literature,[15] he embarked on his first experiment.

He had been invited by Emerson to lecture in America, but when Harriet Martineau and several others sought among their friends two hundred subscribers willing to pay a guinea each to hear Carlyle, he found himself launched on his new career in London. A comfortable four months away from his first appearance, he jocularly minimized the difficulties of public speaking. Once furnished with a subject and the "impudence . . . to lecture at all," one needed only "to turn up

---

[6] *Letters* 10:134, July 27, 1838.

[7] Froude, *Life in London* 1:136.

[8] Fox, *Memories*, 117.

[9] *Letters* 8:42, TC to Ralph Waldo Emerson, February 3, 1835.

[10] *Letters* 9:109, TC to Jean Carlyle Aitken, December 29, 1836.

[11] *Letters* 9:343, TC to John A. Carlyle, November 7, 1837.

[12] *Letters* 9:164, TC to Alexander Carlyle, March 5, 1837.

[13] FitzGerald, *Letters* 3:651.

[14] *Letters* 9:164, TC to Alexander Carlyle, March 5, 1837.

[15] J. A. Froude (*Life in London* 1:98–99) and David Alec Wilson (*Carlyle on Cromwell*, 7) follow the printed 1837 prospectus which lists six lectures. However, Carlyle's letter of May 19, 1837, to his mother (*Letters* 9:206) makes it clear that he gave an unscheduled seventh lecture.

any tub, and get upon it, and open your mouth!" he wrote to Jane Wilson.[16] His misgivings about authorship, which were deeper than the problem of how to make a living from it, had to be temporarily laid aside or, as the months passed, replaced with more immediate anxieties about lecturing. "Heaven only knows what I shall say," he fretted as all public speakers tend to do. "I feel as if I were to be flung overboard, and bid swim or drown."[17]

Many literary figures had preceded and many were to follow him onto the public platform, among them Coleridge, Hazlitt, De Quincey, Sydney Smith, Thackeray, and Dickens. The first half of the century was replete with speakers and audiences who had got hold of the "strange opinion," as Dr. Johnson called it, "that every thing should be taught by lectures."[18] The whole world, said Carlyle, cried "Lecture! . . . Lecture on German Literature, on European Literature, on the French Revolution, on Things in General!" As he followed the world's advice, he felt the lack of three things: "I want knowledge, of my audience, of myself; I want impudence, I want health."[19] He remained diffident rather than impudent, his health was always a worry, but he began to acquire knowledge of his audience and of himself as a lecturer.

As the first day approached, he speculated that his likely audience would "surely be the strangest set of people . . . that ever I talked to."[20] Obviously apprehensive, he determined "to take it as coolly as possible: it is neither death nor men's lives whether I speak well or speak ill, or even decline to speak at all, and do nothing but *gasp*."[21] At times he could not help worrying that on the day of the lecture he might have to say that "it has become entirely impossible for me to talk to you about German or any Literature or terrestrial thing; . . . be kind enough to cover me under a tub . . . and to go your ways all with my blessing!"[22] After the lecture he recalled his "furious determination" not to "break down,"[23] that his tongue had been as "dry as charcoal" and that he had been obliged to "stumble in, and start."[24]

[16] *Letters* 9:115, January 15, 1837.
[17] *Letters* 9:175, TC to John A. Carlyle, March 21, 1837.
[18] Boswell, *Life of Johnson*, 356.
[19] *Letters* 9:378, TC to John Sterling, December 25, 1837.
[20] *Letters* 9:196, TC to Alexander Carlyle, April 23, 1837.
[21] *Letters* 9:199, TC to Margaret A. Carlyle, April 28, 1837.
[22] *Letters* 9:200, TC to Margaret A. Carlyle, April 28, 1837.
[23] Froude, *Life in London* 1:103.
[24] *Letters* 9:215, TC to John A. Carlyle, May 30, 1837.

His sponsor, who was "deaf as a Post,"[25] the "poor Miss Martineau," who two years later "not only lost her ear-trumpet, but her health,"[26] was infected by Carlyle's "unconcealable nervousness," which reflected itself in his "broken speech" and the way his fingers "picked at the desk before him." As "he scarcely slept," and "grew more dyspeptic and nervous every day," she concluded that "no fame and no money . . . could counterbalance the misery which the engagement caused him."[27] However, if Carlyle lacked, as the *Times* said, the "mere technicalities of public speaking," he revealed many of the art's "higher and nobler attributes, gathering self-possession as he proceeded."[28]

The "pecuniary net-result" of his first efforts in 1837 was £135 once expenses had been deducted.[29] It may seem now a modest sum, but to Carlyle at that time it offered financial safety. Better still, another course of lectures was soon proposed that promised to yield at least as much, and the thrifty family might live a year off the proceeds, and be virtually immune to fortune. "Life and labour were now made possible on honest terms, and literary recognition, if it was to come at all, could be waited for without starvation."[30] There was no further talk in Cheyne Row of emigrating or roaming Europe. Lecturing bought Carlyle time, and saved him for a literary career.

Carlyle learned the craft of lecturing as he went along, and his second series in 1838, on the history of literature, found him in not quite "such a dreadful fry" as he had been the previous year.[31] Jane noted that although he was as "white as a pocket handkerchief" he made "no gasping and spluttering" as he had done in the earlier lectures.[32] For his part, Carlyle wrote in his journal, he felt at times like a man "singing through a fleece of wool," and he was frustrated by the sense that while he retained a clear image of his subject, all that his hearers got was a "false impotent scrawl."[33] But the lectures ended with fireworks, with people weeping and applauding. To his

---

[25] *Letters* 9:102, TC to John A. Carlyle, December 2, 1836.
[26] *Letters* 11:234, TC to Richard Monckton Milnes, December 28, 1839.
[27] Martineau, *Autobiography* 1:289.
[28] Cited in *Letters* 9:205n.
[29] *Letters* 9:214, TC to John A. Carlyle, May 30, 1837.
[30] Froude, *Life in London* 1:106.
[31] *Letters* 10:53, TC to Margaret A. Carlyle, March 30, 1838.
[32] *Letters* 10:72, JWC to Jean Carlyle Aitken, May 1, 1838.
[33] Froude, *Life in London* 1:136–37.

family he wrote that the series had gone on better and better until it "grew at last . . . quite a flaming affair,"[34] and had led people to say he had made "a new profession" for himself.[35] Carlyle's material reward was £300, which was some comfort to a man who "had been haunted by the squalid spectre of beggary."[36] With success, however, the fear of popularity arose again to chill his Puritan bones. "I know not what I should do if I were to become an established *Popular*," he fretted. The beggar's wallet was bad, but not so frightful as popularity, "the darkest curse" God could lay on a man.[37]

Nevertheless, April 1839 found him "again upon the threshold of extempore lecturing," and though he was "no longer driven by Poverty as heretofore," he had felt it best to keep this avenue of employment open.[38] Carlyle's health was uncertain and throughout this series, on the revolutions of modern Europe, he was haunted by a sense of failure. For two days after each lecture he felt "a sentiment of pain and remorse at the poor figure" he believed he had made.[39] Even Jane, who considered herself "a perfectly unprejudiced judge,"[40] did not think he was at his best. To Emerson, however, Carlyle boasted of a newfound confidence. "I care less about" lecturing "than I did; it is not agony, and wretched trembling to the marrow of the bone, as it was the last two times."[41] Jane proffered the more sober assessment that unless her husband could "get *hardened* in this trade, he certainly ought to discontinue it; for no gain or eclat that it can yield, is compensation enough for the martyrdom it is to himself, and thro' him to me."[42] To outward appearance, she conceded, he had got through the series "more smoothly and quite as brilliantly as last year" but in place of his usual "agitation *beforehand*" he had "taken to the new and curious crotchet of being ready to hang himself *after*, in the idea that he has made 'a horrible *pluister* [mess] of it.'"[43] The audience, however, "larger than last year, and even more distinguished," seemed not to notice, broke into "loud plaudits," and was full of

[34] *Letters* 10:93, TC to Margaret A. Carlyle, June 12, 1838.
[35] *Letters* 10:134, TC to John A. Carlyle, July 27, 1838.
[36] Froude, *Life in London* 1:139.
[37] *Letters* 10:54, TC to Margaret A. Carlyle, March 30, 1838.
[38] *Letters* 11:81, TC to Ralph Waldo Emerson, April 13, 1839.
[39] *Letters* 11:100, TC to Margaret A. Carlyle, May 20, 1839.
[40] *Letters* 11:93, JWC to Margaret A. Carlyle, May 5, 1839.
[41] *Letters* 11:81, April 13, 1839.
[42] *Letters* 11:98, JWC to Grace Welsh, May 17, 1839.
[43] *Letters* 11:98, JWC to Grace Welsh, May 17, 1839.

praise.[44] The concluding lecture, according to Jane the "most splendid" Carlyle had yet delivered, ended with even more audience frenzy, and the Carlyles left the hall "in a sort of whirlwind of *'glory.'*"[45]

In the weeks immediately before he began the 1839 series of lectures, Carlyle anticipated that he would perhaps be lecturing "for the *last* time,—at least till I get some inward call to speak,"[46] but instead of retiring, he was in fact, with the series of lectures on heroes, about to advance to his greatest triumph on the public platform.

The success of the lectures on heroes in 1840 was due to several factors. Carlyle's treatment of his earlier lecture subjects had been broad-ranging, discursive, and necessarily thin. He could touch, as Leigh Hunt remarked, "only the mountain-tops."[47] This time there was a specific and clear thesis that bound the six lectures together and forged a unit of what might otherwise have remained miscellaneous essays. The arrangement of his new subject was "not so much historic as didactic,"[48] and it was close to Carlyle's heart. "I am telling the people matters that belong much more to myself this year; which is far more interesting to me," he said,[49] and the series had, therefore, an intensity and a focus lacking from the panoramic surveys of cultural and historical topics he had chosen before. As the *Examiner* forecast on May 3, Carlyle's "six lectures on 'Heroes'" seemed "a subject better adapted to the thoughts and style of the lecturer than any he has treated yet."[50]

Perhaps this accounts for the speed with which the scheme for the lectures took shape in Carlyle's mind. On February 24, 1840, he wrote to his mother, "I think I shall lecture this year too, to my old audience! I seem to have a kind of hold of a *subject*; but it is not yet got into any shape," and to his brother John, three days later, he announced that he seemed to have "got the *primordium* of a subject in me,—tho' not nameable as yet."[51] Within a week after his letter to his mother, he was able to assign to his lectures a theme, a six-fold division of their subject matter, and a central hypothesis about the enduring nature of hero-worship. On March 2 he wrote to John, "I am to talk about gods, prophets, priests, kings, poets, teachers (*six*

---

[44] *Letters* 11:93, TC to Margaret A. Carlyle, May 5, 1839.
[45] *Letters* 11:102, JWC to Margaret A. Carlyle, May 20, 1839.
[46] *Letters* 11:84, TC to John A. Carlyle, April 15, 1839.
[47] Nichol, *Carlyle*, 75.
[48] *Letters* 12:94, TC to John A. Carlyle, April 2, 1840.
[49] *Letters* 12:148, TC to Margaret A. Carlyle, May 20, 1840.
[50] Cited in *Letters* 12:132n.
[51] *Letters* 12:55, TC to Margaret A. Carlyle, February 24, 1840; *Letters* 12:58, TC to John A. Carlyle, February 27, 1840.

sorts of them); and may probably call it 'On the Heroic.' Odin, Mahomet, Cromwell are three of my figures; I mean to shew that 'Hero-worship *never ceases*,' that it is at bottom the main or only kind of worship."[52]

The rapidity with which the plan for the lectures took shape in Carlyle's mind did little to facilitate their actual production. During the third week of March he was still "revolving and tumbling about among my projected 'Lectures,'" which remained "dim and horrible; but I suppose I shall get them worked out."[53] These alternations between a clear sense of purpose and a depressed feeling of confusion and anxiety were the usual accompaniments of Carlyle's efforts at composition. By the end of March he was still complaining that the "Lecture-project hardly advances into clearness; stands waiting for a 'glimpse of health,' which, alas, refuses to arrive."[54] Nevertheless he entertained the thought "of writing them down; then flaming about, over both hemispheres with them (too like a Cagliostroccio!), to earn as much as will buy the smallest peculium of annuity whereon to retire into some hut by the sea-shore."[55] As he wrote to his brother John, it was his daily ride on his horse Citoyenne, an activity to which he turned for exercise and therapy when the lectures began "to oppress me sore," that was "the *recipe*" that brought "clearness of spirits and nerves."[56] By April 1, with a month to go to the opening talk, he invited Emerson to consider his "frightful outlook with a Course of Lectures to give 'On Heroes and Hero-Worship'—from Odin to Rob*t* Burns!"[57] or as he wrote facetiously to Henrietta Stanley, "I seem to be fixed to lecture: 'on Heroes'—from the Creation downwards!—'Sport to you but death to us!' Pity me."[58]

During April Carlyle adopted a strict discipline, "rigorous as Rhadamanthus, that I am to dine *nowhere* till once these unfortunate '*Heroes*' are out of me."[59] "I scribble away at my Lectures; refuse *all invitations* whatsoever."[60] Throughout the month he wrote furiously. Daily "I . . . *splash* down (literally as fas[t] as my pen will go) some kind of paragraph on some point or other of my '*Course*' that has

[52] *Letters* 12:67.
[53] *Letters* 12:77, TC to Margaret A. Carlyle, March 17, 1840; *Letters* 12:79, TC to John A. Carlyle, March 17, 1840.
[54] *Letters* 12:89, TC to John A. Carlyle, March 30, 1840.
[55] *Letters* 12:89, TC to John A. Carlyle, March 30, 1840.
[56] *Letters* 12:94, April 2, 1840.
[57] *Letters* 12:94, April 1, 1840.
[58] *Letters* 12:107, [April 13?, 1840].
[59] *Letters* 12:114, TC to Henrietta Maria Stanley, April 17, 1840.
[60] *Letters* 12:116, TC to Alexander Carlyle, April 22, 1840.

b[een] salient and visible to me; paragraph after paragraph, till at least 4 pages daily are full: in this way I put down legibly, if not something that I shall say, yet something that I might and should say. I can clip the paragrap[h]s out, and string them together any way I like."[61] By May 1, with the first lecture only four days away, Carlyle declared to John that they were "*prepared*, as far as preparation will go; I tremble for Tuesday yet not more than is needful."[62] Jane was unafraid about the lectures, fearful only for the lecturer, for the "subject is a fine one—he has well reflected on it—and has already *clashed* out matter enough on paper to carry him triumphan[t]ly thro."[63]

II. THE LECTURES ON HEROES

Of the lectures on heroes themselves, presented in days innocent of the now-ubiquitous tape recorder, we can form only a limited impression, though some glimpses are afforded by those who attended and took an interest in the proceedings. Samuel Wilberforce, who did attend, was asked by Richard Chenevix Trench, later archbishop of Dublin, to supply some of Carlyle's sayings and passed on to him a rumor that the first lecture had been a failure, "as indeed they always are, unless he works himself up into the true Berserker fury, which on that occasion (though it would have been one of the meetest) he certainly failed to do."[64] Carlyle himself felt he had not got much more than a tenth of his meaning across to his audience but fancied he should do better in his next attempt, "though Mahomet is not a very intimate friend to any of us."[65] In fact by common accord the second lecture was what Carlyle himself claimed for it, "the *best* I ever delivered." If anything it was "far *too good*," he ruefully complained, for it had "shivered" his "nerves all in pieces" and made it impossible for him to sleep.[66] The subject of this lecture fully engaged Carlyle's passion against the injustice of historical testimony. He gave "a larger audience than ever . . . to know that the poor Arab had points about him which it were good for all of them to imitate,"[67] indeed that Muḥammad "is a better Christian, with his 'bastard Christianity,'

---

[61] *Letters* 12:114–15, TC to John A. Carlyle, April 18, 1840.
[62] *Letters* 12:128.
[63] *Letters* 12:113, JWC to Margaret A. Carlyle, April 15, 1840.
[64] Trench, *Letters and Memorials* 1:248–49.
[65] Froude, *Life in London* 1:181.
[66] *Letters* 12:142, TC to Alexander Carlyle, May 12, 1840.
[67] Froude, *Life in London* 1:181.

than the most of us shovel-hatted."[68] Despite this provocative tone, or more likely because of it, "the people seemed greatly astonished and greatly pleased. I vomited forth on them like wild Annandale grapeshot. They laughed, applauded, &c."[69] Henry Crabb Robinson, among others, felt the force of Carlyle's presentation. The lecture, he wrote, "gave great satisfaction, for it had uncommon thoughts, and was delivered with unusual animation," Carlyle declaring his conviction that "Mahomet was no mere sensualist, or vulgar impostor, but a real reformer."[70]

By such challenging claims Carlyle no doubt expected to surprise his listeners, who mainly represented the English political and religious establishment, for he set out not only to vindicate a supposed Arab impostor, but to defend a Puritan regicide, a Scottish preacher who had insulted his queen, and a Corsican general who had tried to invade England. By and large, his audience reacted to his provocations with approval rather than outrage. There were naturally some exceptions. On May 9, the *Globe*, which criticized Carlyle's "germanised" thought, also pointed to his affection for some "mighty great ruffians."[71] William Thomson, later Archbishop of York, responding to the published lectures, was roused to object. "Such a menagerie!" he said of Carlyle's heroes. "Elisha, Cyprian, George Herbert, Robert Nelson, Charles I. on one side: Mahomet, Luther, Shakspeare, Rousseau, Cromwell, on the other. Who will weigh the list of the Syncretist with the list of the Churchman?"[72] Frederick Denison Maurice reported that among his clerical colleagues, Sewell was denouncing Carlyle, "and Whewell is very indignant, and believes he is doing the greatest mischief. Hare has much the same opinion." Though Maurice was himself somewhat alarmed at the "wild pantheistic rant" of Carlyle's lecture, he consoled himself with the thought that however much Carlyle "may abuse Churchmen, he will be better able than most men to make us feel our need of a Church." The lecture itself was "by far the most animated and vehement I ever heard from him. It was a passionate defence of Mahomet from all the charges that have been brought against him, and a general panegyric upon him and his doctrine."[73]

---

[68] *Letters* 12:183, TC to Ralph Waldo Emerson, July 2, 1840.
[69] Froude, *Life in London* 1:181.
[70] Robinson, *Diary* 2:287.
[71] Cited in *Letters* 12:157n.
[72] Cited in Seigel, *Critical Heritage*, 177, 176.
[73] Maurice, *Life* 1:280, 283, 279, 282.

Records of audience reaction to the third and fourth lectures, on the hero as poet and priest, are much scantier than those for the first two lectures, but records of the final two, on the hero as man of letters and king, are the most abundant we have, because of the attendance at these last two lectures of Caroline Fox, whose journal not only provides a clear summary of the talks, but a graphic portrait of the lecturer:

> Carlyle soon appeared, and looked as if he felt a well-dressed London crowd scarcely the arena for him to figure in as a popular lecturer. He is a tall, robust-looking man; rugged simplicity and indomitable strength are in his face, and such a glow of genius in it,—not always smouldering there, but flashing from his beautiful grey eyes, from the remoteness of their deep setting under that massive brow. His manner is very quiet, but he speaks like one tremendously convinced of what he utters, and who had much—very much—in him that was quite unutterable, quite unfit to be uttered to the uninitiated ear; and when the Englishman's sense of beauty or truth exhibited itself in vociferous cheers, he would impatiently, almost contemptuously, wave his hand, as if that were not the sort of homage which Truth demanded. He began in a rather low nervous voice, with a broad Scotch accent, but it soon grew firm, and shrank not abashed from its great task.[74]

When it was over Carlyle for once agreed with popular opinion: "The people seem agreed, and I partly think so too, that it was my *best* course of Lectures."[75] In the "fire of the moment" he "all but decided on setting out for America . . . and preaching far and wide . . . on 'Heroes, Hero-Worship and the Heroic.'" But the sterner side of his nature reasserted itself, "the fire of determination died away again," and Carlyle turned his back on a lecturing career at the moment of his greatest lecturing triumph.[76] The calculation of April, that "it will be better *not* to try it any more in future years," hardened into

---

[74] Fox, *Memories*, 105.
[75] *Letters* 12:151, TC to Margaret A. Carlyle, May 23, 1840.
[76] *Letters* 12:184, TC to Ralph Waldo Emerson, July 2, 1840.

certainty.[77] Only financial compulsion could drive him once more onto the platform. "Four times spitted on the spear's point like a Surinam *fire-fly* to give light to the fashionable classes: this is enough of times!"[78] He resolved instead to remain in the brick Babylon of London and to "write down" the lectures.[79] Accordingly, he spent the summer of 1840 transcribing his notes into book form.

III. THE BOOK

The process of conversion was not easy, for the lectures, "wanting all the unction of personal sincerity expressed by voice and face," looked "entirely dull and tame on paper."[80] Records of the first lecture, prepared by a reporter hired by Fraser, were "like soda-water with the gas out of it," so Carlyle decided to write out the lectures himself "if not what was said, yet what might and should have been said."[81] The problem of getting the lecture notes into this perfected form was essentially one of style. Carlyle felt this should be "low-pitched, as like talk as possible," or "somewhat in the style of *speech;* as they were, or rather as they might have been . . . delivered."[82]

The style he sought was that of the ideal lecture, and in this Carlyle succeeded so well that it is easy for readers to forget that the book is no entirely reliable guide to the way the lectures sounded to his original audience. For that we have to rely on hearsay, and the few reports which have come down to us.[83] Perhaps he did speak "as graphically as his 'French Revolution,'"[84] or as Frederic Harrison said, roll forth "Latter-Day Pamphlets by the hour together in the very words, with all the nicknames, expletives, and ebullient tropes that were so familiar to us in print, with the full voice, the Dumfries burr, and the kindling eye which all his friends recall." But the answer to Harrison's rhetorical question "Could printed essay and spoken words be so absolutely the same?"[85] is, in fact, No, they could not,

[77] *Letters* 12:98, TC to Alexander Carlyle, April 8, 1840.
[78] *Letters* 12:141, TC to Thomas Ballantyne, May 11, 1840; see *On Heroes,* 167, and note at 167.9.
[79] *Letters* 12:167, TC to Jean Carlyle Aitken, June 15, 1840.
[80] *Letters* 12:210, TC to John A. Carlyle, August 1, 1840.
[81] *Letters* 12:144, TC to Henry Cole, May 14, 1840.
[82] *Letters* 12:230, TC to John A. Carlyle, August 23, 1840; *Letters* 12:168, TC to Jean Carlyle Aitken, June 15, 1840.
[83] See, for example, the report, "however imperfect," of the first lecture in the *Tablet,* May 16, 1840, 12–13; and *Letters* 12:145n.
[84] Reid, *Life of Milnes* 1:220.
[85] Harrison, *Memories,* 99–100.

as the manuscript fragments of his other writings, notably *Latter-Day Pamphlets* and *Past and Present*, clearly prove.[86] It is easy to be misled, as Wilde was, into thinking that "Carlyle's stormy rhetoric" sprang from enthusiasm. But "even prophets correct their proofs."[87] Whenever Carlyle writes down his thought as it first arose, in the language of his ordinary speech, it lacks much of the literary embellishment of its published version. Carlyle actually roughens his language into growls, barks, and quixotic wrenchings to emulate the strain inherent in the process of thought, and he retains these signs to convey the struggle by which his finished style has been achieved. His style resembles speech in its dramatic immediacy, but Carlyle arrived at his invented language as a deliberate artistic strategy, no less than Wordsworth had done in inventing a poetic version of the language of "ordinary men." In short, for all its colloquial vitality, Carlyle's written prose was the result of considerable artifice and careful contrivance.

Carlyle's account of his experience in writing *On Heroes* bears this out. The labor began in June and ended in September, a period considerably longer than the time he gave to preparing the lectures for oral delivery. By mid-June he had finished the first lecture, ten days later was in sight of completing the second, and confused, "*umgenebelt*," as he was, approached the third.[88] Early July found him "recreating" himself in preparation for this task and confessing that he had no "overplus of heart to the business."[89] Then followed one of his usual outbursts of self-loathing and a familiarly adopted contempt for the enterprise. "These Lectures are pure trash: I could write one of them straight on, if I had a *body* that would stand it. I take ten or twelve days to each; and get into violent extremes of indigestion, this way and that, by means of it."[90] He continued to fret that the lectures seemed "absolutely worth nothing at all,"[91] that they were a "wearisome triviality . . . yet toilsome to produce, which I could like to throw into the fire!" Nothing, he said, "I have ever written pleases me so ill. They have nothing *new*, nothing that to me is not *old*."[92]

[86] See Goldberg and Seigel, eds., *Carlyle's Latter-Day Pamphlets*, lxxii–lxxviii; Calder, *The Writing of* Past and Present, 120–97.

[87] Wilde, "Mr. Pater's Last Volume," 229.

[88] *Letters* 12:167, TC to John A. Carlyle, June 15, 1840; *Letters* 12:173, TC to Alexander Carlyle, June 26, 1840; *Letters* 12:180, TC to John A. Carlyle, July 1, 1840.

[89] *Letters* 12:188, TC to Margaret A. Carlyle, July 3, 1840.

[90] *Letters* 12:192, TC to John A. Carlyle, July 15, 1840.

[91] *Letters* 12:210, TC to John A. Carlyle, August 1, 1840.

[92] *Letters* 12:230, TC to John A. Carlyle, August 23, 1840.

The misery of spirit and ill health that accompanied his writing was no doubt real, but it was also, one suspects, part of a creative strategy that acted as a spur to his energies, for, as he noted, "when I once get rightly *ill*, the writing goes along like a fire well *kindled*."[93] Sometimes he was aware of advantages in converting the spoken to the written word. The third lecture, on the hero as poet, "which was far the worst of all as I delivered it, is considerably the best hitherto as written." With improvements, it would in its final shape "do as well as any of the rest."[94] But even with this satisfaction, the predominant feeling was one of painful struggle. As he said of the fourth, it had been finished, "tho' not till after the toughest fight."[95] By the first week in September the writing was completed and ready "for Printing, for *Combustion*, or whatever else. Most probably, after it has lain a while, I shall go over it again, and with certain parings and addings send it to the Press."[96]

IV. The Subject

It is no surprise that Carlyle chose the subject of heroism for his 1840 lectures. The heroic was a central element in his thinking, and was to become, after several anticipatory treatments in "Goethe" (1828), "Schiller" (1831), and *Sartor Resartus* (1833), the "leading principle of all his later social writing."[97] The subject was also a major Victorian preoccupation. Though Carlyle's intensity was his own, his sentiments were widely shared by his fellow Victorians who, said Edmund Gosse, turned admiration "from a virtue into a religion, and called it Hero Worship."[98] One factor behind Victorian hero-worship was the Romantic rediscovery of enthusiasm. In the neoclassical period it had been applied as a term of ridicule to religious zealots who felt themselves literally ἔνθεος (*en-theos*), possessed by God or having God within them. Romantic theory and sensibility converted enthusiasm from an intellectually ludicrous delusion to a sign of emotional depth and power. The characteristic "romantic passions" thus came to include enthusiasm or unfettered admiration, which, according to Ruskin,

---

[93] *Letters* 12:233, TC to Jean Carlyle Aitken, August 25, 1840.
[94] *Letters* 12:192, TC to John A. Carlyle, July 15, 1840; *Letters* 12:194, TC to Margaret A. Carlyle, July 15, 1840.
[95] *Letters* 12:229, TC to John A. Carlyle, August 23, 1840.
[96] *Letters* 12:238, TC to John A. Carlyle, September 5, 1840.
[97] Raymond Williams, *Culture and Society*, 76.
[98] Gosse, "Agony of the Victorian Age," 295.

meant "primarily all the forms of Hero Worship."[99] Despite dissenting voices like those of T. H. Huxley, who considered hero-worship a form of "idolatry,"[100] and Macaulay, who saw it as a certain index to feeble intellect, hero-worship, as Walter Houghton has said, was an essential "nineteenth century phenomenon. At no other time would it have been called 'the basis of all possible good.' . . . In no other age were men so often told to take 'the great ones of the earth' as models for imitation." For the half century from 1830, "the worship of the hero was a major factor in English culture."[101] Carlyle's 1840 lectures were, therefore, an incursion into the mainstream of Victorian thought, and his theory of the hero "merely the final, high doctrine in a movement which had been for some years under way."[102] The doctrine itself would have needed little or no defense at the time. Even religious leaders who opposed Carlyle's thinking on other grounds saw no objection to his advocacy of heroes as such, but only to his failure to select appropriate Christian models. They did not find him lending support to tyrannical arbitrary power, an objection sometimes attributed to him by later commentators preoccupied with the nightmares of recent history.

Carlyle's originality lay in the depth and seriousness of his treatment and the imaginative richness with which he invested the subject. Furthermore, by means of his chosen historical models he attempted to reshape the public perception of Muḥammad, Cromwell, and Knox, while he sought a deeper and more sympathetic understanding of Norse mythology and the figures of Dante and Burns. He also set himself against certain contemporary attitudes to history that, like Disraeli's Coningsby, he felt had destroyed human individuality. Specifically this meant the scientific conception of history as an impersonal play of forces, which found a locus in such "positivistic fabrications" as "Buckle's attempt to discover historical laws."[103] By such reckoning, the individual leader was fundamentally no different from others and was merely in a position to hasten a development which would have eventually taken place in any event.

Carlyle acknowledged the prevalence of such current theories, but he preferred to believe that "Man is heaven-born; not the thrall of

[99] Ruskin, Works 33:292.
[100] Huxley, Life and Letters 1:304.
[101] Houghton, Victorian Frame of Mind, 305, 310; also Thatcher, Nietzsche in England, 12.
[102] Lehman, Carlyle's Theory of the Hero, 132; but see Harrison, Studies in Early Victorian Literature, 55.
[103] Collingwood, Idea of History, 144.

Circumstances, of Necessity, but the victorious subduer thereof."[104] He felt, perhaps wrongly, certainly intensely, that he inhabited an age that "denies the existence" and "the desirableness of great men. Shew our critics a great man, a Luther for example, they begin to what they call 'account' for him. . . . He was the 'creature of the Time,' they say; the Time called him forth, the Time did everything, he nothing—but what we the little critic could have done too!"[105] He shared Coleridge's belief that "all the great . . . things that have been achieved in the world, have been so achieved by individuals," but that the "rage now-a-days is all the other way: the individual is supposed capable of nothing; there must be organisation, classification, machinery . . . as if the capital of national morality could be increased by making a joint stock of it."[106] Such prevailing notions were exactly those Carlyle set out to disprove in his lectures, to posit instead the view that "every advance which humanity had made was due to special individuals supremely gifted in mind and character, whom Providence sent among them at favoured epochs." This was the "principle which he proposed to illustrate in . . . 'Heroes and Hero-Worship.'"[107]

Since criticism of *On Heroes* has often been preoccupied with Carlyle's "theory" of heroism and the heroic principle, it is worth recalling two correctives: René Wellek's estimate that "Carlyle's achievement as a literary historian and critic is surely rather in his portraits . . . than in any wider historical schemes"[108] and Charles Frederick Harrold's comment that Carlyle's interest in history was, in contrast to Fichte's, "pictorial and psychological."[109] Given his focus on individual heroes, the strong visual character of his imagination, his abiding interest in physiognomy, and his constant reference to these subjects throughout the lectures, it seems not only apt, but a view sanctioned by his own practice, to see him as a painter of historical portraits.

As a "physiognomic reader,"[110] Carlyle believed that a person's inner character impressed itself on every action and utterance. He never wavered in his adherence to this ancient belief in the ability to

[104] "Boswell's Life of Johnson" (1832), *Essays* 3:90.
[105] *On Heroes*, 12; also "Signs of the Times" (1829), *Essays* 2:75.
[106] Coleridge, *Table Talk* (July 24, 1832), 187.
[107] Froude, *Life in London* 1:175–76.
[108] Wellek, *Confrontations*, 97; see also Louise Merwin Young, *Carlyle and the Art of History*; Shine, *Carlyle and the Saint-Simonians*; and Wellek's review of both, "Carlyle and the Philosophy of History."
[109] Harrold, *Carlyle and German Thought*, 180, 196.
[110] "Portraits of Knox" (1875), *Essays* 5:320.

find moral and spiritual features reflected in the face and its expressions. He never shared the reservations of Shakespeare's Duncan, that "there's no art / To find the mind's construction in the face,"[111] but rather, like Fielding's Parson Adams, he felt that "Nature generally imprints such a Portraiture of the Mind in the Countenance, that a skilful Physiognomist will rarely be deceived."[112] Carlyle had a "craze for portraits of great men."[113] He saluted the "worthy wonderful Lavater, the wandering Physiognomist"[114] for his shrewd analyses of Diderot[115] and Cagliostro,[116] and in his own work as historian Carlyle invariably attempted to "procure a bodily likeness of the personage inquired after; a good *Portrait* if such exists; failing that, even an indifferent if sincere one." Often, he said, he had found "a Portrait superior in real instruction to half-a-dozen written 'Biographies.'"[117]

From these remarks one can see that Carlyle used *physiognomy* in both its narrowest and its widest signification. Most narrowly it meant that inner character revealed itself in the face. But such inward character also impressed itself on every action and statement, and manifested itself in every form of expression whether in "painting, singing, fighting, ever with the same physiognomy."[118] Actions were thus "physiognomic" of the person. Secondly, since all moral and intellectual faculties were organically linked, "what we call imagination, fancy, understanding, . . . are but different figures of the same Power of Insight, all indissolubly connected with each other, physiognomically related," so that "if we knew one of them, we might know all of them."[119] Finally, Carlyle, following Herder, extends physiognomy to national as well as individual characteristics. It was the critic's job to construe the character of that "national physiognomy" and trace the record of its expression through history.[120]

This bias in favor of dramatic portraiture and a belief in its significance for grasping historical truth was not new to Carlyle at the time of his 1840 lectures. As early as 1822 he had planned to "come out with a kind of Essay on the Civil Wars, . . . not to write a history . . .

---

[111] *Macbeth*, 1.4.11–12.
[112] Henry Fielding, *Joseph Andrews*, 182.
[113] Wylie, *Carlyle*, 387.
[114] "German Poetry" (1831), *Essays* 2:362.
[115] "Diderot" (1833), *Essays* 3:246.
[116] "Count Cagliostro" (1833), *Essays* 3:246.
[117] "Scottish Portraits" (1854), *Essays* 4:404–5.
[118] *History of Literature*, 156.
[119] *On Heroes*, 90–91.
[120] Wellek, *Confrontations*, 98.

but to exhibit if I can some features of the national character as it was then displayed, supporting my remarks by mental portraits, drawn to the best of my ability, of . . . the most distinguished of the actors in this great scene."[121] The plan was not carried out, but it suggests many of the features Carlyle employed in *On Heroes*. The concept of a "mental portrait," a picture derived by penetrating the appearance of a face to the life of the mind behind it, is exactly the type of characterological study Carlyle attempted in 1840.

Physiognomy lay at the heart of his interest in portraiture and it furnishes a guide to his approach to the pictures he offered of his heroes. It is, in many ways, the animating principle of his treatment of the subject of his 1840 lectures. For this reason the illustrations included in this volume not only reflect the importance Carlyle attached to pictorial reference but also have an intimate bearing on the text itself. In preparing for *On Heroes*, he sought out portraits and used them as physiognomic pointers to insights into the characters of his chosen figures. Repeatedly he harped on the "look" of his historical subjects. "In Kranach's best portraits I find the true Luther. A rude, plebeian face; with its huge crag-like brows and bones, the emblem of rugged energy; at first, almost a repulsive face. Yet in the eyes especially there is a wild silent sorrow; . . . giving to the rest the true stamp of nobleness"[122] (see Plate 6). He found confirmatory evidence of his opinion of Rousseau in the philosopher's face, which was "expressive of him. A high, but narrow contracted intensity in it: bony brows; deep, strait-set eyes, in which there is something bewildered-looking,—bewildered, peering with lynx-eagerness."[123] Dante's "painting," which is how Carlyle alludes to the *Divine Comedy*, is "physiognomical of the whole man,"[124] and in the third lecture he pauses over the supposed Giotto portrait, not only to recall its appearance but also to wonder at its provenance and legitimacy[125] (see Plate 5). Norse mythology is "in some sort the Portraiture" of Odin.[126] The "very look of Boswell" signified so much: "In that cocked nose, cocked partly in triumph over his weaker fellow-creatures, partly to snuff-up the smell of coming pleasure, and scent it from afar; in those bag-cheeks, hanging like half-filled wine-skins, still able to contain

[121] *Letters* 2:94, TC to Alexander Carlyle, April 27, 1822.
[122] *On Heroes*, 121.
[123] *On Heroes*, 158.
[124] *On Heroes*, 80.
[125] *On Heroes*, 73–74.
[126] *On Heroes*, 26.

more; in that coarsely-protruded shelf-mouth, that fat dewlapped chin; in all this, who sees not sensuality, pretension, boisterous imbecility enough."[127] Only the truly discerning eye could penetrate the face of the flunky to see his merits. At the end of his life, Carlyle wrote a commentary on a sixteenth-century book of Reformation portraits, in which he confronted the question of the portraits of the Scottish reformer John Knox. He rejected the most widely available picture of Knox as "very difficult indeed to accept as a bodily physiognomy of the man you have elsewhere got an image of,"[128] that is, from Knox's deeds and writings. As he perused the "dead and boiled-looking" Knox of Beza's engraving,[129] Carlyle saw only a man "content to take things as they come, if only they will let him digest his victuals, and sleep in a whole skin"[130] (see Plate 7). Such a picture violated Carlyle's conception of Knox as a magnificent firebrand kindling Scotland to a sacred blaze, and he sought every means at his disposal to rectify the misleading effect of "this poor Icon."[131] He not only offered his own portrait of Knox in *On Heroes*, a verbal picture that presented a more humane and amiable Knox than that supplied by tradition, but he adopted as authentic an alternative portrait that had been published in 1836 for the Society for the Diffusion of Useful Knowledge. This image, which became known as the Somerville portrait, matched Carlyle's own intuitive sense of how Knox looked, and appealed to his theory that external appearance and inner spirit could not be in conflict. In his last essay he set out to prove, mistakenly as it turned out, the authenticity of the Somerville portrait and to establish it as the "one extant Portrait of the hero."[132]

Similarly he denounced, as a chimera spawned by hatred, popular accounts of Cromwell which were not to his mind "portraits of the man,"[133] any more than those academic paintings of the civil war that consist of "an angry man and horse (man presumably intended for Cromwell, but not like him),—man, with heavy flapping Spanish cloak, etc., and no hat to his head, firing a pistol over his shoulder." What, he asked, "can be the use of such things, except to persons who have turned their back on real interests, and gone wool-gathering in search

---

[127] "Boswell's Life of Johnson" (1832), *Essays* 3:69–70.
[128] "Portraits of Knox" (1875), *Essays* 5:318.
[129] *Essays* 5:328.
[130] *Essays* 5:319.
[131] *Essays* 5:319.
[132] Kaplan, *Thomas Carlyle*, 516–17.
[133] *On Heroes*, 182.

of imaginary?"[134] And earlier, in reviewing the nine volumes of Varnhagen von Ense's *Memoirs*, Carlyle studied the portrait of Rahel Levin, von Ense's wife, that "woman of true genius,"[135] and then wrote a twelve-line physiognomic analysis of it.[136] During the writing of *The French Revolution*, Carlyle also "dug out" a series of engraved portraits that affected his conception of the participants. "Mirabeau's ugliness is now a kind of truth for me; Danton suffered dreadfully, on physiognomic survey; alas, his *energy* looks too like that of some Game Chicken or Dutch Sam, true heroism never dwelt in *such* a tabernacle. I fear Thiers has quite misled me. Lafayette looks puppyish; Robespierre like a narrow, exasperated, exacerbated Methodist Precentor . . . ; Camille Desmoulins is full of spirit, talent, half-blackguard gaiety."[137]

A vivid sense of the actuality and the living presence of the past excited Carlyle's imagination and governed his conception of history. It led to his fascination with faces and also places, wherever some vestige of the past could still be detected by direct observation. When Edward FitzGerald undertook some excavations at Naseby, the famous battlefield lying on his family's estate, Carlyle impressed upon him that his own picture of the battle had been "gathered with industry from some seven or eight eye-witnesses, looking at the business with their own eyes from seven or eight different sides" and that no "'theory,' by what Professor soever, can be of any use to me in comparison."[138] The opening of a burial heap, he wrote, "blazes strangely in my thoughts: these are the very jawbones that were clenched together in deadly rage, on this very ground, 197 years ago! It brings the matter home to one, with a strange veracity,—as if for the first time one saw it to be no fable and theory but a dire fact. I will beg for a tooth and a bullet; authenticated by your own eyes and word of honour!"[139] Such objects as Carlyle's bullet are, in the words of Vladimir Nabokov, "transparent things, through which the past shines."[140] If such objects give a fleeting glimpse of the past, it is a past constantly sliding into obscurity. "How pale, thin, ineffectual do the great figures we would fain summon from History rise before us! . . . The great spirits that have gone before us can survive only as

[134] "Scottish Portraits" (1854), *Essays* 4:410.
[135] "Varnhagen von Ense" (1838), *Essays* 4:109.
[136] *Essays* 4:107–8.
[137] *Letters* 6:331–32, TC to John Stuart Mill, February 22, 1833.
[138] *Letters* 15:90, TC to Edward FitzGerald, September 18, 1842.
[139] *Letters* 15:101–2, TC to Edward FitzGerald, September 24, 1842.
[140] Nabokov, *Transparent Things*, 1.

disembodied Voices; their form and distinctive aspect, outward and even in many respects inward, . . . has passed into another sphere; from which only History, in scanty memorials, can evoke some faint resemblance of it."[141] It was this Carlylean "feeling for the poetic value of all historical facts" that attracted the historian G. M. Trevelyan,[142] and earlier Elizabeth Barrett Browning, who praised Carlyle's "great power of re-production" that enabled him to "bring back his man from the grave of years, not like a ghost, but with all his vital flesh as well as his thoughts about him."[143]

V. THE HEROES

Carlyle's book resists easy schematization. Nevertheless, his own tripartite arrangement of the subject, as suggested by the book's full title, provides a convenient framework for discussion, while at the same time reminding us that he understood there to be close connections between the hero, the attitude of hero-worship, and the historical environment in which the hero worked out his life.

Within Carlyle's collection of heroes one can distinguish several groupings. The heroes of the first two lectures, Odin and Muḥammad, whose teachings would have struck his Victorian audience as arcane (and, in the case of paganism, almost unrecognizable as a system of religious belief), enabled Carlyle to illustrate his conviction that genuine religious feeling is grounded in the permanent fact of hero-worship rather than in any outward framework of myths subject by their very nature to constant historical revision.

Since the impulse to hero-worship was the essence not only of outmoded "Paganism" but of "far higher . . . religions,"[144] the seemingly outlandish myths of the Norsemen offered a clear parallel to nineteenth-century Christianity, which was itself outgrowing its original mythology by stripping off the vesture of supernatural belief. The "Mythus of the Christian Religion" did not look in the nineteenth century "as it did in the eighth" and it was the task of Carlyle's era to "embody the divine Spirit of that Religion in a new Mythus" appropriate to itself.[145] In selecting Odin as his representative divinity in place of Jesus, the "greatest of all Heroes,"[146] just as he chose

[141] "Schiller" (1831), *Essays* 2:166–67.
[142] Trevelyan, *Autobiography*, 13.
[143] Cited in Seigel, *Critical Heritage*, 243–44.
[144] *On Heroes*, 11.
[145] *Sartor*, 2.9.154.
[146] *On Heroes*, 12.

Muḥammad in place of Moses and the Biblical prophets, Carlyle provoked his audience to think afresh about the evolution of their own religion while his indirection took him clear of giving offense or of becoming entangled in theological difficulties. Equally, through his treatment of Islam and Scandinavian paganism he could stress the shared nature of all religious experience and the centrality of hero-worship itself.

Aside from his designated role in this larger strategy, Muḥammad also belongs to that group of heroes who had been vilified by history. The major figures of Muḥammad and Cromwell, and the minor ones of Boswell and Knox, imposed on Carlyle a task not unlike that of a picture restorer who must first erase the dull film that has obscured the original image before the portrait can emerge. Carlyle's aim in these portraits was to show his heroes in a true light, freed from the "falsifying *nimbus*" of their fame and the obscuring lies of their detractors.[147]

There was daring in this venture into intellectual history, for he sought to overturn the traditional Western view of the prophet of Islam as impostor, fraud, and even Antichrist. It was in his 1838 lectures on literature that he first expressed his opinion that Muḥammad was "no imposter at all,"[148] and David Alec Wilson speculates that the surprised response of his audience on that occasion may have led Carlyle to return to the subject in 1840.[149] That medieval Christendom held so adverse a view of the founder of Islam is hardly surprising given that Islamic forces were dominant on every frontier of the Holy Roman Empire. This opinion of Muḥammad and his religion persisted in the later internecine disputes of the Reformation in which it was customary for both Catholic and Protestant parties to discredit each other's doctrines by charging them with affinities to Islam; it was perpetuated by the attempts of eighteenth-century skepticism to discredit all religion as irrational superstition, which gave rise to such works as Voltaire's *Le Fanatisme ou Mahomet le prophète* (1741). Even the partial rehabilitation of Muḥammad's reputation at the hands of Gibbon, "the smoothly shaven historian so ironically civil to Christianity,"[150] was undertaken for the ulterior purpose of scoring points against Christianity.[151]

[147] "Sir Walter Scott" (1838), *Essays* 4:35.
[148] *History of Literature*, 112.
[149] Wilson, *Carlyle on Cromwell*, 33.
[150] Hardy, *Jude the Obscure*, 65.
[151] See Watt, "Carlyle on Muhammad," 247–54; apRoberts, *Ancient Dialect*, 87–101; and Nash, "Thomas Carlyle and Islam," 9–22.

It was against the weight of this long adverse tradition that Carlyle proposed to move in his second lecture. He knew he was attempting a revision of current prejudices, but he hoped to sweep away as an absurdity the belief that teachings that were a "life-guidance" for which millions had lived and died were "a miserable piece of spiritual leg-erdemain."[152] Humphrey Prideaux, among others, had represented the Qur'ān "as a mere bundle of juggleries; chapter after chapter got up to excuse and varnish the author's successive sins, forward his ambitions and quackeries."[153] To Carlyle, the hypothesis that Mu-hammad was a "Falsehood incarnate, that his religion is a mere mass of quackery and fatuity," was no longer tenable.[154] But that view was still current. The eminent churchman William Thomson remained unconvinced by Carlyle, preferring to think Muhammad might be "an impostor for all his millions of dupes," and he speculated that the prophet's "preternatural communings" were either "dyspeptic visions" or "*mendacia salubria*, wholesome lies, used . . . to make firm the feeble tottering faith of invalid adherents."[155]

It was then no vain boast that led Carlyle to say "it was altogether a new kind of thing" his audience was hearing.[156] Muhammad's claim of "supreme Prophethood" dragged "along with it such a coil of fables, impurities, intolerances, as makes it a questionable step for me here and now to say, as I have done, that Mahomet was a true Speaker at all, and not rather an ambitious charlatan, perversity and simula-crum," he added in his next lecture.[157] In spite of such reservations, he did come out and publicly declare his conviction, the "first strong affirmation in the whole of European literature, medieval and mod-ern, of a belief in the sincerity of Muhammad." He was furthermore "the first writer in either east or west to attempt to fathom the inner experience of the founder of Islam. Others in Europe had seen in Muhammad's ideas an expression of the essence of all true religions. Even Goethe seems to have been concerned mainly with Muhammad's historical achievement. Carlyle alone was interested in the man, the human person, grappling with the problems of human life and destiny that are common to all men." That is the view of a distinguished modern Arabist, W. Montgomery Watt, who adds that in the picture Carlyle presents of the prophet there "is perhaps more of Carlyle than

[152] *On Heroes*, 39.
[153] *On Heroes*, 57.
[154] *On Heroes*, 38.
[155] Cited in Seigel, *Critical Heritage*, 180.
[156] Froude, *Life in London* 1:181.
[157] *On Heroes*, 95.

Muhammad. Yet in its essence Carlyle's conception . . . is a true one, and one that is still of value in its broad outlines to the historian of to-day."[158] In fact, the revolution in historical estimates of Muḥammad since the latter part of the nineteenth century must be attributed in large measure to the influence of Carlyle's lecture. The unstinting praise modern scholarship has offered Carlyle in this particular area is the more surprising in that he came to the subject late and without any specialized skills, yet he managed to seize upon and articulate the essential truths that had eluded most of the trained scholars who preceded him. It is a conspicuous vindication of his own theory of hero-worship, with its collateral notion that it takes a heroic spirit to recognize one.

The second major portrait that needed restoration was that of Cromwell. Carlyle intended to "sweep off all the royalist cobwebs" that had obscured Cromwell's "fair fame."[159] While many of the anti-Royalists of the civil war—Eliot, Pym, Hampden, Ludlow, Hutchinson, and Vane—had been "as good as canonized" by popular opinion, and "admitted to be a kind of Heroes," Cromwell alone seemed to Carlyle "to hang yet on the gibbet, and find no hearty apologist anywhere."[160] Carlyle had decided to become Cromwell's "apologist" by the time of his lecture, and within a few months of its completion he had collected an "immense stock of reading about English Puritanism and Oliver Cromwell."[161]

Even during his prodigious researches into the civil war correspondence at the British Museum, which led to the publication in 1845 of *Oliver Cromwell's Letters and Speeches*, the problem remained the same he had set himself in the lectures, the fashioning of a true portrait of the Protector free from historical distortion and the blur of mediocre reporting. It was no easy task. In September he wrote, "I am now over head and ears in *Cromwellean* Books; studying, for perhaps the fourth time in my life, to see if it be possible to get any credible face-to-face acquaintance with our English Puritan period; or whether it must be left forever a mere hearsay and echo to one?"[162] As Carlyle noted in December 1840, "Poor Oliver lies like grains of gold dust scattered under continents of cinders and rubbish. I fear much I shall never be able to collect him: our greatest man irrecoverably

---

[158] Watt, "Carlyle on Muhammad," 247, 253–54.
[159] Hallam Tennyson, *Memoir* 1:226.
[160] *On Heroes*, 178–79.
[161] *Letters* 12:283, TC to Thomas Ballantyne, October 8, 1840.
[162] *Letters* 12:267, TC to Ralph Waldo Emerson, September 26, 1840.

lost to History!"[163] It was specifically during the twelve months that included his researches for the sixth lecture that Carlyle came "actually, as it were, to *see* that this Cromwell was one of the greatest souls ever born of the English kin; a great amorphous semi-articulate *Baresark;* very interesting to me."[164] The lecture in which Carlyle employed the same terms to describe Cromwell was, therefore, an important stage in developing an interest he had shown in the period and its main figures since 1822 when he had planned a brief study of it.

It was a daring plan to take this last of the Puritans down from the gibbet of infamy, and Carlyle knew that there was an element of rashness in his being "among the first that ever ventured to pronounce" Cromwell "not a knave and liar, but a genuinely honest man!"[165] Probably it was the first time since Milton that a voice of undisputed literary genius had been heard in support of the Puritans, for the history of the civil war had been written by Cromwell's enemies. Though the Puritans were, in Macaulay's succinct phrase, "the conquerors, their enemies were the painters." Nor was the question of literary skill irrelevant, for with the major exception of Milton, the Puritan side showed little regard for literature as such, and thereby forfeited a valuable means of claiming the attention of posterity. The best book on the Puritan side, as Macaulay noted, is probably "the charming narrative of Mrs. Hutchinson," but ranged against it are "the most authoritative and the most popular historical works in our language, that of Clarendon, and that of Hume."[166]

Carlyle recognized that the eighteenth century had done most to enshrine the view of Cromwell as a falsity, hated alike by the Tories of the period because he overthrew the king, and by the Whigs because he overthrew Parliament. "Except for a couple of books, the popular historians of the century followed the Royalist party line, whether the fabrications of James Heath's *Flagellum* (1663) or the rolling periods of the first Earl of Clarendon's *History of the Rebellion* (1702)."[167] Well into the nineteenth century, in fact as late as 1839, the year before Carlyle's lecture, John Forster "held it to be 'indisputably true' that Cromwell had 'lived a hypocrite and died a traitor.'" After reading Carlyle's *Cromwell*, some six years later, Forster

[163] *Letters* 12:345, TC to Mary Rich, December 5, 1840.
[164] *Letters* 12:267, TC to Ralph Waldo Emerson, September 26, 1840.
[165] *On Heroes*, 203.
[166] Macaulay, "Milton" (1825), *Essays* 1:172.
[167] Ashley, *Greatness of Cromwell*, 12.

acknowledged that "'Cromwell was as far removed on the one hand from fanaticism, as on the other from hypocrisy.'" Only "an author of genius" could have succeeded in disturbing "so broadly based and tirelessly repeated a verdict" as that reflected in Forster's earlier comment.[168] In fact Carlyle's own opinion had undergone a similar transformation, and he knew from personal experience the seductive pull of this reiterated and traditional viewpoint. In March 1822 he was reading Clarendon's *History* with some thoughts of writing his own account of the civil war, and it is interesting to note how much at this stage his views conformed to Clarendon's. He thought, for instance, that Charles was "a very good man, though weakish and ill-brought up." Cromwell and his Puritans looked "much like a pack of fanatical knaves—a compound of religious enthusiasm, and of barbarous selfishness; which made them stick at no means for gratifying both the one and the other."[169]

Carlyle was certainly taking up a novel position, though in fairness one should note that Macaulay, who so often traversed the same subject matter, had written a favorable account of Cromwell in 1828 when he reviewed Henry Hallam's *Constitutional History of England*. Hallam was among the "fanatic" theorists Carlyle excoriated in his lecture, who believed that Cromwell "sucked only the dregs of a besotted fanaticism" in contrast to Napoleon to whom "the stores of reason and philosophy were open."[170] Macaulay, however, argued that though "every device has been used to blacken [his reputation], though to praise him would long have been a punishable crime, truth and merit at last prevail. . . . Even to the present day his character, though constantly attacked, and scarcely ever defended, is popular with the great body of our countrymen."[171] Macaulay's efforts to rectify the imbalance of historical report about Cromwell preceded Carlyle's, as did John Robertson's attempted vindication in 1839,[172] though they were on a much smaller scale and, for Carlyle, lacking in passion.

Carlyle also tried to set to rights what he denounced as "sorrowful theories" about Dante, Luther, Knox, and Boswell. In each instance, some aspects of the traditionally received portraits were in need of restoration. He set out to show that Knox was "no hateful man" or

[168] Ashley, *Greatness of Cromwell*, 13–14.
[169] *Two Notebooks*, 17.
[170] Cited in Macaulay, "Hallam's Constitutional History" (1828), *Essays* 1:51.
[171] Macaulay, *Essays* 1:54.
[172] *London and Westminster Review* 33 (October 1839): 181–256. See *Letters* 10:251n.

"gloomy, spasmodic, shrieking fanatic,"[173] but one whose brusque encounters with the queen were forced upon him by duty and principle. He sought to dispel the "terrestrial libel" which held that the *Divine Comedy* was Dante's splenetic attempt to put those in Hell "whom he could not be avenged upon on earth."[174] Likewise he rejected the often repeated canard, originating with Leo X, that Luther's attack on indulgences derived from purely mercenary motives, because his order had lost to the Dominicans the lucrative prerogative of dispensing papal pardons.[175]

As for Boswell, the world had written him off as a sycophant. Carlyle conceded his many weaknesses, yet wondered why, with so many glittering and wealthy people who would have better rewarded his sycophancy,[176] he should have attached himself to the "great dusty irascible Pedagogue in his mean garret."[177] Poor Bozzy, whose mind Macaulay likened to one of those "creepers which the botanists call parasites,"[178] had nevertheless discerned the greatness that lay in the impoverished giant of Gough Street. Macaulay saw no "more certain indication of a weak and ill-regulated intellect than that propensity which, for want of a better name, we will venture to christen Boswellism."[179] Carlyle admired what Macaulay scorned. Since *"Bad* is by its nature negative, and can do *nothing,"* it was the falsest possible hypothesis to imagine that "it were the very fact of his being among the worst men in this world" that had enabled Boswell "to write one of the best books therein!"[180]

VI. The Artist as Hero

Dante and Shakespeare have a special place in Carlyle's schema and a particular relevance to his subject. One might think that in comparison with heroes working in what modern jargon calls the "real world," or in the sphere of religious and moral conflict, Carlyle's two representative poets would seem to be less significant or influential. This is particularly so since Carlyle was reluctant to endorse fully the formulation he found in Goethe and Schiller that the beautiful exceeded

---

[173] *On Heroes*, 129.
[174] *On Heroes*, 81.
[175] *On Heroes*, 113.
[176] "Boswell's Life of Johnson" (1832), *Essays* 3:72.
[177] *On Heroes*, 157.
[178] Macaulay, "Samuel Johnson" (1856), *Miscellaneous Works* 7:98.
[179] Macaulay, "Milton" (1825), *Essays* 1:193.
[180] "Boswell's Life of Johnson" (1832), *Essays* 3:76.

the good,[181] so that a defense of art along purely aesthetic lines was
not possible. What he offers in fact is a variation on the traditional *ars
longa, vita brevis* theme. Toward the conclusion of his section on
Dante, Carlyle recalls that within a hundred years of Muḥammad's
death the Arabians were "at Grenada and at Delhi; Dante's Italians
seem to be yet very much where they were. Shall we say, then, Dante's
effect on the world was small in comparison? Not so: his arena is far
more restricted; but also it is far nobler, clearer;—perhaps not less but
more important." The wisdom of Muḥammad was for mass consump-
tion and was, therefore, cast in a dialect crude and inconsistent, whereas
Dante "speaks to the noble, the pure and great, in all times and
places. Neither does he grow obsolete, as the other does. . . . Dante,
one calculates, may long survive Mahomet."[182] Carlyle stresses the
durability and the universality of art, for "even in Arabia . . . Mahomet
will have exhausted himself and become obsolete, while this Shakspeare,
this Dante may still be young;—while this Shakspeare may still pretend to be a Priest of Mankind, of Arabia as of other places, for
unlimited periods to come!"[183]

A collateral issue Carlyle raises is the criterion to be used for
gauging effectiveness. "The uses of this Dante?" he asks, invoking the
terminology of the utilitarians, and thus provocatively establishing
that the question cannot be put in such a form without absurdity, for
the value of Dante exists in "a way that 'utilities' will not succeed well
in calculating! We will not estimate the Sun by the quantity of gas-
light it saves us; Dante shall be invaluable, or of no value."[184] As to
Shakespeare, what item would we not surrender rather than him?
"Will you give up your Indian Empire or your Shakspeare?" he asked
his fashionable audience. "Indian Empire will go, at any rate, some
day," he judged prophetically, "but this Shakspeare does not go, he
lasts forever with us; we cannot give up our Shakspeare!"[185] Carlyle
concludes this comparison that plays upon the difference between the
immediately powerful and the spiritually enduring with a discussion
of Dante and the Russian czar. Despite his command of infinite bayonets and his binding so vast an area together politically, the czar is still
a "dumb monster" who must learn to speak. "His cannons and Cossacks will all have rusted into nonentity, while that Dante's voice is

---

[181] See note to "The Hero as Poet" at 70.15–17.
[182] *On Heroes*, 85.
[183] *On Heroes*, 95.
[184] *On Heroes*, 85.
[185] *On Heroes*, 96.

still audible. The Nation that has a Dante is bound together as no dumb Russia can be."[186]

The very qualities that produce lasting work unite the great artist with other forms of heroism. For "the Poet who could merely sit on a chair, and compose stanzas, would never make a stanza worth much. He could not sing the Heroic warrior, unless he himself were at least a Heroic warrior too."[187] By *hero-king* Carlyle does not mean "sovereign" in the literal sense, but all "able men." Thus Shakespeare is an "English King, whom no time or chance, Parliament or combination of Parliaments, can dethrone!"[188] Luther's role in the Reformation required a "kingly faculty,"[189] and Knox maintained a "virtual Presidency and Sovereignty" over Scotland.[190]

In the Carlylean meritocracy, men of letters and poets may equally belong to the heroic fraternity. Johnson was, through the influence of his books, effectively the "Primate of England,"[191] and there was no "chancellor, king, senator" in England so momentous as Burns.[192] Skeptics might question whether power would have "changed the rustic rake and thirsty exciseman into a Nero or Caligula,"[193] but the idea of Burns as a statesman retained its appeal for Carlyle, as his friend Tennyson remembered.[194] The artist-hero combines the politician, thinker, legislator, and philosopher; "in one or the other degree, he could have been, he is all these." The reverse is true too, for there is something of the poet in all other heroes. Napoleon has words in him "like Austerlitz Battles," the marshals of Louis XIV were "poetical men," and Mirabeau must have been a great writer had the course of his life led him that way.[195]

VII. The Unsung Hero

One of the critical puzzles of *On Heroes* is the absence of Goethe from Carlyle's roster, for he was to Carlyle the most triumphant example of the modern man of letters as hero, "the first of the

[186] *On Heroes*, 97.
[187] *On Heroes*, 67–68.
[188] *On Heroes*, 97.
[189] *On Heroes*, 118.
[190] *On Heroes*, 128.
[191] *On Heroes*, 140.
[192] "Varnhagen von Ense's Memoirs" (1838), *Essays* 4:116–17.
[193] William Thomson, cited in Seigel, *Critical Heritage*, 181.
[194] Hallam Tennyson, *Memoir* 1:279.
[195] *On Heroes*, 68.

moderns"[196] who had personally inspired Carlyle and "convincingly proclaimed" to him the possibility of heroism even in his own "scandalous" generation.[197] Although Carlyle's ostensible reason for neglecting Goethe was the sheer difficulty of making him fully understood by an English audience,[198] fifteen years later G. H. Lewes would acknowledge Carlyle as the man who "first taught England to appreciate Goethe."[199] In his 1828 essay on Goethe, Carlyle had conceded that his "countrymen" had heard "much of Goethe; but heard, for the most part, what excited and perplexed rather than instructed them." There was then little hope of making Goethe properly known but "only to prove that he is worthy of being known."[200] But for this problem, Carlyle's "chosen specimen of the Hero as Literary Man would be this Goethe," he told his audience in 1840.[201] There is no reason to discount the difficulty raised by Carlyle, yet one remembers that it did not deter him from extensive presentations in essay form of Richter, Schiller, and other German authors no better known in England than Goethe. Nor did Carlyle hesitate in *On Heroes* to present to his London audience the little-understood figures of Odin and Muḥammad. It is true that with his translations and writings on Goethe he felt by 1834 that his labors in the field of German literature had come, if not to an end, at least to a temporary halt, and that his mission of making German literature better known in England had been fulfilled. But three years later he made Goethe the subject of his unscheduled seventh lecture in the 1837 series on German literature, and he spoke on Goethe again in the final lecture of the 1838 series.

One possible explanation for the omission of Goethe, and for what appears on the surface to be a curious lapse, may lie in the intellectual structure of *On Heroes*. In it, Carlyle offers no modern example of the hero as writer. Yet on the stage before their eyes his audience had in their lecturer a clear picture of the inspired writer. With Burns, Rousseau, and Johnson, he came no closer to his own age than the end of the eighteenth century, and all three of these writers were in Carlyle's view crippled by living in an age "all calculated for strangling of heroisms."[202] Yet the implications of what he was saying

[196] *Reminiscences*, 282.
[197] *Letters* 8:39, TC to Ralph Waldo Emerson, February 3, 1835.
[198] *On Heroes*, 136.
[199] Lewes, *Life of Goethe*, ix.
[200] "Goethe" (1828), *Essays* 1:199, 209.
[201] *On Heroes*, 136.
[202] "The Opera" (1852), *Essays* 4:402.

about these heroes carried over from past history into the present world in which he himself struggled to find a prophetic voice. No self-portrait being directly possible, he had to associate himself with his heroic models by extension, by implication, by analogy, and sometimes by way of contrast. To insert Goethe would have been to deal explicitly with a connection which Carlyle preferred to leave unstated but strongly implied.

There is no doubt that by the time of his lectures Carlyle conceived of himself as a writer in the heroic tradition he was describing. Yet when he began lecturing in 1837, Carlyle was unsure whether "there ought to be any such thing as a literary man,"[203] and he doubted whether such a role was compatible with honesty, "Book-writing" being "in a ruined state for all men except quacks."[204] But in the process of preparing and delivering his 1840 lectures, Carlyle clarified his ideas on the literary hero. As he thought about authorship in the context of heroes, and brought his chosen exemplars before his own mind and his audience, he recognized a line of literary kings into which he might fit himself. Rather than money-grubbing quacks, he now conceived writers to be, as he had once, more optimistically, believed, "the only Sovereigns of the world in these days,"[205] a "perpetual priesthood" appointed to interpret the "Divine Idea"[206] and to carry the prophetic torch as "the Fire-pillars in this dark pilgrimage of mankind."[207] Upon the writer, if worthy, devolved by direct lineal descent the mantle of the prophet and the scepter of the sovereign. In the tradition of heroism that Carlyle was establishing, he himself was the latest avatar. Thus while *On Heroes* deals with six types of heroes, "it points inexorably toward a seventh hero—the hero as oneself."[208] In fact, the association of Carlyle with his heroes was sometimes made by his contemporaries. Declaring that Carlyle was "himself the hero, as literary man," Thoreau found in his writing a "direct and effectual teaching . . . almost like Mahomet, like Luther."[209] Modern critics have discerned the same tendency. Wellek suggests that if we "read Carlyle on Jean Paul we feel as if he were speaking of himself," Watt finds a good

---

[203] Froude, *Life in London* 1:130.
[204] *Letters* 9:109, TC to Jean Carlyle Aitken, December 29, 1836.
[205] *Two Notebooks*, 184.
[206] "State of German Literature" (1827), *Essays* 1:58.
[207] "Schiller" (1831), *Essays* 2:166.
[208] Rosenberg, *Seventh Hero*, 202.
[209] Cited in Seigel, *Critical Heritage*, 288, 285.

deal of Carlyle in his portrait of Muḥammad, and Fred Kaplan considers that Carlyle in his last essay "created a portrait of Knox that was unwitting self-portraiture."[210]

Carlyle's presence among his heroes takes many forms. As he struggled to bring his heroic portraits into clear focus he often transferred to himself images he had applied to them. Carlyle's description of brave Samuel Johnson, "a Hercules with the burning Nessus'-shirt on him,"[211] or of Mirabeau, to whom he applied the same classical image,[212] expressed Carlyle's perception of his own predicament and heroic struggles. After completing his lectures on heroes, Carlyle complained that none could "unwrap the baleful Nessus shirt of perpetual pain and isolation in which I am . . . swathed," recalling his earlier and more hopeful vow to make it "almost my sole rule of life: to *clear* myself of Cants and formulas, as of poisonous Nessus' shirts; to *strip* them off me, . . . and follow, were it down to Hades, what I myself know and see."[213] The tragic image of Burns sacrificed to popular adulation with which Carlyle closed the fifth lecture—the poet as a fire-fly on a spit, an allusion to Richter—returned in his letters, now applied to his own predicament as a popular lecturer.[214] A more subtle example of indirect self-definition lies in the relationship of Carlyle's prophet and writer to reality. The sincere writer, like the prophet, saw through trend, fashion, falsehood. The "great Mystery of Existence . . . glared in upon him" as on Muḥammad in the desert fastnesses.[215] The true writer could also be defined by reverse analogy, as in the essay on Sir Walter Scott (1838) where Carlyle defines his own conception of the writer's role by analyzing the limitations of his subject. "The great Mystery of Existence was not great to him; did not drive him into rocky solitudes to wrestle with it for an answer."[216] What Scott is not, Carlyle perceives himself and his heroes to be, for as Meredith observed, "the spirit of the prophet was in him" and he had only contempt for "mere literary aptitude."[217]

---

[210] Wellek, *Confrontations*, 64; Watt, "Carlyle on Muhammad," 254; Kaplan, *Thomas Carlyle*, 513.

[211] *On Heroes*, 153.

[212] *French Revolution* 2:3.7.140.

[213] Froude, *Life in London* 1:185; *Letters* 8:253, TC to JWC, November 22, 1835.

[214] *Letters* 12:141, TC to Thomas Ballantyne, May 11, 1840; see above, p. xxxi; *On Heroes*, 167; and note at 167.9.

[215] *On Heroes*, 47.

[216] "Sir Walter Scott" (1838), *Essays* 4:36.

[217] Meredith, *Letters* 2:661.

Whether his heroes were a partial projection of himself or he an extension of them—ideal selves, or exemplary models for the role he felt himself to be following as heroic and prophetic writer—his very selection of them was the affirmation of a kind of identity. "Show me the man you honour," he wrote, and "I know by that symptom . . . what kind of man you yourself are. For you show me there what your ideal of manhood is; what kind of man you long inexpressibly to be."[218] A. J. P. Taylor has proposed the thesis that the hero Carlyle worshipped "was his own opposite." For he denounced long books, but "no one wrote longer"; he admired honest manual toil but did none himself; he preached the virtues of humble obscurity yet lived and became famous "writing successful books for rich industrialists. The rage in his books is rage against himself. The hero that he worshipped was his own opposite—silent, imperturbable, a man of action."[219] His heroes may have represented his opposite self, his suppressed self, or the artistic mask he adopted in his writings and through which he was able to speak in a certain way. Certainly his estimate of them was highly personal, and he felt there to be a series of connections which linked them to him. The strongest of these links was the view of language which they shared.

VIII. The Heroic Voice

In Caroline Fox's picture of Carlyle as a man "convinced of what he utters, and who had much . . . in him that was quite unutterable,"[220] we catch a glimpse of Carlyle assuming an attitude to speech held by many of his heroes. None of Carlyle's true heroes is eager to speak, but must be forced to do so, compelled by destiny to undertake what is at hand. Only the speech that the speaker is reluctant to speak is worth hearing. The ground plan of his lectures, Carlyle insisted in his concluding talk, was rough-hewn, "I have had to tear it up in the rudest manner in order to get into it at all," and he thanked his distinguished audience for listening patiently to his "rude words."[221] In short, Carlyle, concluding the most eloquent lectures he ever gave, affected an awkwardness and darkness of utterance that associated him with the very strengths he had attributed to his greatest heroes.

His rude style recalls Cromwell's blurted utterances to the Long Parliament, the incondite jumble of Muḥammad's Qur'ān, the taci-

---

[218] Pamphlets, 255.
[219] Taylor, Englishmen, 23.
[220] Fox, Memories, 105; see above, p. xxx.
[221] On Heroes, 209.

turn and rugged simplicity of the speech of Luther and of Knox. Like them he must struggle to bring his words into being out of chaos. His models serve to define his role as he finds himself caught in the act of defining theirs. Their past struggles with surrounding events and howling inner confusion correspond to his struggle to clear the mountains of debris that encumber their memories. It is only by his own heroic effort of intellect that he can bring himself and his listeners to grasp the essential character of his heroes.[222]

The difficulties confronting the Carlylean hero in speaking his mind stem from several sources. As the message is revelatory, and therefore totally new, there can be nothing rehearsed about it, and the speaker is as much astounded by his message as his auditors. The message being God-given, in character if not in literal fact, there is an implicit lack of control, since the speaker is not truly the author but more the vehicle of its expression. Furthermore, he does not frame his speech to delight his audience, entertain, or even take very much account of them. His reason for speaking is not a reason at all but a form of compulsion to discharge a message and unburden himself. Since the message does not precede its utterance, it cannot be rehearsed, and consequently it can have none of the reassuring familiarity of proverbial or generalized wisdom, "what oft was thought but ne'er so well expressed." The half-mad incoherence of Cromwell and the towering awkwardness of Richter are in a continuous tradition uniting Moses and Longinus with such self-denying orators and truth speakers as Marc Antony, the stammering Billy Budd, and, at the more trivial end of the same tradition, the tongue-tied cowboy of Hollywood films.

Such a definition of speech as Carlyle proposes excludes self-conscious oratory, the elegant formulation, and the bon mot. In fact it deliberately shuns them for much the same reasons that led Paul to address the sophisticated Greeks of Corinth "not with wisdom of words."[223] The picture Carlyle offers of Cromwell, the great *"dumb* Prophet"[224] making speeches that are "incondite in phrase and conception,"[225] no doubt reflects the great Puritan's distaste for Cavalier ornament, but it also corresponds to Carlyle's own views of language and lecturing. Cromwell's declaration to Parliament, "I never did affect, nor do, nor I hope shall" propose "to have played the

---

[222] See Murray Baumgarten, "Revolution as Context," 188–89.
[223] 1 Corinthians 1:17.
[224] *On Heroes*, 204.
[225] *Cromwell* 3:167.

Orator,"[226] insists on the same distrust of fine speaking as animated the Puritanically descended Carlyle. Fine speaking is, almost by definition for Carlyle, false speaking. If *hypocrisy*—from *hypocritēs*, "the Greek word for 'actor'"—"be the first, second, and third thing in eloquence," he wrote, "then why have *it* at all? Why not insist, as a first and inexorable condition, that all speech be a reality; that every speaker be verily what he pretends or play-acts to be?" He then offers the contrast of Cromwell's speeches: "So soon as by long scanning you can read them clearly, nowhere in the world did I find such persuasion, such powers of compelling belief, there and then, if you did really hear with open ear and heart."[227] In parallel terms Carlyle finds Luther's quartos "not well written," yet in no other books could he discern "a more robust, genuine, . . . noble faculty."[228]

Cromwell's speeches are difficult to read; that is their merit, the guarantee of their authenticity. "Practical Heroes . . . do not speak in blank-verse. . . . Useless to look here for a Greek Temple with its porticoes and entablatures, and *styles*. But the Alp Mountain, with its chasms and cataracts and shaggy pine-forests, and huge granite masses rooted in the Heart of the World: this too is worth looking at, to some."[229] As in the case of pagan mythology, "superior sincerity . . . consoles us for the total want of old Grecian grace."[230] Carlyle applies a similar set of images to Richter. His is "not an articulate voice, but like the sound of cataracts falling among the wild pine-forests! It goes deep in the human heart."[231] And Luther was great, "not as a hewn obelisk; but as an Alpine mountain."[232] The Classical/Gothic antithesis provided Walt Whitman with the terms he used to describe Carlyle in 1881 as "neither Latin nor Greek, but altogether Gothic. Rugged, mountainous, volcanic."[233]

These images glance backward most immediately to the Romantic crags and chasms of the *Prelude*, Gray's Alpine torrents and cliffs "pregnant with religion and poetry,"[234] and more distantly to the tradition of Longinus and the eighteenth-century sublime. Through such contrasting images Carlyle formulates an aesthetic doctrine that

---

[226] *Cromwell* 3:169.
[227] Froude, *Life in London* 2:385.
[228] *On Heroes*, 119.
[229] *Cromwell* 3:167–68.
[230] *On Heroes*, 27.
[231] *History of Literature*, 222.
[232] *On Heroes*, 122.
[233] Cited in Seigel, *Critical Heritage*, 456.
[234] Gray, *Correspondence* 1:128.

shuns facility as much as classical grace. Carlyle expresses in positive terms what a contemporary journalist perceived only pejoratively when he contrasted Carlyle's "uncouth" manner with the more "polished deportment" fashionable audiences were accustomed to.[235] What emerges is an aesthetic contrast between smooth classicism and rough-hewn Gothic integrity. Roughness, organic form, and veracity are Carlyle's central criteria, not conventional polish, fluency, or grace. Works like Thiers's history of the French Revolution may convey a "superficial air of order" but "inwardly, it is waste, inorganic,"[236] in diametric contrast to Cromwell's outwardly confused and jumbled speech that was lit by an inner clarity. Cromwell's speeches are "chaotic," but the superficial histories and biographies of him, however smoothly written, "are far more *obscure.*"[237] Carlyle further extends the distinction into a contrast between creation and manufacture. Creation is inherently difficult for the prophet and the writer whose message is heavily charged with meaning. It "cannot be easy; your Jove has severe pains, and fire-flames, in the head out of which an armed Pallas is struggling! As for manufacture," he contemptuously observes, "that is a different matter."[238]

IX. History and Hero-worship

The most frequent critical issues raised by *On Heroes* are the problem of structure presented by the last two lectures and the attempt to resolve apparent contradictions in Carlyle's theory of heroism. The first problem is that the general chronological movement Carlyle traces throughout *On Heroes* is interrupted by his penultimate lecture on the eighteenth-century "man of letters." This is followed in the final lecture by a return to the seventeenth century for an extended account of Cromwell and his times. A strictly chronological arrangement would have put Cromwell after Luther, thus substituting the sixth for the fifth lecture, and would have concluded the series with the eighteenth century and the few words Carlyle devoted to that "portentous mixture" of quack and hero, Napoleon.[239] Carlyle's failure to do so has disconcerted numerous critics, who contend that as Cromwell is not a "modern hero," his "presence in the final lecture

---

235 Cited in Wilson, *Carlyle on Cromwell*, 86.
236 "Parliamentary History of the French Revolution" (1837), *Essays* 4:3.
237 *On Heroes*, 201.
238 "Sir Walter Scott" (1838), *Essays* 4:80.
239 *On Heroes*, 204.

smashes the general chronological pattern," leading to the "collapse of the general framework" of the book.[240] Had Carlyle's overriding concern been with chronology, such objections would be irresistible.

However, the chronological framework was essentially artificial, a matter of convenience suggested by the six-part format of the lectures. Thematically and polemically it is probably more useful to regard the last two lectures as a continuous unit, since they are, after all, bound together by Carlyle's conception of modernity. Both the man of letters and the king, as Carlyle defines them, are modern forms of heroism. Carlyle's Cromwell is a "post-revolutionary King who comes to impose an order upon Sansculotism. He is . . . a King of the future, not of the past, and the fact that England had its revolution in the seventeenth century does not matter in this essentially philosophical development."[241] Taking this view of the series, Cromwell is still out of time, but he is not out of place. He stands as a shining example to Carlyle's nineteenth-century audience, and beyond that to the world Carlyle wished to address, of heroic possibility. Monarchs were in fact fleeing their thrones in the decade of Carlyle's lecture, but what Carlyle meant by the king as a modern hero was the "Able-man" of whom Cromwell was modern history's best example. Cromwell embodied Carlyle's hope that despite the dismal showing of heroism in the eighteenth century, some revolutionary revival of the heroic spirit was still possible. Cromwell as hero is not for Carlyle a distant historical figure separated by two hundred years from Carlyle and his audience. Carlyle's view of history was less concerned with the pastness of the past than with its continuing presence. He actively sought the effect produced on Friedrich Althaus: "It is just as if we were not modern descendants, divided from them by a gulf of two hundred years of history, but rather contemporaries of those men and parties, the Roundheads and the Cavaliers, the Independents and the Levellers, . . . Charles I and Cromwell."[242] Carlyle viewed history as exemplary and valued it for its relevance. Thus, he wrote to Emerson, "do the two centuries stand related to me, the seventeenth *worthless* except precisely in so far as it can be made the *nineteenth*."[243] Not only is history seen as *magister vitae*, but it is only worthwhile if it is preoccupied with what is alive and relevant. In this way Cromwell could speak to the nineteenth century as could no hero from the eighteenth.

[240] LaValley, *Carlyle and the Idea of the Modern*, 251.
[241] Culler, *Victorian Mirror of History*, 70.
[242] Clubbe, *Two Reminiscences*, 104.
[243] *Letters* 15:57, August 29, 1842.

By ignoring the prophets of Israel and Greece, and by beginning his historical survey with Odin, a figure lying in mythological prehistory, Carlyle had clearly abandoned any strictly calibrated chronological scheme before he started his lectures on heroes, preferring instead a scheme broadly suggestive and representative of heroic types and societies. This scheme has a thematic depth and a conceptual unity lacking from the strictly chronological ordering of his previous lecture series.

Though Carlyle did not allow chronology to become the determining factor in *On Heroes*, his schema does imply an evolutionary process in the history of ideas and beliefs. Paganism is the "infant Thought of man,"[244] while the replacement of the divine hero by the divinely inspired prophet represents a "second phasis of Hero-worship."[245] This forward movement is deflected from time to time by historical countercurrents. As society advances and becomes more sophisticated it makes certain heroic forms obsolete. The hero as god and prophet are the "productions of old ages; not to be repeated in the new. They presuppose a certain rudeness of conception, which the progress of mere scientific knowledge puts an end to."[246] Later Carlyle adds poets and priests to the list of outmoded heroic forms, so that the only two modern forms of heroism are those described in his two final lectures, the man of letters and king. Not only are older heroic forms made obsolete, but as society advances the role of the hero diminishes, though the full effects of this restrictive process are not felt until Carlyle brings the modern period into the center of his discussion.

In contrast to the buoyant evolutionary vision of Darwin, Carlyle's historical pattern presents a pessimistic, descending scale. The heroic form contracts with time, and evolving social conditions make it increasingly difficult for the heroic spirit to manifest itself, so that as Carlyle nears his own age he is forced to concentrate on the conditions that inhibit the growth of heroism. In 1840 he entertained some hope that this pattern might be reversed, but by 1850 he saw heroic values actually inverted, so that George Hudson the Railway "king" became, in *Latter-Day Pamphlets*, the object of veneration for a Mammon-worshipping society, in place of the Cromwell who had been the central figure of his final lecture. Two years later, yielding still further to a sense of pessimism, his answer to the question "Why heroes are not born now, why heroisms are not done now?" was that

[244] *On Heroes*, 18.
[245] *On Heroes*, 37.
[246] *On Heroes*, 67.

the world had become a place "all calculated for strangling of hero-isms. At every ingress into life, the genius of the world lies in wait for heroisms, and by seduction or compulsion unweariedly does its ut-most to pervert them or extinguish them."[247]

Yet another configuration in the pattern of history Carlyle weaves is marked by revolutionary outbreaks in which essentially idolatrous beliefs are violently destroyed and replaced by genuine vision. Many of Carlyle's heroes are necessary iconoclasts. Muḥammad breaks the wooden idols of Arabia just as Luther offers the "first stroke of honest demolition" to a papacy "grown false and idolatrous," while Puri-tanism resists the hollow ceremonies of Laud, and the French Revo-lution burns up the imposture of the age of reason. On the wide spectrum of history, the Reformation was the potential begetter of a "new genuine sovereignty" because it too was a revolt against "*false sovereigns.*"[248]

The problem of consistency in Carlyle's theory of heroism most often turns on his heroes' relation to ordinary people and to the historical situation. The problem of the hero in history stems from the paradox that allows Carlyle to combine "a determinist view of history with a belief in willed effort." He both exhorts and condemns "men as though they were wholly responsible for their views and actions, yet he holds too that they are trapped in history." It is, of course, true that "more systematic minds than Carlyle's have been baffled by this problem."[249]

On the evidence of *On Heroes* alone, Carlyle's answer to the ques-tion, Do heroes create historical events? is both yes and no. Their superior insights, and the actions based on them, crystallize what is merely latent. Heroes provide a dramatic impetus to events. They are not merely creatures of the age in which they live. At the same time they do not act in a vacuum or in social isolation. Others feel more dimly what they perceive most sharply. Their effect upon others is like that of a catalyst or, in Carlyle's metaphor, a lightning rod or conduc-tor. There is then a dynamic balance between human will and the forces of the age. The difficulty Carlyle confronts and acknowledges is thus more of a true paradox than a flat contradiction.

In rejecting materialistic theories of history Carlyle stressed the importance of the individual, but he was not blind to the fact that the hero was restricted and conditioned by surrounding forces. In *On*

[247] "The Opera" (1852), *Essays* 4:402.
[248] *On Heroes*, 106.
[249] Daiches, "Carlyle: The Paradox Reconsidered," 380.

Heroes he says that history is at bottom the "Biography of great men,"[250] but elsewhere he wrote that history was the aggregate of innumerable biographies. This aggregate includes the legion of those whose only record may be the date of their birth in parish registers. From time to time some incident may illuminate one of them, like the poor rustic who shared food and shoes with Charles I or the foolish laird who became famous because he recognized a hero in the form of an eccentric writer in a garret in Gough Street.

The Carlylean hero does not create history out of titanic will, but rather responds to the monitions and the forces alive in his world. The "Reformation simply could not help coming," but Luther was its voice and its instrument. Had his resolution failed at the Diet of Worms, the course of modern history "had all been otherwise!"[251] But Luther, like all Carlyle's heroes, is initially reluctant to assume the burden of conflict and does so only when drawn into the ring of action by moral compulsion. A parallel can be seen in the life of Luther's modern-day counterpart, Dietrich Bonhoeffer, who with his "somewhat ponderous, theologically orientated mind . . . was . . . edged, inch by inch . . . into becoming an authentic hero of his time."[252] Cromwell's mission too is launched only in response to events he did not himself shape. "After twelve years silent waiting, all England stirs itself; there is to be once more a Parliament." Only then did Cromwell throw "down his ploughs" and hasten onto the stage of history.[253] Before a prophet like Muḥammad can arise, "many men must have begun dimly to doubt" the value of old forms of worship.[254] What the hero says, "all men were not far from saying."[255] The hero is thus time-bound and culture-bound, but hears more clearly than others the promptings of the age and directs its struggles. It is this ability to recognize reality in the midst of convention and falsehood that raises the hero to the heroic level. The hero's distinguishing mark is an informing intelligence, an insight that reveals, as it does to Luther, "the awful realities of things."[256] A Knox cannot live "but by fact,"[257] or a Muḥammad evade a reality that "glared in

---

[250] *On Heroes*, 26.
[251] *On Heroes*, 116.
[252] Muggeridge, *Third Testament*, 189.
[253] *On Heroes*, 194.
[254] *On Heroes*, 105.
[255] *On Heroes*, 20.
[256] *On Heroes*, 105.
[257] *On Heroes*, 127.

upon him."[258] For the hero, "fly as he will . . . cannot get out of the awful presence of this Reality."[259]

The effect the hero achieves is like that of the inspired poet, "the *original* man, the Seer; whose shaped spoken Thought awakes the slumbering capability of all into Thought."[260] The hero sums up and completes a general will and impulse; his actions merely authenticate a commonly held sentiment. These relations between heroes and those to whom they speak are reciprocal. To shudder at the hell of Dante is to become a poet; we are all poets when we read a poem well, all heroes when we recognize heroism.

As Carlyle traces the development of the religious sentiment he calls hero-worship, the eighteenth century is thrown into prominence by way of contrast. The towering heroes of earlier periods were the beneficiaries of eras of strenuous faith. The eighteenth century is a spiritual wasteland and even the status of its heroes is sadly diminished. Rousseau, philosophical harbinger of the French Revolution, is a *"contracted* Hero,"[261] Voltaire is a "withered Pontiff of Encyclopedism,"[262] helping to kill superstition, but unable to provide a positive alternative to the system of beliefs he had undermined. Even Johnson could offer only the advice of "Moral Prudence" and the rejection of cant,[263] while Napoleon's heroism was tainted by an admixture of quackery. The eighteenth century is, in this sense, thematically crucial, for there Carlyle traces the societal beginnings of the paralysis that had penetrated his own time. Earlier heroes contended with adversities enough. The banished Locke wrote his *Essay Concerning Human Understanding* in a Dutch garret, Milton was impoverished and endangered when he wrote *Paradise Lost*, and Cervantes was maimed and imprisoned yet finished his work. All possessed what Burns and more modern heroes lacked—they lived in a period "in which heroism and devotedness were still practised, or at least not yet disbelieved in."[264] For them it was not true, as Carlyle could say of his own time, that the godhead had been replaced by an "iron, ignoble circle of Necessity" and that all "Heroic Action is paralysed."[265] However, even the arid soil of the eighteenth century could not

[258] *On Heroes*, 47.
[259] *On Heroes*, 40.
[260] *On Heroes*, 20.
[261] *On Heroes*, 159.
[262] *On Heroes*, 14.
[263] *On Heroes*, 156.
[264] "Burns" (1828), *Essays* 1:312–13.
[265] "Characteristics" (1831), *Essays* 3:30.

entirely extinguish hero-worship. Boswell was a "practical witness, or real *martyr*, to this high everlasting truth."[266] The skeptical French worshipped their Voltaire; the "old antediluvian feeling," forcing itself "into unexpected shapes, asserts its existence in the newest man: and the Chaldeans or old Persians, with their Zerdusht, differ only in vesture and dialect from the French, with their Voltaire."[267] Precisely because of the cramped conditions of modern spiritual life, hero-worship becomes the "one fixed point in modern revolutionary history."[268]

Though Carlyle derived the idea of hero-worship from history, it was for him essentially an article of faith. He found it "cheering to consider that no sceptical logic, or general triviality, insincerity and aridity of any Time and its influences can destroy this noble inborn loyalty and worship."[269] The feeling for it might decline, might attach itself to unworthy objects, but hero-worship remained an unfailing fact of human experience and the basis of social organization. "Veneration of great men is perennial in the nature of man. . . . Show the dullest clodpole, show the haughtiest featherhead, that a soul higher than himself is actually here; were his knees stiffened into brass, he must down and worship." Hero-worship was the primary creed and would prove to be the ultimate creed of mankind. Like the protean hero, "changing in shape, but in essence unchangeable,"[270] hero-worship was the guarantee of social survival even in an age pulled apart by social disruptions, revolutionary tendencies, and false ideologies. The darkness of unbelief would promote revolutions, but Carlyle saw in the "indestructibility of Hero-worship the everlasting adamant lower than which the confused wreck of revolutionary things cannot fall." In his own revolutionary time the ruin would "get down so far; *no* farther."[271] The perennial feeling of hero-worship "waits, even in these dead days, only for occasions to unfold it, and inspire all men with it, and again make the world alive!"[272]

Hero-worship is just as important as the heroism it admires and fosters by its acknowledgment. To recognize the hero is itself a form of heroism, and is possible only "by being ourselves of heroic mind."[273] Carlyle's lectures themselves were a demonstration of hero-worship in

---

[266] "Boswell's Life of Johnson" (1832), *Essays* 3:74.
[267] "Goethe's Works" (1832), *Essays* 2:391.
[268] *On Heroes*, 15.
[269] *On Heroes*, 14.
[270] "Sir Walter Scott" (1838), *Essays* 4:24.
[271] *On Heroes*, 14–15.
[272] "Boswell's Life of Johnson" (1832), *Essays* 3:74.
[273] *Past and Present*, 35.

action. Through his own heroic vision of the past which he asked his audience to grasp, he made it possible to put the question to them, "why may not every one of us be a Hero?"[274] What he sought was a heroic audience, the microcosm of a heroic society, that had once existed "as a practised fact."[275] What was needed to summon it again into existence was not only a hero "but a world fit for him,"[276] an exhortation recalled perhaps in David Lloyd George's appeal, in a speech in September 1914, "to make Britain a fit country for heroes to live in."[277] This was one of the aims of the lectures, to make society receptive to the idea of the hero, to make it ready to "be worthy." Then, and only then, we shall "be as good as sure of his arriving; sure of many things, let him arrive or not."[278] As he looked back over modern history, Carlyle saw events moving toward some yet unrealized goal. "In all this wild revolutionary work, from Protestantism downwards, I see the blessedest result preparing itself: not abolition of Hero-worship, but rather what I would call a whole World of Heroes. . . . A world all sincere, a believing world." In this hope, the past was the prophetic guarantor of the future world he anticipated, for such a world had already been, and its "like will again be,—cannot help being."[279] Like Tennyson's Ulysses, he gestured his audience to the prospect of the Happy Isles where all heroes dwell, "and will dwell: thither, all ye heroic-minded!"[280]

X. THE RESPONSE TO ON HEROES

In June 1841 John Ruskin wrote from Geneva to enquire about "these Carlyle lectures." People, he said, are "making a fuss about them, and from what I see in the reviews, they seem absolute bombast."[281] Given the feeble and scanty reports of the lectures that filtered through to him, this reaction was reasonable enough, as was Ruskin's conclusion that Carlyle sounded remarkably like Dickens's Horatio Sparkins. Ruskin compared Carlyle's, "What *is* it? Ay, what? At bottom we do not yet know; we can never know at all,"[282] which had been quoted in one of the reviews that had reached him, to

[274] *On Heroes*, 109.
[275] *On Heroes*, 124.
[276] *On Heroes*, 186.
[277] Bartlett, *Familiar Quotations*, 866.
[278] *Past and Present*, 260.
[279] *On Heroes*, 109.
[280] *Past and Present*, 37.
[281] Ruskin, *Works* 36:25.
[282] *On Heroes*, 8.

Sparkins's "And after all, sir, what is man? . . . I say, we know that we exist. . . . What more do we know?"[283] In the summer of 1842, however, Ruskin was able to read the book for himself at Chamonix. Evidently the impact of the written work was enough to efface his original bad impression, for in 1854, in his "Addresses on Decorative Colour," he made his first public admission that Carlyle was the man to whom he "owed more than to any other living writer" and he quoted extensively from Carlyle's first lecture on divinity. In a letter published in 1867 Ruskin said, "I only speak of myself together with him as a son might speak of his father and himself, not on any term of other equality." In 1878 he was still making use of *On Heroes*, for he wrote to Carlyle, calling him "My dearest Papa," to say he was studying him along with Gibbon on Muḥammad.[284]

Edward FitzGerald greeted the first edition of *On Heroes* with derision. "No new books," he wrote to Frederick Tennyson on March 21, 1841, "(except a perfectly insane one of Carlyle, who is becoming very obnoxious now that he is become popular.)" A few days later he wrote to W. H. Thompson: "Have you read poor Carlyle's raving book about heroes? Of course you have—or I would ask you to buy my copy. I don't like to live with it in the house. It smoulders."[285] By 1876 he had revised his estimate. To C. E. Norton he recalled that he had heard Carlyle lecture: "I heard his 'Heroes' which now seems to me one of his best Books"; and he speculated on "what a Fortune" Carlyle might have made by "showing himself about as a Lecturer, as Thackeray and Dickens did."[286]

One measure of the book is the variety and quality of the minds it affected. Richard Garnett claims that *On Heroes* was "echoed by all the best minds" of Carlyle's day and that it destroyed the "shallow sneer" that "no one is a hero to his valet-de-chambre."[287] Of course, it is not always possible to separate *On Heroes* from other works that represented Carlyle in the public mind, for when *On Heroes* was first published Carlyle's name "was running like wildfire through the British Islands and through English-speaking America; there was the utmost avidity for his books . . . especially among the young men; phrases from them were in all young men's mouths."[288] Carlyle's influence at the old universities was considerable. Macaulay, warily regarding the

[283] Dickens, *Sketches by Boz*, 360; see Ruskin, *Works* 36:25.
[284] Ruskin, *Works* 12:507; 17:476; 37:248–49.
[285] FitzGerald, *Letters* 1:272, 276.
[286] FitzGerald, *Letters* 3:650–51.
[287] Garnett, *Life of Carlyle*, 102.
[288] Masson, *Carlyle Personally*, 67.

Oxford of 1859 where his nephew was an undergraduate, feared that he was living in the "midst of an atmosphere reeking with Carlylism,"[289] although in 1843 *On Heroes* in particular seems to have run afoul of Oxford's academic authorities. Responding with unconcealed amazement to a report on conditions at the university by Henry Cary, the Dante translator who had just retired from the British Museum, Elizabeth Barrett Browning wrote, "Carlyle's Hero-worship to be cast out!! Is it not the open confession that nobody there is a hero, or wishes to be a hero, or cares for anybody who *is*? I think so."[290] The editors of her letters to Mary Russell Mitford surmise that the "rejection of Carlyle's book may have been based on objections to the 'romanticism' of his chapter on the Hero as Divinity or, more generally, on the anti-dogmatic and anti-establishment cast of his religious ideas."[291]

Carlyle's appeal was not confined to the Victorian intelligentsia. He was also, in Yeats's words, the "chief inspirer of self-educated men in the 'eighties and early 'nineties,"[292] a fact reflected in Samuel Butler's *The Way of All Flesh* (1903), where Ernest Pontifex is assured that he will "make a kind of Carlyle sort of a man some day."[293] Nor was the influence of this book confined to the English-speaking world, as the innumerable editions of the work in languages ranging from Chinese to Hebrew testify. Vincent van Gogh wrote to his brother Theo in 1883 that he had "read a very beautiful little book of Carlyle's: 'Heroes and Hero-worship.'"[294] Van Gogh's diaries and letters refer quite frequently to Carlyle, in whose work he found "much more of love for mankind than bitter criticism. Carlyle has learned a great deal from Goethe, but even more from a certain MAN who did not write books himself but whose words, though not written down, still remain—I mean Jesus."[295]

From the first appearance of *On Heroes* in book form, in 1841, the response of reviewers was tied to the fluctuations in Carlyle's general reputation, and also to broad trends in the climate of opinion. Both of these factors shaped critical reaction to the book's contents. The main topic raised by contemporary reviewers was the "great man"

---

[289] Macaulay, *Letters* 6:206.
[290] Browning, *Letters* 2:176.
[291] Browning, *Letters* 2:177–78n.
[292] Yeats, *Autobiographies*, 264.
[293] Butler, *Way of All Flesh*, 358.
[294] Van Gogh, *Letters to His Brother* 2:314.
[295] Van Gogh, *Letters to an Artist*, 138.

view of history, which came under suspicion initially from the democratic side of the Victorian political spectrum. It was also questioned by clerical and scientific critics for somewhat different reasons. The gospel of heroes met resistance from nineteenth-century liberalism for ignoring the masses; from Engels, at least, among nineteenth-century Marxists for being too religious and mystical; from some segments of the established church for being too radical; and later from some twentieth-century democrats for being too tyrannical. Over succeeding decades, this central idea tended also to run afoul of other theoretical fashions in politics, science, and history.

On the political front, *On Heroes* has been assailed for being on the extreme political right, and proto-fascist, and equally on the extreme left as a close relative of militant Chartism. On the whole the main complaint of nineteenth-century democrats was made in the name of the excluded many, against the perceived exclusivity of Carlyle's heroes, whereas early and mid-twentieth-century democrats directed their complaints against Carlyle's assumed ideological affinities with fascism. In either case, criticism tended to fix upon Carlyle's two statements in "The Hero as Divinity," that the "History of the world is but the Biography of great men," and that universal history "is at bottom the History of the Great Men who have worked here."[296] This clear enunciation of the "great man theory of history" has frequently been taken out of context or simply left to stand as Carlyle's last or only word on the subject. One needs to recall that ten years earlier, in "On History" (1830), he had offered a more democratic and broadly based conception of history: "Social Life is the aggregate of all the individual men's Lives who constitute society; History is the essence of innumerable Biographies."[297] Even in *On Heroes* itself the "innumerable biographies" are not discounted, but for obvious reasons they are off center stage. However, their presence is implied in the reciprocating relationship between hero and hero-worshipper and in the ordinary deficient mortal's representative, Boswell.

One of the earliest democratically inspired objections to *On Heroes* came from the Italian patriot Giuseppe Mazzini, who knew Carlyle. History, insisted Mazzini, directly confuting Carlyle, "is not the biography of great men." Great men are the priests of the religion of humanity but no priest "is equal in the balance to the whole religion of which he is a minister." For Mazzini, Carlyle comprehended "only

[296] *On Heroes*, 26, 3.
[297] "On History" (1830), *Essays* 2:86.

the individual; the true sense of the unity of the human race escapes him."[298] Thus the

> nationality of Italy in his eyes is the glory of having produced Dante . . . of Germany that of having given birth to Luther. . . . The shadow thrown by these gigantic men appears to eclipse from his view every trace of the national thought of which these men were only the interpreters and prophets, and of the people, who alone are its depository.[299]

The consequence of Carlyle's perceived inability to recognize any collective life or aim condemned him to "regard as the offspring of individual impulse, deeds, which others recognise as having derived their source or inspiration from the wants and desires of the multitude." In the "name of the democratic spirit of the age," declared Mazzini, "I protest against such views."[300]

Mazzini's response is a typical one, recurring frequently in later estimates of *On Heroes*, whether sympathetic or hostile. Whitman too articulated the undemocratic implications of Carlyle's hero theory: "The great masses of humanity stand for nothing—at least nothing but nebulous raw material; only the big planets and shining suns for him."[301] It was an inevitable consequence of Carlyle's exalting his heroes that he should appear to diminish his fellows, for "if Gulliver is to be a giant, he must go to Lilliput." Yet as Leslie Stephen pointed out, one may accept that the "chosen few tower above the average" and still "hold to the superior wisdom of the mass." Not that Carlyle accepted the doctrine that "though a man may be wiser than anybody there is something wiser than he—namely, everybody."[302]

Lord Morley kept these familiar objections alive in the latter part of the nineteenth century. In his general account of Carlyle's thought he also points to Carlyle's "deficiency of sympathy with masses of men," and his willingness to "fall down before the individual." For Morley's Carlyle the "victorious hero is the true Paraclete. . . . This is really the kernel," he says, "of the Carlylean doctrine. The whole human race toils and moils, straining and energising, doing and suffering things multitudinous and unspeakable under the sun, in order that like the aloe-tree it may once in a hundred years produce a

---

[298] Mazzini, *Essays*, 126, 124.
[299] Mazzini, *Essays*, 125.
[300] Mazzini, *Essays*, 152–53, 125.
[301] Whitman, *Prose Works* 1:256.
[302] Stephen, *Hours in a Library* 4:268.

flower. It is this hero that age offers to age, and the wisest worship him."[303]

Although their relationship cooled somewhat in later years, John Stuart Mill was by his own acknowledgment "during a long period one of [Carlyle's] most fervent admirers." Carlyle's works were one of the channels through which he "received the influences which enlarged my early narrow creed."[304] By natural sympathy Mill was drawn to Carlyle's hero theory as an account of individual genius, but characteristically he qualified it with the standard checks and balances formula of nineteenth-century political liberalism. "Hero worship, as Carlyle calls it, is doubtless a fine thing," he wrote, "but then it must be the worship not of a hero but of heroes. . . . One hero and sage is necessary to correct another."[305] In his 1832 speculations on genius, Mill anticipated the Carlylean thought frequently asserted in *On Heroes*, and particularly in "The Hero as King,"[306] that in the modern age the hero might be becoming an endangered species and that society was perhaps supplying its "deficiency of giants" by "the united efforts of a constantly increasing multitude of dwarfs."[307] Mill was as much concerned at the tyranny of the majority, the "collective mediocrity," as he was by the tyranny of the despot. He freely acknowledged that "the initiation of all wise or noble things" came from individuals, "generally at first from some one individual. The honour and glory of the average man," he wrote in terms reminiscent of Carlyle's hero-worshipper, "is that he is capable of following that initiative; that he can respond internally to wise and noble things, and be led to them with his eyes open." Of course, Mill made it clear that he was not "countenancing the sort of 'hero-worship' which applauds the strong man of genius for forcibly seizing on the government of the world and making it do his bidding in spite of itself."[308]

Matthew Arnold read and responded favorably to Carlyle when he was at Oxford as an undergraduate in 1841. Among the many voices in the air at that time was the "puissant voice of Carlyle," a voice that still haunted Arnold's memory forty years later.[309] He shared Carlyle's

---

[303] Morley, *Critical Miscellanies* 1:186, 189–90.
[304] Mill, *Autobiography and Literary Essays*, 183, 181.
[305] Mill, *Letters* 2:384.
[306] See note at 174.34–35.
[307] Mill, *Autobiography and Literary Essays*, 330.
[308] Mill, "On Liberty," *Essays on Politics*, 268–69.
[309] See Arnold's "Emerson" in *Philistinism in England and America*, 165–66; Kathleen Tillotson, "Matthew Arnold and Carlyle," 218–25, which re-creates the atmosphere at Oxford in the 1840s; and David J. DeLaura, "Arnold and Carlyle," 104–29, which deals with the ambivalence of Arnold's response to the older writer.

perception of the unheroic spirit of the modern age. In his assessment of the dispiriting condition of modernity, Arnold noted, in a letter to Arthur Clough, "the absence of great *natures*" and "the unavoidable contact with millions of small ones"—a Carlylean point about the decline of heroism. However, in the same letter, Carlyle, once the "beloved man," had become for Arnold one of the "moral despera-does," and a part of the problem.[310] One might have thought that Arnold's diagnosis of the age, which is compatible with Carlyle's, and his comparable yearning for a heroic temper to replace modern en-ervation would predispose him to a more enthusiastic view of Carlyle's heroes. But Arnold's changing estimates of Carlyle reveal that as time went on he felt Carlyle could not save him from those very conditions that Carlyle had first exposed and brought to his attention. With Clough, Arnold felt that Carlyle had led his contemporaries "out into the desert," and "left us there."[311]

In Thomas Hughes's novel *Tom Brown at Oxford* (1861), Tom is a "sedulous believer" in "hero worship," a fact that probably reflects popular opinion at Oxford when Hughes himself was there some twenty years earlier in the decade of Carlyle's lectures, although the novel also contains allusions to Carlyle's later works. A fellow student describes Tom as longing for the "rule of the ablest man. . . . To find your ablest man, and then give him power, and obey him—that you hold to be about the highest act of wisdom which a nation can be capable of?"[312] Tom eagerly assents to the proposition, whose terms are drawn largely from Carlyle's lecture on the hero as king. The heroic governor as an alternative to Victorian democracy had an obvious appeal to those Victorians who associated democratic aspiration with revolutionary turmoil and mob violence. For many people the Char-tist movement in the 1840s awakened memories of the French Revo-lution and provided an immediate focus and urgency to Carlylean calls for the emergence of new Cromwells and Napoleons. They shared Carlyle's hope that the heroic leader would be a bulwark against social disintegration, and that hero-worship, by evoking loyalty for a common leader, would counteract the antisocial forces of personal rather than communal ambition.

[310] Arnold, *Letters to Clough*, 75, 111.
[311] Arnold, *Letters to Clough*, 47.
[312] Hughes, *Tom Brown at Oxford*, 405.

Some Victorians who were willing to follow Carlyle in his admiration for earlier strongmen, including Cromwell and Napoleon, drew back from his later support of Dr. Francia and Governor Eyre, fearing, as John Davidson did later, that Carlylean hero-worship pointed to the "dull hell of the drill-sergeant and the knout."[313] These later enthusiasms are often represented as aspects of Carlylean degeneration, the corruption through age and frustration of his more vigorous early ideas. However, it has also been argued, most recently by Raymond Williams, that even the heroes of Carlyle's 1840 lectures reflect his "steady withdrawal from genuinely social thinking into the preoccupations with personal power."[314] Out of isolation and a sense of frustration, combined with a belief in his superior insight into the problems of his time, Carlyle creates "the image of the hero, 'the strong man who stands alone,' . . . the leader possessed by vision, who shall be listened to, revered, obeyed." This image is often explained in terms of personal psychology—Carlyle's "impotence projecting itself as power"—but, as Williams points out, this is to ignore both the general nature of the phenomenon and the question of the ends for which the power is wanted. In Carlyle's case these "purposes are positive and ennobling," but as Williams sees it Carlyle's tragedy is that he succumbs at last to the disease he was among the first to diagnose. Thus Carlyle's judgment of early Victorian society in "Signs of the Times," "we worship and follow after Power,"[315] returns to his later efforts "as a mocking echo."[316]

Whatever Carlyle's own relationship, politically and psychologically, to his heroes, *On Heroes* seemed somewhat reactionary to many, certainly the more fervent of nineteenth-century democrats. To certain elements in the established church, however, it appeared politically subversive. By a curious coincidence, observed William Thomson in a review in the *Christian Remembrancer* of 1843, all Carlyle's heroes "offend against magistrate, priest, or law." This high Tory sentiment led Thomson to the estimate that in Carlyle's work "true heroism, it seems, is a nearer relation to chartism, and corn-law-leaguerism, than most persons suspect."[317] The supposed affinities of *On Heroes* with the far left and the Chartist agitation of the 1840s was

[313] Davidson, *Theatocrat*, 14–15.
[314] Raymond Williams, *Culture and Society*, 83.
[315] "Signs of the Times" (1829), *Essays* 2:79.
[316] Raymond Williams, *Culture and Society*, 77.
[317] Cited in Seigel, *Critical Heritage*, 186, 185.

a critical aberration of the decade itself, and was only overshadowed in the history of the book's reception by later political claims of its affinities with the far right and with twentieth-century fascism.

An important if odd feature of the critical response to *On Heroes* is how much of it has focused not on what Carlyle actually wrote but rather on what he was assumed to have written. Sometimes this results from importing into the discussion of *On Heroes* expressions from later works or actions. Thus T. H. Huxley, writing in 1866 to Charles Kingsley over the Governor Eyre case, characterized his opponents as "hero-worshippers who believe that the world is to be governed by its great men, who are to lead the little ones, justly if they can; but if not, unjustly drive or kick them the right way."[318] This sentiment appears nowhere in *On Heroes*, and is a gross parody of isolated statements in "Occasional Discourse on the Negro Question" (1849) and *Latter-Day Pamphlets* (1850), but Huxley, while not naming *On Heroes*, evokes its central doctrine to disparage Carlyle, who supported Governor Eyre's brutal suppression of an uprising in Jamaica in 1865. A similar example of telescoping appears in Leonard Woolf's claim that Carlyle's "bias towards savagery is shown not only by his theory of hero-worship, but by the heroes whom he worshipped." They were, in Woolf's view, "all ruffians, the best of them belonging to that class of great conquerors who have always been . . . the greatest pests in human history."[319] It hardly needs pointing out that Woolf's "ruffians" are not members of the team Carlyle assembled in *On Heroes*, and it comes as no surprise to discover that for Woolf the worst of Carlyle's heroes is Governor Eyre. Another factor in the often blurred reaction to *On Heroes* may be the vehemence of Carlyle's conversation, in which he expressed himself with more exaggeration and violence than he did in print. As his prominence grew, his every gesture of impatience, every extempore utterance, was preserved and given weight. If we can rely on Margaret Fuller's record of an encounter between Mazzini and Carlyle in 1846, "all Carlyle's talk that evening was a defence of mere force, success the test of right. If people would not behave well, put collars round their necks. Find a hero, and let them be his slaves. It was very Titanic and Anticelestial." Mazzini, she reports, "after some efforts to remonstrate, became very sad."[320]

---

[318] Huxley, *Life and Letters* 1:304.
[319] Woolf, *Quack*, 123–24.
[320] Cited in Froude, *Life in London* 1:402.

Whatever the value of these speculations, the fact remains that no evidence can in any way be derived from *On Heroes* itself for the belief that Carlyle's hero represents unbridled force, the doctrine that might is right, or the notion that the only criterion for the hero is success. Nor do such parodies take into account Carlyle's belief that only a man who conforms to the law of God's universe can "in the long-run have any 'might,'"[321] for "Moral Force . . . is the parent of all other Force."[322] Thus Carlyle's heroes are not "Nietzschean supermen . . . beyond good and evil, but rather instruments of God's will, executors of a decree which is not of their choosing."[323] Such determined misconceptions of Carlyle's views may have come from his conversation, fairly reported or not: Darwin, after having met Carlyle, noted that "in his eyes might was right,"[324] and in 1881 Lord Acton remarked that the "doctrine of heroes, the doctrine that will is above law, comes next in atrocity to the doctrine that the flag covers the goods."[325] Nevertheless, a decade earlier Sir Leslie Stephen had been at pains to expose the shallowness of the frequently made charge that "Carlyle was a cynic who believed in nothing but brute force." He wondered how a "doctrine . . . implying an unqualified belief in the absolute supremacy of right" could "get itself transmuted into an appearance of the opposite, of being a kind of Hobbism, deducing all morality from sheer force?"[326] It was too often assumed that Carlyle espoused the cause of unregulated power, or, as A. R. Orage put it, "the Prussian error of identifying Might with Right."[327] It was an error that was to reappear with renewed vehemence in estimates of Carlyle in the period of the two world wars.

Stephen's attempts at correction reveal that there were many Victorian anticipations of the sort of objections to Carlyle's hero-worship that were to become popular in the 1940s and 1950s. Charles Reade's bitter comment in *"It Is Never Too Late to Mend"* (1856), that the brutal prison governor Hawes after committing a series of atrocities against prisoners "bade fair to become one of Mr. Carlyle's great men," provides one such example.[328] The *Southern Literary*

---

[321] *Life of Sterling*, 192.
[322] "Signs of the Times" (1829), *Essays* 2:73.
[323] Wellek, *Confrontations*, 100.
[324] Reported by Acton, *History of Freedom*, 223.
[325] Acton, *Letters to Mary Gladstone*, 70.
[326] Stephen, *Hours in a Library* 4:252, 254.
[327] Orage, *Readers and Writers*, 22.
[328] Reade, *"It Is Never Too Late to Mend"* 1:256.

Messenger, reviewing Carlyle's *Latter-Day Pamphlets* in 1850, noted that the very word "heroism" was for Carlyle's admirers like the "Shibboleth of the Illuminati—it unlocks all," and deduced that there could be no mistaking that his "monstrous" opinions advocated "pure unadulterated despotism."[329] Such critics have been misled, in G. K. Chesterton's view, "by those hasty and choleric passages" in which Carlyle "sometimes expressed a preference for mere violence, passages which were a great deal more connected with his temperament than with his philosophy." From this misreading they have "finally imbibed the notion that Carlyle's theory of hero worship was a theory of terrified submission to stern and arrogant men."[330] In view of later twentieth-century attempts to associate Carlyle's hero with the Nazi *Führerprinzip*, it is interesting to note that it was essentially cautious Victorian liberalism that promoted the charge of despotism against Carlyle. Friedrich Engels, whose view of Carlyle was much more favorable than that of the liberals, objected to Carlyle's hero not because of his unchecked power but because he was the product of Carlyle's religious outlook on life; a messiah rather than a dictator, a god rather than a man.[331]

The rise of twentieth-century fascism produced a political climate in which Carlyle's ideas, and predominantly the idea of the hero, could be transformed to brutal purposes. As Carlyle's theories of heroic authority stimulated the appetites of a new constituency of readers, the rapprochements between Carlylean ideas and the theories of emerging fascism were expressed in a series of articles, both for and against him. As early as 1920, Guido Fornelli published articles on Carlyle's conception of history that served as a basis for his fuller study, *Tommaso Carlyle: la nuova aristocrazia*. Even the politically precise George Orwell succumbed to the spirit of the age in linking Carlyle with modern fascism. Reviewing Alfred Noyes's *The Edge of the Abyss* in the *Observer* in 1944, he described Carlyle as "one of the founders of the modern worship of power and success, . . . who applauded the third German war of aggression as vociferously as Pound did the fifth." Later in that same year he described Carlyle bowing

---

[329] *Southern Literary Messenger* (June 16, 1850), 330, 339.

[330] Chesterton, *Twelve Types*, 132.

[331] See a review by Engels in *Neue Rheinische Zeitung. Politisch-Ökonomische Revue*, IV (April, 1850), reprinted in Marx and Engels, *Werke* 7:255–65. For an overview of Engels' response to Carlyle, see his comments in *The Condition of the Working Class in England*, and Steven Marcus, *Engels, Manchester, and the Working Class*.

"down before German militarism" and "worshipping power and successful cruelty."[332] Carlyle was seen in the light of recent history as a "prophet with a sinister message. . . . His views on social and political problems, divested of their moral appeal by the march of time, are revealed to be those of a fascist in their essential implications."[333]

If British Fascists, as G. M. Trevelyan suggested, "had nothing to do with the long-forgotten opinions of Carlyle but with the living doctrine and practice of Mussolini,"[334] there is no doubt that Carlyle was well remembered and read avidly in Nazi Germany. In the closing days of the war in the underground bunker below the Chancellery, Goebbels read to Hitler from Carlyle's *History of Frederick the Great*, "one of the Fuehrer's favorite books."[335] The "cult of heroes" was fashionable in Germany in the late 1920s,[336] and Carlyle's *On Heroes* was "required reading" for students during the Nazi era.[337] Nazi propagandists saw in Carlyle a respectable support for their beliefs. His admiration for strong leaders and obedience and his friendship for Germany all found enthusiastic echoes in a spate of publications produced during the early Nazi period. Many of these are chronicled in G. B. Tennyson's excellent survey of Carlyle studies, which offers one of the best treatments of this aspect of Carlyle's influence.[338]

The mass of such misleading tracts, directly or indirectly, and no doubt the atmosphere of the war itself, produced a somewhat shrill response from anti-Nazis, who berated Carlyle for having been admired by Nazis. The central role accorded Carlyle's hero-worship in this debate is indicated by such titles as "The Hero and the Führer," "Carlyle Rules the Reich," and "Carlyle and Kaiser-Worship." Significantly, though Professor Herbert Grierson's 1930 lecture "Carlyle and the Hero" was balanced in all other respects, its title was changed on publication in 1933 to *Carlyle and Hitler* because "the recent happenings in Germany illustrate the conditions which lead up to, or at least make possible, the emergence of the Hero as Carlyle chiefly thought of him." In the ominous years before the war, Carlyle's teachings and particularly his "cult of the Hero" had "acquired a new interest and significance from the social and political condition of

---

[332] Orwell, *Collected Essays* 3:100, 222.
[333] Schapiro, "Carlyle, Prophet of Fascism," 97.
[334] Trevelyan, *Carlyle: An Anthology*, 5.
[335] Shirer, *Rise and Fall of the Third Reich*, 1108.
[336] Speer, *Inside the Third Reich*, 12.
[337] G. I. Morris, "Divine Hitler," cited in G. B. Tennyson, "The Carlyles," 78.
[338] G. B. Tennyson, "The Carlyles," 77–80.

England and Europe to-day."[339] In response to the same political climate, Leonard Woolf had judged that Carlyle's hero-worship "anticipates Nietzsche and the fascists by providing a philosophical excuse for political magic, war, slavery, intolerance, and the destruction of any vestiges of liberty or democracy."[340] By 1940, with the war raging in earnest, Grierson was ready to proclaim that Carlyle's "hero is well on the way to become a Hitler or a Stalin." He argued that Carlyle's "increasing impatience with democracy" put him "on his way to the Führer, the leader who has become his own policy, who, however he may have begun with the help of . . . popular or influential support, retains that leadership by dint of secret police, concentration camps, and the murder of inconvenient individuals."[341] More sober estimates acknowledge that whatever elements in Carlyle's writing appealed to twentieth-century authoritarianism, it is still a "long way from Victorian anti-democratic currents of thought to the horrors of Germany under Hitler."[342]

The tendency to blame Carlyle for some of his unsavory latter-day admirers and to accuse him of begetting or harboring their political vices is, as John Rosenberg has neatly described it, "guilt by a-historical association." Besides, as Rosenberg points out, the finest scene in *On Heroes* focuses on Luther and "portrays not the worship of authority but its defiance," and he concludes that the book "Carlyle actually wrote is not the proto-Nazi tract he is popularly supposed to have written."[343] Ernst Cassirer's *The Myth of the State* (1946) rejects the imputations of Carlylean fascism fashionable in the 1940s: "to charge Carlyle with all the consequences that have been drawn from his theory would be against all the rules of historical objectivity."[344] This, together with Rosenberg's comments and the carefully documented history of this aspect of Carlylean criticism in G. B. Tennyson's bibliography, should have served to correct such critical aberrations. But, as Tennyson notes, even though the historical circumstances that led to so many of these charges being laid at Carlyle's door have receded, the Nazi "ghost continues to haunt the old premises."[345] Perhaps the best antidote of all is to read *On Heroes* itself. For, as

---

[339] Grierson, *Carlyle and Hitler*, 5, 21.
[340] Woolf, *Quack*, 123.
[341] Grierson, "The Hero and the Führer," 105, 102–3.
[342] Clive, *Not by Fact Alone*, 87.
[343] John Rosenberg, *Carlyle and the Burden of History*, 115.
[344] Cassirer, *Myth of the State*, 216.
[345] G. B. Tennyson, "The Carlyles," 80.

Basil Willey observed in 1949, to do so is to realize that Carlyle's heroes

> are not all Führers: they are also the Prophets—Buddha, Mahomet, Christ; the poets—Dante, Shakespeare, Goethe, Burns; the men of letters—Johnson or Rousseau. True, they are above all the kings, soldiers, and governors: Caesar, Cromwell, Frederick, Napoleon; but Cromwell was the chief of Heroes, because he was the soldier of God. I do not think that Carlyle would have mistaken Hitler for a Cromwell, any more than Plato would have mistaken him for a Philosopher-king.[346]

On a broader intellectual scale, and in an attempt to fit the Carlylean hero into the history of ideas, Bertrand Russell attributes the Carlylean "cult of the hero" to the philosophical movement beginning with Rousseau. "Byron was the poet of this movement; Fichte, Carlyle, and Nietzsche were its philosophers." Russell sees hero-worship as an offshoot of liberalism, in which he distinguishes two schools, "the hardheaded and the soft-hearted." The first "developed, through Bentham, Ricardo, and Marx, by logical stages into Stalin," the second "through Fichte, Byron, Carlyle, and Nietzsche, into Hitler." Russell conceded that such a formulation was "too schematic to be quite true,"[347] but others have been less reserved in making the same connection. Chesterton, for one, suggested that out of Carlyle "flows most of the philosophy of Nietzsche,"[348] a point echoed decades later by Professor Grierson. Thus the Carlylean hero is seen to foreshadow the Nietzschean *Übermensch* as an influence on Nazi theory.

It is, of course, a double irony that Nietzsche, who regarded Carlyle as a humbug and "muddle-head,"[349] should have been identified with the very man whose theories he tried to distance himself from, and also that he should have suffered with him an almost identical fate at the hands of hostile critics and fascist admirers. For Nietzsche, like Carlyle, fell victim to serious misrepresentation by virtue of his adoption by the Nazis; such unscrupulous attempts were made to identify him with Nazi aspirations as Richard Oehler's *Friedrich Nietzsche und die Deutsche Zukunft* (1935), to say nothing of the efforts of his

---

[346] Willey, *Nineteenth Century Studies*, 130.
[347] Russell, *History of Western Philosophy*, 600, 642.
[348] Chesterton, *Twelve Types*, 137.
[349] Nietzsche, *The Dawn of Day*, 264.

pro-Nazi sister Elisabeth who informed Hitler that he was what her brother meant by an *Übermensch*. In the words of Walter Kaufmann, "no other German writer of equal stature has been so thoroughly opposed to all proto-nazism. . . . If some Nazi writers cited him . . . it was at the price of incredible misquotation and exegetical acrobatics."[350] Nor were the Nazis the only ones to misread him. George Bernard Shaw inveighed against the glib assumption held in England that Nietzsche had "gained his European reputation by a senseless glorification of selfish bullying" and equally the mistaken belief that his own use of Nietzsche's *Übermensch* meant that he expected the world to be saved by "the despotism of a single Napoleonic Superman."[351] In fact Nietzsche's own favorite example of the *Übermensch* was "not Napoleon, but Goethe."[352] As for Carlyle leading to Nietzsche, Nietzsche could not have done more to discourage such a view and to separate his own theory of the *Übermensch* from Carlyle's heroes. The word *overman*, he wrote, had been everywhere misunderstood. A consequence was that some "scholarly oxen" had even suspected him of following "the 'hero worship' of that unconscious and involuntary counterfeiter, Carlyle, which I have repudiated so maliciously."[353] Nietzsche credits Carlyle with having "discovered" the formulae of "romantic prostration before 'genius' and 'hero,' so foreign to the spirit of enlightenment."[354] Carlyle was "lured by the craving for a strong faith" and at the same time the "feeling of his incapacity for it," which made him, in Nietzsche's eyes, a "typical romantic." Thus Carlyle "drugs something in himself with the fortissimo of his veneration of men of strong faith."[355]

In addition to changing political currents, intellectual forces both in science, especially evolutionary theory, and in history were also moving sympathy away from the "great man theory of history." Herbert Spencer was perhaps the first to approach the doctrine from the point of view of Darwinian theory, and in doing so he found the great man theory an impediment to the scientific study of social phenomena. In *The Study of Sociology* (1873) Spencer cites Carlyle's statement in *On Heroes* that "Universal History . . . is at bottom the History of the

[350] Kaufmann, "Introduction," *Portable Nietzsche*, 14; see also Jaspers, *Nietzsche and Christianity*, vii.
[351] Shaw, "First Aid to Critics," 162.
[352] Lloyd-Jones, *Blood for the Ghosts*, 166.
[353] Nietzsche, *Ecce Homo*, 261.
[354] Nietzsche, *Dawn of Day*, 257.
[355] Nietzsche, *Twilight of the Idols*, 521.

Great Men who have worked" in the world[356] as the popular view in which most people are educated. That "class which sees in the course of civilization little else than a record of remarkable persons and their doings" was, in Spencer's view, "unprepared to interpret sociological phenomena scientifically."[357] If for Spencer the hero theory was an impediment to serious social study, to John Addington Symonds it appeared as an irrelevance. "If there is truth in the Hegelian Darwinian theory of Evolution," he wrote in 1884, "we have no room left for caprice, for Carlylean Heroes,"[358] echoing the Benthamite worldview against which Carlyle had written.

Carlyle's historical style inspired Oscar Wilde to exclaim, "How great he was! He made history a song for the first time in our language. He was our English Tacitus."[359] But this view of Carlyle was a minority one. For at least in the academic study of history, fashions at the end of the nineteenth century were running counter to the sort of history produced by Carlyle. In general the response to historical elements in Carlyle's *On Heroes* was affected by the reaction, rampant at the end of the last century, against what was scornfully called "literary history." Carlyle and Macaulay were among the earliest major casualties of this "scientific" reaction within the discipline. A personal graph of this change in historical approach can be observed in G. M. Trevelyan's brief "Autobiography of an Historian." He recalls being given at Harrow in the 1890s doses of "the modern type of scientific history" as an antidote to Gibbon, Macaulay, and Carlyle. A few years later at Cambridge he was told by the Regius Professor of History that "history was a science and had nothing to do with literature" and that "Carlyle and Macaulay were charlatans."[360]

Another perceived impediment to the scientific study of society was subjectivity, or what Spencer called "automorphic interpretation." In his attempt to show how subjective factors balk the proper scientific estimate of rulers, Spencer chose the warped conceptions long held of Charles I and Cromwell.[361] He did not, of course, credit Carlyle with in any way effecting the change to a more accurate estimate of those two historical figures, though it would have been fair and reasonable to do so. W. C. Abbott, whose 1937 edition of

---

[356] *On Heroes*, 3.
[357] Spencer, *Study of Sociology*, 26.
[358] Symonds, *Letters* 2:964.
[359] Mikhail, *Wilde* 2:378.
[360] Trevelyan, *Autobiography*, 12, 17.
[361] Spencer, *Study of Sociology*, 104, 159–60.

Cromwell's letters brought Carlyle up to date by adding some seven hundred items and omitting the discredited Squire papers, acknowledges that Carlyle's work on Cromwell "helped to inspire so much historical interest and investigation in that period."[362] After Cromwell's death "a simulacrum or false image of him was set up by his enemies" which lasted as a "butt for popular reprobation for nearly two centuries." If people now take "a more unprejudiced view" of Cromwell, the work Carlyle started in his final lecture has had much to do with it.[363] Carlyle's picture of Cromwell, said Leslie Stephen, "has at least exploded once for all the simple-minded 'hypocrisy' theory, as the essay upon Johnson destroyed the ingenious doctrine that a man could write a good book simply because he was a fool." Carlyle "has done more than any writer to make such barren and degrading explanations impossible for all serious thinkers."[364]

As for Muḥammad, it is equally true that most nineteenth-century readers "who do not condemn the Arabian prophet unheard, derive what favourable notions of him they have, not from Gibbon, but from Carlyle." R. Bosworth Smith recalled in 1874 the "shock of surprise, the epoch in our intellectual and religious life, when we found that [Carlyle] chose for his 'Hero as prophet,' not Moses, or Elijah, or Isaiah, but the so-called impostor Mohammed!"[365] It should be remembered that when Carlyle was delivering his lectures upon hero-worship

> it was thought proper to explain Mahometanism . . .
> as a simple imposture. Carlyle still speaks like a man
> advancing a disputed theory when he urges . . . that
> to explain the power of Mahomet's sword, you must
> explain the force which wielded the sword; and that
> the ingenious hypothesis of a downright cheat will by
> no means serve the turn. This doctrine is now gen-
> erally accepted, unless by a few clever people who
> still cherish the wire-pulling heresy which makes his-
> tory a puppet-show manipulated by ingenious scoun-
> drels, instead of a vast co-operation of organic forces.[366]

[362] Abbott, *Writings and Speeches of Cromwell* 1:xvi.
[363] Trevelyan, *Autobiography*, 174.
[364] Stephen, *Hours in a Library* 4:263.
[365] Smith, *Mohammed*, 87.
[366] Stephen, *Hours in a Library* 4:262–63.

Certainly, as Richard Garnett noted, since Carlyle wrote, no one "has cast a stone at Mahomet."[367] In the portraits of both Cromwell and Muḥammad, Carlyle succeeded in his avowed objective of altering current prejudices. In doing so he took essentially a religious position revised into new terms.

> Every hero conveys . . . a new revelation to mankind. . . . You may recognise it, as the Puritan recognised the authority of his Bible, by the spontaneous witness of your higher nature, and you will recognise it so long as you have not given yourself up to believe a lie. And if you demand some external proofs, you must be referred, not to some particular signs and wonders, but to what you may, if you please, call the 'success' of the message. . . . The hero may be confounded with the sham, . . . but they differ for all that, and the true man recognises the difference as the religious man knows the hypocrite from the saint.[368]

Carlyle's general effect on nineteenth-century fiction, not only on its subject matter but on its form, began to be most strongly felt in the decade of his lectures on heroes. "Although the novel of the forties makes no clear break with the past, anyone reading the major novelists in chronological order would be more struck by change than continuity," and one of the main reasons for this, according to Kathleen Tillotson, is "the influence of Carlyle." In "Dickens, Thackeray, and Kingsley alone there is material for a full-length study,"[369] several of which have appeared since Tillotson's view was first aired.[370]

---

[367] Garnett, *Life of Carlyle*, 102.

[368] Stephen, *Hours in a Library* 4:260–61.

[369] Tillotson, *Novels*, 150, 153.

[370] To the three novelists cited one should add Disraeli, George Eliot, Hardy, Meredith, who claimed the introductory chapter of the *Egoist* was "in the vein of Carlyle" (Meredith, *Letters* 3:1295), Charles Reade, Butler, Kipling, Conan Doyle, Melville, and Twain, all of whose connections with Carlyle have been the subject of recent scholarship. Similarly Carlyle's influence on the poets Arnold, the Brownings, Clough, Tennyson, and Whitman, among others, has been explored, as well as his connection with playwrights, controversialists, and critics such as Ruskin, Morris, Shaw, and Chesterton. See Tarr, *Bibliography of English-Language Criticism;* and G. B. Tennyson, "The Carlyles."

Carlyle's influence was protean, his interaction with other writers and thinkers extensive, and his effect upon the imagination of the whole century profound. The heroic theme was central to that influence. Thoreau goes so far as to say that "all of Carlyle's works might well enough be embraced under the title of . . . *On Heroes, Hero-worship, and the Heroic in History.* Of this department, he is the Chief Professor in the World's University, and even leaves Plutarch behind."[371] This judgment was echoed by the skeptical George Bernard Shaw: "Carlyle, with his vein of peasant inspiration, apprehended the sort of greatness that places the true hero of history so far beyond the mere *preux chevalier.* . . . This one ray of perception became Carlyle's whole stock-in-trade; and it sufficed to make a literary master of him."[372]

[371] Cited in Seigel, *Critical Heritage,* 298.
[372] Shaw, *Three Plays,* xxxiv.

NOTE ON THE TEXT

On Heroes, Hero-Worship, and the Heroic in History was published eight times during Carlyle's lifetime in editions in which he is known or has been claimed to have participated. The manuscript from which the earliest of these editions was typeset is lost. With the exception of two pages of corrected proofs for the first edition, discussed below, no other documents that could provide direct evidence of authorial intervention, such as printer's copies or proof sheets with revisions indicated in Carlyle's hand, are known to survive. Therefore, the only documentary evidence for the text of *On Heroes* is the eight versions of the work that are embodied in those eight lifetime editions.

The text of *On Heroes* that we present in this volume is a critical text. That is to say, it does not correspond in detail to any of the extant authoritative texts. These source texts differ among themselves: none were free of typographical errors; there were changes in spelling that reflect the regularization and modernization of British orthography during the three decades that separate the earliest from the last version; there were other minor changes, in punctuation for example, that may have been introduced by Carlyle's printers or editorial assistants on their own authority; and there is evidence that Carlyle himself ordered revisions in each version except the last. Faced with these differences among the various editions of *On Heroes*, and the virtual absence of conclusive, holographic evidence that Carlyle made or did not make any particular change, our goal has nevertheless been to produce a text that includes *only* those changes that we can confidently attribute to the author, rather than to his typesetters, proofreaders, or editors. This criterion obliges us to err on the side of *excluding* some possibly authorial changes, since some undecidable cases very likely represent changes made by Carlyle, but it has the effect of ensuring that as much as possible of the text is what Carlyle wrote, even though we may not have included all his later revisions.

The evidence of the source texts has been assembled by the process of collation: comparing the earliest edition, as a baseline, with each of the others in turn and recording each point of difference, or variant. These variants from the first edition are then assembled in tabular form as a historical collation, showing for each variant the edition or editions in which it occurs. The complete Historical Collation of *On Heroes* is given in the textual apparatus of this volume, beginning on page 445, and the history of the text that it reveals is summarized in the discussion of the various editions below. In addition to providing the reader with all the textual evidence on which the present edition is based, the Historical Collation will enable a reader interested in any particular source text to reconstruct it in detail.

Collation confirms that each new edition of *On Heroes* was typeset from a copy of the most recent previous edition. From Carlyle's correspondence we know that it was his usual practice, when a new edition of one of his works was being prepared, to supply his printers with such a copy, in which he had entered his revisions by hand. (At least this was his practice through the 1852 Fourth Edition of *On Heroes*. The issues raised by the versions of *On Heroes* included in the three lifetime collected editions, beginning in 1858, are dealt with below.) There were then further opportunities for Carlyle or others to make alterations in the text of each edition during the process of typesetting and proofreading. In preparing the present critical edition, it was the work of editorial judgment to distinguish between those variants that most probably represent Carlyle's own revisions and those that might have been introduced by typesetters or by proofreaders other than Carlyle.

It might seem that such judgments should be based on a prior literary analysis of Carlyle's preferred style, diction, and usage, so that for each variant the editors would consider whether or not the change in the text conformed to such authorial preferences, whether, in other words, a given variant was "Carlylean" in its literary effect. However, such a procedure would be impossible for several reasons.

First, it would not be possible to formulate a set of rules that would adequately embody Carlyle's stylistic preferences. The evidence will not support being reduced to such rules: each punctuation mark, for example, has its unique context, and there is no reason to suppose that Carlyle's stylistic choices were sufficiently regular and unchanging. Second, to the extent that a variant reading seems to be more consistent with Carlyle's style elsewhere than the earlier reading, to that extent the variant might well be the work of a proofreader other than the author, since proofreaders in every age must consider consistency a desideratum. Third, it is clearly impossible to reach any reliable and usefully detailed conclusions about Carlyle's stylistic preferences by studying a text that is not reliably Carlylean; in other words, the work of establishing a text that can claim to be, as nearly as possible, authorial in every detail—the task of the present editors— must obviously precede the work of characterizing in detail the author's style, a task for which we have provided the materials but that we leave to others.

To establish the present text, therefore, we began by noting that the 1841 first edition, although not, of course, a perfect copy of the lost manuscript—as proved by the handful of self-evident typographical errors it contains—is closer to that manuscript (the only version of the text that was authorial in every detail) than any of the other source texts, all of which descend from it. We therefore chose the first edition as our copy-text.

For each variant reading disclosed by collation in later editions, it was necessary to consider whether the best explanation for the variant is authorial revision or whether, on the other hand, we could not confidently attribute the change to the author rather than to a typesetter or to a proofreader other than the author. If the former, we emended our text to include the revision. If the latter, we followed the first edition copy-text at that place. Consider two extreme examples:

In the 1846 Third Edition (and the 1846 American edition; see below), 11 words in Lecture VI on Cromwell's assumption of the protectorship are replaced by 280 words (beginning at 199.33[1]). Even ignoring the biographical fact that, since the appearance of the Second Edition of *On Heroes* in 1842, Carlyle had been engaged in research on Cromwell for his documentary biography, *Oliver Cromwell's Letters and Speeches* (1845; Second Edition, 1846), it is obvious that no one but Carlyle could or would have authored this revision. To fail to include this passage in our text would be (from the point of view of establishing an authorial text) to deny Carlyle the right to amplify in 1846 what he had written in 1841, and (from the point of view of establishing a complete, historically relevant text) to omit a page of text that has been part of the work for all readers since 1846.

On the other hand, consider the multitude of spelling changes found in every lifetime edition, which illustrate the trend toward regularization and "modernization" of English orthography that began in America with the publication of Noah Webster's *Blue-Backed Speller* in 1783 and continued through the nineteenth century in Britain. Although it is possible that Carlyle's own orthographic preferences evolved in step with the times (and the continuing publication of his *Collected Letters* will provide further evidence on this point), it is at least as likely that these spelling variants represent silent—perhaps unconscious—emendations by the various typesetters employed by Carlyle's printers. We know that typesetters and proofreaders then

---

[1] Numbers in this form are page and line numbers in the present edition. See the textual apparatus at the corresponding place for the details of the variants referred to in this Note.

and now routinely "correct" what they perceive as misspellings in ordinary prose texts and impose "house style" preferred spellings when variant forms of a word are currently acceptable. There is no reason to think that Carlyle was strongly committed to the somewhat old-fashioned spellings that appear in the first edition of *On Heroes* ("Shakspeare," as Carlyle spells it in all lifetime editions of all his writings, is the exception that proves the rule; the spelling of proper names is the business of the author—or the modern copy editor—not of typesetters or proofreaders), but there is good reason to think that the first-edition spellings were *Carlyle's* spellings, or as close to them as we can get lacking the manuscript, and there is no reason to believe that any of the subsequent modernizations of them in later editions are Carlyle's revisions. Therefore, to include these modernizations in our text (as distinct from our Historical Collation, where they can all be found) would be to deprive the text of the interesting features of Carlyle's original spelling, with no evidence that the author's intention was being followed and no gain in intelligibility.

As these two clear-cut examples show, our task was to distinguish between those alterations in the text that more probably represent authorial revision, which we therefore accept as emendations, and those that typesetters or proofreaders might have considered themselves authorized to make, which we therefore cannot confidently vouch for as authorial and which we accordingly list in the Historical Collation but do not include in our critical text. Although each variant must be examined individually and in the context of the entire collation (as well as in the context of whatever external evidence from biographical sources can be brought to bear), we can say that, in general, the former category includes especially changes in the wording of the text, but also such matters as the spelling of proper names and significant changes in punctuation that could not plausibly have seemed called for by rules of usage or house style. The latter category includes changes in such minor—and rule-governed—aspects of the text as spelling, capitalization, word division, and routine punctuation.[2]

The present critical text therefore follows the first edition of *On Heroes* as copy-text, but has been emended to follow the reading of one or more of the later editions in four categories of cases: First, in a few places, such as "eartnestness" at 34.26, the reading of the first

---

[2] This policy of giving precedence to variants in wording over variants in spelling and punctuation is not a reflection of any prejudice on our part as editors for "content" over "form" or any such abstract principle. It is rather our application of a distinction made by both authors and printers in the

edition is evidently the result of a typographical error. All such errors were corrected in the 1842 Second Edition, and these corrections have been adopted. Second, because the 1846 American edition and the 1846 British Third Edition were set from "identical" printer's copies—two copies of the 1842 Second Edition marked for revision by Carlyle himself—it follows that, with a few exceptions, new readings that are found in both of the 1846 editions must be attributed to the author and so have been adopted.[3] Exceptions are considered individually in the Discussion of Editorial Decisions, which begins on page 431. Third, variants found in any of the British lifetime editions that constitute a change in the wording of the text—that is, variants that amount to the deletion, the substitution, or, as in the great majority of such changes in *On Heroes*, the addition of one or more words—may be regarded as almost certainly authorial revisions, and have in general been adopted as emendations. Exceptions to this rule have been made only where the change can more probably be attributed to typographical error or to a proofreader "correcting" Carlyle's grammar. Such exceptions are also explained in the Discussion of Editorial Decisions. Fourth, a few changes of punctuation have for various reasons been accepted as authorial (e.g., 166.10 and 172.33); these are all treated fully in the Discussion of Editorial Decisions.

The critical text that we have constructed according to this policy is presented as clear text; that is, no editorial symbols or other indications of emendations appear on the page. A list of all emendations of the copy-text is given in the textual apparatus beginning on page 421. No attempt has been made to reproduce non-textual design features of the copy-text (typeface, lineation, pagination, etc.), but the titles and running heads, including the dates of the original lectures, appear as they do in the first four British editions. A "Summary" and an index, prepared under Carlyle's supervision, first appeared in the 1858 Uniform Edition and were retained in all subsequent editions. We have included both as an appendix to the present text.

---

nineteenth century, a distinction between the creative "wording as content," which was, as a matter of historical fact, ordinarily the exclusive domain of authors, and the rule-bound "formal" aspects of a text, which printers saw as within their province to "correct." Specialists will recognize, and nonspecialists may be interested to know, that this editorial procedure is the one suggested by W. W. Greg in his influential essay "The Rationale of Copy-Text" (1949). For a thoughtful exposition of Greg's position, including a useful discussion of some of its critics' arguments, see G. Thomas Tanselle, "Greg's Theory of Copy-Text" (1975).

[3] See the discussion of the 1846 American edition below, pp. xcv–xcviii.

SOURCES OF THE TEXT

Using the first edition as the standard of collation,[4] we have recorded all variant readings to be found in six subsequent British editions in which Carlyle has been claimed to have participated—the Second Edition of 1842, the Third Edition of 1846, the Fourth Edition of 1852, the Uniform Edition of 1858, the Library Edition of 1870, and the People's Edition of 1872—as well as the historically and textually interesting authorized American edition of 1846.[5] The

[4] The copy of the 1841 first edition, Tarr A12.1.a, used as the standard of collation is owned by Michael Goldberg and is deposited, along with the other materials of the Strouse Edition, in the Norman and Charlotte Strouse Collection of Thomas Carlyle, housed in Special Collections, McHenry Library, University of California, Santa Cruz. This copy (Copy A [PR4426.A1 1841 c. 5]) was compared with another copy of the first edition in the Strouse Collection (Copy E [PR4426.A1 1841 c. 1]) using a Hinman Collator. No textual variants were found. One character that was partially broken in Copy A (on page 45, line 22 of that edition, the first character on that line) was whole in Copy E, and one character, correctly positioned in Copy A (on page 82, line 26, again the first character), was found shifted into the left margin in Copy E. Three other copies of the first edition in the Strouse Collection ([PR4426.A1 1841 c. 2–4]) were judged by the conservators of the Collection too fragile to be submitted to the Hinman Collator. These were compared by eye with the other two copies. No textual differences were found; the shifted character was discovered in intermediate positions, and the broken character in intermediate stages of breakage, suggesting that the two copies that had been machine collated bracketed, in order of printing, the three that could not be. Only 1,000 copies of the first edition were printed. See Tarr, *Descriptive Bibliography*, 89.

[5] The following copies of editions subsequent to the first edition were collated in the preparation of the present text: the 1842 British Second Edition, Tarr A12.3.a, in the University Library of the University of British Columbia (PR4426.A2.1842); the 1846 British Third Edition, Tarr A12.3.b, in the University of Michigan Libraries [Rare Book Room PR4426.A1.1846a]; the 1846 American edition, Tarr A12.6.a, in the Bibliothèque Nationale du Québec (824.82.C22hh); the 1852 British Fourth Edition, Tarr A12.3.c, in Special Collections, Thomas Cooper Library, University of South Carolina; the 1858 Uniform Edition, Tarr D2.a, in the Strouse Collection, McHenry Library, University of California, Santa Cruz (PR4426.A1.1858 v. 6); the 1870 Library Edition, Tarr D3.a$_1$, in the Northern Regional Library Facility of the University of California (952c.1869 v. 12); the 1872 People's Edition, Tarr D4.a$_1$, owned by K. J. Fielding and deposited in the Strouse Collection; and an undated reprint of the People's Edition, Tarr D4.b, in the Strouse Collection (PR4426.A1.1870 v. 13). In addition the 1897 Centenary Edition (see Dyer, *Bibliography*, 60, 108) in the library of San Jose State University (PR4420.E98 v. 5), was collated, although the variants in this posthumous edition are not included in the Historical Collation (see below, p. cii).

Historical Collation provides the complete record of these variants, but it is appropriate here to make some general remarks about the various editions.

THE CORRECTED PROOF PAGES

The earliest extant form of the complete text of *On Heroes* is the British first edition of 1841. Of earlier versions of the text, the only known extant fragments are two proof pages, corresponding to pages 25 and 26 of the first edition (15.13–16.14 of the present edition), in the collection of Carlyle House, Chelsea (see Plate 3). No other proof sheets, manuscript pages, or printer's copies of *On Heroes* are known to survive.

On these two proof pages, six corrections are marked in Carlyle's hand, all of which were incorporated into the text of the first edition and, of course, into the present text: a comma and dash are replaced by a full stop after "ways" (15.19), "geyrers" is corrected to "geysers" (15.28), "of" is inserted (15.33), "Saemund" is changed to "Sæmund" in two places (16.1 and 16.8), and a comma is added (16.8). On the other hand, two commas appear in the first edition (both at 15.14) that had neither been set in proof nor indicated for insertion on the proof pages that survive. Since no other revisions were ordered for that or adjacent lines on the extant proof pages, and since the lineation of the proof pages exactly corresponds to that of the published edition, there would have been no occasion to reset that line unless the author ordered the change on some subsequent set of proofs. Therefore these commas, too, have been included in the present text.

THE 1841 FIRST EDITION

Although the manuscript of *On Heroes* was completed in September 1840 (see Introduction, p. xxxiii), Carlyle was in no hurry to publish. By the beginning of October, negotiations had begun with James Fraser, Carlyle's publisher:

> Jane en[g]ages herself in selling my *Ms.* Lectures to Fraser! *She* can do it better, she thinks. I incline to decide that if I can get no money for them, I will *not* print them. *Cui bono?* To loose the jaw of all the gomerils [fools] in England![6]

[6] *Letters* 12:273, TC to John A. Carlyle, October 3, 1840.

Six weeks later there had been no progress in the negotiations (the Carlyles were asking for £150, which Fraser maintained would leave no profit for him[7]) nor in Carlyle's attitude to the book:

> Jane has had a long negociation with Fraser about publishing the *Lectures* for a sum of money down; money down is a thing Fraser stands aghast at,— . . . the negociation has ended; the *Ms.* has come *back*. . . . There is happily no haste to publish the thing at all. I consider it a paltry thing; really care not if it were burnt: till some stronger temptation outward or inward arise, we will let it lie there.[8]

A month after that, Carlyle's attitude was improving, though there had been no better offer from Fraser:

> My Lectures are never yet gone to Press. I am *sweer* [reluctant] about publishing them; expecting a great quantity of useless cackle if I do; and not being either tempted by money, or necessitated by the want of it, to set them forth till my own time,—which latter is a great blessing. I begin to find it probable that they *will* be printed now, some time in the course of the winter. We shall see.[9]

It was not until late January 1841 that Carlyle accepted Fraser's terms. As Carlyle wrote to his brother on January 26:

> In the course of last week I bargained with Fraser for my Lecture-Book. £75 the dog would give me no more; but he also gives a £75 for a thousand *Sartors*, the edition of that being run out too: so we go on printing *both*, with all imaginable velocity; and I am to have £150 for the two. We must be content. "4 sheets of each, 8 of both" are to come to me every week *credat Judaeus!* I am very busy *revising* the Lectures; am now thro' the First. I design to make

---

[7] *Letters* 12:277, Jane Welsh Carlyle to Anna Brownell Jameson, [October 6?, 1840].
[8] *Letters* 12:326, TC to John A. Carlyle, November 16, 1840.
[9] *Letters* 12:365, TC to Alexander Carlyle, December 16, 1840.

few changes. In five or six weeks I may fairly expect the quit of the concern;—free for another.[10]

In fact, both books were published exactly six weeks later, but those weeks were filled with much stressful work. The next day he wrote,

> Today I have finished my revisal of *Mahomet:* very poor stuff. I am in a terrible fright too about certain leaves of the end of *Odin*, which I thought to have found here; but which I *hope* are at the Printer's! I must go and see. No Proofsheet as yet.[11]

By February 5, the proofreading was well under way:

> Proofsheets have much occupied me. We are now far into the second Lecture: the First needed very heavy correction; paragraphs to be added &c: twice I sat a whole day; sometimes like the *cooking of a cucumber*, after getting something all ready with great labour, I flung it out of window, as the best course! We are thro' all that now, in tolerable fashion. I find these Lectures not so bad a thing. Nothing new in them for *me;* but much like to be new enough for many others.[12]

The next day he reassured his mother, "already we are almost as good as half done,"[13] but twelve days later he complained happily to her:

> I am kept in a perpetual *Kippitch* [confusion] with the Printers at present. But they are getting on very swiftly and well; both the Books are *two-thirds* done; I think we shall be almost thro', at the end of next week. I like my *Lecture* Book considerably better as I go on with it in clear *type:* it is a *gowsterous* [boisterous] determined speaking out of the truth about several things; the people will be no worse for it at present! The astonishment of many of them is likely to be considerable.[14]

---

[10] *Letters* 13:24, TC to John A. Carlyle, January 26, 1841.
[11] *Letters* 13:27, TC to John A. Carlyle, January 27, 1841.
[12] *Letters* 13:29, TC to John A. Carlyle, February 5, 1841.
[13] *Letters* 13:32, TC to Margaret A. Carlyle, February 6, 1841.
[14] *Letters* 13:38, TC to Margaret A. Carlyle, February 18, 1841.

On February 24 he was "nearly done,"[15] and by March 2 he was completely finished with the proofs and had collapsed "under the frightfullest despotism of Influenza":

> *Sartor* and the Hero-*Lectures* are both printed, and away from me. With great pleasure I bequeath them both to the Prince of the Power of the Air to work *his* good pleasure with them: it is not probable that he dislikes them much worse than I do,—under many points of view.[16]

Finally, by March 9, the two books were bound and Carlyle was directing Fraser to send copies of *On Heroes* to Scottish relatives and friends.[17]

The first edition of *On Heroes* was printed by "Robson, Levey, and Franklyn" of 46 St. Martin's Lane.[18] Carlyle's association with these printers had begun in 1837, when Fraser gave the third volume of *The French Revolution* to be printed by the firm of "Levey, Robson, and Franklyn" because the firm of James Moyes was making slow progress on the first two volumes.[19] When the work on *The French Revolution* was completed, Carlyle wrote to Fraser concerning "the Robsons," saying that "they are accurate punctual Printers, and have been extremely helpful to me in this business."[20] In 1839 Carlyle wrote to Fraser, "I am glad you have given the *Meister* to Robson; my imagination has all along represented him as a paragon in comparison with the others. We shall see."[21] In 1840 Robson's firm printed the third, fourth, and fifth volumes of the first British edition of *Critical and Miscellaneous Essays*, and in June 1841 Carlyle told Emerson that Fraser's British edition of "*Emerson's Essays*, the Book so-called" was "in the hands of that invaluable Printer, Robson, who did the *Miscellanies*."[22] In August 1841, Carlyle wrote Emerson,

---

[15] *Letters* 13:46, TC to John Stuart Mill, February 24, 1841.
[16] *Letters* 13:48, TC to John Sterling, March 2, 1841.
[17] *Letters* 13:54, TC to John A. Carlyle, March 9, 1841.
[18] According to the printer's imprint on p. ii. On the last page of the first edition another printer's imprint gives the firm's name as "Levey, Robson, and Franklyn."
[19] *Letters* 9:129–30, TC to John Stuart Mill, January 28, 1837.
[20] *Letters* 9:201, TC to James Fraser, May 1, 1837.
[21] *Letters* 11:176, TC to James Fraser, August 24, 1839. The reference is to the second edition of Carlyle's translation of *Wilhelm Meister's Apprenticeship and Travels* (Tarr A2.3.I–III.a).
[22] *Letters* 13:163, TC to Ralph Waldo Emerson, June 25, 1841.

> Three sheets of the *Essays* lay waiting for me at my
> Mother's, for correction; needing as good as none. The
> type and shape is the same a[s that] of late *Lectures on
> Heroes*. Robson the Printer, who is a very punctual
> intelligent man, a scholar withal, undertook to be him-
> self the Corrector of the other sheets: I hope that you
> will find them "exactly conformable to the text, *minus*
> mere typographical blunders and the more salient
> American spellings (labor for labour &c)."[23]

In the last sentence, Carlyle is apparently quoting Robson himself,[24] and the quotation illustrates the extent to which the printer,
while taking no doubt justified pride in the exactness of his transcrip-
tion, at the same time felt himself authorized to emend, silently but
for this blanket notice, what he considered "blunders" and to conform spellings to contemporary British norms.

By 1843 Carlyle was congratulating himself for having found
Robson, though the credit would seem to belong to Fraser: "He is
a good clever man my Printer, whom I discovered several years ago,
and whom I have insisted on sticking to ever since. They say, 'He is
a little dearer.'—'Well,' I answer, 'ought he not; being considerably
better?'"[25] The printing of each edition of *On Heroes* during Carlyle's
lifetime continued to be done by the firm with which Charles Robson, Carlyle's "paragon" among printers, was associated.[26]

---

[23] *Letters* 13:218–19, TC to Ralph Waldo Emerson, August 18, 1841.

[24] *Letters* 13:219n.

[25] *Letters* 16:96, TC to Margaret A. Carlyle, March 24, 1843.

[26] Between the 1841 first edition and the 1842 Second Edition, the firm of
"Robson, Levey, and Franklyn" apparently left its office on St. Martin's
Lane. The 1842 colophon gives the firm's address as "Great New Street,
Fetter Lane." (The London Post Office directory for 1842 locates the firm
at 24 Great New Street, Fetter Lane. In 1843 it moved to number 23.)
In the 1846 Third Edition, the name of the firm is given as "Levey,
Robson, and Franklyn," still at "Great New Street, Fetter Lane." In the
1852 Fourth Edition as well as the 1858 Uniform Edition, the colophon
reads, "Printed by Robson, Levey, and Franklyn, Great New Street and
Fetter Lane." By the 1870 Library Edition, the printer's imprint reads,
"Robson and Sons, Printers, Pancras Road, N.W."; the 1872 People's
Edition has the same. The undated reprint of the People's Edition we
examined carries the colophon "Bungay: Clay and Taylor, Printers" although it is clear that at least some of the 1872 plates were still being used
in its production and were showing signs of wear. The 1897 Centenary
Edition was "Printed by T. and A. Constable, Printers to Her Majesty at
the Edinburgh University Press."

THE 1842 SECOND EDITION

On February 25, 1842, Carlyle wrote to John Forster, who was acting as intermediary with Carlyle's new publishers, "Pray thank Messrs
Chapman and Hall; and say that the Book on *Heroes* lies *ready* here,
whenever Robson's devil comes for it; and that the large and *cheap-
priced* edition (since you and they recommend it) is the one we will
prefer. Let them consult Robson therefore; I particularly wish and request that Robson may be printer."[27] The "Book" lying ready would
have been a copy of the first edition of *On Heroes*, marked for revision
by Carlyle, and ready to serve as the printer's copy for the Second
Edition.

Five days later Carlyle wrote again to Forster: "The Printer has got
the Book, and will proceed on it, I calculate, rapidly and satisfactorily
without farther aid of mine. I have gone over it all, in these two days,
and made it what it is finally to be. Robson can be depended on for
correctness."[28] This last suggests that Carlyle, having marked his
ordered revisions in the printer's copy, intended to leave the proofreading to Robson. The circumstances of Carlyle's life at this period
make it unlikely that he would have had time for this task—his mother-
in-law died suddenly on February 25, Carlyle was in Scotland by
March 5 and did not return to London until May 7—and the absence
of any further mention in his correspondence of his working on the
Second Edition virtually excludes the possibility that he read proofs.[29]

Beginning with the Second Edition of 1842, all British editions of
On Heroes were published by Chapman and Hall, James Fraser having died in October 1841. In the Second, Third, and Fourth Editions
the same font is used as in the first, and the lineation of the first
edition is followed where possible. However, whereas the first edition
has a normal page of twenty-eight lines, the Second, Third, and
Fourth Editions have twenty-nine lines on a normal page.

The Second Edition makes several corrections of apparent errors
in the first edition, ranging from the correction of typographical errors (e.g., "eartnestness" at 34.26) and inferable misreadings of the

[27] *Letters* 14:50, TC to John Forster, February 25, 1842.
[28] *Letters* 14:56, TC to John Forster, March 2, 1842.
[29] Carlyle wrote from Scotland to Forster in London on March 14: "I know
not what [more] you can at this moment accomplish for me, if it were not
perhaps that you stept over to Robson the Printer (New Street, Fetter Lane)
some day, and saw with your own eyes that he was proceeding,—as indeed
I doubt not he is doing, in a satisfactory manner" (*Letters* 14:71–72).

manuscript (e.g., "desires" for "devises" at 101.32; other instances at 147.10 and 202.21), to the change of a reference to "Mr. Hamilton's" writings on Tibet to "Mr. Turner's" (6.19) and the correction of Luther's daughter's name from Margaret to Magdalene (120.35 and 121.2). Also, one mysterious revision, for which only Carlyle could have been responsible, changes a correct reference to Luther's "Patmos" as "the Wartburg" in the first edition to an apparently incorrect reference to "the Castle of Coburg" in the Second (121.4; see note). On the other hand, the Second Edition contains five new typographical errors (at 55.3, 66.9, 89.21, 102.27, and 114.6), two of which ("*abkar*" for "*akbar*" at 55.3 and again at 66.9) were followed in the Third Edition and in the 1846 American edition and were not corrected until the Fourth Edition in 1852.

Besides the obviously deliberate correction of errors, the Second Edition contains some seventy separate alterations in the wording of the text (including changes in the spelling of proper names) plainly attributable to the author, including significant revisions of passages in each of the lectures. Whole sentences are added in three places (at 56.27, 128.17, and 141.14), and many phrases are amplified, sometimes by the addition of several lines of text (e.g., 120.1 and 147.22). Some changes of wording are very minor (e.g., "only" for "merely" at 33.23—the opposite change occurs at 102.32—or "There" for "These" at 137.2) but for most of these variants in wording in the Second Edition—as in later editions—the most probable explanation is revision intended by Carlyle.

Along with these alterations of wording, the Second Edition contains nearly 150 variations in punctuation and spelling (including capitalization, word division, and the like). These are difficult to characterize. For example, colons in the first edition are changed to semi-colons in the second, or vice versa, some twenty times. Some patterns in these minor variants do emerge. For example, in the first edition "shew" (or "shewn," "shews," and so on) occurs thirty-three times, and "show" fifteen times. ("Show" is always used as a noun, "shew" indifferently as noun or verb.) In the Second Edition, in what seems a failed attempt at consistency, "shew" occurs forty-six times, and "show" twice. Similarly, "woe" occurs four times in the first edition, "wo" three times. All three occurrences of "wo" in the first edition are changed to "woe" in the Second. Also, it may be thought to be a pattern that more than twice as many commas are added in the Second Edition (twenty-six) as are deleted (twelve).

Some of these changes in punctuation and spelling were very likely among the revisions indicated by Carlyle in the printer's copy for this edition, but, unlike changes of wording, it is seldom possible to be confident that any given variant was introduced by the author rather than by Robson or another typesetter or proofreader in his shop. We must consider the historical context of nineteenth-century publishing, in which printers, as members of a skilled craft that was striving for recognition as a profession, when correcting their own proofs, might have considered themselves to be authorized by the evolving norms of style and usage to "correct" such aspects of a text as spelling, word division, punctuation, and perhaps even grammar.

On the other hand, there is reason to believe that in revising and in proofreading his texts, Carlyle concerned himself, far more than most authors do, with correcting and revising his punctuation, capitalization, and to some degree hyphenation. Indeed, when the documentary evidence exists to establish Carlyle as the most likely agent of such changes (as in the case of new variants that appear in both 1846 editions, as explained below), we adopt them as emendations of the copy-text. In addition, we have the evidence of a remarkable document recently obtained by the Strouse Collection—a complete set of "press proofs" for the 1841 second book edition of *Sartor Resartus*, which was typeset and proofread simultaneously with the first edition of *On Heroes* (see pp. lxxxviii–lxxxix above). These proofs were extensively marked, by more than one hand, and among the changes are many corrections and revisions by Carlyle (though not *exclusively* by Carlyle) of the punctuation and capitalization, while most of the spelling changes are in another hand, probably that of the printer's proofreader. It is indeed tempting to regard this rare holographic evidence as the basis for adopting more of the later variants in punctuation and capitalization than the documentary evidence for *On Heroes* otherwise warrants. Unfortunately the *Sartor* proofs afford, at best, an argument by analogy that Carlyle also made such changes in *On Heroes*. They can give us no assurance that Carlyle made, when revising *On Heroes* in 1842 or later, the kind of changes he manifestly did sometimes make when marking proofs for *Sartor* in 1841, and of course they can give us no guidance at all with respect to particular variants. We have therefore *not* relied, in our editing of *On Heroes*, on this detailed documentary evidence of printing-house practice, preserved in these proofs for *Sartor Resartus*, but will of course do so in editing that work for the Strouse Edition.

THE 1846 BRITISH THIRD EDITION

The British Third Edition was evidently set from a copy of the Second Edition, as it reproduces nearly all of the variants of that edition. At the same time, it introduces over ninety additional alterations of wording, including some major revisions of passages on Cromwell in Lecture VI that reflect Carlyle's study of the Civil War for his *Oliver Cromwell's Letters and Speeches.*

Like the Second Edition, the Third contains over 150 changes of punctuation and spelling. So far as there is a pattern among these, it lies in an extended regularization of Carlyle's orthography. Verbs ending in *-ize* in the first edition are changed to *-ise*, consonants are doubled before such suffixes as *-est*, silent *e*'s are dropped before such suffixes as *-able*, and so on. In addition to the changes of wording and of punctuation and spelling, seven typographical errors appear in the Third Edition, including a cluster of five between 77.11 and 95.2, suggesting a less than usually careful typesetter or proofreader. Three of these errors were followed in the Fourth Edition, and one, "or" for "our" at 83.5, was sufficiently plausible to escape detection in all subsequent British editions. The evidence of Carlyle's correspondence is explicit that he did not himself read proofs of this edition (see the discussion of the 1846 American edition below).

Another feature of the Third Edition should be noted, though it is not textual and has not been recorded in the apparatus. Beginning in 1846, in both the British Third Edition and the American edition and continuing through all British lifetime editions, quotations that extend for more than one line (for example the quotation from Novalis at 11.2–6 of the present text) are marked by a left inverted comma, i.e., an opening single quotation mark, at the beginning of each line of the quotation. This style, the ancestor of the modern practice of indenting multi-line quotations from both margins while omitting quotation marks, we take to be a non-textual design feature.

THE 1846 AMERICAN EDITION

The American edition of 1846 was published by Wiley and Putnam in New York, "Stereotyped by T. B. Smith, 216 William St." Although at least three pirated American versions of *On Heroes* had appeared earlier, the first within a month of the publication of the first British edition, this was the first authorized American publication. It bears the following "Imprimatur":

> This Book, "HEROES AND HERO-WORSHIP," I have read over and revised into a correct state for Messrs. WILEY & PUTNAM, of New York, who are hereby authorised, they and they only, so far as I can authorise them, to print and vend the same in the United States.
>
> THOMAS CARLYLE.
>
> *London, June* 18, 1846.

Collation discloses that the 1846 American edition contains about half of the new variants found in the British Third Edition of the same year, including nearly all the changes of wording. But in many of the places where the British edition shows changes in spelling and punctuation, the American follows the 1842 British Second Edition. From this data, we can immediately conclude that the 1846 American edition was set from some version of the text later than the 1842 Second Edition but earlier than the 1846 British Third. The textual evidence supports the hypothesis that both 1846 editions were set from the same printer's copy, a copy of the Second Edition marked with his revisions by Carlyle.

In fact, Carlyle's correspondence for this period[30] reveals that the author marked his revisions in one copy of the Second Edition, to serve as the printer's copy for the American edition, and then *duplicated* his markings in another copy of the Second Edition for his London printers. In 1846 Carlyle was entering into a comprehensive agreement with Wiley and Putnam, the New York publishers, to publish all of his books in America, and George Putnam himself was in London, where he negotiated the agreement with Carlyle personally. On April 28, Carlyle wrote to Edward Chapman, his British publisher, asking him to "send me a Copy of the *Hero-worship* and of the *F. Revolution* . . . for I have to revise them at any rate for the American people. I find *Hero-worship* will be the one to begin with;—and there is no Copy here fit for my purpose."[31] Soon after this, Carlyle agreed with Chapman on the publication of a third edition of *On Heroes* in London, and must have obtained from him a second copy of the Second Edition, to be marked for the setting of the new British edition. On May 3, Carlyle wrote to his brother John to report on

---

[30] The complete evidence will be found in volume 20 of the *Letters*, forthcoming in 1992.

[31] Letter of TC to Edward Chapman, April 28, 1846, in General Manuscripts, Department of Rare Books and Special Collections, Princeton University Libraries. Published with permission of Princeton University Library.

a meeting with Putnam, adding, "Chapman was here yesterday to settle about a new Edition of *Heroes* and the *Miscellanies* for the English Market: we have not yet come to close quarters about the *monies*."[32] In another letter to John on May 20, Carlyle reported that he had finished "*revising* those old Books of mine, *Heroes, Sartor* &c for the Yankees, and some of them for both Yankees and English."[33] On June 15, he wrote to George Putnam, "I have had two of the books, *Sartor* and *Heroes*, carefully revised for your printer. Copies for him are now in readiness precisely identical with those that our English printer will bring out."[34] In fact, the printer's copy for the new British edition was already being typeset, as Carlyle wrote to Chapman on June 17, "*Heroes* has been in Robson's hands for a good while," adding, "I do not design to trouble him with any Proofsheets."[35] On June 18, Carlyle wrote to Emerson, "Yesterday Putnam was here, and we made our bargain, and are to have it signed this day at his shop. . . . I have given Putnam two Books (*Heroes* & *Sartor*) ready, corrected."[36] The "Imprimatur" for the American edition of *On Heroes*, quoted above, was dated the same day.

To summarize, between April 18 and May 20, 1846, Carlyle prepared two copies of the Second Edition, marked with "precisely identical" revisions.[37] One of these copies was sent to his London printer "a good while" before the middle of June. The other was given or sent to his American publisher on June 17 or soon thereafter, Carlyle taking no further part in the American publication. It follows that it is often possible to reconstruct, at those points in the text where identical new variants appear in both the British and American editions, the revisions that Carlyle must have indicated in both printer's copies. Many of these common readings are changes of wording that in any case would be considered most probably authorial. By contrast,

[32] Letter of TC to John A. Carlyle, May 3, 1846, National Library of Scotland.

[33] Letter of TC to John A. Carlyle, May 20, 1846, National Library of Scotland.

[34] The letter was published in Putnam, *Memoir of G. P. Putnam* 1:183–84.

[35] Letter of TC to Edward Chapman, June 17, 1846, Edinburgh University Library. Carlyle repeated his intention not to read proofs in a letter to John two weeks later: "Our other republications, *Heroes* and the *Miscellanies* are also gone to press. . . . I do not intend to trouble myself with the *proofsheets* for either of these Books" (June 30, 1846, National Library of Scotland).

[36] *Emerson and Carlyle*, 402.

[37] One point where the two copies may *not* have been identical is the revision from "Jena" to "Erlangen" (135.2), which occurs in the British but not the American edition. See Discussion of Editorial Decisions.

the new readings found in the British but *not* in the American edition are nearly all minor changes of punctuation or spelling, and can in general be plausibly explained as having been introduced by the printer in the course of the typesetting and proofreading of the British edition. Thus the new variants that occur in both 1846 editions, whether changes of wording or not, have a strong claim to be considered authorial, and we have in general emended the text to include them. Exceptions to this policy are explained in the Discussion of Editorial Decisions, beginning on page 431.

The "Imprimatur" notwithstanding, the Wiley and Putnam edition as printed contains many egregious corruptions. Of the more than three hundred new variants that appear in it but *not* in the British Third Edition, none can be considered authorial, of course, and nearly all must be the result of typesetters' errors, with the possible exception of a pattern of Americanization of spelling that may have been deliberate. There are almost twenty impossible forms (e.g., "Neutonic" for "Teutonic" at 26.15) and nearly fifty changes of wording, which must all be mistakes, though some (e.g., "picture" for "piece" at 205.18 or "sudden" for "certain" at 64.30) are hard to account for. The more than 250 variants in punctuation and spelling likewise can be explained for the most part as typographical lapses.

THE 1852 FOURTH EDITION

The collation includes the now rare Fourth Edition of 1852. It too was published by Chapman and Hall and printed by Charles Robson's firm, again preserving the style and lineation of the earlier editions and preserving likewise the bulk of the new variants in the British Third Edition, from which it was evidently set. The Fourth Edition contains far fewer new variants, either in wording or in punctuation or spelling, than the Second or Third: twelve changes of wording, of which ten are in Lecture I, and about forty changes of punctuation or spelling.

Most of the alterations of wording in this edition are corrections of errors of reference: "Aristotle" to "Plato" and attendant changes (8.17–8.26), *"Havamal"* to *"Völuspa"* (30.26 and 34.32), *"Childe Etin"* to *"Hynde Etin"* (32.12), and "Sordello" to "Brunetto Latini" (79.31). Of these revisions, all but the last were prompted by a letter to Carlyle from Joseph Neuberg[38] on March 20, 1852. Neuberg was preparing a German translation of *On He-*

[38] On Neuberg see Kaplan, *Thomas Carlyle*, 388.

roes,[39] and wrote with several queries to which Carlyle responded on May 31 and June 1. (For the details of this interesting correspondence, see the notes at 8.17, 19.1-2, 30.26, 31.18, 32.12, 167.6-7, and 177.34.) On July 6, Carlyle again wrote to Neuberg, announcing the publication of the Fourth Edition:

> The edit*n* of *Heroes* is out again; a "copy" not to be procured with*t* difficulty; I have therefore copied the small totality of changes to be made; and have sen[t] it to you. . . . I have introduced, for this fourth edit*n*, the corrections you suggested, and all is ready on my part, but the Bookseller (in this downbreak of the old modes of trade) seems to pause in a kind of amaze*t*, uncertain rather *how* to shape himself,—forecasting in the distance what he calls "a *general cheap edition*."[40]

No pattern emerges from the few changes of punctuation and spelling introduced by the Fourth Edition. Five new typographical errors appear, only one of which was not corrected in the Uniform Edition of 1858.

THE 1858 UNIFORM EDITION

The Uniform Edition of 1857-58, the first collected edition of Carlyle's works, includes *On Heroes*, bound together with *Sartor Resartus*, as volume 6, published in 1858. Although the Uniform Edition was also published by Chapman and Hall and printed by Robson, Levey, and Franklyn, it is set in a smaller typeface, in longer lines, and with more lines to the page than the earlier editions of *On Heroes*. This version contains over five hundred new variants, of which only three amount to changes of wording, the addition of one word in Lecture II (46.35) and the substitution of one word in Lecture I and one in Lecture III (16.4 and 94.36). The many changes of punctuation and spelling, on the other hand, are unmistakable signs of an editor's activity throughout, and it is known from external evidence that Carlyle had at least one and possibly several editorial assistants working on the preparation of *On Heroes*, as well as other works, for the Uniform Edition.

---

[39] *Thomas Carlyle über Helden, Heldenverehrung und das Heldenthümliche in der Geschichte*, Berlin, 1853 (Tarr A12.7.a).

[40] These letters between Carlyle and Neuberg are all in the National Library of Scotland.

Alexander Gilchrist, Henry Larkin, Joseph Neuberg,[41] and especially Vernon Lushington[42] variously helped Carlyle in the preparation of the Uniform Edition, creating chapter summaries and indexes and probably assisting with proofreading. Although neither the extent nor the division of these helpers' editorial responsibilities can now be determined, the significant fact for the history of the text of *On Heroes* is that, beginning with this edition, there are known to have been others besides Carlyle and his printers who were involved in the preparation of the published text.

The collation offers what we take to be evidence of that editorial activity. For example, over 320 hyphens were added to the text of *On Heroes* in the Uniform Edition, of which more than 260 join verbs to following prepositions at every opportunity, as if in parody of Carlyle's occasional "Germanic" hyphenation. Carlyle's spelling is further regularized: in the 1852 edition, the spelling "shew" had continued to be used forty-three times, while "show" occurred four times (one instance of "shew" was revised out of the text in 1846,[43] and two instances of "shew" became "show" in 1852, presumably by typesetter's slip), but in the Uniform Edition, and thereafter, the spelling is "show" on all forty-seven occasions.[44] The other patterns of orthographic regularization begun in the 1846 Third Edition are made consistent throughout the Uniform Edition text: "symbolises" for "symbolizes" (7.29), "lovable" for "loveable" (10.26), and so on. Relatively few alterations of punctuation occur. Five new variants are clearly the result of typographical errors, none surviving into the 1870 Library Edition.

THE 1870 LIBRARY EDITION

In 1870, *On Heroes* was published as volume 12 of the Library Edition of 1869–71, which generally follows the wording, punctuation, and spelling of the Uniform Edition. Six apparently deliberate changes of wording appear (at 10.6, 93.3, 100.14, 107.30, 151.14, and 198.10), two of which could well have been the result of a printer's or editorial assistant's effort to regularize Carlyle's grammar (at 107.30 and 198.10). The rest have been adopted. Preliminary collation of *Sartor Resartus* shows a similar pattern of minor changes of wording in the

---

[41] Kaplan, *Thomas Carlyle*, 414–16.
[42] K. J. Fielding, "Vernon Lushington," 16.
[43] In the long revision beginning at 182.25.
[44] See Murray Baumgarten, "Mind is a Muscle," 43–105.

Library Edition of that work, adding weight to the rather meager evidence of authorial involvement in this edition of *On Heroes*.

On May 20, 1871, Thomas's brother John Carlyle, who lived nearby and was a daily visitor, wrote to their friend the American financier Charles Butler (1802–1897) reporting on Thomas's activities:

> He has got the whole of his works published in what is called the "Library Edition" of thirty volumes; corrected the final proofs himself, making no alterations at all, only rectifying errors wherever he could discover any. A "People's Edition" in the same number of volumes has been begun, but he has no charge of it at all, the printers merely having to follow the Library Edition which is stereotyped.[45]

Among nearly two hundred changes of punctuation and spelling in the Library Edition there are eighteen new paragraph breaks. Twenty changes involve moving question marks and exclamation points from the inside to the outside of closing quotation marks. Other new variants are of even less interest. Eight obvious errors appear, of which four are the changes from "euphuism" to "euphemism" at 179.38, 180.12, 180.14, and 187.1. These four errors were continued in the 1872 People's Edition.

The 1872 People's Edition

The last authorized publication of *On Heroes* in Carlyle's lifetime was as volume 13 (1872) of the People's Edition of 1871–74, and its many reprints that continued to be produced at least through 1901.[46] The People's Edition was clearly based on the Library Edition, preserving most of its punctuation and spelling, but it is a complete resetting, not using the "stereotyped" plates of the Library Edition, contrary to the implication in John Carlyle's letter to Butler quoted above. The type in the People's Edition is considerably smaller, and the lineation and pagination do not correspond.

Except for the correction of "Schwiednitz" to "Schweidnitz" at 125.9, which we take to be authorial (or at any rate the fulfillment of the author's intention), the over thirty new variants of the People's

---

[45] Unpublished letter in the collection of the Edinburgh University Library.
[46] A table on the verso of the title leaf of a 1901 reprint of the *On Heroes* volume gives the number of copies year by year, showing that 130,000 copies had been printed since 1872 (Tarr, *Descriptive Bibliography*, 451).

Edition are no more than the usual result of compositorial activity, including four obvious new typographical errors (e.g., "Thunger-god" at 31.24). In the *On Heroes* volume at least, the collation of the People's Edition confirms John Carlyle's statement that the author had "no charge of it at all."

THE CENTENARY EDITION

Although the posthumous publication of *On Heroes* as volume 5 (1897) of the Centenary Edition of Carlyle's Collected Works—edited by H. D. Traill and published by Chapman and Hall, 1896–99—has no textual authority, we decided to collate it in the preparation of this first volume of the Strouse Edition. Through its widespread availability, the Centenary Edition has acquired the status of the standard edition of Carlyle and has been taken as the copy-text for some modern editions of individual titles, including *On Heroes*. It has, in that sense, become part of the history of the text. On the other hand, the quality of its text had never been investigated. We have not included in the Historical Collation the more than four hundred new variants found in the Centenary Edition,[47] but a number of generalizations about its text are now possible.

The Centenary Edition of *On Heroes* unfortunately used as its copy-text the 1872 People's Edition, in accordance with the general nineteenth-century editorial practice of accepting the last lifetime edition of a work as the definitive text. Moreover, the copy used by the editor was not an original issue of the People's Edition but a later reprint. An undated reprint of the People's Edition of *On Heroes* that we examined[48] contains twenty variants from the original issue, though it was clearly printed using many of the original plates, which show signs of wear. Eight of these variants consist of missing punctuation at line-ends caused by worn or broken type. In three of these places the Centenary Edition is also unpunctuated; in another place where punctuation is necessary the Centenary supplied a comma where all editions through 1872 had a period. A serious typographical error in the reprint not found in the original issue of the People's Edition, "halt, articulating" for "half-articulating" at 65.9, is followed in the Centenary Edition.

[47] The collation of the Centenary Edition is available on request to interested scholars.

[48] See note 5 above. The variants found in this reprint are not included in the Historical Collation.

Some of the errors in the People's Edition and its reprint are corrected by the Centenary, but at least twelve new typographical errors are committed.[49] Aside from these apparent errors, over four hundred new variants appear, of which only the nine instances in which "farther" has been changed to "further" could be considered to amount to changes of wording. "Forever" is changed to "for ever" thirty-five times, and Carlyle's spelling of "Brobdignag" is corrected to "Brobdingnag" in three places (19.3, 32.5, and 34.25).[50]

For the rest, more than half of the variants in the Centenary Edition consist of the substitution of single quotation marks for double quotation marks, destroying Carlyle's deliberate distinction between the two in favor of modern British style. In *On Heroes*, Carlyle uses single quotation marks to indicate common expressions or implied speech, e.g.,

> We call that fire of the black thunder-cloud 'electricity,'
> and lecture learnedly about it. (9.4–6)

On the other hand, he uses double quotation marks to indicate fictional or actual speech or dialogue, e.g.,

> Those are critics of small vision, I think, who cry: "See,
> is it not the sticks that made the fire?" (13.16–17)

This pattern was maintained through all the lifetime editions of *On Heroes* with little change. The Centenary Edition, on the other hand, imposes modern British style on all quotations, using single quotation marks everywhere, except double quotation marks for quotes within quotes (the reverse of standard American practice). Thus Carlyle's double quotation marks are changed to singles in 224 places (counting left and right quotation marks as separate variants) and singles are changed to doubles in four places.

In general, then, the Centenary Edition inaccurately attempts to reproduce the text of the last lifetime edition, regardless of whether its readings were authorial, and it arbitrarily imposes a style of its own on spelling and punctuation. As a result the edition of Carlyle's works that has been most respectfully and generally used is textually the worst.

---

[49] For the record, the changes of wording in the Centenary Edition, which must be taken to be either typographical errors or unjustifiable editorial emendations, are as follows: "take" is omitted at 33.30, "some" is omitted at 40.25, "in" is substituted for "as" at 80.19, "earthly" for "earthy" at 89.21, "this" for "his" at 137.35, "wilderness" for "wildernesses" at 138.32, "wild" for "wide" at 187.14, and "now" is added after "not" at 189.29.

[50] See Discussion of Editorial Decisions at 19.3.

PLATES

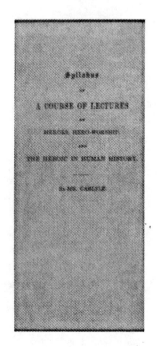

PLATE 1. The syllabus for Carlyle's 1840 lecture
series on heroes. Beinecke Library.

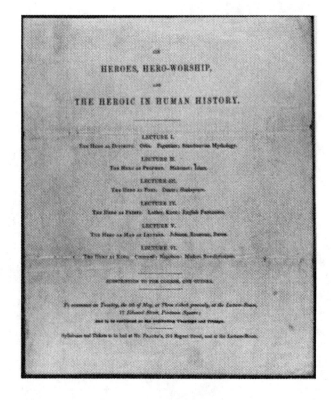

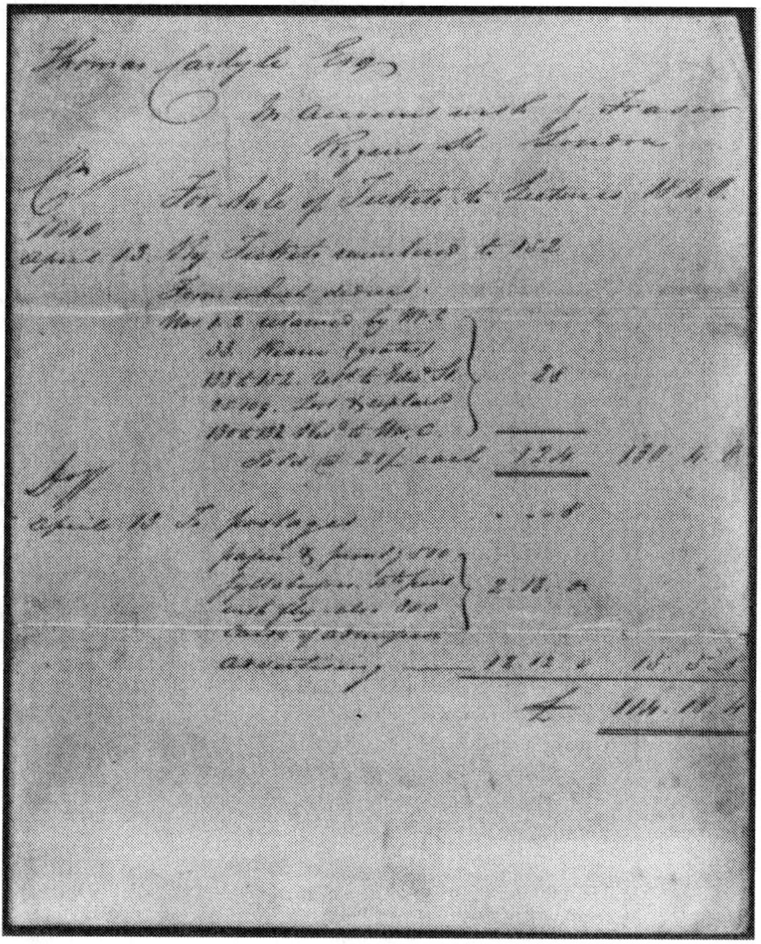
Thomas Carlyle Esq
In Account with J. Fraser
Regent St London
Cr. For Sale of Tickets to Lectures 1840.
1840
April 13. By Tickets numbered to 152
From which deduct:
Sold @ 21/- each

PLATE 2. The receipt for Carlyle's lecture fee.
Beinecke Library.

Revise

Pagan religions have struggled, as they could, to set forth. I think Scandinavian Paganism to us here is more interesting than any other. It is, for one thing, the latest; it continued in these regions of Europe till the eleventh century; eight hundred years ago the Norwegians were still worshippers of Odin. It is interesting also as the creed of our fathers; the men whose blood still runs in our veins, whom doubtless we still resemble in so many ways, strange: they did believe that, while we believe so differently. Let us look a little at this poor Norse creed, for many reasons. We have tolerable means to do it; for there is another point of interest in these Scandinavian mythologies: that they have been preserved so well.

In that strange island Iceland,—burst up, the geologists say, by fire from the bottom of the sea; a wild land of barrenness and lava; swallowed many months of every year in black tempests, yet with a wild gleaming beauty in summer-time; towering up there, stern and grim, in the North Ocean; with its snow-jokuls, roaring geysers, sulphur pools and horrid volcanic chasms, like the waste chaotic battle-field of Frost and Fire;—where of all places we least looked for Literature or written memorials, the record of these things was written down. On

c

the seabord of this wild land is a rim of grassy
country, where cattle can subsist, and men by
means of them and what the sea yields; and it
seems they were poetic men these, men who had
deep thoughts in them, and uttered musically
their thoughts. Much would be lost had Iceland not been burst up from the sea, not been
discovered by the Northmen! The old Norse
Poets were many of them natives of Iceland.

Sæmund, one of the early Christian Priests
there, who perhaps had a lingering fondness for
Paganism, collected certain of their old Pagan
songs, just about becoming obsolete then,—
Poems or Chaunts of a mythic, prophetic, mostly
all of a religious character: this is what Norse
critics call the *Elder* or Poetic *Edda*. *Edda*,
a word of uncertain etymology, is thought to
signify *Ancestress*. Snorro Sturleson, an Iceland gentleman, an extremely notable personage,
educated by this Sæmund's grandson, took in
hand next, near a century afterwards to put
together, among several other books he wrote, a
kind of Prose Synopsis of the whole Mythology;
elucidated by new fragments of traditionary verse.
A work constructed really with great ingenuity,
native talent, what one might call unconscious
art; altogether a perspicuous clear work, pleasant reading still: this is the *Younger* or Prose

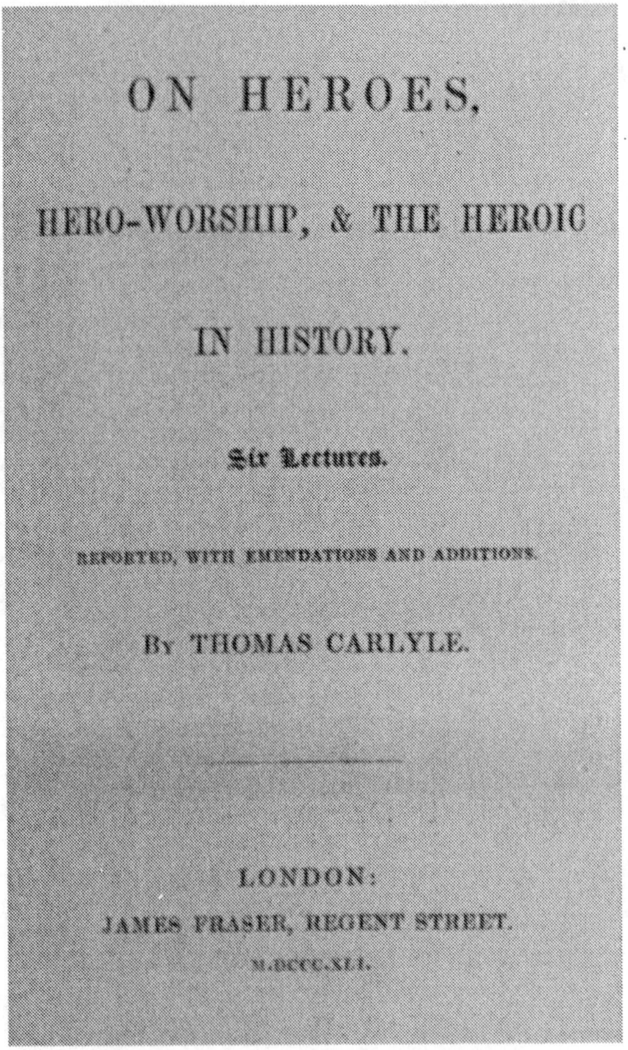

ON HEROES,

HERO-WORSHIP, & THE HEROIC

IN HISTORY.

Six Lectures.

REPORTED, WITH EMENDATIONS AND ADDITIONS.

By THOMAS CARLYLE.

LONDON:

JAMES FRASER, REGENT STREET.

M.DCCC.XLI.

PLATE 4. The title page of the first edition of *On Heroes*. Strouse Collection, University Libraries, University of California, Santa Cruz.

PLATE 5. The portrait of Dante "commonly attributed to Giotto" (see 73.35–36 and note) was not actually by Giotto. Carlyle's source was almost certainly an engraving prepared for Raffael Morghen by Stefano Tofanelli (*left*) from a lost original that some critics have identified as the "Yale" Dante (*above*). A copy of the engraving, which Carlyle owned at his death, is quite likely to be the one that Carlyle mentions receiving from his brother John in 1834 (*Letters* 7:109). Another version of the same portrait, engraved by R. Young, appears as the frontispiece of John Carlyle's edition of the *Inferno* (1849). James Jackson Jarves Collection, Yale University Art Gallery.

PLATE 6. "In Kranach's best portraits I find the true
Luther" (121.28–29). One of the finest of Cranach's
portraits that captures the qualities Carlyle discerned
in Luther is this watercolor on parchment, circa
1532. Collection of The Duke of Buccleuch and
Queensberry, K. T., Boughton House, Kettering,
England.

IOANNES CNOXVS.

PLATE 7. This picture of Knox, published in
Theodore Beza's *Icones* (1580), was rejected by
Carlyle on physiognomic grounds, as being
irreconcilable with the man who kindled Scotland to
a blaze of religious fervor. "Here," he wrote, "is a
gentleman seemingly of a quite eupeptic, not to say
stolid and thoughtless frame of mind; much at his
ease in Zion, and content to take things as they
come, if only they will let him digest his victuals, and
sleep in a whole skin" ("Portraits of John Knox"
[1875], *Essays* 5:319; the engraving itself appears as
an illustration at 5:318). Carlyle preferred a portrait
painted for Lord Somerville in about 1760 from an
earlier engraving, "the only probable likeness of
[Knox], anywhere known to exist" (*Essays* 5:361), but
few now share his confidence about its authenticity.

JAMES BOSWELL Esq.
In the dress of an Armed Corsican Chief, as he appeared at
Shakespeare's Jubilee, at Stratford upon Avon September 1769.

PLATE 8. Boswell in the costume of a Corsican chief
at the Shakespeare Jubilee at Stratford (see 192.17–18
and note). The picture accompanied Boswell's
anonymous account of the masquerade in the *London
Magazine* for September 1769, p. 455, which began:
"One of the most remarkable masks upon this
occasion was James Boswell, Esq; in the dress of an
armed Corsican chief. He entered the amphitheatre
about twelve o'clock. He wore a short dark-coloured
coat of coarse cloth, scarlet waistcoat and breeches,
and black spatterdashes & his cap or bonnet was of
black cloth; on the front of it was embroidered in
gold letters, Viva La Liberta; and on one side of it
was a handsome blue feather and cockade, so that it
had an elegant, as well as a warlike appearance."

PLATE 9. Robert Burns, the subject of Carlyle's review essay of 1828 and one of the figures of his lecture on the hero as man of letters. Painting by Alexander Nasmyth. National Portrait Gallery, London.

PLATE 10. A portrait of Cromwell by Sir Peter Lely
that Carlyle saw in September 1842 in Cromwell's
own Sidney Sussex College, Cambridge. It remained
his favorite image of the man whose reputation
Carlyle worked hard to rehabilitate both in *On Heroes*
and in *Oliver Cromwell's Letters and Speeches* (1845).
Cromwell "is not a *quack*," Carlyle wrote to John
Forster in 1842, "he rather seems to me a *god:* but
how shall I ever convince *you* of that!" (*Letters*
15:70). By kind permission of the Master and Fellows
of Sidney Sussex College, Cambridge.

PLATE 11. Ten years after his Cromwell lecture,
Carlyle urged the erection of a statue to Cromwell,
but it was not until 1901 that this monument to the
Lord Protector was finally put up in St. Ives,
Huntingdonshire. Photo by Michael K. Goldberg.

On Heroes,
Hero-Worship, & the Heroic
in History.

Six Lectures.

Reported, With Emendations and Additions.

By Thomas Carlyle.

LECTURE I.

[Tuesday, 5th May, 1840.]

THE HERO AS DIVINITY. ODIN. PAGANISM: SCANDINAVIAN MYTHOLOGY.

WE have undertaken to discourse here for a little on Great Men, their manner of appearance in our world's business, how they have shaped themselves in the world's history, what ideas men formed of them, what work they did;—on Heroes, namely, and on their reception and performance; what I call Hero-worship and the Heroic in human affairs. Too evidently this is a large topic; deserving quite other treatment than we can expect to give it at present. A large topic; indeed, an illimitable one; wide as Universal History itself. For, as I take it, Universal History, the history of what man has accomplished in this world, is at bottom the History of the Great Men who have worked here. They were the leaders of men, these great ones; the modellers, patterns, and in a wide sense creators, of whatsoever the general mass of men contrived to do or to attain; all things that we see standing accomplished in the world are properly the outer material result, the practical realisation and embodiment, of Thoughts that dwelt in the Great Men sent into the world: the soul of the whole world's history, it may justly be considered, were the history of these. Too clearly it is a topic we shall do no justice to in this place!

One comfort is, that Great Men, taken up in any way, are profitable company. We cannot look, however imperfectly, upon a great man, without gaining something by him. He is the living light-fountain, which it is good and pleasant to be near. The light which enlightens, which has enlightened the darkness of the world: and this not as a kindled lamp only, but rather as a natural luminary shining

3

by the gift of Heaven; a flowing light-fountain, as I say, of native
original insight, of manhood and heroic nobleness;—in whose radiance all souls feel that it is well with them. On any terms whatsoever,
you will not grudge to wander in such neighbourhood for a while.
These Six classes of Heroes, chosen out of widely distant countries
and epochs, and in mere external figure differing altogether, ought,
if we look faithfully at them, to illustrate several things for us. Could
we see *them* well, we should get some glimpses into the very marrow
of the world's history. How happy, could I but, in any measure, in
such times as these, make manifest to you the meanings of Heroism;
the divine relation (for I may well call it such) which in all times
unites a Great Man to other men; and thus, as it were, not exhaust
my subject, but so much as break ground on it! At all events, I must
make the attempt.

It is well said, in every sense, that a man's religion is the chief fact
with regard to him. A man's, or a nation of men's. By religion I do
not mean here the church-creed which he professes, the articles of
faith which he will sign and, in words or otherwise, assert; not this
wholly, in many cases not this at all. We see men of all kinds of
professed creeds attain to almost all degrees of worth or worthless-
ness under each or any of them. This is not what I call religion, this
profession and assertion; which is often only a profession and assertion from the outworks of the man, from the mere argumentative
region of him, if even so deep as that. But the thing a man does
practically believe (and this is often enough *without* asserting it even
to himself, much less to others); the thing a man does practically lay
to heart, and know for certain, concerning his vital relations to this
mysterious Universe, and his duty and destiny there, that is in all
cases the primary thing for him, and creatively determines all the rest.
That is his *religion;* or, it may be, his mere scepticism and *no-religion:*
the manner it is in which he feels himself to be spiritually related to
the Unseen World or No-world; and I say, if you tell me what that
is, you tell me to a very great extent what the man is, what the kind
of things he will do is. Of a man or of a nation we inquire, therefore,
first of all, What religion they had? Was it Heathenism,—plurality of
gods, mere sensuous representation of this Mystery of Life, and for
chief recognised element therein Physical Force? Was it Christianism;

faith in an Invisible, not as real only, but as the only reality; Time, through every meanest moment of it, resting on Eternity; Pagan empire of Force displaced by a nobler supremacy, that of Holiness? Was it Scepticism, uncertainty and inquiry whether there was an Unseen World, any Mystery of Life except a mad one;—doubt as to all this, or perhaps unbelief and flat denial? Answering of this question is giving us the soul of the history of the man or nation. The thoughts they had were the parents of the actions they did; their feelings were parents of their thoughts: it was the unseen and spiritual in them that determined the outward and actual;—their religion, as I say, was the great fact about them. In these Discourses, limited as we are, it will be good to direct our survey chiefly to that religious phasis of the matter. That once known well, all is known. We have chosen as the first Hero in our series, Odin the central figure of Scandinavian Paganism; an emblem to us of a most extensive province of things. Let us look, for a little, at the Hero as Divinity, the oldest primary form of Heroism.

Surely it seems a very strange-looking thing this Paganism; almost inconceivable to us in these days. A bewildering, inextricable jungle of delusions, confusions, falsehoods, and absurdities, covering the whole field of Life! A thing that fills us with astonishment, almost, if it were possible, with incredulity,—for truly it is not easy to understand that sane men could ever calmly, with their eyes open, believe and live by such a set of doctrines. That men should have worshipped their poor fellow-man as a God, and not him only, but stocks and stones, and all manner of animate and inanimate objects; and fashioned for themselves such a distracted chaos of hallucinations by way of Theory of the Universe: all this looks like an incredible fable. Nevertheless it is a clear fact that they did it. Such hideous inextricable jungle of misworships, misbeliefs, men, made as we are, did actually hold by, and live at home in. This is strange. Yes, we may pause in sorrow and silence over the depths of darkness that are in man; if we rejoice in the heights of purer vision he has attained to. Such things were and are in man; in all men; in us too.

Some speculators have a short way of accounting for the Pagan religion: mere quackery, priestcraft, and dupery, say they; no sane man ever did believe it,—merely contrived to persuade other men, not worthy of the name of sane, to believe it! It will be often our duty to protest against this sort of hypothesis about men's doings and history; and I here, on the very threshold, protest against it in reference to Paganism, and to all other *isms* by which man has ever for a length of time striven to walk in this world. They have all had a truth in them, or men would not have taken them up. Quackery and dupery do abound; in religions, above all in the more advanced decaying stages of religions, they have fearfully abounded: but quackery was never the originating influence in such things; it was not the health and life of such things, but their disease, the sure precursor of their being about to die! Let us never forget this. It seems to me a most mournful hypothesis, that of quackery giving birth to any faith even in savage men. Quackery gives birth to nothing; gives death to all things. We shall not see into the true heart of anything, if we look merely at the quackeries of it; if we do not reject the quackeries altogether; as mere diseases, corruptions, with which our and all men's sole duty is to have done with them, to sweep them out of our thoughts as out of our practice. Man everywhere is the born enemy of lies. I find Grand Lamaism itself to have a kind of truth in it. Read the candid, clear-sighted, rather sceptical Mr. Turner's *Account of his Embassy* to that country, and see. They have their belief, these poor Thibet people, that Providence sends down always an Incarnation of Himself into every generation. At bottom some belief in a kind of Pope! At bottom still better, belief that there is a *Greatest* Man; that *he* is discoverable; that, once discovered, we ought to treat him with an obedience which knows no bounds! This is the truth of Grand Lamaism; the 'discoverability' is the only error here. The Thibet Priests have methods of their own of discovering what Man is Greatest, fit to be supreme over them. Bad methods: but are they so much worse than our methods,—of understanding him to be always the eldest-born of a certain genealogy? Alas, it is a difficult thing to find good methods for!——We shall begin to have a chance of understanding Paganism, when we first admit that to its followers it was, at one time, earnestly true. Let us consider it very certain that men did believe in Paganism; men with open eyes, sound senses, men made altogether like ourselves; that we, had we been there, should have believed in it. Ask now, What Paganism could have been?

Another theory, somewhat more respectable, attributes such things to Allegory. It was a play of poetic minds, say these theorists;

a shadowing forth, in allegorical fable, in personification, and visual form, of what such poetic minds had known and felt of this Universe. Which agrees, add they, with a primary law of human nature, still everywhere observably at work, though in less important things, That what a man feels intensely, he struggles to speak out of him, to see represented before him in visual shape, and as if with a kind of life and historical reality in it. Now doubtless there is such a law, and it is one of the deepest in human nature; neither need we doubt that it did operate fundamentally in this business. The hypothesis which ascribes Paganism wholly or mostly to this agency, I call a little more respectable; but I cannot yet call it the true hypothesis. Think, would *we* believe, and take with us as our life-guidance, an allegory, a poetic sport? Not sport but earnest is what we should require. It is a most earnest thing to be alive in this world; to die is not sport for a man. Man's life never was a sport to him; it was a stern reality, altogether a serious matter to be alive! I find, therefore, that though these Allegory-theorists are on the way towards truth in this matter, they have not reached it either. Pagan Religion is indeed an Allegory, a Symbol of what men felt and knew about the Universe; and all Religions are symbols of that, altering always as that alters: but it seems to me a radical perversion, and even *in*version, of the business, to put that forward as the origin and moving cause, when it was rather the result and termination. To get beautiful allegories, a perfect poetic symbol, was not the want of men; but to know what they were to believe about this Universe, what course they were to steer in it; what, in this mysterious Life of theirs, they had to hope and to fear, to do and to forbear doing. The *Pilgrim's Progress* is an Allegory, and a beautiful, just and serious one: but consider whether Bunyan's Allegory could have *preceded* the Faith it symbolizes! The Faith had to be already there, standing believed by everybody;—of which the Allegory could *then* become a shadow; and, with all its seriousness, we may say a *sportful* shadow, a mere play of the Fancy, in comparison with that awful Fact and scientific certainty, which it poetically strives to emblem. The Allegory is the product of the certainty, not the producer of it; not in Bunyan's nor in any other case. For Paganism, therefore, we have still to inquire, Whence came that scientific certainty, the parent of such a bewildered heap of allegories, errors and confusions? How was it, what was it?

Surely it were a foolish attempt to pretend 'explaining,' in this place, or in any place, such a phenomenon as that far-distant distracted cloudy imbroglio of Paganism,—more like a cloudfield, than a distant continent of firm-land and facts! It is no longer a reality, yet it was one. We ought to understand that this seeming cloudfield was once a reality; that not poetic allegory, least of all that dupery and deception was the origin of it. Men, I say, never did believe idle songs, never risked their soul's life on allegories: men, in all times, especially in early earnest times, have had an instinct for detecting quacks, for detesting quacks. Let us try if, leaving out both the quack-theory and the allegory one, and listening with affectionate attention to that far-off confused rumour of the Pagan ages, we cannot ascertain so much as this at least, That there was a kind of fact at the heart of them; that they too were not mendacious and distracted, but in their own poor way true and sane!

You remember that fancy of Plato's, of a man who had grown to maturity in some dark distance, and was brought on a sudden into the upper air to see the sun rise. What would his wonder be, his rapt astonishment at the sight we daily witness with indifference! With the free open sense of a child, yet with the ripe faculty of a man, his whole heart would be kindled by that sight, he would discern it well to be Godlike, his soul would fall down in worship before it. Now, just such a childlike greatness was in the primitive nations. The first Pagan Thinker among rude men, the first man that began to think, was precisely this child-man of Plato's. Simple, open as a child, yet with the depth and strength of a man. Nature had as yet no name to him; he had not yet united under a name the infinite variety of sights, sounds, shapes and motions, which we now collectively name Universe, Nature, or the like,—and so with a name dismiss it from us. To the wild deep-hearted man all was yet new, not veiled under names or formulas; it stood naked, flashing in on him there, beautiful, awful, unspeakable. Nature was to this man, what to the Thinker and Prophet it forever is, *preter*natural. This green flowery rock-built earth, the trees, the mountains, rivers, many-sounding seas;—that great deep sea of azure that swims overhead; the winds sweeping through it; the black cloud fashioning itself together, now pouring out fire, now hail and rain: what *is* it? Ay, what? At bottom we do not yet know; we can never know at all. It is not by our superior insight

that we escape the difficulty; it is by our superior levity, our inatten-
tion, our *want* of insight. It is by *not* thinking that we cease to
wonder at it. Hardened round us, encasing wholly every notion we
form, is a wrappage of traditions, hearsays, mere *words*. We call that
fire of the black thunder-cloud 'electricity,' and lecture learnedly
about it, and grind the like of it out of glass and silk: but *what* is it?
What made it? Whence comes it? Whither goes it? Science has done
much for us; but it is a poor science that would hide from us the great
deep sacred infinitude of Nescience, whither we can never penetrate,
on which all science swims as a mere superficial film. This world, after
all our science and sciences, is still a miracle; wonderful, inscrutable,
magical and more, to whosoever will *think* of it.

That great mystery of TIME, were there no other; the illimitable,
silent, never-resting thing called Time, rolling, rushing on, swift,
silent, like an all-embracing ocean-tide, on which we and all the
Universe swim like exhalations, like apparitions which *are*, and then
are not: this is forever very literally a miracle; a thing to strike us
dumb,—for we have no word to speak about it. This Universe, ah
me!—what could the wild man know of it; what can we yet know?
That it is a Force, and thousandfold Complexity of Forces; a Force
which is *not we*. That is all; it is not we, it is altogether different from
us. Force, Force, everywhere Force; we ourselves a mysterious Force
in the centre of that. 'There is not a leaf rotting on the highway but
has Force in it: how else could it rot?' Nay surely, to the Atheistic
Thinker, if such a one were possible, it must be a miracle too, this
huge illimitable whirlwind of Force, which envelopes us here; never-
resting whirlwind, high as Immensity, old as Eternity. What is it?
God's Creation, the religious people answer; it is the Almighty God's!
Atheistic science babbles poorly of it, with scientific nomenclatures,
experiments and what not, as if it were a poor dead thing, to be
bottled up in Leyden jars, and sold over counters: but the natural
sense of man, in all times, if he will honestly apply his sense, pro-
claims it to be a living thing,—ah, an unspeakable, godlike thing;
towards which the best attitude for us, after never so much science,
is awe, devout prostration and humility of soul; worship if not in
words, then in silence.

But now I remark farther: What in such a time as ours it requires
a Prophet or Poet to teach us, namely, the stripping off of those poor
undevout wrappages, nomenclatures and scientific hearsays,—this, the

ancient earnest soul, as yet unencumbered with these things, did for itself. The world, which is now divine only to the gifted, was then divine to whosoever would turn his eye upon it. He stood bare before it face to face. 'All was Godlike or God:'—Jean Paul still finds it so; the giant Jean Paul, who has power to escape out of hearsays: but there then were no hearsays. Canopus shining down over the desert, with its blue diamond brightness (that wild blue spirit-like brightness, far brighter than we ever witness here), would pierce into the heart of the wild Ishmaelitish man, whom it was guiding through the solitary waste there. To his wild heart, with all feelings in it, with no *speech* for any feeling, it might seem a little eye, that Canopus, glancing out on him from the great deep Eternity; revealing the inner Splendour to him. Cannot we understand how these men *worshipped* Canopus; became what we call Sabeans, worshipping the stars? Such is to me the secret of all forms of Paganism. Worship is transcendent wonder; wonder for which there is now no limit or measure; that is worship. To these primeval men, all things and everything they saw exist beside them were an emblem of the Godlike, of some God.

And look what perennial fibre of truth was in that. To us also, through every star, through every blade of grass, is not a God made visible, if we will open our minds and eyes? We do not worship in that way now: but is it not reckoned still a merit, proof of what we call a 'poetic nature,' that we recognise how every object has a divine beauty in it; how every object still verily is 'a window through which we may look into Infinitude itself?' He that can discern the loveliness of things, we call him Poet, Painter, Man of Genius, gifted, loveable. These poor Sabeans did even what he does,—in their own fashion. That they did it, in what fashion soever, was a merit: better than what the entirely stupid man did, what the horse and camel did,—namely, nothing!

But now if all things whatsoever that we look upon are emblems to us of the Highest God, I add that more so than any of them is man such an emblem. You have heard of St. Chrysostom's celebrated saying, in reference to the Shekinah, or Ark of Testimony, visible Revelation of God, among the Hebrews: "The true Shekinah is Man!" Yes, it is even so: this is no vain phrase; it is veritably so. The essence of our being, the mystery in us that calls itself "I,"—ah, what words have we for such things?—is a breath of Heaven; the Highest

Being reveals himself in man. This body, these faculties, this life of ours, is it not all as a vesture for that Unnamed? 'There is but one temple in the Universe,' says the devout Novalis, 'and that is the Body of Man. Nothing is holier than that high form. Bending before men is a reverence done to this Revelation in the Flesh. We touch Heaven when we lay our hand on a human body!' This sounds much like a mere flourish of rhetoric; but it is not so. If well meditated, it will turn out to be a scientific fact; the expression, in such words as can be had, of the actual truth of the thing. *We* are the miracle of miracles,—the great inscrutable mystery of God. We cannot understand it, we know not how to speak of it; but we may feel and know, if we like, that it is verily so.

Well; these truths were once more readily felt than now. The young generations of the world, who had in them the freshness of young children, and yet the depth of earnest men, who did not think that they had finished off all things in Heaven and Earth by merely giving them scientific names, but had to gaze direct at them there, with awe and wonder: they felt better what of divinity is in man and Nature;—they, without being mad, could *worship* Nature, and man more than anything else in Nature. Worship, that is, as I said above, admire without limit: this, in the full use of their faculties, with all sincerity of heart, they could do. I consider Hero-worship to be the grand modifying element in that ancient system of thought. What I called the perplexed jungle of Paganism sprang, we may say, out of many roots: every admiration, adoration of a star or natural object, was a root or fibre of a root; but Hero-worship is the deepest root of all; the tap-root, from which in a great degree all the rest were nourished and grown.

And now if worship even of a star had some meaning in it, how much more might that of a Hero! Worship of a Hero is transcendent admiration of a Great Man. I say great men are still admirable; I say there is, at bottom, nothing else admirable! No nobler feeling than this of admiration for one higher than himself dwells in the breast of man. It is to this hour, and at all hours, the vivifying influence in man's life. Religion I find stand upon it; not Paganism only, but far higher and truer religions,—all religion hitherto known. Hero-worship, heartfelt prostrate admiration, submission, burning, boundless, for a noblest godlike Form of Man,—is not that the germ of

Christianity itself? The greatest of all Heroes is One—whom we do
not name here! Let sacred silence meditate that sacred matter; you
will find it the ultimate perfection of a principle extant throughout
man's whole history on earth.

Or coming into lower, less *un*speakable provinces, is not all
Loyalty akin to religious Faith also? Faith is loyalty to some inspired
Teacher, some spiritual Hero. And what therefore is loyalty proper,
the life-breath of all society, but an effluence of Hero-worship, submissive admiration for the truly great? Society is founded on Hero-
worship. All dignities of rank, on which human association rests, are
what we may call a *Hero*archy (Government of Heroes),—or a Hierarchy, for it is 'sacred' enough withal! The Duke means *Dux*, Leader;
King is *Kön-ning, Kan-ning*, Man that *knows* or *cans*. Society everywhere is some representation, not *in*supportably inaccurate, of a
graduated Worship of Heroes;—reverence and obedience done to
men really great and wise. Not *in*supportably inaccurate, I say! They
are all as bank-notes, these social dignitaries, all representing gold;—
and several of them, alas, always are *forged* notes. We can do with
some forged false notes; with a good many even: but not with all, or
the most of them forged! No: there have to come revolutions then;
cries of Democracy, Liberty and Equality, and I know not what:—the
notes being all false, and no gold to be had for *them*, people take to
crying in their despair that there is no gold, that there never was
any!—'Gold,' Hero-worship, *is* nevertheless, as it was always and
everywhere, and cannot cease till man himself ceases.

I am well aware that in these days Hero-worship, the thing I call
Hero-worship, professes to have gone out, and finally ceased. This,
for reasons which it will be worth while some time to inquire into,
is an age that as it were denies the existence of great men; denies the
desirableness of great men. Shew our critics a great man, a Luther for
example, they begin to what they call 'account' for him; not to
worship him, but take the dimensions of him,—and bring him out to
be a little kind of man! He was the 'creature of the Time,' they say;
the Time called him forth, the Time did everything, he nothing—but
what we the little critic could have done too! This seems to me but
melancholy work. The Time call forth? Alas, we have known Times
call loudly enough for their great man; but not find him when they
called! He was not there; Providence had not sent him; the Time,

calling its loudest, had to go down to confusion and wreck because he would not come when called. For if we will think of it, no Time need have gone to ruin, could it have *found* a man great enough, a man wise and good enough: wisdom to discern truly what the Time wanted, valour to lead it on the right road thither; these are the salvation of any Time. But I liken common languid Times, with their unbelief, distress, perplexity, with their languid doubting characters and embarrassed circumstances, impotently crumbling down into ever worse distress towards final ruin;—all this I liken to dry dead fuel, waiting for the lightning out of Heaven that shall kindle it. The great man, with his free force direct out of God's own hand, is the lightning. His word is the wise healing word which all can believe in. All blazes round him now, when he has once struck on it, into fire like his own. The dry mouldering sticks are thought to have called him forth. They did want him greatly; but as to calling him forth—!—Those are critics of small vision, I think, who cry: "See, is it not the sticks that made the fire?" No sadder proof can be given by a man of his own littleness than disbelief in great men. There is no sadder symptom of a generation than such general blindness to the spiritual lightning, with faith only in the heap of barren dead fuel. It is the last consummation of unbelief. In all epochs of the world's history, we shall find the Great Man to have been the indispensable saviour of his epoch;—the lightning, without which the fuel never would have burnt. The History of the World, I said already, was the Biography of Great Men.

Such small critics do what they can to promote unbelief and universal spiritual paralysis; but happily they cannot always completely succeed. In all times it is possible for a man to arise great enough to feel that they and their doctrines are chimeras and cobwebs. And what is notable, in no time whatever can they entirely eradicate out of living men's hearts a certain altogether peculiar reverence for Great Men; genuine admiration, loyalty, adoration, however dim and perverted it may be. Hero-worship endures forever while man endures. Boswell venerates his Johnson, right truly even in the Eighteenth century. The unbelieving French believe in their Voltaire; and burst out round him into very curious Hero-worship, in that last act of his life, when they 'stifle him under roses.' It has always seemed to me extremely curious this of Voltaire. Truly, if Christianity be the highest instance of Hero-worship, then we may find here in Voltairism one of the lowest! He whose life was that of a kind of Antichrist, does again on this side exhibit a curious contrast. No people ever were so little prone to admire at all as those French of Voltaire. *Persiflage* was the character of their whole mind; adoration had nowhere a place in it. Yet see! The old man of Ferney comes up to Paris; an old, tottering, infirm man of eighty-four years. They feel that he too is a kind of Hero; that he has spent his life in opposing error and injustice, delivering Calases, unmasking hypocrites in high places;—in short that *he* too, though in a strange way, has fought like a valiant man. They feel withal that, if *persiflage* be the great thing, there never was such a *persifleur*. He is the realized ideal of every one of them; the thing they are all wanting to be; of all Frenchmen the most French. *He* is properly their god,—such god as they are fit for. Accordingly all persons, from the Queen Antoinette to the Douanier at the Porte St. Denis, do they not worship him? People of quality disguise themselves as tavern-waiters. The Maitre de Poste, with a broad oath, orders his Postilion: "*Va bon train;* thou art driving M. de Voltaire." At Paris his carriage is 'the nucleus of a comet, whose train fills whole streets.' The ladies pluck a hair or two from his fur, to keep it as a sacred relic. There was nothing highest, beautifullest, noblest in all France, that did not feel this man to be higher, beautifuller, nobler.

Yes, from Norse Odin to English Samuel Johnson, from the divine Founder of Christianity to the withered Pontiff of Encyclopedism, in all times and places, the Hero has been worshipped. It will ever be so. We all love great men; love, venerate and bow down submissive before great men: nay can we honestly bow down to anything else? Ah, does not every true man feel that he is himself made higher by doing reverence to what is really above him? No nobler or more blessed feeling dwells in man's heart. And to me it is very cheering to consider that no sceptical logic, or general triviality, insincerity and aridity of any Time and its influences can destroy this noble inborn loyalty and worship that is in man. In times of unbelief, which soon have to become times of revolution, much down-rushing, sorrowful decay and ruin is visible to everybody. For myself in these days, I seem to see in this indestructibility of Hero-worship the everlasting adamant lower than which the confused wreck of revolutionary things cannot fall. The confused wreck of things crumbling and even crashing and tumbling all round us in these revolutionary ages, will get down so far; *no* farther. It is an eternal corner-stone, from which they can begin to build themselves up again. That man, in some sense or other, worships Heroes; that we all of us reverence and must ever reverence Great Men: this is, to me, the living rock amid all rushings down whatsoever;—the one fixed point in modern revolutionary history, otherwise as if bottomless and shoreless.

So much of truth, only under an ancient obsolete vesture, but the spirit of it still true, do I find in the Paganism of old nations. Nature is still divine, the revelation of the workings of God; the Hero is still worshipable: this, under poor cramped incipient forms, is what all Pagan religions have struggled, as they could, to set forth. I think Scandinavian Paganism, to us here, is more interesting than any other. It is, for one thing, the latest; it continued in these regions of Europe till the eleventh century; eight hundred years ago the Norwegians were still worshippers of Odin. It is interesting also as the creed of our fathers; the men whose blood still runs in our veins, whom doubtless we still resemble in so many ways. Strange: they did believe that, while we believe so differently. Let us look a little at this poor Norse creed, for many reasons. We have tolerable means to do it; for there is another point of interest in these Scandinavian mythologies: that they have been preserved so well.

In that strange island Iceland,—burst up, the geologists say, by fire from the bottom of the sea; a wild land of barrenness and lava; swallowed many months of every year in black tempests, yet with a wild gleaming beauty in summer-time; towering up there, stern and grim, in the North Ocean; with its snow-jokuls, roaring geysers, sulphur-pools and horrid volcanic chasms, like the waste chaotic battle-field of Frost and Fire;—where of all places we least looked for Literature or written memorials, the record of these things was written down. On the seabord of this wild land is a rim of grassy country, where cattle can subsist, and men by means of them and of what the sea yields; and it seems they were poetic men these, men who had deep thoughts in them, and uttered musically their thoughts. Much would be lost had Iceland not been burst up from the sea, not been discovered by the Northmen! The old Norse Poets were many of them natives of Iceland.

Sæmund, one of the early Christian Priests there, who perhaps had a lingering fondness for Paganism, collected certain of their old Pagan songs, just about becoming obsolete then,—Poems or Chaunts of a mythic, prophetic, mostly all of a religious character: that is what Norse critics call the *Elder* or Poetic *Edda*. *Edda*, a word of uncertain etymology, is thought to signify *Ancestress*. Snorro Sturleson, an Iceland gentleman, an extremely notable personage, educated by this Sæmund's grandson, took in hand next, near a century afterwards, to put together, among several other books he wrote, a kind of Prose Synopsis of the whole Mythology; elucidated by new fragments of traditionary verse. A work constructed really with great ingenuity, native talent, what one might call unconscious art; altogether a perspicuous clear work, pleasant reading still: this is the *Younger* or Prose *Edda*. By these and the numerous other *Sagas*, mostly Icelandic, with the commentaries, Icelandic or not, which go on zealously in the North to this day, it is possible to gain some direct insight even yet; and see that old Norse system of Belief, as it were, face to face. Let us forget that it is erroneous Religion; let us look at it as old Thought, and try if we cannot sympathise with it somewhat.

The primary characteristic of this old Northland Mythology I find to be Impersonation of the visible workings of Nature. Earnest simple recognition of the workings of Physical Nature, as a thing wholly miraculous, stupendous and divine. What we now lecture of as Science, they wondered at, and fell down in awe before, as Religion. The dark hostile Powers of Nature they figure to themselves as '*Jötuns*,' Giants, huge shaggy beings of a demonic character. Frost, Fire, Sea-tempest; these are Jötuns. The friendly Powers again, as Summer-heat, the Sun, are Gods. The empire of this Universe is divided between these two; they dwell apart, in perennial internecine feud. The Gods dwell above in Asgard, the Garden of the Asen or Divinities; Jötunheim, a distant dark chaotic land, is the Home of the Jötuns.

Curious all this; and not idle or inane, if we will look at the foundation of it! The power of *Fire*, or *Flame*, for instance, which we designate by some trivial chemical name, thereby hiding from ourselves the essential character of wonder that dwells in it as in all things, is with these old Northmen, Loke, a most swift subtle *Demon*, of the brood of the Jötuns. The savages of the Ladrones Islands too (say some Spanish voyagers) thought Fire, which they never had seen before, was a devil or god, that bit you sharply when you touched it, and that lived upon dry wood. From us too, no Chemistry, if it had not Stupidity to help it, would hide that Flame is a wonder. What *is* Flame?—*Frost* the old Norse Seer discerns to be a monstrous Hoary Jötun, the Giant *Thrym, Hrym;* or *Rime,* the old word now nearly obsolete here, but still used in Scotland to signify hoar-frost. *Rime* was not then as now a dead chemical thing, but a living Jötun or Devil; the monstrous Jötun *Rime* drove home his Horses at night, sat 'combing their manes,'—which Horses were *Hail-Clouds,* or fleet *Frost-winds.* His Cows—No, not his, but a kinsman's, the Giant Hymir's Cows are *Ice-bergs:* this Hymir 'looks at the rocks' with his devil-eye, and they *split* in the glance of it.

Thunder was not then mere Electricity, vitreous or resinous; it was the God Donner (Thunder) or Thor,—God also of beneficent Summer-heat. The thunder was his wrath; the gathering of the black clouds is the drawing down of Thor's angry brows; the fire-bolt bursting out of Heaven is the all-rending Hammer flung from the hand of Thor: he urges his loud chariot over the mountain-tops,— that is the peal: wrathful he 'blows in his red beard;' that is the rustling stormblast before the thunder begin. Balder again, the White God, the beautiful, the just and benignant (whom the early Christian Missionaries found to resemble Christ), is the Sun,—beautifullest of visible things; wondrous too, and divine still, after all our Astronomies and Almanacs! But perhaps the notablest god we hear tell of is one of whom Grimm the German Etymologist finds trace: the God *Wünsch,* or Wish. The God *Wish;* who could give us all that we *wished!* Is not this the sincerest and yet rudest voice of the spirit of man? The *rudest* ideal that man ever formed; which still shews itself in the latest forms of our spiritual culture. Higher considerations have to teach us that the God *Wish* is not the true God.

Of the other Gods or Jötuns I will mention only for etymology's sake, that Sea-tempest is the Jötun *Aegir,* a very dangerous Jötun;— and now to this day, on our river Trent, as I learn, the Nottingham bargemen, when the River is in a certain flooded state (a kind of backwater, or eddying swirl it has, very dangerous to them), call it *Eager;* they cry out, "Have a care, there is the *Eager* coming!" Curious; that word surviving, like the peak of a submerged world!

The *oldest* Nottingham bargemen had believed in the God Aegir. Indeed our English blood too in good part is Danish, Norse; or rather, at bottom, Danish and Norse and Saxon have no distinction, except a superficial one,—as of Heathen and Christian, or the like. But all over our Island we are mingled largely with Danes proper,—from the incessant invasions there were: and this, of course, in a greater proportion along the east coast; and greatest of all, as I find, in the North Country. From the Humber upwards, all over Scotland, the speech of the common people is still in a singular degree Icelandic; its Germanism has still a peculiar Norse tinge. They too are 'Normans,' Northmen,—if that be any great beauty!—

Of the chief god, Odin, we shall speak by and by. Mark at present so much; what the essence of Scandinavian and indeed of all Paganism is: a recognition of the forces of Nature as godlike, stupendous, personal Agencies,—as Gods and Demons. Not inconceivable to us. It is the infant Thought of man opening itself, with awe and wonder, on this ever-stupendous Universe. To me there is in the Norse System something very genuine, very great and manlike. A broad simplicity, rusticity, so very different from the light gracefulness of the old Greek Paganism, distinguishes this Scandinavian System. It is Thought; the genuine Thought of deep, rude, earnest minds, fairly opened to the things about them; a face-to-face and heart-to-heart inspection of the things,—the first characteristic of all good Thought in all times. Not graceful lightness, half-sport, as in the Greek Paganism; a certain homely truthfulness and rustic strength, a great rude sincerity, discloses itself here. It is strange, after our beautiful Apollo statues and clear smiling mythuses, to come down upon the Norse Gods 'brewing ale' to hold their feast with Aegir, the Sea-Jötun; sending out Thor to get the cauldron for them in the Jötun country; Thor, after many adventures, clapping the Pot on his head, like a huge hat, and walking off with it,—quite lost in it, the ears of the Pot reaching down to his heels! A kind of vacant hugeness, large awkward gianthood, characterises that Norse System; enormous force, as yet altogether untutored, stalking helpless with large uncertain strides. Consider only their primary mythus of the Creation. The Gods, having got the Giant Ymer slain, a Giant made by 'warm winds,' and much confused work, out of the conflict of Frost and Fire,—determined on constructing a world with him. His blood made the Sea; his flesh was the Land, the Rocks his bones; of his eyebrows they formed Asgard their Gods'-dwelling; his scull was the great blue vault of Immensity, and the brains of it became the Clouds. What a Hyper-Brobdignagian business! Untamed Thought, great, giantlike, enormous;—to be tamed in due time into the compact greatness, not giantlike, but godlike and stronger than gianthood, of the Shakspeares, the Goethes!—Spiritually as well as bodily these men are our progenitors.

I like, too, that representation they have of the Tree Igdrasil. All Life is figured by them as a Tree. Igdrasil, the Ash-tree of Existence, has its roots deep down in the kingdoms of Hela or Death; its trunk reaches up heaven-high, spreads its boughs over the whole Universe: it is the Tree of Existence. At the foot of it, in the Death-kingdom, sit Three *Nornas*, Fates,—the Past, Present, Future; watering its roots from the Sacred Well. Its 'boughs,' with their buddings and disleafings,—events, things suffered, things done, catastrophes,—stretch through all lands and times. Is not every leaf of it a biography, every fibre there an act or word? Its boughs are Histories of Nations. The rustle of it is the noise of Human Existence, onwards from of old. It grows there, the breath of Human Passion rustling through it;—or stormtost, the stormwind howling through it like the voice of all the gods. It is Igdrasil, the Tree of Existence. It is the past, the present, and the future; what was done, what is doing, what will be done; 'the infinite conjugation of the verb *To do*.' Considering how human things circulate, each inextricably in communion with all,—how the word I speak to you today is borrowed, not from Ulfila the Mœsogoth only, but from all men since the first man began to speak,—I find no similitude so true as this of a Tree. Beautiful; altogether beautiful and great. The '*Machine* of the Universe,'—alas, do but think of that in contrast!

Well, it is strange enough this old Norse view of Nature; different enough from what we believe of Nature. Whence it specially came, one would not like to be compelled to say very minutely! One thing we may say: It came from the thoughts of Norse men;—from the thought, above all, of the *first* Norse man who had an original power of thinking. The First Norse 'man of genius,' as we should call him! Innumerable men had passed by, across this Universe, with a dumb vague wonder, such as the very animals may feel; or with a painful, fruitlessly inquiring wonder, such as men only feel;—till the great Thinker came, the *original* man, the Seer; whose shaped spoken Thought awakes the slumbering capability of all into Thought. It is ever the way with the Thinker, the spiritual Hero. What he says, all men were not far from saying, were longing to say. The Thoughts of all start up, as from painful enchanted sleep, round his Thought; answering to it, Yes, even so! Joyful to men as the dawning of day from night;—*is* it not, indeed, the awakening for them from no-being into being, from death into life? We still honour such a man; call him Poet, Genius, and so forth: but to these wild men he was a very magician, a worker of miraculous unexpected blessing for them; a Prophet, a God!—Thought once awakened does not again slumber; unfolds itself into a System of Thought; grows, in man after man, generation after generation,—till its full stature is reached, and *such* System of Thought can grow no farther, but must give place to another.

For the Norse people, the Man now named Odin, and Chief Norse God, we fancy, was such a man. A Teacher, and Captain of soul and of body; a Hero, of worth *im*measurable; admiration for whom, transcending the known bounds, became adoration. Has he not the power of articulate Thinking; and many other powers, as yet miraculous? So, with boundless gratitude, would the rude Norse heart feel. Has he not solved for them the Sphinx-enigma of this Universe; given assurance to them of their own destiny there. By him they know now what they have to do here, what to look for hereafter. Existence has become articulate, melodious by him; he first has made Life alive!— We may call this Odin the origin of Norse Mythology: Odin, or whatever name the First Norse Thinker bore while he was a man among men. His view of the Universe once promulgated, a like view starts into being in all minds; grows, keeps ever growing, while it continues credible there. In all minds it lay written, but invisibly, as in sympathetic ink; at his word it starts into visibility in all. Nay, in every epoch of the world, the great event, parent of all others, is it not the arrival of a Thinker in the world!—

One other thing we must not forget; it will explain, a little, the confusion of these Norse Eddas. They are not one coherent System of Thought; but properly the *summation* of several successive systems. All this of the old Norse Belief which is flung out for us, in one level of distance in the Edda, like a Picture painted on the same canvass, does not at all stand so in the reality. It stands rather at all manner of distances and depths, of successive generations since the Belief first began. All Scandinavian thinkers, since the first of them, contributed to that Scandinavian System of Thought; in ever new elaboration and addition, it is the combined work of them all. What history it had, how it changed from shape to shape, by one thinker's contribution after another, till it got to the full final shape we see it under in the *Edda*, no man will now ever know: *its* Councils of Trebisond, Councils of Trent, Athanasiuses, Dantes, Luthers, are sunk without echo in the dark night! Only that it had such a history we can all know. Wheresoever a thinker appeared, there in the thing he thought of was a contribution, accession, a change or revolution made. Alas, the grandest 'revolution' of all, the one made by the man Odin himself, is not this too sunk for us like the rest! Of Odin what history? Strange rather to reflect that he *had* a history! That this Odin, in his wild Norse vesture, with his wild beard and eyes, his rude Norse speech and ways, was a man like us; with our sorrows, joys, with our limbs, features;—intrinsically all one as we; and did such a work! But the work, much of it, has perished; the worker, all to the name. "*Wednes*day," men will say tomorrow; Odin's day! Of Odin there exists no history: no document of it; no guess about it worth repeating.

Snorro indeed, in the quietest manner, almost in a brief business style, writes down, in his *Heimskringla*, how Odin was a heroic Prince, in the Black-Sea region, with Twelve Peers, and a great people straitened for room. How he led these *Asen* (Asiatics) of his out of Asia; settled them in the North parts of Europe, by warlike conquest; invented Letters, Poetry and so forth,—and came by and by to be worshipped as Chief God by these Scandinavians, his Twelve Peers made into Twelve Sons of his own, Gods like himself: Snorro has no doubt of this. Saxo Grammaticus, a very curious Northman of that same century, is still more unhesitating; scruples not to find out a historical fact in every individual mythus, and writes it down as a terrestrial event in Denmark or elsewhere. Torfæus, learned and cautious, some centuries later, assigns by calculation a *date* for it: Odin, he says, came into Europe about the Year 70 before Christ. Of all which, as grounded on mere uncertainties, found to be untenable now, I need say nothing. Far, very far beyond the Year 70! Odin's date, adventures, whole terrestrial history, figure and environment, are sunk from us forever into unknown thousands of years.

Nay Grimm, the German Antiquary, goes so far as to deny that any man Odin ever existed. He proves it by etymology. The word *Wuotan*, which is the original form of *Odin*, a word spread, as name of their chief Divinity, over all the Teutonic Nations everywhere; this word, which connects itself, according to Grimm, with the Latin *vadere*, with the English *wade* and such like,—means primarily *Movement*, Source of Movement, Power; and is the fit name of the highest god, not of any man. The word signifies Divinity, he says, among the old Saxon, German and all Teutonic Nations; the adjectives formed from it all signify *divine*, *supreme*, or something pertaining to the chief god. Like enough! We must bow to Grimm in matters etymo-logical. Let us consider it fixed that *Wuotan* means *Wading*, force of *Movement*. And now still, what hinders it from being the name of a Heroic Man and *Mover*, as well as of a god? As for the adjectives, and words formed from it,—did not the Spaniards in their universal admiration for Lope, get into the habit of saying 'a Lope flower,' 'a Lope *dama*,' if the flower or woman were of surpassing beauty? Had this lasted, *Lope* would have grown, in Spain, to be an adjective signifying *godlike* also. Indeed Adam Smith, in his *Essay on Language*, surmises that all adjectives whatsoever were formed precisely in that way: some very green thing, chiefly notable for its greenness, got the appellative name *Green*, and then the next thing remarkable for that quality, a tree for instance, was named the *green* tree,—as we still say 'the *steam* coach,' 'four-horse coach,' or the like. All primary adjectives, according to Smith, were formed in this way; were at first substantives and things. We cannot annihilate a man for etymologies like that! Surely there was a First Teacher and Captain; surely there must have been an Odin, palpable to the sense at one time; no adjective, but a real Hero of flesh and blood! The voice of all tradition, history or echo of history, agrees with all that thought will teach one about it, to assure us of this.

How the man Odin came to be considered a *god*, the chief god?—that surely is a question which nobody would wish to dogmatise upon. I have said, his people knew no *limits* to their admiration of him; they had as yet no scale to measure admiration by. Fancy your own generous heart's-love of some greatest man expanding till it *transcended* all bounds, till it filled and overflowed the whole field of your thought! Or what if this man Odin,—since a great deep soul, with the afflatus and mysterious tide of vision and impulse rushing on him he knows not whence, is ever an enigma, a kind of terror and wonder to himself,—should have felt that perhaps *he* was divine; that *he* was some effluence of the 'Wuotan,' '*Movement*,' Supreme Power and Divinity, of whom to his rapt vision all Nature was the awful Flame-image; that some effluence of *Wuotan* dwelt here in him! He was not necessarily false; he was but mistaken, speaking the truest he knew. A great soul, any sincere soul, knows not *what* he is,—alternates between the highest height and the lowest depth; can, of all things, the least measure—Himself! What others take him for, and what he guesses that he may be; these two items strangely act on one another, help to determine one another. With all men reverently admiring him; with his own wild soul full of noble ardours and affections, of whirlwind chaotic darkness and glorious new light; a divine Universe bursting all into godlike beauty round him, and no man to whom the like ever had befallen, what could he think himself to be? "Wuotan?" All men answered, "Wuotan!"—

And then consider what mere Time will do in such cases; how if a man was great while living, he becomes tenfold greater when dead. What an enormous *camera-obscura* magnifier is Tradition! How a thing grows in the human Memory, in the human Imagination, when love, worship and all that lies in the human Heart, is there to encourage it. And in the darkness, in the entire ignorance; without date or document, no book, no Arundel-marble; only here and there some dumb monumental cairn. Why, in thirty or forty years, were there no books, any great man would grow *mythic*, the contemporaries, who had seen him, being once all dead. And in three hundred years, and in three thousand years—!—To attempt *theorising* on such matters would profit little: they are matters which refuse to be *theoremed* and diagramed; which Logic ought to know that she *cannot* speak of. Enough for us to discern, far in the uttermost distance, some gleam as of a small real light shining in the centre of that enormous camera-obscura image; to discern that the centre of it all was not a madness and nothing, but a sanity and something.

This light, kindled in the great dark vortex of the Norse Mind, dark but living, waiting only for light: this is to me the centre of the whole. How such light will then shine out, and with wondrous thousandfold expansion spread itself, in forms and colours, depends not on *it*, so much as on the National Mind recipient of it. The colours and forms of your light will be those of the *cut-glass* it has to shine through.—Curious to think how, for every man, any the truest fact is modelled by the nature of the man! I said, The earnest man, speaking to his brother men, must always have stated what seemed to him a *fact*, a real Appearance of Nature. But the way in which such Appearance or fact shaped itself,—what sort of *fact* it became for him,—was and is modified by his own laws of thinking; deep, subtle, but universal, ever-operating laws. The world of Nature, for every man, is the Fantasy of Himself; this world is the multiplex 'Image of his own Dream.' Who knows to what unnameable subtleties of spiritual law all these Pagan Fables owe their shape! The number *Twelve*, divisiblest of all, which could be halved, quartered, parted into three, into six, the most remarkable number,—this was enough to determine the *Signs of the Zodiac*, the number of Odin's *Sons*, and innumerable other Twelves. Any vague rumour of number had a tendency to settle itself into Twelve. So with regard to every other matter. And quite unconsciously too,—with no notion of building up 'Allegories!' But the fresh clear glance of those First Ages would be prompt in discerning the secret relations of things, and wholly open to obey these. Schiller finds in the *Cestus of Venus* an everlasting æsthetic truth as to the nature of all Beauty; curious:—but he is careful not to insinuate that the old Greek Mythists had any notion of lecturing about the 'Philosophy of Criticism!'— —On the whole, we must leave those boundless regions. Cannot we conceive that Odin was a reality? Error indeed, error enough: but sheer falsehood, idle fables, allegory aforethought,—we will not believe that our Fathers believed in these.

Odin's *Runes* are a significant feature of him. Runes, and the miracles of 'magic' he worked by them, make a great feature in tradition. Runes are the Scandinavian Alphabet; suppose Odin to have been the inventor of Letters, as well as 'magic,' among that people! It is the greatest invention man has ever made, this of marking down the unseen thought that is in him by written characters. It is a kind of second speech, almost as miraculous as the first. You remember the astonishment and incredulity of Atahualpa the Peruvian King; how he made the Spanish Soldier who was guarding him scratch *Dios* on his thumb-nail, that he might try the next soldier with it, to ascertain whether such a miracle was possible. If Odin brought Letters among his people, he might work magic enough!

Writing by Runes has some air of being original among the Norsemen; not a Phenician Alphabet, but a native Scandinavian one. Snorro tells us farther that Odin invented Poetry; the music of human speech, as well as that miraculous runic marking of it. Transport yourselves into the early childhood of nations; the first beautiful morning-light of our Europe, when all yet lay in fresh young radiance as of a great sunrise, and our Europe was first beginning to think, to be! Wonder, hope; infinite radiance of hope and wonder, as of a young child's thoughts, in the hearts of these strong men! Strong sons of Nature; and here was not only a wild Captain and Fighter; discerning with his wild flashing eyes what to do, with his wild lion-heart daring and doing it; but a Poet too, all that we mean by a Poet, Prophet, great devout Thinker and Inventor,—as the truly Great Man ever is. A Hero is a Hero at all points; in the soul and thought of him first of all. This Odin, in his rude semi-articulate way, had a word to speak. A great heart laid open to take in this great Universe, and man's Life here, and utter a great word about it. A Hero, as I say, in his own rude manner; a wise, gifted, noble-hearted man. And now, if we still admire such a man beyond all others, what must these wild Norse souls, first awakened into thinking, have made of him! To them, as yet without names for it, he was noble and noblest; Hero, Prophet, God; *Wuotan*, the greatest of all. Thought is Thought, however it speak or spell itself. Intrinsically, I conjecture, this Odin must have been of the same sort of stuff as the greatest kind of men. A great thought in the wild deep heart of him! The rough words he articulated, are they not the rudimental roots of those English words we still use? He worked so, in that obscure element. But he was as a *light* kindled in it; a light of Intellect, rude Nobleness of heart, the only kind of lights we have yet; a Hero, as I say: and he had to shine there, and make his obscure element a little lighter,—as is still the task of us all.

We will fancy him to be the Type-Norseman; the finest Teuton whom that race had yet produced. The rude Norse heart burst up into *boundless* admiration round him; into adoration. He is as a root of so many great things; the fruit of him is found growing, from deep thousands of years, over the whole field of Teutonic Life. Our own Wednesday, as I said, is it not still Odin's Day? Wednesbury, Wansborough, Wanstead, Wandsworth: Odin grew into England too, these are still leaves from that root! He was the Chief God to all the Teutonic Peoples: their Pattern Norseman;—in such way did *they* admire their Pattern Norseman; that was the fortune he had in the world.

Thus if the man Odin himself have vanished utterly, there is this huge Shadow of him which still projects itself over the whole History of his People. For this Odin once admitted to be God, we can understand well that the whole Scandinavian Scheme of Nature, or dim No-scheme, whatever it might before have been, would now begin to develope itself altogether differently, and grow thenceforth in a new manner. What this Odin saw into, and taught with his runes and his rhymes, the whole Teutonic People laid to heart and carried forward. His way of thought became their way of thought:—such, under new conditions, is the history of every great thinker still. In gigantic confused lineaments, like some enormous camera-obscura shadow thrown upwards from the dead deeps of the Past, and covering the whole Northern Heaven, is not that Scandinavian Mythology in some sort the Portraiture of this man Odin? The gigantic image of *his* natural face, legible or not legible there, expanded and confused in that manner! Ah, Thought, I say, is always Thought. No great man lives in vain. The History of the world is but the Biography of great men.

To me there is something very touching in this primeval figure of Heroism; in such artless, helpless, but hearty entire reception of a Hero by his fellow-men. Never so helpless in shape, it is the noblest of feelings, and a feeling in some shape or other perennial as man himself. If I could shew in any measure, what I feel deeply for a long time now, That it is the vital element of manhood, the soul of man's history here in our world,—it would be the chief use of this discoursing at present. We do not now call our great men Gods, nor admire *without* limit; ah no, *with* limit enough! But if we have no great men, or do not admire at all,—that were a still worse case.

This poor Scandinavian Hero-worship, that whole Norse way of looking at the Universe, and adjusting oneself there, has an indestructible merit for us. A rude childlike way of recognising the divineness of Nature, the divineness of Man; most rude, yet heartfelt, robust, giantlike; betokening what a giant of a man this child would yet grow to! It was a truth, and is none. Is it not as the half-dumb stifled voice of the long-buried generations of our own Fathers, calling out of the depths of ages to us, in whose veins their blood still runs: "This then, this is what *we* made of the world: this is all the image and notion we could form to ourselves of this great mystery of a Life and Universe. Despise it not. You are raised high above it, to large free scope of vision; but you too are not yet at the top. No, your notion too, so much enlarged, is but a partial, imperfect one; that matter is a thing no man will ever, in time or out of time, comprehend; after thousands of years of ever-new expansion, man will find himself but struggling to comprehend again a part of it: the thing is larger than man, not to be comprehended by him; an Infinite thing!"

The essence of the Scandinavian, as indeed of all Pagan Mythologies, we found to be recognition of the divineness of Nature; sincere communion of man with the mysterious invisible Powers visibly seen at work in the world round him. This, I should say, is more sincerely done in the Scandinavian than in any Mythology I know. Sincerity is the great characteristic of it. Superior sincerity (far superior) consoles us for the total want of old Grecian grace. Sincerity, I think, is better than grace. I feel that these old Northmen were looking into Nature with open eye and soul: most earnest, honest; childlike, and yet manlike; with a greathearted simplicity and depth and freshness, in a true, loving, admiring, unfearing way. A right valiant, true old race of men. Such recognition of Nature one finds to be the chief element of Paganism: recognition of Man, and his Moral Duty, though this too is not wanting, comes to be the chief element only in purer forms of religion. Here, indeed, is a great distinction and epoch in Human Beliefs; a great landmark in the religious development of Mankind. Man first puts himself in relation with Nature and her Powers, wonders and worships over those; not till a later epoch does he discern that all Power is Moral, that the grand point is the distinction for him of Good and Evil, of *Thou shalt* and *Thou shalt not*.

With regard to all these fabulous delineations in the *Edda*, I will remark, moreover, as indeed was already hinted, that most probably they must have been of much newer date; most probably, even from the first, were comparatively idle for the old Norsemen, and as it were a kind of Poetic sport. Allegory and Poetic Delineation, as I said above, cannot be religious Faith; the Faith itself must first be there, then Allegory enough will gather round it, as the fit body round its soul. The Norse Faith, I can well suppose, like other Faiths, was most active while it lay mainly in the silent state, and had not yet much to say about itself, still less to sing.

Among those shadowy *Edda* matters, amid all that fantastic congeries of assertions, and traditions, in their musical Mythologies, the main practical belief a man could have was probably not much more than this: of the *Valkyrs* and the *Hall of Odin;* of an inflexible *Destiny*, and that the one thing needful for a man was *to be brave.* The *Valkyrs* are Choosers of the Slain; a Destiny inexorable, which it is useless trying to bend or soften, has appointed who is to be slain: this was a fundamental point for the Norse believer;—as indeed it is for all earnest men everywhere, for a Mahomet, a Luther, for a Napoleon too. It lies at the basis this for every such man; it is the woof out of which his whole system of thought is woven. The *Valkyrs;* and then that these *Choosers* lead the brave to a heavenly *Hall of Odin;* only the base and slavish being thrust elsewhither, into the realms of Hela the Death-goddess: I take this to have been the soul of the whole Norse Belief. They understood in their heart that it was indispensable to be brave; that Odin would have no favour for them, but despise and thrust them out, if they were not brave. Consider too whether there is not something in this! It is an everlasting duty, valid in our day as in that, the duty of being brave. *Valour* is still *value.* The first duty for a man is still that of subduing *Fear.* We must get rid of Fear; we cannot act at all till then. A man's acts are slavish, not true but specious; his very thoughts are false, he thinks too as a slave and coward, till he have got Fear under his feet. Odin's creed, if we disentangle the real kernel of it, is true to this hour. A man shall and must be valiant; he must march forward, and quit himself like a man,—trusting imperturbably in the appointment and *choice* of the upper Powers; and, on the whole, not fear at all. Now and always, the completeness of his victory over Fear will determine how much of a man he is.

It is doubtless very savage that kind of valour of the old Northmen. Snorro tells us they thought it a shame and misery not to die in battle; and if natural death seemed to be coming on, they would cut wounds in their flesh, that Odin might receive them as warriors slain. Old kings, about to die, had their body laid into a ship; the ship sent forth, with sails set and slow fire burning it; that, once out at sea, it might blaze up in flame, and in such manner bury worthily the old hero, at once in the sky and in the ocean! Wild bloody valour; yet valour of its kind; better, I say, than none. In the old Sea-kings too, what an indomitable rugged energy! Silent, with closed lips, as I fancy them, unconscious that they were specially brave; defying the wild ocean with its monsters, and all men and things;—progenitors of our own Blakes and Nelsons. No Homer sang these Norse Sea-kings; but Agamemnon's was a small audacity, and of small fruit in the world, to some of them;—to Hrolf's of Normandy, for instance! Hrolf, or Rollo Duke of Normandy, the wild Sea-king, has a share in governing England at this hour.

Nor was it altogether nothing, even that wild sea-roving and battling, through so many generations. It needed to be ascertained which was the *strongest* kind of men; who were to be ruler over whom. Among the Northland Sovereigns, too, I find some who got the title *Wood-cutter;* Forest-felling Kings. Much lies in that. I suppose at bottom many of them were forest-fellers as well as fighters, though the Skalds talk mainly of the latter,—misleading certain critics not a little; for no nation of men could ever live by fighting alone; there could not produce enough come out of that! I suppose the right good fighter was oftenest also the right good forest-feller,—the right good improver, discerner, doer and worker in every kind; for true valour, different enough from ferocity, is the basis of all. A more legitimate kind of valour that; shewing itself against the untamed Forests and dark brute Powers of Nature, to conquer Nature for us. In the same direction have not we their descendants since carried it far? May such valour last forever with us!

That the man Odin, speaking with a Hero's voice and heart, as with an impressiveness out of Heaven, told his People the infinite importance of Valour, how man thereby became a god; and that his People, feeling a response to it in their own hearts, believed this message of his, and thought it a message out of Heaven, and him a Divinity for telling it them: this seems to me the primary seed-grain of the Norse Religion, from which all manner of mythologies, symbolic practices, speculations, allegories, songs and sagas would naturally grow. Grow,—how strangely! I called it a small light shining and shaping in the huge vortex of Norse darkness. Yet the darkness itself was *alive;* consider that. It was the eager inarticulate uninstructed Mind of the whole Norse People, longing only to become articulate, to go on articulating ever farther! The living doctrine grows, grows;—like a Banyan-tree; the first *seed* is the essential thing: any branch strikes itself down into the earth, becomes a new root; and so, in endless complexity, we have a whole wood, a whole jungle, one seed the parent of it all. Was not the whole Norse Religion, accordingly, in some sense, what we called 'the enormous shadow of this man's likeness?' Critics trace some affinity in some Norse mythuses, of the Creation and such like, with those of the Hindoos. The Cow Adumbla, 'licking the rime from the rocks,' has a kind of Hindoo look. A Hindoo Cow, transported into frosty countries. Probably enough; indeed we may say undoubtedly, these things will have a kindred with the remotest lands, with the earliest times. Thought does not die, but only is changed. The first man that began to think in this Planet of ours, he was the beginner of all. And then the second man, and the third man;—nay every true Thinker to this hour is a kind of Odin, teaches men *his* way of thought, spreads a shadow of his own likeness over sections of the History of the World.

Of the distinctive poetic character or merit of this Norse Mythology I have not room to speak; nor does it concern us much. Some wild Prophecies we have, as the *Völuspa* in the *Elder Edda;* of a rapt, earnest, sibylline sort. But they were comparatively an idle adjunct of the matter, men who as it were but toyed with the matter, these later Skalds; and it is *their* songs chiefly that survive. In later centuries, I suppose, they would go on singing, poetically symbolizing, as our modern Painters paint, when it was no longer from the innermost heart, or not from the heart at all. This is everywhere to be well kept in mind.

Gray's fragments of Norse Lore, at any rate, will give one no notion of it;—any more than Pope will of Homer. It is no square-built gloomy palace of black ashlar marble, shrouded in awe and horror, as Gray gives it us: no; rough as the North rocks, as the Iceland deserts, it is; with a heartiness, homeliness, even a tint of goodhumour and robust mirth in the middle of these fearful things. The strong old Norse heart did not go upon theatrical sublimities; they had not time to tremble. I like much their robust simplicity; their veracity, directness of conception. Thor 'draws down his brows' in a veritable Norse rage; 'grasps his hammer till the *knuckles grow white*.' Beautiful traits of pity too, an honest pity. Balder 'the white God' dies; the beautiful, benignant; he is the Sungod. They try all Nature for a remedy; but he is dead. Frigga, his mother, sends Hermoder to seek or see him: nine days and nine nights he rides, through gloomy deep valleys, a labyrinth of gloom; arrives at the Bridge with its gold roof: the Keeper says, "Yes, Balder did pass here; but the Kingdom of the Dead is down yonder, far towards the North." Hermoder rides on; leaps Hell-gate, Hela's gate; does see Balder, and speak with him: Balder cannot be delivered. Inexorable! Hela will not, for Odin or any God, give him up. The beautiful and gentle has to remain there. His Wife had volunteered to go with him, to die with him. They shall forever remain there. He sends his ring to Odin; Nanna his wife sends her *thimble* to Frigga, as a remembrance.—Ah me!—

For indeed Valour is the fountain of Pity too;—of Truth, and all that is great and good in man. The robust homely vigour of the Norse heart attaches one much, in these delineations. Is it not a trait of right honest strength, says Uhland, who has written a fine *Essay* on Thor, that the old Norse heart finds its friend in the Thunder-god? That it is not frightened away by his thunder; but finds that Summer-heat, the beautiful noble summer, must and will have thunder withal! The Norse heart *loves* this Thor and his hammer-bolt; sports with him. Thor is Summer-heat; the god of Peaceable Industry as well as Thunder. He is the Peasant's friend; his true henchman and attendant is Thialfi, *Manual Labour*. Thor himself engages in all manner of rough manual work, scorns no business for its plebeianism; is ever and anon travelling to the country of the Jötuns, harrying those chaotic Frost-monsters, subduing them, at least straitening and damaging them. There is a great broad humour in some of these things.

Thor, as we saw above, goes to Jötun-land, to seek Hymir's Cauldron, that the Gods may brew beer. Hymir the huge Giant enters, his grey beard all full of hoar-frost; splits pillars with the very glance of his eye; Thor, after much rough tumult, snatches the Pot, claps it on his head; the 'handles of it reach down to his heels.' The Norse Skald has a kind of loving sport with Thor. This is the Hymir whose cattle, the critics have discovered, are Ice-bergs. Huge untu‑ tored Brobdignag genius,—needing only to be tamed down; into Shakspeares, Dantes, Goethes! It is all gone now, that old Norse work,—Thor the Thundergod changed into Jack the Giant-killer: but the mind that made it is here yet. How strangely things grow, and die, and do not die! There are twigs of that great world-tree of Norse Belief, still curiously traceable. This poor Jack of the Nursery, with his miraculous shoes of swiftness, coat of darkness, sword of sharpness, he is one. *Hynde Etin*, and still more decisively *Red Etin of Ireland*, in the Scottish Ballads, these are both derived from Norseland; *Etin* is evidently a *Jötun*. Nay, Shakspeare's *Hamlet* is a twig too of this same world-tree; there seems no doubt of that. Hamlet, *Amleth*, I find, is really a mythic personage; and his Tragedy, of the poisoned Father, poisoned asleep by drops in his ear, and the rest, is a Norse mythus! Old Saxo, as his wont was, made it a Danish history; Shak‑ speare, out of Saxo, made it what we see. That is a twig of the world-tree that has *grown*, I think;—by nature or accident that one has grown!

In fact, these old Norse songs have a *truth* in them, an inward perennial truth and greatness,—as, indeed, all must have that can very long preserve itself by tradition alone. It is a greatness not of mere body and gigantic bulk, but a rude greatness of soul. There is a sublime uncomplaining melancholy traceable in these old hearts. A great free glance into the very deeps of thought. They seem to have seen, these brave old Northmen, what Meditation has taught all men in all ages, That this world is after all but a shew,—a phenomenon or appearance, no real thing. All deep souls see into that,—the Hindoo Mythologist, the German Philosopher,—the Shakspeare, the earnest Thinker wherever he may be:

'We are such stuff as Dreams are made of!'

One of Thor's expeditions, to Utgard (the *Outer* Garden, central seat of Jötun-land), is remarkable in this respect. Thialfi was with him, and Loke. After various adventures, they entered upon Giant-land; wandered over plains, wild uncultivated places, among stones and trees. At nightfall they noticed a house; and as the door, which indeed formed one whole side of the house, was open, they entered. It was a simple habitation; one large hall, altogether empty. They staid there. Suddenly in the dead of the night loud noises alarmed them. Thor grasped his hammer; stood in the door, prepared for fight. His companions within ran hither and thither in their terror, seeking some outlet in that rude hall; they found a little closet at last, and took refuge there. Neither had Thor any battle: for, lo, in the morning it turned out that the noise had been only the *snoring* of a certain enormous but peaceable Giant, the Giant Skrymir, who lay peaceably sleeping near by; and this that they took for a house was merely his *Glove*, thrown aside there; the door was the Glove-wrist; the little closet they had fled into was the Thumb! Such a glove;— I remark too that it had not fingers as ours have, but only a thumb, and the rest undivided: a most ancient, rustic glove!

Skrymir now carried their portmanteau all day; Thor, however, had his own suspicions, did not like the ways of Skrymir; determined at night to put an end to him as he slept. Raising his hammer, he struck down into the Giant's face a right thunderbolt blow, of force to rend rocks. The Giant merely awoke; rubbed his cheek, and said, Did a leaf fall? Again Thor struck, so soon as Skrymir again slept; a better blow than before; but the Giant only murmured, Was that a grain of sand? Thor's third stroke was with both his hands (the 'knuckles white' I suppose), and seemed to dint deep into Skrymir's visage; but he merely checked his snore, and remarked, There must be sparrows roosting in this tree, I think; what is that they have dropt?—At the gate of Utgard, a place so high, that you had to 'strain your neck bending back to see the top of it,' Skrymir went his ways. Thor and his companions were admitted; invited to take share in the games going on. To Thor, for his part, they handed a Drinking-horn; it was a common feat, they told him, to drink this dry at one draught. Long and fiercely, three times over, Thor drank; but made hardly any impression. He was a weak child, they told him: could he lift that Cat he saw there? Small as the feat seemed, Thor with his whole godlike strength could not; he bent up the creature's back, could not raise its feet off the ground, could at the utmost raise one foot. Why, you are no man, said the Utgard people; there is an Old Woman that will wrestle you! Thor, heartily ashamed, seized this haggard Old Woman; but could not throw her.

And now on their quitting Utgard, the chief Jötun, escorting them politely a little way, said to Thor: "You are beaten then:—yet be not so much ashamed; there was deception of appearance in it. That Horn you tried to drink was the *Sea;* you did make it ebb; but who could drink that, the bottomless! The Cat you would have lifted,—why, that is the *Midgard-snake,* the Great World-serpent, which, tail in mouth, girds and keeps up the whole created world; had you torn that up, the world must have rushed to ruin. As for the Old Woman, she was *Time,* Oid Age, Duration: with her what can wrestle? No man nor no god with her; gods or men, she prevails over all! And then those three strokes you struck,—look at these *three valleys;* your three strokes made these!" Thor looked at his attendant Jötun: it was Skrymir;—it was, say Norse critics, the old chaotic rocky *Earth* in person, and that glove-*house* was some Earth-cavern! But Skrymir had vanished; Utgard with its skyhigh gates, when Thor grasped his hammer to smite them, had gone to air; only the Giant's voice was heard mocking: "Better come no more to Jötunheim!"—

This is of the allegoric period, as we see, and half play, not of the prophetic and entirely devout: but as a mythus, is there not real antique Norse gold in it? More true metal, rough from the Mimerstithy, than in many a famed Greek mythus *shaped* far better! A great broad Brobdignag grin of true humour is in this Skrymir; mirth resting on earnestness and sadness, as the rainbow on black tempest: only a right valiant heart is capable of that. It is the grim humour of our own Ben Jonson, rare old Ben; runs in the blood of us, I fancy; for one catches tones of it, under a still other shape, out of the American Backwoods.

That is also a very striking conception that of the *Ragnarök,* Consummation, or *Twilight of the Gods.* It is in the *Völuspa* Song; seemingly a very old, prophetic idea. The Gods and Jötuns, the divine Powers and the chaotic brute ones, after long contest and partial victory by the former, meet at last in universal world-embracing wrestle and duel; World-serpent against Thor, strength against strength; mutually extinctive; and ruin, 'twilight' sinking into darkness, swallows the created Universe. The old Universe with its Gods is sunk; but it is not final death: there is to be a new Heaven and a new Earth; a higher supreme God, and Justice to reign among men. Curious: this law of mutation, which also is a law written in man's inmost thought, had been deciphered by these old earnest Thinkers in their rude style; and how, though all dies, and even gods die, yet all death is but a Phœnix fire-death, and new-birth into the Greater and the Better! It is the fundamental Law of Being for a creature made of Time, living in this Place of Hope. All earnest men have seen into it; may still see into it.

And now, connected with this, let us glance at the *last* mythus of the appearance of Thor; and end there. I fancy it to be the latest in date of all these fables; a sorrowing protest against the advance of Christianity,—set forth reproachfully by some Conservative Pagan. King Olaf has been harshly blamed for his over-zeal in introducing Christianity; surely I should have blamed him far more for an under-zeal in that! He paid dear enough for it; he died by the revolt of his Pagan people, in battle, in the year 1033, at Stickelstad, near that Drontheim, where the chief Cathedral of the North has now stood for many centuries, dedicated gratefully to his memory as *Saint* Olaf. The mythus about Thor is to this effect. King Olaf, the Christian Reform King, is sailing with fit escort along the shore of Norway, from haven to haven; dispensing justice, or doing other royal work: on leaving a certain haven, it is found that a stranger, of grave eyes and aspect, red beard, of stately robust figure, has stept in. The courtiers address him; his answers surprise by their pertinency and depth: at length he is brought to the King. The stranger's conversation here is not less remarkable, as they sail along the beautiful shore; but after some time, he addresses King Olaf thus: "Yes, King Olaf, it is all beautiful, with the sun shining on it there; green, fruitful, a right fair home for you; and many a sore day had Thor, many a wild fight with the rock Jötuns, before he could make it so. And now you seem minded to put away Thor. King Olaf, have a care!" said the stranger, drawing down his brows;—and when they looked again, he was nowhere to be found.—This is the last appearance of Thor on the stage of this world!

Do we not see well enough how the Fable might arise, without unveracity on the part of any one: it is the way most Gods have come to appear among men: thus if in Pindar's time 'Neptune was seen

once at the Nemean Games,' what was this Neptune too but a
'stranger of noble grave aspect,'—*fit* to be 'seen!' There is something
pathetic, tragic for me, in this last voice of Paganism. Thor is
vanished, the whole Norse world has vanished; and will not return
ever again. In like fashion to that, pass away the highest things. All
things that have been in this world, all things that are or will be in
it, have to vanish: we have our sad farewell to give them.

That Norse Religion, a rude but earnest, sternly impressive
Consecration of Valour (so we may define it), sufficed for these old
valiant Northmen. Consecration of Valour is not a *bad* thing! We will
take it for good, so far as it goes. Neither is there no use in *knowing*
something about this old Paganism of our Fathers. Unconsciously,
and combined with higher things, it is in *us* yet, that old Faith withal!
To know it consciously, brings us into closer and clearer relation with
the Past,—with our own possessions in the Past. For the whole Past,
as I keep repeating, is the possession of the Present; the Past had
always something *true*, and is a precious possession. In a different
time, in a different place, it is always some other *side* of our common
Human Nature that has been developing itself. The actual True is the
sum of all these; not any one of them by itself constitutes what of
Human Nature is hitherto developed. Better to know them all than
misknow them. "To which of these Three Religions do you specially
adhere?" inquires Meister of his Teacher. "To all the Three!" answers
the other: "To all the Three; for they by their union first constitute
the True Religion."

LECTURE II.

[Friday, 8th May, 1840.]

THE HERO AS PROPHET. MAHOMET: ISLAM.

FROM the first rude times of Paganism among the Scandinavians in the North, we advance to a very different epoch of religion, among a very different people: Mahometanism among the Arabs. A great change; what a change and progress is indicated here, in the universal condition and thoughts of men!

The Hero is not now regarded as a God among his fellow-men; but as one God-inspired, as a Prophet. It is the second phasis of Hero-worship: the first or oldest, we may say, has passed away without return; in the history of the world there will not again be any man, never so great, whom his fellow-men will take for a god. Nay we might rationally ask, Did any set of human beings ever really think the man they *saw* there standing beside them a god, the maker of this world? Perhaps not: it was usually some man they remembered, or *had* seen. But neither can this, any more, be. The Great Man is not recognised henceforth as a god any more.

It was a rude gross error, that of counting the Great Man a god. Yet let us say that it is at all times difficult to know *what* he is, or how to account of him and receive him! The most significant feature in the history of an epoch is the manner it has of welcoming a Great Man. Ever, to the true instincts of men, there is something godlike in him. Whether they shall take him to be a god, to be a prophet, or what they shall take him to be? that is ever a grand question; by their way of answering that, we shall see, as through a little window, into the very heart of these men's spiritual condition. For at bottom the Great

Man, as he comes from the hand of Nature, is ever the same kind of thing: Odin, Luther, Johnson, Burns; I hope to make it appear that these are all originally of one stuff; that only by the world's reception of them, and the shapes they assume, are they so immeasurably diverse. The worship of Odin astonishes us,—to fall prostrate before the Great Man, into *deliquium* of love and wonder over him, and feel in their hearts that he was a denizen of the skies, a god! This was imperfect enough: but to welcome, for example, a Burns as we did, was that what we can call perfect? The most precious gift that Heaven can give to the Earth; a man of 'genius' as we call it; the Soul of a Man actually sent down from the skies with a God's-message to us,— this we waste away as an idle artificial firework, sent to amuse us a little, and sink it into ashes, wreck and ineffectuality: *such* reception of a Great Man I do not call very perfect either! Looking into the heart of the thing, one may perhaps call that of Burns a still uglier phenomenon, betokening still sadder imperfections in mankind's ways, than the Scandinavian method itself! To fall into mere un-reasoning *deliquium* of love and admiration, was not good; but such unreasoning, nay irrational, supercilious no-love at all is perhaps still worse!—It is a thing forever changing, this of Hero-worship; different in each age, difficult to do well in any age. Indeed the heart of the whole business of the age, one may say, is to do it well.

We have chosen Mahomet not as the most eminent Prophet; but as the one we are freest to speak of. He is by no means the truest of Prophets; but I do esteem him a true one. Farther, as there is no danger of our becoming, any of us, Mahometans, I mean to say all the good of him I justly can. It is the way to get at his secret: let us try to understand what *he* meant with the world; what the world meant and means with him, will then be a more answerable question. Our current hypothesis about Mahomet, that he was a scheming Impostor, a Falsehood incarnate, that his religion is a mere mass of quackery and fatuity, begins really to be now untenable to any one. The lies, which well-meaning zeal has heaped round this man, are disgraceful to ourselves only. When Pococke inquired of Grotius, Where the proof was of that story of the pigeon, trained to pick peas from Mahomet's ear, and pass for an angel dictating to him? Grotius answered that there was no proof! It is really time to dismiss all that. The word this man spoke has been the life-guidance now of one hundred and eighty millions of men these twelve hundred years. These hundred and eighty millions were made by God as well as we. A greater number of God's creatures believe in Mahomet's word, at this hour, than in any other word whatever. Are we to suppose that it was a miserable piece of spiritual legerdemain, this which so many creatures of the Almighty have lived by and died by? I, for my part, cannot form any such supposition. I will believe most things sooner than that. One would be entirely at a loss what to think of this world at all, if quackery so grew and were sanctioned here.

Alas, such theories are very lamentable. If we would attain to knowledge of anything in God's true Creation, let us disbelieve them wholly! They are the product of an Age of Scepticism; they indicate the saddest spiritual paralysis, and mere death-life of the souls of men: more godless theory, I think, was never promulgated in this Earth. A false man found a religion? Why, a false man cannot build a brick house! If he do not know and follow *truly* the properties of mortar, burnt clay and what else he works in, it is no house that he makes, but a rubbish-heap. It will not stand for twelve centuries, to lodge a hundred and eighty millions; it will fall straightway. A man must conform himself to Nature's laws, *be* verily in communion with Nature and the truth of things, or Nature will answer him, No, not at all! Speciosities are specious—ah me!—a Cagliostro, many Cagliostros, prominent world-leaders, do prosper by their quackery, for a day. It is like a forged bank-note; they get it passed out of *their* worthless hands: others, not they, have to smart for it. Nature bursts up in fire-flames, French Revolutions and such like, proclaiming with terrible veracity that forged notes are forged.

But of a Great Man especially, of him I will venture to assert that it is incredible he should have been other than true. It seems to me the primary foundation of him, and of all that can lie in him, this. No Mirabeau, Napoleon, Burns, Cromwell, no man adequate to do any thing, but is first of all in right earnest about it; what I call a sincere man. I should say *sincerity*, a deep, great, genuine sincerity, is the first characteristic of all men in any way heroic. Not the sincerity that calls itself sincere; ah no, that is a very poor matter indeed;—a shallow braggart conscious sincerity; oftenest self-conceit mainly. The Great Man's sincerity is of the kind he cannot speak of, is not conscious of: nay, I suppose, he is conscious rather of *in*sincerity; for what man can walk accurately by the law of truth for one day? No, the Great Man does not boast himself sincere, far from that; perhaps does not ask himself if he is so: I would say rather, his sincerity does not depend on himself; he cannot help being sincere! The great Fact of Existence is great to him. Fly as he will, he cannot get out of the awful presence of this Reality. His mind is so made; he is great by that, first of all. Fearful and wonderful, real as Life, real as Death, is this Universe to him. Though all men should forget its truth, and walk in a vain show, he cannot. At all moments the Flame-image glares in upon him; undeniable, there, there!—I wish you to take this as my primary definition of a Great Man. A little man may have this, it is competent to all men that God has made: but a Great Man cannot be without it.

Such a man is what we call an *original* man; he comes to us at first hand. A messenger he, sent from the Infinite Unknown with tidings to us. We may call him Poet, Prophet, God;—in one way or other, we all feel that the words he utters are as no other man's words. Direct from the Inner Fact of things;—he lives, and has to live, in daily communion with that. Hearsays cannot hide it from him; he is blind, homeless, miserable, following hearsays; *it* glares in upon him. Really his utterances, are they not a kind of 'revelation;'—what we must call such for want of some other name? It is from the heart of the world that he comes; he is portion of the primal reality of things. God has made many revelations: but this man too, has not God made him, the latest and newest of all? The 'inspiration of the Almighty giveth *him* understanding:' we must listen before all to him.

This Mahomet, then, we will in no wise consider as an Inanity and Theatricality, a poor conscious ambitious schemer; we cannot conceive him so. The rude message he delivered was a real one withal; an earnest confused voice from the unknown Deep. The man's words were not false, nor his workings here below: no Inanity and Simulacrum; a fiery mass of Life cast up from the great bosom of Nature herself. To *kindle* the world; the world's Maker had ordered it so. Neither can the faults, imperfections, insincerities even, of Mahomet, if such were never so well proved against him, shake this primary fact about him.

On the whole, we make too much of faults; the details of the business hide the real centre of it. Faults? The greatest of faults, I should say, is to be conscious of none. Readers of the Bible above all, one would think, might know better. Who is called there 'the man according to God's own heart?' David, the Hebrew King, had fallen into sins enough; blackest crimes; there was no want of sins. And thereupon the unbelievers sneer and ask, Is this your man according to God's heart? The sneer, I must say, seems to me but a shallow one. What are faults, what are the outward details of a life; if the inner secret of it, the remorse, temptations, true, often-baffled, never-ended struggle of it, be forgotten? 'It is not in man that walketh to direct his steps.' Of all acts is not, for a man, *repentance* the most divine? The deadliest sin, I say, were that same supercilious consciousness of no sin;—that is death; the heart so conscious is divorced from sincerity, humility and fact; is dead: it is 'pure' as dead dry sand is pure. David's life and history, as written for us in those Psalms of his, I consider to be the truest emblem ever given of a man's moral progress and warfare here below. All earnest souls will ever discern in it the faithful struggle of an earnest human soul towards what is good and best. Struggle often baffled, sore baffled, down as into entire wreck; yet a struggle never ended; ever, with tears, repentance, true unconquerable purpose, begun anew. Poor human nature! Is not a man's walking, in truth, always that: 'a succession of falls?' Man can do no other. In this wild element of a Life, he has to struggle onwards; now fallen, deep-abased; and ever, with tears, repentance, with bleeding heart, he has to rise again, struggle again still onwards. That his struggle *be* a faithful unconquerable one: that is the question of questions. We will put up with many sad details, if the soul of it were true. Details by themselves will never teach us what it is. I believe we mis-estimate Mahomet's faults even as faults: but the secret of him will never be got by dwelling there. We will leave all this behind us; and assuring ourselves that he did mean some true thing, ask candidly, what it was or might be.

These Arabs Mahomet was born among are certainly a notable people. Their country itself is notable; the fit habitation for such a race. Savage inaccessible rock-mountains, great grim deserts, alternating with beautiful strips of verdure: wherever water is, there is greenness, beauty; odoriferous balm-shrubs, date-trees, frankincense-trees. Consider that wide waste horizon of sand, empty, silent, like a sandsea, dividing habitable place from habitable. You are all alone there, left alone with the Universe; by day a fierce sun blazing down on it with intolerable radiance; by night the great deep Heaven with its stars. Such a country is fit for a swift-handed, deep-hearted race of men. There is something most agile, active, and yet most meditative, enthusiastic in the Arab character. The Persians are called the French of the East; we will call the Arabs Oriental Italians. A gifted noble people; a people of wild strong feelings, and of iron restraint over these: the characteristic of noblemindedness, of genius. The wild Bedouin welcomes the stranger to his tent, as one having right to all that is there; were it his worst enemy, he will slay his foal to treat him, will serve him with sacred hospitality for three days, will set him fairly on his way;—and then, by another law as sacred, kill him if he can. In words too, as in action. They are not a loquacious people, taciturn rather; but eloquent, gifted when they do speak. An earnest, truthful kind of men. They are, as we know, of Jewish kindred: but with that deadly terrible earnestness of the Jews they seem to combine something graceful, brilliant, which is not Jewish. They had 'Poetic contests' among them before the time of Mahomet. Sale says, at Ocadh, in the South of Arabia, there were yearly fairs, and there, when the merchandising was done, Poets sang for prizes:—the wild people gathered to hear that.

One Jewish quality these Arabs manifest; the outcome of many or of all high qualities: what we may call religiosity. From of old they had been zealous worshippers, according to their light. They worshipped the stars, as Sabeans; worshipped many natural objects,— recognised them as symbols, immediate manifestations, of the Maker of Nature. It was wrong; and yet not wholly wrong. All God's works are still in a sense symbols of God. Do we not, as I urged, still account it a merit to recognise a certain inexhaustible significance, 'poetic beauty,' as we name it, in all natural objects whatsoever? A man is a poet, and honoured, for doing that, and speaking or singing it,—a kind of diluted worship. They had many Prophets these Arabs; Teachers each to his tribe, each according to the light he had. But

indeed, have we not from of old the noblest of proofs, still palpable
to every one of us, of what devoutness and noble-mindedness had
dwelt in these rustic thoughtful peoples? Biblical critics seem agreed
that our own Book of Job was written in that region of the world.
I call that, apart from all theories about it, one of the grandest things
ever written with pen. One feels, indeed, as if it were not Hebrew;
such a noble universality, different from noble patriotism or sectari-
anism, reigns in it. A noble Book; all men's Book! It is our first,
oldest statement of the never-ending Problem,—man's destiny and
God's ways with him here in this earth. And all in such free flowing
outlines; grand in its sincerity, in its simplicity; in its epic melody, and
repose of reconcilement. There is the seeing eye, the mildly understanding heart. So *true*, every way; true eyesight and vision for all
things; material things no less than spiritual: the Horse,—'hast thou
clothed his neck with *thunder?*'—he '*laughs* at the shaking of the
spear!' Such living likenesses were never since drawn. Sublime sorrow,
sublime reconciliation; oldest choral melody as of the heart of
mankind;—so soft, and great; as the summer midnight, as the world
with its seas and stars! There is nothing written, I think, in the Bible
or out of it, of equal literary merit.—

To the idolatrous Arabs one of the most ancient universal objects
of worship was that Black Stone, still kept in the building called
Caabah, at Mecca. Diodorus Siculus mentions this Caabah in a way
not to be mistaken, as the oldest, most honoured temple in his time;
that is, some half-century before our Era. Silvestre de Sacy says there
is some likelihood that the Black Stone is an aerolite. In that case,
some man might *see* it fall out of Heaven! It stands now beside the
Well Zemzem; the Caabah is built over both. A Well is in all places
a beautiful affecting object, gushing out like life from the hard
earth;—still more so in those hot dry countries, where it is the first
condition of being. The Well Zemzem has its name from the bub-
bling sound of the waters, *zem-zem;* they think it is the Well which
Hagar found with her little Ishmael in the wilderness: the aerolite and
it have been sacred now, and had a Caabah over them, for thousands
of years. A curious object that Caabah! There it stands at this hour,
in the black cloth-covering the Sultan sends it yearly; 'twenty-seven
cubits high;' with circuit, with double circuit of pillars, with festoon-
rows of lamps and quaint ornaments: the lamps will be lighted again

this night,—to glitter again under the stars. An authentic fragment of
the oldest Past. It is the *Keblah* of all Moslem: from Delhi all onwards
to Morocco, the eyes of innumerable praying men are turned towards
it, five times, this day and all days: one of the notablest centres in the
Habitation of Men.

It had been from the sacredness attached to this Caabah Stone and
Hagar's Well, from the pilgrimings of all tribes of Arabs thither, that
Mecca took its rise as a Town. A great town once, though much
decayed now. It has no natural advantage for a town; stands in a
sandy hollow amid bare barren hills, at a distance from the sea; its
provisions, its very bread, have to be imported. But so many pilgrims
needed lodgings: and then all places of pilgrimage do, from the first,
become places of trade. The first day pilgrims meet, merchants have
also met: where men see themselves assembled for one object, they
find that they can accomplish other objects which depend on meeting
together. Mecca became the Fair of all Arabia. And thereby indeed
the chief staple and warehouse of whatever Commerce there was
between the Indian and the Western countries, Syria, Egypt, even
Italy. It had at one time a population of 100,000; buyers, forwarders
of those Eastern and Western products; importers for their own
behoof of provisions and corn. The government was a kind of irreg-
ular aristocratic republic, not without a touch of theocracy. Ten Men
of a chief tribe, chosen in some rough way, were Governors of Mecca,
and Keepers of the Caabah. The Koreish were the chief tribe in
Mahomet's time; his own family was of that tribe. The rest of the
Nation, fractioned and cut asunder by deserts, lived under similar
rude patriarchal governments by one or several: herdsmen, carriers,
traders, generally robbers too; being oftenest at war, one with another, or with all: held together by no open bond, if it were not this
meeting at the Caabah, where all forms of Arab Idolatry assembled
in common adoration;—held mainly by the *inward* indissoluble bond
of a common blood and language. In this way had the Arabs lived for
long ages, unnoticed by the world; a people of great qualities, unconsciously waiting for the day when they should become notable to all
the world. Their Idolatries appear to have been in a tottering state;
much was getting into confusion and fermentation among them.
Obscure tidings of the most important Event ever transacted in this
world, the Life and Death of the Divine Man in Judea, at once the
symptom and cause of immeasurable change to all people in the

world, had in the course of centuries reached into Arabia too; and could not but, of itself, have produced fermentation there.

It was among this Arab people, so circumstanced, in the year 570 of our Era, that the man Mahomet was born. He was of the family of Hashem, of the Koreish tribe as we said; though poor, connected with the chief persons of his country. Almost at his birth he lost his Father; at the age of six years his Mother too, a woman noted for her beauty, her worth and sense: he fell to the charge of his Grandfather, an old man, a hundred years old. A good old man: Mahomet's Father, Abdallah, had been his youngest favourite son. He saw in Mahomet, with his old life-worn eyes, a century old, the lost Abdallah come back again, all that was left of Abdallah. He loved the little orphan Boy greatly; used to say, They must take care of that beautiful little Boy, nothing in their kindred was more precious than he. At his death, while the boy was still but two years old, he left him in charge to Abu Thaleb the eldest of the Uncles, as to him that now was head of the house. By this Uncle, a just and rational man as everything betokens, Mahomet was brought up in the best Arab way.

Mahomet, as he grew up, accompanied his Uncle on trading journeys and such like; in his eighteenth year one finds him a fighter following his Uncle in war. But perhaps the most significant of all his journeys is one we find noted as of some years' earlier date: a journey to the Fairs of Syria. The young man here first came in contact with a quite foreign world,—with one foreign element of endless moment to him: the Christian Religion. I know not what to make of that 'Sergius, the Nestorian Monk,' whom Abu Thaleb and he are said to have lodged with; or how much any monk could have taught one still so young. Probably enough it is greatly exaggerated, this of the Nestorian Monk. Mahomet was only fourteen; had no language but his own: much in Syria must have been a strange unintelligible whirlpool to him. But the eyes of the lad were open; glimpses of many things would doubtless be taken in, and lie very enigmatic as yet, which were to ripen in a strange way into views, into beliefs and insights one day. These journeys to Syria were probably the beginning of much to Mahomet.

One other circumstance we must not forget: that he had no school-learning; of the thing we call school-learning none at all. The art of writing was but just introduced into Arabia; it seems to be the true opinion that Mahomet never could write! Life in the Desert, with its experiences, was all his education. What of this infinite Universe he, from his dim place, with his own eyes and thoughts, could take in, so much and no more of it was he to know. Curious, if we will reflect on it, this of having no books. Except by what he could see for himself, or hear of by uncertain rumour of speech in the obscure Arabian Desert, he could know nothing. The wisdom that had been before him or at a distance from him in the world, was in a manner as good as not there for him. Of the great brother souls, flame-beacons through so many lands and times, no one directly communicates with this great soul. He is alone there, deep down in the bosom of the Wilderness; has to grow up so,—alone with Nature and his own Thoughts.

But, from an early age, he had been remarked as a thoughtful man. His companions named him '*Al Amin*, The Faithful.' A man of truth and fidelity; true in what he did, in what he spake and thought. They noted that *he* always meant something. A man rather taciturn in speech; silent when there was nothing to be said; but pertinent, wise, sincere, when he did speak; always throwing light on the matter. This is the only sort of speech *worth* speaking! Through life we find him to have been regarded as an altogether solid, brotherly, genuine man. A serious, sincere character; yet amiable, cordial, companionable, jocose even;—a good laugh in him withal: there are men whose laugh is as untrue as anything about them; who cannot laugh. One hears of Mahomet's beauty: his fine sagacious honest face, brown florid complexion, beaming black eyes;—I somehow like too that vein on the brow, which swelled up black, when he was in anger: like the '*horse-shoe* vein' in Scott's *Redgauntlet*. It was a kind of feature in the Hashem family, this black swelling vein in the brow; Mahomet had it prominent, as would appear. A spontaneous, passionate, yet just, true-meaning man! Full of wild faculty, fire and light; of wild worth, all uncultured; working out his life-task in the depths of the Desert there.

How he was placed with Kadijah, a rich Widow, as her Steward, and travelled in her business, again to the Fairs of Syria; how he managed all, as one can well understand, with fidelity, adroitness; how her gratitude, her regard for him grew: the story of their marriage is altogether a graceful intelligible one, as told us by the Arab authors. He was twenty-five; she forty, though still beautiful. He seems to have lived in a most affectionate, peaceable, wholesome way with this wedded benefactress; loving her truly, and her alone. It goes greatly against the impostor-theory, the fact that he lived in this entirely unexceptionable, entirely quiet and commonplace way, till the heat of his years was done. He was forty before he talked of any mission from Heaven. All his irregularities, real and supposed, date from after his fiftieth year, when the good Kadijah died. All his 'ambition,' seemingly, had been, hitherto, to live an honest life; his 'fame,' the mere good-opinion of neighbours that knew him, had been sufficient hitherto. Not till he was already getting old, the prurient heat of his life all burnt out, and *peace* growing to be the chief thing this world could give him, did he start on the 'career of ambition;' and, belying all his past character and existence, set up as a wretched empty charlatan to acquire what he could now no longer enjoy! For my share, I have no faith whatever in that.

Ah no: this deep-hearted Son of the Wilderness, with his beaming black eyes, and open social deep soul, had other thoughts in him than ambition. A silent great soul; he was one of those who cannot *but* be in earnest; whom Nature herself has appointed to be sincere. While others walk in formulas and hearsays, contented enough to dwell there, this man could not screen himself in formulas; he was alone with his own soul and the reality of things. The great Mystery of Existence, as I said, glared in upon him; with its terrors, with its splendours; no hearsays could hide that unspeakable fact, "Here am I!" Such *sincerity*, as we named it, has in very truth something of divine. The word of such a man is a Voice direct from Nature's own Heart. Men do and must listen to that as to nothing else;—all else is wind in comparison. From of old, a thousand thoughts, in his pilgrimings and wanderings, had been in this man: What am I? What *is* this unfathomable Thing I live in, which men name Universe? What is Life; what is Death! What am I to believe? What am I to do? The grim rocks of Mount Hara, of Mount Sinai, the stern sandy solitudes answered not. The great Heaven rolling silent overhead, with its blue-glancing stars, answered not. There was no answer. The man's own soul, and what of God's inspiration dwelt there, had to answer!

It is the thing which all men have to ask themselves; which we too have to ask, and answer. This wild man felt it to be of *infinite* moment; all other things of no moment whatever in comparison. The jargon of argumentative Greek Sects, vague traditions of Jews, the stupid routine of Arab Idolatry: there was no answer in these. A Hero, as I repeat, has this first distinction, which indeed we may call first and last, the Alpha and Omega of his whole Heroism, That he looks through the shews of things into *things*. Use and wont, respectable hearsay, respectable formula: all these are good, or are not good. There is something behind and beyond all these, which all these must correspond with, be the image of, or they are—*Idolatries;* 'bits of black wood pretending to be God:' to the earnest soul a mockery and abomination. Idolatries never so gilded, waited on by heads of the Koreish, will do nothing for this man. Though all men walk by them, what good is it? The great Reality stands glaring there upon *him*. He there has to answer it, or perish miserably. Now, even now, or else through all Eternity never! Answer it; *thou* must find an answer.— Ambition? What could all Arabia do for this man; with the crown of Greek Heraclius, of Persian Chosroes, and all crowns in the Earth;— what could they all do for him? It was not of the Earth he wanted to hear tell; it was of the Heaven above and of the Hell beneath. All crowns and sovereignties whatsoever, where would *they* in a few brief years be? To be Shiek of Mecca or Arabia, and have a bit of gilt wood put into your hand,—will that be one's salvation? I decidedly think, not. We will leave it altogether, this impostor-hypothesis, as not credible; not very tolerable even, worthy chiefly of dismissal by us.

Mahomet had been wont to retire yearly, during the month Ramadhan, into solitude and silence; as indeed was the Arab custom; a praiseworthy custom, which such a man, above all, would find natural and useful. Communing with his own heart, in the silence of the mountains; himself silent; open to the 'small still voices:' it was a right natural custom! Mahomet was in his fortieth year, when having withdrawn to a cavern in Mount Hara, near Mecca, during this Ramadhan, to pass the month in prayer, and meditation on those great questions, he one day told his wife Kadijah, who with his household was with him or near him this year, That by the unspeakable special favour of Heaven he had now found it all out; was in doubt and darkness no longer, but saw it all. That all these Idols and Formulas were nothing, miserable bits of wood; that there was One God in and over all; and we must leave all Idols, and look to Him.

That God is great; and that there is nothing else great! He is the Reality. Wooden Idols are not real; He is real. He made us at first, sustains us yet; we and all things are but the shadow of Him; a transitory garment veiling the Eternal Splendour. 'Allah akbar, God is great;'—and then also 'Islam,' That we must submit to God. That our whole strength lies in resigned submission to Him, whatsoever He do to us. For this world, and for the other! The thing He sends to us, were it death and worse than death, shall be good, shall be best; we resign ourselves to God.—'If this be Islam,' says Goethe, 'do we not all live in Islam?' Yes, all of us that have any moral life; we all live so. It has ever been held the highest wisdom for a man not merely to submit to Necessity,—Necessity will make him submit,—but to know and believe well that the stern thing which Necessity had ordered was the wisest, the best, the thing wanted there. To cease his frantic pretension of scanning this great God's-World in his small fraction of a brain; to know that it had verily, though deep beyond his soundings, a Just Law, that the soul of it was Good;—that his part in it was to conform to the Law of the Whole, and in devout silence follow that; not questioning it, obeying it as unquestionable.

I say, this is yet the only true morality known. A man is right and invincible, virtuous and on the road towards sure conquest, precisely while he joins himself to the great deep Law of the World, in spite of all superficial laws, temporary appearances, profit-and-loss calculations; he is victorious while he cooperates with that great central Law, not victorious otherwise;—and surely his first chance of cooperating with it, or getting into the course of it, is to know with his whole soul that it is; that it is good, and alone good! This is the soul of Islam; it is properly the soul of Christianity,—for Islam is definable as a confused form of Christianity; had Christianity not been, neither had it been. Christianity also commands us, before all, to be resigned to God. We are to take no counsel with flesh and blood; give ear to no vain cavils, vain sorrows and wishes: to know that we know nothing; that the worst and cruellest to our eyes is not what it seems; that we have to receive whatsoever befals us as sent from God above, and say, It is good and wise, God is great! "Though He slay me, yet will I trust in Him." Islam means in its way Denial of Self, Annihilation of Self. This is yet the highest Wisdom that Heaven has revealed to our Earth.

Such light had come, as it could, to illuminate the darkness of this wild Arab soul. A confused dazzling splendour as of life and Heaven, in the great darkness which threatened to be death: he called it revelation and the angel Gabriel;—who of us yet can know what to call it? It is the 'inspiration of the Almighty' that giveth us understanding. To *know;* to get into the truth of anything, is ever a mystic act,—of which the best Logics can but babble on the surface. 'Is not Belief the true god-announcing Miracle?' says Novalis.—That Mahomet's whole soul, set in flame with this grand Truth vouchsafed him, should feel as if it were important and the only important thing, was very natural. That Providence had unspeakably honoured *him* by revealing it, saving him from death and darkness; that he therefore was bound to make known the same to all creatures: this is what was meant by 'Mahomet is the Prophet of God;' this too is not without its true meaning.—

The good Kadijah, we can fancy, listened to him with wonder, with doubt; at length she answered: Yes, it was *true* this that he said. One can fancy too the boundless gratitude of Mahomet; and how of all the kindnesses she had done him, this of believing the earnest struggling word he now spoke was the greatest. 'It is certain,' says Novalis, 'my Conviction gains infinitely, the moment another soul will believe in it.' It is a boundless favour.—He never forgot this good Kadijah. Long afterwards, Ayesha his young favourite wife, a woman who indeed distinguished herself among the Moslem, by all manner of qualities, through her whole long life; this young brilliant Ayesha was, one day, questioning him: "Now am not I better than Kadijah? She was a widow; old, and had lost her looks: you love me better than you did her?"—"No, by Allah!" answered Mahomet: "No, by Allah! She believed in me when none else would believe. In the whole world I had but one friend, and she was that!"—Seid, his Slave, also believed in him; these with his young Cousin Ali, Abu Thaleb's son, were his first converts.

He spoke of his Doctrine to this man and that; but the most treated it with ridicule, with indifference: in three years, I think, he had gained but thirteen followers. His progress was slow enough. His encouragement to go on, was altogether the usual encouragement that such a man in such a case meets. After some three years of small success, he invited forty of his chief kindred to an entertainment; and there stood up and told them what his pretension was: that he had this thing to promulgate abroad to all men; that it was the highest thing, the one thing: which of them would second him in that? Amid the doubt and silence of all, young Ali, as yet a lad of sixteen, impatient of the silence, started up, and exclaimed in passionate fierce language, That he would! The assembly, among whom was Abu Thaleb, Ali's Father, could not be unfriendly to Mahomet; yet the sight there, of one unlettered elderly man, with a lad of sixteen, deciding on such an enterprise against all mankind, appeared ridiculous to them; the assembly broke up in laughter. Nevertheless it proved not a laughable thing; it was a very serious thing! As for this young Ali, one cannot but like him. A noble-minded creature, as he shews himself, now and always afterwards; full of affection, of fiery daring. Something chivalrous in him; brave as a lion; yet with a grace, a truth and affection worthy of Christian knighthood. He died by assassination in the Mosque at Bagdad; a death occasioned by his own generous fairness, confidence in the fairness of others: he said, If the wound proved not unto death, they must pardon the Assassin; but if it did, then they must slay him straightway, that so they two in the same hour might appear before God, and see which side of that quarrel was the just one!

Mahomet naturally gave offence to the Koreish, Keepers of the Caabah, superintendents of the Idols. One or two men of influence had joined him: the thing spread slowly, but it was spreading. Naturally he gave offence to everybody: Who is this that pretends to be wiser than we all; that rebukes us all, as mere fools and worshippers of wood! Abu Thaleb the good Uncle spoke with him: Could he not be silent about all that; believe it all for himself, and not trouble others, anger the chief men, endanger himself and them all, talking of it? Mahomet answered: If the Sun stood on his right hand and the Moon on his left, ordering him to hold his peace, he could not obey! No: there was something in this Truth he had got which was of Nature herself; equal in rank to Sun, or Moon, or whatsoever thing Nature had made. It would speak itself there, so long as the Almighty allowed it, in spite of Sun and Moon, and all Koreish and all men and things. It must do that, and could do no other. Mahomet answered so; and, they say, 'burst into tears.' Burst into tears: he felt that Abu Thaleb was good to him; that the task he had got was no soft, but a stern and great one.

He went on speaking to who would listen to him; publishing his Doctrine among the pilgrims as they came to Mecca; gaining adherents in this place and that. Continual contradiction, hatred, open or secret danger attended him. His powerful relations protected Mahomet himself; but by and by, on his own advice, all his adherents had to quit Mecca, and seek refuge in Abyssinia over the sea. The Koreish grew ever angrier; laid plots, and swore oaths among them, to put Mahomet to death with their own hands. Abu Thaleb was dead, the good Kadijah was dead. Mahomet is not solicitous of sympathy from us; but his outlook at this time was one of the dismallest. He had to hide in caverns, escape in disguise; fly hither and thither; homeless, in continual peril of his life. More than once it seemed all over with him; more than once it turned on a straw, some rider's horse taking fright or the like, whether Mahomet and his Doctrine had not ended there, and not been heard of at all. But it was not to end so.

In the thirteenth year of his mission, finding his enemies all banded against him, forty sworn men, one out of every tribe waiting to take his life, and no continuance possible at Mecca for him any longer, Mahomet fled to the place then called Yathreb, where he had gained some adherents; the place they now call Medina, or '*Medinat al Nabi*, the City of the Prophet,' from that circumstance. It lay some 200 miles off, through rocks and deserts; not without great difficulty, in such mood as we may fancy, he escaped thither, and found welcome. The whole East dates its era from this Flight, *Hegira* as they name it: the Year 1 of this Hegira is 622 of our era, the fifty-third of Mahomet's life. He was now becoming an old man; his friends sinking round him one by one; his path desolate, encompassed with danger: unless he could find hope in his own heart, the outward face of things was but hopeless for him. It is so with all men in the like case. Hitherto Mahomet had professed to publish his Religion by the way of preaching and persuasion alone. But now, driven foully out of his native country, since unjust men had not only given no ear to his earnest Heaven's-message, the deep cry of his heart, but would not even let him live if he kept speaking it,—the wild Son of the Desert resolved to defend himself, like a man and Arab. If the Koreish will have it so, they shall have it. Tidings, felt to be of infinite moment to them and all men, they would not listen to these; would trample them down by sheer violence, steel and murder: well, let steel try it then! Ten years more this Mahomet had; all of fighting, of breathless impetuous toil and struggle; with what result we know.

Much has been said of Mahomet's propagating his Religion by the sword. It is no doubt far nobler what we have to boast of the Christian Religion, that it propagated itself peaceably in the way of preaching and conviction. Yet withal, if we take this for an argument of the truth or falsehood of a religion, there is a radical mistake in it. The sword indeed: but where will you get your sword! Every new opinion, at its starting, is precisely in a *minority of one*. In one man's head alone, there it dwells as yet. One man alone of the whole world believes it; there is one man against all men. That *he* take a sword, and try to propagate with that, will do little for him. You must first get your sword! On the whole, a thing will propagate itself as it can. We do not find, of the Christian Religion either, that it always disdained the sword, when once it had got one. Charlemagne's conversion of the Saxons was not by preaching. I care little about the sword: I will allow a thing to struggle for itself in this world, with any sword or tongue or implement it has, or can lay hold of. We will let it preach, and pamphleteer, and fight, and to the uttermost bestir itself, and do, beak and claws, whatsoever is in it; very sure that it will, in the long-run, conquer nothing which does not deserve to be conquered. What is better than itself, it cannot put away, but only what is worse. In this great Duel, Nature herself is umpire, and can do no wrong: the thing which is deepest-rooted in Nature, what we call *truest*, that thing and not the other will be found growing at last.

Here however, in reference to much that there is in Mahomet and his success, we are to remember what an umpire Nature is; what a greatness, composure of depth and tolerance there is in her. You take wheat to cast into the Earth's bosom: your wheat may be mixed with chaff, chopped straw, barn-sweepings, dust and all imaginable rubbish; no matter: you cast it into the kind just Earth; she grows the wheat,—the whole rubbish she silently absorbs, shrouds *it* in, says nothing of the rubbish. The yellow wheat is growing there; the good Earth is silent about all the rest,—has silently turned all the rest to some benefit too, and makes no complaint about it! So everywhere in Nature. She is true and not a lie; and yet so great, and just, and motherly, in her truth. She requires of a thing only that it *be* genuine of heart; she will protect it if so; will not, if not so. There is a soul of truth in all the things she ever gave harbour to. Alas, is not this the history of all highest Truth that comes or ever came into the world? The *body* of them all is imperfection, an element of light *in* darkness: to us they have to come embodied in mere Logic, in some merely *scientific* Theorem of the Universe; which *cannot* be complete; which cannot but be found, one day, *in*complete, erroneous, and so die and disappear. The body of all Truth dies; and yet in all, I say, there is a soul which never dies; which in new and ever-nobler embodiment lives immortal as man himself! It is the way with Nature. The genuine essence of Truth never dies. That it be genuine, a voice from the great Deep of Nature, there is the point at Nature's judgment-seat. What *we* call pure or impure, is not with her the final question. Not how much chaff is in you; but whether you have any wheat. Pure? I might say to many a man: Yes, you are pure; pure enough; but you are chaff,—insincere hypothesis, hearsay, formality; you never were in contact with the great heart of the Universe at all; you are properly neither pure nor impure; you *are* nothing, Nature has no business with you.

Mahomet's Creed we called a kind of Christianity; and really, if we look at the wild rapt earnestness with which it was believed and laid to heart, I should say a better kind than that of those miserable Syrian Sects, with their vain janglings about *Homoiousion* and *Homoousion*, the head full of worthless noise, the heart empty and dead! The truth of it is embedded in portentous error and falsehood; but the truth of it makes it be believed, not the falsehood: it succeeded by its truth. A bastard kind of Christianity, but a living kind; with a heart-life in it; not dead, chopping barren logic merely! Out of all that rubbish of Arab idolatries, argumentative theologies, traditions, subtleties, rumours and hypotheses of Greeks and Jews, with their idle wire-drawings, this wild man of the Desert, with his wild sincere heart, earnest as death and life, with his great flashing natural eyesight, had seen into the kernel of the matter. Idolatry is nothing: these Wooden Idols of yours, 'ye rub them with oil and wax, and the flies stick on them,'—these are wood, I tell you! They can do nothing for you;

they are an impotent blasphemous pretence; a horror and abomination, if ye knew them. God alone is; God alone has power; He made us, He can kill us and keep us alive: *"Allah akbar,* God is great." Understand that His will is the best for you; that howsoever sore to flesh and blood, you will find it the wisest, best: you are bound to take it so; in this world and in the next, you have no other thing that you can do!—And now if the wild idolatrous men did believe this, and with their fiery hearts lay hold of it to do it, in what form soever it came to them, I say it was well worthy of being believed. In one form or the other, I say it is still the one thing worthy of being believed by all men. Man does hereby become the high-priest of this Temple of a World. He is in harmony with the Decrees of the Author of this World; cooperating with them, not vainly withstanding them: I know, to this day, no better definition of Duty than that same. All that is *right* includes itself in this of cooperating with the real Tendency of the World: you succeed by this (the World's Tendency will succeed), you are good, and in the right course there. *Homoiousion, Homoousion,* vain logical jangle, then or before or at any time, may jangle itself out, and go whither and how it likes: this is the *thing* it all struggles to mean, if it would mean anything. If it do not succeed in meaning this, it means nothing. Not that Abstractions, logical Propositions, be correctly worded or incorrectly; but that living concrete Sons of Adam do lay this to heart: that is the important point. Islam devoured all these vain jangling Sects; and I think had right to do so. It was a Reality, direct from the great Heart of Nature once more. Arab idolatries, Syrian formulas, whatsoever was not equally real, had to go up in flame,—mere dead *fuel,* in various senses, for this which was *fire.*

It was during these wild warfarings and strugglings, especially after the Flight to Mecca, that Mahomet dictated at intervals his Sacred Book, which they name *Koran,* or *Reading,* 'Thing to be read.' This is the Work he and his disciples made so much of, asking all the world, Is not that a miracle? The Mahometans regard their Koran with a reverence which few Christians pay even to their Bible. It is admitted everywhere as the standard of all law and all practice; the thing to be gone upon in speculation and life: the message sent direct out of Heaven, which this Earth has to conform to, and walk by; the thing to be read. Their Judges decide by it; all Moslem are bound to study it, seek in it for the light of their life. They have mosques where it is all read daily; thirty relays of priests take it up in succession, get through the whole each day. There, for twelve hundred years, has the voice of this Book, at all moments, kept sounding through the ears and the hearts of so many men. We hear of Mahometan Doctors that had read it seventy thousand times!

Very curious: if one sought for 'discrepancies of national taste,' here surely were the most eminent instance of that! We also can read the Koran; our Translation of it, by Sale, is known to be a very fair one. I must say, it is as toilsome reading as I ever undertook. A wearisome confused jumble, crude, incondite; endless iterations, longwindedness, entanglement; most crude, incondite;—insupportable stupidity, in short! Nothing but a sense of duty could carry any European through the Koran. We read in it, as we might in the State-Paper Office, unreadable masses of lumber, that perhaps we may get some glimpses of a remarkable man. It is true we have it under disadvantages: the Arabs see more method in it than we. Mahomet's followers found the Koran lying all in fractions, as it had been written down at first promulgation; much of it, they say, on shoulder-blades of mutton, flung pellmell into a chest: and they published it, without any discoverable order as to time or otherwise;—merely trying, as would seem, and this not very strictly, to put the longest chapters first. The real beginning of it, in that way, lies almost at the end; for the earliest portions were the shortest. Read in its historical sequence it perhaps would not be so bad. Much of it, too, they say, is rhythmic; a kind of wild chaunting song, in the original. This may be a great point; much perhaps has been lost in the Translation here. Yet with every allowance, one feels it difficult to see how any mortal ever could consider this Koran as a Book written in Heaven, too good for the Earth; as a well-written book, or indeed as a *book* at all; and not a bewildered rhapsody; *written*, so far as writing goes, as badly as almost any book ever was! So much for national discrepancies, and the standard of taste.

Yet I should say, it was not unintelligible how the Arabs might so love it. When once you get this confused coil of a Koran fairly off your hands, and have it behind you at a distance, the essential type of it begins to disclose itself; and in this there is a merit quite other than the literary one. If a book come from the heart, it will contrive to reach other hearts; all art and authorcraft are of small amount to that. One would say the primary character of the Koran is this of its *genuineness*, of its being a *bonâ-fide* book. Prideaux, I know, and others have represented it as a mere bundle of juggleries; chapter after chapter got up to excuse and varnish the author's successive sins, forward his ambitions and quackeries: but really it is time to dismiss all that. I do not assert Mahomet's continual sincerity: who is continually sincere? But I confess I can make nothing of the critic, in these times, who would accuse him of deceit *prepense;* of conscious deceit generally, or perhaps at all;—still more, of living in a mere element of conscious deceit, and writing this Koran as a forger and juggler would have done! Every candid eye, I think, will read the Koran far otherwise than so. It is the confused ferment of a great rude human soul; rude, untutored, that cannot even read; but fervent, earnest, struggling vehemently to utter itself in words. With a kind of breathless intensity he strives to utter himself; the thoughts crowd on him pellmell; for very multitude of things to say he can get nothing said. The meaning that is in him shapes itself into no form of composition, is stated in no sequence, method, or coherence;— they are not *shaped* at all, these thoughts of his; flung out unshaped, as they struggle and tumble there, in their chaotic inarticulate state. We said 'stupid:' yet natural stupidity is by no means the character of Mahomet's Book; it is natural uncultivation rather. The man has not studied speaking; in the haste and pressure of continual fighting, has not time to mature himself into fit speech. The panting breathless haste and vehemence of a man struggling in the thick of battle for life and salvation; this is the mood he is in! A headlong haste; for very magnitude of meaning he cannot get himself articulated into words. The successive utterances of a soul in that mood, coloured by the various vicissitudes of three-and-twenty years; now well uttered, now worse: this is the Koran.

For we are to consider Mahomet, through these three-and-twenty years, as the centre of a world wholly in conflict. Battles with the Koreish and Heathen, quarrels among his own people, backslidings of his own wild heart; all this kept him in a perpetual whirl, his soul knowing rest no more. In wakeful nights, as one may fancy, the wild soul of the man, tossing amid these vortices, would hail any light of a decision for them as a veritable light from Heaven; *any* making up of his mind, so blessed, indispensable for him there, would seem the inspiration of a Gabriel. Forger and juggler? No, no! This great fiery heart, seething, simmering like a great furnace of thoughts, was not a juggler's. His Life was a Fact to him; this God's Universe an awful Fact and Reality. He has faults enough. The man was an uncultured semi-barbarous Son of Nature, much of the Bedouin still clinging to him: we must take him for that. But for a wretched Simulacrum, a hungry Impostor without eyes or heart, practising for a mess of pottage such blasphemous swindlery, forgery of celestial documents, continual high-treason against his Maker and Self, we will not and cannot take him.

Sincerity, in all senses, seems to me the merit of the Koran; what had rendered it precious to the wild Arab men. It is, after all, the first and last merit in a book; gives rise to merits of all kinds,—nay, at bottom, it alone can give rise to merit of any kind. Curiously, through these incondite masses of tradition, vituperation, complaint, ejaculation in the Koran, a vein of true direct insight, of what we might almost call poetry, is found straggling. The body of the Book is made up of mere tradition, and as it were vehement enthusiastic extempore preaching. He returns forever to the old stories of the Prophets as they went current in the Arab memory: how Prophet after Prophet, the Prophet Abraham, the Prophet Hud, the Prophet Moses, Christian and other real and fabulous Prophets, had come to this Tribe and to that, warning men of their sin; and been received by them even as he Mahomet was,—which is a great solace to him. These things he repeats ten, perhaps twenty times; again and ever again, with wearisome iteration; has never done repeating them. A brave Samuel Johnson, in his forlorn garret, might con over the Biographies of Authors in that way! This is the great staple of the Koran. But curiously, through all this, comes ever and anon some glance as of the real thinker and seer. He has actually an eye for the world, this Mahomet: with a certain directness and rugged vigour, he brings home still, to our heart, the thing his own heart has been opened to. I make but little of his praises of Allah, which many praise; they are borrowed I suppose mainly from the Hebrew, at least they are far surpassed there. But the eye that flashes direct into the heart of things, and *sees* the truth of them; this is to me a highly interesting object. Great Nature's own gift; which she bestows on all; but which only one in the thousand does not cast sorrowfully away: it is what I call sincerity of vision; the test of a sincere heart. Mahomet can work no miracles; he often answers impatiently: I can work no miracles. I? 'I am a Public Preacher;' appointed to preach this doctrine to all creatures. Yet the world, as we can see, had really from of old been all one great miracle to him. Look over the world, says he; is it not wonderful, the work of Allah; wholly 'a sign to you,' if your eyes were open! This Earth, God made it for you; 'appointed paths in it;' you can live in it, go to and fro on it.—The clouds in the dry country of Arabia, to Mahomet they are very wonderful: Great clouds, he says, born in the deep bosom of the Upper Immensity, where do they come from! They hang there, the great black monsters; pour down their rain-deluges 'to revive a dead earth,' and grass springs, and 'tall leafy palm-trees with their date-clusters hanging round. Is not that a sign?' Your cattle too,—Allah made them: serviceable dumb creatures; they change the grass into milk; you have your clothing from them, very strange creatures; they come ranking home at evening time, 'and,' adds he, 'and are a credit to you!' Ships also,—he talks often about ships: Huge moving mountains, they spread out their cloth wings, go bounding through the water there, Heaven's wind driving them; anon they lie motionless, God has withdrawn the wind, they lie dead, and cannot stir! Miracles? cries he: What miracle would you have? Are not you yourselves there? God made *you*, 'shaped you out of a little clay.' Ye were small once; a few years ago ye were not at all. Ye have beauty, strength, thoughts, 'ye have compassion on one another.' Old age comes on you, and grey hairs; your strength fades into feebleness; ye sink down, and again are not. 'Ye have compassion on one another:' this struck me much: Allah might have made you having no compassion on one another,—how had it been then! This is a great direct thought, a glance at first-hand into the very fact of things. Rude vestiges of poetic genius, of whatsoever is best and truest, are visible in this man. A strong untutored intellect; eyesight, heart: a strong wild man,—might have shaped himself into Poet, King, Priest, any kind of Hero.

To his eyes it is forever clear that this world wholly is miraculous. He sees what, as we said once before, all great thinkers, the rude Scandinavians themselves, in one way or other, have contrived to see:

That this so solid-looking material world is, at bottom, in very deed, Nothing; is a visual and tactual Manifestation of God's power and presence,—a shadow hung out by Him on the bosom of the void Infinite; nothing more. The mountains, he says, these great rock-mountains, they shall dissipate themselves 'like clouds;' melt into the Blue as clouds do, and not be! He figures the Earth, in the Arab fashion, Sale tells us, as an immense Plain or flat Plate of ground, the mountains are set on that to *steady* it. At the Last Day, they shall disappear 'like clouds;' the whole Earth shall go spinning, whirl itself off into wreck, and as dust and vapour vanish in the Inane. Allah withdraws his hand from it, and it ceases to be. The universal empire of Allah, presence everywhere of an unspeakable Power, a Splendour, and a Terror not to be named, as the true force, essence and reality, in all things whatsoever, was continually clear to this man. What a modern talks of by the name, Forces of Nature, Laws of Nature; and does not figure as a divine thing; not even as one thing at all, but as a set of things, undivine enough,—saleable, curious, good for propelling steam-ships! With our Sciences and Cyclopædias, we are apt to forget the *divineness*, in those laboratories of ours. We ought not to forget it! That once well forgotten, I know not what else were worth remembering. Most sciences, I think, were then a very dead thing; withered, contentious, empty;—a thistle in late autumn. The best science, without this, is but as the dead *timber;* it is not the growing tree and forest,—which gives ever-new timber among other things! Man cannot *know* either, unless he can *worship* in some way. His knowledge is a pedantry, and dead thistle, otherwise.

Much has been said and written about the sensuality of Mahomet's Religion; more than was just. The indulgences, criminal to us, which he permitted, were not of his appointment; he found them practised, unquestioned from immemorial time in Arabia; what he did was to curtail them, restrict them, not on one but on many sides. His Religion is not an easy one; with rigorous fasts, lavations, strict complex formulas, prayers five times a day, and abstinence from wine, it did not 'succeed by being an easy religion.' As if indeed any religion, or cause holding of religion, could succeed by that! It is a calumny on men to say that they are roused to heroic action by ease, hope of pleasure, recompense,—sugar-plums of any kind, in this world or the next! In the meanest mortal there lies something nobler.

The poor swearing soldier, hired to be shot, has his 'honour of a soldier,' different from drill-regulations and the shilling a day. It is not to taste sweet things, but to do noble and true things, and vindicate himself under God's Heaven as a god-made Man, that the poorest son of Adam dimly longs. Shew him the way of doing that, the dullest daydrudge kindles into a hero. They wrong man greatly who say he is to be seduced by ease. Difficulty, abnegation, martyrdom, death are the *allurements* that act on the heart of man. Kindle the inner genial life of him, you have a flame that burns up all lower considerations. Not happiness, but something higher: one sees this even in the frivolous classes, with their 'point of honour' and the like. Not by flattering our appetites; no, by awakening the Heroic that slumbers in every heart, can any Religion gain followers.

Mahomet himself, after all that can be said about him, was not a sensual man. We shall err widely if we consider this man as a common voluptuary, intent mainly on base enjoyments,—nay on enjoyments of any kind. His household was of the frugalest; his common diet barley-bread and water: sometimes for months there was not a fire once lighted on his hearth. They record with just pride that he would mend his own shoes, patch his own cloak. A poor, hard-toiling, ill-provided man; careless of what vulgar men toil for. Not a bad man, I should say; something better in him than *hunger* of any sort,—or these wild Arab men, fighting and jostling three and twenty years at his hand, in close contact with him always, would not have reverenced him so! They were wild men, bursting ever and anon into quarrel, into all kinds of fierce sincerity; without right worth and manhood, no man could have commanded them. They called him Prophet, you say? Why, he stood there face to face with them; bare, not enshrined in any mystery; visibly clouting his own cloak, cobbling his own shoes; fighting, counselling, ordering in the midst of them: they must have seen what kind of a man he *was*, let him be *called* what you like! No emperor with his tiaras was obeyed as this man in a cloak of his own clouting. During three and twenty years of rough actual trial. I find something of a veritable Hero necessary for that, of itself.

His last words are a prayer; broken ejaculations of a heart struggling up, in trembling hope, towards its Maker. We cannot say that his religion made him *worse;* it made him better; good, not bad.

Generous things are recorded of him: when he lost his Daughter, the thing he answers is, in his own dialect, every way sincere, and yet equivalent to that of Christians, 'The Lord giveth, and the Lord taketh away; blessed be the name of the Lord.' He answered in like manner of Seid, his emancipated well-beloved Slave, the second of the believers. Seid had fallen in the War of Tabûc, the first of Mahomet's fightings with the Greeks. Mahomet said, It was well; Seid had done his Master's work, Seid had now gone to his Master: it was all well with Seid. Yet Seid's daughter found him weeping over the body;—the old gray-haired man melting in tears! "What do I see?" said she.—"You see a friend weeping over his friend."—He went out for the last time into the mosque, two days before his death; asked, If he had injured any man? Let his own back bear the stripes. If he owed any man? A voice answered, "Yes, me three drachms," borrowed on such an occasion. Mahomet ordered them to be paid: "Better be in shame now," said he, "than at the Day of Judgment."— You remember Kadijah, and the "No, by Allah!" Traits of that kind shew us the genuine man, the brother of us all, brought visible through twelve centuries,—the veritable Son of our common Mother.

Withal I like Mahomet for his total freedom from cant. He is a rough self-helping son of the wilderness; does not pretend to be what he is not. There is no ostentatious pride in him; but neither does he go much upon humility: he is there as he can be, in cloak and shoes of his own clouting; speaks plainly to all manner of Persian Kings, Greek Emperors, what it is they are bound to do; knows well enough, about himself, 'the respect due unto thee.' In a life-and-death war with Bedouins, cruel things could not fail; but neither are acts of mercy, of noble natural pity and generosity, wanting. Mahomet makes no apology for the one, no boast of the other. They were each the free dictate of his heart; each called for, there and then. Not a mealy-mouthed man! A candid ferocity, if the case call for it, is in him; he does not mince matters! The War of Tabûc is a thing he often speaks of: his men refused, many of them, to march on that occasion; pleaded the heat of the weather, the harvest, and so forth; he can never forget that. Your harvest? It lasts for a day. What will become of your harvest through all Eternity? Hot weather? Yes, it was hot; but 'Hell will be hotter!' Sometimes a rough sarcasm turns up: He says to the unbelievers, Ye shall have the just measure of your deeds at that Great Day. They will be weighed out to you; ye shall not have short weight!—Everywhere he fixes the matter in his eye; he *sees* it: his heart, now and then, is as if struck dumb by the greatness of it. 'Assuredly,' he says: that word, in the Koran, is written down sometimes as a sentence by itself: 'Assuredly.'

No *Dilettantism* in this Mahomet; it is a business of Reprobation and Salvation with him, of Time and Eternity: he is in deadly earnest about it! Dilettantism, hypothesis, speculation, a kind of amateur-search for Truth, toying and coquetting with Truth: this is the sorest sin. The root of all other imaginable sins. It consists in the heart and soul of the man never having been *open* to Truth;—'living in a vain show.' Such a man not only utters and produces falsehoods, but *is* himself a falsehood. The rational moral principle, spark of the Divinity, is sunk deep in him, in quiet paralysis of life-death. The very falsehoods of Mahomet are truer than the truths of such a man. He is the insincere man: smooth-polished, respectable in some times and places; inoffensive, says nothing harsh to anybody; most *cleanly*,—just as carbonic acid is, which is death and poison.

We will not praise Mahomet's moral precepts as always of the superfinest sort; yet it can be said that there is always a tendency to good in them; that they are the true dictates of a heart aiming towards what is just and true. The sublime forgiveness of Christianity, turning of the other cheek when the one has been smitten, is not here: you *are* to revenge yourself, but it is to be in measure, not over much, or beyond justice. On the other hand, Islam, like any great Faith, and insight into the essence of man, is a perfect equalizer of men: the soul of one believer outweighs all earthly kingships; all men, according to Islam too, are equal. Mahomet insists not on the propriety of giving alms, but on the necessity of it: he marks down by law how much you are to give, and it is at your peril if you neglect. The tenth part of a man's annual income, whatever that may be, is the *property* of the poor, of those that are afflicted and need help. Good all this: the natural voice of humanity, of pity and equity dwelling in the heart of this wild Son of Nature speaks *so*.

Mahomet's Paradise is sensual, his Hell sensual: true; in the one and the other there is enough that shocks all spiritual feeling in us. But we are to recollect that the Arabs already had it so; that Mahomet, in whatever he changed of it, softened and diminished all this.

The worst sensualities, too, are the work of doctors, followers of his, not his work. In the Koran there is really very little said about the joys of Paradise; they are intimated rather than insisted on. Nor is it forgotten that the highest joys even there shall be spiritual; the pure Presence of the Highest, this shall infinitely transcend all other joys. He says, 'Your salutation shall be, Peace.' *Salam*, Have Peace!—the thing that all rational souls long for, and seek, vainly here below, as the one blessing. 'Ye shall sit on seats, facing one another: all grudges shall be taken away out of your hearts.' All grudges! Ye shall love one another freely; for each of you, in the eyes of his brothers, there will be Heaven enough!

In reference to this of the sensual Paradise and Mahomet's sensuality, the sorest chapter of all for us, there were many things to be said; which it is not convenient to enter upon here. Two remarks only I shall make, and therewith leave it to your candour. The first is furnished me by Goethe; it is a casual hint of his which seems well worth taking note of. In one of his Delineations, in *Meister's Travels* it is, the hero comes upon a Society of men with very strange ways, one of which was this: "We require," says the Master, "that each of our people shall restrict himself in one direction," shall go right against his desire in one matter, and *make* himself do the thing he does not wish, "should we allow him the greater latitude on all other sides." There seems to me a great justness in this. Enjoying things which are pleasant; that is not the evil: it is the reducing of our moral self to slavery by them that is. Let a man assert withal that he is king over his habitudes; that he could and would shake them off, on cause shewn: this is an excellent law. The Month Ramadhan for the Moslem, much in Mahomet's Religion, much in his own Life, bears in that direction; if not by forethought, or clear purpose of moral improvement on his part, then by a certain healthy manful instinct, which is as good.

But there is another thing to be said about the Mahometan Heaven and Hell. This namely, that, however gross and material they may be, they are an emblem of an everlasting truth, not always so well remembered elsewhere. That gross sensual Paradise of his; that horrible flaming Hell; the great enormous Day of Judgment he perpetually insists on: what is all this but a rude shadow, in the rude Bedouin imagination, of that grand spiritual Fact, and Beginning of Facts, which it is ill for us too if we do not all know and feel: the Infinite Nature of Duty? That man's actions here are of *infinite* moment to him, and never die or end at all; that man, with his little life, reaches upwards high as Heaven, downwards low as Hell, and in his three-score years of Time holds an Eternity fearfully and wonderfully hidden: all this had burnt itself, as in flame-characters, into the wild Arab soul. As in flame and lightning, it stands written there; awful, unspeakable, ever present to him. With bursting earnestness, with a fierce savage sincerity, half-articulating, not able to articulate, he strives to speak it, bodies it forth in that Heaven and that Hell. Bodied forth in what way you will, it is the first of all truths. It is venerable under all embodiments. What is the chief end of man here below? Mahomet has answered this question, in a way that might put some of *us* to shame! He does not, like a Bentham, a Paley, take Right and Wrong, and calculate the profit and loss, ultimate pleasure of the one and of the other; and summing all up by addition and subtraction into a net result, ask you, Whether on the whole the Right does not preponderate considerably? No: it is not *better* to do the one than the other; the one is to the other as life is to death,—as Heaven is to Hell. The one must in nowise be done, the other in nowise left undone. You shall not measure them; they are incommensurable: the one is death eternal to a man, the other is life eternal. Benthamee Utility, virtue by Profit and Loss; reducing this God's-world to a dead brute Steam-engine, the infinite celestial Soul of Man to a kind of Hay-balance for weighing hay and thistles on, pleasures and pains on:—If you ask me which gives, Mahomet or they, the beggarlier and falser view of Man and his Destinies in this Universe, I will answer, It is not Mahomet!— —

On the whole, we will repeat that this Religion of Mahomet's is a kind of Christianity; has a genuine element of what is spiritually highest looking through it, not to be hidden by all its imperfections. The Scandinavian God *Wish*, the god of all rude men,—this has been enlarged into a Heaven by Mahomet; but a Heaven symbolical of sacred Duty, and to be earned by faith and welldoing, by valiant action, and a divine patience which is still more valiant. It is Scandinavian Paganism, and a truly celestial element superadded to that. Call it not false; look not at the falsehood of it, look at the truth of it. For these twelve centuries, it has been the religion and life-guidance of the fifth part of the whole kindred of Mankind. Above all things, it has been a religion heartily *believed*. These Arabs believe their religion, and try to live by it! No Christians, since the early ages, or only perhaps the English Puritans in modern times, have ever stood by their Faith as the Moslem do by theirs,—believing it wholly, fronting Time with it, and Eternity with it. This night the watchman on the streets of Cairo when he cries, "Who goes?" will hear from the passenger, along with his answer, "There is no God but God." *Allah akbar, Islam*, sounds through the souls, and whole daily existence, of these dusky millions. Zealous missionaries preach it abroad among Malays, black Papuans, brutal Idolators;—displacing what is worse, nothing that is better or good.

To the Arab Nation it was as a birth from darkness into light; Arabia first became alive by means of it. A poor shepherd people, roaming unnoticed in its deserts since the creation of the world: a Hero-Prophet was sent down to them with a word they could believe: see, the unnoticed becomes world-notable, the small has grown world-great; within one century afterwards, Arabia is at Grenada on this hand, at Delhi on that;—glancing in valour and splendour and the light of genius, Arabia shines through long ages over a great section of the world. Belief is great, life-giving. The history of a Nation becomes fruitful, soul-elevating, great, so soon as it believes. These Arabs, the man Mahomet, and that one century,—is it not as if a spark had fallen, one spark, on a world of what seemed black unnoticeable sand; but lo, the sand proves explosive powder, blazes heaven-high from Delhi to Grenada! I said, the Great Man was always as lightning out of Heaven; the rest of men waited for him like fuel, and then they too would flame.

LECTURE III.

[Tuesday, 12th May, 1840.]

THE HERO AS POET. DANTE; SHAKSPEARE.

THE Hero as Divinity, the Hero as Prophet, are productions of old ages; not to be repeated in the new. They presuppose a certain rudeness of conception, which the progress of mere scientific knowledge puts an end to. There needs to be, as it were, a world vacant, or almost vacant of scientific forms, if men in their loving wonder are to fancy their fellow man either a god or one speaking with the voice of a god. Divinity and Prophet are past. We are now to see our Hero in the less ambitious, but also less questionable, character of Poet; a character which does not pass. The Poet is a heroic figure belonging to all ages; whom all ages possess, when once he is produced, whom the newest age as the oldest may produce;—and will produce, always when Nature pleases. Let Nature send a Hero-soul; in no age is it other than possible that he may be shaped into a Poet.

Hero, Prophet, Poet,—many different names, in different times and places, do we give to Great Men; according to varieties we note in them, according to the sphere in which they have displayed themselves! We might give many more names, on this same principle. I will remark again, however, as a fact not unimportant to be understood, that the different *sphere* constitutes the grand origin of such distinction; that the Hero can be Poet, Prophet, King, Priest or what you will, according to the kind of world he finds himself born into. I confess, I have no notion of a truly great man that could not be *all* sorts of men. The Poet who could merely sit on a chair, and compose stanzas, would never make a stanza worth much. He could not sing the Heroic warrior, unless he himself were at least a Heroic warrior too. I fancy there is in him the Politician, the Thinker, Legislator, Philosopher;—in one or the other degree, he could have been, he is all these. So too I cannot understand how a Mirabeau, with that great glowing heart, with the fire that was in it, with the bursting tears that were in it, could not have written verses, tragedies, poems, and touched all hearts in that way, had his course of life and education led him thitherward. The grand fundamental character is that of Great Man; that the man be great. Napoleon has words in him which are like Austerlitz Battles. Louis Fourteenth's Marshals are a kind of poetical men withal; the things Turenne says are full of sagacity and geniality, like sayings of Samuel Johnson. The great heart, the clear deep-seeing eye: there it lies; no man whatever, in what province soever, can prosper at all without these. Petrarch and Boccaccio did diplomatic messages, it seems, quite well: one can easily believe it; they had done things a little harder than these! Burns, a gifted song-writer, might have made a still better Mirabeau. Shakspeare,—one knows not what *he* could not have made, in the supreme degree.

True, there are aptitudes of Nature too. Nature does not make all great men, more than all other men, in the self-same mould. Varieties of aptitude doubtless; but infinitely more of circumstance; and far oftenest it is the *latter* only that are looked to. But it is as with common men in the learning of trades. You take any man, as yet a vague capability of a man, who could be any kind of craftsman; and make him into a smith, a carpenter, a mason: he is then and thenceforth that and nothing else. And if, as Addison complains, you sometimes see a street-porter staggering under his load on spindle-shanks, and near at hand a tailor with the frame of a Samson, handling a bit of cloth and small Whitechapel needle,—it cannot be considered that aptitude of Nature alone has been consulted here either!—The Great Man also, to what shall he be bound apprentice? Given your Hero, is he to become Conqueror, King, Philosopher, Poet? It is an inexplicably complex controversial-calculation between the world and him! He will read the world and its laws; the world with its laws will be there to be read. What the world, on *this* matter, shall permit and bid is, as we said, the most important fact about the world.—

Poet and Prophet differ greatly in our loose modern notions of them. In some old languages, again, the titles are synonymous; *Vates* means both Prophet and Poet: and indeed at all times, Prophet and Poet, well understood, have much kindred of meaning. Fundamentally indeed they are still the same; in this most important respect especially, That they have penetrated both of them into the sacred mystery of the Universe; what Goethe calls 'the open secret!' "Which is the great secret?" asks one.—"The *open* secret,"—open to all, seen by almost none! That divine mystery, which lies everywhere in all Beings, 'the Divine Idea of the World, that which lies at the bottom of Appearance,' as Fichte styles it; of which all Appearance, from the starry sky to the grass of the field, but especially the Appearance of Man and his work, is but the *vesture*, the embodiment that renders it visible. This divine mystery *is* in all times and in all places; veritably is. In most times and places it is greatly overlooked; and the Universe, definable always in one or the other dialect, as the realised Thought of God, is considered a trivial, inert, commonplace matter,—as if, says the Satirist, it were a dead thing, which some upholsterer had put together! It could do no good, at present, to *speak* much about this; but it is a pity for every one of us if we do not know it, live ever in the knowledge of it. Really a most mournful pity;—a failure to live at all, if we live otherwise!

But now, I say, whoever may forget this divine mystery, the *Vates*, whether Prophet or Poet, has penetrated into it; is a man sent hither to make it more impressively known to us. That always is his message; he is to reveal that to us,—that sacred mystery which he more than others lives ever present with. While others forget it, he knows it;— I might say, he has been driven to know it; without consent asked of *him*, he finds himself living in it, bound to live in it. Once more, here is no Hearsay, but a direct Insight and Belief; this man too could not help being a sincere man! Whosoever may live in the shows of things, it is for him a necessity of nature to live in the very fact of things. A man, once more, in earnest with the Universe, though all others were but toying with it. He is a *Vates*, first of all, in virtue of being sincere. So far Poet and Prophet, participators in the 'open secret,' are one.

With respect to their distinction again: The *Vates* Prophet, we might say, has seized that sacred mystery rather on the moral side, as

Good and Evil, Duty and Prohibition; the *Vates* Poet on what the Germans call the æsthetic side, as Beautiful, and the like. The one we may call a revealer of what we are to do, the other of what we are to love. But indeed these two provinces run into one another, and cannot be disjoined. The Prophet too has his eye on what we are to love: how else shall he know what it is we are to do? The highest Voice ever heard on this Earth said withal, "Consider the lilies of the field; they toil not, neither do they spin: yet Solomon in all his glory was not arrayed like one of these." A glance, that, into the deepest deep of Beauty. 'The lilies of the field,'—dressed finer than earthly princes, springing up there in the humble furrow-field; a beautiful *eye* looking out on you, from the great inner Sea of Beauty! How could the rude Earth make these, if her Essence, rugged as she looks and is, were not inwardly Beauty?—In this point of view, too, a saying of Goethe's, which has staggered several, may have meaning: 'The Beautiful,' he intimates, 'is higher than the Good; the Beautiful includes in it the Good.' The *true* Beautiful; which however, I have said somewhere, 'differs from the *false*, as Heaven does from Vauxhall!' So much for the distinction and identity of Poet and Prophet.—

In ancient and also in modern periods, we find a few Poets who are accounted perfect; whom it were a kind of treason to find fault with. This is noteworthy; this is right: yet in strictness it is only an illusion. At bottom, clearly enough, there is no perfect Poet! A vein of Poetry exists in the hearts of all men; no man is made altogether of Poetry. We are all poets when we *read* a poem well. The 'imagination that shudders at the Hell of Dante,' is not that the same faculty, weaker in degree, as Dante's own? No one but Shakspeare can embody, out of *Saxo Grammaticus*, the story of *Hamlet* as Shakspeare did: but every one models some kind of story out of it; every one embodies it better or worse. We need not spend time in defining. Where there is no specific difference, as between round and square, all definition must be more or less arbitrary. A man that has *so* much more of the poetic element developed in him as to have become noticeable, will be called Poet by his neighbours. World-Poets too, those whom we are to take for perfect Poets, are settled by critics in the same way. One who rises *so* far above the general level of Poets will, to such and such critics, seem a Universal Poet; as he ought to do. And yet it is, and must be, an arbitrary distinction. All Poets, all men, have some touches of the Universal; no man is wholly made of that. Most Poets are very soon forgotten: but not the noblest Shakspeare or Homer of them can be remembered *forever;*—a day comes when he too is not!

Nevertheless, you will say, there must be a difference between true Poetry and true Speech not poetical: what is the difference? On this point many things have been written, especially by late German Critics, some of which are not very intelligible at first. They say, for example, that the Poet has an *infinitude* in him; communicates an *Unendlichkeit,* a certain character of 'infinitude' to whatsoever he delineates. This, though not very precise, yet on so vague a matter is worth remembering: if well meditated, some meaning will gradually be found in it. For my own part, I find considerable meaning in the old vulgar distinction of Poetry being *metrical,* having music in it, being a Song. Truly, if pressed to give a definition, one might say this as soon as anything else: If your delineation be authentically *musical,* musical not in word only, but in heart and substance, in all the thoughts and utterances of it, in the whole conception of it, then it will be poetical; if not, not.—Musical: how much lies in that! A *musical* thought is one spoken by a mind that has penetrated into the inmost heart of the thing; detected the inmost mystery of it, namely the *melody* that lies hidden in it; the inward harmony of coherence which is its soul, whereby it exists, and has a right to be, here in this world. All inmost things, we may say, are melodious; naturally utter themselves in Song. The meaning of Song goes deep. Who is there that, in logical words, can express the effect music has on us? A kind of inarticulate unfathomable speech, which leads us to the edge of the Infinite, and lets us for moments gaze into that!

Nay all speech, even the commonest speech, has something of song in it: not a parish in the world but has its parish-accent;—the rhythm or *tune* to which the people there *sing* what they have to say! Accent is a kind of chaunting; all men have accent of their own,—though they only *notice* that of others. Observe too how all passionate language does of itself become musical,—with a finer music than the mere accent; the speech of a man even in zealous anger becomes a chaunt, a song. All deep things are Song. It seems somehow the very central essence of us, Song; as if all the rest were but wrappages and hulls! The primal element of us; of us, and of all things. The

Greeks fabled of Sphere-Harmonies: it was the feeling they had of
the inner structure of Nature; that the soul of all her voices and utterances was perfect music. Poetry, therefore, we will call *musical
Thought*. The Poet is he who *thinks* in that manner. At bottom, it
turns still on power of intellect; it is a man's sincerity and depth of
vision that makes him a Poet. See deep enough, and you see musically; the heart of Nature *being* everywhere music, if you can only
reach it.

The *Vates* Poet, with his melodious Apocalypse of Nature, seems
to hold a poor rank among us, in comparison with the *Vates* Prophet;
his function, and our esteem of him for his function, alike slight. The
Hero taken as Divinity; the Hero taken as Prophet; then next the
Hero taken only as Poet: does it not look as if our estimate of the
Great Man, epoch after epoch, were continually diminishing? We take
him first for a god, then for one god-inspired; and now in the next
stage of it, his most miraculous word gains from us only the recognition that he is a Poet, beautiful verse-maker, man of genius, or such
like!—It looks so; but I persuade myself that intrinsically it is not so.
If we consider well, it will perhaps appear that in man still there is the
same altogether peculiar admiration for the Heroic Gift, by what
name soever called, that there at any time was. I should say, if we do
not now reckon a Great Man literally divine, it is that our notions of
God, of the supreme unattainable Fountain of Splendour, Wisdom
and Heroism, are ever rising *higher;* not altogether that our reverence
for these qualities, as manifested in our like, is getting lower. This is
worth taking thought of. Sceptical Dilettantism, the curse of these
ages, a curse which will not last forever, does indeed in this the
highest province of human things, as in all provinces, make sad work;
and our reverence for great men, all crippled, blinded, paralytic as it
is, comes out in poor plight, hardly recognisable. Men worship the
shows of great men; the most disbelieve that there is any reality of
great men to worship. The dreariest, fatalest faith; believing which,
one would literally despair of human things. Nevertheless look, for
example, at Napoleon! A Corsican lieutenant of artillery; that is the
show of *him:* yet is he not obeyed, *worshipped* after his sort, as all the
Tiaraed and Diademed of the world put together could not be? High
duchesses, and ostlers of inns, gather round the Scottish rustic,
Burns;—a strange feeling dwelling in each that they never heard a

man like this; that on the whole this is the man! In the secret heart of these people it still dimly reveals itself, though there is no accredited way of uttering it at present, that this rustic, with his black brows and flashing sun-eyes, and strange words moving laughter and tears, is of a dignity far beyond all others, incommensurable with all others. Do not we feel it so? But now, were Dilettantism, Scepticism, Triviality, and all that sorrowful brood, cast out of us,—as, by God's blessing, they shall one day be; were faith in the shows of things entirely swept out, replaced by clear faith in the *things*, so that a man acted on the impulse of that only, and counted the other non-extant, what a new livelier feeling towards this Burns were it!

Nay here in these ages, such as they are, have we not two mere Poets, if not deified, yet we may say beatified? Shakspeare and Dante are Saints of Poetry; really, if we will think of it, *canonized*, so that it is impiety to meddle with them. The unguided instinct of the world, working across all these perverse impediments, has arrived at such result. Dante and Shakspeare are a peculiar Two. They dwell apart, in a kind of royal solitude; none equal, none second to them: in the general feeling of the world, a certain transcendentalism, a glory as of complete perfection, invests these two. They *are* canonized, though no Pope or Cardinals took hand in doing it! Such, in spite of every perverting influence, in the most unheroic times, is still our indestructible reverence for heroism.—We will look a little at these Two, the Poet Dante and the Poet Shakspeare: what little it is permitted us to say here of the Hero as Poet, will most fitly arrange itself in that fashion.

Many volumes have been written by way of commentary on Dante and his Book; yet, on the whole, with no great result. His Biography is, as it were, irrecoverably lost for us. An unimportant, wandering, sorrowstricken man, not much note was taken of him while he lived; and the most of that has vanished, in the long space that now intervenes. It is five centuries since he ceased writing and living here. After all commentaries, the Book itself is mainly what we know of him. The Book;—and one might add that Portrait commonly attributed to Giotto, which, looking on it, you cannot help inclining to think genuine, whoever did it. To me it is a most touching face; perhaps of all faces that I know, the most so. Lonely there, painted as on vacancy, with the simple laurel wound round it; the deathless sorrow and pain, the known victory which is also deathless;—significant of the whole history of Dante! I think it is the mournfulest face that ever was painted from reality; an altogether tragic, heart-affecting face. There is in it, as foundation of it, the softness, tenderness, gentle affection as of a child; but all this is as if congealed into sharp contradiction, into abnegation, isolation, proud hopeless pain. A soft ethereal soul looking out so stern, implacable, grim-trenchant, as from imprison-ment of thick-ribbed ice! Withal it is a silent pain too, a silent scorn-ful one: the lip is curled in a kind of godlike disdain of the thing that is eating out his heart,—as if it were withal a mean insignificant thing, as if he whom it had power to torture and strangle were greater than it. The face of one wholly in protest, and life-long unsurrendering battle, against the world. Affection all converted into indignation: an implacable indignation; slow, equable, silent, like that of a god! The eye too, it looks out as in a kind of *surprise*, a kind of inquiry, Why the world was of such a sort? This is Dante: so he looks, this 'voice of ten silent centuries,' and sings us 'his mystic unfathom-able song.'

The little that we know of Dante's Life corresponds well enough with this Portrait and this Book. He was born at Florence, in the upper class of society, in the year 1265. His education was the best then going; much school-divinity, Aristotelean logic, some Latin classics,—no inconsiderable insight into certain provinces of things: and Dante, with his earnest intelligent nature, we need not doubt, learned better than most all that was learnable. He has a clear culti-vated understanding, and of great subtlety; this best fruit of educa-tion he had contrived to realize from these scholastics. He knows accurately and well what lies close to him; but, in such a time, with-out printed books or free intercourse, he could not know well what was distant: the small clear light, most luminous for what is near, breaks itself into singular *chiaroscuro* striking on what is far off. This was Dante's learning from the schools. In life, he had gone through the usual destinies; been twice out campaigning as a soldier for the Florentine State, been on embassy; had in his thirty-fifth year, by natural gradation of talent and service, become one of the Chief Magistrates of Florence. He had met in boyhood a certain Beatrice

Portinari, a beautiful little girl of his own age and rank, and grown up thenceforth in partial sight of her, in some distant intercourse with her. All readers know his graceful affecting account of this; and then of their being parted; of her being wedded to another, and of her death soon after. She makes a great figure in Dante's Poem; seems to have made a great figure in his life. Of all beings it might seem as if she, held apart from him, far apart at last in the dim Eternity, were the only one he had ever with his whole strength of affection loved. She died: Dante himself was wedded; but it seems not happily, far from happily. I fancy, the rigorous earnest man, with his keen excitabilities, was not altogether easy to make happy.

We will not complain of Dante's miseries: had all gone right with him as he wished it, he might have been Prior, Podestà, or whatsoever they call it, of Florence, well accepted among neighbours,—and the world had wanted one of the most notable words ever spoken or sung. Florence would have had another prosperous Lord Mayor; and the ten dumb centuries continued voiceless, and the ten other listening centuries (for there will be ten of them and more) had no *Divina Commedia* to hear! We will complain of nothing. A nobler destiny was appointed for this Dante; and he, struggling like a man led towards death and crucifixion, could not help fulfilling it. Give *him* the choice of his happiness! He knew not more than we do what was really happy, what was really miserable.

In Dante's Priorship, the Guelf-Ghibelline, Bianchi-Neri, or some other confused disturbances rose to such a height, that Dante, whose party had seemed the stronger, was with his friends cast unexpectedly forth into banishment; doomed thenceforth to a life of woe and wandering. His property was all confiscated and more; he had the fiercest feeling that it was entirely unjust, nefarious in the sight of God and man. He tried what was in him to get reinstated; tried even by warlike surprisal, with arms in his hand: but it would not do; bad only had become worse. There is a record, I believe, still extant in the Florence Archives, dooming this Dante, wheresoever caught, to be burnt alive. Burnt alive; so it stands, they say: a very curious civic document. Another curious document, some considerable number of years later, is a Letter of Dante's to the Florentine Magistrates, written in answer to a milder proposal of theirs, that he should return on condition of apologizing and paying a fine. He answers, with fixed stern pride, "If I cannot return without calling myself guilty, I will never return, *nunquam revertar.*"

For Dante there was now no home in this world. He wandered from patron to patron, from place to place; proving, in his own bitter words, 'How hard is the path, *Come è duro calle.*' The wretched are not cheerful company. Dante, poor and banished, with his proud earnest nature, with his moody humours, was not a man to conciliate men. Petrarch reports of him that being at Can della Scala's court, and blamed one day for his gloom and taciturnity, he answered in no courtier-like way. Della Scala stood among his courtiers, with mimes and buffoons (*nebulones ac histriones*) making him heartily merry; when turning to Dante, he said: "Is it not strange, now, that this poor fool should make himself so entertaining; while you, a wise man, sit there day after day, and have nothing to amuse us with at all?" Dante answered bitterly: "No, not strange; your Highness is to recollect the Proverb, *Like to Like;*"—given the amuser, the amusee must also be given! Such a man, with his proud silent ways, with his sarcasms and sorrows, was not made to succeed at court. By degrees, it came to be evident to him that he had no longer any resting place, or hope of benefit, in this earth. The earthly world had cast him forth, to wander, wander; no living heart to love him now; for his sore miseries there was no solace here.

The deeper naturally would the Eternal World impress itself on him; that awful reality over which, after all, this Time-world, with its Florences and banishments, only flutters as an unreal shadow. Florence thou shalt never see: but Hell and Purgatory and Heaven thou shalt surely see! What is Florence, Can della Scala, and the World and Life altogether? ETERNITY: thither, of a truth, not elsewhither, art thou and all things bound! The great soul of Dante, homeless on earth, made its home more and more in that awful other world. Naturally his thoughts brooded on that, as on the one fact important for him. Bodied or bodiless, it is the one fact important for all men:— but to Dante, in that age, it was bodied in fixed certainty of scientific shape; he no more doubted of that *Malebolge* Pool, that it all lay there with its gloomy circles, with its *alti guai,* and that he himself should see it, than we doubt that we should see Constantinople if we went thither. Dante's heart, long filled with this, brooding over it in speechless thought and awe, bursts forth at length into 'mystic un-fathomable song;' and this his *Divine Comedy*, the most remarkable of all modern Books, is the result. It must have been a great solace-ment to Dante, and was, as we can see, a proud thought for him at times, that he, here in exile, could do this work; that no Florence, nor no man or men, could hinder him from doing it, or even much help him in doing it. He knew too, partly, that it was great; the greatest a man could do. 'If thou follow thy star, *Se tu segui tua stella*'—so could the Hero, in his forsakenness, in his extreme need, still say to himself: "Follow thou thy star, thou shalt not fail of a glorious haven!" The labour of writing, we find, and indeed could know otherwise, was great and painful for him; he says, This Book 'which has made me lean for many years.' Ah yes, it was won, all of it, with pain and sore toil,—not in sport, but in grim earnest. His Book, as indeed most good Books are, has been written, in many senses, with his heart's blood. It is his whole history this Book. He died after finishing it; not yet very old, at the age of fifty-six;—broken-hearted rather, as is said. He lies buried in his death-city Ravenna: *Hic claudor Dantes patriis extorris ab oris.* The Florentines begged back his body, in a century after; the Ravenna people would not give it. "Here am I Dante laid, shut out from my native shores."

I said, Dante's Poem was a Song: it is Tieck who calls it 'a mystic unfathomable Song;' and such is literally the character of it. Cole-ridge remarks very pertinently somewhere, that wherever you find a sentence musically worded, of true rhythm and melody in the words, there is something deep and good in the meaning too. For body and soul, word and idea, go strangely together, here as everywhere. Song: we said before, it was the Heroic of Speech! All *old* Poems, Homer's and the rest, are authentically Songs. I would say, in strictness, that all right Poems are; that whatsoever is not *sung* is properly no Poem, but a piece of Prose cramped into jingling lines,—to the great injury of the grammar, to the great grief of the reader, for most part! What we want to get at is the *thought* the man had, if he had any: why should he twist it into jingle, if he *could* speak it out plainly? It is only when the heart of him is rapt into true passion of melody, and the very tones of him, according to Coleridge's remark, become musical by the greatness, depth and music of his thoughts, that we can give him right to rhyme and sing; that we call him a Poet, and listen to him as the Heroic of Speakers,—whose speech *is* Song. Pretenders to this are many; and to an earnest reader, I doubt, it is for most part a very melancholy, not to say an insupportable business, that of reading rhyme! Rhyme that had no inward necessity to be rhymed;—it ought to have told us plainly, without any jingle, what it was aiming at. I would advise all men who *can* speak their thought, not to sing it; to understand that, in a serious time, among serious men, there is no vocation in them for singing it. Precisely as we love the true song, and are charmed by it as by something divine, so shall we hate the false song, and account it a mere wooden noise, a thing hollow, superfluous, altogether an insincere and offensive thing.

I give Dante my highest praise when I say of his *Divine Comedy* that it is, in all senses, genuinely a Song. In the very sound of it there is a *canto fermo;* it proceeds as by a chaunt. The language, his simple *terza rima,* doubtless helped him in this. One reads along naturally with a sort of *lilt.* But I add, that it could not be otherwise; for the essence and material of the work are themselves rhythmic. Its depth, and rapt passion and sincerity, makes it musical;—go *deep* enough, there is music everywhere. A true inward symmetry, what one calls an architectural harmony, reigns in it, proportionates it all: architectural; which also partakes of the character of music. The three kingdoms, *Inferno, Purgatorio, Paradiso,* look out on one another like compartments of a great edifice; a great supernatural world-cathedral, piled up there, stern, solemn, awful; Dante's World of Souls! It is, at bottom, the *sincerest* of all Poems; sincerity, here too, we find to be the measure of worth. It came deep out of the author's heart of hearts; and it goes deep, and through long generations, into ours. The people of Verona, when they saw him on the streets, used to say, "*Eccovi l' uom ch' è stato all' Inferno,* See, there is the man that was in Hell!" Ah, yes, he had been in Hell;—in Hell enough, in long severe sorrow and struggle; as the like of him is pretty sure to have been. Commedias that come out *divine,* are not accomplished otherwise. Thought, true labour of any kind, highest virtue itself, is it not the daughter of Pain? Born as out of the black whirlwind;—true *effort,* in fact, as of a captive struggling to free himself: that is Thought. In all ways we are 'to become perfect through *suffering.*'—But, as I say, no work known to me is so elaborated as this of Dante's.

It has all been as if molten, in the hottest furnace of his soul. It had made him 'lean' for many years. Not the general whole only; every compartment of it is worked out, with intense earnestness, into truth, into clear visuality. Each answers to the other; each fits in its place, like a marble stone accurately hewn and polished. It is the soul of Dante, and in this the soul of the middle ages, rendered forever rhythmically visible there. No light task; a right intense one: but a task which is *done*.

Perhaps one would say, *intensity*, with the much that depends on it, is the prevailing character of Dante's genius. Dante does not come before us as a large catholic mind; rather as a narrow, and even sectarian mind: it is partly the fruit of his age and position, but partly too of his own nature. His greatness has, in all senses, concentered itself into fiery emphasis and depth. He is world-great not because he is world-wide, but because he is world-deep. Through all objects he pierces as it were down into the heart of Being. I know nothing so intense as Dante. Consider, for example, to begin with the outermost development of his intensity, consider how he paints. He has a great power of vision; seizes the very type of a thing; presents that and nothing more. You remember that first view he gets of the Hall of Dite: *red* pinnacle, redhot cone of iron glowing through the dim immensity of gloom;—so vivid, so distinct, visible at once and for-ever! It is as an emblem of the whole genius of Dante. There is a brevity, an abrupt precision in him: Tacitus is not briefer, more condensed; and then in Dante it seems a natural condensation, spontaneous to the man. One smiting word; and then there is silence, nothing more said. His silence is more eloquent than words. It is strange with what a sharp decisive grace he snatches the true likeness of a matter; cuts into the matter as with a pen of fire. Plutus, the blustering giant, collapses at Virgil's rebuke; it is 'as the sails sink, the mast being suddenly broken.' Or that poor Brunetto Latini, with the *cotto aspetto*, 'face *baked*,' parched brown and lean; and the 'fiery snow' that falls on them there, a 'fiery snow without wind,' slow, deliberate, never-ending! Or the lids of those Tombs; square sarcoph-aguses, in that silent dim-burning Hall, each with its Soul in torment; the lids laid open there; they are to be shut at the Day of Judgment, through Eternity. And how Farinata rises; and how Cavalcante falls— at hearing of his Son, and the past tense *'fue!'* The very movements

in Dante have something brief; swift, decisive, almost military. It is of
the inmost essence of his genius this sort of painting. The fiery, swift
Italian nature of the man, so silent, passionate, with its quick abrupt
movements, its silent 'pale rages,' speaks itself in these things.

For though this of painting is one of the outermost developments
of a man, it comes like all else from the essential faculty of him; it is
physiognomical of the whole man. Find a man whose words paint you
a likeness, you have found a man worth something; mark his manner
of doing it, as very characteristic of him. In the first place, he could
not have discerned the object at all, or seen the vital type of it, unless
he had, what we may call, *sympathized* with it,—had sympathy in him
to bestow on objects. He must have been *sincere* about it too; sincere
and sympathetic: a man without worth cannot give you the likeness
of any object; he dwells in vague outwardness, fallacy and trivial
hearsay, about all objects. And indeed may we not say that intellect
altogether expresses itself in this power of discerning what an object
is? Whatsoever of faculty a man's mind may have will come out here.
Is it even of business, a matter to be done? The gifted man is he who
sees the essential point, and leaves all the rest aside as surplusage: it
is his faculty too, the man of business's faculty, that he discern the
true *likeness*, not the false superficial one, of the thing he has got to
work in. And how much of *morality* is in the kind of insight we get
of anything; 'the eye seeing in all things what it brought with it the
faculty of seeing!' To the mean eye all things are trivial, as certainly
as to the jaundiced they are yellow. Raphael, the Painters tell us, is the
best of all Portrait-painters withal. No most gifted eye can exhaust
the significance of any object. In the commonest human face there
lies more than Raphael will take away with him.

Dante's painting is not graphic only, brief, true, and of a vividness
as of fire in dark night; taken on the wider scale, it is everyway noble,
and the outcome of a great soul. Francesca and her Lover, what
qualities in that! A thing woven as out of rainbows, on a ground of
eternal black. A small flute-voice of infinite wail speaks there, into our
very heart of hearts. A touch of womanhood in it too; *della bella
persona, che mi fu tolta;* and how, even in the Pit of woe, it is a solace
that *he* will never part from her! Saddest tragedy in these *alti guai.*
And the racking winds, in that *aer bruno,* whirl them away again, to
wail forever!—Strange to think: Dante was the friend of this poor
Francesca's father; Francesca herself may have sat upon the Poet's

knee, as a bright innocent little child. Infinite pity, yet also infinite rigour of law: it is so Nature is made; it is so Dante discerned that she was made. What a paltry notion is that of his *Divine Comedy's* being a poor splenetic impotent terrestrial libel; putting those into Hell whom he could not be avenged upon on earth! I suppose if ever pity, tender as a mother's, was in the heart of any man, it was in Dante's. But a man who does not know rigour cannot pity either. His very pity will be cowardly, egoistic,—sentimentality, or little better. I know not in the world an affection equal to that of Dante. It is a tenderness, a trembling, longing, pitying love: like the wail of Æolean harps, soft, soft; like a child's young heart;—and then that stern, sore-saddened heart! These longings of his towards his Beatrice; their meeting together in the *Paradiso;* his gazing in her pure transfigured eyes, her that had been purified by death so long, separated from him so far:—one likens it to the song of angels; it is among the purest utterances of affection, perhaps the very purest, that ever came out of a human soul.

For the *intense* Dante is intense in all things; he has got into the essence of all. His intellectual insight, as painter, on occasion too as reasoner, is but the result of all other sorts of intensity. Morally great, above all, we must call him; it is the beginning of all. His scorn, his grief are as transcendent as his love;—as indeed, what are they but the *inverse* or *converse* of his love? 'A Dio spiacenti, ed a' nemici sui, Hateful to God and to the enemies of God:' lofty scorn, unappeasable silent reprobation and aversion: '*Non ragionam di lor*, We will not speak of *them,* look only and pass.' Or think of this: 'They have not the *hope* to die, *Non han speranza di morte.*' One day, it had risen sternly benign on the scathed heart of Dante, that he, wretched, never-resting, worn as he was, would full surely *die;* 'that Destiny itself could not doom him not to die.' Such words are in this man. For rigour, earnestness and depth, he is not to be paralleled in the modern world; to seek his parallel we must go into the Hebrew Bible, and live with the antique Prophets there.

I do not agree with much modern criticism, in greatly preferring the *Inferno* to the two other parts of the Divine *Commedia*. Such preference belongs, I imagine, to our general Byronism of taste, and is like to be a transient feeling. The *Purgatorio* and *Paradiso*, especially the former, one would almost say, is even more excellent than it. It is a noble thing that *Purgatorio*, 'Mountain of Purification;' an emblem of the noblest conception of that age. If Sin is so fatal, and Hell is and must be so rigorous, awful, yet in Repentance too is man purified; Repentance is the grand Christian act. It is beautiful how Dante works it out. The *tremolar dell' onde*, that 'trembling' of the ocean-waves, under the first pure gleam of morning, dawning afar on the wandering Two, is as the type of an altered mood. Hope has now dawned; never-dying Hope, if in company still with heavy sorrow. The obscure sojourn of dæmons and reprobate is under foot; a soft breathing of penitence mounts higher and higher, to the Throne of Mercy itself. "Pray for me," the denizens of that Mount of Pain all say to him. "Tell my Giovanna to pray for me," my daughter Giovanna; "I think her mother loves me no more!" They toil painfully up by that winding steep, 'bent down like corbels of a building,' some of them,—crushed together so 'for the sin of pride;' yet nevertheless in years, in ages and æons, they shall have reached the top, which is Heaven's gate, and by Mercy shall have been admitted in. The joy too of all, when one has prevailed; the whole Mountain shakes with joy, and a psalm of praise rises, when one soul has perfected repentance, and got its sin and misery left behind! I call all this a noble embodiment of a true noble thought.

But indeed the Three compartments mutually support one another, are indispensable to one another. The *Paradiso*, a kind of inarticulate music to me, is the redeeming side of the *Inferno;* the *Inferno* without it were untrue. All three make up the true Unseen World, as figured in the Christianity of the Middle Ages; a thing forever memorable, forever true in the essence of it, to all men. It was perhaps delineated in no human soul with such depth of veracity as in this of Dante's; a man *sent* to sing it, to keep it long memorable. Very notable with what brief simplicity he passes out of the every-day reality, into the Invisible one; and in the second or third stanza, we find ourselves in the World of Spirits; and dwell there, as among things palpable, indubitable! To Dante they *were* so; the real world, as it is called, and its facts, was but the threshold to an infinitely higher Fact of a World. At bottom, the one was as *preter*natural as the other. Has not each man a soul? He will not only be a spirit, but is one. To the earnest Dante it is all one visible Fact; he believes it, sees it; is the Poet of it in virtue of that. Sincerity, I say again, is the saving merit, now as always.

Dante's Hell, Purgatory, Paradise, are a symbol withal, an emblematic representation of his Belief about this Universe:—some Critic in a future age, like those Scandinavian ones the other day, who has ceased altogether to think as Dante did, may find this too all an 'Allegory,' perhaps an idle Allegory! It is a sublime embodiment, our sublimest, of the soul of Christianity. It expresses, as in huge worldwide architectural emblems, how the Christian Dante felt Good and Evil to be the two polar elements of this Creation, on which it all turns; that these two differ not by *preferability* of one to the other, but by incompatibility absolute and infinite; that the one is excellent and high as light and Heaven, the other hideous, black as Gehenna and the Pit of Hell! Everlasting Justice, yet with Penitence, with everlasting Pity,—all Christianism, as Dante and the Middle Ages had it, is emblemed here. Emblemed: and yet, as I urged the other day, with what entire truth of purpose; how unconscious of any embleming! Hell, Purgatory, Paradise: these things were not fashioned as emblems; was there, in our Modern European Mind, any thought at all of their being emblems! Were they not indubitable awful facts; the whole heart of man taking them for practically true, all Nature everywhere confirming them? So is it always in these things. Men do not believe an Allegory. The future Critic, whatever his new thought may be, who considers this of Dante to have been all got up as an Allegory, will commit one sore mistake!—Paganism we recognised as a veracious expression of the earnest awe-struck feeling of man towards the Universe; veracious, true once, and still not without worth for us. But mark here the difference of Paganism and Christianism; one great difference. Paganism emblemed chiefly the Operations of Nature; the destinies, efforts, combinations, vicissitudes of things and men in this world: Christianism emblemed the Law of Human Duty, the Moral Law of Man. One was for the sensuous nature; a rude helpless utterance of the *first* Thought of men,—the chief recognised virtue, Courage, Superiority to Fear. The other was not for the sensuous nature, but for the moral. What a progress is here, if in that one respect only!—

And so in this Dante, as we said, had ten silent centuries, in a very strange way, found a voice. The *Divina Commedia* is of Dante's writing; yet in truth *it* belongs to ten Christian centuries, only the finishing of it is Dante's. So always. The craftsman there, the smith with that metal of his, with these tools, with these cunning methods,—how little of all he does is properly *his* work! All past inventive men work there with him;—as indeed with all of us, in all things. Dante is the spokesman of the Middle Ages; the Thought they lived by stands here, in everlasting music. These sublime ideas of his, terrible and beautiful, are the fruit of the Christian Meditation of all the good men who had gone before him. Precious they; but also is not he precious? Much, had not he spoken, would have been dumb; not dead, yet living voiceless.

On the whole, is it not an utterance, this mystic Song, at once of one of the greatest human souls, and of the highest thing that Europe had hitherto realised for itself? Christianism, as Dante sings it, is another than Paganism in the rude Norse mind; another than 'Bastard Christianism' half-articulately spoken in the Arab Desert, seven hundred years before!—The noblest *idea* made *real* hitherto among men, is sung, and emblemed forth abidingly, by one of the noblest men. In the one sense and in the other, are we not right glad to possess it? As I calculate, it may last yet for long thousands of years. For the thing that is uttered from the inmost parts of a man's soul, differs altogether from what is uttered by the outer part. The outer is of the day, under the empire of mode; the outer passes away, in swift endless changes; the inmost is the same yesterday, today and forever. True souls, in all generations of the world, who look on this Dante, will find a brotherhood in him; the deep sincerity of his thoughts, his woes and hopes, will speak likewise to their sincerity; they will feel that this Dante too was a brother. Napoleon in Saint-Helena is charmed with the genial veracity of old Homer. The oldest Hebrew Prophet, under a vesture the most diverse from ours, does yet, because he speaks from the heart of man, speak to all men's hearts. It is the one sole secret of continuing long memorable. Dante, for depth of sincerity, is like an antique Prophet too; his words, like theirs, come from his very heart. One need not wonder if it were predicted that his Poem might be the most enduring thing our Europe has yet made; for nothing so endures as a truly spoken word. All cathedrals, pontificalities, brass and stone, and outer arrangement never so lasting, are brief in comparison to an unfathomable heart-song like this: one feels as if it might survive, still of importance to men, when these had all sunk into new irrecognisable combinations, and had ceased individually to be. Europe has made much; great cities, great empires, encyclopædias, creeds, bodies of opinion and practice: but it has made little of the class of Dante's Thought. Homer yet *is*, veritably present face to face with every open soul of us; and Greece, where is *it*? Desolate for thousands of years; away, vanished; a bewildered heap of stones and rubbish, the life and existence of it all gone. Like a dream; like the dust of King Agamemnon! Greece was; Greece, except in the *words* it spoke, is not.

The uses of this Dante? We will not say much about his 'uses.' A human soul who has once got into that primal element of *Song*, and sung forth fitly somewhat therefrom, has worked in the *depths* of our existence; feeding through long times the life-*roots* of all excellent human things whatsoever,—in a way that 'utilities' will not succeed well in calculating! We will not estimate the Sun by the quantity of gas-light it saves us; Dante shall be invaluable, or of no value. One remark I may make: the contrast in this respect between the Hero-Poet and the Hero-Prophet. In a hundred years, Mahomet, as we saw, had his Arabians at Grenada and at Delhi; Dante's Italians seem to be yet very much where they were. Shall we say, then, Dante's effect on the world was small in comparison? Not so: his arena is far more restricted; but also it is far nobler, clearer;—perhaps not less but more important. Mahomet speaks to great masses of men, in the coarse dialect adapted to such; a dialect filled with inconsistencies, crudities, follies: on the great masses alone can he act, and there with good and with evil strangely blended. Dante speaks to the noble, the pure and great, in all times and places. Neither does he grow obsolete, as the other does. Dante burns as a pure star, fixed there in the firmament, at which the great and the high of all ages kindle themselves: he is the possession of all the chosen of the world for uncounted time. Dante, one calculates, may long survive Mahomet. In this way the balance may be made straight again.

But, at any rate, it is not by what is called their effect on the world, by what *we* can judge of their effect there, that a man and his work are measured. Effect? Influence? Utility? Let a man *do* his work; the fruit of it is the care of Another than he. It will grow its own fruit; and whether embodied in Caliph Thrones and Arabian Conquests, so that it 'fills all Morning and Evening Newspapers,' and all Histories,

which are a kind of distilled Newspapers; or not embodied so at all;—
what matters that? That is not the real fruit of it! The Arabian Caliph,
in so far only as he did something, was something. If the great Cause
of Man, and Man's work in God's Earth, got no furtherance from the
Arabian Caliph, then no matter how many scimetars he drew, how
many gold piastres pocketed, and what uproar and blaring he made
in this world,—*he* was but a loud-sounding inanity and futility; at
bottom, he *was* not at all. Let us honour the great empire of *Silence*,
once more! The boundless treasury which we do *not* jingle in our
pockets, or count up and present before men! It is perhaps, of all
things, the usefulest for each of us to do, in these loud times.— —

As Dante, the Italian man, was sent into our world to embody
musically the Religion of the Middle Ages, the Religion of our
Modern Europe, its Inner Life; so Shakspeare, we may say, embodies
for us the Outer Life of our Europe as developed then, its chivalries,
courtesies, humours, ambitions, what practical way of thinking, acting, looking at the world, men then had. As in Homer we may still
construe Old Greece; so in Shakspeare and Dante, after thousands of
years, what our Modern Europe was, in Faith and in Practice, will still
be legible. Dante has given us the Faith or soul; Shakspeare, in a not
less noble way, has given us the Practice or body. This latter also we
were to have; a man was sent for it, the man Shakspeare. Just when
that chivalry-way of life had reached its last finish, and was on the
point of breaking down into slow or swift dissolution, as we now see
it everywhere, this other sovereign Poet, with his seeing eye, with his
perennial singing voice, was sent to take note of it, to give long-
enduring record of it. Two fit men: Dante, deep, fierce as the central
fire of the world; Shakspeare, wide, placid, far-seeing, as the Sun, the
upper light of the world. Italy produced the one world-voice; we
English had the honour of producing the other.
    Curious enough how, as it were by mere accident, this man came
to us. I think always, so great, quiet, complete and self-sufficing is
this Shakspeare, had the Warwickshire Squire not prosecuted him for
deer-stealing, we had perhaps never heard of him as a Poet! The
woods and skies, the rustic Life of Man in Stratford there, had been
enough for this man! But indeed that strange outbudding of our
whole English Existence, which we call the Elizabethan Era, did not

it too come as of its own accord? The 'Tree Igdrasil' buds and withers by its own laws,—too deep for our scanning. Yet it does bud and wither, and every bough and leaf of it is there, by fixed eternal laws; not a Sir Thomas Lucy but comes at the hour fit for him. Curious, I say, and not sufficiently considered: how every thing does cooperate with all; not a leaf rotting on the highway but is indissoluble portion of solar and stellar systems; no thought, word or act of man but has sprung withal out of all men, and works sooner or later, recognisably or irrecognisably, on all men! It is all a Tree: circulation of sap and influences, mutual communication of every minutest leaf with the lowest talon of a root, with every other greatest and minutest portion of the whole. The Tree Igdrasil, that has its roots down in the Kingdoms of Hela and Death, and whose boughs overspread the highest Heaven!—

In some sense it may be said that this glorious Elizabethan Era with its Shakspeare, as the outcome and flowerage of all which had preceded it, is itself attributable to the Catholicism of the Middle Ages. The Christian Faith, which was the theme of Dante's Song, had produced this Practical Life which Shakspeare was to sing. For Religion then, as it now and always is, was the soul of Practice; the primary vital fact in men's life. And remark here, as rather curious, that Middle-Age Catholicism was abolished, so far as Acts of Parliament could abolish it, before Shakspeare, the noblest product of it, made his appearance. He did make his appearance nevertheless. Nature at her own time, with Catholicism or what else might be necessary, sent him forth; taking small thought of Acts of Parliament. King-Henrys, Queen-Elizabeths go their way; and Nature too goes hers. Acts of Parliament, on the whole, are small, notwithstanding the noise they make. What Act of Parliament, debate at St. Stephen's, on the hustings or elsewhere, was it that brought this Shakspeare into being? No dining at Freemasons' Tavern, opening subscription-lists, selling of shares, and infinite other jangling and true or false endeavouring! This Elizabethan Era, and all its nobleness and blessedness, came without proclamation, preparation of ours. Priceless Shakspeare was the free gift of Nature; given altogether silently;—received altogether silently, as if it had been a thing of little account. And yet, very literally, it is a priceless thing. One should look at that side of matters too.

Of this Shakspeare of ours, perhaps the opinion one sometimes hears a little idolatrously expressed is, in fact, the right one; I think the best judgment not of this country only, but of Europe at large, is slowly pointing to the conclusion, That Shakspeare is the chief of all Poets hitherto; the greatest intellect who, in our recorded world, has left record of himself in the way of Literature. On the whole, I know not such a power of vision, such a faculty of thought, if we take all the characters of it, in any other man. Such a calmness of depth; placid joyous strength; all things imaged in that great soul of his so true and clear, as in a tranquil unfathomable sea! It has been said, that in the constructing of Shakspeare's Dramas there is, apart from all other 'faculties' as they are called, an understanding manifested, equal to that in Bacon's *Novum Organum*. That is true; and it is not a truth that strikes every one. It would become more apparent if we tried, any of us for himself, how, out of Shakspeare's dramatic materials, *we* could fashion such a result! The built house seems all so fit,—every-way as it should be, as if it came there by its own law and the nature of things,—we forget the rude disorderly quarry it was shaped from. The very perfection of the house, as if Nature herself had made it, hides the builder's merit. Perfect, more perfect than any other man, we may call Shakspeare in this: he discerns, knows as by instinct, what condition he works under, what his materials are, what his own force and its relation to them is. It is not a transitory glance of insight that will suffice; it is deliberate illumination of the whole matter; it is a calmly *seeing* eye; a great intellect, in short. How a man, of some wide thing that he has witnessed, will construct a narrative, what kind of picture and delineation he will give of it,—is the best measure you could get of what intellect is in the man. Which circumstance is vital and shall stand prominent; which unessential, fit to be suppressed; where is the true *beginning*, the true sequence and ending? To find out this, you task the whole force of insight that is in the man. He must *understand* the thing; according to the depth of his understanding, will the fitness of his answer be. You will try him so. Does like join itself to like; does the spirit of method stir in that confusion, so that its embroilment becomes order? Can the man say, *Fiat lux*, Let there be light; and out of chaos make a world? Precisely as there is *light* in himself, will he accomplish this.

Or indeed we may say again, it is in what I called Portrait-painting, delineating of men and things, especially of men, that Shakspeare is great. All the greatness of the man comes out decisively here. It is unexampled, I think, that calm creative perspicacity of Shakspeare. The thing he looks at reveals not this or that face of it, but its inmost heart and generic secret: it dissolves itself as in light before him, so that he discerns the perfect structure of it. Creative, we said: poetic creation, what is this too but *seeing* the thing sufficiently? The *word* that will describe the thing follows, of itself, from such clear intense sight of the thing. And is not Shakspeare's *morality*, his valour, candour, tolerance, truthfulness; his whole victorious strength and greatness, which can triumph over such obstructions, visible there too? Great as the world! No *twisted*, poor convex-concave mirror, reflecting all objects with its own convexities and concavities; a perfectly *level* mirror;—that is to say withal, if we will understand it, a man justly related to all things and men, a good man. It is truly a lordly spectacle how this great soul takes in all kinds of men and objects, a Falstaff, an Othello, a Juliet, a Coriolanus; sets them all forth to us in their round completeness; loving, just, the equal brother of all. *Novum Organum*, and all the intellect you will find in Bacon, is of a quite secondary order; earthy, material, poor in comparison with this. Among modern men, one finds, in strictness, almost nothing of the same rank. Goethe alone, since the days of Shakspeare, reminds me of it. Of him too you say that he *saw* the object; you may say what he himself says of Shakspeare: 'His characters are like watches with dial-plates of transparent crystal; they shew you the hour like others, and the inward mechanism also is all visible.'

The seeing eye! It is this that discloses the inner harmony of things; what Nature meant, what musical idea Nature has wrapped up in these often rough embodiments. Something she did mean. To the seeing eye that something were discernible. Are they base, miserable things? You can laugh over them, you can weep over them; you can in some way or other genially relate yourself to them;—you can, at lowest, hold your peace about them, turn away your own and others' face from them, till the hour come for practically exterminating and extinguishing them! At bottom, it is the Poet's first gift, as it is all men's, that he have intellect enough. He will be a Poet if he have: a

Poet in word; or failing that, perhaps still better, a Poet in act.
Whether he write at all; and if so, whether in prose or in verse, will
depend on accidents: who knows on what extremely trivial accidents,—perhaps on his having had a singing-master, on his being
taught to sing in his boyhood! But the faculty which enables him to
discern the inner heart of things, and the harmony that dwells there
(for whatsoever exists has a harmony in the heart of it, or it would
not hold together and exist), is not the result of habits or accidents,
but the gift of Nature herself; the primary outfit for a Heroic Man in
what sort soever. To the Poet, as to every other, we say first of all,
See. If you cannot do that, it is of no use to keep stringing rhymes
together, jingling sensibilities against each other, and *name* yourself
a Poet; there is no hope for you. If you can, there is, in prose or verse,
in action or speculation, all manner of hope. The crabbed old Schoolmaster used to ask, when they brought him a new pupil, "But are ye
sure he's *not a dunce?*" Why, really one might ask the same thing, in
regard to every man proposed for whatsoever function; and consider
it as the one inquiry needful: Are ye sure he's not a dunce? There is,
in this world, no other entirely fatal person.

For, in fact, I say the degree of vision that dwells in a man is a
correct measure of the man. If called to define Shakspeare's faculty,
I should say superiority of Intellect, and think I had included all
under that. What indeed are faculties? We talk of faculties as if they
were distinct, things separable; as if a man had intellect, imagination,
fancy, &c., as he has hands, feet and arms. That is a capital error.
Then again, we hear of a man's 'intellectual nature,' and of his 'moral
nature,' as if these again were divisible, and existed apart. Necessities
of language do perhaps prescribe such forms of utterance; we must
speak, I am aware, in that way, if we are to speak at all. But words
ought not to harden into things for us. It seems to me, our appre-
hension of this matter is, for most part, radically falsified thereby. We
ought to know withal, and to keep forever in mind, that these divi-
sions are at bottom but *names;* that man's spiritual nature, the vital
Force which dwells in him, is essentially one and indivisible; that what
we call imagination, fancy, understanding, and so forth, are but different figures of the same Power of Insight, all indissolubly connected
with each other, physiognomically related; that if we knew one of

them, we might know all of them. Morality itself, what we call the moral quality of a man, what is this but another *side* of the one vital Force whereby he is and works? All that a man does is physiognomical of him. You may see how a man would fight, by the way in which he sings; his courage, or want of courage, is visible in the word he utters, in the opinion he has formed, no less than in the stroke he strikes. He is *one;* and preaches the same Self abroad in all these ways.

Without hands a man might have feet, and could still walk: but, consider it,—without morality, intellect were impossible for him; a thoroughly immoral *man* could not know anything at all! To know a thing, what we can call knowing, a man must first *love* the thing, sympathize with it: that is, be *virtuously* related to it. If he have not the justice to put down his own selfishness at every turn, the courage to stand by the dangerous-true at every turn, how shall he know? His virtues, all of them, will lie recorded in his knowledge. Nature with her truth remains to the bad, to the selfish and the pusillanimous, forever a sealed book: what such can know of Nature is mean, superficial, small; for the uses of the day merely.—But does not the very Fox know something of Nature? Exactly so: it knows where the geese lodge! The human Reynard, very frequent everywhere in the world, what more does he know but this and the like of this? Nay, it should be considered too, that if the Fox had not a certain vulpine *morality*, he could not even know where the geese were, or get at the geese! If he spent his time in splenetic atrabiliar reflexions on his own misery, his ill usage by Nature, Fortune and other Foxes, and so forth; and had not courage, promptitude, practicality, and other suitable vulpine gifts and graces, he would catch no geese. We may say of the Fox too, that his morality and insight are of the same dimensions; different faces of the same internal unity of vulpine life!— These things are worth stating, for the contrary of them acts with manifold very baleful perversion, in this time: what limitations, modifications they require, your own candour will supply.

If I say, therefore, that Shakspeare is the greatest of Intellects, I have said all concerning him. But there is more in Shakspeare's intellect than we have yet seen. It is what I call an unconscious intellect; there is more virtue in it than he himself is aware of. Novalis beautifully remarks of him, that those Dramas of his are Products of

Nature too, deep as Nature herself. I find a great truth in this saying. Shakspeare's Art is not Artifice; the noblest worth of it is not there by plan or precontrivance. It grows up from the deeps of Nature, through this noble sincere soul, who is a voice of Nature. The latest generations of men will find new meanings in Shakspeare, new elucidations of their own human being; 'new harmonies with the infinite structure of the Universe; concurrences with later ideas, affinities with the higher powers and senses of man.' This well deserves meditating. It is Nature's highest reward to a true simple great soul, that he get thus to be *a part of herself.* Such a man's works, whatsoever he with utmost conscious exertion and forethought shall accomplish, grow up withal *un*consciously, from the unknown deeps in him;—as the oak-tree grows from the Earth's bosom, as the mountains and waters shape themselves; with a symmetry grounded on Nature's own laws, conformable to all Truth whatsoever. How much in Shakspeare lies hid; his sorrows, his silent struggles known to himself; much that was not known at all, not speakable at all: like *roots*, like sap and forces working under ground! Speech is great; but Silence is greater.

Withal the joyful tranquillity of this man is notable. I will not blame Dante for his misery: it is as battle without victory; but true battle,—the first, indispensable thing. Yet I call Shakspeare greater than Dante, in that he fought truly, and did conquer. Doubt it not, he had his own sorrows: those *Sonnets* of his will even testify expressly in what deep waters he had waded, and swum struggling for his life;—as what man like him ever failed to have to do? It seems to me a heedless notion, our common one, that he sat like a bird on the bough; and sang forth, free and offhand, never knowing the troubles of other men. Not so; with no man is it so. How could a man travel forward from rustic deer-poaching to such tragedy-writing, and not fall in with sorrows by the way? Or, still better, how could a man delineate a Hamlet, a Coriolanus, a Macbeth, so many suffering heroic hearts, if his own heroic heart had never suffered?—And now, in contrast with all this, observe his mirthfulness, his genuine overflowing love of laughter! You would say, in no point does he *exaggerate* but only in laughter. Fiery objurgations, words that pierce and burn, are to be found in Shakspeare: yet he is always in measure here; never what Johnson would remark as a specially 'good hater.'

But his laughter seems to pour from him in floods; he heaps all manner of ridiculous nicknames on the butt he is bantering, tumbles and tosses him in all sorts of horse-play; you would say, with his whole heart laughs. And then, if not always the finest, it is always a genial laughter. Not at mere weakness, at misery or poverty; never. No man who *can* laugh, what we call laughing, will laugh at these things. It is some poor character only *desiring* to laugh, and have the credit of wit, that does so. Laughter means sympathy; good laughter is not 'the crackling of thorns under the pot.' Even at stupidity and pretension this Shakspeare does not laugh otherwise than genially. Dogberry and Verges tickle our very hearts; and we dismiss them covered with explosions of laughter: but we like the poor fellows only the better for our laughing; and hope they will get on well there, and continue Presidents of the City-watch.—Such laughter, like sunshine on the deep sea, is very beautiful to me.

We have no room to speak of Shakspeare's individual works; though perhaps there is much still waiting to be said on that head. Had we, for instance, all his Plays reviewed as *Hamlet*, in *Wilhelm Meister*, is! A thing which might, one day, be done. August Wilhelm Schlegel has a remark on his Historical Plays, *Henry Fifth* and the others, which is worth remembering. He calls them a kind of National Epic. Marlborough, you recollect, said, he knew no English History but what he had learned from Shakspeare. There are really, if we look to it, few as memorable Histories. The great salient points are admirably seized; all rounds itself off, into a kind of rhythmic coherence: it is, as Schlegel says, *epic;*—as indeed all delineation by a great thinker will be. There are right beautiful things in those Pieces, which indeed together form one beautiful thing. That battle of Agincourt strikes me as one of the most perfect things, in its sort, we anywhere have of Shakspeare's. The description of the two hosts: the worn-out, jaded English; the dread hour, big with destiny, when the battle shall begin; and then that deathless valour: "Ye good yeomen, whose limbs were made in England!" There is a noble Patriotism in it,—far other than the 'indifference' you sometimes hear ascribed to Shakspeare. A true English heart breathes, calm and strong, through the whole business; not boisterous, protrusive; all the better for that. There is a sound in it like the ring of steel. This man too had a right stroke in him, had it come to that!

But I will say, of Shakspeare's works generally, that we have no full impress of him there; even as full as we have of many men. His works are so many windows, through which we see a glimpse of the world that was in him. All his works seem, comparatively speaking, cursory, imperfect, written under cramping circumstances; giving only here and there a note of the full utterance of the man. Passages there are that come upon you like splendour out of Heaven; bursts of radiance, illuminating the very heart of the thing: you say, "That is *true*, spoken once and forever; wheresoever and whensoever there is an open human soul, that will be recognised as true!" Such bursts, however, make us feel that the surrounding matter is not radiant; that it is, in part, temporary, conventional. Alas, Shakspeare had to write for the Globe Playhouse: his great soul had to crush itself, as it could, into that and no other mould. It was with him, then, as it is with us all. No man works save under conditions. The sculptor cannot set his own free Thought before us; but his Thought as he could translate it into the stone that was given, with the tools that were given. *Disjecta membra* are all that we find of any Poet, or of any man.

Whoever looks intelligently at this Shakspeare may recognise that he too was a *Prophet*, in his way; of an insight analogous to the Prophetic, though he took it up in another strain. Nature seemed to this man also divine; *un*speakable, deep as Tophet, high as Heaven: 'We are such stuff as Dreams are made of!' That scroll in Westminster Abbey, which few read with understanding, is of the depth of any Seer. But the man sang; did not preach, except musically. We called Dante the melodious Priest of Middle-Age Catholicism. May we not call Shakspeare the still more melodious Priest of a *true* Catholicism, the 'Universal Church' of the Future and of all times? No narrow superstition, harsh asceticism, intolerance, fanatical fierceness or perversion: a Revelation, so far as it goes, that such a thousandfold hidden beauty and divineness dwells in all Nature; which let all men worship as they can! We may say without offence, that there rises a kind of universal Psalm out of this Shakspeare too; not unfit to make itself heard among the still more sacred Psalms. Not in disharmony with these, if we understood them, but in harmony!—I cannot call this Shakspeare a 'Sceptic,' as some do; his indifference to the creeds and theological quarrels of his time misleading them. No: neither un-patriotic, though he says little about his Patriotism; nor sceptic, though he says little about his Faith. Such 'indifference' was the fruit of his greatness withal: his whole heart was in his own grand sphere of worship (we may call it such); these other controversies, vitally important to other men, were not vital to him.

But call it worship, call it what you will, is it not a right glorious thing, and set of things, this that Shakspeare has brought us? For myself, I feel that there is actually a kind of sacredness in the fact of such a man being sent into this Earth. Is he not an eye to us all; a blessed heaven-sent Bringer of Light?—And, at bottom, was it not perhaps far better that this Shakspeare, every way an unconscious man, was *conscious* of no Heavenly message? He did not feel, like Mahomet, because he saw into those internal Splendours, that he specially was the 'Prophet of God:' and was he not greater than Mahomet in that? Greater; and also, if we compute strictly, as we did in Dante's case, more successful. It was intrinsically an error that notion of Mahomet's, of his supreme Prophethood; and has come down to us inextricably involved in error to this day; dragging along with it such a coil of fables, impurities, intolerances, as makes it a questionable step for me here and now to say, as I have done, that Mahomet was a true Speaker at all, and not rather an ambitious charlatan, perversity and simulacrum, no Speaker, but a Babbler! Even in Arabia, as I compute, Mahomet will have exhausted himself and become obsolete, while this Shakspeare, this Dante may be still young;—while this Shakspeare may still pretend to be a Priest of Mankind, of Arabia as of other places, for unlimited periods to come! Compared with any speaker or singer one knows, even with Æschylus or Homer, why should he not, for veracity and universality, last like them? He is *sincere* as they; reaches deep down like them, to the universal and perennial. But as for Mahomet, I think it had been better for him *not* to be so conscious! Alas, poor Mahomet; all that he was *conscious* of was a mere error; a futility and triviality,—as indeed such ever is. The truly great in him too was the unconscious: that he was a wild Arab lion of the desert, and did speak out with that great thunder-voice of his, not by words which he *thought* to be great, but by actions, by feelings, by a history which *were* great! His

Koran has become a stupid piece of prolix absurdity; we do not believe, like him, that God wrote that! The Great Man here too, as always, is a Force of Nature; whatsoever is truly great in him springs up from the *in*articulate deeps.

Well: this is our poor Warwickshire Peasant, who rose to be Manager of a Playhouse, so that he could live without begging; whom the Earl of Southampton cast some kind glances on; whom Sir Thomas Lucy, many thanks to him, was for sending to the Treadmill! We did not account him a god, like Odin, while he dwelt with us;— on which point there were much to be said. But I will say rather, or repeat: In spite of the sad state Hero-worship now lies in, consider what this Shakspeare has actually become among us. Which Englishman we ever made, in this land of ours, which million of Englishmen, would we not give up rather than the Stratford Peasant? There is no regiment of highest Dignitaries that we would sell him for. He is the grandest thing we have yet done. For our honour among foreign nations, as an ornament to our English Household, what item is there that we would not surrender rather than him? Consider now, if they asked us, Will you give up your Indian Empire or your Shakspeare, you English; never have had any Indian Empire, or never have had any Shakspeare? Really it were a grave question. Official persons would answer doubtless in official language; but we, for our part too, should not we be forced to answer: Indian Empire, or no Indian Empire; we cannot do without Shakspeare! Indian Empire will go, at any rate, some day; but this Shakspeare does not go, he lasts forever with us; we cannot give up our Shakspeare!

Nay, apart from spiritualities; and considering him merely as a real, marketable, tangibly useful possession. England, before long, this Island of ours, will hold but a small fraction of the English: in America, in New Holland, east and west to the very Antipodes, there will be a Saxondom covering great spaces of the Globe. And now, what is it that can keep all these together into virtually one Nation, so that they do not fall out and fight, but live at peace, in brotherlike intercourse, helping one another? This is justly regarded as the greatest practical problem, the thing all manner of sovereignties and governments are here to accomplish: what is it that will accomplish this? Acts of Parliament, administrative prime-ministers cannot.

America is parted from us, so far as Parliament could part it. Call it not fantastic, for there is much reality in it: Here, I say, is an English King, whom no time or chance, Parliament or combination of Parliaments, can dethrone! This King Shakspeare, does not he shine, in crowned sovereignty, over us all, as the noblest, gentlest, yet strongest of rallying-signs; *in*destructible; really more valuable in that point of view, than any other means or appliance whatsoever? We can fancy him as radiant aloft over all the Nations of Englishmen, a thousand years hence. From Paramatta, from New York, wheresoever, under what sort of Parish-Constable soever, English men and women are, they will say to one another: "Yes, this Shakspeare is ours; we produced him, we speak and think by him; we are of one blood and kind with him." The most common-sense politician too, if he pleases, may think of that.

Yes, truly, it is a great thing for a Nation that it get an articulate voice; that it produce a man who will speak forth melodiously what the heart of it means! Italy, for example, poor Italy lies dismembered, scattered asunder, not appearing in any protocol or treaty as a unity at all; yet the noble Italy is actually *one:* Italy produced its Dante; Italy can speak! The Czar of all the Russias, he is strong, with so many bayonets, Cossacks and cannons; and does a great feat in keeping such a tract of Earth politically together; but he cannot yet speak. Something great in him, but it is a dumb greatness. He has had no voice of genius, to be heard of all men and times. He must learn to speak. He is a great dumb monster hitherto. His cannons and Cossacks will all have rusted into nonentity, while that Dante's voice is still audible. The Nation that has a Dante is bound together as no dumb Russia can be.—We must here end what we had to say of the *Hero-Poet*.

LECTURE IV.

[Friday, 15th May, 1840.]

THE HERO AS PRIEST. LUTHER; REFORMATION:
KNOX; PURITANISM.

OUR present discourse is to be of the Great Man as Priest. We have repeatedly endeavoured to explain that all sorts of Heroes are intrinsically of the same material; that given a great soul, open to the Divine Significance of Life, then there is given a man fit to speak of this, to sing of this, to fight and work for this, in a great, victorious, enduring manner; there is given a Hero,—the outward shape of whom will depend on the time and the environment he finds himself in. The Priest too, as I understand it, is a kind of Prophet; in him too there is required to be a light of inspiration, as we must name it. He presides over the worship of the people; is the Uniter of them with the Unseen Holy. He is the spiritual Captain of the people; as the Prophet is their spiritual King with many captains: he guides them heavenward, by wise guidance through this Earth and its work. The ideal of him is, that he too be what we can call a voice from the unseen Heaven; interpreting, even as the Prophet did, and in a more familiar manner unfolding the same to men. The unseen Heaven,— the 'open secret of the Universe,' which so few have an eye for! He is the Prophet shorn of his more awful splendour; burning with mild equable radiance, as the enlightener of daily life. This, I say, is the ideal of a Priest. So in old times; so in these, and in all times. One knows very well that, in reducing ideals to practice, great latitude of tolerance is needful; very great. But a Priest who is not this at all, who does not any longer aim or try to be this, is a character—of whom we had rather not speak in this place.

Luther and Knox were by express vocation Priests, and did faithfully perform that function in its common sense. Yet it will suit us
better here to consider them chiefly in their historical character, rather
as Reformers than Priests. There have been other Priests perhaps
equally notable, in calmer times, for doing faithfully the office of a
Leader of Worship; bringing down, by faithful heroism in that kind,
a light from Heaven into the daily life of their people; leading them
forward, as under God's guidance, in the way wherein they were to
go. But when this same *way* was a rough one, of battle, confusion and
danger, the spiritual Captain who led through that, becomes, especially to us who live under the fruit of his leading, more notable than
any other. He is the warfaring and battling Priest; who led his people,
not to quiet faithful labour as in smooth times, but to faithful valor-
ous conflict, in times all violent, dismembered: a more perilous service, and a more memorable one, be it higher or not. These two men
we will account our best Priests, inasmuch as they were our best Reformers. Nay I may ask, Is not every true Reformer, by the nature of
him, a *Priest* first of all? He appeals to Heaven's invisible justice
against Earth's visible force; knows that it, the invisible, is strong and
alone strong. He is a believer in the divine truth of things; a *seer*,
seeing through the shows of things; a worshipper, in one way or the
other, of the divine truth of things: a Priest, that is. If he be not first
a Priest, he will never be good for much as a Reformer.

Thus then, as we have seen Great Men, in various situations,
building up Religions, heroic Forms of human Existence in this
world, Theories of Life worthy to be sung by a Dante, Practices of
Life by a Shakspeare,—we are now to see the reverse process; which
also is necessary, which also may be carried on in the Heroic manner.
Curious how this should be necessary: yet necessary it is. The mild
shining of the Poet's light has to give place to the fierce lightning of
the Reformer: unfortunately the Reformer too is a personage that
cannot fail in History! The Poet indeed, with his mildness, what is he
but the product and ultimate adjustment of Reform, or Prophecy,
with its fierceness? No wild Saint Dominics and Thebaid Eremites,
there had been no melodious Dante; rough Practical Endeavour,
Scandinavian and other, from Odin to Walter Raleigh, from Ulfila to
Cranmer, enabled Shakspeare to speak. Nay the finished Poet, I

remark sometimes, is a symptom that his epoch itself has reached perfection and is finished; that before long there will be a new epoch, new Reformers needed.

Doubtless it were finer, could we go along always in the way of *music;* be tamed and taught by our Poets, as the rude creatures were by their Orpheus of old. Or failing this rhythmic *musical* way, how good were it could we get so much as into the *equable* way; I mean, if *peaceable* Priests, reforming from day to day, would always suffice us! But it is not so; even this latter has not yet been realised. Alas, the battling Reformer too is, from time to time, a needful and inevitable phenomenon. Obstructions are never wanting: the very things that were once indispensable furtherances become obstructions; and need to be shaken off, and left behind us,—a business often of enormous difficulty. It is notable enough, surely, how a Theorem or spiritual Representation, so we may call it, which once took-in the whole Universe, and was completely satisfactory in all parts of it to the highly discursive acute intellect of Dante, one of the greatest in the world,—had in the course of another century become dubitable to common intellects; become deniable; and is now, to every one of us, flatly incredible, obsolete as Odin's Theorem! To Dante, human Existence, and God's ways with men, were all well represented by those *Malebolges, Purgatorios;* to Luther not well. How was this? Why could not Dante's Catholicism continue; but Luther's Protestantism must needs follow? Alas, nothing will *continue.*

I do not make much of 'Progress of the Species,' as handled in these times of ours; nor do I think you would care to hear much about it. The talk on that subject is too often of the most extravagant, confused sort. Yet I may say, the fact itself seems certain enough; nay we can trace out the inevitable necessity of it in the nature of things. Every man, as I have stated somewhere, is not only a learner but a doer: he learns with the mind given him what has been; but with the same mind he discovers farther, he invents and devises somewhat of his own. Absolutely without originality there is no man. No man whatever believes, or can believe, exactly what his grandfather believed: he enlarges somewhat, by fresh discovery, his view of the Universe, and consequently his Theorem of the Universe,—which is an *infinite* Universe, and can never be embraced wholly or finally by any view or Theorem, in any conceivable enlargement: he enlarges somewhat, I say; finds somewhat that was credible to his grandfather incredible to him, false to him, inconsistent with some new thing he has discovered or observed. It is the history of every man; and in the history of Mankind we see it summed up into great historical amounts,—revolutions, new epochs. Dante's Mountain of Purgatory does *not* stand 'in the ocean of the other Hemisphere,' when Columbus has once sailed thither! Men find no such thing extant in the other Hemisphere. It is not there. It must cease to be believed to be there. So with all beliefs whatsoever in this world,—all Systems of Belief, and Systems of Practice that spring from these.

If we add now the melancholy fact that when Belief waxes uncertain, Practice too becomes unsound, and errors, injustices and miseries everywhere more and more prevail, we shall see material enough for revolution. At all turns, a man who will *do* faithfully, needs to believe firmly. If he have to ask at every turn the world's suffrage; if, he cannot dispense with the world's suffrage, and make his own suffrage serve, he is a poor eye-servant; the work committed to him will be *mis*done. Every such man is a daily contributor to the inevitable downfal. Whatsoever work he does, dishonestly, with an eye to the outward look of it, is a new offence, parent of new misery to somebody or other. Offences accumulate till they become insupportable; and are then violently burst through, cleared off as by explosion. Dante's sublime Catholicism, incredible now in theory, and defaced still worse by faithless, doubting and dishonest practice, has to be torn asunder by a Luther; Shakspeare's noble Feudalism, as beautiful as it once looked and was, has to end in a French Revolution. The accumulation of offences is, as we say, too literally *exploded*, blasted asunder volcanically; and there are long troublous periods, before matters come to a settlement again.

Surely it were mournful enough to look only at this face of the matter, and find in all human opinions and arrangements merely the fact that they were uncertain, temporary, subject to the law of death! At bottom, it is not so: all death, here too we find, is but of the body, not of the essence or soul; all destruction, by violent revolution or howsoever it be, is but new creation on a wider scale. Odinism was *Valour*; Christianism was *Humility*, a nobler kind of Valour. No thought that ever dwelt honestly as true in the heart of man but *was* an honest insight into God's truth on man's part, and *has* an essential truth in it which endures through all changes, an everlasting possession for us all. And, on the other hand, what a melancholy notion is that, which has to represent all men, in all countries and times except our own, as having spent their life in blind condemnable error, mere lost Pagans, Scandinavians, Mahometans, only that we might have the true ultimate knowledge! All generations of men were lost and wrong, only that this present little section of a generation might be saved and right. They all marched forward there, all generations since the beginning of the world, like the Russian soldiers into the ditch of Schweidnitz Fort, only to fill up the ditch with their dead bodies, that we might march over and take the place! It is an incredible hypothesis.

Such incredible hypothesis we have seen maintained with fierce emphasis; and this or the other poor individual man, with his sect of individual men, marching as over the dead bodies of all men, towards sure victory: but when he too, with his hypothesis and ultimate infallible credo, sank into the ditch, and became a dead body, what was to be said?—Withal, it is an important fact in the nature of man, that he tends to reckon his own insight as final, and goes upon it as such. He will always do it, I suppose, in one or the other way; but it must be in some wider, wiser way than this. Are not all true men that live, or that ever lived, soldiers of the same army; enlisted, under Heaven's captaincy, to do battle against the same enemy, the empire of Darkness and Wrong? Why should we misknow one another, fight not against the enemy but against ourselves, from mere difference of uniform? All uniforms shall be good, so they hold in them true valiant men. All fashions of arms, the Arab turban and swift scimetar, Thor's strong hammer smiting down *Jötuns*, shall be welcome. Luther's battle-voice, Dante's march-melody, all genuine things are with us, not against us. We are all under one Captain, soldiers of the same host.—Let us now look a little at this Luther's fighting; what kind of battle it was, and how he comported himself in it. Luther too was of our spiritual Heroes; a Prophet to his country and time.

As introductory to the whole, a remark about Idolatry will perhaps be in place here. One of Mahomet's characteristics, which indeed belongs to all Prophets, is unlimited implacable zeal against Idolatry.

It is the grand theme of Prophets: Idolatry, the worshipping of dead Idols as the Divinity, is a thing they cannot away with, but have to denounce continually, and brand with inexpiable reprobation; it is the chief of all the sins they see done under the sun. This is worth noting. We will not enter here into the theological question about Idolatry. Idol is *Eidolon*, a thing seen, a symbol. It is not God, but a Symbol of God; and perhaps one may question whether any the most benighted mortal ever took it for more than a Symbol. I fancy, he did not think that the poor image his own hands had made *was* God; but that God was emblemed by it, that God was in it some way or other. And now in this sense, one may ask, Is not all worship whatsoever a worship by Symbols, by *eidola*, or things seen? Whether *seen*, rendered visible as an image or picture to the bodily eye; or visible only to the inward eye, to the imagination, to the intellect: this makes a superficial, but no substantial difference. It is still a Thing Seen, significant of Godhood; an Idol. The most rigorous Puritan has his Confession of Faith, and intellectual Representation of Divine things, and worships thereby; thereby is worship first made possible for him. All creeds, liturgies, religious forms, conceptions that fitly invest religious feelings, are in this sense *eidola*, things seen. All worship whatsoever must proceed by Symbols, by Idols:—we may say, all Idolatry is comparative, and the worst Idolatry is only *more* idolatrous.

Where then lies the evil of it? Some fatal evil must lie in it, or earnest prophetic men would not on all hands so reprobate it. Why is Idolatry so hateful to Prophets? It seems to me as if, in the worship of those poor wooden symbols, the thing that had chiefly provoked the Prophet, and filled his inmost soul with indignation and aversion, was not exactly what suggested itself to his own thought, and came out of him in words to others, as the thing. The rudest heathen that worshipped Canopus, or the Caabah Black-stone, he, as we saw, was superior to the horse that worshipped nothing at all! Nay there was a kind of lasting merit in that poor act of his; analogous to what is still meritorious in Poets: recognition of a certain endless *divine* beauty and significance in stars and all natural objects whatsoever. Why should the Prophet so mercilessly condemn him? The poorest mortal worshipping his Fetish, while his heart is full of it, may be an object of pity, of contempt and avoidance, if you will; but cannot surely be an object of hatred. Let his heart *be* honestly full of it, the whole space of his dark narrow mind illuminated thereby; in one word, let him entirely *believe* in his Fetish,—it will then be, I should say, if not well with him, yet as well as it can readily be made to be, and you will leave him alone, unmolested there.

But here enters the fatal circumstance of Idolatry, that, in the era of the Prophets, no man's mind *is* any longer honestly filled with his Idol, or Symbol. Before the Prophet can arise who, seeing through it, knows it to be mere wood, many men must have begun dimly to doubt that it was little more. Condemnable Idolatry is *insincere* Idolatry. Doubt has eaten out the heart of it: a human soul is seen clinging spasmodically to an Ark of the Covenant, which it half-feels now to have become a Phantasm. This is one of the balefulest sights. Souls are no longer *filled* with their Fetish; but only pretend to be filled, and would fain make themselves feel that they are filled. "You do not believe," said Coleridge; "you only believe that you believe." It is the final scene in all kinds of Worship and Symbolism; the sure symptom that death is now nigh. It is equivalent to what we call Formulism, and Worship of Formulas, in these days of ours. No more immoral act can be done by a human creature; for it is the beginning of all immorality, or rather it is the impossibility henceforth of any morality whatsoever: the innermost moral soul is paralyzed thereby, cast into fatal magnetic sleep! Men are no longer *sincere* men. I do not wonder that the earnest man denounces this, brands it, prosecutes it with inextinguishable aversion. He and it, all good and it, are at death-feud. Blameable Idolatry is *Cant*, and even what one may call Sincere-Cant. Sincere-Cant: that is worth thinking of! Every sort of Worship ends with this phasis.—I find Luther to have been a Breaker of Idols, no less than any other Prophet. The wooden gods of the Koreish, made of timber and bees'-wax, were not more hateful to Mahomet than Tetzel's Pardons of Sin, made of sheepskin and ink, were to Luther. It is the property of every Hero, in every time, in every place and situation, that he come back to reality; that he stand upon things, and not shows of things. According as he loves, and venerates, articulately or with deep speechless thought, the awful realities of things, so will the hollow shows of things, however regular, decorous, accredited by Koreishes or Conclaves, be intolerable and detestable to him. Protestantism too is the work of a Prophet:

the prophet-work of that sixteenth century. The first stroke of honest demolition to an ancient thing grown false and idolatrous; preparatory afar off to a new thing, which shall be true, and authentically divine!—

At first view it might seem as if Protestantism were entirely destructive to this that we call Hero-worship, and represent as the basis of all possible good, religious or social, for mankind. One often hears it said that Protestantism introduced a new era, radically different from any the world had ever seen before: the era of 'private judgment,' as they call it. By this revolt against the Pope, every man became his own Pope; and learnt, among other things, that he must never trust any Pope, or spiritual Hero-captain, any more! Whereby, is not spiritual union, all hierarchy and subordination among men, henceforth an impossibility? So we hear it said.—Now I need not deny that Protestantism was a revolt against spiritual sovereignties, Popes and much else. Nay I will grant that English Puritanism, revolt against earthly sovereignties, was the second act of it; that the enormous French Revolution itself was the third act, whereby all sovereignties earthly and spiritual were, as might seem, abolished or made sure of abolition. Protestantism is the grand root from which our whole subsequent European History branches out. For the spiritual will always body itself forth in the temporal history of men; the spiritual is the beginning of the temporal. And now, sure enough, the cry is everywhere for Liberty and Equality, Independence and so forth; instead of *Kings*, Ballot-boxes and Electoral suffrages: it seems made out that any Hero-sovereign, or loyal obedience of men to a man, in things temporal or things spiritual, has passed away forever from the world. I should despair of the world altogether, if so. One of my deepest convictions is, that it is not so. Without sovereigns, true sovereigns, temporal and spiritual, I see nothing possible but an anarchy; the hatefulest of things. But I find Protestantism, whatever anarchic democracy it have produced, to be the beginning of new genuine sovereignty and order. I find it to be a revolt against *false* sovereigns; the painful but indispensable first preparative for *true* sovereigns getting place among us! This is worth explaining a little.

Let us remark, therefore, in the first place, that this of 'private judgment' is, at bottom, not a new thing in the world, but only new at that epoch of the world. There is nothing generically new or peculiar in the Reformation; it was a return to Truth and Reality in opposition to Falsehood and Semblance, as all kinds of Improvement and genuine Teaching are and have been. Liberty of private judgment, if we will consider it, must at all times have existed in the world. Dante had not put out his eyes, or tied shackles on himself; he was at home in that Catholicism of his, a free-seeing soul in it,— if many a poor Hogstraten, Tetzel and Dr. Eck had now become slaves in it. Liberty of judgment? No iron chain, or outward force of any kind, could ever compel the soul of a man to believe or to disbelieve: it is his own indefeasible light, that judgment of his; he will reign, and believe there, by the grace of God alone! The sorriest sophistical Bellarmine, preaching sightless faith and passive obedience, must first, by some kind of *conviction*, have abdicated his right to be convinced. His 'private judgment' indicated that, as the adviseablest step *he* could take. The right of private judgment will subsist, in full force, wherever true men subsist. A true man *believes* with his whole judgment, with all the illumination and discernment that is in him, and has always so believed. A false man, only struggling to 'believe that he believes,' will naturally manage it in some other way. Protestantism said to this latter, Woe! and to the former, Well done! At bottom, it was no new saying; it was a return to all old sayings that ever had been said. Be genuine, be sincere: that was, once more, the meaning of it. Mahomet believed with his whole mind; Odin with his whole mind,—he, and all *true* Followers of Odinism. They, by their private judgment, had 'judged'—*so*.

And now I venture to assert, that the exercise of private judgment, faithfully gone about, does by no means necessarily end in selfish independence, isolation; but rather ends necessarily in the opposite of that. It is not honest inquiry that makes anarchy; but it is error, insincerity, half-belief, and untruth that makes it. A man protesting against error is on the way towards uniting himself with all men that believe in truth. There is no communion possible among men who believe only in hearsays. The heart of each is lying dead; has no power of sympathy even with *things*,—or he would believe *them* and not hearsays. No sympathy even with things; how much less with his fellow-men! He cannot unite with men; he is an anarchic man. Only in a world of sincere men is unity possible;—and there, in the long-run, it is as good as *certain*.

For observe one thing, a thing too often left out of view, or rather altogether lost sight of in this controversy: That it is not necessary a man should himself have *discovered* the truth he is to believe in, and never so *sincerely* to believe in. A Great Man, we said, was always sincere, as the first condition of him. But a man need not be great in order to be sincere; that is not the necessity of Nature and all Time, but only of certain corrupt unfortunate epochs of Time. A man can believe, and make his own, in the most genuine way, what he has received from another;—and with boundless gratitude to that other! The merit of *originality* is not novelty; it is sincerity. The believing man is the original man; whatsoever he believes he believes it for himself, not for another. Every son of Adam can become a sincere man, an original man, in this sense; no mortal is doomed to be an insincere man. Whole ages, what we call ages of Faith, are original,— all men in them, or the most of men in them, sincere. These are the great and fruitful ages: every worker, in all spheres, is a worker not on semblance but on substance; every work issues in a result: the general sum of such work is great; for all of it, as genuine, tends towards one goal; all of it is *additive*, none of it subtractive. There is true union, true kingship, loyalty, all true and blessed things, so far as the poor Earth can produce blessedness for men. Hero-worship? Ah me, that a man be self-subsistent, original, true, or what we call it, is surely the farthest in the world from indisposing him to rever- ence and believe other men's truth! It only disposes, necessitates and invincibly compels him to *dis*believe other men's dead formulas, hearsays and untruths. A man embraces truth with his eyes open, and because his eyes are open: does he need to shut them before he can love his Teacher of truth? He alone can love, with a right gratitude and genuine loyalty of soul, the Hero-Teacher who has delivered him out of darkness into light. Is not such a one a true Hero, and Serpent- queller; worthy of all reverence! The black monster, Falsehood, our one enemy in this world, lies prostrate by his valour; it was he that conquered the world for us!—See, accordingly, was not Luther himself reverenced as a true Pope, or Spiritual Father, *being* verily such? Napoleon, from amid boundless revolt of Sansculottism, be- came a King. Hero-worship never dies, nor can die. Loyalty and Sovereignty are everlasting in the world:—and there is this in them, that they are grounded not on garnitures and semblances, but on realities and sincerities. Not by shutting your eyes, your 'private judgment;' no, but by opening them, and by having something to see! Luther's message was deposition and abolition to all false Popes and Potentates, but life and strength, though afar off, to new genuine ones.

All this of Liberty and Equality, Electoral Suffrages, Independence and so forth, we will take, therefore, to be a temporary phenomenon, by no means a final one. Though likely to last a long time, with sad enough embroilments for us all, we must welcome it, as the penalty of sins that are past, the pledge of inestimable benefits that are coming. In all ways, it behoved men to quit simulacra and return to fact; cost what it might, that did behove to be done. With spurious Popes, and believers having no private judgment,—quacks pretending to command over dupes,—what can you do? Misery and mischief only. You cannot make an association out of insincere men; you cannot build an edifice except by plummet and level,—at *right*-angles to one another! In all this wild revolutionary work, from Protestant-ism downwards, I see the blessedest result preparing itself: not abo-lition of Hero-worship, but rather what I would call a whole World of Heroes. If Hero mean *sincere man*, why may not every one of us be a Hero? A world all sincere, a believing world: the like has been; the like will again be,—cannot help being. That were the right sort of Worshippers for Heroes: never could the truly Better be so rever-enced as where all were True and Good!—But we must hasten to Luther and his Life.

Luther's birthplace was Eisleben in Saxony; he came into the world there on the 10th of November, 1483. It was an accident that gave this honour to Eisleben. His parents, poor mine-labourers in a village of that region, named Mohra, had gone to the Eisleben Winter-Fair: in the tumult of this scene the Frau Luther was taken with travail, found refuge in some poor house there, and the boy she bore was named MARTIN LUTHER. Strange enough to reflect upon it. This poor Frau Luther, she had gone with her husband to make her small merchandisings; perhaps to sell the lock of yarn she had been spinning, to buy the small winter-necessaries for her narrow hut or household: in the whole world, that day, there was not a more en-tirely unimportant-looking pair of people than this Miner and his

Wife. And yet what were all Emperors, Popes and Potentates, in comparison? There was born here, once more, a Mighty Man; whose light was to flame as the beacon over long centuries and epochs of the world; the whole world and its history was waiting for this man. It is strange, it is great. It leads us back to another Birth-hour, in a still meaner environment, Eighteen Hundred years ago,—of which it is fit that we *say* nothing, that we think only in silence; for what words are there! The Age of Miracles past? The Age of Miracles is forever here!—

I find it altogether suitable to Luther's function in this Earth, and doubtless wisely ordered to that end by the Providence presiding over him and us and all things, that he was born poor, and brought up poor, one of the poorest of men. He had to beg, as the school-children in those times did; singing for alms and bread, from door to door. Hardship, rigorous Necessity was the poor boy's companion; no man nor no thing would put-on a false face to flatter Martin Luther. Among things, not among the shows of things, had he to grow. A boy of rude figure, yet with weak health, with his large greedy soul, full of all faculty and sensibility, he suffered greatly. But it was his task to get acquainted with *realities*, and keep acquainted with them, at whatever cost: his task was to bring the whole world back to reality, for it had dwelt too long with semblance! A youth nursed up in wintry whirlwinds, in desolate darkness and difficulty, that he may step forth at last from his stormy Scandinavia, strong as a true man, as a god: a Christian Odin,—a right Thor once more, with his thunder-hammer, to smite asunder ugly enough *Jötuns* and Giant-monsters!

Perhaps the turning incident of his life, we may fancy, was that death of his friend Alexis, by lightning, at the gate of Erfurt. Luther had struggled up through boyhood, better and worse; displaying in spite of all hindrances the largest intellect, eager to learn: his father judging doubtless that he might promote himself in the world, set him upon the study of Law. This was the path to rise; Luther, with little will in it either way, had consented: he was now nineteen years of age. Alexis and he had been to see the old Luther people at Mansfeldt; were got back again near Erfurt, when a thunderstorm came on; the bolt struck Alexis, he fell dead at Luther's feet. What

is this Life of ours;—gone in a moment, burnt up like a scroll, into
the blank Eternity! What are all earthly preferments, Chancellorships,
Kingships? They lie shrunk together—there! The Earth has opened
on them; in a moment they are not, and Eternity is. Luther, struck
to the heart, determined to devote himself to God, and God's service
alone. In spite of all dissuasions from his father and others, he became
a Monk in the Augustine Convent at Erfurt.

This was probably the first light-point in the history of Luther, his
purer will now first decisively uttering itself; but, for the present, it
was still as one light-point in an element all of darkness. He says he
was a pious monk, *ich bin ein frommer Mönch gewesen;* faithfully,
painfully struggling to work out the truth of this high act of his; but
it was to little purpose. His misery had not lessened; had rather, as
it were, increased into infinitude. The drudgeries he had to do, as
novice in his Convent, all sorts of slave-work, were not his grievance:
the deep earnest soul of the man had fallen into all manner of black
scruples, dubitations; he believed himself likely to die soon, and far
worse than die. One hears with a new interest for poor Luther that,
at this time, he lived in terror of the unspeakable misery; fancied that
he was doomed to eternal reprobation. Was it not the humble sincere
nature of the man? What was he, that he should be raised to Heaven!
He that had known only misery, and mean slavery: the news was too
blessed to be credible. It could not become clear to him how, by
fasts, vigils, formalities and mass-work, a man's soul could be saved.
He fell into the blackest wretchedness; had to wander staggering as
on the verge of bottomless Despair.

It must have been a most blessed discovery, that of an old Latin
Bible which he found in the Erfurt Library about this time. He had
never seen the Book before. It taught him another lesson than that
of fasts and vigils. A brother monk too, of pious experience, was
helpful. Luther learned now that a man was saved not by singing
masses, but by the infinite grace of God: a more credible hypothesis.
He gradually got himself founded, as on the rock. No wonder he
should venerate the Bible, which had brought this blessed help to
him. He prized it as the Word of the Highest must be prized by such
a man. He determined to hold by that; as through life and to death
he firmly did.

This then is his deliverance from darkness, his final triumph over darkness, what we call his conversion; for himself the most important of all epochs. That he should now grow daily in peace and clearness; that, unfolding now the great talents and virtues implanted in him, he should rise to importance in his Convent, in his country, and be found more and more useful in all honest business of life, is a natural result. He was sent on missions by his Augustine Order, as a man of talent and fidelity fit to do their business well: the Elector of Saxony, Friedrich, named the Wise, a truly wise and just prince, had cast his eye on him as a valuable person; made him Professor in his new University of Wittenberg, Preacher too at Wittenberg; in both which capacities, as in all duties he did, this Luther, in the peaceable sphere of common life, was gaining more and more esteem with all good men.

It was in his twenty-seventh year that he first saw Rome; being sent thither, as I said, on mission from his Convent. Pope Julius the Second, and what was going on at Rome, must have filled the mind of Luther with amazement. He had come as to the Sacred City, throne of God's Highpriest on Earth; and he found it—what we know! Many thoughts it must have given the man; many which we have no record of, which perhaps he did not himself know how to utter. This Rome, this scene of false priests, clothed not in the beauty of holiness, but in far other vesture, is *false:* but what is it to Luther? A mean man he, how shall he reform a world? That was far from his thoughts. A humble, solitary man, why should he at all meddle with the world? It was the task of quite higher men than he. His business was to guide his own footsteps wisely through the world. Let him do his own obscure duty in it well; the rest, horrible and dismal as it looks, is in God's hand, not in his.

It is curious to reflect what might have been the issue, had Roman Popery happened to pass this Luther by; to go on in its great wasteful orbit, and not come athwart his little path, and force him to assault it! Conceivable enough that, in this case, he might have held his peace about the abuses of Rome; left Providence, and God on high, to deal with them! A modest quiet man; not prompt he to attack irreverently persons in authority. His clear task, as I say, was to do his own duty; to walk wisely in this world of confused wickedness, and save his own soul alive. But the Roman Highpriesthood did come athwart him: afar off at Wittenberg he, Luther, could not get lived in honesty for it; he remonstrated, resisted, came to extremity; was struck at, struck again, and so it came to wager of battle between them! This is worth attending to, in Luther's history. Perhaps no man of so humble, peaceable a disposition ever filled the world with contention. We cannot but see that he would have loved privacy, quiet diligence in the shade; that it was against his will he ever became a notoriety. Notoriety: what would that do for him? The goal of his march through this world was the Infinite Heaven; an indubitable goal for him: in a few years, he should either have attained that, or lost it forever! We will say nothing at all, I think, of that sorrowfulest of theories, of its being some mean shopkeeper grudge, of the Augustine Monk against the Dominican, that first kindled the wrath of Luther, and produced the Protestant Reformation. We will say to the people who maintain it, if indeed any such exist now, Get first into the sphere of thought by which it is so much as possible to judge of Luther, or of any man like Luther, otherwise than distractedly; we may then begin arguing with you.

The Monk Tetzel, sent out carelessly in the way of trade, by Leo Tenth,—who merely wanted to raise a little money, and for the rest seems to have been a Pagan rather than a Christian, so far as he was anything,—arrived at Wittenberg, and drove his scandalous trade there. Luther's flock bought Indulgences; in the confessional of his Church, people pleaded to him that they had already got their sins pardoned. Luther, if he would not be found wanting at his own post, a false sluggard and coward at the very centre of the little space of ground that was his own and no other man's, had to step forth against Indulgences, and declare aloud that *they* were a futility and sorrowful mockery, that no man's sins could be pardoned by *them*. It was the beginning of the whole Reformation. We know how it went; forward from this first public challenge of Tetzel, on the last day of October 1517, through remonstrance and argument;—spreading ever wider, rising ever higher; till it became unquenchable, and enveloped all the world. Luther's heart's-desire was to have this grief and other griefs amended; his thought was still far other than that of introducing separation in the Church, or revolting against the Pope, Father of Christendom.—The elegant Pagan Pope cared little about this Monk and his doctrines; wished, however, to have done with the noise of him: in a space of some three years, having tried various softer methods, he thought good to end it by *fire*. He dooms the Monk's writings to be burnt by the hangman, and his body to be sent bound to Rome—probably for a similar purpose. It was the way they had ended with Huss, with Jerome, the century before. A short argument, fire. Poor Huss: he came to that Constance Council, with all imaginable promises and safe-conducts; an earnest, not rebellious kind of man: they laid him instantly in a stone dungeon 'three feet wide, six feet high, seven feet long;' *burnt* the true voice of him out of this world; choked it in smoke and fire. That was *not* well done!

I, for one, pardon Luther for now altogether revolting against the Pope. The elegant Pagan, by this fire-decree of his, had kindled into noble just wrath the bravest heart then living in this world. The bravest, if also one of the humblest, peaceablest; it was now kindled. These words of mine, words of truth and soberness, aiming faithfully, as human inability would allow, to promote God's truth on Earth, and save men's souls, you, God's vicegerent on earth, answer them by the hangman and fire? You will burn me and them, for answer to the God's-message they strove to bring you? *You* are not God's vicegerent; you are another's than his, I think! I take your Bull, as an emparchmented Lie, and burn *it*. You will do what you see good next; this is what I do.—It was on the tenth of December 1520, three years after the beginning of the business, that Luther 'with a great concourse of people,' took this indignant step of burning the Pope's fire-decree 'at the Elster-Gate of Wittenberg.' Wittenberg looked on 'with shoutings;' the whole world was looking on. The Pope should not have provoked that 'shout!' It was the shout of the awakening of nations. The quiet German heart, modest, patient of much, had at length got more than it could bear. Formulism, Pagan Popism, and other Falsehood and corrupt Semblance had ruled long enough: and here once more was a man found who durst tell all men that God's-world stood not on semblances but on realities; that Life was a truth, and not a lie!

At bottom, as was said above, we are to consider Luther as a Prophet Idol-breaker; a bringer back of men to reality. It is the function of great men and teachers. Mahomet said, These idols of yours are wood; you put wax and oil on them, the flies stick on them: they are not God, I tell you, they are black wood! Luther said to the

Pope, This thing of yours that you call a Pardon of Sins, it is a bit of rag-paper with ink. It *is* nothing else; it, and so much like it, is nothing else. God alone can pardon sins. Popeship, spiritual Fatherhood of God's Church, is that a vain semblance, of cloth and parchment? It is an awful fact. God's Church is not a semblance, Heaven and Hell are not semblances. I stand on this, since you drive me to it. Standing on this, I a poor German Monk am stronger than you all. I stand solitary, friendless, but on God's Truth; you with your tiaras, triple-hats, with your treasuries and armories, thunders spiritual and temporal, stand on the Devil's Lie, and are not so strong!—

The Diet of Worms, Luther's appearance there on the 17th of April 1521, may be considered as the greatest scene in Modern European History; the point, indeed, from which the whole subsequent history of civilization takes its rise. After multiplied negotiations, disputations, it had come to this. The young Emperor Charles Fifth, with all the Princes of Germany, Papal nuncios, dignitaries spiritual and temporal, are assembled there: Luther is to appear and answer for himself, whether he will recant or not. The world's pomp and power sits there on this hand: on that, stands up for God's Truth, one man, the poor miner Hans Luther's Son. Friends had reminded him of Huss, advised him not to go; he would not be advised. A large company of friends rode out to meet him, with still more earnest warnings; he answered, "Were there as many Devils in Worms as there are roof-tiles, I would on." The people, on the morrow, as he went to the Hall of the Diet, crowded the windows and housetops, some of them calling out to him, in solemn words, not to recant: "Whosoever denieth me before men!" they cried to him,—as in a kind of solemn petition and adjuration. Was it not in reality our petition too, the petition of the whole world, lying in dark bondage of soul, paralysed under a black spectral Nightmare and triple-hatted Chimera, calling itself Father in God, and what not: "Free us; it rests with thee; desert us not!" Luther did not desert us. His speech, of two hours, distinguished itself by its respectful, wise and honest tone; submissive to whatsoever could lawfully claim submission, not submissive to any more than that. His writings, he said, were partly his own, partly derived from the Word of God. As to what was his own, human infirmity entered into it; unguarded anger, blindness, many things doubtless which it were a blessing for him could he abolish altogether. But as to what stood on sound truth and the Word of God, he could not recant it. How could he? "Confute me," he concluded, "by proofs of Scripture, or else by plain just arguments: I cannot recant otherwise. For it is neither safe nor prudent to do aught against conscience. Here stand I; I can do no other: God assist me!"—It is, as we say, the greatest moment in the Modern History of Men. English Puritanism, England and its Parliaments, Americas, and vast work these two centuries; French Revolution, Europe and its work everywhere at present: the germ of it all lay there: had Luther in that moment done other, it had all been otherwise! The European World was asking him: Am I to sink ever lower into falsehood, stagnant putrescence, loathsome accursed death; or, with whatever paroxysm, to cast the falsehoods out of me, and be cured and live?—

Great wars, contentions, and disunion followed out of this Reformation; which last down to our day, and are yet far from ended. Great talk and crimination has been made about these. They are lamentable, undeniable; but after all, what has Luther or his cause to do with them? It seems strange reasoning to charge the Reformation with all this. When Hercules turned the purifying river into King Augeas's stables, I have no doubt the confusion that resulted was considerable all around: but I think it was not Hercules's blame; it was some other's blame! The Reformation might bring what results it liked when it came, but the Reformation simply could not help coming. To all Popes and Popes' advocates, expostulating, lamenting and accusing, the answer of the world is: Once for all, your Popehood has become untrue. No matter how good it was, how good you say it is, we cannot believe it; the light of our whole mind, given us to walk by from Heaven above, finds it henceforth a thing unbelievable. We will not believe it, we will not try to believe it,—we dare not! The thing is *untrue;* we were traitors against the Giver of all Truth, if we durst pretend to think it true. Away with it; let whatsoever likes come in the place of it: with *it* we can have no farther trade!—Luther and his Protestantism is not responsible for wars; the false Simulacra that forced him to protest, they are responsible. Luther did what every man that God has made has not only the right, but lies under the sacred duty, to do: answered a Falsehood when it questioned him,

Dost thou believe me?—No!—At what cost soever, without counting of costs, this thing behoved to be done. Union, organisation spiritual and material, a far nobler than any Popedom or Feudalism in their truest days, I never doubt, is coming for the world; sure to come. But on Fact alone, not on Semblance and Simulacrum, will it be able either to come, or to stand when come. With union grounded on falsehood, and ordering us to speak and act lies, we will not have anything to do. Peace? A brutal lethargy is peaceable, the noisome grave is peaceable. We hope for a living peace, not a dead one!

And yet, in prizing justly the indispensable blessings of the New, let us not be unjust to the Old. The Old *was* true, if it no longer is. In Dante's days it needed no sophistry, self-blinding or other dishonesty, to get itself reckoned true. It was good then; nay there is in the soul of it a deathless good. The cry of 'No Popery,' is foolish enough in these days. The speculation that Popery is on the increase, building new chapels, and so forth, may pass for one of the idlest ever started. Very curious: to count up a few Popish chapels, listen to a few Protestant logic-choppings,—to much dull-droning drowsy inanity that still calls itself Protestant, and say: See, Protestantism is *dead;* Popism is more alive than it, will be alive after it!—Drowsy inanities, not a few, that call themselves Protestant are dead; but *Protestantism* has not died yet, that I hear of! Protestantism, if we will look, has in these days produced its Goethe, its Napoleon; German Literature and the French Revolution; rather considerable signs of life! Nay, at bottom, what else is alive *but* Protestantism? The life of most else that one meets is a galvanic one merely,—not a pleasant, not a lasting sort of life!

Popery can build new chapels; welcome to do so, to all lengths. Popery cannot come back, any more than Paganism can,—*which* also still lingers in some countries. But, indeed, it is with these things, as with the ebbing of the sea: you look at the waves oscillating hither, thither on the beach; for *minutes* you cannot tell how it is going: look in half an hour where it is,—look in half a century where your Popehood is! Alas, would there were no greater danger to our Europe than the poor old Pope's revival! Thor may as soon try to revive.—And withal this oscillation has a meaning. The poor old Popehood will not die away entirely, as Thor has done, for some time yet; nor ought it. We may say, the Old never dies till this happen, Till all the soul of good that was in it have got itself transfused into the practical New. While a good work remains capable of being done by the Romish form; or, what is inclusive of all, while a *pious life* remains capable of being led by it, just so long, if we consider, will this or the other human soul adopt it, go about as a living witness of it. So long it will obtrude itself on the eye of us who reject it, till we in our practice too have appropriated whatsoever of truth was in it. Then, but also not till then, it will have no charm more for any man. It lasts here for a purpose. Let it last as long as it can.—

Of Luther I will add now, in reference to all these wars and bloodshed, the noticeable fact that none of them began so long as he continued living. The controversy did not get to fighting so long as he was there. To me it is proof of his greatness in all senses, this fact. How seldom do we find a man that has stirred up some vast commotion, who does not himself perish, swept away in it. Such is the usual course of revolutionists. Luther continued, in a good degree, sovereign of this greatest revolution; all Protestants, of what rank or function soever, looking much to him for guidance: and he held it peaceable, continued firm at the centre of it. A man to do this must have a kingly faculty: he must have the gift to discern at all turns where the true heart of the matter lies, and to plant himself courageously on that, as a strong true man, that other true men may rally round him there. He will not continue leader of men otherwise. Luther's clear deep force of judgment, his force of all sorts, of *silence*, of tolerance and moderation, among others, are very notable in these circumstances.

Tolerance, I say; a very genuine kind of tolerance: he distinguishes what is essential, and what is not; the unessential may go very much as it will. A complaint comes to him that such and such a Reformed Preacher 'will not preach without a cassock.' Well, answers Luther, what harm will a cassock do the man? 'Let him have a cassock to preach in; let him have three cassocks if he find benefit in them!' His conduct in the matter of Karlstadt's wild image-breaking; of the Anabaptists; of the Peasants' War, shews a noble strength, very differ-ent from spasmodic violence. With sure prompt insight he discriminates what is what: a strong just man, he speaks forth what is the wise course, and all men follow him in that. Luther's Written Works give similar testimony of him. The dialect of these speculations is now grown obsolete for us; but one still reads them with a singular attraction. And indeed the mere grammatical diction is still legible enough; Luther's merit in literary history is of the greatest: his dialect became the language of all writing. They are not well written, these Four-and-twenty Quartos of his; written hastily, with quite other than literary objects. But in no Books have I found a more robust, genuine, I will say noble faculty of a man than in these. A rugged honesty, homeliness, simplicity; a rugged sterling sense and strength. He flashes out illumination from him; his smiting idiomatic phrases seem to cleave into the very secret of the matter. Good humour too, nay tender affection, nobleness, and depth: this man could have been a Poet too! He had to *work* an Epic Poem, not write one. I call him a great Thinker; as indeed his greatness of heart already betokens that.

Richter says of Luther's words, 'his words are half-battles.' They may be called so. The essential quality of him was that he could fight and conquer; that he was a right piece of human Valour. No more valiant man, no mortal heart to be called *braver*, that one has record of, ever lived in that Teutonic Kindred, whose character is valour. His defiance of the 'Devils' in Worms was not a mere boast, as the like might be if now spoken. It was a faith of Luther's that there were Devils, spiritual denizens of the Pit, continually besetting men. Many times, in his writings, this turns up; and a most small sneer has been grounded on it by some. In the room of the Wartburg where he sat translating the Bible, they still shew you a black spot on the wall; the strange memorial of one of these conflicts. Luther sat translating one of the Psalms; he was worn down with long labour, with sickness, abstinence from food: there rose before him some hideous indefinable Image, which he took for the Evil One, to forbid his work: Luther started up, with fiend-defiance; flung his inkstand at the spectre, and it disappeared! The spot still remains there; a curious monument of several things. Any apothecary's apprentice can now tell us what we are to think of this apparition, in a scientific sense: but the man's heart that dare rise defiant, face to face, against Hell itself, can give no higher proof of fearlessness. The thing he will quail before, exists

not on this Earth or under it.—Fearless enough! 'The Devil is aware,'
writes he on one occasion, 'that this does not proceed out of fear in
me. I have seen and defied innumerable Devils. Duke George,' of
Leipzig, a great enemy of his, 'Duke George is not equal to one
Devil,'—far short of a Devil! 'If I had business at Leipzig, I would
ride into Leipzig, though it rained Duke-Georges for nine days
running.' What a reservoir of Dukes to ride into!—

At the same time, they err greatly who imagine that this man's
courage was ferocity, mere coarse disobedient obstinacy and savagery,
as many do. Far from that. There may be an absence of fear which
arises from the absence of thought or affection, from the presence of
hatred and stupid fury. We do not value the courage of the tiger
highly! With Luther it was far otherwise; no accusation could be
more unjust than this of mere ferocious violence brought against
him. A most gentle heart withal, full of pity and love, as indeed the
truly valiant heart ever is. The tiger before a *stronger* foe—flies: the
tiger is not what we call valiant, only fierce and cruel. I know few
things more touching than those soft breathings of affection, soft as
a child's or a mother's, in this great wild heart of Luther. So honest,
unadulterated with any cant; homely, rude in their utterance; pure as
water welling from the rock. What, in fact, was all that downpressed
mood of despair and reprobation, which we saw in his youth, but the
outcome of preeminent thoughtful gentleness, affections too keen
and fine? It is the course such men as the poor Poet Cowper fall into.
Luther, to a slight observer, might have seemed a timid, weak man;
modesty, affectionate shrinking tenderness the chief distinction of
him. It is a noble valour which is roused in a heart like this, once
stirred up into defiance; all kindled into a heavenly blaze.

In Luther's *Table-talk*, a posthumous Book of anecdotes and
sayings collected by his friends, the most interesting now of all the
Books proceeding from him, we have many beautiful unconscious
displays of the man, and what sort of nature he had. His behaviour
at the deathbed of his little Daughter, so still, so great and loving, is
among the most affecting things. He is resigned that his little
Magdalene should die, yet longs inexpressibly that she might live;—
follows, in awestruck thought, the flight of her little soul through
those unknown realms. Awestruck; most heartfelt, we can see; and

sincere,—for after all dogmatic creeds and articles, he feels what nothing it is that we know, or can know: His little Magdalene shall be with God, as God wills; for Luther too that is all; *Islam* is all.

Once, he looks out from his solitary Patmos, the Castle of Coburg, in the middle of the night: The great vault of Immensity, long flights of clouds sailing through it,—dumb, gaunt, huge:—who supports all that? "None ever saw the pillars of it; yet it is supported." God supports it. We must know that God is great, that God is good; and trust, where we cannot see.—Returning home from Leipzig once, he is struck by the beauty of the harvest-fields: How it stands, that golden yellow corn, on its fair taper stem, its golden head bent, all rich and waving there,—the meek Earth, at God's kind bidding, has produced it once again; the bread of man!—In the garden at Wittenberg one evening at sunset, a little bird has perched for the night: That little bird, says Luther, above it are the stars and deep Heaven of worlds; yet it has folded its little wings; gone trustfully to rest there as in its home: the Maker of it has given it too a home!— —Neither are mirthful turns wanting: there is a great free human heart in this man. The common speech of him has a rugged nobleness, idiomatic, expressive, genuine; gleams here and there with beautiful poetic tints. One feels him to be a great brother man. His love of Music, indeed, is not this, as it were, the summary of all these affections in him? Many a wild unutterability he spoke forth from him in the tones of his flute. The Devils fled from his flute, he says. Death-defiance on the one hand, and such love of music on the other: I could call these the two opposite poles of a great soul; between these two all great things had room.

Luther's face is to me expressive of him; in Kranach's best portraits I find the true Luther. A rude, plebeian face; with its huge crag-like brows and bones, the emblem of rugged energy; at first, almost a repulsive face. Yet in the eyes especially there is a wild silent sorrow; an unnameable melancholy, the element of all gentle and fine affections; giving to the rest the true stamp of nobleness. Laughter was in this Luther, as we said; but tears also were there. Tears also were appointed him; tears and hard toil. The basis of his life was Sadness, Earnestness. In his latter days, after all triumphs and victories, he expresses himself heartily weary of living; he considers that God alone

can and will regulate the course things are taking, and that perhaps
the Day of Judgment is not far. As for him, he longs for one thing:
that God would release him from his labour, and let him depart and
be at rest. They understand little of the man who cite this in *dis*credit
of him!—I will call this Luther a true Great Man; great in intellect,
in courage, affection and integrity; one of our most loveable and
precious men. Great, not as a hewn obelisk; but as an Alpine mountain,—so simple, honest, spontaneous, not setting up to be great at
all; there for quite another purpose than being great! Ah yes, unsub-
duable granite, piercing far and wide into the Heavens;—yet in the
clefts of it fountains, green beautiful valleys with flowers! A right
Spiritual Hero and Prophet; once more, a true Son of Nature and
Fact, for whom these centuries, and many that are to come yet, will
be thankful to Heaven.

The most interesting phasis which the Reformation anywhere
assumes, especially for us English, is that of Puritanism. In Luther's
own country, Protestantism soon dwindled into a rather barren affair:
not a religion or faith, but rather now a theological jangling of
argument, the proper seat of it not the heart; the essence of it sceptical contention: which indeed has jangled more and more, down to
Voltairism itself,—through Gustavus-Adolphus contentions onward
to French-Revolution ones! But in our Island there arose a Puritanism, which even got itself established as a Presbyterianism and National Church among the Scotch; which came forth as a real business
of the heart; and has produced in the world very notable fruit. In
some senses, one may say it is the only phasis of Protestantism that
ever got to the rank of being a Faith, a true heart-communication
with Heaven, and of exhibiting itself in History as such. We must
spare a few words for Knox; himself a brave and remarkable man; but
still more important as Chief Priest and Founder, which one may
consider him to be, of the Faith that became Scotland's, New
England's, Oliver Cromwell's. History will have something to say
about this, for some time to come!
We may censure Puritanism as we please; and no one of us, I
suppose, but would find it a very rough defective thing. But we, and
all men, may understand that it was a genuine thing; for Nature has
adopted it, and it has grown, and grows. I say sometimes, that all

goes by wager of battle in this world; that *strength*, well understood, is the measure of all worth. Give a thing time; if it can succeed, it is a right thing. Look now at American Saxondom; and at that little Fact of the sailing of the Mayflower, two hundred years ago, from Delft Haven in Holland! Were we of open sense as the Greeks were, we had found a Poem here; one of Nature's own Poems, such as she writes in broad facts over great continents. For it was properly the beginning of America: there were straggling settlers in America before, some material as of a body was there; but the soul of it was first this. These poor men, driven out of their own country, not able well to live in Holland, determine on settling in the New World. Black untamed forests are there, and wild savage creatures; but not so cruel as Star-chamber hangmen. They thought the Earth would yield them food, if they tilled honestly; the everlasting Heaven would stretch, there too, overhead; they should be left in peace, to prepare for Eternity by living well in this world of Time; worshipping in what they thought the true, not the idolatrous way. They clubbed their small means together; hired a ship, the little ship Mayflower, and made ready to set sail. In *Neal's History of the Puritans*[1] is an account of the ceremony of their departure: solemnity, we might call it rather, for it was a real act of worship. Their minister went down with them to the beach, and their brethren whom they were to leave behind; all joined in solemn prayer, That God would have pity on His poor children, and *go* with them into that waste wilderness, for He also had made that, He was there also as well as here.—Hah! These men, I think, had a work! The weak thing, weaker than a child, becomes strong one day, if it be a true thing. Puritanism was only despicable, laughable then; but nobody can manage to laugh at it now. Puritanism has got weapons and sinews; it has fire-arms, war-navies; it has cunning in its ten fingers, strength in its right arm: it can steer ships, fell forests, remove mountains;—it is one of the strongest things under this sun at present!

In the history of Scotland too, I can find properly but one epoch: we may say, it contains nothing of world-interest at all but this Reformation by Knox. A poor barren country, full of continual broils, dissensions, massacrings; a people in the last state of rudeness and

[1] Neal (London, 1755), i. 490.

destitution, little better perhaps than Ireland at this day. Hungry fierce barons, not so much as able to form any arrangement with each other *how to divide* what they fleeced from these poor drudges; but obliged, as the Columbian Republics are at this day, to make of every alteration a revolution; no way of changing a ministry but by hanging the old ministers on gibbets: this is a historical spectacle of no very singular significance! 'Bravery' enough, I doubt not; fierce fighting in abundance: but not braver or fiercer than that of their old Scandinavian Sea-king ancestors; *whose* exploits we have not found worth dwelling on! It is a country as yet without a soul; nothing developed in it but what is rude, external, semi-animal. And now at the Reformation, the internal life is kindled, as it were, under the ribs of this outward material death. A cause, the noblest of causes kindles itself, like a beacon set on high; high as Heaven, yet attainable from Earth;—whereby the meanest man becomes not a Citizen only, but a Member of Christ's visible Church; a veritable Hero, if he prove a true man!

Well; this is what I mean by a whole 'nation of heroes;' a *believing* nation. There needs not a great soul to make a hero; there needs a god-created soul which will be true to its origin; that will be a great soul! The like has been seen, we find. The like will be again seen, under wider forms than the Presbyterian: there can be no lasting good done till then.—Impossible! say some. Possible? Has it not *been*, in this world, as a practised fact? Did Hero-worship fail in Knox's case? Or are we made of other clay now? Did the Westminster Confession of Faith add some new property to the soul of man? God made the soul of man. He did not doom any soul of man to live as a Hypothesis and Hearsay, in a world filled with such, and with the fatal work and fruit of such!— —

But to return: This that Knox did for his Nation, I say, we may really call a resurrection as from death. It was not a smooth business; but it was welcome surely, and cheap at that price, had it been far rougher. On the whole, cheap at any price;—as life is. The people began to *live*: they needed first of all to do that, at what cost and costs soever. Scotch Literature and Thought, Scotch Industry; James Watt, David Hume, Walter Scott, Robert Burns: I find Knox and the Reformation acting in the heart's core of every one of these persons and phenomena; I find that without the Reformation they would not have been. Or what of Scotland? The Puritanism of Scotland became that of England, of New England. A tumult in the High Church of Edinburgh spread into a universal battle and struggle over all these realms;—there came out, after fifty years struggling, what we all call the 'Glorious Revolution,' a Habeas-Corpus Act, Free Parliaments, and much else!—Alas, is it not too true what we said, That many men in the van do always, like Russian soldiers, march into the ditch of Schweidnitz, and fill it up with their dead bodies, that the rear may pass over them dry-shod, and gain the honour? How many earnest rugged Cromwells, Knoxes, poor Peasant Covenanters, wrestling, battling for very life, in rough miry places, have to struggle, and suffer, and fall, greatly censured, bemired,—before a beautiful Revolution of Eighty-eight can step over them in official pumps and silk-stockings, with universal three-times-three!

It seems to me hard measure that this Scottish man, now after three hundred years, should have to plead like a culprit before the world; intrinsically for having been, in such way as it was then possible to be, the bravest of all Scotchmen! Had he been a poor Half-and-half, he could have crouched into the corner, like so many others; Scotland had not been delivered; and Knox had been without blame. He is the one Scotchman to whom, of all others, his country and the world owe a debt. He has to plead that Scotland would forgive him for having been worth to it any million 'unblameable' Scotchmen that need no forgiveness! He bared his breast to the battle; had to row in French galleys, wander forlorn in exile, in clouds and storms; was censured, shot at through his windows; had a right sore fighting life: if this world were his place of recompense, he had made but a bad venture of it. I cannot apologize for Knox. To him it is very indifferent, these two hundred and fifty years or more, what men say of him. But we, having got above all those details of his battle, and living now in clearness on the fruits of his victory, we for our own sake ought to look through the rumours and controversies enveloping the man, into the man himself.

For one thing, I will remark that this post of Prophet to his Nation was not of his seeking; Knox had lived forty years quietly obscure, before he became conspicuous. He was the son of poor parents; had got a college-education; become a Priest; adopted the Reformation, and seemed well content to guide his own steps by the light of it, nowise unduly intruding it on others. He had lived as Tutor in gentlemen's families; preaching when any body of persons wished to hear his doctrine: resolute he to walk by the truth, and speak the truth when called to do it; not ambitious of more; not fancying himself capable of more. In this entirely obscure way he had reached the age of forty; was with the small body of Reformers who were standing siege in St. Andrew's Castle,—when one day in their chapel, the Preacher after finishing his exhortation to these fighters in the forlorn hope, said suddenly, That there ought to be other speakers, that all men who had a priest's heart and gift in them ought now to speak;—which gifts and heart one of their own number, John Knox the name of him, had: Had he not? said the Preacher, appealing to all the audience: What then is *his* duty? The people answered affirmatively; it was a criminal forsaking of his post, if such a man held the word that was in him silent. Poor Knox was obliged to stand up; he attempted to reply; he could say no word;—burst into a flood of tears, and ran out. It is worth remembering, that scene. He was in grievous trouble for some days. He felt what a small faculty was his for this great work. He felt what a baptism he was called to be baptized withal. He 'burst into tears.'

Our primary characteristic of a Hero, that he is sincere, applies emphatically to Knox. It is not denied anywhere that this, whatever might be his other qualities or faults, is among the truest of men. With a singular instinct he holds to the truth and fact; the truth alone is there for him, the rest a mere shadow and deceptive nonentity. However feeble, forlorn the reality may seem, on that and that only *can* he take his stand. In the Galleys of the River Loire, whither Knox and the others, after their Castle of St. Andrew's was taken, had been sent as Galley-slaves,—some officer or priest, one day, presented them an Image of the Virgin Mother, requiring that they, the blasphemous heretics, should do it reverence. Mother? Mother of God? said Knox, when the turn came to him: This is no Mother of God: this is "a *pented bredd*,"—a piece of wood, I tell you, with paint on it! She is fitter for swimming, I think, than for being worshipped, added Knox: and flung the thing into the river. It was not very cheap jesting there:

but come of it what might, this thing to Knox was and must continue nothing other than the real truth; it was a *pented bredd:* worship it he would not. He told his fellow-prisoners, in this darkest time, to be of courage; the Cause they had was the true one, and must and would prosper; the whole world could not put it down. Reality is of God's making; it is alone strong. How many *pented bredds,* pretending to be real, are fitter to swim than to be worshipped!—This Knox cannot live but by fact: he clings to reality as the shipwrecked sailor to the cliff. He is an instance to us how a man, by sincerity itself, becomes heroic: it is the grand gift he has. We find in Knox a good honest intellectual talent, no transcendent one;—a narrow, inconsiderable man, as compared with Luther: but in heartfelt instinctive adherence to truth, in *sincerity,* as we say, he has no superior; nay, one might ask, What equal he has? The heart of him is of the true Prophet cast. "He lies there," said the Earl of Morton at his grave, "who never feared the face of man." He resembles, more than any of the moderns, an Old-Hebrew Prophet. The same inflexibility, intolerance, rigid narrow-looking adherence to God's truth, stern rebuke in the name of God to all that forsake truth: an Old-Hebrew Prophet in the guise of an Edinburgh Minister of the Sixteenth Century. We are to take him for that; not require him to be other.

Knox's conduct to Queen Mary, the harsh visits he used to make in her own palace, to reprove her there, have been much commented upon. Such cruelty, such coarseness fills us with indignation. On reading the actual narrative of the business, what Knox said, and what Knox meant, I must say one's tragic feeling is rather disappointed. They are not so coarse, these speeches; they seem to me about as fine as the circumstances would permit! Knox was not there to do the courtier; he came on another errand. Whoever, reading these colloquies of his with the Queen, thinks they are vulgar insolences of a plebeian priest to a delicate high lady, mistakes the purport and essence of them altogether. It was unfortunately not possible to be polite with the Queen of Scotland, unless one proved untrue to the Nation and Cause of Scotland. A man who did not wish to see the land of his birth made a hunting-field for intriguing ambitious Guises, and the Cause of God trampled under foot of Falsehoods, Formulas and the Devil's Cause, had no method of making himself agreeable!

"Better that women weep," said Morton, "than that bearded men be forced to weep." Knox was the constitutional opposition-party in Scotland: the Nobles of the country, called by their station to take that post, were not found in it; Knox had to go, or no one. The hapless Queen;—but the still more hapless Country, if *she* were made happy! Mary herself was not without sharpness enough, among her other qualities: "Who are you," said she once, "that presume to school the nobles and sovereign of this realm?"—"Madam, a subject born within the same," answered he. Reasonably answered! If the 'subject' have truth to speak, it is not the 'subject's' footing that will fail him here.—

We blame Knox for his intolerance. Well, surely it is good that each of us be as tolerant as possible. Yet, at bottom, after all the talk there is and has been about it, what is tolerance? Tolerance has to tolerate the *un*essential; and to see well what that is. Tolerance has to be noble, measured, just in its very wrath, when it can tolerate no longer. But, on the whole, we are not altogether here to tolerate! We are here to resist, to control and vanquish withal. We do not 'tolerate' Falsehoods, Thieveries, Iniquities, when they fasten on us; we say to them, Thou art false, thou art not tolerable! We are here to extinguish Falsehoods, and put an end to them, in some wise way! I will not quarrel so much with the way; the doing of the thing is our great concern. In this sense, Knox was, full surely, intolerant.

A man sent to row in French Galleys, and such like, for teaching the Truth in his own land, cannot always be in the mildest humour! I am not prepared to say that Knox had a soft temper; nor do I know that he had what we call an ill temper. An ill nature he decidedly had not. Kind honest affections dwelt in the much-enduring, hard-worn, ever-battling man. That he *could* rebuke Queens, and had such weight among those proud turbulent Nobles, proud enough whatever else they were; and could maintain to the end a kind of virtual Presidency and Sovereignty in that wild realm, he who was only 'a subject born within the same:' this of itself will prove to us that he was found, close at hand, to be no mean acrid man; but at heart, a healthful, strong, sagacious man. Such alone can bear rule in that kind. They blame him for pulling down cathedrals, and so forth, as if he were a seditious rioting demagogue: precisely the reverse is seen to be the fact, in regard to cathedrals and the rest of it, if we examine! Knox wanted no pulling down of stone edifices; he wanted leprosy and darkness to be thrown out of the lives of men. Tumult was not his element; it was the tragic feature of his life that he was forced to dwell so much in that. Every such man is the born enemy of Disorder; hates to be in it: but what then? Smooth Falsehood is not Order; it is the general sumtotal of *Dis*order. Order is *Truth,*—each thing standing on the basis that belongs to it: Order and Falsehood cannot subsist together.

Withal, unexpectedly enough, this Knox has a vein of drollery in him; which I like much, in combination with his other qualities. He has a true eye for the ridiculous. His *History*, with its rough earnestness, is curiously enlivened with this. When the two Prelates, entering Glasgow Cathedral, quarrel about precedence; march rapidly up, take to hustling one another, twitching one another's rochets, and at last flourishing their crosiers like quarter-staves, it is a great sight for him every way! Not mockery, scorn, bitterness alone; though there is enough of that too. But a true, loving, illuminating laugh mounts up over the earnest visage; not a loud laugh; you would say, a laugh in the *eyes* most of all. An honesthearted, brotherly man; brother to the high, brother also to the low; sincere in his sympathy with both. He had his pipe of Bourdeaux too, we find, in that old Edinburgh house of his; a cheery social man, with faces that loved him! They go far wrong who think this Knox was a gloomy, spasmodic, shrieking fanatic. Not at all: he is one of the solidest of men. Practical, cautious-hopeful, patient; a most shrewd, observing, quietly discerning man. In fact, he has very much the type of character we assign to the Scotch at present: a certain sardonic taciturnity is in him; insight enough; and a stouter heart than he himself knows of. He has the power of holding his peace over many things which do not vitally concern him,—"They? what are they?" But the thing which does vitally concern him, that thing he will speak of; and in a tone the whole world shall be made to hear: all the more emphatic for his long silence.

This Prophet of the Scotch is to me no hateful man!—He had a sore fight of an existence; wrestling with Popes and Principalities; in defeat, contention, life-long struggle; rowing as a galley-slave, wandering as an exile. A sore fight: but he won it. "Have you hope?" they asked him in his last moment, when he could no longer speak. He lifted his finger, 'pointed upwards with his finger,' and so died. Honour to him. His works have not died. The letter of his work dies, as of all men's; but the spirit of it never.

One word more as to the letter of Knox's work. The unforgiveable offence in him is, that he wished to set up Priests over the head of Kings. In other words, he strove to make the Government of Scotland a *Theocracy*. This indeed is properly the sum of his offences; the essential sin, for which what pardon can there be? It is most true, he did, at bottom, consciously or unconsciously, mean a Theocracy, or Government of God. He did mean that Kings and Prime Ministers, and all manner of persons, in public or private, diplomatising or whatever else they might be doing, should walk according to the Gospel of Christ, and understand that this was their Law, supreme over all laws. He hoped once to see such a thing realised; and the Petition, *Thy Kingdom come*, no longer an empty word. He was sore grieved when he saw greedy worldly Barons clutch hold of the Church's property; when he expostulated that it was not secular property, that it was spiritual property, and should be turned to *true* churchly uses, education, schools, worship;—and the Regent Murray had to answer, with a shrug of the shoulders, "It is a devout imagination!" This was Knox's scheme of right and truth; this he zealously endeavoured after, to realise it. If we think his scheme of truth was too narrow, was not true; we may rejoice that he could not realise it; that it remained, after two centuries of effort, unrealisable, and is a 'devout imagination' still. But how shall we blame *him* for struggling to realise it? Theocracy, Government of God, is precisely the thing to be struggled for! All Prophets, zealous Priests, are there for that purpose. Hildebrand wished a Theocracy; Cromwell wished it, fought for it; Mahomet attained it. Nay, is it not what all zealous men, whether called Priests, Prophets, or whatsoever else called, do essentially wish, and must wish? That right and truth, or God's Law, reign supreme among men, this is the Heavenly Ideal (well-named in Knox's time, and nameable in all times, a revealed 'Will of God'); towards which the Reformer will insist that all be more and more approximated. All true Reformers, as I said, are by the nature of them Priests, and strive for a Theocracy.

How far such Ideals can ever be introduced into Practice, and at what point our impatience with their non-introduction ought to begin, is always a question. I think we may say safely, Let them introduce themselves as far as they can contrive to do it! If they are the true faith of men, all men ought to be more or less impatient always where they are not found introduced. There will never be wanting Regent-Murrays enough to shrug their shoulders, and say, "A devout imagination!" We will praise the Hero-Priest rather, who does what is in *him* to bring them in; and wears out, in toil, calumny, contradiction, a noble life, to make a God's Kingdom of this Earth. The Earth will not become too godlike!

LECTURE V.

[Tuesday, 19th May, 1840.]

THE HERO AS MAN OF LETTERS. JOHNSON, ROUSSEAU, BURNS.

HERO-GODS, Prophets, Poets, Priests are forms of Heroism that belong to the old ages, make their appearance in the remotest times; some of them have ceased to be possible long since, and cannot any more shew themselves in this world. The Hero as *Man of Letters*, again, of which class we are to speak today, is altogether a product of these new ages; and so long as the wondrous art of *Writing*, or of Ready-writing which we call *Printing*, subsists, he may be expected to continue, as one of the main forms of Heroism for all future ages. He is, in various respects, a very singular phenomenon.

He is new, I say; he has hardly lasted above a century in the world yet. Never, till about a hundred years ago, was there seen any figure of a Great Soul living apart in that anomalous manner; endeavouring to speak forth the inspiration that was in him by Printed Books, and find place and subsistence by what the world would please to give him for doing that. Much had been sold and bought, and left to make its own bargain in the marketplace; but the inspired wisdom of a Heroic Soul never till then, in that naked manner. He, with his copy-rights and copy-wrongs, in his squalid garret, in his rusty coat; ruling (for this is what he does), from his grave, after death, whole nations and generations who would, or would not, give him bread while living,—is a rather curious spectacle! Few shapes of Heroism can be more unexpected.

Alas, the Hero from of old has had to cramp himself into strange shapes: the world knows not well at any time what to do with him, so foreign is his aspect in the world! It seemed absurd to us that men, in their rude admiration, should take some wise great Odin for a god, and worship him as such; some wise great Mahomet for one god-inspired, and religiously follow his Law for twelve centuries: but that a wise great Johnson, a Burns, a Rousseau, should be taken for some idle nondescript, extant in the world to amuse idleness, and have a few coins and applauses thrown him, that he might live thereby; *this* perhaps, as before hinted, will one day seem a still absurder phasis of things!—Meanwhile, since it is the spiritual always that determines the material, this same Man-of-Letters Hero must be regarded as our most important modern person. He, such as he may be, is the soul of all. What he teaches, the whole world will do and make. The world's manner of dealing with him is the most significant feature of the world's general position. Looking well at his life, we may get a glance as deep as is readily possible for us into the life of those singular centuries which have produced him, in which we ourselves live and work.

There are genuine Men of Letters, and not genuine; as in every kind there is a genuine and a spurious. If *Hero* be taken to mean genuine, then I say the Hero as Man of Letters will be found discharging a function for us which is ever honourable, ever the highest; and was once well known to be the highest. He is uttering forth, in such way as he has, the inspired soul of him; all that a man, in any case, can do. I say *inspired;* for what we call 'originality,' 'sincerity,' 'genius,' the heroic quality we have no good name for, signifies that. The Hero is he who lives in the inward sphere of things, in the True, Divine and Eternal, which exists always, unseen to most, under the Temporary, Trivial: his being is in that; he declares that abroad, by act or speech as it may be, in declaring himself abroad. His life, as we said before, is a piece of the everlasting heart of Nature herself: all men's life is,—but the weak many know not the fact, and are untrue to it, in most times; the strong few are strong, heroic, perennial, because it cannot be hidden from them. The Man of Letters, like every Hero, is there to proclaim this in such sort as he can. Intrinsically it is the same function which the old generations named a man Prophet, Priest, Divinity for doing; which all manner of Heroes, by speech or by act, are sent into the world to do.

Fichte the German Philosopher delivered, some forty years ago at Erlangen, a highly remarkable Course of Lectures on this subject: '*Ueber das Wesen des Gelehrten*, On the Nature of the Literary Man.' Fichte, in conformity with the Transcendental Philosophy, of which he was a distinguished teacher, declares first, That all things which we see or work with in this Earth, especially we ourselves and all persons, are as a kind of vesture or sensuous Appearance; that under all there lies, as the essence of them, what he calls the 'Divine Idea of the World;' this is the Reality which 'lies at the bottom of all Appearance.' To the mass of men no such Divine Idea is recognisable in the world; they live merely, says Fichte, among the superficialities, practicalities and shews of the world, not dreaming that there is anything divine under them. But the Man of Letters is sent hither specially that he may discern for himself, and make manifest to us, this same Divine Idea: in every new generation it will manifest itself in a new dialect; and he is there for the purpose of doing that. Such is Fichte's phraseology; with which we need not quarrel. It is his way of naming what I here, by other words, am striving imperfectly to name; what there is at present no name for: The unspeakable Divine Significance, full of splendour, of wonder and terror, that lies in the being of every man, of every thing,—the Presence of the God who made every man and thing. Mahomet taught this in his dialect; Odin in his: it is the thing which all thinking hearts, in one dialect or another, are here to teach. Fichte calls the Man of Letters, therefore, a Prophet, or as he prefers to phrase it, a Priest, continually unfolding the Godlike to men: Men of Letters are a perpetual Priesthood, from age to age, teaching all men that a God is still present in their life; that all 'Appearance,' whatsoever we see in the world, is but as a vesture for the 'Divine Idea of the World,' for 'that which lies at the bottom of Appearance.' In the true Literary Man there is thus ever, acknowledged or not by the world, a sacredness: he is the light of the world; the world's Priest;—guiding it, like a sacred Pillar of Fire, in its dark pilgrimage through the waste of Time. Fichte discriminates with sharp zeal the *true* Literary Man, what we here call the *Hero* as Man of Letters, from multitudes of false unheroic. Whoever lives not wholly in this Divine Idea, or living partially in it, struggles not, as for the one good, to live wholly in it,—he is, let him live where else he like, in what pomps and prosperities he like, no Literary Man; he is, says Fichte, a 'Bungler, *Stümper*.' Or at best, if he belong to the prosaic provinces, he may be a 'Hodman;' Fichte even calls him elsewhere a 'Nonentity,' and has in short no mercy for him, no wish that *he* should continue happy among us! This is Fichte's notion of the Man of Letters. It means, in its own form, precisely what we here mean.

In this point of view, I consider that, for the last hundred years, by far the notablest of all Literary Men is Fichte's countryman, Goethe. To that man too, in a strange way, there was given what we may call a life in the Divine Idea of the World; vision of the inward divine mystery: and strangely, out of his Books, the world rises imaged once more as godlike, the workmanship and temple of a God. Illuminated all, not in fierce impure fire-splendour as of Mahomet, but in mild celestial radiance;—really a Prophecy in these most unprophetic times; to my mind, by far the greatest, though one of the quietest, among all the great things that have come to pass in them! Our chosen specimen of the Hero as Literary Man would be this Goethe. And it were a very pleasant plan for me here, to discourse of his heroism: for I consider him to be a true Hero; heroic in what he said and did, and perhaps still more in what he did not say and did not do; to me a noble spectacle: a great heroic ancient man, speaking and keeping silence as an ancient Hero, in the guise of a most modern, high-bred, high-cultivated Man of Letters! We have had no such spectacle; no man capable of affording such, for the last hundred and fifty years. But at present, such is the general state of knowledge about Goethe, it were worse than useless to attempt speaking of him in this case. Speak as I might, Goethe, to the great majority of you, would remain problematic, vague; no impression but a false one could be realised. Him we must leave to future times. Johnson, Burns, Rousseau, three great figures from a prior time, from a far inferior state of circumstances, will suit us better here. Three men of the Eighteenth Century; the conditions of their life far more resemble what those of ours still are in England, than what Goethe's in Germany were. Alas, these men did not conquer like him; they fought bravely, and fell. They were not heroic bringers of the light, but heroic seekers of it. They lived under galling conditions; struggling as under mountains of impediment, and could not unfold themselves into clearness, or victorious interpretation of that 'Divine Idea.' It is rather the *Tombs* of three Literary Heroes that I have to shew you. There are the monumental heaps, under which three spiritual giants lie buried. Very mournful, but also great and full of interest for us. We will linger by them for a while.

Complaint is often made, in these times, of what we call the disorganised condition of society: how ill many arranged forces of society fulfil their work; how many powerful forces are seen working in a wasteful, chaotic, altogether unarranged manner. It is too just a complaint, as we all know. But perhaps if we look at this of Books and the Writers of Books, we shall find here, as it were, the summary of all other disorganization;—a sort of *heart*, from which and to which all other confusion circulates in the world! Considering what Book-writers do in the world, and what the world does with Book-writers, I should say, It is the most anomalous thing the world at present has to shew.—We should get into a sea far beyond sounding, did we attempt to give account of this: but we must glance at it for the sake of our subject. The worst element in the life of these three Literary Heroes was, that they found their business and position such a chaos. On the beaten road there is tolerable travelling; but it is sore work, and many have to perish, fashioning a path through the impassable!

Our pious Fathers, feeling well what importance lay in the speaking of man to men, founded churches, made endowments, regulations; everywhere in the civilised world there is a Pulpit, environed with all manner of complex dignified appurtenances and furtherances, that therefrom a man with the tongue may, to best advantage, address his fellow-men. They felt that this was the most important thing; that without this there was no good thing. It is a right pious work, that of theirs; beautiful to behold! But now with the art of Writing, with the art of Printing, a total change has come over that business. The Writer of a Book, is not he a Preacher preaching, not to this parish or that, on this day or that, but to all men in all times and places? Surely it is of the last importance that *he* do his work right, whoever do it wrong;—that the *eye* report not falsely, for then all the other members are astray! Well; how he may do his work, whether he do it right or wrong, or do it at all, is a point which no man in the world has taken the pains to think of. To a certain shopkeeper, trying to get some money for his books, if lucky, he is of some importance; to no other man of any. Whence he came, whither he is bound, by what ways he arrived, by what he might be furthered on his course, no one asks. He is an accident in society. He wanders like a wild Ishmaelite, in a world of which he is as the spiritual light, either the guidance or the misguidance!

Certainly the Art of Writing is the most miraculous of all things man has devised. Odin's *Runes* were the first form of the work of a Hero; *Books*, written words, are still miraculous *Runes*, the latest form! In Books lies the *soul* of the whole Past Time; the articulate audible voice of the Past, when the body and material substance of it has altogether vanished like a dream. Mighty fleets and armies, harbours and arsenals, vast cities, high-domed, many-engined,—they are precious, great: but what do they become? Agamemnon, the many Agamemnons, Pericleses, and their Greece; all is gone now to some ruined fragments, dumb mournful wrecks and blocks: but the Books of Greece! There Greece, to every thinker, still very literally lives; can be called up again into life. No magic *Rune* is stranger than a Book. All that Mankind has done, thought, gained or been: it is lying as in magic preservation in the pages of Books. They are the chosen possession of men.

Do not Books still accomplish *miracles*, as *Runes* were fabled to do? They persuade men. Not the wretchedest circulating-library novel, which foolish girls thumb and con in remote villages, but will help to regulate the actual practical weddings and households of those foolish girls. So 'Celia' felt, so 'Clifford' acted: the foolish Theorem of Life, stamped into those young brains, comes out as a solid Practice one day. Consider whether any *Rune* in the wildest imagination of Mythologist ever did such wonders as, on the actual firm Earth, some Books have done! What built St. Paul's Cathedral? Look at the heart of the matter, it was that divine HEBREW Book,— the word partly of the man Moses, an outlaw tending his Midianitish herds, four thousand years ago, in the wildernesses of Sinai! It is the strangest of things, yet nothing is truer. With the art of Writing, of which Printing is a simple, an inevitable and comparatively insignificant corollary, the true reign of miracles for mankind commenced. It related, with a wondrous new contiguity and perpetual closeness, the Past and Distant with the Present in time and place; all times and all places with this our actual Here and Now. All things were altered for men; all modes of important work of men: teaching, preaching, governing, and all else.

To look at Teaching, for instance. Universities are a notable, respectable product of the modern ages. Their existence too is modified, to the very basis of it, by the existence of Books. Universities arose while there were yet no Books procurable; while a man, for a single Book, had to give an estate of land. That, in those circumstances, when a man had some knowledge to communicate, he should do it by gathering the learners round him, face to face, was a necessity for him. If you wanted to know what Abelard knew, you must go and listen to Abelard. Thousands, as many as thirty thousand, went to hear Abelard and that metaphysical theology of his. And now for any other teacher who had also something of his own to teach, there was a great convenience opened: so many thousands eager to learn were already assembled yonder; of all places the best place for him was that. For any third teacher it was better still; and grew ever the better, the more teachers there came. It only needed now that the King took notice of this new phenomenon; combined or agglomerated the various schools into one school; gave it edifices, privileges, encouragements, and named it *Universitas*, or School of all Sciences: the University of Paris, in its essential characters, was there. The model of all subsequent Universities; which down even to these days, for six centuries now, have gone on to found themselves. Such, I conceive, was the origin of Universities.

It is clear, however, that with this simple circumstance, facility of getting Books, the whole conditions of the business from top to bottom were changed. Once invent Printing, you metamorphosed all Universities, or superseded them! The teacher needed not now to gather men personally round him, that he might *speak* to them what he knew: print it in a Book, and all learners far and wide, for a trifle, had it each at his own fireside, much more effectually to learn it!— Doubtless there is still peculiar virtue in Speech; even writers of Books may still, in some circumstances, find it convenient to speak also,— witness our present meeting here! There is, one would say, and must ever remain while man has a tongue, a distinct province for Speech as well as for Writing and Printing. In regard to all things this must remain; to Universities among others. But the limits of the two have nowhere yet been pointed out, ascertained; much less put in practice: the University which would completely take in that great new fact, of the existence of Printed Books, and stand on a clear footing for the Nineteenth Century as the Paris one did for the Thirteenth, has not yet come into existence. If we think of it, all that a University, or final highest School can do for us, is still but what the first School began doing,—teach us to *read*. We learn to *read*, in various languages, in various sciences; we learn the alphabet and letters of all manner of Books. But the place where we are to get knowledge, even theoretic knowledge, is the Books themselves! It depends on what we read, after all manner of Professors have done their best for us. The true University of these days is a Collection of Books.

But to the Church itself, as I hinted already, all is changed, in its preaching, in its working, by the introduction of Books. The Church is the working recognised Union of our Priests or Prophets, of those who by wise teaching guide the souls of men. While there was no Writing, even while there was no Easy-writing, or *Printing*, the preaching of the voice was the natural sole method of performing this. But now with Books!—He that can write a true Book, to persuade England, is not he the Bishop and Archbishop, the Primate of England and of all England? I many a time say, the writers of Newspapers, Pamphlets, Poems, Books, these *are* the real working effective Church of a modern country. Nay, not only our preaching, but even our worship, is not it too accomplished by means of Printed Books? The noble sentiment which a gifted soul has clothed for us in melodious words, which brings melody into our hearts,—is not this essentially, if we will understand it, of the nature of worship? There are many, in all countries, who, in this confused time, have no other method of worship. He who, in any way, shews us better than we knew before that a lily of the fields is beautiful, does he not shew it us as an effluence of the Fountain of all Beauty; as the *handwriting*, made visible there, of the great Maker of the Universe? He has sung for us, made us sing with him, a little verse of a sacred Psalm. Essentially so. How much more he who sings, who says, or in any way brings home to our heart the noble doings, feelings, darings and endurances of a brother man! He has verily touched our hearts as with a live coal *from the altar*. Perhaps there is no worship more authentic. Literature, so far as it is Literature, is an 'apocalypse of Nature,' a revealing of the 'open secret.' It may well enough be named, in Fichte's style, a 'continuous revelation' of the Godlike in the Terrestrial and Common. The Godlike does ever, in very truth, endure there; is brought out, now in this dialect, now in that, with various degrees of clearness: all true gifted Singers and Speakers are, consciously or unconsciously, doing so. The dark stormful indignation of a Byron, so wayward and perverse, may have touches of it; nay, the withered mockery of a French sceptic,—his mockery of the False, a love and worship of the True. How much more the sphere-harmony of a Shakspeare, of a Goethe; the cathedral-music of a Milton! They are something, too, those humble genuine lark-notes of a Burns,—skylark, starting from the humble furrow, far overhead into the blue depths, and singing to us so genuinely there! For all true singing is of the nature of worship; as indeed all true *working* may be said to be,—whereof such *singing* is but the record, and fit melodious representation, to us. Fragments of a real 'Church Liturgy' and 'body of Homilies,' strangely disguised from the common eye, are to be found weltering in that huge froth-ocean of Printed Speech we loosely call Literature! Books are our Church too.

Or turning now to the Government of men. Witenagemote, old Parliament, was a great thing. The affairs of the nation were there deliberated and decided; what we were to *do* as a nation. But does not, though the name Parliament subsists, the parliamentary debate go on now, everywhere and at all times, in a far more comprehensive way, *out* of Parliament altogether? Burke said there were Three Estates in Parliament; but, in the Reporters' Gallery yonder, there sat a *Fourth Estate* more important far than they all. It is not a figure of speech, or a witty saying; it is a literal fact,—very momentous to us in these times. Literature is our Parliament too. Printing, which comes necessarily out of Writing, I say often, is equivalent to Democracy: invent Writing, Democracy is inevitable. Writing brings Printing; brings universal every-day extempore Printing, as we see at present. Whoever can speak, speaking now to the whole nation, becomes a power, a branch of government, with inalienable weight in law-making, in all acts of authority. It matters not what rank he has, what revenues or garnitures: the requisite thing is, that he have a tongue which others will listen to; this and nothing more is requisite.

The nation is governed by all that has tongue in the nation: Democracy is virtually *there*. Add only that whatsoever power exists will have itself by and by organised; working secretly under bandages, obscurations, obstructions, it will never rest till it get to work free, unincumbered, visible to all. Democracy virtually extant will insist on becoming palpably extant.—

On all sides, are we not driven to the conclusion that, of the things which man can do or make here below, by far the most momentous, wonderful and worthy are the things we call Books! Those poor bits of rag-paper with black ink on them;—from the Daily Newspaper to the sacred Hebrew BOOK, what have they not done, what are they not doing!—For indeed, whatever be the outward form of the thing (bits of paper, as we say, and black ink), is it not verily, at bottom, the highest act of man's faculty that produces a Book? It is the *Thought* of man; the true thaumaturgic virtue; by which man works all things whatsoever. All that he does, and brings to pass, is the vesture of a Thought. This London City, with all its houses, palaces, steamengines, cathedrals, and huge immeasurable traffic and tumult, what is it but a Thought, but millions of Thoughts made into One;—a huge immeasurable Spirit of a THOUGHT, embodied in brick, in iron, smoke, dust, Palaces, Parliaments, Hackney Coaches, Katherine Docks, and the rest of it! Not a brick was made but some man had to *think* of the making of that brick.—The thing we called 'bits of paper with traces of black ink,' is the *purest* embodiment a Thought of man can have. No wonder it is, in all ways, the activest and noblest.

All this, of the importance and supreme importance of the Man of Letters in modern Society, and how the Press is to such a degree superseding the Pulpit, the Senate, the *Senatus Academicus* and much else, has been admitted for a good while; and recognised often enough, in late times, with a sort of sentimental triumph and wonderment. It seems to me, the Sentimental by and by will have to give place to the Practical. If Men of Letters *are* so incalculably influential, actually performing such work for us from age to age, and even from day to day, then I think we may conclude that Men of Letters will not always wander like unrecognised unregulated Ishmaelites among us! Whatsoever thing, as I said above, has virtual unnoticed power will cast off its wrappages, bandages, and step forth one day with palpably articulated, universally visible power. That one man wear the clothes, and take the wages, of a function which is done by quite another: there can be no profit in this; this is not right, it is wrong. And yet, alas, the *making* of it right,—what a business, for long times to come! Sure enough, this that we call Organisation of the Literary Guild is still a great way off, incumbered with all manner of complexities. If you asked me what were the best possible organisation for the Men of Letters in modern society; the arrangement, of furtherance and regulation, grounded the most accurately on the actual facts of their position and of the world's position,—I should beg to say that the problem far exceeded my faculty! It is not one man's faculty; it is that of many successive men turned earnestly upon it, that will bring out even an approximate solution. What the best arrangement were, none of us could say. But if you ask, Which is the worst? I answer: This which we now have, that Chaos should sit umpire in it; this is the worst. To the best, or any good one, there is yet a long way.

One remark I must not omit, That royal or parliamentary grants of money are by no means the chief thing wanted! To give our Men of Letters stipends, endowments, and all furtherance of cash, will do little towards the business. On the whole, one is weary of hearing about the omnipotence of money. I will say rather that, for a genuine man, it is no evil to be poor; that there ought to be Literary Men poor,—to shew whether they are genuine or not! Mendicant Orders, bodies of good men doomed to *beg*, were instituted in the Christian Church; a most natural and even necessary development of the spirit of Christianity. It was itself founded on Poverty, on Sorrow, Contradiction, Crucifixion, every species of worldly Distress and Degradation. We may say that he who has not known those things, and learned from them the priceless lessons they have to teach, has missed a good opportunity of schooling. To beg, and go barefoot, in coarse woollen cloak with a rope round your loins, and be despised of all the world, was no beautiful business;—nor an honourable one in any eye, till the nobleness of those who did so had made it honoured of some! Begging is not in our course at the present time: but for the rest of it, who will say that a Johnson is not perhaps the better for being poor? It is needful for him, at all rates, to know that outward profit, that success of any kind is *not* the goal he has to aim at. Pride, vanity, ill-conditioned egoism of all sorts, are bred in his heart, as in every heart; need, above all, to be cast out of his heart,—to be, with whatever pangs, torn out of it, cast forth from it, as a thing worthless. Byron, born rich and noble, made out even less than Burns, poor and plebeian. Who knows but, in that same 'best possible organisation' as yet far off, Poverty may still enter as an important element? What if our Men of Letters, men setting up to be Spiritual Heroes, were still *then*, as they now are, a kind of 'involuntary monastic order;' bound still to this same ugly Poverty,—till they had tried what was in it too, till they had learned to make it too do for them! Money, in truth, can do much, but it cannot do all. We must know the province of it, and confine it there; and even spurn it back, when it wishes to get farther.

Besides, were the money-furtherances, the proper season for them, the fit assigner of them, all settled,—how is the Burns to be recognised that merits these? He must pass through the ordeal, and prove himself. *This* ordeal; this wild welter of a chaos which is called Literary Life: this too is a kind of ordeal! There is clear truth in the idea that a struggle from the lower classes of society, towards the upper regions and rewards of society, must ever continue. Strong men are born there, who ought to stand elsewhere than there. The manifold, inextricably complex, universal struggle of these constitutes, and must constitute, what is called the progress of society. For Men of Letters, as for all other sorts of men. How to regulate that struggle? There is the whole question. To leave it as it is, at the mercy of blind Chance; a whirl of distracted atoms, one cancelling the other; one of the thousand arriving saved, nine hundred and ninety-nine lost by the way; your royal Johnson languishing inactive in garrets, or harnessed to the yoke of Printer Cave, your Burns dying brokenhearted as a Gauger, your Rousseau driven into mad exasperation, kindling French Revolutions by his paradoxes: this, as we said, is clearly enough the *worst* regulation. The *best*, alas, is far from us!

And yet there can be no doubt but it is coming; advancing on us, as yet hidden in the bosom of centuries: this is a prophecy one can risk. For so soon as men get to discern the importance of a thing, they do infallibly set about arranging it, facilitating, forwarding it; and rest not till, in some approximate degree, they have accomplished that. I say, of all Priesthoods, Aristocracies, Governing Classes at present extant in the world, there is no class comparable for importance to that Priesthood of the Writers of Books. This is a fact which he who runs may read,—and draw inferences from. "Literature will take care of itself," answered Mr. Pitt, when applied to for some help for Burns. "Yes," adds Mr. Southey, "it will take care of itself; *and of you too*, if you do not look to it!"

The result to individual Men of Letters is not the momentous one; they are but individuals, an infinitesimal fraction of the great body; they can struggle on, and live or else die, as they have been wont. But it deeply concerns the whole society, whether it will set its *light* on high places, to walk thereby; or trample it under foot, and scatter it in all ways of wild waste (not without conflagration), as heretofore! Light is the one thing wanted for the world. Put wisdom in the head of the world, the world will fight its battle victoriously, and be the best world man can make it. I called this anomaly of a disorganic Literary Class the heart of all other anomalies, at once product and parent; some good arrangement for that would be as the *punctum saliens* of a new vitality and just arrangement for all. Already, in some European countries, in France, in Prussia, one traces some beginnings of an arrangement for the Literary Class; indicating the gradual possibility of such. I believe that it is possible; that it will have to be possible.

By far the most interesting fact I hear about the Chinese is one on which we cannot arrive at clearness, but which excites endless curiosity even in the dim state: this namely, that they do attempt to make their Men of Letters their Governors! It would be rash to say, one understood how this was done, or with what degree of success it was done. All such things must be very *un*successful; yet a small degree of success is precious; the very attempt how precious! There does seem to be, all over China, a more or less active search everywhere to discover the men of talent that grow up in the young generation. Schools there are for every one: a foolish sort of training, yet still a sort. The youths who distinguish themselves in the lower school are promoted into favourable stations in the higher, that they may still more distinguish themselves,—forward and forward: it appears to be out of these that the Official Persons, and incipient Governors, are taken. These are they whom they *try* first, whether they can govern or not. And surely with the best hope; for they are the men that have already shewn intellect. Try them, they have not governed or administered as yet; perhaps they cannot; but there is no doubt they *have* some understanding,—without which no man can! Neither is Understanding a *tool*, as we are too apt to figure; 'it is a *hand* which can handle any tool.' Try these men: they are of all others the best worth trying.—Surely there is no kind of government, constitution, revolution, social apparatus or arrangement, that I know of in this world, so promising to one's scientific curiosity as this. The man of intellect at the top of affairs: this is the aim of all constitutions and revolutions, if they have any aim. For the man of true intellect, as I assert and believe always, is the noblehearted man withal, the true, just, humane and valiant man. Get *him* for governor, all is got; fail to get him, though you had Constitutions plentiful as blackberries, and a Parliament in every village, there is nothing yet got!—

These things look strange, truly; and are not such as we commonly speculate upon. But we are fallen into strange times; these things will require to be speculated upon; to be rendered practicable, to be in some way put in practice. These, and many others. On all hands of us, there is the announcement, audible enough, that the old Empire of Routine has ended; that to say a thing has long been, is no reason for its continuing to be. The things which have been are fallen into decay, are fallen into incompetence; large masses of mankind, in every society of our Europe, are no longer capable of living at all by the things which have been. When millions of men can no longer by their utmost exertion gain food for themselves, and 'the third man for thirty-six weeks each year is short of third-rate potatoes,' the things which have been must decidedly prepare to alter themselves!—I will now quit this of the organisation of Men of Letters.

Alas, the evil that pressed heaviest on those Literary Heroes of ours was not the want of organisation for Men of Letters, but a far deeper one; out of which, indeed, this and so many other evils for the Literary Man, and for all men, had, as from their fountain, taken rise. That our Hero as Man of Letters had to travel without highway, companionless, through an inorganic chaos,—and to leave his own life and faculty lying there, as a partial contribution towards *pushing* some highway through it: this, had not his faculty itself been so perverted and paralysed, he might have put up with, might have considered to be but the common lot of Heroes. His fatal misery was the *spiritual paralysis,* so we may name it, of the age in which his life lay; whereby his life too, do what he might, was half-paralysed! The Eighteenth was a *Sceptical* Century; in which little word there is a whole Pandora's Box of miseries. Scepticism means not intellectual Doubt alone, but moral Doubt; all sorts of *in*fidelity, insincerity, spiritual paralysis. Perhaps, in few centuries that one could specify since the world began, was a life of Heroism more difficult for a man. That was not an age of Faith,—an age of Heroes! The very possibility of Heroism had been, as it were, formally abnegated in the minds of all. Heroism was gone forever; Triviality, Formulism and Commonplace were come forever. The 'age of miracles' had been, or perhaps had not been; but it was not any longer. An effete world; wherein Wonder, Greatness, Godhood could not now dwell;—in one word, a godless world!

How mean, dwarfish are their ways of thinking, in this time,—compared not with the Christian Shakspeares and Miltons, but with the old Pagan Skalds, with any species of believing men. The living TREE Igdrasil, with the melodious prophetic waving of its world-wide boughs, deep-rooted as Hela, has died out into the clanking of a World-MACHINE. 'Tree' and 'machine:' contrast these two things. I, for my share, declare the world to be no Machine; I say that it does *not* go by wheel-and-pinion 'motives,' self-interests, checks, balances; that there is something far other in it than the clank of spinning-jennies, and parliamentary majorities; and, on the whole, that it is not a machine at all!—The old Norse Heathen had a truer notion of God's-world than these poor Machine-Sceptics: the old Heathen Norse were *sincere* men. But for these poor Sceptics there was no sincerity, no truth. Half-truth and hearsay was called truth. Truth, for most men, meant plausibility; to be measured by the number of votes you could get. They had lost any notion that sincerity was possible, or of what sincerity was. How many Plausibilities asking, with unaffected surprise and the air of offended virtue, What! am not I sincere? Spiritual Paralysis, I say, nothing left but a Mechanical life, was the characteristic of that century. For the common man, unless happily he stood *below* his century and belonged to another prior one, it was impossible to be a Believer, a Hero; he lay buried, unconscious, under these baleful influences. To the strongest man, only with infinite struggle and confusion was it possible to work himself half-loose; and lead as it were, in an enchanted, most tragical way, a spiritual death-in-life, and be a Half-Hero!

Scepticism is the name we give to all this; as the chief symptom, as the chief origin of all this. Concerning which so much were to be said! It would take many Discourses, not a small fraction of one Discourse, to state what one feels about that Eighteenth Century and its ways. As indeed this, and the like of this, which we now call Scepticism, is precisely the black malady and life-foe, against which all teaching and discoursing since man's life began has directed itself: the battle of Belief against Unbelief is the never-ending battle! Neither is it in the way of crimination that one would wish to speak. Scepticism, for that century, we must consider as the decay of old ways of believ-ing, the preparation afar off for new better and wider ways,—an inevitable thing. We will not blame men for it; we will lament their hard fate. We will understand that destruction of old *forms* is not destruction of everlasting *substances;* that Scepticism, as sorrowful and hateful as we see it, is not an end but a beginning.

The other day speaking, without prior purpose that way, of Bentham's theory of man and man's life, I chanced to call it a more beggarly one than Mahomet's. I am bound to say, now when it is once uttered, that such is my deliberate opinion. Not that one would mean offence against the man Jeremy Bentham, or those who respect and believe him. Bentham himself, and even the creed of Bentham, seems to me comparatively worthy of praise. It is a determinate *being* what all the world, in a cowardly half-and-half manner, was tending to be. Let us have the crisis; we shall either have death or the cure. I call this gross, steamengine Utilitarianism an approach towards new Faith. It was a laying down of cant; a saying to oneself: "Well then, this world is a dead iron machine, the god of it Gravitation and selfish Hunger; let us see what, by checking and balancing, and good adjust-ment of tooth and pinion, can be made of it!" Benthamism has something complete, manful, in such fearless committal of itself to what it finds true; you may call it Heroic, though a Heroism with its *eyes* put out! It is the culminating point, and fearless ultimatum, of what lay in the half-and-half state, pervading man's whole existence in that Eighteenth Century. It seems to me, all deniers of Godhood, and all lip-believers of it, are bound to be Benthamites, if they have courage and honesty. Benthamism is an *eyeless* Heroism: the Human Species, like a hapless blinded Samson grinding in the Philistine Mill, clasps convulsively the pillars of its Mill; brings huge ruin down, but ultimately deliverance withal. Of Bentham I meant to say no harm.

But this I do say, and would wish all men to know and lay to heart, that he who discerns nothing but Mechanism in the Universe, has in the fatalest way missed the secret of the Universe altogether. That all Godhood should vanish out of men's conception of this Universe seems to me precisely the most brutal error,—I will not disparage Heathenism by calling it a Heathen error,—that men could fall into. It is not true; it is false at the very heart of it. A man who thinks so will think *wrong* about all things in the world; this original sin will vitiate all other conclusions he can form. One might call it the most lamentable of Delusions,—not forgetting Witchcraft itself! Witchcraft worshipped at least a living Devil; but this worships a dead iron Devil; no God, not even a Devil!—Whatsoever is noble, divine, inspired, drops thereby out of life. There remains everywhere in life a despicable *caput-mortuum;* the mechanical hull, all soul fled out of it. How can a man act heroically? The 'Doctrine of Motives' will teach him that it is, under more or less disguise, nothing but a wretched love of Pleasure, fear of Pain; that Hunger, of applause, of cash, of whatsoever victual it may be, is the ultimate fact of man's life. Atheism, in brief;—which does indeed frightfully punish itself. The man, I say, is become spiritually a paralytic man; this godlike Universe a dead mechanical Steamengine, all working by motives, checks, balances, and I know not what; wherein, as in the detestable belly of some Phalaris'-Bull of his own contriving, he the poor Phalaris sits miserably dying!—

Belief I define to be the healthy act of a man's mind. It is a mysterious indescribable process that of getting to believe;—indescribable, as all vital acts are. We have our mind given us, not that it may cavil and argue, but that it may see into something, give us clear belief and understanding about something, whereon we are then to proceed to act. Doubt, truly, is not itself a crime. Certainly we do not rush out, clutch up the first thing we find, and straightway believe that! All manner of doubt, inquiry, σκέψις as it is named, about all manner of objects, dwells in every reasonable mind. It is the mystic working of the mind, on the object it is *getting* to know and believe.

Belief comes out of all this, above ground, like the tree from its hidden *roots*. But now if, even on common things, we require that a man keep his doubts *silent*, and not babble of them till they in some measure become affirmations or denials; how much more in regard to the highest things, impossible to speak of in words at all! That a man parade his doubt, and get to imagine that debating and logic (which means at best only the manner of *telling* us your thought, your belief or disbelief, about a thing) is the triumph and true work of what intellect he has: alas, this is as if you should *overturn* the tree, and instead of green boughs, leaves and fruits, shew us ugly taloned roots turned up into the air,—and no growth, only death and misery going on!

For the Scepticism, as I said, is not intellectual only; it is moral also; a chronic atrophy and disease of the whole soul. A man lives by believing something; not by debating and arguing about many things. A sad case for him when all that he can manage to believe is something he can button in his pocket, and with one or the other organ eat and digest! Lower than that he will not get. We call those ages in which he gets so low the mournfulest, sickest and meanest of all ages. The world's heart is palsied, sick: how can any limb of it be whole? Genuine Acting ceases in all departments of the world's work; dexterous Similitude of Acting begins. The world's wages are pocketed, the world's work is not done. Heroes have gone out; Quacks have come in. Accordingly, what Century, since the end of the Roman world, which also was a time of scepticism, simulacra and universal decadence, so abounds with Quacks as that Eighteenth? Consider them, with their tumid sentimental vapouring about virtue, benevolence,—the wretched Quack-squadron, Cagliostro at the head of them! Few men were without quackery; they had got to consider it a necessary ingredient and amalgam for truth. Chatham, our brave Chatham himself, comes down to the House, all wrapt and bandaged; he "has crawled out in great bodily suffering," and so on;—*forgets*, says Walpole, that he is acting the sick man; in the fire of debate, snatches his arm from the sling, and oratorically swings and brandishes it! Chatham himself lives the strangest mimetic life, half-hero, half-quack, all along. For indeed the world is full of dupes; and you have to gain the *world's* suffrage! How the duties of the world will be done in that case, what quantities of error, which means failure, which means sorrow and misery, to some and to many, will gradually accumulate in all provinces of the world's business, we need not compute.

It seems to me, you lay your finger here on the heart of the world's maladies, when you call it a Sceptical World. An insincere world; a godless untruth of a world! It is out of this, as I consider, that the whole tribe of social pestilences, French Revolutions, Chartisms, and what not, have derived their being,—their chief necessity to be. This must alter. Till this alter, nothing can beneficially alter. My one hope of the world, my inexpugnable consolation in looking at the miseries of the world, is that this is altering. Here and there one does now find a man who knows, as of old, that this world is a Truth, and no Plausibility and Falsity; that he himself is alive, not dead or paralytic; and that the world is alive, instinct with Godhood, beautiful and awful, even as in the beginning of days! One man once knowing this, many men, all men, must by and by come to know it. It lies there clear, for whosoever will take the *spectacles* off his eyes and honestly look, to know! For such a man the Unbelieving Century, with its unblessed Products, is already past; a new century is already come. The old unblessed Products and Performances, as solid as they look, are Phantasms, preparing speedily to vanish. To this and the other noisy, very great-looking Simulacrum with the whole world huzzahing at its heels, he can say, composedly stepping aside: Thou art not *true;* thou art not extant, only semblant; go thy way!—Yes, hollow Formulism, gross Benthamism, and other unheroic atheistic Insincerity is visibly and even rapidly declining. An unbelieving Eighteenth Century is but an exception,—such as now and then occurs. I prophesy that the world will once more become *sincere;* a believing world; with *many* Heroes in it, a Heroic World! It will then be a victorious world; never till then.

Or indeed what of the world and its victories? Men speak too much about the world. Each one of us here, let the world go how it will, and be victorious or not victorious, has he not a Life of his own to lead? One Life; a little gleam of Time between two Eternities; no second chance to us forevermore! It were well for *us* to live not as fools and simulacra, but as wise and realities. The world's being saved will not save us; nor the world's being lost destroy us. We should look to ourselves: there is great merit here in the 'duty of staying at home!'

And, on the whole, to say truth, I never heard of 'worlds' being 'saved' in any other way. That mania of saving worlds is itself a piece of the Eighteenth Century with its windy sentimentalism. Let us not follow it too far. For the saving of the *world* I will trust confidently to the Maker of the world; and look a little to my own saving, which I am more competent to!—In brief, for the world's sake, and for our own, we will rejoice greatly that Scepticism, Insincerity, Mechanical Atheism, with all their poison-dews, are going, and as good as gone.

Now it was under such conditions, in those times of Johnson, that our Men of Letters had to live. Times in which there was properly no truth in life. Old Truths had fallen nigh dumb; the new lay yet hidden, not trying to speak. That Man's Life here below was a Sincerity and Fact, and would forever continue such, no new intimation in that dusk of the world, had yet dawned. No intimation; not even any French Revolution,—which we define to be a Truth once more, though a Truth clad in hellfire! How different was the Luther's pilgrimage, with its assured goal, from the Johnson's girt with mere traditions, suppositions, grown now incredible, unintelligible! Mahomet's Formulas were of 'wood waxed and oiled,' and could be *burnt* out of one's way: poor Johnson's were far more difficult to burn.—The strong man will ever find *work*, which means difficulty, pain, to the full measure of his strength. But to make out a victory, in those circumstances of our poor Hero as Man of Letters, was perhaps more difficult than in any. Not obstruction, disorganisation, Bookseller Osborne and Fourpence-halfpenny a day; not this alone; but the light of his own soul was taken from him. No landmark on the Earth; and, alas, what is that to having no loadstar in the Heaven! We need not wonder that none of those Three men rose to victory. That they fought truly, is the highest praise. With a mournful sympathy we will contemplate, if not three living victorious Heroes, as I said, the Tombs of three fallen Heroes! They fell for us too; making a way for us. There are the mountains which they hurled abroad in their confused War of the Giants; under which, their strength and life spent, they now lie buried.

I have already written of these three Literary Heroes, expressly or incidentally; what I suppose is known to most of you; what need not be spoken or written a second time. They concern us here as the singular *Prophets* of that singular age; for such they virtually were; and the aspect they and their world exhibit, under this point of view, might lead us into reflexions enough! I call them, all three, Genuine Men more or less; faithfully, for most part unconsciously, struggling to be genuine, and plant themselves on the everlasting truth of things. This to a degree that eminently distinguishes them from the poor artificial mass of their contemporaries; and renders them worthy to be considered as Speakers, in some measure, of the everlasting truth, as Prophets in that age of theirs. By Nature herself a noble necessity was laid on them to be so. They were men of such magnitude that they could not live on unrealities,—clouds, froth and all inanity gave way under them: there was no footing for them but on firm earth; no rest or regular motion for them, if they got not footing there. To a certain extent, they were Sons of Nature once more in an age of Artifice; once more, Original Men.

As for Johnson, I have always considered him to be, by nature, one of our great English souls. A strong and noble man; so much left undeveloped in him to the last: in a kindlier element what might he not have been,—Poet, Priest, sovereign Ruler! On the whole, a man must not complain of his 'element,' of his 'time,' or the like; it is thriftless work doing so. His time is bad: well then, he is there to make it better!—Johnson's youth was poor, isolated, hopeless, very miserable. Indeed, it does not seem possible that, in any the favourablest outward circumstances, Johnson's life could have been other than a painful one. The world might have had more of profitable *work* out of him, or less; but his *effort* against the world's work could never have been a light one. Nature, in return for his nobleness, had said to him, Live in an element of diseased sorrow. Nay, perhaps the sorrow and the nobleness were intimately and even inseparably connected with each other. At all events, poor Johnson had to go about girt with continual hypochondria, physical and spiritual pain. Like a Hercules with the burning Nessus'-shirt on him, which shoots in on him dull incurable misery: the Nessus'-shirt not to be stript off, which is his own natural skin! In this manner, *he* had to live. Figure him there, with his scrofulous diseases, with his great greedy heart, and unspeakable chaos of thoughts; stalking mournful as a stranger in this Earth; eagerly devouring what spiritual thing he could come at: school-languages and other merely grammatical stuff, if there were nothing better! The largest soul that was in all England; and provision made for it of 'fourpence-halfpenny a day.' Yet a giant invincible

soul; a true man's. One remembers always that story of the shoes at
Oxford: the rough, seamy-faced, rawboned College Servitor stalking
about, in winter-season, with his shoes worn out; how the charitable
Gentleman Commoner secretly places a new pair at his door; and the
rawboned Servitor, lifting them, looking at them near, with his dim
eyes, with what thoughts,—pitches them out of window! Wet feet,
mud, frost, hunger or what you will; but not beggary: we cannot
stand beggary! Rude stubborn self-help here; a whole world of
squalor, rudeness, confused misery and want, yet of nobleness and
manfulness withal. It is a type of the man's life, this pitching away of
the shoes. An original man;—not a secondhand, borrowing or begging man. Let us stand on our own basis, at any rate! On such shoes
as we ourselves can get. On frost and mud, if you will, but honestly
on that;—on the reality and substance which Nature gives *us*, not on
the semblance, on the thing she has given another than us!—

And yet with all this rugged pride of manhood and self-help, was
there ever soul more tenderly affectionate, loyally submissive to what
was really higher than he? Great souls are always loyally submissive,
reverent to what is over them; only small mean souls are otherwise.
I could not find a better proof of what I said the other day, That the
sincere man was by nature the obedient man; that only in a World of
Heroes was there loyal Obedience to the Heroic. The essence of
originality is not that it be *new:* Johnson believed altogether in the
old; he found the old opinions credible for him, fit for him; and in
a right heroic manner, lived under them. He is well worth study in
regard to that. For we are to say that Johnson was far other than a
mere man of words and formulas; he was a man of truths and facts.
He stood by the old formulas; the happier was it for him that he
could so stand: but in all formulas that *he* could stand by, there
needed to be a most genuine substance. Very curious how, in that
poor Paper-age, so barren, artificial, thick-quilted with Pedantries,
Hearsays, the great Fact of this Universe glared-in forever, wonderful, indubitable, unspeakable, divine-infernal, upon this man too!
How he harmonised his Formulas with it, how he managed at all
under such circumstances: that is a thing worth seeing. A thing 'to
be looked at with reverence, with pity, with awe.' That Church of St.
Clement Danes, where Johnson still *worshipped* in the era of Voltaire,
is to me a venerable place.

It was in virtue of his *sincerity*, of his speaking still in some sort from the heart of Nature, though in the current artificial dialect, that Johnson was a Prophet. Are not all dialects 'artificial?' Artificial things are not all false;—nay every true Product of Nature will infallibly *shape* itself; we may say all artificial things are, at the starting of them, *true*. What we call 'Formulas' are not in their origin bad; they are indispensably good. Formula is *method*, habitude; found wherever man is found. Formulas fashion themselves as Paths do, as beaten Highways, leading towards some sacred or high object, whither many men are bent. Consider it. One man, full of heartfelt earnest impulse, finds out a way of doing somewhat,—were it of uttering his soul's reverence for the Highest, were it but of fitly saluting his fellow-man. An inventor was needed to do that, a *poet;* he has articulated the dim-struggling thought that dwelt in his own and many hearts. This is his way of doing that; these are his footsteps, the beginning of a 'Path.' And now see: the second man travels naturally in the footsteps of his foregoer, it is the *easiest* method. In the footsteps of his foregoer; yet with improvements, with changes where such seem good; at all events with enlargements, the Path ever *widening* itself as more travel it;—till at last there is a broad Highway whereon the whole world may travel and drive. While there remains a City or Shrine, or any Reality to drive to, at the farther end, the Highway shall be right welcome! When the City is gone, we will forsake the Highway. In this manner all Institutions, Practices, Regulated Things in the world have come into existence, and gone out of existence. Formulas all begin by being *full* of substance; you may call them the *skin*, the articulation into shape, into limbs and skin, of a substance that is already there: *they* had not been there otherwise. Idols, as we said, are not idolatrous till they become doubtful, empty for the worshipper's heart. Much as we talk against Formulas, I hope no one of us is ignorant withal of the high significance of *true* Formulas; that they were, and will ever be, the indispensablest furniture of our habitation in this world.— —

Mark, too, how little Johnson boasts of his 'sincerity.' He has no suspicion of his being particularly sincere,—of his being particularly anything! A hard-struggling, weary-hearted man, or 'scholar' as he calls himself, trying hard to get some honest livelihood in the world, not to starve, but to live—without stealing! A noble unconsciousness is in him. He does not 'engrave *Truth* on his watch-seal;' no, but he stands by truth, speaks by it, works and lives by it. Thus it ever is. Think of it once more. The man whom Nature has appointed to do great things is, first of all, furnished with that openness to Nature which renders him incapable of being *in*sincere! To his large, open, deep-feeling heart Nature is a Fact: all hearsay is hearsay; the unspeakable greatness of this Mystery of Life, let him acknowledge it or not, nay even though he seem to forget it or deny it, is ever present to *him*,—fearful and wonderful, on this hand and on that. He has a basis of sincerity; unrecognised, because never questioned or capable of question. Mirabeau, Mahomet, Cromwell, Napoleon: all the Great Men I ever heard of have this as the primary material of them. Innumerable commonplace men are debating, are talking everywhere their commonplace doctrines, which they have learned by logic, by rote, at second-hand: to that kind of man all this is still nothing. He must have truth; truth which *he* feels to be true. How shall he stand otherwise? His whole soul, at all moments, in all ways, tells him that there is no standing. He is under the noble necessity of being true. Johnson's way of thinking about this world is not mine, any more than Mahomet's was: but I recognise the everlasting element of heart-*sincerity* in both; and see with pleasure how neither of them remains ineffectual. Neither of them is as *chaff* sown; in both of them is something which the seed-field will *grow*.

Johnson was a Prophet to his people; preached a Gospel to them,—as all like him always do. The highest Gospel he preached we may describe as a kind of Moral Prudence: 'in a world where much is to be done and little is to be known,' see how you will *do* it! A thing well worth preaching. 'A world where much is to be done and little is to be known:' do not sink yourselves in boundless bottomless abysses of Doubt, of wretched godforgetting Unbelief;—you were miserable then, powerless, mad: how could you *do* or work at all? Such Gospel Johnson preached and taught;—coupled, theoretically and practically, with this other great Gospel, 'Clear your mind of Cant!' Have no trade with Cant: stand on the cold mud in the frosty weather, but let it be in your own *real* torn shoes: 'that will be bet ter for you,' as Mahomet says! I call this, I call these two things *joined together*, a great Gospel, the greatest perhaps that was possible at that time.

Johnson's Writings, which once had such currency and celebrity, are now as it were disowned by the young generation. It is not wonderful; Johnson's opinions are fast becoming obsolete: but his style of thinking and of living, we may hope, will never become obsolete. I find in Johnson's Books the indisputablest traces of a great intellect and great heart;—ever welcome, under what obstructions and perversions soever. They are *sincere* words, those of his; he means things by them. A wondrous buckram style,—the best he could get to then; a measured grandiloquence, stepping or rather stalking along in a very solemn way, grown obsolete now; sometimes a tumid *size* of phraseology not in proportion to the contents of it: all this you will put up with. For the phraseology, tumid or not, has always *something within it*. So many beautiful styles, and books, with *nothing* in them;—a man is a *male*factor to the world who writes such! *They* are the avoidable kind!—Had Johnson left nothing but his *Dictionary*, one might have traced there a great intellect, a genuine man. Looking to its clearness of definition, its general solidity, honesty, insight and successful method, it may be called the best of all Dictionaries. There is in it a kind of architectural nobleness; it stands there like a great solid square-built edifice, finished, symmetrically complete: you judge that a true Builder did it.

One word, in spite of our haste, must be granted to poor Bozzy. He passes for a mean, inflated, gluttonous creature; and was so in many senses. Yet the fact of his reverence for Johnson will ever remain noteworthy. The foolish conceited Scotch Laird, the most conceited man of his time, approaching in such awestruck attitude the great dusty irascible Pedagogue in his mean garret there: it is a genuine reverence for Excellence; a *worship* for Heroes, at a time when neither Heroes nor worship were surmised to exist. Heroes, it would seem, exist always, and a certain worship of them! We will also take the liberty to deny altogether that of the witty Frenchman, That no man is a Hero to his valet-de-chambre. Or if so, it is not the Hero's blame, but the Valet's: that his soul, namely, is a mean *valet*-soul! He expects his Hero to advance in royal stage-trappings, with measured step, trains borne behind him, trumpets sounding before him. It should stand rather, No man can be a *Grand-Monarque* to his valet-de-chambre. Strip your Louis Quatorze of his king-gear, and there *is* left nothing but a poor forked radish with a head fantastically carved;—admirable to no valet. The Valet does not know a Hero when he sees him! Alas, no: it requires a kind of *Hero* to do that;—and one of the world's wants, in *this* as in other senses, is for most part want of such.

On the whole, shall we not say, that Boswell's admiration was well bestowed; that he could have found no soul in all England so worthy of bending down before? Shall we not say, of this great mournful Johnson too, that he guided his difficult confused existence wisely; led it *well*, like a right valiant man? That waste chaos of Authorship by Trade; that waste chaos of Scepticism in religion and politics, in life-theory and life-practice; in his poverty, in his dust and dimness, with the sick body and the rusty coat: he made it do for him, like a brave man. Not wholly without a loadstar in the Eternal; he had still a loadstar, as the brave all need to have: with his eye set on that, he would change his course for nothing in these confused vortices of the lower sea of Time. 'To the Spirit of Lies, bearing death and hunger, he would in no wise strike his flag.' Brave old Samuel: *ultimus Romanorum!*

Of Rousseau and his Heroism I cannot say so much. He is not what I call a strong man. A morbid, excitable, spasmodic man; at best, intense rather than strong. He had not 'the talent of Silence,' an invaluable talent; which few Frenchmen, or indeed men of any sort in these times, excel in! The suffering man ought really 'to consume his own smoke;' there is no good in emitting *smoke* till you have made it into *fire*,—which, in the metaphorical sense too, all smoke is capable of becoming! Rousseau has not depth or width, not calm force for difficulty; the first characteristic of true greatness. A fundamental mistake to call vehemence and rigidity strength! A man is not strong who takes convulsion-fits; though six men cannot hold him then. He that can walk under the heaviest weight without staggering, he is the strong man. We need forever, especially in these loud-shrieking days, to remind ourselves of that. A man who cannot *hold his peace*, till the time come for speaking and acting, is no right man.

Poor Rousseau's face is to me expressive of him. A high, but narrow contracted intensity in it: bony brows; deep, strait-set eyes, in which there is something bewildered-looking,—bewildered, peering with lynx-eagerness. A face full of misery, even ignoble misery, and also of the antagonism against that; something mean, plebeian there, redeemed only by *intensity:* the face of what is called a Fanatic,—a sadly *contracted* Hero! We name him here because, with all his drawbacks, and they are many, he has the first and chief characteristic of a Hero: he is heartily *in earnest*. In earnest, if ever man was; as none of these French Philosophes were. Nay, one would say, of an earnestness too great for his otherwise sensitive, rather feeble nature; and which indeed in the end drove him into the strangest incoherences, almost delirations. There had come, at last, to be a kind of madness in him: his Ideas *possessed* him like demons; hurried him so about, drove him over steep places!—

The fault and misery of Rousseau was what we easily name by a single word, *Egoism;* which is indeed the source and summary of all faults and miseries whatsoever. He had not perfected himself into victory over mere Desire; a mean Hunger, in many sorts, was still the motive principle of him. I am afraid he was a very vain man; hungry for the praises of men. You remember Genlis's experience of him. She took Jean Jacques to the Theatre; he bargaining for a strict incognito,—"*He* would not be seen there for the world!" The curtain did happen nevertheless to be drawn aside: the Pit recognised Jean Jacques, but took no great notice of him! He expressed the bitterest indignation; gloomed all evening, spake no other than surly words. The glib Countess remained entirely convinced that his anger was not at being seen, but at not being applauded when seen. How the whole nature of the man is poisoned; nothing but suspicion, self-isolation, fierce moody ways! He could not live with anybody. A man of some rank from the country, who visited him often, and used to sit with him, expressing all reverence and affection for him, comes one day; finds Jean Jacques full of the sourest unintelligible humour. "Monsieur," said Jean Jacques, with flaming eyes, "I know why you come here. You come to see what a poor life I lead; how little is in my poor pot that is boiling there. Well, look into the pot! There is half a pound of meat, one carrot and three onions; that is all: go and tell the whole world that, if you like, Monsieur!"—A man of this sort was far gone. The whole world got itself supplied with anecdotes, for light laughter, for a certain theatrical interest, from these perversions and contorsions of poor Jean Jacques. Alas, to him they were not laughing or theatrical; too real to him! The contorsions of a dying gladiator: the crowded amphitheatre looks on with entertainment; but the gladiator is in agonies and dying.

And yet this Rousseau, as we say, with his passionate appeals to Mothers, with his *Contrat-social*, with his celebrations of Nature, even of savage life in Nature, did once more touch upon Reality, struggle towards Reality; was doing the function of a Prophet to his Time. As *he* could, and as the Time could! Strangely through all that defacement, degradation and almost madness, there is in the inmost heart of poor Rousseau a spark of real heavenly fire. Once more, out of the element of that withered mocking Philosophism, Scepticism, and Persiflage, there has arisen in this man the ineradicable feeling and knowledge that this Life of ours is *true;* not a Scepticism, Theorem, or Persiflage, but a Fact, an awful Reality. Nature had made that revelation to him; had ordered him to speak it out. He got it spoken out; if not well and clearly, then ill and dimly,—as clearly as he could. Nay what are all errors and perversities of his, even those stealings of ribbons, aimless confused miseries and vagabondisms, if we will interpret them kindly, but the blinkard dazzlement and staggerings to and fro of a man sent on an errand he is too weak for, by a path he cannot yet find? Men are led by strange ways. One should have tolerance for a man, hope of him; leave him to try yet what he will do. While life lasts, hope lasts for every man.

Of Rousseau's literary talents, greatly celebrated still among his countrymen, I do not say much. His Books, like himself, are what I call unhealthy; not the good sort of Books. There is a sensuality in Rousseau. Combined with such an intellectual gift as his, it makes pictures of a certain gorgeous attractiveness: but they are not genuinely poetical. Not white sunlight: something *operatic;* a kind of rosepink, artificial bedizenment. It is frequent, or rather it is universal, among the French since his time. Madame de Staël has something of it; St. Pierre; and down onwards to the present astonishing convulsionary 'Literature of Desperation,' it is everywhere abundant. That same *rosepink* is not the right hue. Look at a Shakspeare, at a Goethe, even at a Walter Scott! He who has once seen into this, has seen the difference of the True from the Sham-True, and will discriminate them ever afterwards.

We had to observe in Johnson how much good a Prophet, under all disadvantages and disorganisations, can accomplish for the world.

In Rousseau we are called to look rather at the fearful amount of evil which, under such disorganisation, may accompany the good. Historically it is a most pregnant spectacle, that of Rousseau. Banished into Paris garrets, in the gloomy company of his own Thoughts and Necessities there; driven from post to pillar; fretted, exasperated till the heart of him went mad, he had grown to feel deeply that the world was not his friend nor the world's law. It was expedient, if any way possible, that such a man should *not* have been set in flat hostility with the world. He could be cooped into garrets, laughed at as a maniac, left to starve like a wild beast in his cage;—but he could not be hindered from setting the world on fire. The French Revolution found its Evangelist in Rousseau. His semi-delirious speculations on the miseries of civilised life, the preferability of the savage to the civilised, and such like, helped well to produce a whole delirium in France generally. True, you may well ask, What could the world, the governors of the world, do with such a man? Difficult to say what the governors of the world could do with him! What he could do with them is unhappily clear enough,—*guillotine* a great many of them! Enough now of Rousseau.

It was a curious phenomenon, in the withered, unbelieving, secondhand Eighteenth Century, that of a Hero starting up, among the artificial pasteboard figures and productions, in the guise of a Robert Burns. Like a little well in the rocky desert places,—like a sudden splendour of Heaven in the artificial Vauxhall! People knew not what to make of it. They took it for a piece of the Vauxhall fire-work; alas, it *let* itself be so taken, though struggling half-blindly, as in bitterness of death, against that! Perhaps no man had such a false reception from his fellow-men. Once more a very wasteful life-drama was enacted under the sun.

The tragedy of Burns's life is known to all of you. Surely we may say, if discrepancy between place held and place merited constitute perverseness of lot for a man, no lot could be more perverse than Burns's. Among those secondhand acting-figures, *mimes* for most part, of the Eighteenth Century, once more a giant Original Man; one of those men who reach down to the perennial Deeps, who take rank with the Heroic among men: and he was born in a poor Ayrshire hut. The largest soul of all the British lands came among us in the shape of a hard-handed Scottish Peasant.—His Father, a poor toiling man, tried various things; did not succeed in any; was involved in continual difficulties. The Steward, Factor as the Scotch call him, used to send letters and threatenings, Burns says, 'which threw us all into tears.' The brave hard-toiling, hard-suffering Father, his brave heroine of a wife; and those children, of whom Robert was one! In this Earth, so wide otherwise, no shelter for *them*. The letters 'threw us all into tears:' figure it. The brave Father, I say always;—a *silent* Hero and Poet; without whom the son had never been a speaking one! Burns's Schoolmaster came afterwards to London, learnt what good society was; but declares that in no meeting of men did he ever enjoy better discourse than at the hearth of this peasant. And his poor 'seven acres of nursery-ground,'—not that, nor the miserable patch of clay-farm, nor anything he tried to get a living by, would prosper with him; he had a sore unequal battle all his days. But he stood to it valiantly; a wise, faithful, unconquerable man;—swallowing down how many sore sufferings daily into silence; fighting like an unseen Hero,—nobody publishing newspaper-paragraphs about his nobleness; voting pieces of plate to him! However, he was not lost; nothing is lost. Robert is there; the outcome of him,—and indeed of many generations of such as him.

This Burns appeared under every disadvantage: uninstructed, poor, born only to hard manual toil; and writing, when it came to that, in a rustic special dialect, known only to a small province of the country he lived in. Had he written, even what he did write, in the general language of England, I doubt not he had already become universally recognised as being, or capable to be, one of our greatest men. That he should have tempted so many to penetrate through the rough husk of that dialect of his, is proof that there lay something far from common within it. He has gained a certain recognition, and is continuing to do so over all quarters of our wide Saxon world: wheresoever a Saxon dialect is spoken, it begins to be understood, by personal inspection of this and the other, that one of the most considerable Saxon men of the Eighteenth century was an Ayrshire Peasant named Robert Burns. Yes, I will say, here too was a piece of the right Saxon stuff: strong as the Harz-rock, rooted in the depths of the world;—rock, yet with wells of living softness in it! A wild impetuous whirlwind of passion and faculty slumbered quiet there;

such heavenly *melody* dwelling in the heart of it. A noble rough genuineness; homely, rustic, honest; true simplicity of strength; with its lightning-fire, with its soft dewy pity;—like the old Norse Thor, the Peasant-god!—

Burns's Brother Gilbert, a man of much sense and worth, has told me that Robert, in his young days, in spite of their hardship, was usually the gayest of speech; a fellow of infinite frolic, laughter, sense, and heart; far pleasanter to hear there, stript cutting peats in the bog, or such like, than he ever afterwards knew him. I can well believe it. This basis of mirth ('*fond gaillard,*' as old Marquis Mirabeau calls it), a primal-element of sunshine and joyfulness, coupled with his other deep and earnest qualities, is one of the most attractive characteristics of Burns. A large fund of Hope dwells in him; spite of his tragical history, he is not a mourning man. He shakes his sorrows gallantly aside; bounds forth victorious over them. It is as the lion shaking 'dew-drops from his mane;' as the swift-bounding horse, that *laughs* at the shaking of the spear.—But indeed, Hope, Mirth, of the sort like Burns's, are they not the outcome properly of warm generous affection,—such as is the beginning of all to every man?

You would think it strange if I called Burns the most gifted British soul we had in all that century of his: and yet I believe the day is coming when there will be little danger in saying so. His writings, all that he *did* under such obstructions, are only a poor fragment of him. Professor Stewart remarked very justly, what indeed is true of all Poets good for much, that his poetry was not any particular faculty; but the general result of a naturally vigorous original mind expressing itself in that way. Burns's gifts, expressed in conversation, are the theme of all that ever heard him. All kinds of gifts: from the gracefulest utterances of courtesy, to the highest fire of passionate speech; loud floods of mirth, soft wailings of affection, laconic emphasis, clear piercing insight: all was in him. Witty duchesses celebrate him as a man whose speech 'led them off their feet.' This is beautiful: but still more beautiful that which Mr. Lockhart has recorded, which I have more than once alluded to, How the waiters and ostlers at inns would get out of bed, and come crowding to hear this man speak! Waiters and ostlers:—they too were men, and here was a man! I have heard much about his speech; but one of the best things I ever heard of it was, last year, from a venerable gentleman long familiar with him,

That it was speech distinguished by always *having something in it*.
"He spoke rather little than much," this old man told me; "sat rather
silent in those early days, as in the company of persons above him;
and always when he did speak, it was to throw new light on the
matter." I know not why any one should ever speak otherwise!—But
if we look at his general force of soul, his healthy *robustness* every way,
the rugged downrightness, penetration, generous valour and manfulness that was in him,—where shall we readily find a better gifted man?

Among the great men of the Eighteenth Century, I sometimes feel
as if Burns might be found to resemble Mirabeau more than any
other. They differ widely in vesture; yet look at them intrinsically.
There is the same burly thicknecked strength of body as of soul;—
built, in both cases, on what the old Marquis calls a *fond gaillard*. By
nature, by course of breeding, indeed by nation, Mirabeau has much
more of bluster; a noisy, forward, unresting man. But the characteristic of Mirabeau too is veracity and sense, power of true *insight*,
superiority of vision. The thing that he says is worth remembering.
It is a flash of insight into some object or other: so do both these men
speak. The same raging passions; capable too in both of manifesting
themselves as the tenderest noble affections. Wit, wild laughter,
energy, directness, sincerity: these were in both. The types of the two
men are not dissimilar. Burns too could have governed, debated in
National Assemblies; politicised, as few could. Alas, the courage
which had to exhibit itself in capture of smuggling schooners in the
Solway Frith; in keeping *silence* over so much, where no good speech,
but only inarticulate rage was possible: this might have bellowed
forth Ushers de Brézé and the like; and made itself visible to all men,
in managing of kingdoms, in ruling of great ever-memorable epochs!
But they said to him reprovingly, his Official Superiors said, and
wrote: 'You are to work, not think.' Of your *thinking*-faculty, the
greatest in this land, we have no need; you are to gauge beer there;
for that only are *you* wanted. Very notable;—and worth mentioning,
though we know what is to be said and answered! As if Thought,
Power of Thinking, were not, at all times, in all places and situations
of the world, precisely the thing that *was* wanted. The fatal man, is
he not always the *un*thinking man, the man who cannot think and *see*;
but only grope, and hallucinate, and *mis*see the nature of the thing
he works with? He missees it, mis*takes* it, as we say; takes it for one

thing, and it *is* another thing,—and leaves him standing like a Futility there! He is the fatal man; unutterably fatal, put in the high places of men.—"Why complain of this?" say some. "Strength is mournfully denied its arena; that was true from of old." Doubtless; and the worse for the *arena*, answer I! *Complaining* profits little; stating of the truth may profit. That a Europe, with its French Revolution just breaking out, finds no need of a Burns except for gauging beer,—is a thing I, for one, cannot *rejoice* at!—

Once more we have to say here that the chief quality of Burns is the *sincerity* of him. So in his Poetry, so in his Life. The Song he sings is not of fantasticalities; it is of a thing felt, really there; the prime merit of this, as of all in him, and of his Life generally, is truth. The Life of Burns is what we may call a great tragic sincerity. A sort of savage sincerity,—not cruel, far from that; but wild, wrestling naked with the truth of things. In that sense, there is something of the savage in all great men.

Hero-worship,—Odin, Burns? Well; these Men of Letters too were not without a kind of Hero-worship: but what a strange condition has that got into now! The waiters and ostlers of Scotch inns, prying about the door, eager to catch any word that fell from Burns, were doing unconscious reverence to the Heroic. Johnson had his Boswell for worshipper. Rousseau had worshippers enough; princes calling on him in his mean garret; the great, the beautiful doing reverence to the poor moonstruck man. For himself a most portentous contradiction; the two ends of his life not to be brought into harmony. He sits at the tables of grandees; and has to copy music for his own living. He cannot even get his music copied: "By dint of dining out," says he, "I run the risk of dying by starvation at home." For his worshippers too a most questionable thing! If doing Hero-worship well or badly be the test of vital well-being or illbeing to a generation, can we say that *these* generations are very first-rate?—And yet our heroic Men of Letters do teach, govern, are kings, priests, or what you like to call them; intrinsically there is no preventing it by any means whatever. The world *has* to obey him who thinks and sees in the world. The world can alter the manner of that; can either have it as blessed continuous summer-sunshine, or as unblessed black thunder and tornado,—with unspeakable difference of profit for the world! The manner of it is very alterable; the matter and fact of it is not alterable by any power under the sky. Light; or, failing that, lightning: the world can take its choice. Not whether we call an Odin god, prophet, priest or what we call him; but whether we believe the word he tells us: there it all lies. If it be a true word, we shall have to believe it; believing it, we shall have to do it. What *name* or welcome we give him or it, is a point that concerns ourselves mainly. *It*, the new Truth, new deeper revealing of the Secret of this Universe, is verily of the nature of a message from on high; and must and will have itself obeyed.— —

My last remark is on that notablest phasis of Burns's history,—his visit to Edinburgh. Often it seems to me as if his demeanour there were the highest proof he gave of what a fund of worth and genuine manhood was in him. If we think of it, few heavier burdens could be laid on the strength of a man. So sudden; all common *Lionism*, which ruins innumerable men, was as nothing to this. It is as if Napoleon had been made a King of, not gradually, but at once from the Artillery Lieutenancy in the Regiment La Fère. Burns, still only in his twenty-seventh year, is no longer even a ploughman; he is flying to the West Indies to escape disgrace and a jail. This month he is a ruined peasant, his wages seven pounds a year, and these gone from him: next month he is in the blaze of rank and beauty, handing down jewelled Duchesses to dinner; the cynosure of all eyes! Adversity is sometimes hard upon a man; but for one man who can stand prosperity, there are a hundred that will stand adversity. I admire much the way in which Burns met all this. Perhaps no man one could point out, was ever so sorely tried, and so little forgot himself. Tranquil, unastonished; not abashed, not inflated, neither awkwardness nor affectation: he feels that *he* there is the man Robert Burns; that the 'rank is but the guinea-stamp;' that the celebrity is but the candle-light, which will shew *what* man, not in the least make him a better or other man! Alas, it may readily, unless he look to it, make him a *worse* man; a wretched inflated windbag,—inflated till he *burst*, and become a *dead* lion; for whom, as some one has said, 'there is no resurrection of the body:' worse than a living dog!—Burns is admirable here.

And yet, alas, as I have observed elsewhere, these Lion-hunters were the ruin and death of Burns. It was they that rendered it impossible for him to live! They gathered round him in his Farm;

hindered his industry; no place was remote enough from them. He could not get his Lionism forgotten, honestly as he was disposed to do so. He falls into discontents, into miseries, faults; the world getting ever more desolate for him; health, character, peace of mind, all gone;—solitary enough now. It is tragical to think of! These men came but to *see* him; it was out of no sympathy with him, nor no hatred to him. They came to get a little amusement: they got their amusement;—and the Hero's life went for it!

Richter says, in the Island of Sumatra there is a kind of 'Light-chafers,' large Fire-flies, which people stick upon spits, and illuminate the ways with at night. Persons of condition can thus travel with a pleasant radiance, which they much admire. Great honour to the Fire-flies! But—!—

LECTURE VI.

THE HERO AS KING. CROMWELL, NAPOLEON:
MODERN REVOLUTIONISM.

WE come now to the last form of Heroism; that which we call
Kingship. The Commander over Men; he to whose will our wills are
to be subordinated, and loyally surrender themselves, and find their
welfare in doing so, may be reckoned the most important of Great
Men. He is practically the summary for us of *all* the various figures
of Heroism; Priest, Teacher, whatsoever of earthly or of spiritual
dignity we can fancy to reside in a man, embodies itself here, to
command over us, to furnish us with constant practical teaching, to
tell us for the day and hour what we are to *do*. He is called *Rex*,
Regulator, *Roi:* our own name is still better; King, *Könning*, which
means *Can*-ning, Able-man.

Numerous considerations, pointing towards deep, questionable,
and indeed unfathomable regions, present themselves here: on the
most of which we must resolutely for the present forbear to speak at
all. As Burke said that perhaps fair *Trial by Jury* was the soul of
Government, and that all legislation, administration, parliamentary
debating, and the rest of it, went on, in order 'to bring twelve
impartial men into a jury-box;'—so, by much stronger reason, may I
say here, that the finding of your *Able-man*, and getting him invested
with the *symbols of ability*, with dignity, worship (*worth*-ship), royalty,
kinghood, or whatever we call it, so that *he* may actually have room
to guide according to his faculty of doing it,—is the business, well or
ill accomplished, of all social procedure whatsoever in this world!
Hustings-speeches, Parliamentary motions, Reform Bills, French

Revolutions, all mean at heart this; or else nothing. Find in any country the Ablest Man that exists there; raise *him* to the supreme place, and loyally reverence him: you have a perfect government for that country; no ballot-box, parliamentary eloquence, voting, constitution-building, or other machinery whatsoever can improve it a whit. It is in the perfect state; an ideal country. The Ablest Man; he means also the truest-hearted, justest, the Noblest Man: what he *tells us to do* must be precisely the wisest, fittest, that we could anywhere or anyhow learn;—the thing which it will in all ways behove us, with right loyal thankfulness, and nothing doubting, to do! Our *doing* and life were then, so far as government could regulate it, well regulated; that were the ideal of constitutions.

Alas, we know very well that Ideals can never be completely embodied in practice. Ideals must ever lie a very great way off; and we will right thankfully content ourselves with any not intolerable approximation thereto! Let no man, as Schiller says, too querulously 'measure by a scale of perfection the meagre product of reality' in this poor world of ours. We will esteem him no wise man; we will esteem him a sickly, discontented, foolish man. And yet, on the other hand, it is never to be forgotten that Ideals do exist; that if they be not approximated to at all, the whole matter goes to wreck! Infallibly. No bricklayer builds a wall *perfectly* perpendicular, mathematically this is not possible; a certain degree of perpendicularity suffices him; and he, like a good bricklayer, who must have done with his job, leaves it so. And yet if he sway *too much* from the perpendicular; above all, if he throw plummet and level quite away from him, and pile brick on brick heedless, just as it comes to hand—! Such bricklayer, I think, is in a bad way. *He* has forgotten himself: but the Law of Gravitation does not forget to act on him; he and his wall rush down into confused welter of ruin!—

This is the history of all rebellions, French Revolutions, social explosions in ancient or modern times. You have put the too *Un*able Man at the head of affairs! The too ignoble, unvaliant, fatuous man. You have forgotten that there is any rule, or natural necessity whatever, of putting the Able Man there. Brick must lie on brick as it may and can. Unable Simulacrum of Ability, *quack*, in a word, must adjust himself with quack, in all manner of administration of human things;—which accordingly lie unadministered, fermenting into unmeasured masses of failure, of indigent misery: in the outward, and in the inward or spiritual, miserable millions stretch out the hand for their due supply, and *it* is not there. The 'law of gravitation' acts; Nature's laws do none of them forget to act. The miserable millions burst forth into Sansculottism, or some other sort of madness: bricks and bricklayer lie as a fatal chaos!—

Much sorry stuff, written some hundred years ago or more, about the 'Divine right of Kings,' moulders unread now in the Public Libraries of this country. Far be it from us to disturb the calm process by which it is disappearing harmlessly from the earth, in those repositories! At the same time, not to let the immense rubbish go without leaving us, as it ought, some soul of it behind,—I will say that it did mean something; something true, which it is important for us and all men to keep in mind. To assert that in whatever man you chose to lay hold of (by this or the other plan of clutching at him); and clapt a round piece of metal on the head of, and called King,—there straightway came to reside a divine virtue, so that *he* became a kind of god, and a Divinity inspired him with faculty and right to rule over you to all lengths: this,—what can we do with this but leave it to rot silently in the Public Libraries? But I will say withal, and that is what these Divine-right men meant, That in Kings, and in all human Authorities, and relations that men god-created can form among each other, there is verily either a Divine Right or else a Diabolic Wrong; one or the other of these two! For it is false altogether, what the last Sceptical Century taught us, that this world is a steamengine. There is a God in this world; and a God's-sanction, or else the violation of such, does look out from all ruling and obedience, from all moral acts of men. There is no act more moral between men than that of rule and obedience. Wo to him that claims obedience when it is not due; wo to him that refuses it when it is! God's law is in that, I say, however the Parchment-laws may run: there is a Divine Right or else a Diabolic Wrong at the heart of every claim that one man makes upon another.

It can do none of us harm to reflect on this: in all the relations of life it will concern us; in Loyalty and Royalty, the highest of these. I esteem the modern error, That all goes by self-interest and the checking and balancing of greedy knaveries, and that in short there is nothing divine whatever in the association of men, a still more despicable error, natural as it is to an unbelieving century, than that of a 'divine right' in people *called* Kings. I say, Find me the true *Könning*, King, or Able-man, and he *has* a divine right over me. That we knew in some tolerable measure how to find him, and that all men were ready to acknowledge his divine right when found: this is precisely the healing which a sick world is everywhere, in these ages, seeking after! The true King, as guide of the practical, has ever something of the Pontiff in him,—guide of the spiritual, from which all practice has its rise. This too is a true saying, That the *King* is head of the *Church*.—But we will leave the Polemic stuff of a dead century to lie quiet on its book-shelves.

Certainly it is a fearful business, that of having your Able-man to *seek*, and not knowing in what manner to proceed about it! That is the world's sad predicament in these times of ours. They are times of revolution, and have long been. The bricklayer with his bricks, no longer heedful of plummet or the law of gravitation, have toppled, tumbled, and it all welters as we see! But the beginning of it was not the French Revolution; that is rather the *end*, we can hope. It were truer to say, the *beginning* was three centuries farther back: in the Reformation of Luther. That the thing which still called itself Christian Church had become a Falsehood, and brazenly went about pretending to pardon men's sins for metallic coined money, and to do much else which in the everlasting truth of Nature it did *not* now do: here lay the vital malady. The inward being wrong, all outward went ever more and more wrong. Belief died away; all was Doubt, Disbelief. The builder *cast away* his plummet; said to himself, "What is gravitation? Brick lies on brick there!" Alas, does it not still sound strange to many of us, the assertion that there *is* a God's-truth in the business of god-created men; that all is not a kind of grimace, an 'expediency,' diplomacy, one knows not what!—

From that first necessary assertion of Luther's, "You, self-styled *Papa*, you are no Father in God at all; you are—a Chimera, whom I know not how to name in polite language!"—from that onwards to the shout which rose round Camille Desmoulins in the Palais-Royal, "*Aux armes!*" when the people had burst up against *all* manner of Chimeras,—I find a natural historical sequence. That shout too, so frightful, half-infernal, was a great matter. Once more the voice of awakened nations;—starting confusedly, as out of nightmare, as out of death-sleep, into some dim feeling that Life was real; that God's-world was not an expediency and diplomacy! Infernal;—yes, since they would not have it otherwise. Infernal, since not celestial or terrestrial! Hollowness, insincerity *has* to cease; sincerity of some sort has to begin. Cost what it may, reigns of terror, horrors of French Revolution or what else, we have to return to truth. Here is a Truth, as I said: a Truth clad in hellfire, since they would not but have it so!—

A common theory among considerable parties of men in England and elsewhere used to be, that the French Nation had, in those days, as it were gone *mad;* that the French Revolution was a general act of insanity, a temporary conversion of France and large sections of the world into a kind of Bedlam. The Event had risen and raged; but was a madness and nonentity,—gone now happily into the region of Dreams and the Picturesque!—To such comfortable philosophers, the Three Days of July, 1830, must have been a surprising phenomenon. Here is the French Nation risen again, in musketry and death-struggle, out shooting and being shot, to make that same mad French Revolution good! The sons and grandsons of those men, it would seem, persist in the enterprise: they do not disown it; they will have it made good; will have themselves shot, if it be not made good! To philosophers who had made up their life-system on that 'madness' quietus, no phenomenon could be more alarming. Poor Niebuhr, they say, the Prussian Professor and Historian, fell broken-hearted in consequence; sickened, if we can believe it, and died of the Three Days! It was surely not a very heroic death;—little better than Racine's, dying because Louis Fourteenth looked sternly on him once. The world had stood some considerable shocks in its time; might have been expected to survive the Three Days too, and be found turning on its axis after even them! The Three Days told all mortals that the old French Revolution, mad as it might look, was not a transitory ebullition of Bedlam, but a genuine product of this Earth where we all live; that it was verily a Fact, and that the world in general would do well everywhere to regard it as such.

Truly, without the French Revolution, one would not know what to make of an age like this at all. We will hail the French Revolution, as shipwrecked mariners might the sternest rock, in a world otherwise all of baseless sea and waves. A true Apocalypse, though a terrible one, to this false withered artificial time; testifying once more that Nature is *preter*natural, if not divine, then diabolic; that Semblance is not Reality; that it has to become Reality, or the world will take fire under it,—burn *it* into what it is, namely Nothing! Plausibility has ended; empty Routine has ended; much has ended. This, as with a Trump of Doom, has been proclaimed to all men. They are the wisest who will learn it soonest. Long confused generations before it be learned; peace impossible till it be! The earnest man, surrounded, as ever, with a world of inconsistencies, can await patiently, patiently strive to do *his* work, in the midst of that. Sentence of Death is written down in Heaven against all that; sentence of Death is now proclaimed on the Earth against it: this he with his eyes may see. And surely, I should say, considering the other side of the matter, what enormous difficulties lie there, and how fast, fearfully fast, in all countries, the inexorable demand for solution of them is pressing on,—he may easily find other work to do than labouring in the Sansculottic province at this time of day!

To me, in these circumstances, that of 'Hero-worship' becomes a fact inexpressibly precious; the most solacing fact one sees in the world at present. There is an everlasting hope in it for the management of the world. Had all traditions, arrangements, creeds, societies that men ever instituted, sunk away, this would remain. The certainty of Heroes being sent us; our faculty, our necessity, to reverence Heroes when sent: it shines like a pole-star through smoke-clouds, dust-clouds, and all manner of down-rushing and conflagration.

Hero-worship would have sounded very strange to those workers and fighters in the French Revolution. Not reverence for Great Men; not any hope, or belief, or even wish, that Great Men could again appear in the world! Nature, turned into a 'Machine,' was as if effete now; could not any longer produce Great Men:—I can tell her, she may give up the trade altogether, then; we cannot do without Great Men!—But neither have I any quarrel with that of 'Liberty and Equality;' with the faith that, wise great men being impossible, a level immensity of foolish small men would suffice. It was a natural faith then and there. "Liberty and Equality; no Authority needed any longer. Hero-worship, reverence for *such* Authorities, has proved false, is itself a falsehood; no more of it! We have had such *forgeries*, we will now trust nothing. So many base plated coins passing in the market, the belief has now become common that no gold any longer exists,—and even that we can do very well without gold!"—I find this, among other things, in that universal cry of Liberty and Equality; and find it very natural, as matters then stood.

And yet surely it is but the *transition* from false to true. Considered as the whole truth, it is false altogether;—the product of entire sceptical blindness, as yet only *struggling* to see. Hero-worship exists forever, and everywhere: not Loyalty alone; it extends from divine adoration down to the lowest practical regions of life. 'Bending before men,' if it is not to be a mere empty grimace, better dispensed with than practised, is Hero-worship; a recognition that there does dwell in that presence of our brother something divine; that every created man, as Novalis said, is a 'revelation in the Flesh.' They were Poets too, that devised all those graceful courtesies which make life noble! Courtesy is not a falsehood or grimace; it need not be such. And Loyalty, religious Worship itself, are still possible; nay still inevitable.

May we not say, moreover, while so many of our late Heroes have worked rather as revolutionary men, that nevertheless every Great Man, every genuine man, is by the nature of him a son of Order, not of Disorder? It is a tragical position for a true man to work in revolutions. He seems an anarchist; and indeed a painful element of anarchy does encumber him at every step,—him to whose whole soul anarchy is hostile, hateful. His mission is Order; every man's is. He is here to make what was disorderly, chaotic, into a thing ruled, regular. He is the missionary of Order. Is not all work of man in this world a *making of Order*? The carpenter finds rough trees; shapes them, constrains them into square fitness, into purpose and use. We are all born enemies of Disorder: it is tragical for us all to be concerned in image-breaking and down-pulling; for the Great Man, *more* a man than we, it is doubly tragical.

Thus too all human things, maddest French Sansculottisms, do and must work towards Order. I say, there is not a *man* in them, raging in the thickest of the madness, but is impelled withal, at all moments, towards Order. His very life means that; Disorder is dissolution, death. No chaos but it seeks a *centre* to revolve round. While man is man, some Cromwell or Napoleon is the necessary finish of a

Sansculottism.—Curious: in those days when Hero-worship was the most incredible thing to every one, how it does come out neverthe-less, and assert itself practically, in a way which all have to credit. Divine *right*, take it on the great scale, is found to mean divine *might* withal! While old false Formulas are getting trampled everywhere into destruction, new genuine Substances unexpectedly unfold them-selves indestructible. In rebellious ages, when Kingship itself seems dead and abolished, Cromwell, Napoleon step forth again as Kings. The history of these men is what we have now to look at, as our last phasis of Heroism. The old ages are brought back to us; the manner in which Kings were made, and Kingship itself first took rise, is again exhibited in the history of these Two.

We have had many civil-wars in England; wars of Red and White Roses, wars of Simon de Montfort; wars enough, which are not very memorable. But that war of the Puritans has a significance which belongs to no one of the others. Trusting to your candour, which will suggest on the other side what I have not room to say, I will call it a section once more of that great universal war which alone makes up the true History of the World,—the war of Belief against Unbelief! The struggle of men intent on the real essence of things, against men intent on the semblances and forms of things. The Puritans, to many, seem mere savage Iconoclasts, fierce destroyers of Forms; but it were more just to call them haters of *untrue* Forms. I hope we know how to respect Laud and his King as well as them. Poor Laud seems to me to have been weak and ill-starred, not dishonest; an unfortunate Pedant rather than anything worse. His 'Dreams' and superstitions, at which they laugh so, have an affectionate, loveable kind of char-acter. He is like a College-Tutor, whose whole world is forms, College-rules; whose notion is that these are the life and safety of the world. He is placed suddenly, with that unalterable luckless notion of his, at the head not of a College but of a Nation, to regulate the most complex deep-reaching interests of men. He thinks they ought to go by the old decent regulations; nay that their salvation will lie in extending and improving these. Like a weak man, he drives with spasmodic vehemence towards his purpose; cramps himself to it, heeding no voice of prudence, no cry of pity: He will have his College-rules obeyed by his Collegians; that first; and till that, noth-ing. He is an ill-starred Pedant, as I said. He would have it the world was a College of that kind, and the world *was not* that. Alas, was not his doom stern enough? Whatever wrongs he did, were they not all frightfully avenged on him?

It is meritorious to insist on forms; Religion and all else naturally clothes itself in forms. Everywhere the *formed* world is the only habitable one. The naked formlessness of Puritanism is not the thing I praise in the Puritans; it is the thing I pity,—praising only the spirit which had rendered that inevitable! All substances clothe themselves in forms: but there are suitable true forms, and then there are untrue unsuitable. As the briefest definition, one might say, Forms which *grow* round a substance, if we rightly understand that, will correspond to the real nature and purport of it, will be true, good; forms which are consciously *put* round a substance, bad. I invite you to reflect on this. It distinguishes true from false in Ceremonial Form, earnest solemnity from empty pageant, in all human things.

There must be a veracity, a natural spontaneity in forms. In the commonest meeting of men, a person making, what we call, 'set speeches,' is not he an offence? In the mere drawing-room, whatsoever courtesies you see to be grimaces, prompted by no spontaneous reality within, are a thing you wish to get away from. But suppose now it were some matter of vital concernment, some transcendent matter (as Divine Worship is), about which your whole soul, struck dumb with its excess of feeling, knew not how to *form* itself into utterance at all, and preferred formless silence to any utterance there possible,—what should we say of a man coming forward to represent or utter it for you in the way of upholsterer-mummery? Such a man,— let him depart swiftly, if he love himself! You have lost your only son; are mute, struck down, without even tears: an importunate man importunately offers to celebrate Funeral Games for him in the manner of the Greeks! Such mummery is not only not to be accepted; it is hateful, unendurable. It is what the old Prophets called 'Idolatry,' worshipping of hollow *shows;* what all earnest men do and will reject. We can partly understand what those poor Puritans meant. Laud dedicating that St. Catherine Creed's Church, in the manner we have it described; with his multiplied ceremonial bowings, gesticulations, exclamations: surely it is rather the rigorous formal *Pedant,* intent on his 'College-rules,' than the earnest Prophet, intent on the essence of the matter!

Puritanism found *such* forms insupportable; trampled on such forms;—we have to excuse it for saying, No form at all rather than such! It stood preaching in its bare pulpit, with nothing but the Bible in its hand. Nay, a man preaching from his earnest *soul* into the earnest *souls* of men: is not this virtually the essence of all Churches whatsoever? The nakedest, savagest reality, I say, is preferable to any semblance, however dignified. Besides, it will clothe itself with *due* semblance by and by, if it be real. No fear of that; actually no fear at all. Given the living *man*, there will be found *clothes* for him; he will find himself clothes. But the suit-of-clothes pretending that *it* is both clothes and man—! We cannot 'fight the French' by three hundred thousand red uniforms; there must be *men* in the inside of them! Semblance, I assert, must actually *not* divorce itself from Reality. If Semblance do,—why then there must be men found to rebel against Semblance, for it has become a lie! These two Antagonisms at war here, in the case of Laud and the Puritans, are as old nearly as the world. They went to fierce battle over England in that age; and fought out their confused controversy to a certain length, with many results for all of us.

In the age which directly followed that of the Puritans, their cause or themselves were little likely to have justice done them. Charles Second and his Rochesters were not the kind of men you would set to judge what the worth or meaning of such men might have been. That there could be any faith or truth in the life of a man, was what these poor Rochesters, and the age they ushered in, had forgotten. Puritanism was hung on gibbets,—like the bones of the leading Puritans. Its work nevertheless went on accomplishing itself. All true work of a man, hang the author of it on what gibbet you like, must and will accomplish itself. We have our *Habeas-Corpus*, our free Representation of the People; acknowledgment, wide as the world, that all men are, or else must, shall, and will become, what we call *free* men;—men with their life grounded on reality and justice, not on tradition, which has become unjust and a chimera! This in part, and much besides this, was the work of the Puritans.

And indeed, as these things became gradually manifest, the character of the Puritans began to clear itself. Their memories were, one after another, taken *down* from the gibbet; nay a certain portion of them are now, in these days, as good as canonized. Eliot, Hampden,

Pym, nay Ludlow, Hutchinson, Vane himself, are admitted to be a kind of Heroes; political Conscript Fathers, to whom in no small degree we owe what makes us a free England: it would not be safe for anybody to designate these men as wicked now. Few Puritans of note but find their apologists somewhere, and have a certain reverence paid them by earnest men. One Puritan, I think, and almost he alone, our poor Cromwell, seems to hang yet on the gibbet, and find no hearty apologist anywhere. Him neither saint nor sinner will acquit of great wickedness. A man of ability, infinite talent, courage, and so forth: but he betrayed the Cause! Selfish ambition, dishonesty, duplicity; a fierce, coarse, hypocritical *Tartufe;* turning all that noble Struggle for constitutional Liberty into a sorry farce played for his own benefit: this and worse is the character they give of Cromwell. And then there come contrasts with Washington and others; above all, with these noble Pyms and Hampdens, whose noble work he stole for himself, and ruined into a futility and deformity.

This view of Cromwell seems to me the not unnatural product of a century like the Eighteenth. As we said of the Valet, so of the Sceptic: He does not know a Hero when he sees him! The Valet expected purple mantles, gilt sceptres, bodyguards and flourishes of trumpets: the Sceptic of the Eighteenth century looks for regulated respectable Formulas, 'Principles,' or what else he may call them; a style of speech and conduct which has got to seem 'respectable,' which can plead for itself in a handsome articulate manner, and gain the suffrages of an enlightened sceptical Eighteenth century! It is, at bottom, the same thing that both the Valet and he expect: the garnitures of some *acknowledged* royalty, which *then* they will acknowledge! The King coming to them in the rugged *un*formulistic state shall be no King.

For my own share, far be it from me to say or insinuate a word of disparagement against such characters as Hampden, Eliot, Pym; whom I believe to have been right worthy and useful men. I have read diligently what books and documents about them I could come at;—with the honestest wish to admire, to love, and worship them like Heroes; but I am sorry to say, if the real truth must be told, with very indifferent success! At bottom, I found that it would not do. They are very noble men these; step along in their stately way, with their measured euphuisms, philosophies, parliamentary eloquences, Ship-monies, *Monarchies of Man;* a most constitutional, unblameable, dignified set of men. But the heart remains cold before them; the fancy alone endeavours to get up some worship of them. What man's heart does, in reality, break forth into any fire of brotherly love for these men? They are become dreadfully dull men! One breaks down often enough in the constitutional eloquence of the admirable Pym, with his 'seventhly and lastly.' You find that it may be the admirablest thing in the world, but that it is heavy,—heavy as lead, barren as brick clay; that, in a word, for you there is little or nothing now surviving there! One leaves all these Nobilities standing in their niches of honour: the rugged outcast Cromwell, he is the man of them all, in whom one still finds human stuff. The great savage *Baresark:* he could write no euphuistic *Monarchy of Man;* did not speak, did not work with glib regularity; had no straight story to tell for himself anywhere. But he stood bare, not cased in euphuistic coat-of-mail; he grappled like a giant, face to face, heart to heart, with the naked truth of things! That, after all, is the sort of man for one. I plead guilty to valuing such a man beyond all other sorts of men. Smooth-shaven Respectabilities not a few one finds, that are not good for much. Small thanks to a man for keeping his hands clean, who would not touch the work but with gloves on!

Neither, on the whole, does this constitutional tolerance of the Eighteenth century for the other happier Puritans seem to be a very great matter. One might say, it is but a piece of Formulism and Scepticism like the rest. They tell us, It was a sorrowful thing to consider that the foundation of our English Liberties should have been laid by 'Superstition.' These Puritans came forward with Calvinistic incredible Creeds, Anti-Laudisms, Westminster Confessions; demanding, chiefly of all, that they should have liberty to *worship* in their own way. Liberty to *tax* themselves: that was the thing they should have demanded! It was Superstition, Fanaticism, disgraceful ignorance of Constitutional Philosophy to insist on the other thing!— Liberty to *tax* oneself? Not to pay out money from your pocket except on reason shewn? No century, I think, but a rather barren one would have fixed on that as the first right of man! I should say, on the contrary, A just man will generally have better cause than *money* in what shape soever, before deciding to revolt against his Government. Ours is a most confused world; in which a good man will be thankful to see any kind of Government maintain itself in a not insupportable manner: and here in England, to this hour, if he is not ready to pay a great many taxes which *he* can see very small reason in, it will not go well with him, I think! He must try some other climate than this. Taxgatherer? Money? He will say: "Take my money, since you *can*, and it is so desirable to you; take it,—and take yourself away with it; and leave me alone to my work here. *I* am still here; can still work, after all the money you have taken from me!" But if they come to him, and say, "Acknowledge a Lie; pretend to say you are worshipping God, when you are not doing it: believe not the thing that *you* find true, but the thing that I find, or pretend to find true!" He will answer: "No; by God's help, No! You may take my purse; but I cannot have my moral Self annihilated. The purse is any Highwayman's who might meet me with a loaded pistol: but the Self is mine and God my Maker's; it is not yours; and I will resist you to the death, and revolt against you, and on the whole front all manner of extremities, accusations and confusions, in defence of that!"—

Really, it seems to me the one reason which could justify revolting, this of the Puritans. It has been the soul of all just revolts among men. Not *Hunger* alone produced even the French Revolution; no, but the feeling of the insupportable all-pervading *Falsehood* which had now embodied itself in Hunger, in universal material Scarcity and Nonentity, and thereby become *indisputably* false in the eyes of all! We will leave the Eighteenth century with its 'liberty to tax itself.' We will not astonish ourselves that the meaning of such men as the Puritans remained dim to it. To men who believe in no reality at all, how shall a *real* human soul, the intensest of all realities, as it were the Voice of this world's Maker still speaking to *us*,—be intelligible? What it cannot reduce into constitutional doctrines relative to 'taxing,' or other the like material interest, gross, palpable to the sense, such a century will needs reject as an amorphous heap of rubbish. Hampdens, Pyms and Ship-money will be the theme of much constitutional eloquence, striving to be fervid;—which will glitter, if not as fire does, then as *ice* does: and the irreducible Cromwell will remain a chaotic mass of 'Madness,' 'Hypocrisy,' and much else.

From of old, I will confess, this theory of Cromwell's falsity has been incredible to me. Nay, I cannot believe the like, of any Great Man whatever. Multitudes of Great Men figure in History as false selfish men; but if we will consider it, they are but *figures* for us, unintelligible shadows: we do not see into them as men that could have existed at all. A superficial unbelieving generation only, with no eye but for the surfaces and semblances of things, could form such notions of Great Men. Can a great soul be possible without a *con-science* in it, the essence of all *real* souls, great or small?—No, we cannot figure Cromwell as a Falsity and Fatuity; the longer I study him and his career, I believe this the less. Why should we? There is no evidence of it. Is it not strange that, after all the mountains of calumny this man has been subject to, after being represented as the very prince of liars, who never, or hardly ever, spoke truth, but always some cunning counterfeit of truth, there should not yet have been one falsehood brought clearly home to him? A prince of liars, and no lie spoken by him. Not one that I could yet get sight of. It is like Pococke asking Grotius, Where is your *proof* of Mahomet's Pigeon? No proof!—Let us leave all these calumnious chimeras, as chimeras ought to be left. They are not portraits of the man; they are dis-tracted phantasms of him, the joint product of hatred and darkness.

Looking at the man's life with our own eyes, it seems to me, a very different hypothesis suggests itself. What little we know of his earlier obscure years, distorted as it has come down to us, does it not all betoken an earnest, affectionate, sincere kind of man? His nervous melancholic temperament indicates rather a seriousness *too* deep for him. Of those stories of 'Spectres;' of the white Spectre in broad daylight, predicting that he should be King of England, we are not bound to believe much;—probably no more than of the other black Spectre, or Devil in person, to whom the Officer *saw* him sell himself before Worcester Fight! But the mournful, over-sensitive, hypochon-driac humour of Oliver, in his young years, is otherwise indisputably known. The Huntingdon Physician told Sir Philip Warwick himself, He had often been sent for at midnight; Mr. Cromwell was full of hypochondria, thought himself near dying, and "had fancies about the Town-cross." These things are significant. Such an excitable deep-feeling nature, in that rugged stubborn strength of his, is not the symptom of falsehood; it is the symptom and promise of quite other than falsehood!

The young Oliver is sent to study Law; falls, or is said to have fallen, for a little period, into some of the dissipations of youth; but if so, speedily repents, abandons all this: not much above twenty, he is married, settled as an altogether grave and quiet man. 'He pays back what money he had won at gambling,' says the story;—he does not think any gain of that kind could be really *his*. It is very interesting, very natural, this 'conversion,' as they well name it; this awakening of a great true soul from the worldly slough, to see into the awful *truth* of things;—to see that Time and its shows all rested on Eternity, and this poor Earth of ours was the threshold either of Heaven or of Hell! Oliver's life at St. Ives and Ely as a sober industrious Farmer, is it not altogether as that of a true and devout man? He has renounced the world and its ways; *its* prizes are not the thing that can enrich him. He tills the earth; he reads his Bible; daily assembles his servants round him to worship God. He comforts persecuted ministers, is fond of preachers; nay, can himself preach,—exhorts his neighbours to be wise, to redeem the time. In all this, what 'hypocrisy,' 'ambition,' 'cant,' or other falsity? The man's hopes, I do believe, were fixed on the other Higher World; his aim to get well *thither* by walking well through his humble course in *this* world. He courts no notice: what could notice here do for him? 'Ever in his great Taskmaster's eye.'—It is striking, too, how he comes out once into public view; he, since no other is willing to come: in resistance to a public grievance. I mean, in that matter of the Bedford Fens. No one else will go to law with Authority; therefore he will. That matter once settled, he returns back into obscurity, to his Bible and his Plough. 'Gain influence?' His influence is the most legitimate; derived from personal knowledge of him, as a just, religious, reasonable and determined man. In this way he has lived till past forty; old age is now in view of him, and the earnest portal of Death and Eternity;—it was at this point that he suddenly became 'ambitious!' I do not interpret his Parliamentary mission in that way!

His successes in Parliament, his successes through the war, are honest successes of a brave man; who has more resolution in the heart of him, more light in the head of him than other men. His prayers to God; his spoken thanks to the God of Victory, who had preserved him safe, and carried him forward so far, through the furious clash of a world all set in conflict, through desperate-looking envelopments at Dunbar; through the death-hail of so many battles; mercy after mercy; to the 'crowning mercy' of Worcester Fight: all this is good and genuine for a deephearted Calvinistic Cromwell. Only to vain unbelieving Cavaliers, worshipping not God but their own 'love-locks,' frivolities and formalities, living quite apart from contemplations of God, living *without* God in the world, need it seem hypocritical.

Nor will his participation in the King's death involve him in condemnation with us. It is a stern business killing of a King! But if you once go to war with him, it lies *there;* this and all else lies there. Once at war, you have made wager of battle with him: it is he to die, or else you. Reconciliation is problematic; may be possible, or, far more likely, is impossible. It is now pretty generally admitted that the Parliament, having vanquished Charles First, had no way of making any tenable arrangement with him. The large Presbyterian party, apprehensive now of the Independents, were most anxious to do so; anxious indeed as for their own existence; but it could not be. The unhappy Charles, in those final Hampton-Court negotiations, shews himself as a man fatally incapable of being dealt with. A man who, once for all, could not and would not *understand:*—whose thought did not in any measure represent to him the real fact of the matter; nay, worse, whose *word* did not at all represent his thought. We may say this of him without cruelty, with deep pity rather: but it is true and undeniable. Forsaken there of all but the *name* of Kingship, he still, finding himself treated with outward respect as a King, fancied that he might play off party against party, and smuggle himself into his old power by deceiving both. Alas, they both *discovered* that he was deceiving them. A man whose *word* will not inform you at all what he means or will do, is not a man you can bargain with. You must get out of that man's way, or put him out of yours! The Presbyterians, in their despair, were still for believing Charles, though found false, unbelievable again and again. Not so Cromwell: "For all our fighting," says he, "we are to have a little bit of paper?" No!—

In fact, everywhere we have to note the decisive practical *eye* of this man; how he drives towards the practical and practicable; has a genuine insight into what *is* fact. Such an intellect, I maintain, does not belong to a false man: the false man sees false shows, plausibilities, expediencies: the true man is needed to discern even practical truth. Cromwell's advice about the Parliament's Army, early in the contest, How they were to dismiss their city-tapsters, flimsy riotous persons, and choose substantial yeomen, whose heart was in the work, to be soldiers for them: this is advice by a man who *saw*. Fact answers, if you see into Fact! Cromwell's *Ironsides* were the embodiment of this insight of his; men fearing God; and without any other fear. No more conclusively genuine set of fighters ever trod the soil of England, or of any other land.

Neither will we blame greatly that word of Cromwell's to them; which was so blamed: "If the King should meet me in battle, I would kill the King." Why not? These words were spoken to men who stood as before a Higher than Kings. They had set more than their own lives on the cast. The Parliament may call it, in official language, a fighting '*for* the King:' but we, for our share, cannot understand that. To us it is no dilettante work, no sleek officiality; it is sheer rough death and earnest. They have brought it to the calling forth of *War;* horrid internecine fight, man grappling with man in fire-eyed rage,— the *infernal* element in man called forth, to try it by that! *Do* that therefore; since that is the thing to be done.—The successes of Cromwell seem to me a very natural thing! Since he was not shot in battle, they were an inevitable thing. That such a man, with the eye to see, with the heart to dare, should advance, from post to post, from victory to victory, till the Huntingdon Farmer became, by whatever name you might call him, the acknowledged Strongest Man in England, virtually the King of England, requires no magic to explain it!—

Truly it is a sad thing for a people, as for a man, to fall into Scepticism, into dilettantism, insincerity; not to know a Sincerity when they see it. For this world, and for all worlds, what curse is so fatal? The heart lying dead, the eye cannot see. What intellect remains is merely the *vulpine* intellect. That a true *King* be sent them is of small use; they do not know him when sent. They say scornfully, Is this your King? The Hero wastes his heroic faculty in bootless contradiction from the unworthy; and can accomplish little. For himself he does accomplish a heroic life, which is much, which is all; but for the world he accomplishes comparatively nothing. The wild rude Sincerity, direct from Nature, is not glib in answering from the witness-box: in your small-debt *pie-powder* court, he is scouted as a counterfeit. The vulpine intellect 'detects' him. For being a man worth any thousand men, the response your Knox, your Cromwell gets, is an argument for two centuries whether he was a man at all. God's greatest gift to this Earth is sneeringly flung away. The miraculous talisman is a paltry plated coin, not fit to pass in the shops as a common guinea.

Lamentable this! I say, this must be remedied. Till this be remedied in some measure, there is nothing remedied. 'Detect quacks?' Yes do, for Heaven's sake; but know withal the men that are to be trusted! Till we know that, what is all our knowledge; how shall we even so much as 'detect?' For the vulpine sharpness, which considers itself to be knowledge, and 'detects' in that fashion, is far mistaken. Dupes indeed are many: but, of all *dupes*, there is none so fatally situated as he who lives in undue terror of being duped. The world does exist; the world has truth in it, or it would not exist! First recognise what is true, we shall *then* discern what is false; and properly never till then.

'Know the men that are to be trusted:' alas, this is yet, in these days, very far from us. The sincere alone can recognise sincerity. Not a Hero only is needed, but a world fit for him; a world not of *Valets;*—the Hero comes almost in vain to it otherwise! Yes, it is far from us: but it must come; thank God, it is visibly coming. Till it do come, what have we? Ballot-boxes, suffrages, French Revolutions:— if we are as Valets, and do not know the Hero when we see him, what good are all these? A heroic Cromwell comes; and for a hundred and fifty years he cannot have a vote from us. Why, the insincere, unbelieving world is the *natural property* of the Quack, and of the Father of Quacks and Quackeries! Misery, confusion, unveracity are alone possible there. By ballot-boxes we alter the *figure* of our Quack; but the substance of him continues. The Valet-World *has* to be governed by the Sham-Hero, by the King merely *dressed* in King-gear. It is his; he is its! In brief, one of two things: We shall either learn to know a Hero, a true Governor and Captain, somewhat better, when we see him; or else go on to be forever governed by the Unheroic;—had we ballot-boxes clattering at every street-corner, there were no remedy in these.

Poor Cromwell,—great Cromwell! The inarticulate Prophet; Prophet who could not *speak*. Rude, confused, struggling to utter himself, with his savage depth, with his wild sincerity; and he looked so strange, among the elegant Euphuisms; dainty little Falklands, didactic Chillingworths, diplomatic Clarendons! Consider him. An outer hull of chaotic confusion, visions of the Devil, nervous dreams, almost semi-madness; and yet such a clear determinate man's-energy working in the heart of that. A kind of chaotic man. The ray as of pure starlight and fire, working in such an element of boundless hypochondria, *un*formed black of darkness! And yet withal this hypochondria, what was it but the very greatness of the man? The depth and tenderness of his wild affections; the quantity of *sympathy* he had with things,—the quantity of insight he would yet get into the heart of things, the mastery he would yet get over things: this was his hypochondria. The man's misery, as man's misery always does, came of his greatness. Samuel Johnson too is that kind of man. Sorrow-stricken, half-distracted; the wide element of mournful *black* enveloping him,—wide as the world. It is the character of a prophetic man; a man with his whole soul *seeing* and struggling to see.

On this ground, too, I explain to myself Cromwell's reputed confusion of speech. To himself the internal meaning was sun-clear; but the material with which he was to clothe it in utterance was not there. He had *lived* silent; a great unnamed sea of Thought round him all his days; and in his way of life little call to attempt *naming* or uttering that. With his sharp power of vision, resolute power of action, I doubt not he could have learned to write Books withal, and speak fluently enough;—he did harder things than writing of Books. This kind of man is precisely he who is fit for doing manfully all things you will set him on doing. Intellect is not speaking and log-icizing; it is seeing and ascertaining. Virtue, *Vir-tus*, manhood, *hero*-hood, is not fairspoken immaculate regularity; it is first of all, what the Germans well name it, *Tugend* (*Taugend*, *dow*-ing or *Dough*ti-ness), Courage and the Faculty to *do*. This basis of the matter Cromwell had in him.

One understands moreover how, though he could not speak in Parliament, he might *preach*, rhapsodic preaching; above all, how he might be great in extempore prayer. These are the free outpouring utterances of what is in the heart: method is not required in them; warmth, depth, sincerity are all that is required. Cromwell's habit of prayer is a notable feature of him. All his great enterprises were commenced with prayer. In dark inextricable-looking difficulties, his

Officers and he used to assemble, and pray alternately, for hours, for days, till some definite resolution rose among them, some 'door of hope,' as they would name it, disclosed itself. Consider that. In tears, in fervent prayers, and cries to the great God, to have pity on them, to make His light shine before them. They, armed Soldiers of Christ, as they felt themselves to be; a little band of Christian Brothers, who had drawn the sword against a great black devouring world not Christian, but Mammonish, Devilish,—they cried to God in their straits, in their extreme need, not to forsake the Cause that was His. The light which now rose upon them,—how could a human soul, by any means at all, get better light? Was not the purpose so formed like to be precisely the best, wisest, the one to be followed without hesitation any more? To them it was as the shining of Heaven's own Splendour in the waste-howling darkness; the Pillar of Fire by night, that was to guide them on their desolate perilous way. *Was* it not such? Can a man's soul, to this hour, get guidance by any other method than intrinsically by that same,—devout prostration of the earnest struggling soul before the Highest, the Giver of all Light; be such *prayer* a spoken, articulate, or be it a voiceless, inarticulate one? There is no other method. 'Hypocrisy?' One begins to be weary of all that. They who call it so, have no right to speak on such matters. They never formed a purpose, what one can call a purpose. They went about balancing expediencies, plausibilities; gathering votes, advices; they never were alone with the *truth* of a thing at all.— Cromwell's prayers were likely to be 'eloquent,' and much more than that. His was the heart of a man who *could* pray.

But indeed his actual Speeches, I apprehend, were not nearly so ineloquent, incondite, as they look. We find he was, what all speakers aim to be, an impressive speaker, even in Parliament; one who, from the first, had weight. With that rude passionate voice of his, he was always understood to *mean* something, and men wished to know what. He disregarded eloquence, nay despised and disliked it; spoke always without premeditation of the words he was to use. The Reporters, too, in those days, seem to have been singularly candid; and to have given the Printer precisely what they found on their own note-paper. And withal, what a strange proof is it of Cromwell's being the premeditative ever-calculating hypocrite, acting a play before the world, That to the last he took no more charge of his Speeches! How came he not to study his words a little, before flinging them out to the public? If the words were true words, they could be left to shift for themselves.

But with regard to Cromwell's 'lying,' we will make one remark. This, I suppose, or something like this, to have been the nature of it. All parties found themselves deceived in him; each party understood him to be meaning *this*, heard him even say so, and behold he turns out to have been meaning *that!* He was, cry they, the chief of liars. But now, intrinsically, is not all this the inevitable fortune, not of a false man in such times, but simply of a superior man? Such a man must have *reticences* in him. If he walk wearing his heart upon his sleeve for daws to peck at, his journey will not extend far! There is no use for any man's taking up his abode in a house built of glass. A man always is to be himself the judge how much of his mind he will shew to other men; even to those he would have work along with him. There are impertinent inquiries made: your rule is, to leave the inquirer *un*informed on that matter; not, if you can help it, *mis*informed, but precisely as dark as he was! This, could one hit the right phrase of response, is what the wise and faithful man would aim to answer in such a case.

Cromwell, no doubt of it, spoke often in the dialect of small subaltern parties; uttered to them a *part* of his mind. Each little party thought him all its own. Hence their rage, one and all, to find him not of their party, but of his own party! Was it his blame? At all seasons of his history, he must have felt, among such people, how, if he explained to them the deeper insight he had, they must either have shuddered aghast at it, or believing it, their own little compact hypothesis must have gone wholly to wreck. They could not have worked in his province any more; nay perhaps they could not now have worked in their own province. It is the inevitable position of a great man among small men. Small men, most active, useful, are to be seen everywhere, whose whole activity depends on some conviction which to you is palpably a limited one; imperfect, what we call an *error*. But would it be a kindness always, is it a duty always or often, to disturb them in that? Many a man, doing loud work in the world, stands only on some thin traditionality, conventionality; to him indubitable, to you incredible: break that beneath him, he sinks to endless depths! "I might have my hand full of truth," said Fontenelle, "and open only my little finger."

And if this be the fact even in matters of doctrine, how much more in all departments of practice. He that cannot withal *keep his mind to himself* cannot practise any considerable thing whatever. And we call it 'dissimulation,' all this? What would you think of calling the general of an army a dissembler because he did not tell every corporal and private soldier, who pleased to put the question, what his thoughts were about everything?—Cromwell, I should rather say, managed all this in a manner we must admire for its perfection. An endless vortex of such questioning 'corporals' rolled confusedly round him through his whole course; whom he did answer. It must have been as a great true-seeing man that he managed this too. Not one proved falsehood, as I said; not one! Of what man that ever wound himself through such a coil of things will you say so much?—

But, in fact, there are two errors, widely prevalent, which pervert to the very basis our judgments formed about such men as Cromwell; about their 'ambition,' 'falsity,' and such like. The first is what I might call substituting the *goal* of their career for the course and starting-point of it. The vulgar Historian of a Cromwell fancies that he had determined on being Protector of England, at the time when he was ploughing the marsh lands of Cambridgeshire. His career lay all mapped out; a program of the whole drama; which he then step by step dramatically unfolded, with all manner of cunning, deceptive dramaturgy, as he went on,—the hollow, scheming Ὑποκριτής or Play-actor that he was! This is a radical perversion; all but universal in such cases. And think for an instant how different the fact is! How much does one of *us* foresee of his own life? Short way ahead of us it is all dim; an *un*wound skein of possibilities, of apprehensions, attemptabilities, vague-looming hopes. This Cromwell had *not* his life lying all in that fashion of Program, which he needed then, with that unfathomable cunning of his, only to enact dramatically, scene after scene! Not so. We see it so; but to him it was in no measure so. What absurdities would fall away of themselves, were this one undeniable fact kept honestly in view by History! Historians indeed will tell you that they do keep it in view;—but look whether such is practically the fact! Vulgar History, as in this Cromwell's case, omits it altogether; even the best kinds of History only remember it now and then. To remember it duly, with rigorous perfection, as in the fact it *stood*, requires indeed a rare faculty; rare, nay impossible. A very Shakspeare for faculty; or more than Shakspeare; who could *enact* a brother man's biography, see with the brother man's eyes at all points of his course what things *he* saw; in short, *know* his course and him, as few 'Historians' are like to do. Half or more of all the thick-plied perversions which distort our image of Cromwell, will disappear, if we honestly so much as try to represent them so; in sequence, as they *were;* not in the lump, as they are thrown down before us.

But a second error, which I think the generality commit, refers to this same 'ambition' itself. We exaggerate the ambition of Great Men; we mistake what the nature of it is. Great Men are not ambitious in that sense; he is a small poor man that is ambitious so. Examine the man who lives in misery because he does not shine above other men; who goes about producing himself, pruriently anxious about his gifts and claims; struggling to force everybody, as it were begging everybody for God's sake, to acknowledge him a great man, and set him over the heads of men! Such a creature is among the wretchedest sights seen under this sun. A *great* man? A poor morbid prurient empty man; fitter for the ward of a hospital, than for a throne among men. I advise you to keep out of his way. He cannot walk on quiet paths; unless you will look at him, wonder at him, write paragraphs about him, he cannot live. It is the *emptiness* of the man, not his greatness. Because there is nothing in himself, he hungers and thirsts that you would find something in him. In good truth, I believe no great man, not so much as a genuine man who had health and real substance in him of whatever magnitude, was ever much tormented in this way.

Your Cromwell, what good could it do him to be 'noticed' by noisy crowds of people? God his Maker already noticed him. He, Cromwell, was already there; no notice would make *him* other than he already was. Till his hair was grown grey; and Life from the downhill slope was all seen to be limited, not infinite but finite, and all a measurable matter *how* it went,—he had been content to plough the ground, and read his Bible. He in his old days could not support it any longer, without selling himself to Falsehood, that he might ride in gilt carriages to Whitehall, and have clerks with bundles of papers haunting him, "Decide this, decide that," which in utmost sorrow of heart no man can perfectly decide! What could gilt carriages do for this man? From of old, was there not in his life a weight of meaning, a terror and a splendour as of Heaven itself? His existence there as man, set him beyond the need of gilding. Death, Judgment and Eternity: these already lay as the background of whatsoever he thought or did. All his life lay begirt as in a sea of nameless Thoughts, which no speech of a mortal could name. God's Word, as the Puritan prophets of that time had read it: this was great, and all else was little to him. To call such a man 'ambitious,' to figure him as the prurient windbag described above, seems to me the poorest solecism. Such a man will say: "Keep your gilt carriages and huzzaing mobs, keep your red-tape clerks, your influentialities, your important businesses. Leave me alone, leave me alone; there is *too much of life* in me already!" Old Samuel Johnson, the greatest soul in England in his day, was not ambitious. 'Corsica Boswell' flaunted at public shows with printed ribbons round his hat; but the great old Samuel staid at home. The world-wide soul wrapt up in its thoughts, in its sorrows;—what could paradings, and ribbons in the hat, do for it?

Ah yes, I will say again: The great *silent* men! Looking round on the noisy inanity of the world, words with little meaning, actions with little worth, one loves to reflect on the great Empire of *Silence*. The noble silent men, scattered here and there, each in his department; silently thinking, silently working; whom no Morning Newspaper makes mention of! They are the salt of the Earth. A country that has none or few of these is in a bad way. Like a forest which had no *roots;* which had all turned into leaves and boughs;—which must soon wither and be no forest. Wo for us if we had nothing but what we can *shew,* or speak. Silence, the great Empire of Silence: higher than the stars; deeper than the Kingdoms of Death! It alone is great; all else is small.—I hope we English will long maintain our *grand talent pour le silence.* Let others that cannot do without standing on barrel-heads, to spout, and be seen of all the market-place, cultivate speech exclusively,—become a most green forest without roots! Solomon says, There is a time to speak; but also a time to keep silence. Of some great silent Samuel, not urged to writing, as old Samuel Johnson says he was, by *want of money,* and nothing other, one might ask, "Why do not you too get up and speak; promulgate your system, found your sect?"—"Truly," he will answer, "I am *continent* of my thought hitherto; happily I have yet had the ability to keep it in me, no compulsion strong enough to speak it. My 'system' is not for promulgation first of all; it is for serving myself to live by. That is the great purpose of it to me. And then the 'honour?' Alas, yes;—but as Cato said of the statue: So many statues in that Forum of yours, may it not be better if they ask, Where is Cato's statue?"— —

But now, by way of counterpoise to this of Silence, let me say that there are two kinds of ambition; one wholly blameable, the other laudable and inevitable. Nature has provided that the great silent Samuel shall not be silent too long. The selfish wish to shine over others, let it be accounted altogether poor and miserable. 'Seekest thou great things, seek them not:' this is most true. And yet, I say, there is an irrepressible tendency in every man to develope himself according to the magnitude which Nature has made him of; to speak out, to act out, what Nature has laid in him. This is proper, fit, inevitable; nay it is a duty, and even the summary of duties for a man. The meaning of life here on earth might be defined as consisting in this: To unfold your *self*, to work what thing you have the faculty for. It is a necessity for the human being, the first law of our existence. Coleridge beautifully remarks that the infant learns to *speak* by this necessity it feels.—We will say therefore, To decide about ambition, whether it is bad or not, you have two things to take into view. Not the coveting of the place alone, but the fitness of the man for the place withal: that is the question. Perhaps the place was *his;* perhaps he had a natural right, and even obligation, to seek the place! Mirabeau's ambition to be Prime Minister, how shall we blame it, if he were 'the only man in France that could have done any good there?' Hopefuler perhaps had he not so clearly *felt* how much good he could do! But a poor Necker, who could do no good, and had even felt that he could do none, yet sitting broken-hearted because they had flung him out, and he was now quit of it, well might Gibbon mourn over him.—Nature, I say, has provided amply that the silent great man shall strive to speak withal; *too* amply, rather!

Fancy, for example, you had revealed to the brave old Samuel Johnson, in his shrouded-up existence, that it was possible for him to do a priceless divine work for his country and the whole world. That

the perfect Heavenly Law might be made Law on this Earth, that the
prayer he prayed daily, 'Thy kingdom come,' was at length to be
fuifilled! If you had convinced his judgment of this; that it was
possible, practicable; that he the mournful silent Samuel was called to
take a part in it! Would not the whole soul of the man have flamed
up into a divine clearness, into noble utterance and determination to
act; casting all sorrows and misgivings under his feet, counting all
affliction and contradiction small,—the whole dark element of his
existence blazing into articulate radiance of light and lightning? It
were a true ambition this! And think now how it actually was with
Cromwell. From of old, the sufferings of God's Church, true zealous
Preachers of the truth flung into dungeons, whipt, set on pillories,
their ears cropt off, God's Gospel-cause trodden under foot of the
unworthy: all this had lain heavy on his soul. Long years he had
looked upon it, in silence, in prayer; seeing no remedy on Earth;
trusting well that a remedy in Heaven's goodness would come,—that
such a course was false, unjust, and could not last forever. And now
behold the dawn of it; after twelve years silent waiting, all England
stirs itself; there is to be once more a Parliament, the Right will get
a voice for itself: inexpressible well-grounded hope has come again
into the Earth. Was not such a Parliament worth being a member of?
Cromwell threw down his ploughs, and hastened thither. He spoke
there,—rugged bursts of earnestness, of a self-seen truth, where we
get a glimpse of them. He worked there; he fought and strove, like
a strong true giant of a man, through cannon-tumult and all else,—
on and on, till the Cause *triumphed*, its once so formidable enemies
all swept from before it, and the dawn of hope had become clear light
of victory and certainty. That *he* stood there as the strongest soul of
England, the undisputed Hero of all England,—what of this? It was
possible that the Law of Christ's Gospel could now establish itself in
the world! The Theocracy which John Knox in his pulpit might dream
of as a 'devout imagination,' this practical man, experienced in the
whole chaos of most rough practice, dared to consider as capable of
being *realised*. Those that were highest in Christ's Church, the
devoutest wisest men, were to rule the land: in some considerable
degree, it might be so and should be so. Was it not *true*, God's truth?
And if *true*, was it not then the very thing to do? The strongest

practical intellect in England dared to answer, Yes! This I call a noble true purpose: is it not, in its own dialect, the noblest that could enter into the heart of Statesman or man? For a Knox to take it up was something; but for a Cromwell, with his great sound sense and experience of what our world *was*,—History, I think, shews it only this once in such a degree. I account it the culminating point of Protestantism; the most heroic phasis that 'Faith in the Bible' was appointed to exhibit here below. Fancy it: that it were made manifest to one of us, how we could make the Right supremely victorious over Wrong, and all that we had longed and prayed for, as the highest good to England and all lands, an attainable fact!

Well, I must say, the *vulpine* intellect, with its knowingness, its alertness and expertness in 'detecting hypocrites,' seems to me a rather sorry business. We have had but one such Statesman in England; one man, that I can get sight of, who ever had in the heart of him any such purpose at all. One man, in the course of fifteen hundred years; and this was his welcome. He had adherents by the hundred or the ten; opponents by the million. Had England rallied all round him,—why, then, England might have been a *Christian* land! As it is, vulpine knowingness sits yet at its hopeless problem, 'Given a world of Knaves, to educe an Honesty from their united action;'—how cumbrous a problem you may see in Chancery Law-Courts, and some other places! Till at length, by Heaven's just anger, but also by Heaven's great grace, the matter begins to stagnate; and this problem is becoming to all men a *palpably* hopeless one.—

But with regard to Cromwell and his purposes: Hume, and a multitude following him, come upon me here with an admission that Cromwell *was* sincere at first; a sincere 'Fanatic' at first, but gradually became a 'Hypocrite' as things opened round him. This of the Fanatic-Hypocrite is Hume's theory of it; extensively applied since,—to Mahomet and many others. Think of it seriously, you will find something in it; not much, not all, very far from all. Sincere hero-hearts do not sink in this miserable manner. The Sun flings forth impurities, gets balefully incrusted with spots; but it does not quench itself, and become no Sun at all, but a mass of Darkness! I will venture to say that such never befel a great deep Cromwell; I think, never. Nature's own lion-hearted Son; Antæus-like, his strength is got by *touching the Earth*, his Mother; lift him up from the Earth, lift him up into Hypocrisy, Inanity, his strength is gone. We will not assert that Cromwell was an immaculate man; that he fell into no faults, no insincerities among the rest. He was no dilettante professor of 'perfections,' 'immaculate conducts.' He was a rugged Orson, rending his rough way through actual true *work*,—doubtless with many a *fall* therein. Insincerities, faults, very many faults daily and hourly: it was too well known to him; known to God and him! The Sun was dimmed many a time; but the Sun had not himself grown a Dimness. Cromwell's last words, as he lay waiting for death, are those of a Christian heroic man. Broken prayers to God, that He would judge him and this Cause, He since man could not, in justice yet in pity. They are most touching words. He breathed out his wild great soul, its toils and sins all ended now, into the presence of his Maker, in this manner.

I, for one, will not call the man a Hypocrite! Hypocrite, mummer, the life of him a mere theatricality; empty barren quack, hungry for the shouts of mobs? The man had made obscurity do very well for him till his head was grey; and now he *was*, there as he stood recognised unblamed, the virtual King of England. Cannot a man do without King's Coaches and Cloaks? Is it such a blessedness to have clerks forever pestering you with bundles of papers in red tape? A simple Diocletian prefers planting of cabbages; a George Washington, no very immeasurable man, does the like. One would say, it is what any genuine man could do; and would do. The instant his real work were out in the matter of Kingship,—away with it!

Let us remark, meanwhile, how indispensable everywhere a *King* is, in all movements of men. It is strikingly shewn, in this very War, what becomes of men when they cannot find a Chief Man, and their enemies can. The Scotch Nation was all but unanimous in Puritanism; zealous and of one mind about it, as in this English end of the Island was always far from being the case. But there was no great Cromwell among them; poor tremulous, hesitating, diplomatic Argyles and such like: none of them had a heart true enough for the truth, or durst commit himself to the truth. They had no leader; and the scattered Cavalier party in that country had one: Montrose, the noblest of all the Cavaliers; an accomplished, gallant-hearted, splendid man; what one may call the Hero-Cavalier. Well, look at it: on the one hand subjects without a King; on the other a King without subjects! The subjects without King can do nothing; the subjectless King can do something. This Montrose, with a handful of Irish or Highland savages, few of them so much as guns in their hand, dashes at the drilled Puritan armies like a wild whirlwind; sweeps them, time after time, some five times over, from the field before him. He was at one period, for a short while, master of all Scotland. One man; but he was a man: a million zealous men, but *without* the one; they against him were powerless! Perhaps of all the persons in that Puritan struggle, from first to last, the single indispensable one was verily Cromwell. To see and dare, and decide; to be a fixed pillar in the welter of uncertainty;—a King among them, whether they called him so or not.

Precisely here, however, lies the rub for Cromwell. His other proceedings have all found advocates, and stand generally justified; but this dismissal of the Rump Parliament and assumption of the Protectorship, is what no one can pardon him. He had fairly grown to be King in England, Chief Man of the victorious party in England: but it seems he could not do without the King's Cloak, and sold himself to perdition in order to get it. Let us see a little how this was.

England, Scotland, Ireland, all lying now subdued at the feet of the Puritan Parliament, the practical question arose, What was to be done with it? How will you govern these Nations, which Providence in a wondrous way has given up to your disposal? Clearly those hundred surviving members of the Long Parliament, who sit there as supreme authority, cannot continue forever to sit. What *is* to be done?—It was a question which theoretical constitution-builders may find easy to answer; but to Cromwell, looking there into the real practical facts of it, there could be none more complicated. He asked of the Parliament, What it was they would decide upon? It was for the Parliament to say. Yet the Soldiers too, however contrary to Formula, they who had purchased this victory with their blood, it seemed to them that they also should have something to say in it! We will not "for all our fighting have nothing but a little piece of paper." We understand that the Law of God's Gospel, to which He through us has given the victory, shall establish itself, or try to establish itself, in this land!

For three years, Cromwell says, this question had been sounded in the ears of the Parliament. They could make no answer; nothing but talk, talk. Perhaps it lies in the nature of parliamentary bodies; perhaps no Parliament could in such case make any answer but even that of talk, talk! Nevertheless the question must and shall be answered. You sixty men there, becoming fast odious, even despicable, to the whole nation, whom the nation already call Rump Parliament, *you* cannot continue to sit there: who or what then is to follow? 'Free Parliament,' right of Election, Constitutional Formulas of one sort or the other,—the thing is a hungry Fact coming on us, which we must answer or be devoured by it! And who are you that prate of Constitutional Formulas, rights of Parliament? You have had to kill your King, to make Pride's Purges, to expel and banish by the law of the stronger whosoever would not let your Cause prosper: there are but fifty or three-score of you left there, debating in these days. Tell us what we shall do; not in the way of Formula, but of practicable Fact!

How they did finally answer, remains obscure to this day. The diligent Godwin himself admits that he cannot make it out. The likeliest is, that this poor Parliament still would not, and indeed could not dissolve and disperse; that when it came to the point of actually dispersing, they again, for the tenth or twentieth time, adjourned it,—and Cromwell's patience failed him. But we will take the favourablest hypothesis ever started for the Parliament; the favourablest, though I believe it is not the true one, but too favourable. According to this version: At the uttermost crisis, when Cromwell and his Officers were met on the one hand, and the fifty or sixty Rump Members on the other, it was suddenly told Cromwell that the Rump in its despair *was* answering in a very singular way; that in their splenetic envious despair, to keep out the Army at least, these men were hurrying through the House a kind of Reform Bill,—Parliament to be chosen by the whole of England; equable electoral division into districts; free suffrage, and the rest of it! A very questionable, or indeed for *them* an unquestionable thing. Reform Bill, free suffrage of Englishmen? Why, the Royalists themselves, silenced indeed but not exterminated, perhaps out*number* us; the great numerical majority of England was always indifferent to our Cause, merely looked at it and submitted to it. It is in weight and force, not by counting of heads, that we are the majority! And now with your Formulas and Reform Bills, the whole matter, sorely won by our swords, shall again launch itself to sea; become a mere hope, and likelihood, *small* even as a likelihood? And it is not a likelihood; it is a certainty, which we have won, by God's strength and our own right hands, and do now hold *here*. Cromwell walked down to these refractory Members; interrupted them in that rapid speed of their Reform Bill;—ordered them to begone, and talk there no more.—Can we not forgive him? Can we not understand him? John Milton, who looked on it all near at hand, could applaud him. The Reality had swept the Formulas away before it. I fancy, most men who were Realities in England might see into the necessity of that.

The strong daring man, therefore, has set all manner of Formulas and logical superficialities against him; has dared appeal to the genuine Fact of this England, Whether it will support him or not? It is curious to see how he struggles to govern in some constitutional way; find some Parliament to support him; but cannot. His first Parliament, the one they call Barebones's Parliament, is, so to speak, a *Convocation of the Notables*. From all quarters of England the leading Ministers and chief Puritan Officials nominate the men most distinguished by religious reputation, influence and attachment to the true Cause: these are assembled to shape out a plan. They sanctioned what was past; shaped as they could what was to come. They were scornfully called *Barebones's Parliament:* the man's name, it seems, was not *Barebones*, but Barbone,—a good enough man. Nor was it a jest, their work; it was a most serious reality,—a trial on the part of these Puritan Notables how far the Law of Christ could become the Law of this England. There were men of sense among them, men of some quality; men of deep piety I suppose the most of them were. They failed, it seems, and broke down, endeavouring to reform the Court of Chancery! They dissolved themselves, as incompetent; delivered up their power again into the hands of the Lord General Cromwell, to do with it what he liked and could. What *will* he do with it! The Lord General Cromwell, 'Commander-in-chief of all the Forces raised and to be raised;' he hereby sees himself, at this unexampled juncture, as it were the one available Authority left in England, nothing between

England and utter Anarchy but him alone. Such is the undeniable Fact of his position and England's, there and then. What will he do with it! After deliberation, he decides that he will *accept* it; will formally, with public solemnity, say and vow before God and men, "Yes, the Fact is so, and I will do the best I can with it!" Protectorship, Instrument of Government,—these are the external forms of the thing; worked out and sanctioned as they could in the circumstances be, by the Judges, by the leading Official people, 'Council of Officers and Persons of interest in the Nation:' and as for the thing itself, undeniably enough, at the pass matters had now come to, there *was* no alternative but Anarchy or that. Puritan England might accept it or not; but Puritan England was, in real truth, saved from suicide thereby!—I believe the Puritan People did, in an inarticulate, grumbling, yet on the whole grateful and real way, accept this anomalous act of Oliver's; at least, he and they together made it good, and always better to the last. But in their Parliamentary *articulate* way, they had their difficulties, and never knew fully what to say to it!—

Oliver's second Parliament, properly his *first* regular Parliament, chosen by the rule laid down in the Instrument of Government, did assemble, and worked;—but got, before long, into bottomless questions as to the Protector's *right*, as to 'usurpation,' and so forth; and had at the earliest legal day to be dismissed. Cromwell's concluding Speech to these men is a remarkable one. So likewise to his third Parliament, in similar rebuke for their pedantries and obstinacies. Most rude, chaotic, all these Speeches are; but most earnest-looking. You would say, it was a sincere helpless man; not used to *speak* the great inorganic thought of him, but to act it rather! A helplessness of utterance, in such bursting fulness of meaning. He talks much about 'births of Providence:' All these changes, so many victories and events, were not forethoughts, and theatrical contrivances of men, of *me* or of men; it is blind blasphemers that will persist in calling them so! He insists with a heavy sulphurous wrathful emphasis on this. As he well might! As if a Cromwell in that dark huge game he had been playing, the world wholly thrown into chaos round him, had *foreseen* it all, and played it all off like a precontrived puppetshow by wood and wire! These things were foreseen by no man, he says; no man could tell what a day would bring forth: they were 'births of Providence,' God's finger guided us on, and we came at last to clear height of victory, God's Cause triumphant in these Nations; and you as a Parliament could assemble together, and say in what manner all this could be *organised*, reduced into rational feasibility among the affairs of men. You were to help with your wise counsel in doing that. "You have had such an opportunity as no Parliament in England ever had." Christ's Law, the Right and True, was to be in some measure made the Law of this land. In place of that, you have got into your idle pedantries, constitutionalities, bottomless cavillings and questionings about written laws for *my* coming here;—and would send the whole matter into Chaos again, because I have no Notary's parchment, but only God's voice from the battle-whirlwind, for being President among you! That opportunity is gone; and we know not when it will return. You have had your constitutional Logic; and Mammon's Law, not Christ's Law rules yet in this land. "God be judge between you and me!" These are his final words to them: Take you your constitution-formulas in your hand; and I my *in*formal struggles, purposes, realities and acts; and "God be judge between you and me!"—

We said above what shapeless, involved chaotic things the printed Speeches of Cromwell's are. *Wilfully* ambiguous, unintelligible, say the most: a hypocrite shrouding himself in confused Jesuistic jargon! To me they do not seem so. I will say rather, they afforded the first glimpses I could ever get into the reality of this Cromwell, nay into the possibility of him. Try to believe that he means something, search lovingly what that may be: you will find a real *speech* lying imprisoned in these broken rude tortuous utterances; a meaning in the great heart of this inarticulate man! You will, for the first time, begin to see that he was a man; not an enigmatic chimera, unintelligible to you, incredible to you. The Histories and Biographies written of this Cromwell, written in shallow sceptical generations that could not know or conceive of a deep believing man, are far more *obscure* than Cromwell's Speeches. You look through them only into the infinite vague of Black and the Inane. 'Heats and jealousies,' says Lord Clarendon himself: 'heats and jealousies,' mere crabbed whims, theories, and crotchets; these induced slow sober quiet Englishmen to lay down their ploughs and work; and fly into red fury of confused war against the best-conditioned of Kings! *Try* if you can find that true. Scepticism writing about Belief may have great gifts; but it is really *ultra vires* there. It is Blindness laying down the Laws of Optics.—

Cromwell's third Parliament split on the same rock as his second. Ever the constitutional Formula: How came *you* there? Shew us some Notary parchment! Blind pedants:—"Why, surely the same power which makes you a Parliament, that, and something more, made me a Protector!" If my Protectorship is nothing, what in the name of wonder is your Parliamenteership, a reflex and creation of that?—

Parliaments having failed, there remained nothing but the way of Despotism. Military Dictators, each with his district, to *coerce* the Royalist and other gainsayers, to govern them, if not by act of Parliament, then by the sword. Formula shall *not* carry it, while the Reality is here! I will go on, protecting oppressed Protestants abroad, appointing just judges, wise managers, at home, cherishing true Gospel ministers; doing the best I can to make England a Christian England, greater than old Rome, the Queen of Protestant Christianity; I, since you will not help me; I while God leaves me life!—Why did he not give it up; retire into obscurity again, since the Law would not acknowledge him? cry several. That is where they mistake. For him there was no giving of it up! Prime Ministers have governed countries, Pitt, Pombal, Choiseul; and their word was a law while it held: but this Prime Minister was one that *could not get resigned.* Let him once resign, Charles Stuart and the Cavaliers waited to kill him; to kill the Cause *and* him. Once embarked, there is no retreat, no return. This Prime Minister could *retire* no-whither except into his tomb.

One is sorry for Cromwell in his old days. His complaint is incessant of the heavy burden Providence has laid on him. Heavy; which he must bear till death. Old Colonel Hutchinson, as his wife relates it, Hutchinson his old battle-mate, coming to see him on some indispensable business, much against his will,—Cromwell 'follows him to the door,' in a most fraternal, domestic, conciliatory style; begs that he would be reconciled to him, his old brother in arms; says how much it grieves him to be misunderstood, deserted by true fellow soldiers, dear to him from of old: the rigorous Hutchinson, cased in his Republican formula, sullenly goes his way.—And the man's head now white; his strong arm growing weary with its long work! I think always too of his poor Mother, now very old, living in that Palace of his; a right brave woman; as indeed they lived all an honest God-fearing Household there: if she heard a shot go off, she thought it was her son killed. He had to come to her at least once a day that she might see with her own eyes that he was yet living. The poor old Mother!— —What had this man gained; what had he gained? He had a life of sore strife and toil, to his last day. Fame, ambition, place in History? His dead body was hung in chains; his 'place in History'—place in History forsooth—has been a place of ignominy, accusation, blackness and disgrace; and here, this day, who knows if it is not rash in me to be among the first that ever ventured to pronounce him not a knave and liar, but a genuinely honest man! Peace to him. Did he not, in spite of all, accomplish much for us? *We* walk smoothly over his great rough heroic life; step over his body sunk in the ditch there. We need not *spurn* it, as we step on it!—Let the Hero rest. It was not to *men's* judgment that he appealed; nor have men judged him very well.

Precisely a century and a year after this of Puritanism had got itself hushed up into decent composure, and its results made smooth, in 1688, there broke out a far deeper explosion, much more difficult to hush up, known to all mortals, and like to be long known, by the name of French Revolution. It is properly the third and final act of Protestantism; the explosive confused return of mankind to Reality and Fact, now that they were perishing of Semblance and Sham. We call our English Puritanism the second act: "Well then, the Bible is true; let us go by the Bible!" "In Church," said Luther; "In Church and State," said Cromwell, "let us go by what actually *is* God's Truth." Men have to return to reality; they cannot live on semblance. The French Revolution, or third act, we may well call the final one; for lower than that savage *Sansculottism* men cannot go. They stand there on the nakedest haggard Fact, undeniable in all seasons and circumstances; and may and must begin again confidently to build up from that. The French explosion, like the English one, got its King,— who had no Notary parchment to shew for himself. We have still to glance for a moment at Napoleon, our second modern King.

Napoleon does by no means seem to me so great a man as Cromwell. His enormous victories which reached over all Europe, while Cromwell abode mainly in our little England, are but as the high *stilts* on which the man is seen standing; the stature of the man is not altered thereby. I find in him no such *sincerity* as in Cromwell; only a far inferior sort. No silent walking, through long years, with the Awful, Unnameable of this Universe; 'walking with God,' as he called it; and faith and strength in that alone: *latent* thought and valour, content to lie latent, then burst out as in blaze of Heaven's lightning! Napoleon lived in an age when God was no longer believed; the meaning of all Silence, Latency, was thought to be Nonentity: he had to begin not out of the Puritan Bible, but out of poor Sceptical *Encyclopédies*. This was the length the man carried it. Meritorious to get so far. His compact, prompt, every-way articulate character is in itself perhaps small, compared with our great chaotic *in*articulate Cromwell's. Instead of '*dumb* Prophet struggling to speak,' we have a portentous mixture of the Quack withal! Hume's notion of the Fanatic-Hypocrite, with such truth as it has, will apply much better to Napoleon, than it did to Cromwell, to Mahomet or the like,— where indeed taken strictly it has hardly any truth at all. An element of blameable ambition shews itself, from the first, in this man; gets the victory over him at last, and involves him and his work in ruin.

'False as a bulletin' became a proverb in Napoleon's time. He makes what excuse he could for it: that it was necessary to mislead the enemy, to keep up his own men's courage, and so forth. On the whole, there are no excuses. A man in no case has liberty to tell lies. It had been in the long-run *better* for Napoleon too if he had not told any. In fact, if a man have any purpose reaching beyond the hour and day, meant to be found extant *next* day, what good can it ever be to promulgate lies? The lies are found out; ruinous penalty is exacted for them. No man will believe the liar next time even when he speaks truth, when it is of the last importance that he be believed. The old cry of wolf!—A Lie is *no*-thing; you cannot of nothing make something; you make *nothing* at last, and lose your labour into the bargain.

Yet Napoleon *had* a sincerity: we are to distinguish between what is superficial and what is fundamental in insincerity. Across these outer manœuvrings and quackeries of his, which were many and most blameable, let us discern withal that the man had a certain instinctive ineradicable feeling for reality; and did base himself upon fact, so long as he had any basis. He has an instinct of Nature better than his culture was. His *savans*, Bourrienne tells us, in that voyage to Egypt were one evening busily occupied arguing that there could be no

God. They had proved it, to their satisfaction, by all manner of logic. Napoleon looking up into the stars, answers, "Very ingenious, Messieurs: but *who made* all that?" The Atheistic logic runs off from him like water; the great Fact stares him in the face: "Who made all that?" So too in Practice: he, as every man that can be great, or have victory in this world, sees, through all entanglements, the practical heart of the matter; drives straight towards that. When the steward of his Tuileries Palace was exhibiting the new upholstery, with praises, and demonstration how glorious it was, and how cheap withal, Napoleon, making little answer, asked for a pair of scissors, clipt one of the gold tassels from a window-curtain, put it in his pocket, and walked on. Some days afterwards, he produced it at the right moment, to the horror of his upholstery functionary: it was not gold but tinsel! In Saint Helena, it is notable how he still, to his last days, insists on the practical, the real. "Why talk and complain; above all, why quarrel with one another? There is no *result* in it; it comes to nothing that one can *do*. Say nothing, if one can do nothing!" He speaks often so, to his poor discontented followers; he is like a piece of silent strength in the middle of their morbid querulousness there.

And accordingly was there not what we can call a *faith* in him, genuine so far as it went? That this new enormous Democracy asserting itself here in the French Revolution is an insuppressible Fact, which the whole world, with its old forces and institutions, cannot put down: this was a true insight of his, and took his conscience and enthusiasm along with it,—a *faith*. And did he not interpret the dim purport of it well? '*La carrière ouverte aux talens*, The implements to him who can handle them:' this actually is the truth, and even the whole truth; it includes whatever the French Revolution or any Revolution could mean. Napoleon, in his first period, was a true Democrat. And yet by the nature of him, fostered too by his military trade, he knew that Democracy, if it were a true thing at all, could not be an anarchy: the man had a heart-hatred for anarchy. On that Twentieth of June (1792), Bourrienne and he sat in a coffee-house, as the mob rolled by: Napoleon expresses the deepest contempt for persons in authority that they do not restrain this rabble. On the Tenth of August he wonders why there is no man to command these poor Swiss; they would conquer if there were. Such a faith in

Democracy, yet hatred of anarchy, it is that carries Napoleon through all his great work. Through his brilliant Italian Campaigns, onwards to the Peace of Leoben, one would say, his inspiration is: 'Triumph to the French Revolution; assertion of it against these Austrian Simulacra that pretend to call it a Simulacrum!' Withal, however, he feels, and has a right to feel, how necessary a strong Authority is; how the Revolution cannot prosper or last without such. To bridle in that great devouring, self-devouring French Revolution; to *tame* it, so that its intrinsic purpose can be made good, that it may become *organic*, and be able to live among other organisms and *formed* things, not as a wasting destruction alone: is not this still what he partly aimed at, as the true purport of his life; nay what he actually managed to do? Through Wagrams, Austerlitzes; triumph after triumph,—he triumphed so far. There was an eye to see in this man, a soul to dare and do. He rose naturally to be the King. All men saw that he *was* such. The common soldiers used to say on the march: "These babbling *Avocats*, up at Paris; all talk and no work! What wonder it runs all wrong? We shall have to go and put our *Petit Caporal* there!" They went, and put him there; they and France at large. Chief-consulship, Emperorship, victory over Europe;—till the poor Lieutenant of *La Fère*, not unnaturally, might seem to himself the greatest of all men that had been in the world for some ages.

But at this point, I think, the fatal charlatan-element got the upper hand. He apostatised from his old faith in Facts, took to believing in Semblances; strove to connect himself with Austrian Dynasties, Popedoms, with the old false Feudalities which he once saw clearly to be false;—considered that *he* would found "his Dynasty" and so forth; that the enormous French Revolution meant only that! The man was 'given up to strong delusion, that he should believe a lie;' a fearful but most sure thing. He did not know true from false now when he looked at them,—the fearfulest penalty a man pays for yielding to untruth of heart. *Self* and false ambition had now become his god: *self*-deception once yielded to, *all* other deceptions follow naturally more and more. What a paltry patchwork of theatrical paper-mantles, tinsel and mummery, had this man wrapt his own great reality in, thinking to make it more real thereby! His hollow Pope's-*Concordat*, pretending to be a re-establishment of Catholicism, felt by himself to be the method of extirpating it, "*la vaccine de la religion:*" his cere-monial Coronations, consecrations by the old Italian Chimera in Notre-Dame,—"wanting nothing to complete the pomp of it," as Augereau said, "nothing but the half-million of men who had died to put an end to all that!" Cromwell's Inauguration was by the Sword and Bible; what we must call a genuinely *true* one. Sword and Bible were borne before him, without any chimera: were not these the *real* emblems of Puritanism; its true decoration and insignia? It had used them both in a very real manner, and pretended to stand by them now! But this poor Napoleon mistook: he believed too much in the *Dupeability* of men; saw no fact deeper in man than Hunger and this! He was mistaken. Like a man that should build upon cloud: his house and he fall down in confused wreck, and depart out of the world.

Alas, in all of us this charlatan-element exists; and *might* be devel-oped, were the temptation strong enough. 'Lead us not into temp-tation!' But it is fatal, I say, that it *be* developed. The thing into which it enters as a cognisable ingredient is doomed to be altogether tran-sitory; and, however huge it may *look*, is in itself small. Napoleon's working, accordingly, what was it with all the noise it made? A flash as of gunpowder wide-spread; a blazing-up as of dry heath. For an hour the whole Universe seems wrapt in smoke and flame; but only for an hour. It goes out: the Universe with its old mountains and streams, its stars above and kind soil beneath, is still there.

The Duke of Weimar told his friends always, To be of courage; this Napoleonism was *unjust*, a falsehood, and could not last. It is true doctrine. The heavier this Napoleon trampled on the world, holding it tyrannously down, the fiercer would the world's recoil against him be, one day. Injustice pays itself with frightful compound-interest. I am not sure but he had better have lost his best park of artillery, or had his best regiment drowned in the sea, than shot that poor German Bookseller, Palm! It was a palpable tyrannous murderous injustice, which no man, let him paint an inch thick, could make out to be other. It burnt deep into the hearts of men, it and the like of it; suppressed fire flashed in the eyes of men, as they thought of it,— waiting their day! Which day *came:* Germany rose round him.—What Napoleon *did* will in the long-run amount to what he did *justly;* what Nature with her laws will sanction. To what of reality was in him; to

that and nothing more. The rest was all smoke and waste. *La carrière
ouverte aux talens:* that great true Message, which has yet to articulate and fulfil itself everywhere, he left in a most inarticulate state. He
was a great *ébauche*, a rude-draught never completed; as indeed what
great man is other? Left in *too* rude a state, alas!

His notions of the world, as he expresses them there at St. Helena,
are almost tragical to consider. He seems to feel the most unaffected
surprise that it has all gone so; that he is flung out on the rock here,
and the World is still moving on its axis. France is great, and all-great;
and at bottom, he is France. England itself, he says, is by Nature only
an appendage of France; 'another Isle of Oleron to France.' So it was
by Nature, by Napoleon-Nature; and yet look how in fact—HERE AM
I! He cannot understand it: inconceivable that the reality has not
corresponded to his program of it; that France was not all-great, that
he was not France. 'Strong delusion,' that he should believe the thing
to be which *is* not! The compact, clear-seeing, decisive Italian nature
of him, strong, genuine, which he once had, has enveloped itself, half
dissolved itself, in a turbid atmosphere of French Fanfaronade. The
world was not disposed to be trodden down underfoot; to be bound
into masses, and built together, as *he* liked, for a pedestal to France
and him: the world had quite other purposes in view! Napoleon's
astonishment is extreme. But alas, what help now? He had gone that
way of his; and Nature also had gone her way. Having once parted
with Reality, he tumbles helpless in Vacuity; no rescue for him. He
had to sink there, mournfully as man seldom did; and break his great
heart, and die,—this poor Napoleon: a great implement too soon
wasted, till it was useless: our last Great Man!

Our last, in a double sense. For here finally these wide roamings of
ours through so many times and places, in search and study of
Heroes, are to terminate. I am sorry for it: there was pleasure for me
in this business, if also much pain. It is a great subject, and a most
grave and wide one, this which, not to be too grave about it, I have
named *Hero-worship.* It enters deeply, as I think, into the secret of
Mankind's ways and vitalest interests in this world, and is well worth
explaining at present. With six months, instead of six days, we might
have done better. I promised to break ground on it; I know not

whether I have even managed to do that. I have had to tear it up in the rudest manner in order to get into it at all. Often enough, with these abrupt utterances thrown out isolated, unexplained, has your tolerance been put to the trial. Tolerance, patient candour, all-hoping favour and kindness, which I will not speak of at present. The accomplished and distinguished, the beautiful, the wise, something of what is best in England, have listened patiently to my rude words. With many feelings, I heartily thank you all; and say, Good be with you all!

THE END.

APPENDIX:
1858 SUMMARY AND INDEX

A "Summary" and an "Index" of On Heroes *were prepared under Carlyle's supervision for the 1858 Uniform Edition (see Note on the Text, pp. lxxxv, c) and were included in the two subsequent lifetime collected editions. Both are presented here, their texts as they appeared in the 1858 edition, their page references renumbered to correspond to the present edition as nearly as possible.*

SUMMARY.

LECTURE I.

HEROES: Universal History consists essentially of their United Biographies. Religion not a man's church-creed, but his practical *belief* about himself and the Universe: Both with Men and Nations it is the One fact about them which creatively determines all the rest. Heathenism: Christianity: Modern Scepticism. The Hero as Divinity. Paganism a fact; not Quackery, nor Allegory: Not to be pretentiously 'explained;' to be looked at as old Thought, and with sympathy. (p. 3).—Nature no more seems divine, except to the Prophet or Poet, because men have ceased to *think:* To the Pagan Thinker, as to a child-man, all was either Godlike or God. Canopus: Man. Hero-worship the Basis of Religion, Loyalty, Society. A Hero, not the 'creature of the time:' Hero-worship, indestructible. Johnson: Voltaire. (8).—Scandinavian Paganism, the Religion of our Fathers. Iceland, the home of the Norse Poets, described. The *Edda*. The primary characteristic of Norse Paganism, the impersonation of the visible workings of Nature. Jötuns and the Gods. Fire: Frost: Thunder: The Sun: Sea-Tempest. Mythus of the Creation: The Life-Tree Igdrasil. The modern '*Machine* of the Universe.' (15).—The Norse Creed, as recorded, the summation of several successive systems: Originally the shape given to the national thought by their first 'Man of Genius.' Odin: He has no history or date; but was no mere adjective, but a man of flesh and blood. How deified. The World of Nature, to every man a Fantasy of Himself. (19).—Odin the inventor of Runes, of Letters and Poetry. His reception as a Hero: The pattern

213

Norse-Man; a God: His shadow over the whole History of his People. (24).—The essence of Norse Paganism, not so much Morality, as a sincere recognition of Nature: Sincerity better than Gracefulness. The Allegories, the after-creations of the Faith. Main practical Belief: Hall of Odin: Valkyrs: Destiny: Necessity of Valour. Its worth: Their Sea-Kings, Wood-cutter Kings, our spiritual Progenitors. The growth of Odinism. (27).—The strong simplicity of Norse lore quite unrecognised by Gray. Thor's veritable Norse rage: Balder, the white Sun-god. How the old Norse heart loves the Thunder-god, and sports with him: Huge Brobdignag genius, needing only to be tamed-down, into Shakspeares, Goethes. Truth in the Norse Songs: This world a show. Thor's Invasion of Jötunheim. The Ragnarök, or Twilight of the Gods: The Old must die that the New and Better may be born. Thor's last appearance. The Norse Creed a Consecration of Valour. It and the whole Past a possession of the Present. (30).

LECTURE II.

THE HERO AS PROPHET. MAHOMET: ISLAM.

THE HERO no longer regarded as a God, but as one God-inspired. All Heroes primarily of the same stuff; differing according to their reception. The welcome of its Heroes, the truest test of an epoch. Odin: Burns. (p. 37).—Mahomet a True Prophet; not a scheming Imposter. A Great Man, and therefore first of all a sincere man: No man to be judged merely by his faults. David the Hebrew King. Of all acts for man *repentance* the most divine: The deadliest sin, a supercilious consciousness of none. (38).—Arabia described. The Arabs always a gifted people; of wild strong feelings, and of iron restraint over these. Their Religiosity: Their Star-worship: Their Prophets and inspired men; from Job downwards. Their Holy Places. Mecca, its site, history and government. (41).—Mahomet. His youth: His fond Grandfather. Had no book-learning: Travels to the Syrian Fairs; and first comes in contact with the Christian Religion. An altogether solid, brotherly, genuine man: A good laugh, and a good flash of anger in him withal. (45).—Marries Kadijah. Begins his Prophet-career at forty years of age. *Allah Akbar;* God is great: *Islam;* we must *submit* to God. Do we not all live in Islam? Mahomet, 'the Prophet of God.' (46).—The good Kadijah believes in him: Mahomet's gratitude. His slow progress: Among forty of his kindred, young Ali alone joined him. His good Uncle expostulates with him: Mahomet, bursting into tears, persists in his mission. The Hegira. Propagating by the sword: First get your sword: A thing will propagate itself as it can. Nature a just umpire. Mahomet's Creed unspeakably better than the wooden idolatries, and jangling Syrian Sects extirpated by it. (50).—The Koran, the universal standard of Mahometan life: An imperfectly, badly written, but genuine book: Enthusiastic extempore preaching, amid the hot haste of wrestling with flesh-and-blood and spiritual enemies. Its direct poetic insight. The World, Man, human Compassion; all wholly miraculous to Mahomet. (55).—His religion did not succeed by 'being easy:' None can. The sensual part of it not of Mahomet's making. He himself, frugal; patched his own clothes; proved a hero in a rough actual trial of twenty-three years. Traits of his generosity, and resignation. His total freedom from cant. (60).— His moral precepts not always of the superfinest sort; yet is there always a tendency to good in them. His Heaven and Hell sensual, yet not altogether so. Infinite Nature of Duty. The evil of sensuality, in the *slavery* to pleasant things, not in the enjoyment of them. Mahometanism, a religion heartily *believed*. To the Arab Nation it was as a birth from darkness into light: Arabia first became alive by means of it. (63).

LECTURE III.

THE HERO AS POET. DANTE; SHAKSPEARE.

THE HERO as Divinity or Prophet, inconsistent with the modern progress of science: The Hero Poet, a figure common to all ages. All Heroes at bottom the same: The different *sphere* constituting the grand distinction: Examples. Varieties of aptitude. (p. 243).—Poet and Prophet meet in *Vates:* Their Gospel the same, for the Beautiful and the Good are one. All men somewhat of poets; and the highest Poets far from perfect. Prose, and Poetry or *musical Thought.* Song, a kind of inarticulate unfathomable speech: All deep things are Song.

The Hero as Divinity, as Prophet, and then only as Poet, no indication that our estimate of the Great Man is diminishing: The Poet seems to be losing caste, but it is rather that our notions of God are rising higher. (69).—Shakspeare and Dante, Saints of Poetry. Dante: His history, in his Book and Portrait. His scholastic education, and its fruit of subtlety. His miseries: Love of Beatrice: His marriage not happy. A banished man: Will never return, if to plead guilty be the condition. His wanderings: *"Come è duro calle."* At the Court of Della Scala. The great soul of Dante, homeless on earth, made its home more and more in Eternity. His mystic, unfathomable Song. Death: Buried at Ravenna. (73).—His Divina Commedia, a Song: Go *deep* enough, there is music everywhere. The sincerest of Poems: It has all been as if molten, in the hottest furnace of his soul. Its Intensity; and Pictorial power. The three parts make-up the true Unseen World of the Middle Ages: How the Christian Dante felt Good and Evil to be the two polar elements of this Creation. Paganism and Christianism. (77).—Ten silent centuries found a voice in Dante. The thing that is uttered from the inmost parts of a man's soul, differs altogether from what is uttered by the outer. The 'uses' of Dante: We will not estimate the Sun, by the quantity of gas it saves us. Mahomet and Dante contrasted. Let a man *do* his work; the *fruit* of it is the care of Another than he. (83).—As Dante embodies musically the Inner Life of the Middle Ages, so does Shakspeare embody the Outer Life which grew therefrom. The strange outbudding of English Existence which we call 'Elizabethan Era.' Shakspeare the chief of all Poets: His calm, all-seeing Intellect: His marvellous Portrait-painting. (86).—The Poet's first gift, as it is all men's, that he have intellect enough,—that he be able to *see*. Intellect the summary of all human gifts: Human intellect and vulpine intellect contrasted. Shakspeare's instinctive unconscious greatness: His works a part of Nature, and partaking of her inexhaustible depth. Shakspeare greater than Dante; in that he not only sorrowed, but triumphed over his sorrows. His mirthfulness, and genuine overflowing love of laughter. His Historical Plays, a kind of National Epic. The Battle of Agincourt: A noble Patriotism, far other than the 'indifference' sometimes ascribed to him. His works, like so many windows, through which we see glimpses of the world that is in him. (89).—Dante the melodious Priest of Middle Age Catholicism: Out of this Shakspeare too there rises a kind of Universal Psalm, not unfit to make itself heard among still more sacred Psalms. Shakspeare an 'unconscious Prophet;' and therein greater and truer than Mahomet. This poor Warwickshire Peasant, worth more to us than a whole regiment of highest Dignitaries: Indian Empire, or Shakspeare,—which? An English King, whom no time or chance can dethrone: A rallying-sign and bond of brotherhood for all Saxondom: Wheresoever English men and women are, they will say to one another, 'Yes, this Shakspeare is *ours!*' (94).

LECTURE IV.

THE HERO AS PRIEST. LUTHER; REFORMATION: KNOX; PURITANISM.

THE PRIEST, a kind of Prophet; but more familiar, as the daily en- lightener of daily life. A true Reformer, he who appeals to Heaven's invisible justice against Earth's visible force. The finished Poet often a symptom that his epoch itself has reached perfection, and finished. Alas, the battling Reformer, too, is at times a needful and inevitable phenomenon: Offences *do* accumulate, till they become insupport- able. Forms of Belief, modes of life must perish; yet the good of the Past survives, an everlasting possession for us all. (p. 99).—Idols, or visible recognised Symbols, common to all Religions: Hateful only when insincere: The property of every Hero, that he come back to sincerity, to reality: Protestantism, and 'private judgment.' No living communion possible among men who believe only in hearsays. The Hero-Teacher, who delivers men out of darkness into light. Not abolition of Hero-worship, does Protestantism mean; but rather a whole World of Heroes, of *sincere*, believing men. (103).—Luther; his obscure, seemingly-insignificant birth. His youth schooled in adversity and stern reality. Becomes a Monk. His religious despair: Discovers a Latin Bible: No wonder he should venerate the Bible. He visits Rome. Meets the Pope's fire by fire. At the Diet of Worms: The greatest moment in the modern History of men. (109).—The Wars that followed, are not to be charged to the Reformation. The Old Religion, once true: The cry of 'No Popery,' foolish enough in these days. Protestantism not dead: German Literature and the French Revolution, rather considerable signs of life! (116).—How Luther held the sovereignty of the Reformation and kept Peace while he lived. His written Works: Their rugged homely strength: His dialect became the language of all writing. No mortal heart to be called *braver*, ever lived in that Teutonic Kindred, whose character is valour: Yet a most gentle heart withal, full of pity and love, as the truly valiant heart ever is: Traits of character from his Table-Talk: His daughter's Death-bed: The miraculous in Nature. His love of Music. His Portrait. (118).—Puritanism, the only phasis of Protestantism that ripened into a living faith: Defective enough, but genuine. Its fruit in the world. The sailing of the Mayflower from Delft Haven, the beginning of American Saxondom. In the history of Scotland, properly but one epoch of world-interest,—the Reformation by Knox: A 'nation of heroes;' a *believing* nation. The Puritanism of Scotland became that of England, of New England. (122).—Knox, 'guilty' of being the bravest of all Scotchmen: Did not seek the post of Prophet. At the siege of St. Andrew's Castle. Emphatically a sincere man. A Galley-slave on the River Loire. An Old-Hebrew Prophet, in the guise of an Edinburgh Minister of the Sixteenth Century. (125).— Knox and Queen Mary: 'Who are you, that presume to school the nobles and sovereign of this realm?'—'Madam, a subject born within the same.' His intolerance,—of falsehoods and knaveries. Not a mean acrid man; else he had never been virtual President and Sovereign of Scotland. His unexpected vein of drollery: A cheery social man; practical, cautious-hopeful, patient. His 'devout imagination' of a Theocracy, or Government of God. Hildebrand wished a Theocracy; Cromwell wished it, fought for it: Mahomet attained it. In one form or other, it is the one thing to be struggled for. (127).

LECTURE V.

THE HERO AS MAN OF LETTERS. JOHNSON, ROUSSEAU, BURNS.

THE HERO as Man of Letters, altogether a product of these new ages: A Heroic Soul in very strange guise. Literary Men; genuine and spurious. Fichte's 'Divine Idea of the World:' His notion of the True Man of Letters. Goethe, the Pattern Literary Hero. (p. 133).—The disorganised condition of Literature, the summary of all other modern disorganisations. The Writer of a true Book, our true modern Preacher. Miraculous influence of Books: The Hebrew Bible. Books are now our actual University, our Church, our Parliament. With Books, Democracy is inevitable. *Thought* the true thaumaturgic influence, by which man works all things whatsoever. (137).—Organisation of the 'Literary Guild:' Needful discipline; 'priceless lessons' of Poverty. The Literary Priesthood, and its importance to society. Chinese Literary Governors. Fallen into strange times; and strange things need to be speculated upon. (142).—An age of Scepticism: The very possibility of Heroism formally abnegated. Benthamism, an *eyeless* Heroism. Scepticism, Spiritual Paralysis, Insincerity: Heroes gone-out; Quacks come-in. Our brave Chatham himself lived the strangest mimetic life, all along. Violent remedial revulsions: Chartisms, French Revolutions: The Age of Scepticism, passing away. Let each Man look to the mending of his own Life. (146).—Johnson, one of our Great English Souls. His miserable Youth and Hypochondria: Stubborn Self-help. His loyal submission to what is really higher than himself. How he stood by the old Formulas: Not less original for that. Formulas; their Use and Abuse. Johnson's unconscious sincer-ity. His Twofold Gospel, a kind of Moral Prudence and clear Hatred of Cant. His writings, sincere and full of substance. Architectural nobleness of his Dictionary. Boswell, with all his faults, a true hero-worshiper of a true Hero. (152).— Rousseau, a morbid, excitable, spasmodic man; intense rather than strong. Had not the invaluable 'talent of Silence.' His Face, expressive of his character. His Egoism: Hungry for the praises of men. His books: Passionate appeals, which did once more struggle towards Reality: A Prophet to his Time; as he could, and as the Time could. Rosepink, and artificial bedizenment. Fretted, exasperated, till the heart of him went mad: He could be cooped, starving, into garrets; laughed at as a maniac; but he could not be hindered from setting the world on fire. (158).—Burns, a genuine Hero, in a withered, unbelieving, secondhand Century. The largest soul of all the British lands, came among us in the shape of a hard-handed Scottish Peasant. His heroic Father and Mother, and their sore struggle through life. His rough, untutored dialect: Affectionate joyousness: His writings, a poor fragment of him. His conversational gifts: High duchesses and low ostlers alike fascinated by him. (161).—Resemblance between Burns and Mirabeau. Official Superiors: The greatest 'thinking-faculty' in this land superciliously dispensed with. Hero-worship under strange conditions. The notablest phasis of Burns's history, his visit to Edinburgh. For one man who can stand prosperity, there are a hundred that will stand adversity. Literary Lionism. (164).

LECTURE VI.

THE HERO AS KING. CROMWELL, NAPOLEON: MODERN REVOLUTIONISM.

THE KING, the most important of Great Men; the summary of *all* the various figures of Heroism. To enthrone the Ablest Man, the true business of all Social procedure: The Ideal of Constitutions. Tolerable and intolerable approximations. Divine Rights and Diabolic Wrongs. (p. 169).—The world's sad predicament; that of having its Able-Man to *seek*, and not knowing in what manner to proceed about it. The era of Modern Revolutionism dates from Luther. The French Revolution, no mere act of General Insanity: Truth clad in hell-fire; the Trump of Doom to Plausibilities and empty Routine. The cry of 'Liberty and Equality' at bottom the repudiation of sham Heroes. Hero-worship exists forever and everywhere; from divine adoration down to the common courtesies of man and man: The soul of Order, to which all things, Revolutions included, work. Some Cromwell or Napoleon, the necessary finish of a Sansculottism. The manner in which Kings were made, and Kingship itself first took rise. (172).— Puritanism, a section of the universal war of Belief against Make-believe. Laud, a weak ill-starred Pedant; in his spasmodic vehemence, heeding no voice of prudence, no cry of pity. Universal necessity for true Forms: How to distinguish between True and False. The nakedest reality, preferable to any empty semblance, however dignified. (176).—The work of the Puritans. The Sceptical Eighteenth Century, and its constitutional estimate of Cromwell and his associates. No wish to disparage such characters as Hampden, Eliot, Pym; a most constitutional, unblamable, dignified set of men. The rugged outcast Cromwell, the man of them all in whom one still finds human stuff. The One thing worth revolting for. (178).—Cromwell's 'hypocrisy,' an impossible theory. His pious Life as a Farmer until forty years of age. His public successes, honest successes of a brave man. His participation in the King's death, no ground of condemnation. His eye for facts, no hypocrite's gift. His Ironsides, the embodiment of this insight of his. (181).—Know the men that may be trusted: Alas, this is yet, in these days, very far from us. Cromwell's hypochondria: His reputed confusion of speech: His habit of prayer. His Speeches unpremeditated and full of meaning. His *reticences;* called 'lying' and 'dissimulation:' Not one falsehood proved against him. (185).—Foolish charge of 'ambition.' The great Empire of Silence: Noble silent men, scattered here and there, each in his department; silently thinking, silently hoping, silently working. Two kinds of ambition; one wholly blamable, the other laudable, inevitable: How it actually was with Cromwell. (190).—Hume's Fanatic-Hypocrite Theory: How indispensable everywhere a *King* is, in all movements of men. Cromwell, as King of Puritanism, of England. Constitutional palaver: Dismissal of the Rump Parliament. Cromwell's Parliaments, and Protectorship: Parliaments having failed, there remained nothing for him but the way of Despotism. His closing days: His poor old Mother. It was not to men's judgments that he appealed; nor have men judged him very well. (195).—The French Revolution, the 'third act' of Protestantism. Napoleon, infected with the Quackeries of his age: Had a kind of Sincerity,—an instinct towards the *practical.* His *faith,*—'the Tools to him that can handle them,'—the whole truth of Democracy. His heart-hatred of Anarchy. Finally, his quackeries got the upper hand: He would found a 'Dynasty:' Believed wholly in the dupeability of Men. This Napoleonism was *unjust,* a falsehood; and could not last. (203).

1858 INDEX.

223

---

[1] [Reference is made to two different quotes from Novalis on belief that occurred on consecutive pages in the 1858 edition.]

[2] [Conjectural. All three lifetime editions that include this index refer at this point to approximately page 87 in this edition, which seems to be an error. In the earliest version of the index in the 1858 edition, the reference is to page "261." An emendation to "281" gives the present reference.]

NOTES

(Complete citations for all works referred to by page number will be found in the list of works cited, beginning on page 393.)

Notes to Lecture I. The Hero as Divinity.

Sources: Early in 1840, about a month before the precise subject matter of the lectures was fixed in his mind, Carlyle was "reading Scandinavian things" (*Letters* 12:32n). His interest had been excited by reading *Friþjóf's Saga*, in the 1825 retelling by the Swedish poet Esaias Tegnér (1782–1846) of the fourteenth-century saga of the same title (*Letters* 12:32n). Reading it in George Stephens's translation, *Frithiof's Saga, a Legend of the North* (1839)—"'translated,' it is said, 'from *Björner's Kämpa Dater'*" (*Letters* 12:33n)—Carlyle expressed some skepticism about Tegnér's "modern aqueous" and sentimental version of the original "right old block of Swedish *iron*" (*Letters* 12:28). The saga made such an impression on Carlyle that he wrote a summary of it two years later (K. J. Fielding, "Carlyle and Esaias Tegnér: An Unpublished MS").

"The old *Saga* of *Frithiof*" gave Carlyle "a great appetite" for more such material (*Letters* 12:28). His fascination for these Norse sagas and his desire to try them in the original are attested to by his having "some thoughts of learning Danish" (*Letters* 12:35n), as he had wanted to learn Arabic for the sake of the Qūr'ān and did study Italian for his reading of Dante. On February 4, 1840, he wrote to Richard Monckton Milnes to ask his friend John Kemble to recommend a Danish grammar in English, French, or German. He also wanted to know from Kemble, who had studied philology with Jacob Grimm, whether Peter Erasmus Müller's *Sagabibliothek med Anmærkninger og indledende Afhandlinger* (1817–20) was available in German (*Letters* 12:28). (Carlyle persisted in this linguistic interest, later acquiring a copy of *A Grammar of the Icelandic or Old Norse Tongue*, translated from the Swedish of Erasmus Rask by George Webbe Dasent [London, 1843]. This work is bound together with Rask's *Danish Grammar for Englishmen* [1847]. Carlyle's copy is in the Strouse Collection.) In his journal, he notes borrowing the *Heims Kringla, eller Snorre Sturlusons*, edited by J. Peringskiöld (1697) from Hensleigh Wedgwood (*Letters* 12:32n). In these readings Carlyle found nothing that interested him "more than old Snorro" (*Letters* 12:34n).

Later in February, Carlyle was still "puddling in the *Norse* matters" (*Letters* 12:49). He read with enjoyment Paul Henri Mallet's *L'introduction à l'histoire de Dannemarc, où l'on traite de la religion, des loix, des moeurs, et des usages des anciens Danois* (1755–56). Other "Scandinavian things" Carlyle looked at included Ebenezer Henderson's *Iceland; or the Journal of a Residence in that Island, during the years 1814 and 1815* (1818); Sir George Steuart Mackenzie's *Travels in the Island of Iceland* (1811); G. Gordon MacDougall's translation of Captain W. A. Graah's *Narrative of an Expedition to the East Coast of Greenland* (1837); "Lindl's *Faroe Isles*," presumably meaning the Rev. Jørgen Jørgensen Landt's *A Description of the Feroe Islands, Containing an Account of Their Situation, Climate, and Productions* (1810); Dr. John Jamieson's *Hermes Scythicus; or, the Radical Affinities of the Greek and Latin Languages to the Gothic* (1814); the Rev. James Johnstone's translation of *The Norwegian Account of Haco's Expedition against Scotland* A.D. *1263* (1782) and his volume *Antiquitates Celto-Normanicae* (1786) (*Letters* 12:32–33n). Many of these works on Norse matters were read by Carlyle before he had fixed upon the topic of his lecture series.

3.5. Hero-worship: The subject of heroes and hero-worship took shape gradually in Carlyle's mind from 1824, and there are numerous anticipations of the concept in his essays; for example, "Sir Walter Scott" ([1838], *Essays* 4:24): "Understand it well, this of 'hero-worship' was the primary creed, . . . and will be the ultimate and final creed of mankind." He considered hero-worship the basis of society and "a chief aim of Education" ("Goethe's Works" [1832], *Essays* 2:395). It was not only a property of past heroic ages but a perennial power in the human heart that "waits, even in these dead days, only for occasions to unfold it, and inspire all men with it, and again make the world alive!" ("Boswell's Life of Johnson" [1832], *Essays* 3:74).

Carlyle's thinking on the subject was influenced specifically by Fichte's *Über das Wesen des Gelehrten* (1806), Goethe's *Wilhelm Meisters Lehrjahre* (1796, translated by Carlyle in 1824), and D. Heynig's *Theorie der Sämmtlichen Religionsarten* (1799), and more generally by various works of the English Romantics. The term itself he may have derived from David Hume's *The Natural History of Religion* (1757), which considers hero-worship to be a form of polytheism arising from a tendency to "deify mortals" of superior ability (40). Despite antecedent treatments, literary interest in hero-worship was essentially a nineteenth-century phenomenon. See Lehman, *Carlyle's Theory of the Hero*, 130–70.

3.9–11. Universal History . . . is . . . the History of the Great Men who have worked here: This and the later statement in *On Heroes*, "The History of the world is but the Biography of great men" (26.24–25 below), are frequently quoted and often misrepresented as Carlyle's exclusive view of the subject. See, however, his view of history as "the essence of innumerable Biographies" ("Biography" [1832], *Essays* 3:46), and compare as a possible source the opening paragraph of Henry Fielding's *Jonathan Wild:* "The Lives of [great and eminent Men] may be justly and properly styled the Quintessence of History."

3.22–23. The light which enlightens: An echo of John 1:9: "*That* was the true Light, which lighteth every man that cometh into the world."

4.16. a man's religion is the chief fact: A point made in a letter to Emerson on May 13, 1835: "Man *lives* by Belief" (*Letters* 8:121).

4.17–18. By religion I do not mean here the church-creed which he professes: The association of religion not with ritual, liturgy, or creed but with practicality echoes *Sartor*, 3.2.170–73, and anticipates *Past and Present*, 3.11.196, and "Hudson's Statue," *Pamphlets*, 7.255–60. William Allingham reports Carlyle as saying, "I have for many years strictly avoided going to church, or having anything to do with Mumbo-Jumbo" (*Diary*, 217). But compare apRoberts, *Ancient Dialect*, 1–7, 73–86.

5.14–15. Odin the central figure of Scandinavian Paganism: Odin was the principal deity of both Scandinavian and Teutonic paganism. Odin and twelve other Aesir were chief deities, but Odin's supremacy is considered by Jacob Grimm to show a tendency toward monotheism (*Teutonic Mythology* 1:164). In Old German he was known as *Wuotan*, in Anglo-Saxon, *Woden*. Carlyle follows an anglicized spelling of the Norse *Óðinn*. The name signifies "fury" or "frenzy." Among the ancient Germans Odin was also identified with the Roman Mercurius, with whom he shared the office of captain of the dead.

5.25–26. stocks and stones: Possibly recalling Milton's "On the Late Massacre in Piedmont" (line 4): "When all our fathers worshipped stocks and stones." According to the *Concise Scots Dictionary* (672), *stock* is a "block of wood, log; a tree-stump." Compare Deuteronomy 29:17: "And ye have seen their abominations, and their idols, wood and stone."

5.35–36. Some speculators have a short way of accounting for the Pagan religion: In defending paganism against the charge of quackery, Carlyle is reverting to a position he took in defense of Greek polytheism in his 1838 lecture series on the history of literature (*History of Literature*, 12; see the note on Sources for "The Hero as Poet," p. 279 below). Among the speculators he probably had in mind is David Hume, particularly in *The Natural History of Religion* (1757).

5.38. It will be often our duty: See Introduction, pp. xli–xlvi.

6.19. Mr. Turner's *Account*: *An Account of an Embassy to the Court of the Teshoo Lama, in Tibet; Containing a Narrative of a Journey Through Bootan, and Part of Tibet* (1800), by Captain Samuel Turner. The expedition was launched in 1783 on behalf of the East India Company on the recommendation of Turner's cousin, Warren Hastings. Turner arrived to "joyful tidings of the Lama's re-appearance in the world," an infant lama having been discovered in the valley of Painom; he was assured that "the present and the late Teshoo Lama, were one and the same" (238). Turner's book contains only sparse details of Tibetan religion (in part 2, chapter 4). In the first edition of *On Heroes*, Carlyle referred not to Turner's *Account* but to Francis Buchanan Hamilton's *An Account of the Kingdom of Nepal and of the territories annexed to this dominion by the House of Gorkha* (1819); see textual apparatus. Presumably Carlyle's knowledge of Tibetan religious practices was derived from these published sources, though he may also have been aware of the expeditions by George Bogle and Alexander Hamilton in 1774 and Thomas Manning in 1811.

6.26–27. The Thibet Priests have methods: According to a twentieth-century Dalai Lama, a dying lama would often designate the place and circumstances of his rebirth. Three or four years following the lama's death, the Tashi Lama and fifteen other high priests would indicate where the reincarnated lama was to be discovered. Their inquiries would produce several candidates whose miraculous births had occurred at the right place and time. At the age of four, the prospective lama was required to prove himself by recognizing religious items he had owned in his former existence and recounting events of his previous life. The boy would also exhibit physical signs that would distinguish him from ordinary mortals. See Bell, *Tibet*, 50–53.

6.30. eldest-born of a certain genealogy: By 1866, however, Carlyle thought there was "a great deal more in genealogy than is generally believed at present. . . . It goes for a great deal, the hereditary principle,—in Government as in other things" ("Inaugural Address at Edinburgh" [1866], *Essays* 4:463–64).

6.37–38. Another theory . . . attributes such things to Allegory: In *History of Literature* (11–12), Carlyle had likewise rejected the allegorical theory as implausible, preferring euhemerism, the explanation of myths as traditional accounts of historical persons and events, which corresponds more closely to the doctrine of hero-worship. Hume, in section 5 of his *Natural History of Religion*, discusses the creation of fable and allegory among vulgar polytheists, and Mallet, one of Carlyle's chief sources, saw in Eddic tales a "spirit of allegory" (*Northern Antiquities* 1:91).

7.27. *Pilgrim's Progress*: *The Pilgrim's Progress from this World to that Which is to Come* (1678) by John Bunyan (1628–1688).

8.17. that fancy of Plato's: An imperfect recollection of *Phaedo* 109 and the allegory of the cave from *Republic* 7. Until the Fourth Edition (1852), all editions read "Aristotle's" here and at 8.26 below; see textual apparatus. On March 20, 1852, Joseph Neuberg, who was then preparing a German translation of *On Heroes*, wrote to Carlyle with a number of queries (see Note on the Text, pp. xcviii–xcix), among them: "*page 11*. 'that fancy of *Aristotle's*,' about a man brought up in the dark.—I remember such a fancy of *Plato's*, I believe in the *Republic*; should *Aristotle* have had it too? and should not *Plato's* be considered the original?" Carlyle replied, on May 31, "p. 11. (*Aristotle's* fancy), I have very little doubt *Plato* is the word,—tho' Plato's 'fancy,' too, in his *Republic*, does not too well suit (if I remember now) what is there said of the Sun and the man. However, *say* 'Plato,' beyond doubt. I read the thing, forty years ago, in some poor Book or other, neither Aristotle nor Plato; and have ignorantly but now irremediably, twisted it to my own uses a little." The page references in his letter show that Neuberg was working from a copy of the 1841 first edition.

9.4. hearsays: One of Carlyle's leitmotivs. Aside from the conventional meaning, Carlyle applied the term pejoratively to connote abstraction, as in the "faint hearsays" of some histories, which he contrasted to the animated history he found in Scott's historical novels ("Sir Walter Scott" [1838], *Essays* 4:78). He also condemned "the common English mode of writing" which "has to do with what I call *hearsays* of things; and the great business for me . . . is recording the *presence*, bodily concrete coloured presence of things" (*Letters* 9:15; see also *Letters* 12:267).

9.6. **grind the like of it out of glass and silk**: Early experiments with electricity involved the rubbing of fur or silk against amber (Greek, *ēlektron*), sulfur, or glass to produce electrostatic charges. In 1768, for example, Jesse Ramsden, an English instrument maker, built an electrostatic generator consisting of a large glass disk, driven by a hand crank, that rubbed against leather pads covered with silk.

9.20-21. **a Force which is *not we***: Carlyle's phrasing probably derives from the *Ich* and *Nicht-Ich* of Fichte, as recalled in "Novalis" ([1829], *Essays* 2:25). It is also an anticipation of Matthew Arnold's celebrated and sometimes criticized definition of God as "*The Eternal, not ourselves, that makes for righteousness*" (*God and the Bible*, 156).

9.23-24. **'There is not a leaf rotting . . .'**: "The withered leaf is not dead and lost, there are Forces in and around it, though working in inverse order; else how could it *rot*?" (*Sartor*, 1.11.56). The idea is also found in *Wilhelm Meister* 1:2.1.106.

9.31. **Leyden jars**: Devices for storing electrical charges, invented at the University of Leyden in the eighteenth century and used in early experiments with electricity. Benjamin Franklin proved that atmospheric electricity was identical with the electrostatic charge on a Leyden jar. The young Carlyle published two long letters on Franklin's theory of electricity in the *Dumfries and Galloway Courier* in June 1815 (see *Letters* 1:59 and Tarr, *Descriptive Bibliography*, 415).

10.4. **'All was Godlike or God'**: A quotation from Jean Paul Richter's *Life of Quintus Fixlein* (1796), which Carlyle translated: "I look up to the starry sky . . . and all is godlike or God" (*German Romance* 2:331). See also "Jean Paul Friedrich Richter" (1827), *Essays* 1:24.

10.6. **Canopus**: Star in the southern constellation of Argo, second only to Sirius in brilliance. It served Arab travelers in the desert as a southern pole star.

10.9. Ishmaelitish: Of the tribe of Ishmael, the son of Abraham and Hagar, who was cast out with his mother at Sarah's insistence (Genesis 17:20 and 21:9ff). Arabs claim descent from Ishmael. Beginning his career in London in 1834, Carlyle thought himself "fated to be an Ishmaelite, his hand against every man and every man's hand against him" (Froude, *Life in London* 1:11, echoing Genesis 16:12).

10.14. Sabeans: Inhabitants of the kingdom of Saba, in pre-Islamic Arabia, described by the historian Diodorus Siculus (3.46–47). The Sabeans are referred to in the Bible; for example, Job 1:15, Isaiah 45:14, and Joel 3:8. The kingdom of Saba, or Sheba, appears in Psalms 72:10, while the story of Solomon and the queen of Sheba is described in 1 Kings 10:1–13, 2 Chronicles 9:1–12, and Chapter 27 of the Qur'ān, which closely follows the account given in the Aggadic Targum Sheni. The polytheistic religion of the Sabeans focused on a triad of deities: the Venus star, the moon god, and the sun goddess. The moon god, essentially a national deity whose cult unified the Sabean tribes, was worshipped under the name Ilmugah; the term "children of Ilmugah" was synonymous with "citizens of Saba." See George Sale's "Preliminary Discourse" to the *Korân* (15–17).

10.24–25. 'a window . . . into Infinitude itself': "All objects are as windows, through which the philosophic eye looks into Infinitude itself" (*Sartor*, 1.11.57).

10.33. St. Chrysostom's: Saint John Chrysostom (347?–407), the "golden-mouthed" preacher of the early Greek church. In "Count Cagliostro" ([1833], *Essays* 3:296), Carlyle dubbed the fraudulent adventurer "Pinchbeckostom, or Mouth-of-Pinchbeck," after Christopher Pinchbeck, the eighteenth-century inventor of a zinc-copper alloy resembling gold that was often used in cheap jewelry.

10.34. the Shekinah, or Ark of Testimony: The Shekinah was not the ark itself but the divine Presence around it. The term was often adopted in Rabbinic exegesis to designate the holy Presence in those biblical passages where it is described as a cloud or glory (Exodus 40:34), a presence or a face (Exodus 33:14). It is also a favored term in the Kabbalah (see Scholem, *Major Trends in Jewish Mysticism*, 111ff). The "Ark of Testimony" was the wooden chest into which Moses placed the tables of law (Exodus 25:10–16, 40:20; Numbers 7:89).

10.35–36. "The true Shekinah is Man!": Echoing *Sartor*, 1.10.52: "Well said Saint Chrysostom, with his lips of gold, 'the true SHEKINAH is Man.'" Carlyle's allusion is not taken directly from Chrysostom but from Sterne's *Tristram Shandy*, 5.1.239: "MAN ... the *miracle* of nature, as Zoroaster ... called him——the SHEKINAH of the divine presence, as Chrysostom——the *image* of God, as Moses——the *ray* of divinity, as Plato——the *marvel of marvels*, as Aristotle ...," which is a playful adaptation of the opening paragraph of Burton's *Anatomy of Melancholy* (1621). The source in Chrysostom may be: "Augustior quippe est homo magisque venerandus, quam Ecclesia. Non enim propter parietes mortuus est Christus, sed propter ista Spiriti Sancti templa" (Surely man is more venerable, greater, more to be reverenced than the Church. For not on account of walls did Christ die, but on account of those dwelling places of the Holy Spirit; *Collected Works* 4:351). Though Chrysostom does not use the postbiblical Hebrew noun *shĕkhīnāh*, in rabbinic exegesis it was frequently adopted as a synonym for "the dwelling place of the Holy Spirit."

10.37. the mystery in us that calls itself "I": Possibly a recollection of "Jean Paul Friedrich Richter" ([1830], *Essays* 2:111): "Never shall I forget that inward occurrence ... wherein I witnessed the birth of my Self-consciousness. ... I was standing, a very young child, in the outer door, ... when all at once the internal vision, 'I am a ME (*ich bin ein Ich*),' came like a flash from heaven before me." Compare the final passage in Coleridge's *Biographia Literaria:* "It is Night, sacred Night! the upraised Eye views only the starry Heaven which manifests itself alone: and the outward Beholding is fixed on the sparks twinkling in the aweful depth, though Suns of other Worlds, only to preserve the Soul steady and collected in its pure *Act* of inward Adoration to the great I AM, and to the filial WORD that re-affirmeth it from Eternity to Eternity, whose choral Echo is the Universe" (*Biographia Literaria* 2:247–48).

11.2–6. 'There is but one temple in the Universe. ... We touch Heaven when we lay our hand on a human body!': Novalis, *Schriften* 2:126: "Es giebt nur Einen Tempel in der Welt, und das ist der menschliche Körper. Nichts ist heiliger als diese hohe Gestalt. Das Bücken vor Menschen ist eine Huldigung dieser Offenbarung im Fleisch. Man berührt den Himmel, wenn man einen Menschenleib betastet." "'There is but one temple in the universe,' says Novalis, 'and that is the body of man'" (Froude, *First Forty Years* 2:87; see also "Novalis" [1829], *Essays* 2:39). Novalis was adapting Paul, "Know ye not that ye are the temple of God" (1 Corinthians 3:16). Along with the debt to Novalis, Harrold sees the "reverence" passage in chapter 11 of Goethe's *Wilhelm Meisters Wanderjahre* as Carlyle's "unmistakeable source" here (*Carlyle and German Thought*, 193).

11.3. the devout Novalis: Baron Friedrich Leopold von Hardenberg (1772–1801), German poet who wrote under the pseudonym Novalis. He also wrote the influential novels *Heinrich von Ofterdingen* (1799) and *Die Lehrlinge zu Sais* (*The Disciples at Sais*; 1798–99).

11.4–5. Bending before . . . this Revelation in the Flesh: "Bending before men is a reverence done to this Revelation in the Flesh" ("Novalis" [1829], *Essays* 2:39). Carlyle also quotes the passage in "Goethe's Works" (1832), *Essays* 2:390; *Sartor*, 3.6.190–91; and *Past and Present*, 2.16.124.

12.1. The greatest of all Heroes: Jesus.

12.13. *Kön-ning, Kan-ning*: This etymology of *king*, though popular with Carlyle (see, for example, *French Revolution* 1:1.2.9; *Sartor*, 3.7.198; and "The Hero as King" at 169.10–11 below), is now discredited. *King* is derived from the Anglo-Saxon *cyning*, meaning "tribe" or "people" as in *kin*, rather than the Anglo-Saxon *cunnan*, meaning "to know" as in *ken*. See, among others, *Sweet's Anglo-Saxon Reader* (314, 113); Bosworth's *Compendious Anglo-Saxon Dictionary* (64, 62); F. Holthausen, *Altenglisches Etymologisches Wörterbuch* (67, 63); and Jacob and Wilhelm Grimm's *Deutsches Wörterbuch* (1691). Though lacking sound philological basis, Carlyle's imaginative etymological speculations perfectly suit his rhetorical and ideological purposes in these lectures.

13.10. lightning out of Heaven: See also "The Hero as Prophet" at 66.27. Kathleen Tillotson points to this image in Arnold's "The Scholar-Gipsy" (lines 120 and 171) and also to echoes of Carlyle's first lecture in "Stanzas from the Grande Chartreuse" and *Balder Dead* (Tillotson, "Matthew Arnold and Carlyle," 217, 234).

13.37. 'stifle him under roses': Describing Voltaire's triumphal reception in Paris in 1778, Carlyle finds a dramatic justice in the fact that Voltaire, "who had all his life hungered and thirsted after public

favour, should at length die by excess of it; should find the door of
his Heaven-on-earth unexpectedly thrown wide open, and enter there,
only to be, as he himself said, 'smothered under roses'" ("Voltaire"
[1829], *Essays* 1:437; compare "Goethe's Works" [1832], *Essays* 2:391).
An engraving of the "Crowning of Voltaire" hung in the Carlyles' house
at 24 Cheyne Row (*Carlyle's House, Chelsea: Illustrated Catalogue*, 24).

The details of Voltaire's reception in Paris were mostly derived
from the *Mémoires sur Voltaire et sur ses Ouvrages* (1826), including
accounts by Voltaire's secretaries Longchamp and Wagnière and by
the Marquise du Châtelet, which Carlyle reviewed in 1829 for the
Foreign Review (*Essays* 1:396–468). These, especially the account by
Longchamp, are now thought to be unreliable (see for instance Noyes,
Voltaire, 350–54). Carlyle's treatment of Voltaire here should be
compared not only with his 1829 essay but with his account in *Frederick*, which is less dependent on Longchamp.

14.2. **Antichrist**: Carlyle adds Voltaire to the more familiar roster of
suggested Antichrists, which has included the Samaritan sorcerer Simon Magus (Acts 8:9–24); the Roman emperors Caligula, Nero, and
Diocletian; Muḥammad; and, during the Reformation, both Luther
and the Pope. The term, which appears in the New Testament only
in the Epistles of John, is used to designate the false Christs whose
presence is to herald the ending of the world.

14.4. *Persiflage*: Light raillery or banter. Carlyle calls Voltaire "the greatest
of all *Persifleurs*" ("Voltaire" [1829], *Essays* 1:436). See Henry Crabb
Robinson's comments on Carlyle's "admirable article on Voltaire," which
represented him in the character "of a *persifleur*" (*Diary* 2:284–85).

14.6. **Ferney**: The village on the French-Swiss border where Voltaire
lived in near exile from 1759 until his triumphal return to Paris where
he died. See note at 13.37 above.

14.9. **delivering Calases**: Calas was a Huguenot who in 1762 was
tortured because of a false accusation that he had murdered his own
son to stop him from turning Catholic. To escape further persecution
the family fled to Geneva, where they were protected by Voltaire. In
"Voltaire" ([1829], *Essays* 1:439), Carlyle describes how a woman in
the street pointed to Voltaire, saying, "'*C'est le sauveur des Calas.*'"
Carlyle's source for this incident, which occurred in 1778, is Condorcet, *Oeuvres* 4:112.

14.12. **the realized ideal**: Carlyle titled the second chapter of *French Revolution* "Realised Ideals." The chapter deals with the French political and social atmosphere between 1744 and 1774.

14.15–16. **the Douanier at the Porte St. Denis**: When stopped at the customs barrier in Paris, according to Carlyle's translation of Wagnière, Voltaire declared, "'I believe there is nothing contraband here except myself.'" One of the guards recognized Voltaire and, "all gazing with the greatest astonishment mingled with respect, begged M. de Voltaire to pass on whither he pleased" ("Voltaire" [1829], *Essays* 1:438).

14.17. **tavern-waiters**: At the Golden Cross tavern in Dijon, people of distinction dressed as waiters that they might serve Voltaire at supper ("Voltaire" [1829], *Essays* 1:438).

14.18. **"*Va bon train;* thou art driving M. de Voltaire"**: "The Maître-de-poste ordered his postillion to yoke better horses, and said to him with a broad oath: '*Va bon train, crève mes chevaux, je m'en f——; tu mènes M. de Voltaire!*'" (Go like the wind. Don't spare the horses. I don't give a damn. You are driving M. Voltaire!; "Voltaire" [1829], *Essays* 1:438).

14.19–20. **'the nucleus of a comet, whose train fills whole streets'**: Voltaire's carriage "was as the nucleus of a comet, whose train extended over whole districts of the city" ("Voltaire" [1829], *Essays* 1:439).

14.20. **The ladies pluck a hair or two from his fur**: Carlyle translates Wagnière: "On his entering the playhouse, a crowd of more elegance, and seized with true enthusiasm for genius, surrounded him: the ladies, above all, threw themselves in his way, and stopped it, the better to look at him; some were seen squeezing forward to touch his clothes; some plucking hair from his fur" ("Voltaire" [1829], *Essays* 1:441). Compare *Julius Caesar*, 3.2.136: "beg a hair of him for memory."

14.24. **the withered Pontiff of Encyclopedism**: Referring to Voltaire, who was one of the contributors to the *Encyclopédie* of Diderot and D'Alembert, published 1751–77 (see note at 204.7–8 below). *Withered* suggests both Carlyle's response to the skeptical and rational spirit of the enterprise and Voltaire's appearance. Dr. John Moore, who visited Voltaire in 1776, described the philosopher as being like "a skeleton" (Noyes, *Voltaire*, 561). See "The Hero as Man of Letters" at 141.9 below and note.

15.28. snow-jokuls: *Jökull* is Icelandic for "glacier."

15.28. geysers: *Geyser*, or "boiling spring," is derived from the Icelandic *geysa* meaning "to rage."

15.29–30. chaotic battle-field of Frost and Fire: In the Old Norse creation myth, chaos was *Ginnungagap*, at the southern end of which was the abode of Fire (*Múspell*) and at the northern end the land of frost (*Niflheimr*).

16.1. Sæmund: Sæmund Sigfússon (1056–1133), medieval priest, poet, and historian, to whom was sometimes ascribed the thirteenth-century collection of tales and songs known as the *Elder* or *Poetic Edda*. Brynjólf Sveinsson (1605–1675) discovered the codex containing the *Poetic Edda* in 1643, and, believing it to be a compilation of Sæmund Sigfússon, titled it *Edda Sæmundi multiscii* (Edda of Sæmund the Learned). Carlyle follows Mallet in regarding Sæmund as the compiler of these poems (*Northern Antiquities* 2:151). Modern scholars tend to the view of Lee Hollander (*The Poetic Edda*, xii): "The connection of Sæmundr with the *Poetic Edda* has no documentary evidence whatever. Moreover, it is inherently improbable."

16.5. *Elder* or Poetic *Edda*: The *Elder Edda* is distinguished from the *Prose Edda*, attributed to Snorri Sturluson. Carlyle notes that some philologists have derived the word from Oddi in southwest Iceland, "where *Saemund Sigfusson* (elder Edda) had his abode" (*Letters* 12:33n), a suggestion adopted by Eirík Magnússon (see Hollander, *Poetic Edda*, xiii). Still others have derived it from Old Norse *óðr* meaning "poem." *Edda* may also be translated as "poetics." See Young, *Prose Edda*, 8; Hollander, *Poetic Edda*, xiii.

16.6. Snorro Sturleson: Snorri Sturluson (1179–1241), Icelandic historian generally regarded as the author of the *Prose Edda* (1220?) and the *Heimskringla* (1223–35?). The *Prose Edda* is an "Ars Poetica" containing rules for verse making and poetic diction, and it includes a summary of the Scandinavian myths. Carlyle read the *Heimskringla*, a history of the kings of Norway, in the edition of G. Olafsson, revised by J. Peringskiöld, *Heims Kringla, eller Snorre*

Sturlusons (1697), which he had borrowed from Hensleigh Wedgwood (*Letters* 12:32n). Carlyle said it is "built out of these old Sagas; and has in it a great deal of poetic fire, . . . and, in a word, deserves, were it once well-edited, . . . to be reckoned among the great history-books of the world" ("Early Kings of Norway." [1875], *Essays* 5:201).

16.14. *Sagas*: From the Old Norse for "saw" or "saying." Prose narratives of medieval Iceland and Scandinavia. In his journal of January 21, 1840, Carlyle wrote: "Reading Scandinavian things; set on by *Frithiof's* Saga" (*Letters* 12:32n).

16.25–26. '*Jötuns*,' Giants: According to Jacob Grimm in *Teutonic Mythology* (2:519), the "oldest and most comprehensive" term for "giant" in Norse is not *jötunn* but *iötunn*, which is cognate with the Anglo-Saxon *eoten* and the Old English *etin*, and he conjectures that it may be derived from the Norse verb *eta*, to eat, and might therefore be rendered by "πολυφάγος, devourer." Swinburne recalled this passage when he wrote to William Bell Scott, March 1, 1881, on learning of Carlyle's death: "Let us hope he is and will remain happier and more contented among 'the Fire-Jötuns'" (*Swinburne Letters* 4:201).

16.30. Asgard: The abode of the gods or Æsir, an enormous enclosure connected to the human world by the bridge Bifrost. *Gar, gard*, and its cognates in Indo-European languages usually signify an enclosure, as in Old Norse *Miðgarð*, *Útgarð*, and *Ásgarð*, hence the English verb *gird*. The further relationship to the English *garden* is implied by Carlyle's "Garden of the Asen." Asgard was not eternal but doomed to ruin with the destruction of the gods. See the note on *Ragnarök* at 34.31 below.

16.37. Loke: According to Snorri Sturluson, one of the sons of the giant Fárbauti and a giantess, Luafey. In Scandinavian mythology, Loki is evil and fickle, the counterpart of the devil in Christianity. Jacob Grimm records the view of Rask that Loki is "akin to Finn. *lokki*, wolf; some may think it an abbrev. of Lucifer!" (*Teutonic Mythology* 4:1362). The name has also been linked to *logi* ("flame"), and *loka* ("to shut"), which is the root of the English *lock*.

16.38. Ladrones Islands: Magellan's discovery of the Ladrones or Mariana Islands in 1521 was described by his companion Antonio Pigafetta in *Le voyage et navigation aux isles de Mollucque* (1525). In that account Pigafetta makes no mention of fire being unknown to the islanders. In fact, this suggestion was first made 180 years later by the Jesuit Father Le Gobien, in his *Histoire des Isles Marianes* (1700), who claimed that the islanders had "never seen fire" and at first regarded it "as a kind of animal which attached itself to the wood on which it fed" (cited by Tylor, see below). This latter detail may derive from a similar claim made regarding the Egyptians by Herodotus (3.16). The whole matter is described by Tylor, *Researches into the Early History of Mankind*, 246–47.

17.6. *Thrym, Hrym; or Rime*: The "Lay of Thrym" (*Þrymskviða*) in the *Elder Edda* describes how the giant Thrym was slain by Thor in Jötunheim for stealing the god's hammer. The Icelandic for "rime" or "hoarfrost" is *hrím*, not *thrym*.

17.11–12. the Giant Hymir: The Norse poem *Hymiskviða* relates how Thor fished for the Miðgarð snake and encountered and slew the sea giant Hymir. That Hymir "'looks at the rocks'" and splits them is presumably an imprecise rendering of section 1, stanza 12 of *Hymiskviða*. See *Edda: Die Lieder des Codex regius* 1:90.

17.15. Thor: Thor (*Þór*) was the second most important god in the Scandinavian pantheon, after Odin. Thor, with his hammer Mjöllnir, is the thunder god; he is also associated with agriculture. "The Edda calls him expressly the most valiant of the sons of Odin" and the "defender and avenger of the gods" (Mallet, *Northern Antiquities* 1:81–82). Carlyle frequently linked Thor and Robert Burns: "Burns, remarkable modern Thor, a Peasant god of these sunk ages" (*Frederick* 1:395); "This new Norse Thor had to put-up with what was going; to gauge ale, and be thankful" (*Pamphlets*, 3.119). See "The Hero as Man of Letters" at 163.3 below and note.

17.20. 'blows in his red beard': According to Jacob Grimm there is a traditional association in the sagas of Thor's red beard and lightning. When "the god is angry, he blows in his red beard, and thunder peals through the clouds" (*Teutonic Mythology* 1:177). The *Flateyjarbók* reveals how by blowing out his beard Thor raised a tempest against Ólaf Tryggvason.

17.21–23. Balder . . . found to resemble Christ: The second son of Odin and Frigg, Baldr was fair-skinned, wise, and merciful. Apart from personal qualities, the main resemblances between Baldr and Christ lie in the story of Baldr's descent into Hela, and the prophecy that he would return from death to inaugurate a new heaven and earth. Sir James Frazer, in *The Golden Bough*, links Baldr with other resurrected gods such as Osiris, Thammuz, and Adonis. The resemblances between Christ and Baldr were noticed in the Viking age, and the ending of the *Vǫluspá* in the *Hauksbǫk* version is read by some scholars as "an adumbration of the coming of Christ . . . but at present the best scholarship" regards such traces of Christianity in the poem as interpolations (Hollander, *Poetic Edda*, 1, 13n).

17.27. *Wünsch*: "The sum total of well-being and blessedness, the fulness of all graces, seems in our ancient language to have been expressed by a single word, whose meaning has since been narrowed down; it was named *wunsch* (wish) . . . , perfection in whatever kind, what we should call the Ideal" (Jacob Grimm, *Teutonic Mythology* 1:138; see also 4:1328).

17.33. *Aegir*: The name of the giant *Ægir* is Old Norse for "sea, ocean." Finn Magnusen derives *Ægir* from the verb *aga*, "to flow" (cited by I. A. Blackwell in his revised edition of Mallet, *Northern Antiquities*, 546). According to Jacob Grimm, *Oegir*, who "bears the name of the terrible," also signifies the sea. "The boisterous element awakened awe, and the sense of a god's immediate presence" (Jacob Grimm, *Teutonic Mythology* 1:237). Carlyle's connection here of the *eager* on the Trent with the sea giant *Ægir* is adopted by Grimm (4:1361). Carlyle correctly identifies *eager* as a provincial English survival of this word, meaning a sea wave or tidal bore on a river.

18.27–28. 'brewing ale': In "The Lay of Hymir" (Hollander, *Poetic Edda*, 83–89).

18.35. **primary mythus of the Creation**: As given in Snorri Sturluson's *Edda*, the giant Ymir appears out of melting ice when the hot winds from Múspell meet the cold vapors of Niflheimr, two regions on the outskirts of Ginnungagap, the central chaos (see the note at 15.29–30 above). Ymir was fed on milk from the cow Auðumbla (see 30.14 below), which licked salty blocks of rime into the shape of a man, Búri, grandfather of Odin and his two brothers, Vili and Vé. These gods slew Ymir and formed the earth out of his parts.

19.1–2. of his eyebrows they formed Asgard their Gods'-dwelling: In his letter to Carlyle of March 20, 1852 (see Note on the Text, pp. xcviii–xcix), Joseph Neuberg suggested, "Was it not rather *Mid*gard, *mens'*-dwelling, that was formed out of those materials? So, at least, I learn from *Simrock's Edda* page 246 & 247." (Neuberg was referring to *Die Edda, die ältere und jungere*, translated and edited by Karl Simrock [Stuttgart, 1851].) Carlyle replied to Neuberg on May 31, "Follow *Simrock*; my knowledge is vague, and quite second hand." But this passage was unchanged in the 1852 Fourth Edition (or any later version), although Carlyle did revise that edition elsewhere in response to other suggestions by Neuberg in the same letter (see notes at 8.17 above and 30.26 and 32.12 below).

19.3–4. Hyper-Brobdignagian: From *Gulliver's Travels*, part 2, where Gulliver encounters the giants of Brobdingnag. The deviation from Swift's spelling here and at 32.5 and 34.25 below was not exclusive to Carlyle. See, for example, Pope's *Epistle to Burlington*, line 104.

19.9. Tree Igdrasil: The ash tree Yggdrasill, whose branches extended over the world and whose three roots reached the realms of the Æsir, the Hrímþursar (frost-giants), and the underworld. Hollander explains the name as "Ygg's ('the Terrible One's,' Óthin's) Horse ('the gallows')" (Hollander, *Poetic Edda*, 36n). The world tree was a favorite image with Carlyle, providing perhaps the central structure of *On Heroes*. See Kusch, "Pattern and Paradox," 148–49, and also the note to "The Hero as Man of Letters" at 147.18–20 below. For Carlyle's "*Igdrasil. From the Norse*," published in 1890, see Tarr, *Descriptive Bibliography*, 436.

19.11. Hela: Hel, the death-goddess of the infernal regions, and in later personification used instead of *Helheimr* for the regions themselves. The dead are sent to her, except for those who fall in battle and people Valhalla. On their conversion to Christianity, the Teutonic nations used the word to denote a place for the punishment of wicked souls, though it originally had no such connotation.

19.14. *Nornas*: Three female deities, Urðr, Verðandi, and Skuld, who fixed the allotted lifetimes of all men. They are often said to represent fate, being, and necessity, as well as the past, present, and future, which Carlyle probably derived from Mallet (*Northern Antiquities*

1:87). There were various other Norns, but the prominence of this trinity reflects the influence of the Parcae of classical mythology.

19.24. 'the infinite conjugation of the verb *To do*': Untraced.

19.26–27. Ulfila the Mœsogoth: Ulfilas, or Wulfila (311?–381?), was consecrated bishop of the Arian Visigoths in 341 and ministered to the Gothic settlements in Moesia and Thrace. In 369 he translated the Bible into Gothic, chiefly from Greek manuscripts. Fragments of his translation are extant in the Codex Argenteum at Uppsala. Carlyle borrowed an edition, probably *Ulfilas Gothische Bibelübersetzung* (1805), from Hensleigh Wedgwood in 1837. That same year he mentioned Ulfilas in his lecture of May 1, the first in his course of lectures on the history of German literature (*Letters* 9:136n; 5:105). According to Carlyle, the translation is "faithfully, and even with a stiff closeness, rendered from the Septuagint; on which account, and being at the same time of such antiquity, it is still valued by the Biblical Critic, as well as by the Philologer" (*German Literature*, 25).

19.29. '*Machine* of the Universe': Possibly alluding to the five-volume *Méchanique céleste* (1798–1827) by Pierre-Simon, Marquis de Laplace (1749–1827). Note Carlyle's reference to "Laplace's Book on the Stars" and the "Mechanism of the Heavens" in *Sartor*, 3.8.204–5; also "Signs of the Times" (1829), *Essays* 2:64.

20.24. the Sphinx-enigma of this Universe: A reference to the riddle of the Theban sphinx, which was solved by Oedipus.

20.33. sympathetic ink: So-called invisible ink, an acid-based ink that remained invisible until heated or treated with chemicals. Dr. Thomas Chalmers told Carlyle that Christianity was "all written in us already, as in *sympathetic ink;* Bible awakens it, and you can read!" (*Reminiscences*, 215).

21.10–11. Councils of Trebisond: The first traces of Christianity in Trabzon, or Trebizond, in northeastern Turkey, date from the reign of Diocletian. In 1260 Trebizond secured a measure of religious independence from Nicaea and Constantinople, but there is no record of a council having met there. Note Carlyle's further references to "Trebisond" in connection with Cagliostro ("Count Cagliostro" [1833], *Essays* 3:254, 276).

21.11. Councils of Trent: The Council of Trent sat between 1545 and 1563. It was summoned into being by Charles V and sought, without success, to heal the schism in Christendom caused by the Protestant Reformation.

21.11. Athanasiuses: An early church father, Athanasius (293?–373) was engaged throughout his life in theological struggles against the Arian heresy, which culminated at the Council of Nicaea. There he formulated the homoousian doctrine, which holds, contrary to Arian formulas, that the Son of God is of the same essence or substance as the Father (see "The Hero as Prophet" at 54.26 below and note). Froude referred to Carlyle as *"Athanasius contra mundum"* (Clubbe, Introduction, *Froude's Life of Carlyle*, 11).

21.22. *"Wednesday"*: Woden's day, from the Old Norse *Óðinsdagr;* Anglo-Saxon, *Wódnesdæg. Woden* is a variant of *Óðinn.* Similarly, *Tuesday* derives from the Old Norse *Týsdagr* (after the god Týr), *Thursday* from Old Norse *Þórsdagr* (after Thor), and *Friday* from Old Norse *Freydagr* (after Freyja) (Mallet, *Northern Antiquities* 1:77–83).

21.26. *Heimskringla*: A title derived from the first words in the saga of the kings of Norway by Snorri Sturluson (see note at 16.6 above). *Heimskringla* means "world's circle." The account of a human Odin occurs in the *Ynglingasaga*, which forms the first section of *Heimskringla*.

21.33. Saxo Grammaticus: (1150?–1216?) Danish poet, historian, and author of the Latin *Historia Danica*, or *Gesta Danorum*. Compare "The Hero as Poet" at 70.28 below.

21.36. Torfæus: Þormóður Torfason (Thormodus Torfæus, 1636–1719), Icelandic scholar, author of the *Orcades* (*Prolegomena in Historiam Norwegicam & Orcadensem*, 1697). Mallet (*Northern Antiquities* 1:19) cites Torfæus's claim that an historical Odin and his followers arrived in Scandinavia from Asia "about 70 years before the birth of Christ." The whole question of the historical Odin, in Saxo and Torfæus, which Carlyle raises here, is probably derived from Mallet's discussion in chapter 2 of *Northern Antiquities* (1:18–35).

22.5. Grimm: Jacob Grimm (1785–1863), German philologist, popularly known for the collection of fairy tales he wrote with his brother Wilhelm (1786–1859). Apart from his massive work on Teutonic mythology, he is known for his work on the mutations of consonants in Germanic languages.

22.5–6. deny that any man Odin ever existed: Grimm questions on etymological grounds the humanity but not the divinity of Odin. Discussing sacred sites, the names of which are compounded with Odin's, he says it is "very unlikely that they should be due to men bearing the same name as the god, instead of to the god himself; Wuotan, Oðinn, as a man's name, does occur, but not often; and the meaning of the second half of the compounds . . . are altogether in favour of their being attributable to the god" (*Teutonic Mythology* 1:157–58). Snorri Sturluson, however, clearly states that Odin settled in Sigtúnir, now Sigtuna near Stockholm, engaged in numerous battles, had many sons, and finally died in his bed in Sweden. See Sturluson, *Heimskringla*, 10–13. Mallet also accepts as "facts" the tradition that "an extraordinary person" named Odin "formerly reigned in the north: that he made great changes in the government" and had "divine honours paid him" (*Northern Antiquities* 1:50).

22.9–10. Latin *vadere*: Though Carlyle says below, "we must bow to Grimm in matters etymological" (22.15–16), he did not in this instance do so, for Grimm derives the Norse Oðinn from the Old High German *watan*, but specifically denies that *watan* is "identical with Lat. vadere" (*Teutonic Mythology* 1:131). Some philologists, however, do connect the two words, and others have associated *Wodan* with the Latin *vates* (Skeat, *Concise Etymological Dictionary*, under "Wednesday").

22.19–20. universal admiration for Lope: Frey Lope Félix de Vega Carpio (1562–1635). See also *History of Literature*, 119.

22.23. *Essay on Language*: *Considerations Concerning the First Formation of Languages* (1761) by Adam Smith (1723–1790) (*Early Writings of Adam Smith*, 225–51). Carlyle is mistaken about Smith's argument (see especially 228–29).

23.23. *camera-obscura*: From the Latin, literally a "dark chamber," a camera consisting of a dark room with an opening or lens through which an image can be projected onto an opposite surface. The device was very popular in the seventeenth century. The first description of a portable reflex camera obscura is contained in *Collegium Curiosum*

(1676–85) by Johannes Christoph Sturm. By the end of the century, a portable model was on sale in London.

23.27. Arundel-marble: The collection of Greek antiquities presented to Oxford University by the Earl of Arundel in 1677. Among them is the Parian Chronicle, which records Greek historical events.

24.12–13. 'Image of his own Dream': From chapter 2 of Novalis's *Lehrlinge zu Saiz*, and translated by Carlyle in "Boswell's Life of Johnson" ([1832], *Essays* 3:76): "Is not that Universe even Himself, the reflex of his own fearful and wonderful being, 'the waste fantasy of his own dream'?"

24.23. *Cestus of Venus*: A magic girdle compelling love, given by Aphrodite to Hera (*Iliad* 14.213–45). Carlyle's reference is specifically to Schiller's essay "Über Anmuth und Wurde," which makes a distinction between charm and beauty.

24.32. Odin's *Runes*: The *Heimskringla* claims Odin as the discoverer of runes, magical inscriptions that conferred immense power on anyone who could inscribe them.

24.39–25.1. Atahualpa the Peruvian King: The last Inca ruler of Peru, imprisoned and, after he had submitted to Christian baptism, garroted by the Spanish explorer Francisco Pizarro. The incident of the writing on thumbnails to which Carlyle alludes is in William Robertson's *History of America* (1777) 3:153–54. The book was "an early favourite" of Carlyle's (Froude, *First Forty Years* 2:358).

25.6. Phenician Alphabet: The alphabet found on clay tablets at Ras Shamra is a Semitic script of thirty signs, representing consonants only, and written like cuneiform. The Phoenician language belonged to the Canaanite group of the Semitic family, which included Hebrew. A version of the Phoenician alphabet was adopted by the Greeks and transmitted to the Romans, from whom it spread throughout the Western world.

28.11. *Valkyrs*: Maidens who served Odin in Valhalla. The Valkyries (Icelandic *Valkyrur*, Anglo-Saxon *Wælcyrigan*) were sent to battlefields, where they chose who must be slain.

28.11. *Hall of Odin*: The chief hall of Ásgarð was Valhalla (*Valhǫll*, "hall of the slain"), the banquet hall of the gods. There were 640 vast portals to Valhalla, where Odin presided over the festivals of the gods and heroes. A brave death entitled the Norse warrior to a seat in Valhalla.

28.12. **the one thing needful**: Echoing Luke 10:42: "But one thing is needful." Perhaps recalled by Dickens in the title of the first chapter of *Hard Times* (1854), "The One Thing Needful." The novel was dedicated to Carlyle. Compare *Letters* 10:231: "An old blind schoolmaster in Annan used to ask with endless anxiety when a new scholar was offered him, 'But are ye sure *he's not a Dunce?*' It is really the one thing needful in a man."

28.26. *Valour* is still *value*: Latin *valor* signifies both "value" and "valor."

28.38-29.1. **Snorro tells us they thought it a shame and misery not to die in battle**: In the *Heimskringla*, Snorri Sturluson says that dying heroes were carried into battle to die, or hurled themselves from cliffs into the sea. Even after the advent of Christianity, Norsemen would call for their armor so that they could travel to the next world in battle harness (Mallet, *Northern Antiquities* 1:175-82).

29.3-4. **the ship sent forth, with sails set and slow fire burning it**: See, for example, the sea burial of Baldr (Jean Young, *Prose Edda*, 82). Father Klaeber in his edition of *Beowulf* (122) notes the prevalence of sea burial in Scandinavia from the fourth to the mid-sixth century. Sometimes the dead were burned in ships, a custom started in Sweden that spread to England. The Sutton Hoo burial ship of the seventh century reflects the modification by Christianity of the pagan custom in Anglo-Saxon England. There are numerous literary illustrations of the practice, among them the sea burials of Scyld Scefing in *Beowulf* (lines 4-52); of King Haki of Sweden in *Ynglingasaga* (chapter 23), the first saga in *Heimskringla;* and, in modern literature, the deaths of Tennyson's *Lady of Shalott* (part 4) and Longfellow's *Hiawatha* (final canto).

29.11. **Blakes and Nelsons**: Robert Blake (1599-1657) commanded Cromwell's navy and was a member of both the Short Parliament and Barebones Parliament (see note at 199.20-21 below). Admiral Horatio Nelson (1758-1805) was the hero of the battles of the Nile and Trafalgar.

29.11. No Homer sang these Norse Sea-kings: See Horace, *Odes*, 4.9.25–28: "vixere fortes ante Agamemnona / multi; sed omnes inlacrimabiles / urgentur ignotique longa / nocte, carent quia vate sacro" (Many heroes lived before Agamemnon, but all are overwhelmed in unending night, unwept, unknown, because they lack a sacred bard).

29.14. Hrolf, or Rollo Duke of Normandy: Hrolf the Ganger (876–932) became the first duke of Normandy and was an ancestor of William the Conqueror. After his banishment from Norway, Hrolf sailed up the Seine to Rouen and by force of arms secured parts of Neustria that were later called Normandy. See Mallet, *Northern Antiquities* 1:222–26; also "Early Kings of Norway" (1875), *Essays* 5:205.

29.19–20. some who got the title *Wood-cutter*: Ólaf Trételgja, the son of King Ingjald. The *Ýnglingasaga* tells how Ólaf and his followers cleared woods near Lake Vænir and called the district Vernaland. Ólaf was contemptuously nicknamed "Wood-cutter" (Sturluson, *Heimskringla*, 42–44). See also Mallet's exaggerated version of the king of Sweden "sirnamed the WOOD-CUTTER, for having grubbed up and cleared vast provinces, and felled the trees" that covered them (*Northern Antiquities* 1:345–46).

29.22. Skalds: *Skáld*, an Old Norse word signifying a "bard" or "court singer." Skaldic poetry deals mostly with the deeds of contemporary kings and warriors. Unlike the writers of the *Elder Edda*, the authors of skaldic poetry were often known by name, the names of around 250 skálds having come down to us. See "The Hero as Man of Letters" at 147.17 below.

30.7. Banyan-tree: An East Indian fig tree whose branches take root and become new trunks.

30.14. Cow Adumbla: Auðumbla or Auðhumla, the primeval cow of the Norse creation myth, who nourished the first being, the giant Ymir (see note at 18.35 above).

30.14. 'licking the rime from the rocks': See Young, *Prose Edda*, 34.

30.26. *Völuspa*: *Vǫluspá*, one of the Poetic Eddas; a sibylline lay containing the whole system of Scandinavian mythology. The *Vǫlu-* or *Vǫlo-spá* is a compound signifying "a song of a prophetess." All

Teutonic tribes had *valas*, or prophetesses. See for instance Tacitus, *History* 4.61, on the Veleda of the Bructeri. Until the 1852 Fourth Edition, all editions read *"Havamal"* here and at 34.32 below (see textual apparatus), but Joseph Neuberg, in his letter of March 20, 1852 (see Note on the Text, pp. xcviii–xcix, and the note at 19.1–2 above), noted: *"page 55.* the *Havamal* described as *prophetic:* 'rapt, earnest, sibylline.'—I find this description to fit the *Völuspa* (the first *Lied* in *Simrock's Edda*) but *not* the *Havamal;* which latter (#13 in *Simrock*) consists of a series of wise saws after the manner of King Solomon, but not what you would call 'sybilline'.—The prophecy of the 'Consummation,' too, ascribed (page 60 of the Hero-Worship) to the *Havamal,* I find not in *it*, but in the said *Völuspa*." Carlyle replied simply, "p. 55 (Havamal, Völuspa) *do do.*"

30.34. Gray's fragments of Norse Lore: Thomas Gray (1716–1771) produced two poems from the Norse, "The Fatal Sisters" and "The Descent of Odin," both of which were composed in 1761 (*Complete Poems of Gray,* 25–34, 211–20). In both poems Gray relied on a Latin translation of the Old Norse by Bartholinus, *Antiquitatum Danicarum de causis contemptae . . . mortis* (1689), and in "The Fatal Sisters" he also drew on the *Orcades* of Torfæus (see note at 21.36 above).

30.35. any more than Pope will of Homer: Carlyle objected to Pope's translation as "a very false, and though ingenious and talented, yet bad translation" (Froude, *First Forty Years* 2:97). While Gray's knowledge of Old Norse might have been unreliable, Pope's knowledge of Greek was undoubted. See Boswell, *Life of Johnson,* 1033.

31.4–6. 'draws down his brows' . . . 'grasps his hammer till the knuckles grow white': See Young, *Prose Edda,* 70.

31.6–7. Balder 'the white God' dies: See Young, *Prose Edda,* 81–82.

31.8. Frigga: Frigg, the wife of Odin and mother of Baldr.

31.9. Hermoder: Hermóðr, one of the sons of Odin, who rides into the land of Hel to bargain for the return of his dead brother Baldr. The name is given as "Hermode" throughout the first and second editions of *On Heroes* (1841 and 1842).

31.11. the Keeper: Móðguðr, "the maiden who kept the bridge" over the river Gjöll, on the way to Hel, where she confronts Hermóðr in his search for the dead Baldr (Young, *Prose Edda*, 83).

31.18. Nanna . . . sends her *thimble* to Frigga: In his letter of March 20, 1852, Joseph Neuberg observed to Carlyle that "according to *Simrock* (page 282) she sends her . . . a cloak. . . . I find no mention of a *thimble*." (The reference is to *Die Edda, die ältere und jungere*, trans. Karl Simrock [Stuttgart, 1851].) Carlyle replied, "(thimble).—I got this from Mallet (Northern Antiquities,—"*ron dez*"), and have since repeatedly seen it different in better authorities; but *liking* the poor thimble, I always kept it."

31.23. Uhland: Johann Ludwig Uhland (1787–1862), German poet and professor of German literature at Tubingen (1830–35), was the author of *Der Mythus von Thor* (1836). Armstrong ("Carlyle and Uhland," 221) traces one possible connection between a section of *Sartor* and Uhland's lines on the death of a child.

31.30. Thialfi, *Manual Labour*: Þjálfi (literally "a delver, digger"), Thor's retainer, a farmer's son he encountered on the journey to Jötunheim, as described in the *Gylfaginning*.

32.2. 'handles of it reach down to his heels': From "The Lay of Hymir": Thor "heaved on his head the heavy kettle: / hard on his heels the handles rang" (Hollander, *Poetic Edda*, 89).

32.10. Jack of the Nursery: A ubiquitous figure in folklore. Carlyle's reference is to the English fairy tale set in Cornwall during the time of King Arthur. It is from his uncle, a three-headed giant, that Jack obtains a magical cap, a rusty sword, a cloak, and the slippers that make him fleet of foot.

32.12. *Hynde Etin*, and still more decisively *Red Etin of Ireland*: Hynde Etin and Red Etin are giants in Scottish folklore. All editions before 1852 mentioned only "*Childe Etin*" here (see textual apparatus). Joseph Neuberg, in his letter of March 20, 1852, queried, "*page 58. 'Childe Etin'*, where can I find some thing about him, with a view to an explanatory note?" Carlyle replied on May 31, "There is a Ballad of *Childe-Etin*, whh I have read in some Scotch collection (hardly *Scott*'s, I think), but cannot say where. I have written to R*t*.

Chambers to tell me; and if his answer, which is already due, come before tomorrow's post go, you shall still have it. . . . Meanwhile here is the *Red Etin of Ireland* (still more decisively a *Jötun*; who changes people into stone; has married the King of Scotland's daughter, and daily beats her;—a truly ugly scoundrel and son of Chaos;—but gets his monstrous heads well cut off at last, by a dextrous pious little fellow (Thor in modern coat): of him you will find lively enough account in a German Book *Geschichte der Volksthümlichen schottischen Liederdichtung, von Eduard Fideler* (2 voll Zerbst, 1846) ii. 261-7;—and this will do for you whatever befal. Fideler (some poor schoolmaster I suppose) gives the *fullest* account of Scotch songwriting I have anywhere seen,—the good faithful soul!"

Carlyle had written to Robert Chambers on May 27, and Chambers replied to him on May 31: "There is no ballad called Childe Etin, but there is one called Hynde Etin, which you will find in Chambers's Scottish Ballads, 1829. . . . In my Popular Rhymes of Scotland the tale of the Red Etin was first printed—a totally different thing from the ballad, as you will see by a copy which I enclose." ("Hynde Etin" in Chambers, ed., *Scottish Ballads*, 193–200; "Red Etin of Ireland" in Chambers, ed., *Popular Rhymes of Scotland*, 89–95.) As promised, Carlyle sent Chamber's reply along to Neuberg on June 1, with the comment, "*Childe* Etin, apparently, is a mistake, and should be Hynde Etin (*Hind* means, drudge, slave): the *baptism* of the child (or rather non-baptism) seems to be the chief *jötunish* feature of the '*Hynde*';—it must have been in Chambers that I read of him. *Red Etin*, which I also send if you can read Scotch, is a much more conspicuously Norse business. He is also, you see, of venerable age as a myth.——On the whole, you had better say, in translating the Text, '*Hynde Etin* in the Scottish Ballads, and still more conspicuously *Red Etin*, are Norse myths: *Etin*' &c. And add what brief Note, manufactured out of these materials, you find suitable."

32.13. Scottish Ballads . . . derived from Norseland: Robert Jamieson in *Popular Ballads and Songs . . . with Translations of Similar Pieces from the Ancient Danish Language . . .* (1806) was the first to point out parallels in incident and language between the ballads of Scotland and those of Scandinavia, a connection also suggested by Mallet.

32.15. Hamlet, *Amleth*: The earliest known reference to the Hamlet story is in a verse preserved in Snorri Sturluson's *Skáldskaparmál*.

Hamlet appears in books 3 and 4 of Saxo Grammaticus's *Gesta Danorum*, where his name is Amlethus, a latinization of *Amlóði*, "an imbecile, weakling." Saxo's story was retold in Belleforest's *Histoires Tragiques* (1576). Shakespeare's *Hamlet* was written in 1600–1601 and first performed in 1602.

32.30–31. the Hindoo Mythologist: A reference to the doctrine of *maya* (illusion) in Hindu mythology. Compare Emerson, *Journals* 16:29–33.

32.31. the German Philosopher: Immanuel Kant (1724–1804) and his school. See note to "The Hero as Man of Letters" at 135.4.

32.33. 'We are such stuff as Dreams are made of!': A variant quotation of *The Tempest*, 4.1.156–57: "We are such stuff / As dreams are made on." Carlyle may have been influenced by George Steevens (1736–1800), whose fifteen-volume edition of Shakespeare (1793) gives the quotation exactly as Carlyle has it, as does Boswell's Malone edition (1821), which includes Steevens's notes.

32.34. One of Thor's expeditions: In Snorri Sturluson's *Edda* (see Young, *Prose Edda*, 69–80). An account is also given in Mallet (*Northern Antiquities* 2:87–91). In January 1840, Carlyle described Mallet's book as a "kind of translation of Snorro's *Edda*, . . . which seems a very ingenious didactic Fiction" (*Letters* 12:35n).

32.34. Utgard: Útgarð, a realm outside Ásgarð, was ruled by the giant Útgarðaloki.

33.28–29. 'strain your neck bending back to see the top of it': Thor and his companions reach Útgarð, a city "so lofty, that one could not look up to the top of it, without throwing one's head quite back upon the shoulders" (Snorri Sturluson, "The Prose Edda," in Mallet, *Northern Antiquities* 2:90; also Jean Young, *Prose Edda*, 73).

34.9. *Midgard-snake*: *Miðgarðormr*, the serpent of Miðgarð. The oceanic snake surrounds Miðgarð, the abode of men, the "middle land" between Niflheimr and Múspellheimr. In Norse legend, Thor tries but fails to kill the Miðgarð snake, but his ultimate success is prophesied in the *Vǫluspá*. See Hollander, *Poetic Edda*, 14.

34.23-24. Mimer-stithy: The forge of Mimer. Carlyle's image is the forge out of which emerged the allegorical tales of Norse mythology. The skálds were called *Ljóðasmiðir*, literally, lay-smiths or verse-smiths. *Stithy* is an archaic term for "anvil" or "forge." Jacob Grimm (*Teutonic Mythology* 1:378) identifies a "smith, *Mímir*" in the *Vilkinasaga*. Carlyle may be associating him with the smith Hephaestus in classical mythology, who makes thunderbolts, and is therefore connected to Thor the thunder-god in the paragraph immediately above.

34.29-30. out of the American Backwoods: What precise example of American humor Carlyle had in mind is impossible to determine. However, he cites observations by Morris Birkbeck about "society in the backwoods of America" in "Burns" ([1828], *Essays* 1:261).

34.31. *Ragnarök*: Literally, "Doom of the Reigners," the twilight of the gods, signaling the end of the world, the destruction of Ásgarð and Miðgarð, and the slaying of the gods by monsters.

35.1-2. a new Heaven and a new Earth: The final part of the *Voluspá* pictures the earth rising a second time, fresh and green from the sea. Compare Revelation 21:1.

35.6. Phœnix fire-death: The phoenix is the legendary Arabian bird that by tradition consumed itself by fire, a new bird rising from the ashes. Herodotus describes the phoenix but confesses, "I myself have never seen it, but only pictures of it, for the bird comes but seldom into Egypt, once in five hundred years, as the people of Heliopolis say" (2.73). Tacitus reported the appearance of a phoenix in Egypt during the reign of Tiberius (*Annals* 6.28). Early Christianity adopted the phoenix as a symbol of immortality and resurrection. The principle of perpetual renewal was also central to post-Kantian philosophy and occurs in the work of Goethe and Fichte. For Carlyle the phoenix was a popular symbol of "palingenetic" change; it occurs frequently in *Sartor*. See, for example, chapter 5 of book 3, which is called "The Phœnix": "Thus is Teufelsdröckh content that old sick Society should be deliberately burnt (alas, with quite other fuel than spicewood); in the faith that she is a Phœnix; and that a new heavenborn young one will rise out of her ashes!" (3.5.189).

35.14. King Olaf: Ólaf II Haraldsson (995?–1030), Saint Ólaf, King of Norway 1016-28. "The new Olaf . . . set himself with all his strength to mend such a state of matters [the relapse into semi-heathenism]. . . . His method was by no means soft; on the contrary, it was hard, rapid, severe. . . . There was a great deal of mauling, vigorous punishing. . . . 'Too severe,' cried many; to whom one answers, 'Perhaps in part *yes*, perhaps also in great part *no*; depends altogether on the previous question, How far the law was the eternal one of the God Almighty in the universe, How far the law merely of Olaf (destitute of right inspiration) left to his own passions and whims?'" ("Early Kings of Norway" [1875], *Essays* 5:260–61).

35.16–17. revolt of his Pagan people: Instigated by the Danish King Cnut, Ólaf's own people revolted and he was driven into exile for two years. His efforts to regain his kingdom led to the battle of Stiklestad, in which he was killed. According to the Anglo-Saxon Chronicle for 1030, "In this year King Olaf was killed in Norway by his own people, and was afterwards holy" (*Anglo-Saxon Chronicle*, 101). Carlyle gives a detailed description of the battle in his "Early Kings of Norway" ([1875], *Essays* 5:280–83). The saga of Saint Ólaf is recorded in the *Heimskringla*. The story of the conflict between the Christianizing king and the displaced pagan god Thor, which Carlyle gives below (35.21–35), concerns not Saint Ólaf but Ólaf Trygvason (968–1000), and is recorded in the so-called Great Olaf Trygvason Saga, not the life of Trygvason in the *Heimskringla*. See *Saga of King Olaf Tryggwason*, 332–33.

35.38–36.1. 'Neptune was seen once at the Nemean Games': Poseidon (Neptune), "who oft cometh from Aegae to the famous Dorian Isthmus, where the joyous bands welcome the god with the music of the flute, and wrestle with all the hardy prowess of their limbs" (Pindar; the passage is from the third strophe of the fifth Nemean ode). The Nemean festival took place in the valley of Nemea near Cleōnae in Argos.

36.22. Three Religions: In Goethe's *Wilhelm Meister's Travels*, religious instruction is given in three stages. "The Religion which depends on reverence for what is above us, we denominate the Ethnic. . . . The Second Religion, which founds itself on reverence for what is around us, we denominate the Philosophical. . . . The Third Religion, grounded on reverence for what is beneath us: this we name the Christian. . . . 'To which of these Religions do you specially adhere?' inquired Wilhelm. 'To all the three,' replied they: 'for in their union they produce what may properly be called the true religion'" (*Wilhelm Meister* 2:10.267–68).

NOTES TO LECTURE II. THE HERO AS PROPHET.

Sources: Carlyle first read Edward Gibbon's *The History of the Decline and Fall of the Roman Empire* (1776–88) during his Kirkcaldy period in 1816 (Froude, *Life in London* 2:461). Chapter 50 of that work deals with the character, doctrines, and history of Muḥammad, and Carlyle drew on it extensively for his picture of the founder of Islam. Supplementary sources of information include Humphry Prideaux's *The True Nature of Imposture Fully Display'd in the Life of Mahomet* (1678), Edward Pococke's *Specimen Historiæ Arabum* (1650), and Hugo Grotius' *De Veritate Christianæ* (1627). In October 1839, Carlyle read the "Arabian Tales by Lane" (Froude, *Life in London* 1:176), being volume one of the first edition of Edward William Lane's *The Thousand and One Nights*...(1839–41). Perhaps Carlyle's most important direct source was the Qur'ān itself, which he was reading in February 1840 "partly with a view to *lecturing*" (*Letters* 12:64). In early March he was still "deep in perusal of the *Koran;* a strange *crowdie* [thick gruel] of a thing" (*Letters* 12:68), which he finished by March 17, about a month and a half before his lecture. Carlyle, who had no Arabic though he was tempted at this stage to learn, knew the Qur'ān in the translation of George Sale (1734; see note on Sale at 42.23 below), whose "Preliminary Discourse" was one of his principal sources. (All citations to the Qur'ān are to Sale's translation, in the absence of a standard English version.) In June 1837, he found "an excellent Arabian thing," Friedrich Rückert's translation into German of al-Ḥarīrī's "Ebu Seid" (*Letters* 9:228), *Die Verwandlungen des Abu Seid von Serug* (1837), which inspired Carlyle to go "searching" through "Sylvestre de Sacy and others" (*Letters* 9:384; see note at 43.25 below). Carlyle's other sources would have included Goethe, whose *West-östlicher Divan* (1819) Carlyle alluded to in this lecture.

The system of transliteration of Arabic names and terms follows that of the Library of Congress as modified by Hanna E. Kassis in *A Concordance of the Qur'an*, xi, xv–xvi.

38.6. *deliquium*: Latin, meaning "a melting" or "swooning."

38.13. *such* reception: See "The Hero as Man of Letters" below at 161.28–29 and also "Burns" (1828), *Essays* 1:258–318.

38.24. Mahomet: Muḥammad (570?–632), the prophet and founder of Islam. Faced with such orthographic variants as "Mahommed, Mohammed, Mâhmet, Moûhmed, Mahômet, Mahmoud," Carlyle, like Macaulay, stuck to the "common practice" in writing *"Mahomet"* (Macaulay, *Letters* 5:195).

38.31–32. a scheming Impostor: The commonly held European view of Muḥammad for many centuries before Carlyle's lecture. Embodied in the title of Prideaux's *The True Nature of Imposture Fully Display'd in the Life of Mahomet* (1678), it is echoed by Gibbon: "A politician will suspect that he secretly smiled (the victorious impostor!) at the enthusiasm of his youth and the credulity of his proselytes" (*Decline and Fall* 5:50.401). Sale notes the "general opinion of Christian writers" that Muḥammad's love of women "sufficiently proves him to have been a wicked man, and consequently an impostor" ("Preliminary Discourse," 41–43). Carlyle had first made the claim that Muḥammad was not an impostor but an intensely sincere teacher two years earlier, in his lecture of May 18, 1838 (*History of Literature*, 112).

38.35–39.1. Pococke inquired of Grotius . . . there was no proof!: The inquiry Carlyle refers to is in *Specimen Historiæ Arabum*, 191ff, by Edward Pococke (1604–1691). In *De Veritate Religionis Christianæ*, 389, Hugo Grotius (1583–1645) had written: "Secuti tamen sunt, qui ei & miracula attribuerent, at qualia? Nempe quæ aut arte humana facile possunt effecta reddi, ut de columba ad aurem advolante" (Yet there followed those who also attributed miracles to him; but what kind of miracles? Why, those of course that can either be easily executed by human skill as in the case of a pigeon flying to his ear). Prideaux also claimed that Muḥammad "bred up *Pigeons* to come to his Ears, to make show thereby, as if the *Holy Ghost* conversed with him" (*True Nature of Imposture*, 42). See also Gibbon, *Decline and Fall* 5:50.400n. Mallet, who was one of Carlyle's sources for the first lecture, associates Odin's pretense of having restored the use of speech to the decapitated head of Mimer with "the Pigeon, which brought to Mahomet the commands of heaven" (*Northern Antiquities* 1:60).

39.24. Cagliostro: Giuseppe Balsamo (1743–1795), the shopkeeper's son who, posing as the Count Cagliostro, deceived a fashionable and credulous European society. He practiced as a physician, necromancer, and alchemist, claiming knowledge of Egyptian magic and occult wisdom. Carlyle devoted an essay to this "King of Quacks" (Froude, *First Forty Years* 2:339) and "born scoundrel" ("Count Cagliostro" [1833], *Essays* 3:266), who spent time in the Bastille for his supposed involvement in the affair of "The Diamond Necklace" ([1837], *Essays* 3:324–402) and was arrested in Rome by the Holy Inquisition.

39.33. **Mirabeau**: Honoré Gabriel Riquetti, Comte de Mirabeau (1749–1791), Carlyle's hero of French revolutionary history, whose *Mémoires* he reviewed in the *Westminster Review* in 1837 (*Essays* 3:403–80). Carlyle considered Mirabeau "of a genius equal in strength . . . to Napoleon's; but a much humaner genius, almost a poetic one" ("Mirabeau" [1837], *Essays* 3:412). See "The Hero as Man of Letters" at 156.10 below and note.

40.11. **walk in a vain show**: Psalms 39:6: "Surely every man walketh in a vain shew."

40.27. **has not God made him**: See 59.24–25 below and note.

40.28–29. **'inspiration . . . understanding'**: Job 32:8: "The inspiration of the Almighty giveth them understanding."

41.6–7. **'the man according to God's own heart'**: 1 Samuel 13:14: "The Lord hath sought him a man after his own heart." Compare Acts 13:22.

41.13–14. **'It is not in man that walketh to direct his steps'**: Jeremiah 10:23.

41.25. **'a succession of falls'**: Possibly echoing Arthur Schopenhauer, "we know our walking to be only a constantly prevented falling" (*World as Will and Representation* 1:311). Carlyle had used the idea in "Sir Walter Scott" ([1838], *Essays* 4:30): Man's "walk, like all walking (say the mechanicians), is a series of *falls*"; also in a letter to Thomas Spedding in August 1839 (*Letters* 11:160). Compare Emerson: "The walking of man and all animals is a falling forward. All our manual labor and works of strength, as prying, splitting, digging, rowing, and so forth, are done by dint of continual falling, and the globe, earth, moon, comet, sun, star, fall forever and ever" (Emerson, "Spiritual Laws" [1841], *Essays*, 80). Also, "They fall successive, and successive rise" (Pope, *Iliad* 1:6.184).

42.10–11. The Persians are called the French of the East: In De Quincey's "Kant on National Character in Relation to the Sense of the Sublime and the Beautiful: A Translation" (1824): "If the Arabs are as it were the Asiatic Spaniards, the *Persians* are the Asiatic Frenchmen. They are good poets, courteous, and of tolerably refined taste" (*Collected Writings of Thomas De Quincey* 14:55).

42.20. Jewish kindred: According to Watt, "the Jewish tribes had many customs identical with those of their pagan Arab neighbours and intermarried with them" (*Muhammad at Medina*, 192).

42.23. Sale: George Sale (1697?–1736). His translation of the Qur'ān into English, *The Korán*, was first published in 1734. It had "no rival in the field" when it appeared, and had "been superseded by no subsequent translations," wrote Sir Edward Denison Ross in his introduction to the 1927 edition (vi). Ross finds that Sale's annotations reflect little direct use of Arabic commentators except for al-Bayḍāwī, and that he relies heavily on Pococke as well as Luigi Marracci's translation published in Padua in 1698.

42.23. at Ocadh: ʿUkāẓ. "To keep up an emulation among their poets, the tribes had, once a year, a general assembly at Ocadh, a place famous on this account. This annual meeting lasted a whole month, during which time they employed themselves, not only in trading, but in repeating their poetical compositions, contending and vying with each other for the prize; whence the place, it is said, took its name" (Sale, "Preliminary Discourse," 30).

42.30. Sabeans: See "The Hero As Divinity" above at 10.14 and note.

43.14–16. the Horse . . . 'laughs at the shaking of the spear!': Carlyle conflates two quotations from Job, only one of which refers to the horse, Job 39:19: "Hast thou given the horse strength? hast thou clothed his neck with thunder?" The second phrase, Job 41:29, "he laugheth at the shaking of a spear," describes Leviathan.

43.22–23. Black Stone . . . in the building called Caabah: The black stone was built into the southeastern corner of the Kaʿbah during renovations to repair flood damage in A.D. 605. Muḥammad assisted in the reconstruction and arbitrated tribal feuding over who should place the sacred stone. See Muir, *Life of Moḥammad*, 27–30, who relies on the accounts of Ibn Hishām, aṭ-Ṭabarī, and Ibn Saʿd. The stone is semicircular, about six inches high and eight inches broad (Muir, *Life of Moḥammad*, 28; Sale, "Preliminary Discourse," 126; Gibbon, *Decline and Fall* 5:50.351). Among numerous observances, pilgrims to Mecca are required to make seven circuits around the Kaʿbah and to greet the black stone (Muir, *Life of Moḥammad*, cii–ciii).

43.23. Mecca: *Makkah*, the birthplace of Muḥammad.

43.23. Diodorus Siculus: The Sicilian historian who flourished under Caesar and Augustus. Carlyle follows Gibbon (*Decline and Fall* 5:50.350) in attributing to Diodorus an early identification of the Kaʿbah. His reference to a temple "revered by all Arabians" (3.44.2) is not as unmistakeable an allusion to the Kaʿbah as Carlyle and Gibbon supposed.

43.25. Silvestre de Sacy: Antoine Isaac Silvestre de Sacy (1758–1838), orientalist, translator, and commentator of, among other works, *Les Séances de Hariri publiées en Arabe, avec un commentaire choisi par M. Le Baron Silvestre de Sacy* (1822). Carlyle searched through de Sacy "tho' with little effect" in December 1837 (*Letters* 9:384), after reading, in June of that year, a German translation of al-Ḥarīrī's book, *Die Verwandlungen des Abu Seid von Serug, oder die Makamen des Hariri* (1837) by Friedrich Rückert (*Letters* 9:228). The "little effect" was doubtless due to the fact that *Les Séances* is in Arabic. However, de Sacy did, in his *Chrestomathie Arabe . . .* (1806), translate into French two of the fifty Assemblies of al-Ḥarīrī. Goethe's *West-östlicher Divan* ends with a dedication to de Sacy (Goethe, *Werke* 2:267).

43.28. Zemzem: *Zamzam*, the well at Mecca, situated on the east side of the Kaʿbah. Muslims are "persuaded it is the very spring which gushed out for the relief of Ishmael, when Hagar his mother wandered with him in the desert" (Sale, "Preliminary Discourse," 127; see also Sale's note to Chapter 14, *Korân*, 249n). The derivation of Zemzem at 43.31–32 below is also given by Sale ("Preliminary Discourse," 127).

43.33. Hagar . . . Ishmael: Hagar, the handmaid of the barren Sarah, became Abraham's concubine and gave birth to Ishmael (Genesis 16, 21:1–21). In Islamic tradition, Hagar is Abraham's true wife, just as Ishmael (*Ismāʿīl*), rather than Isaac, is his favored son.

43.36–37. 'twenty-seven cubits high': "The length of this edifice, from north to south, is twenty-four cubits, its breadth from east to west twenty-three cubits, and its height twenty-seven cubits" (Sale, "Preliminary Discourse," 123). See also Gibbon, *Decline and Fall* 5:50.350.

44.2. *Keblah*: *Qiblah*, "direction of prayer." Jerusalem was the first qiblah of Muḥammad. In a subsequent revelation "Jerusalem was abandoned" and the Kaʿbah became the qiblah of Islam. See Muir, *Life of Mohammad*, 189–90. The Qurʾanic version of these decisions and revelations is given in *Korân*, Chapters 2 (21) and 10 (207), and the change from Jerusalem to Mecca is described by Gibbon (*Decline and Fall*, 5:50.388, 369–70). Carlyle used the term *"Keblah"* in a letter in August 1840 (*Letters* 12:208).

44.19. a population of 100,000: The source of this figure has not been located.

44.22. Ten Men: Sale mentions a prevailing tribal aristocracy at Mecca ("Preliminary Discourse," 13). The early guardians of the Kaʿbah were from the tribe of the Banī Jurham who were displaced in A.D. 207 by the Khuzāʿa tribe who in turn were displaced after A.D. 400 by the "Kinana clan of the Qoraish tribe" (Gaury, *Rulers of Mecca*, 36–37; see next note). "The Government of Mecca . . . was . . . an oligarchy composed of the leading members of the house of Kossay. After the discovery of the sacred well of Zemzem . . . the governing body consisted of ten senators, who were styled Sharifs" (Ali, *Life and Teachings of Mohammed*, 65).

44.24. Koreish: Tribe said to be direct descendants of Ishmael. Muḥammad's father was of the family of Hāshim of the Quraysh tribe (see below at 45.5–6). "The tribe of Koreish, by fraud or force, had acquired the custody of the Caaba: the sacerdotal office devolved through four lineal descents to the grandfather of Mahomet" (Gibbon, *Decline and Fall* 5:50.350).

44.35. Idolatries . . . in a tottering state: Pre-Islamic idolatry is described by Sale ("Preliminary Discourse," 15–21). It included Sabian beliefs that showed some influences of Christianity, especially baptism. The Qurʾān refers to three major tribal idols, Al-Lāt, Al-ʿUzzá, and Manāt, and the Kaʿbah itself contained, according to tradition, 360 idols "of men, eagles, lions, and antelopes" (Gibbon,

Decline and Fall 5:50.351; see also Muir, *Life of Mohammad*, 408). After the conquest of Mecca, Muḥammad purified the temple. As he touched each of them with his staff, the idols of the Kaʿbah fell down (Sale, *Korân*, Chapter 17, 280n).

45.4. in the year 570: Gibbon places Muḥammad's birth in A.D. 569, "four years after the death of Justinian," the "old Arabian calendar" being too "dark and uncertain" to support Benedictine calculations that would "remove the birth of Mahomet to the year of Christ 570, the 10th of November" (*Decline and Fall* 5:50.356–57n). Sale, however, gives the year 570 ("Preliminary Discourse," 39n). Muir suggests the autumn of 570, though the "materials are too vague and discrepant for any close calculation" (*Life of Mohammad*, 5).

45.27. 'Sergius, the Nestorian Monk': A Nestorian monk, known in the east as Baḥīrah, who according to Prideaux assisted Muḥammad in writing at least those sections of the Qurʾān relating to Christianity (*True Nature of Imposture*, 38–42). Carlyle's reservations concerning this story are probably due to Sale's rejection of the theory. See Sale's extensive note to Chapter 16 (*Korân*, 267n).

46.1. Mahomet never could write: Muḥammad could "neither write nor read" (Sale, "Preliminary Discourse," 45). He rejoiced "in the title of *An-Nebi al-Ummi*, or the Illiterate Prophet" (Muir, *Life of Mohammad*, 512; see *Korân*, Chapter 7, 160), and he used this fact as evidence of the divine inspiration of the Qurʾān, since it was inconceivable that a person who "could neither write nor read should be able to compose a book of such excellent doctrine . . . and style" (Sale, "Preliminary Discourse," 45; see also Sale's note to Chapter 16 cited in the preceding note and Gibbon, *Decline and Fall* 5:50.358).

46.15. 'Al Amin, The Faithful': Muḥammad's youthful resistance to the temptations of Mecca led his fellow citizens to award him the title of Al-Amīn, "the Faithful" (Muir, *Life of Mohammad*, 19–20). The title appears to have stuck. See Muir, 29.

46.24–25. One hears of Mahomet's beauty: A "comely, agreeable person" (Sale, "Preliminary Discourse," 44). "According to the tradition of his companions, Mahomet was distinguished by the beauty of his person" (Gibbon, *Decline and Fall* 5:50.357). Muir, following the account of al-Wāqidī, refers to Muḥammad's attractive face and expression, which "gained the confidence and love of strangers, even at first sight" (*Life of Moḥammad*, 510).

46.26-27. vein on the brow: In his journal for October 1839, Carlyle noted of Muḥammad, "the 'vein of anger' between his brows" (Froude, *Life in London* 1:176). See also *Past and Present*, 4.6.288. The same characteristic is noted by Washington Irving in his *Mahomet and His Successors* (192) and Muir (*Life of Moḥammad*, 27).

46.28. 'horse-shoe' vein' in Scott's *Redgauntlet*: A family trait of the Redgauntlets. Sir Robert had a "visible mark of a horse-shoe in his forehead" and his son John, when very angry, seemed to have "that selfsame fearful shape of a horse's shoe in the middle of his brow" (Scott, *Redgauntlet*, 105, 109). See also *Past and Present*, 4.6.288.

46.34. Kadijah: Muḥammad's first wife. His marriage in A.D. 595 to Khadījah bint Khuwaylid ibn Asad was a turning point in the prophet's early career. The traditional account is that the wealthy, twice-married widow invited Muḥammad to act as her agent on a caravan journey to Syria. She was so pleased with his stewardship that she offered to marry him. She was then forty and Muḥammad twenty-five years old. At critical junctures of his life she encouraged him in his prophetic mission. See *Letters* 15:190 and 248 for two references to Khadījah in letters by Jane Welsh Carlyle.

46.38-47.1. the Arab authors: The early biographers whose works are the primary sources for Muḥammad's life include Ibn Isḥāq (d. A.H. 151 [A.D. 773]), Ibn Hishām (d. A.H. 213 [A.D. 835]), al-Wāqidī (d. A.H. 207 [A.D. 829]), his secretary Ibn Saʿd (d. A.H. 230 [A.D. 852]), who wrote fifteen volumes on Muḥammad's companions and successors, and aṭ-Ṭabarī (d. A.H. 310 [A.D. 932]), called by Gibbon the "Livy of the Arabians" (*Decline and Fall* 5:50.428n). See Muir, *Life of Moḥammad*, lxxvi-lxxxvi.

47.23-24. great Mystery of Existence . . . glared in upon him: An almost exact reversal of Carlyle's judgment of Scott, "the great Mystery of Existence was not great to him; did not drive him into rocky solitudes to wrestle with it for an answer" ("Sir Walter Scott" [1838], *Essays* 4:36). See above at 40.12 and 40.23 and below at 48.13, and Introduction, p. li.

47.25-26. "Here am I!": Recalling the words of Moses in response to God's calling to him from the burning bush (Exodus 3:4).

47.33. Mount Hara ... Mount Sinai: It was to a cave in Mount Ḥirā᾿ near Mecca that Muḥammad often retired during the month of Ramaḍān to meditate; the mountain is since called "Jebel Nūr, or Mountain of Light, because Moḥammad is said to have received his first revelation there" (Muir, *Life of Moḥammad*, 37n). See also Sale, "Preliminary Discourse," 42; Gibbon, *Decline and Fall* 5:50.360. Sinai or Horeb in the peninsula between the gulfs of Suez and Aqaba is, by tradition, the mountain on which Moses received the Ten Commandments (Exodus 19).

48.2. jargon of argumentative Greek Sects: Though the sects are not specifically named, nor their "jargon" identified, the Qur᾿ān describes a religious schism that caused the *Rŭm*, the Byzantine Christians, to divide "into various sects" (*Korân*, Chapter 30, 397). Arab idolatry and various Jewish traditions, which Carlyle links together, are likewise objects of attack in the Qur᾿ān.

48.5. Alpha and Omega: Revelation 21:6: "I am Alpha and Omega, the beginning and the end."

48.9-10. 'bits of black wood ... ': Untraced.

48.17. Heraclius ... Chosroes: Heraclius (575?-641), Byzantine emperor 610-41, and Khosrow II Parvīz, king of Persia 590-628. In 627 Muḥammad unsuccessfully attempted their conversion to Islam. See Sale, "Preliminary Discourse," 57, and *Korân*, Chapter 30, 395n; Gibbon, *Decline and Fall* 5:50.395ff. Based on Ibn-al-Athir, Ali gives details of Muḥammad's embassies to Heraclius and Chosroes and their reactions (*Life and Teachings of Mohammed*, 185-86).

48.26. Ramadhan: Ramaḍān, the ninth month of the Muslim year, is observed as a fast from dawn to sunset. See *Korân*, Chapter 2, 26.

48.29. 'small still voices': 1 Kings 19:12: "and after the fire a still small voice" heard by Elijah.

49.4. transitory garment: An idea adapted from Goethe's *Faust*, part 1, line 509. What the *Erdgeist* calls "*the living visible Garment* *of God"* (*Sartor*, 1.8.43; see note to "The Hero as Man of Letters" at 135.6–7 below).

49.4–5. 'Allah akbar, God is great': The phrase proved popular with Carlyle at this period and appears fairly frequently in his letters. See for instance *Letters* 10:215, 11:22, and 13:116.

49.5. 'Islam': Carlyle follows Sale ("Preliminary Discourse," 75): The "word signifies resignation, or submission to the service and commands of God." For a different interpretation see Ali, *Life and Teachings of Mohammed*, 226, and for a more technical discussion of the subject see Jane I. Smith, *Historical and Semantic Study of the Term 'Islām.'*

49.9–10. 'If this be Islam,' says Goethe: "Wenn Islam Gott ergeben heißt, / Im Islam leben und sterben wir alle" (If Islam means devoted to God, we all live and die in Islam; Goethe, "Hikmet Nameh: Buch der Sprüche," verse 40, *West-östlicher Divan* [1819], *Werke* 2:56). Carlyle expressed the same idea in a letter to Geraldine Jewsbury on April 12, 1840: "We are bound to say with the Moslem . . . 'God is Great. *Islam;* I *submit* to God'" (*Letters* 12:106).

49.15. pretension of scanning: An adaptation of Pope's lines: "presume not God to scan, / The proper study of mankind is man" (*An Essay on Man*, Epistle 2, lines 1–2).

49.31. take no counsel with flesh and blood: Galatians 1:16: "I conferred not with flesh and blood."

49.35–36. "Though He slay me, yet will I trust in him.": Job 13:15.

49.36–37. Annihilation of Self: Derived from Novalis: "The true philosophical Act is annihilation of self (*Selbsttödtung*); this is the real beginning of all Philosophy. . . . This Act alone corresponds to all the conditions and characteristics of transcendental conduct" ("Novalis" [1829], *Essays* 2:39). In *Sartor*, Carlyle described "Annihilation of Self" as "the first preliminary moral Act" (2.9.149). Though the phrasing is from Novalis, Carlyle's idea is closer to Goethe's *Entsagen*, and even closer to the Christian ideal of losing one's life to save it (see Matthew 16:24–25).

50.4. Gabriel: According to al-Wāqidī, aṭ-Ṭabarī, and Ibn Hishām, Gabriel appeared to Muḥammad on Mount Ḥirā' and revealed to him the first five lines of the first *Sūrah*, Chapter 96, of the Qur'ān (Muir, *Life of Moḥammad*, 50; Gibbon, *Decline and Fall* 5:50.365; Sale, "Preliminary Discourse," 45, and *Korân*, Chapter 96, 585n). Gabriel was already established in the angelology of both Old and New Testaments as the revealer of divine will, as in his interpretation of the prophetic vision of Daniel (Daniel 8:15–26) and his annunciations of John the Baptist and Jesus (Luke 1:11–19, 1:26–38). To the Persians, Gabriel was *"the angel of revelations"* (Sale, *Korân*, Chapter 2, 15n).

50.5. 'inspiration of the Almighty': See above at 40.28–29 and note.

50.7–8. '. . . god-announcing Miracle': As Carlyle translated for his 1829 essay on Novalis: "Is not real Conviction, this highest function of our soul and personality, the only true God-announcing Miracle?" (*Essays* 2:42).

50.14. 'Mahomet is the Prophet of God': Part of the *Adhān*, or call to prayer, adopted by Muḥammad in A.H. 20 (A.D. 642) in place of the earlier and simpler summons "To public prayer!" and in preference to alternative suggestions that included a horn and a bell or wooden gong (Muir, *Life of Moḥammad*, 195; see also Gibbon, *Decline and Fall* 5:50.420). Sale gives the sequence of calls entoned by the muezzin that includes the twice-uttered statement: "I testify that Mohammed is the Apostle of God" ("Preliminary Discourse," 115n).

50.20–22. 'It is certain,' says Novalis: Carlyle's translation of a passage in Novalis (*Schriften* 2:104): "Es ist gewiss, das eine Meinung sehr viel gewinnt, sobald ich weiss, dass irgend jemand davon übergengt ist, sie wahrhaft annimmt." See also "Characteristics" (1831), *Essays* 3:11; and *Sartor*, 3.2.171. Compare: "Religion has to be made and produced (*gemacht und hervorgebracht*) by the union of a number of persons" ("Novalis" [1829], *Essays* 2:43), and Matthew 18:20. In his journal Carlyle notes: "Religion, as Novalis thinks, is a social thing. Without a church there can be little or no religion. The action of mind on mind is mystical, infinite; religion, worship can hardly . . . support itself without this aid. The derivation of *Schwärmerey* indicates some notion of this in the Germans. To *schwärmen* (to be enthusiastic) means, says Coleridge, to *swarm*, to crowd together and excite one another" (Froude, *First Forty Years* 2:80). Compare

Walter Pater's use of Coleridge's etymological speculation in *Greek Studies*, 56–57.

50.26. **Ayesha was, one day, questioning him:** ʿĀʾishah bint Abī Bakr. The anecdote Carlyle refers to is in Gibbon, *Decline and Fall* 5:50.405. See also Muir, *Life of Moḥammad*, 25. A fiery, independent spirit, ʿĀʾishah is the inspiration of modern Arabic feminism.

50.30–31. **Seid, his Slave:** Zayd ibn Ḥārithah was captured by bandits and sold into slavery when still a child. As a young man he was presented by Khadījah as a gift to Muḥammad shortly after their marriage. His father attempted to ransom Zayd, who preferred to remain with Muḥammad and was adopted by him as his own son. As a freedman he took the name Zayd ibn Muḥammad (Muir, *Life of Moḥammad*, 34–35).

50.31. **young Cousin Ali:** ʿAlī ibn Abī Ṭālib, the self-styled "first of the believers." The story Carlyle quotes of ʿAlī's discipleship is given by Sale as fact ("Preliminary Discourse," 47). Muir, however, regards it as apocryphal (*Life of Moḥammad*, 61n). According to Watt, even if true, "for the Western historian" the claim of ʿAlī "cannot be significant, since ʿAlī was admittedly only nine or ten at the time and a member of Muḥammad's household" (*Muhammad at Mecca*, 86).

51.17. **assassination in the Mosque at Bagdad:** On January 24, 661. After ʿAlī's murder, dissension between his opponents and his adherents led to the first schism in Islam, the split between Shiʾites, the followers of ʿAlī, and Sunnites. For ʿAlī's dying comments at 51.18–22, see Washington Irving, *Mahomet and His Successors*, 422. Irving's book was published after Carlyle's lecture. However, a draft had been completed in 1820 and revised in 1831 before finally appearing in 1849. Carlyle knew Irving and some of his work (see *Letters* 2:134, 137, 142–43, 150, 468, and 3:11). Whether Irving's book was a source for this lecture or not, many of its details were drawn from the translations of "Abulfeda" (Abū al-Fidāʾ), whose work was accessible to Carlyle through the footnotes to chapter 50 of Gibbon's *Decline and Fall*.

51.31. **Mahomet answered:** Sale ("Preliminary Discourse," 47) repeats the anecdote based on "Abulfeda" (Abū al-Fidāʾ). Carlyle's reference to Muḥammad's tears at 52.1–2 is derived from some source other than Sale or Gibbon. Muir suggests that Muḥammad wept not out of gratitude, as Carlyle interprets it, but fear that he was to be abandoned by Abī Ṭālib (*Life of Moḥammad*, 87–88).

52.9. Abyssinia: Ethiopia, the appointed place of refuge for the followers of Muḥammad who were forced to evacuate Mecca in A.D. 615 because of the hostility of the Quraysh. For details surrounding the two emigrations, and the causes behind them, see Sale, "Preliminary Discourse," 48; Muir, *Life of Moḥammad*, 69–70, 86–87.

52.14–17. hide in caverns . . . some rider's horse: The cavern was in Mount Thaur (Jabal al-Thawr), a few miles south of Mecca. A slightly different version of the episode of the rider's horse is given by Ibn Hishām; see Muir, *Life of Moḥammad*, 142, and Ali, *Life and Teachings of Mohammed*, 127, who cites both Ibn-Hishām and Ibn-al-Athir.

52.23. Yathreb: Yathrib, the name for Medina before Muḥammad's retreat there, after which it became known as the city of the prophet, or *Madīnat an-Nabī*. For Islam, it is second to Mecca in sanctity.

52.24–25. 'Medinat al Nabi, the City of the Prophet': "Medina is the usual English form of *al-Madīnah*, the city (or perhaps 'place of justice'); it is said to be a shortening of *Madīnat an-Nabī*, the city of the Prophet" (Watt, *Muhammad at Mecca*, 141).

52.28. The whole East dates its era: Thus A.D. 622, the date of the Hijrah, is considered A.H. 1.

52.28. Hegira: The Latin form for the Arabic *hijrah*.

53.7–8. propagating his Religion by the sword: From Medina in the years 622–32 Muḥammad "was now commanded to propagate his religion by the sword," and in the first months of his reign "the martial apostle fought in person at nine battles or sieges" (Gibbon, *Decline and Fall* 5:50.383). Gibbon also quotes Muḥammad: "The sword . . . is the key of heaven and of hell: a drop of blood shed in the cause of God . . . is of more avail than two months of fasting or prayer" (5:50.384). See also *Korán*, Chapter 47, 489: "When ye encounter the unbelievers, strike off *their* heads, until ye have made a great slaughter." Also Chapters 8 and 9. Ross, however, suggests that the simplicity of Muḥammad's monotheism was "a more potent factor in the spread of Islam than the sword of the Ghazis" (Intro-duction, *Korân*, vii).

53.13. *minority of one*: The phrase, which seems to have originated with Carlyle, appeared a number of times in his correspondence with Emerson (see *Emerson and Carlyle*, 384, 434). Emerson used the phrase "a pretty good minority of one" to describe Carlyle's *Latter-Day Pamphlets* (*Emerson and Carlyle*, 497). The phrase later proved popular; for instance, Herbert Spencer, *Autobiography* (1877); O. W. Holmes in a speech in 1913; George Orwell in *1984*. Compare Thoreau's phrase "majority of one" ("Resistance to Civil Govern-ment," 74). Also see Thoreau's 1847 review essay, "Thomas Carlyle and His Works." After reading the highly favorable review, Carlyle wrote to Emerson, "I like Mr Thoreau very well; and hope yet to hear good and better news of him" (*Emerson and Carlyle*, 422).

53.19–20. conversion of the Saxons: In 777, after victorious cam-paigns against the Saxons and the destruction of the sanctuary of Odin, Charlemagne received the submission of the Saxon confedera-tion, and forcibly baptized many of them, at Paderborn, where he had earlier installed a bishop.

54.26. *Homoiousion* and *Homoousion*: From the Greek *homoios* ("simi-lar") and *ousia* ("substance"), the homoiousian doctrine, propounded by Arius (250?–336), contended that the Son was of similar rather than identical substance to the Father and was, therefore, not eternal. The homoousian doctrine (from *homos*, "same"), first introduced at the Council of Nicaea to correct the error, was formulated by Athanasius (293?–373) and adopted as one of the three creeds of Christendom by the Catholic Church. After re-reading Gibbon in 1877, Carlyle spoke to Froude about the Athanasian controversy and "of the Christian world torn in pieces over a dipthong, and he would ring the changes in broad Annandale on the Homoousion and the Homoiousion. . . . He perceived Christianity itself to have been at stake. If the Arians had won, it would have dwindled away into a legend" (Froude, *Life in London* 2:462).

54.33–34. wiredrawings: Compare *Letters* 9:183.

54.37–38. Idols of yours, 'ye rub them with oil and wax, and the flies stick on them': "The commentators say, that the Arabs used to anoint the images of their gods with some odoriferous composition, and with honey, which the flies eat, though the doors of the temple were carefully shut, getting in at the windows or crevices. Perhaps Mohammed took this argument from the Jews, who pretend that the temple of Jerusalem, and the sacrifices there offered to the true God, were never annoyed by flies (Pirke Aboth, c. 5, Sect. 6, 7); whereas swarms of those insects infested the heathen temples" (Sale, *Korân*, Chapter 22, 334n).

55.31. **Flight to Mecca**: Actually from Mecca to Medina.

55.32. *Koran, or Reading*: Sale derives "Korân" from the verb "karaa [*qara'a*], to read," which signifies "the reading, or rather, that which ought to be read" ("Preliminary Discourse," 60). The chapters of the Qur'ān recorded by his adherents during Muḥammad's lifetime were first collected two years after his death, and the first authorized version was established during the Caliphate of Othman (644–56). The Qur'ān was introduced into Europe in 1143 in a Latin version by Robert of Retina and Hermann of Dalmatia, ultimately printed in Basel in 1543.

55.34. **Is not that a miracle?**: The response, especially of the Meccans, to the Qur'ān and to the selection of Muḥammad as a prophet was, "this is manifest sorcery" (*Korân*, Chapter 10, 199). To the charge that he had "forged" the Qur'ān, Muḥammad challenged his detractors to produce ten chapters comparable to it in doctrine and eloquence (Chapter 11, 211–13), though elsewhere he reduced this to one chapter (Chapter 10, 203).

56.6–7. **We hear of Mahometan Doctors that had read it seventy thousand times!**: Seven thousand, not seventy thousand. Sale, citing Pococke, notes: "It is said that he [Abū Ḥanīfa] read the Korân in the prison where he died, no less than seven thousand times" (Sale, "Preliminary Discourse," 116).

56.8. **'discrepancies of national taste'**: "Here are strange diversities of taste; 'national discrepancies' enough, had we time to investigate them!" ("Goethe" [1828], *Essays* 1:230). Perhaps Carlyle recalled that Francis Jeffrey had pointed to "diversities of National Taste" in his unfavorable review of Carlyle's translation of Goethe's *Wilhelm Meister* in the *Edinburgh Review* (42 [1825]: 409).

56.10–11. **a very fair one:** See note on Sale at 42.23 above.

56.19. **found the Koran lying all in fractions:** Since Muḥammad could not write, he recited the Qurʾanic passages to friends and followers who wrote them on palm leaves, leather, stones, or other available materials. During Muḥammad's prophetic period of twenty-three years, the recorded utterances were never collected or systematically arranged, or preserved in any single depository. During his life many fragments were produced. In his Meccan period Muḥammad must have relied upon the writing ability of Khadījah, ʿAlī, or Abī Bakr, and at Medina he had many Arab amanuenses. After his death, the Qurʾanic fragments were sought out. See Muir, *Life of Moḥammad*, xiv–xv; Gibbon, *Decline and Fall* 5:50.365.

56.20–21. **shoulder-blades of mutton:** "The word of God and of the apostle was diligently recorded by his disciples on palm-leaves and the shoulder-bones of mutton" (Gibbon, *Decline and Fall* 5:50.365).

57.4. **Prideaux:** Humphrey Prideaux (1648–1724), Dean of Norwich and author of *The True Nature of Imposture Fully Display'd in the Life of Mahomet* (1678).

57.10. **deceit** *prepense*: The Qurʾān itself addresses contemporary allegations of its fraudulent composition, for instance Chapters 16, 267; 10, 203. However, the charge of outright imposture "has been increasingly opposed by scholarly opinion" since it was "vigorously attacked by Thomas Carlyle over a hundred years ago" (Watt, *Muḥammad at Medina*, 325). Carlyle ignored the more subtle charge of self-deception, the claim that Muḥammad's revelations closely corresponded to his personal desires. The subject is fully dealt with by Watt, *Muḥammad at Medina*, 324–35.

58.7. **semi-barbarous Son of Nature:** Perhaps suggested by Gibbon's description of Muḥammad as "an illiterate barbarian" (*Decline and Fall* 5:50.358), or perhaps Carlyle uses "Son of Nature" in contrast with the Christian use of "Son of Man" or "Son of God" in reference to Jesus. Compare "The Hero as Man of Letters" at 153.12–14 below: "To a certain extent, they were Sons of Nature once more in an age of Artifice; once more, Original Men."

58.23. the Prophet Hud: See *Korân*, Chapter 11, entitled "Hūd," in which the story of this prophet is told.

59.5. 'I am a Public Preacher': *Korân*, Chapter 11, 212: Noah said, "Verily I am a public preacher unto you." Also Chapter 29, 392: "Signs are in the power of GOD alone; and I am *no more than* a public preacher."

59.8. 'a sign to you': Biblical sources include 1 Samuel 2:34, 2 Kings 19:29, Jeremiah 44:29, and Luke 2:12. Also see an instance in the Qur'ān quoted in the note at 59.26-27 below.

59.9. 'appointed paths in it': Perhaps *Korân*, Chapters 20, 308 and 43, 473: "and hath made you paths therein."

59.14. 'to revive a dead earth': *Korân*, Chapter 25, 357-58: "and we send down pure water from heaven, that we may thereby revive a dead country."

59.14-16. 'tall leafy palm-trees with their date-clusters . . .': *Korân*, Chapter 6, 130: "and palm-trees from whose branches proceed clusters of dates *hanging* close together."

59.16-19. Your cattle too,—Allah made them . . . 'and are a credit to you!': *Korân*, Chapter 16, 257: "He hath likewise created the cattle for you: from them ye have wherewith to keep yourselves warm, and *other* advantages; and of them do ye *also* eat. And they are likewise a credit unto you, when ye drive *them* home *in the evening*, and when ye lead *them* forth to feed *in the morning*."

59.19-20. he talks often about ships: For example, *Korân*, Chapters 16, 257, and 40, 463.

59.24-25. 'shaped you out of a little clay': *Korân*, Chapter 22, 327: "created you of the dust of the ground"; Chapter 6, 118: "of clay"; Chapter 15, 253: "of dried clay, of black mud"; Chapter 55, 513-14: "of dried clay like an earthen vessel." Also see following note.

59.26-27. 'ye have compassion on one another': *Korân*, Chapter 30, 396: "Of his signs *one is*, that he hath created you of dust, and behold, ye *are become* men, spread *over the face of the earth*. And of his signs *another is*, that he hath created you, out of yourselves, wives, that ye may cohabit with them; and hath put love and compassion between you: verily herein are signs unto people who consider."

60.4–5. rock-mountains . . . dissipate themselves 'like clouds': *Korán*, Chapter 27, 376–77: "And thou shalt see the mountains, and shalt think them firmly fixed; but they shall pass away, even as the clouds pass away."

60.7. Sale tells us: "The Mohammedans suppose that the earth, when first created, was smooth and equal, and thereby liable to a circular motion as well as the celestial orbs; and that the angels asking who could be able to stand on so tottering a frame, God fixed it the next morning by throwing the mountains on it" (Sale, *Korán*, Chapter 16, 258n).

60.34. 'succeed by being an easy religion': Untraced.

61.14–15. not a sensual man: Carlyle attempts to refute such claims as those of Prideaux: "The gratifying of his Ambition and his Lust, was the main end of his *Imposture*" (*True Nature of Imposture*, 126), and of Gibbon: "Perfumes and women were the two sensual enjoyments which his nature required and his religion did not forbid" (*Decline and Fall* 5:50.402).

61.17–18. household was of the frugalest; his common diet barley-bread and water: Muir, citing both al-Wāqidī and Ibn Sa'd, indicates the relatively frugal habits of Muḥammad (*Life of Moḥammad*, 511). "What he most relished was a mess of bread cooked with meat, and a dish of dates dressed with butter and milk" (527).

61.19. They record: Both al-Wāqidī and Ibn Sa'd record that Muḥammad cobbled his sandals and mended his clothes. See Muir, *Life of Moḥammad*, 511, 524, and Gibbon, *Decline and Fall* 5:50.402.

61.29. clouting: Patching. Carlyle re-used this detail of Muḥammad "clouting" his own cloak in "Dr. Francia" ([1843], *Essays* 4:305) and in *Past and Present*, 4.6.288.

61.36. His last words: Carlyle probably had in mind Gibbon's version: "O God! . . . pardon my sins . . . Yes, . . . I come, . . . among my fellow-citizens on high" (*Decline and Fall* 5:50.399, ellipses in Gibbon). According to Muir, Muḥammad whispered: "'Lord, grant me pardon; and join me to the companionship on high.' Then at intervals: 'Eternity in Paradise!' 'Pardon!' 'The blessed companionship on high!'" (*Life of Moḥammad*, 495).

62.1. his Daughter: Muḥammad had four daughters by Khadījah, only one of whom survived him. Carlyle probably meant Ruqayyah, the news of whose death awaited Muḥammad on his return to Medina after his victory at Badr in A.D. 624. See Muir, *Life of Moḥammad*, 232.

62.3-4. 'The Lord giveth . . .': Job's response to news of the multiple disasters that had befallen his house: "Naked came I out of my mother's womb, and naked shall I return thither: the Lord gave, and the Lord hath taken away; blessed be the name of the Lord" (Job 1:21).

62.6. War of Tabûc: The expedition to Tabūk in the ninth year of the Hijrah (A.D. 630) followed the year in which Zayd had been slain while leading a Muslim army against the Greeks at Mu'tah. The expedition did not engage in heavy fighting, mainly because of disaffection among the troops (see *Korân*, Chapter 9, and Gibbon, *Decline and Fall* 5:50.396-97).

62.9. Seid's daughter: Muḥammad wept with the grief-stricken daughter of Zayd after he had informed her of her father's death at the battle of Mu'tah. See Gibbon, *Decline and Fall* 5:50.396. The next morning a smiling Muḥammad explained that he had seen Zayd in paradise (Muir, *Life of Moḥammad*, 396n).

62.14. ". . . three drachms": From the pulpit Muḥammad learned of a debt of three drachms of silver (*darāhim*, plural of *dirham*, a small silver coin). He "satisfied the demand, and thanked his creditor for accusing him in this world rather than at the day of judgment" (Gibbon, *Decline and Fall* 5:50.398).

62.26. 'the respect due unto thee': After becoming established at Medina, according to Gibbon, Muḥammad "assumed the exercise of the regal and sacerdotal office." The people had "exalted the fugitive of Mecca to the rank of a sovereign" (Gibbon, *Decline and Fall* 5:50.381-82). His increasing power "may be traced in the reverence and submission prescribed in the Ḳor'ān as due to him" (Muir, *Life of Moḥammad*, 330).

62.37. 'Hell will be hotter!': "Hell is much hotter," Muḥammad's retort to complaints about heat and other difficulties experienced by his troops during the expedition to Tabūk (Gibbon, *Decline and Fall* 5:50.396). The hell reserved for erring Muslims is "Jehennam" (*Jahannam*) (Sale, "Preliminary Discourse," 98–99), the name of which is derived from the Hebrew *Gê' Hinnōm* (Greek *Geenna*, Latin *Gehenna*, as in the Vulgate Matthew 5:22, 5:29, and Epistle to James 3:6; see "The Hero as Poet" at 83.11 below), meaning "Valley of Hinnom," the ravine near Jerusalem where children were burnt alive as a sacrifice to Baal (see Jeremiah.19:2–6).

63.1. weighed out: *Korân*, Chapter 21, 319: "We will appoint just balances for the day of resurrection; neither shall any soul be injured at all: although *the merit or guilt of an action* be of the weight of a grain of mustard-seed *only*, we will produce it *publicly*; and there will be sufficient accountants with us" and Chapter 7, 140: "The weighing *of men's actions* on that day *shall be* just; and they whose balances *laden with their good works* shall be heavy, are those who *shall be* happy; but they whose balances shall be light, are those who have lost their souls."

63.4. 'Assuredly': For example, in Sale's translation "Assuredly" occurs as a separate sentence three times in the short Chapter 96 (585–86), by tradition the first *Sûrah* to be revealed (see note at 50.4 above).

63.11–12. 'living in a vain show': See above at 40.11 and note.

63.18. carbonic acid: A weak acid formed by dissolving carbon dioxide in water. Carlyle no doubt meant carbolic acid, i.e., phenol, a powerful disinfectant derived from coal tar that was applied as an antiseptic in Victorian surgery. Lethal amounts were sometimes absorbed through the wound.

63.22–23. turning of the other cheek: Luke 6:29: "And unto him that smiteth thee on the one cheek offer also the other."

63.24. revenge . . . not over much: *Korân*, Chapter 17, 275: Private revenge for murder is allowed, "but let him not exceed the bounds *of moderation* in putting to death *the murderer in too cruel a manner,* or *by* revenging *his friend's blood on any other than the person who killed him.*"

63.27-28. all men, according to Islam too, are equal: Islam being in concept a world religion, there is "no tribe or race triumphant in the Koran, but absolute equality in Islam" (Campbell, *Masks of God* 3:433).

63.28-29. giving alms: Almsgiving, *zakāt*, is prescribed by Qur'anic law. Voluntary almsgiving, called *ṣadaqah*, is also urged and honored but not legally required. Sale offers a discussion of the subject in section 4 of his "Preliminary Discourse" (118-20).

63.35. Paradise is sensual: *Korân*, Chapter 52, 506, pictures the pious in the afterlife "leaning on couches disposed in order: and we will espouse them unto virgins having large black eyes" (also Chapters 55, 515; 56, 517). These houris (from *ḥūr*, pl. of *ḥawrā'*) were perfect creatures formed not out of clay but of musk. A carnal paradise was, according to Sir Richard Burton, preached only to the ignorant (*Love, War and Fancy*, 105). Sale, however, says that, in depicting the sensual pleasures of Paradise, Muḥammad "chose rather to imitate the indecency of the Magians than the modesty of the Christians" ("Preliminary Discourse," 109).

64.4. the highest joys ... shall be spiritual: *Korân*, Chapter 9, 189: "but goodwill from GOD *shall be their* most excellent *reward*."

64.6. 'Your salutation shall be, Peace': True believers shall in the afterlife have "rivers flowing through gardens of pleasure. Their prayer therein *shall be*, Praise be unto thee, O GOD! and their salutation therein *shall be*, Peace!" (*Korân*, Chapter 10, 200). This single verse, says Burton, "is sufficient refutation" of the claim made either through "ignorance or pious fraud" that the Muslim paradise is "wholly sensual" (*Love, War and Fancy*, 105).

64.8-9. 'Ye shall sit ... all grudges ...': *Korân*, Chapter 56, 517: "These *are* they who shall approach near *unto God*: they shall dwell in gardens of delight. . . . Reposing on couches adorned with gold and precious stones; sitting opposite to one another thereon. . . . They shall not hear therein any vain discourse, or any charge of sin; but only the salutation, Peace! Peace!" Also Chapter 7, 143: "And we will remove all grudges from their minds."

64.19-23. "We require ... greater latitude on all other sides": "Every one that means to live with us must agree to constrain himself in some particular point, if the greater freedom be left him in all other points" (*Wilhelm Meister* 1:15.346).

65.14. Bentham: Jeremy Bentham (1743–1832), political philosopher and writer on ethics and jurisprudence, whose *Introduction to the Principles of Morals and Legislation* (1789) contains a fundamental statement of the doctrine of utilitarianism. He is mainly remembered for applying the principle of utility to ethical decisions, arguing that the "greatest happiness of the greatest number" was the measure of "whatever is right or wrong, useful, useless, or mischievous in human conduct, whether in the field of morals or of politics" (Bentham, *Works* 10:79). Carlyle was consistently hostile to Bentham's philosophy. "What is Jeremy Bentham's significance? Altogether intellectual, logical. I name him as the representative of a class important only for their numbers, intrinsically wearisome, almost pitiable and pitiful. Logic is their sole foundation, no other even recognised as possible; wherefore their system is a *machine* and cannot *grow* or endure" (Froude, *First Forty Years* 2:90). Carlyle attacked Bentham for the effort to establish morality on the basis of happiness, since it undermined religious teaching and Carlyle's own view of the central importance of duty. The parallels in Dickens's work are striking. See K. J. Fielding, "Benthamite Utilitarianism and *Oliver Twist*," 62ff; and Goldberg, "From Bentham to Carlyle: Dickens' Political Development," 61–76.

65.14. Paley: William Paley (1743–1805), the main exponent of theological utilitarianism. In his *Evidences of Christianity* (1794), he finds a proof of God's existence in natural phenomena, and refutes the adaptation of the organism to its circumstances. Carlyle wrote: "To prove the existence of God as Paley has attempted to do . . . is like lighting a lantern to seek for the Sun" (*Two Notebooks*, 103).

65.22–23. Benthamee Utility: A conflation of Bentham and the utilitarian movement of which he was the figurehead. The contemptuous adjectival form was adopted by Carlyle as early as 1836, when he denounced the "Benthamee Gospel,—to me a miserablest chimera" (*Letters* 8:289). When Carlyle pronounced the word "beggarlier" (at 65.26), John Stuart Mill stood up "with an emphatic No!" (Garnett, *Life of Carlyle*, 171). Mill's protest led to Carlyle's qualified apology in the fifth lecture. See "The Hero as Man of Letters" below at 148.19–25 and note at 148.19–20.

65.32. God *Wish*: *Wunsch*, a God principle in Scandinavian paganism that Carlyle learned of from Jacob Grimm's etymological studies. See "The Hero as Divinity" above at 17.27 and note.

66.18. Arabia is at Grenada: After Muḥammad's death in A.D. 632, armies of the first Caliphate swept through the Middle East and North Africa. They invaded Spain in 711. See "The Hero as Poet" below at 85.19 and note.

66.27. lightning out of Heaven: Compare "The Hero as Divinity" above at 13.10.

NOTES TO LECTURE III. THE HERO AS POET.

Sources: With the help of Count Carlo Pepoli (1796–1881), a former professor of philosophy at Bologna who was living in exile in London, Carlyle read Dante every Wednesday night during the summer of 1835 (*Letters* 8:212). Two and a half years later, in preparation for his 1838 lectures on the history of literature, the fifth of which focused on Dante, he was reading the *Inferno* as a matter of daily study and finding the "great and enduring" poem "uphill work" (*Letters* 10:19n). Carlyle may also have discussed Dante with Giuseppi Mazzini, who had been a political exile in London since 1837. In April 1840, Carlyle recommended him to Henry Cole as "a man of true genius, an honourable, brave and gifted man" (*Letters* 12:82). "I like Mazzini," Carlyle wrote to his brother John, on the same day that he finished the manuscript of the third lecture (*Letters* 12:194).

The allusions to the *Divine Comedy* in *On Heroes* are frequently a reprise of passages Carlyle had used in his 1838 lecture on Dante. The 1838 lecture series is known from notes taken by Thomas Chisholm Anstey (1816–1873), "a youth from van Diemen's Land," who presented them to Carlyle in the form of "a manuscript volume. . . . It is one of the strangest things: not a *miniature*, but an entire *large-as-life* only half eaten away as with moths!" (*Letters* 10:121). *Lectures on the History of Literature* (1892), edited by J. Reay Greene, was based on copies of these notes. The original manuscript, now lost, was deposited by Anstey at the Asiatic Society in Bombay, where it was edited and published by R. P. Karkaria, also in 1892. Greene's edition has been cited here, as being more accessible, but interesting variants in Karkaria's edition are noted.

There is no certain evidence as to what editions of the *Divine Comedy* Carlyle may have consulted. In November 1837 Carlyle sought to borrow again a copy of the poem from Leigh Hunt in order to resume his careful reading of it (*Letters* 9:351), but the edition is unknown. In the spring of 1840, when he was preparing the lecture on the hero as poet, Carlyle returned Leigh Hunt's edition, noting that his own, which he would now have to rely on, was "as good as any of the others" (*Letters* 12:90). Once again, neither his "own" nor the "other" editions have been identified. Shine (*Carlyle's Early Reading*, 182) cites the "*Divina comedia di Dante Alleghieri di Firenze*, Foligno, 1472," translated into English verse by H. Boyd in 1802, as the source of Carlyle's reference to Dante in his 1828 essay on Burns. Carlyle himself makes no mention of this edition. Whether he used Boyd's eccentric edition in 1828 is uncertain, but by 1838 or 1839 he had certainly gone beyond what it had to offer. He did know the edition by Henry Francis Cary (1772–1844), for in a preface to the first American publication of that work (1844), the editor acknowledged his debt to Carlyle, "one of the most original thinkers of our time," who had taken the trouble to point out "oversights" in earlier printings (Cary, *The Vision*, 5). Despite such circumstantial evidence, Carlyle's references to Dante in *On Heroes* do not follow either Boyd or Cary, and several idiosyncrasies of translation such as that at 82.13 suggest that Carlyle's translations were largely his own, though he may have received help from his brother John, who published his own edition and prose translation of the *Inferno* in 1849, or from Count Pepoli. John Carlyle's preface acknowledges "the kindness of one highly accomplished friend, whose name I am not allowed to mention: he read over the proofs of the first eight Cantos, and suggested some useful additions and amendments." In the following notes, all quotations and translations from the *Divine Comedy*, other than Carlyle's, are taken from the edition by Charles S. Singleton.

Carlyle is known to have owned a copy of *The Works of Shakespear*, 8 vols. (Edinburgh, 1761), which is probably a reprint of the edition of Hugh Blair (but see the note to "The Hero as Divinity" at 32.33 above). In these notes, references to the plays employ the text and lineation of the *Riverside Shakespeare*.

68.2. Legislator: Though not an admirer of Shelley's poetry, Carlyle echoes Shelley's statement in the *Defence of Poetry* (written 1821, first published 1840): "Poets are the unacknowledged legislators of the world" (80). Carlyle's view of the poet as *vates* (see below at 69.2 and note) may also be found in Shelley's *Defence* (31).

68.4. Mirabeau: Honoré Gabriel Riquetti, Comte de Mirabeau (1749–1791), Carlyle's hero of French revolutionary history. See notes to

"The Hero as Prophet" at 39.33 above and to "The Hero as Man of Letters" at 156.10 below.

68.9. Napoleon has words: An adaptation of a comment about Luther by Richter in *Vorschule der Aesthetik*, "Luther's prose is a half-battle; few deeds are equal to his words" ("Jean Paul Friedrich Richter" [1830], *Essays* 2:148). See "The Hero as Priest" at 119.17 below and note.

68.10. Austerlitz Battles: The battle fought on December 2, 1805, between the French, the Austrians, and the Russians. See "The Hero as King" at 206.13 below and note.

68.10-11. Louis Fourteenth's Marshals . . . the things Turenne says: Henri de La Tour d'Auvergne, Vicomte de Turenne (1611-1675), marshal of France, commanded the armies of Louis XIV. The sayings are in his *Mémoires*, eight editions of which were published in the eighteenth century. Napoleon annotated and added to them with his *Précis des dernières campagnes de Turenne*. See Weygand, *Turenne*, 149-50.

68.14. Petrarch and Boccaccio: Giovanni Boccaccio (1313-1375) undertook various diplomatic services for the city government of Florence after settling there about 1350. Francesco Petrarca (1304-1374) travelled widely in the service of the church and the Visconti family.

68.26. as Addison complains: Joseph Addison (1672-1719). The complaint has not been traced.

69.2. *Vates*: Latin, "prophet," "seer," "bard." "The true Poet is ever, as of old, the Seer; . . . we can still call him a *Vates* and Seer; for he *sees* into this greatest of secrets, 'the open secret'" ("Death of Goethe" [1832], *Essays* 2:377). Compare "Sir Walter Scott" (1838), *Essays* 4:53.

69.7. what Goethe calls 'the open secret!': Carlyle's translation of Goethe's phrase "das öffentliche Geheimnis," as in *Wilhelm Meister's Travels* (*Wilhelm Meister* 2:13.305): "While Nature unfolded the open secret of her beauty, he could not but feel an irresistible attraction towards Art, as towards her most fit expositor." Carlyle's identification here of Goethe's "open secret" with Fichte's "Divine Idea" behind appearances (see following note) was "a fusion of ideas which neither Goethe nor Fichte would have accepted without heavy qualifications"

(Harrold, *Carlyle and German Thought*, 117). Compare "The Hero as Man of Letters" at 141.1-2 below and note.

69.10-11. 'the Divine Idea . . . ,' as Fichte styles it: In *Über das Wesen des Gelehrten*, a series of lectures delivered in 1805, Johann Gottlieb Fichte (1762-1814), the German idealist philosopher and disciple of Kant, said: "The whole material world, . . . and in particular the life of man in this world, are by no means . . . that which they seem to be to the uncultivated and natural sense of man; but there is something higher, which lies concealed behind all natural appearance. This concealed foundation of all appearance may, in its greatest universality, be aptly named *the Divine Idea* [die göttliche Idee]" (Fichte, *Nature of the Scholar*, 210). Compare Emerson's lecture "Shakspeare, or the Poet" in *Representative Men*, 109-25, especially 124; and see "The Hero as Man of Letters" at 135.1-10 below.

69.18. the Satirist: Carlyle himself, in *French Revolution* 1:4.1.212. Compare also *Sartor*, 3.8.202-12.

70.1-2. what the Germans call the æsthetic side: The term "aesthetic" was coined in the eighteenth century by Alexander Gottlieb Baumgarten. His definition of "the science of perception, or aesthetic" concludes his 1735 *Meditationes philosophicae de nonnullis ad poema pertinentibus* (Aschenbrenner and Holther, trans., 78), which formed the basis for his more widely known *Æsthetica* (1750). Carlyle refers to Baumgarten in his *Life of Schiller* (111). Aesthetics was a major preoccupation of German Romantic thought, attracting the attention of Winckelmann, Kant, Lessing, Schiller, Fichte, and Hegel, among others.

70.7-9. "Consider the lilies of the field; . . .": Matthew 6:28-29:

70.15-17. 'The Beautiful . . . is higher than the Good . . .': An idea derived from Goethe and Schiller that had occupied Carlyle's thoughts in February 1831: "I wish I could define to myself the true relation of moral genius to poetic genius; of Religion to Poetry. Are they one and the same, different forms of the same; and if so which is to stand higher, the Beautiful or the Good? Schiller and Goethe seem to say the former, as if it included the latter and might supersede it: how truly I can never well see" (*Two Notebooks*, 188). Basically, Carlyle thought the proposition was "*Sehr einseitig!* [very one-sided] Yet perhaps there is a glimpse of the truth here" (*Two Notebooks*, 204). See also Froude,

First Forty Years 2:93–94. The idea that the beautiful subsumed the good was widespread in German Romantic writing. Specifically, Carlyle may have been alluding to the three volumes of correspondence between Schiller and Goethe that he reviewed for *Fraser's Magazine* ("Schiller" [1831], *Essays* 2:165–215). Similar speculations are also the subject of Schiller's *Briefe über die æsthetische Erziehung des Menschen* (1795), to which Carlyle refers in "Schiller" (*Essays* 2:191–92) and in *Life of Schiller*, 111ff.

70.17–18. **I have said somewhere:** In "Diderot" (1833), *Essays* 3:240: "The true Beautiful (differing from the false, as Heaven does from Vauxhall) comprehends in it the Good."

70.18–19. **Vauxhall:** The Vauxhall Gardens, a popular pleasure resort, were laid out in the mid-seventeenth century on the south bank of the Thames and finally closed in July 1859.

70.25–26. **'imagination that shudders . . .':** Quoting himself: "The imagination, which shudders at the Hell of Dante, is the same faculty, weaker in degree, which called that picture into being" ("Burns" [1828], *Essays* 1:278).

70.28. *Saxo Grammaticus*: (1150?–1216?) Danish poet and historian. See "The Hero as Divinity" at 21.33 above and note.

70.34. **World-Poets:** Carlyle may be recalling and adapting Goethe's term *Weltliteratur*, which first appeared in his *Über Kunst und Altertum* (1827). See Strich, *Goethe and World Literature*, 349. In a letter to Goethe in 1831, Carlyle writes that he has concluded his review of Taylor's *Historic Survey of German Poetry* with some "speculations . . . on what I have named *World-Literature*, after you" (*Letters* 5:220).

71.7–8. **late German Critics:** The German critics Carlyle had in mind, as dealing with the distinction between poetry and speech, must include Franz Horn, whose three-volume work on poetry and oratory, *Die Poesie und Beredsamkeit der Deutschen, von Luthers Zeit bis zur Gegenwart* (1822–24), Carlyle reviewed for the *Edinburgh Review* ("State of German Literature" [1827], *Essays* 1:26–86; see 1:27 for Carlyle's complaint against Horn's overuse of the word *infinite*). According to Carlyle, Germany was the foremost nation "in the practice or science of Criticism. . . . Criticism has assumed a new form in

Germany," of "rigorous scientific inquiry" appealing to principles deduced from philosophy (*Essays* 1:51–52). For his earlier and less favorable estimate of German critics, see *Two Notebooks*, 33.

71.16. musical: Below (77.24–27), Carlyle attributes this thought to Coleridge. In his 1838 lecture Carlyle said that the *Divine Comedy* "was so musical that it got up to the length of singing itself, his soul was in it; and when we read there is a tune which hurries itself along [which hums itself along (Karkaria, 80)]" (*History of Literature*, 92).

72.1. Greeks fabled of Sphere-Harmonies: The Pythagorean belief, repeated by Plato, that on each heavenly sphere there stood a Siren, "borne around in its revolution and uttering one sound, one note, and from all the eight there was the concord of a single harmony" (*Republic* 10.617b). Though Aristotle (*De Cælo* 2.9) scoffed at the idea, Renaissance Platonists adapted it to Christian use by suggesting that the angels who moved the spheres were identical with the Sirens. Carlyle refers to "sphere-melody" in *Sartor* (3.8.210), and Teufelsdröckh, after his conversion, awakens to a new Evangel "like soft streamings of celestial music" (*Sartor*, 2.9.150). In his notebooks, Carlyle said: "The highest melody dwells only in silence (the Sphere melody, the melody of Health)" (*Two Notebooks*, 228).

72.36–37. High duchesses: The Duchess of Gordon was leader of Edinburgh society at the time of Burns's visit. He was also noticed by the Duchess of Atholl. "High duchesses were captivated with the chivalrous ways of the man; recognised that here was the true chivalry" (*Pamphlets*, 5.197). See "The Hero as Man of Letters" at 163.31 below and note.

73.35–36. Portrait commonly attributed to Giotto: The portrait was not by Giotto. Most probably Carlyle had in mind an engraving by Gio Paolo Lorenzi of a Dante portrait by Stefano Tofanelli, which Carlyle owned at the time of his death. The few details Carlyle offers, such as the "simple laurel," match precisely the features of the Tofanelli portrait (see Plate 5). The first identification of Carlyle's description with the Tofanelli painting was made by F. N. Scott in 1903 in a letter in the *Nation*. This suggestion was followed by Paget Toynbee in *Dante in English Literature* (2:498n), and by Richard Holbrook in *Portraits of Dante* (183). All three critics identify the engraver as Raffael Morghen, whose illustration was reproduced in the 1795 Palma edition of the *Divine Comedy*. In February 1834 Carlyle was given a Dante portrait by his brother John (*Letters* 7:109), whose 1849 prose translation of the *Inferno* had as frontispiece the Tofanelli portrait, engraved in some copies by R. Young and in others by J. Halpin. Two months after Carlyle's lecture, while he was preparing the text for publication, a Dante portrait was rediscovered in the Bargello at Florence, formerly the Palazzo de Podestà, where it had been covered over by whitewash. On the authority of Giorgio Vasari (1511–1574), whose work Carlyle was again reading in 1840 (*Letters* 12:90), it was accepted by many Victorians as a Giotto. See W. S. Landor's 1840 letter in the *Examiner*. Modern art historians consider the portrait to have been painted after Giotto's death by his pupils (Battisti, *Giotto*, 21).

74.9. **thick-ribbed ice**: *Measure for Measure*, 3.1.122: "In thrilling region of thick-ribbed ice." In a letter of September 23, 1835, Carlyle uses a similar image: "A grand old Puritan this Dante; depth and Ferocity without limit; implacable, composed; as if *covered* with winter and ice, and like Hecla, his interior is molten fire!" (*Letters* 8:212).

74.18. **'voice of ten silent centuries'**: I.e., the ten centuries of Christianity between the conversion of the emperor Constantine and Dante's poem. Compare below at 75.17 and 83.36.

74.18–19. **'his mystic unfathomable song'**: Quoting Tieck on Novalis: "He, alone among the moderns, resembles the lofty Dante; and sings us, like him, an unfathomable mystic song" ("Novalis" [1829], *Essays* 2:53). See below at 77.1–2, 77.23–24, and 84.11.

74.32. *chiaroscuro*: Striking contrast of light and shadow, especially in painting.

75.4. **wedded to another**: Dante, however, nowhere refers to the marriage of Beatrice Portinari (1266–1290) to the banker Simone de' Bardi in 1287. Paget Toynbee says that in Carlyle's two lectures on Dante "he mistranslates, and misquotes, and puts into Dante's mouth fictitious statements, such as that 'he says he knew Francesca's father,' and that he mentions Beatrice's wedding. These inaccuracies are more marked in the later lecture . . . than in the earlier one, suggesting that Carlyle got up the subject on the first occasion and neglected to refresh his memory afterwards" (*Dante in English Literature* 2:481).

75.13. Prior, Podestà: As Carlyle mentions in the next paragraph, Dante *was* one of the six priors of Florence from June 15 to August 15, 1300. The six members of the *Priore* formed an executive committee of the City Council; they were appointed for two months. The *podestà* was an outsider brought in and made responsible for the maintenance of public order, with soldiers at his disposal. He was obligated to obey the orders of the *Priore*.

75.24. Guelf-Ghibelline, Bianchi-Neri: Guelphs and Ghibellines were opposing factions in medieval Italy. The Guelphs, whom Dante initially supported, favored the Papacy against Imperial authority. The Bianchi and Neri ("Whites" and "Blacks") were factions within the Guelph party of Florence. The Neri, after seizing power in Florence in 1302, banished Dante, fined him in absentia, and later condemned him to death if he returned to the city. During his exile in Northern Italy, Dante converted to the Ghibelline cause. For Carlyle's thoughts on the Guelph-Ghibelline factions, see *History of Literature*, 87.

75.27. banishment: Dante was not exiled during his priorate, but two years later. See following note.

75.33. Florence Archives: "There is still to be seen an act of that time in the archives of Florence, charging all magistrates to burn Dante alive when he should be taken" (*History of Literature*, 88). The document is dated March 10, 1302, and names fourteen others besides Dante.

75.36–76.3. Letter of Dante's . . . *"nunquam revertar"*: Dante's actual words were "nunquam Florentiam introibo." The letter, written probably in May 1315, was not to the Florentine magistrates but to a Florentine friend. The "milder proposal" in the amnesty of May 19, 1315, was that Dante should pay a fine and seek pardon by making an offering at the Baptistery of San Giovanni, conditions he rejected as degrading. "Quod si per nullam talem Florentia introitur, nunquam Florentiam introibo" (But if Florence may be entered by no other path, then I will never enter Florence; Dante, *Epistolae*, 9.4.158).

76.6. 'How hard is the path, . . .': *Paradiso* 17.58–60: "sì come sa di sale / lo pane altrui, e come è duro calle / lo scendere e 'l salir per l'altrui scale" (how salt is the taste of another's bread, and how hard the path to descend and mount by another man's stairs). The passage is also quoted in "Mirabeau" ([1837], *Essays* 3:420). In his *Commentary* on the *Paradiso*, Singleton interprets this, "How bitter is the bread of another, i.e., bread that must be begged" (294). However, by long tradition, the bread of Tuscany, whose principal city was Florence, was salt free. See Carol Field, *Italian Baker*, 110.

76.9. **Petrarch reports**: In his *Rerum Memorandarum Libri* (1343–45), 2.83.98–99. Though probably apocryphal, such anecdotes represent "the popular conception of what Dante was like in ordinary life" (Toynbee, *Dante Alighieri*, 144–45).

76.9. **Can della Scala**: The Ghibelline prince Can Francesco della Scala (1291–1329), called Can Grande, sole Lord of Verona in 1311, to whom Dante dedicated the *Paradiso* (Dante, *Epistolae*, 10.3.169–70). He is thought by some to be the "greyhound" of *Inferno* 1.101–11. Dante praises him in the *Paradiso* (17.76ff).

76.12. *nebulones ac histriones*: Petrarch has "histriones ac nebulones" (actors and worthless people; *Rerum Memorandarum Libri*, 2.83.98).

76.35. *Malebolge*: *Inferno* 18.1: "Luogo è in inferno detto Malebolge" (There is a place in Hell called Malebolge), where the fraudulent, who have abused the privilege of reason, are punished. The name, invented by Dante, is a compound of *malo* (evil) and *bolgia* (pouch). It was sometimes applied by Carlyle to London; see *Letters* 11:24 and 12:112.

76.36. *alti guai*: Literally, deep groans or wails. "Quivi sospiri, pianti e alti guai / risonavan per l'aere sanza stelle" (Here sighs, laments, and loud wailings were resounding through the starless air; *Inferno* 3.22–23). See below at 80.36.

77.8. **'If thou follow thy star, . . . '**: *Inferno* 15.55–56: "Se tu segui tua stella, / non puoi fallire a glorïoso porto" (If you follow your star you cannot fail a glorious port), the opening of Bruno Latini's speech to Dante. Latini had been Dante's schoolmaster and was an adept of judicial astrology. In *History of Literature* (97) Carlyle translates: "His old schoolmaster tells him: 'If thou follow thy star, thou canst not miss a happy harbour.'" Carlyle quoted this passage in a letter, June 23, 1847, to Robert Browning commenting on the poet's marriage (*Mill, Sterling and Browning*, 281).

77.12–13. '. . . made me lean . . .': *Paradiso* 25.1–3: "che 'l poema sacro / al quale ha posto mano e cielo e terra, / sì che m'ha fatto per molti anni macro" (that the sacred poem to which heaven and earth have so set hand that it has made me lean for many years). This passage was suggested to Carlyle by Leigh Hunt. In November 1837, Carlyle recalled it inaccurately and asked Hunt to send him the passage where Dante "speaks about the toil of his *Divine Comedy* having made him grey" (*Letters* 9:351). See also "Sir Walter Scott" (1838), *Essays* 4:80; *Letters* 1:336; and *Past and Present*, 3.12.205.

77.18–19. *Hic claudor Dantes patriis extorris ab oris*: The fifth line of the epitaph Dante was said to have composed for himself, one of two carved on his tomb in Ravenna. It is now known to be the work of an acquaintance, Bernardo Canaccio. For the Latin text and a translation, see Toynbee, *Dante Alighieri*, 106.

77.24–25. Coleridge remarks . . . somewhere: Perhaps a conflation of several remarks in Coleridge's *Table Talk*, which Carlyle read in 1835, and his comment in the *Biographia Literaria* (2:15.14): "'The man that hath not music in his soul' can indeed never be a genuine poet."

78.15. *canto fermo*: The ancient vocal music of the Church, plainsong or Gregorian chant.

78.16. *terza rima*: The measure adopted by Dante for the *Divine Comedy*, also used by Boccaccio and Petrarch. It consists of a series of interlocking three-line stanzas in which the second line of each tercet rhymes with the first and third of the following, e.g., aba bcb cdc.

78.30–31. "*Eccovi l' uom* . . . the man that was in Hell!": Carlyle's version of the anecdote recorded by Boccaccio in his *Trattatello in laude di Dante* (465). See also James Smith, *Lives of Dante*, 42–43.

78.33. Commedias that come out *divine*: Dante's epic was called *La Commedia* (The Comedy) because it had a happy ending in Heaven. The adjective "*Divina*" was first added two centuries after Dante's death in an edition of 1555.

78.37. 'to become perfect through *suffering*': Hebrews 2:10. The Authorized Version reads, "to make the captain of their salvation perfect through sufferings."

79.20–21. **Hall of Dite:** *red* **pinnacle:** Not the hall, but the city of Dis, "la città c'ha nome Dite" (the city that is named Dis), in *Inferno* 8.68. Compare *Aeneid* 6.541, "Ditis magni sub moenia" (under the walls of great Dis). The "*red* pinnacle" (*Inferno* 8.70–72) is more literally "vermilion mosques" ("meschite . . . vermiglie"). They were also commented on by John Carlyle in his translation of the *Inferno* (xxxiii).

79.24. **Tacitus is not briefer:** Cornelius Tacitus (55?–117?), Roman historian whose accounts of the Roman Empire and the Julian emperors are noted for their concise expression.

79.29–31. **Plutus . . . 'suddenly broken':** *Inferno* 7.13–15: "Quali dal vento le gonfiate vele / caggiono avvolte, poi che l'alber fiacca, / tal cadde a terra la fiera crudele" (As sails swollen by the wind fall in a heap when the mainmast snaps, so fell that cruel beast to the ground). Dante apparently did not clearly distinguish between Pluto, the god of the underworld, and Plutus, the god of wealth. See Singleton's *Commentary* on the *Inferno*, 109–10.

79.31. **Brunetto Latini:** Carlyle's reference is to *Inferno* 15.26–27. See also *History of Literature*, 93–94. The figure with the baked face, "cotto aspetto," is Bruno Latini (see note at 77.8 above). In the first three editions of *On Heroes* Carlyle confused him with Sordello, who appears in the *Purgatorio*, cantos 6–9. See textual apparatus.

79.32–33. **'fiery snow':** *Inferno* 14.28–30. Compare *History of Literature*, 93.

79.34–36. **those Tombs . . . to be shut at the Day of Judgment:** *Inferno* 10.1–18. Dante compares the tombs of the Epicureans to the Roman cemetery at Arles in Provence, which still preserves many sarcophagi. See *Inferno* 9.112–21. In *History of Literature* (96), Carlyle noted: "The description is striking of the sarcophaguses in which these people are enclosed, [some red-hot, others brown-hot, (Karkaria, 84)] 'more or less heated' . . . ; the lids are to be kept open till the last day, and are then to be sealed down forever." Carlyle's interpretation of the word *sospeci* (suspended) in this passage is more confident than that of modern scholars. See for example Singleton's *Commentary* on the *Inferno*, 142.

79.36–37. Day of Judgment, through Eternity: *Inferno* 10.10–12. Carlyle's rendering of Dante's reference to "Iosafàt" (Jehoshaphat), the valley where, according to Jewish and Moslem tradition, the Last Judgment is to occur. See Joel 3:12.

79.37. how Farinata rises: Farinata degli Uberti (d. 1264), a Ghibelline noble who took part in the massacre of Guelphs at Montaperti in 1260. The Guelphs, among whom were Dante's ancestors, never forgave him, burning the Farinata palaces and exiling the family. As a follower of Epicurus, he is confined in hell among the heretics (*Inferno* 10.22–51). At 10.35–36, Farinata rises from his sarcophagus "upright with chest and brow thrown back as if he had great scorn of Hell." See also *History of Literature*, 96.

79.37. how Cavalcante falls: *Inferno* 10.52–72. Cavalcante de' Cavalcanti, a Guelph leader who like Farinata was noted for his Epicureanism. His son Guido (1255?–1300) was a poet, friend to Dante, who dedicated the *Vita Nuova* to him, and son-in-law to Farinata. Cavalcante, who had risen to his knees in his sarcophagus to ask news of his son, "fell supine again and showed himself no more" (10.72) when Dante spoke of Guido in the past tense.

79.38. '*fue!*': In fact "ebbe," not "fue." "Di sùbito drizzato gridò: 'Come? / dicesti "elli ebbe"? non viv' elli ancora?'" (Suddenly straightening up, he cried, "How? Did you say 'he had'? Does he not still live?"; *Inferno* 10.67–68).

80.7. physiognomical: Carlyle admired the physiognomical studies of Johann Kaspar Lavater (1741–1801) ("Count Cagliostro" [1833], *Essays* 3:297) and himself relied on the belief that human character was reflected in the face. See, for example, "Scottish Portraits" (1854), *Essays* 4:404–5; "Portraits of John Knox" (1875), *Essays* 5:309–67; and *Mill, Sterling and Browning*, 40; and see the discussion of Carlyle's interest in physiognomy in the Introduction, pp. xxxv–xxxix.

80.11. *sympathized* with it: The value of sympathy to the artist is a central Carlylean theme. See "Biography" (1832), *Essays* 3:57, where he explains that the secret of being "graphic" is "*To have an open loving heart*."

80.23–24. 'the eye seeing in all things what it brought with it the faculty of seeing!': An echo of *French Revolution* 1:1.2.5: "In every object there is inexhaustible meaning; the eye sees in it what the eye brings means of seeing." See also "Count Cagliostro" (1833), *Essays* 3:317. Carlyle states a familiar Romantic formula; compare Blake's letter of August 23, 1799: "As a man is, so he sees. As the eye is formed, such are its powers" (Blake, *Letters*, 62). Their common source is probably Plotinus's first Ennead, sixth Tractate, "On Beauty": "Τὸ γὰρ ὁρῶν πρὸς τὸ ὁρώμενον συγγενὲς καὶ ὅμοιον ποιησάμενον δεῖ ἐπιβάλλειν τῇ θέᾳ" (For one must come to the sight with a seeing power made akin and like to what is seen; 1.6.9).

80.25. Raphael: Raffaello, surnamed Santi or Sanzio, of Urbino (1483–1520), the Renaissance painter.

80.31. Francesca and her Lover: *Inferno* 5.73ff. "There are many of his greatest qualities in the celebrated passage about Francesca. . . . I know nowhere of a more striking passage. . . . It is as tender as the voice of mothers, full of the gentlest pity, though there is much stern tragedy in it. It is very touching" (*History of Literature*, 94; Karkaria [82] has ". . . stern tragedy in it. He appears there both as he was environed outwardly, and as he was in his inward feeling; it is very touching"). Francesca, daughter of Guido da Polenta, lord of Ravenna, made a political marriage with Gianciotto da Rimini but fell in love with his younger brother, Paolo. According to tradition, shortly after the wedding the lovers were surprised and killed by the angry husband. The story is told by Boccaccio in his *Esposizioni* on the *Divine Comedy* (315–17), a series of lectures he delivered in Florence from 1372 to 1374.

80.34–35. *della bella persona*: *Inferno* 5.101–2: "de la bella persona / che me fu tolta" (for the fair form that was taken from me). In the first edition these words from the episode of Francesca and Paolo are given as "questa forma." The words of Francesca do not include "questa forma" as Carlyle must subsequently have recalled, since later editions were corrected. See textual apparatus.

80.36. *he* will never part from her!: Carlyle paraphrases Francesca's words, *Inferno* 5.135: "questi, che mai da me non fia diviso" (this one, who never shall be parted from me).

80.37. *aer bruno*: *Inferno* 2.1: "aere bruno" (dark air); literally "brown air." Similar to the "aere perso" of *Inferno* 5.89, *perso* being a color predominantly black, but mingled with purple.

81.4. terrestrial libel: "Some have regarded the poem as a kind of satire upon his enemies, on whom he revenged himself by putting them into hell. Now, nothing is more unworthy of Dante than such a theory. If he had been of such an ignoble nature, he never could have written the *Divina Commedia*. It was written in the purest spirit of justice" (*History of Literature*, 95).

81.10-11. Æolean harps: Wind harps, which were extremely popular during the Romantic period, as in Coleridge's "Dejection: An Ode" and Shelley's "Ode to the West Wind." In his essay "The Correspondent Breeze: A Romantic Metaphor," M. H. Abrams established the centrality of this image for the English Romantic writers.

81.12-13. their meeting together in the *Paradiso*: Actually the *Purgatorio*, at 30.28ff and 32.1ff.

81.23-24. '*A Dio spiacenti, ed a' nemici sui*, . . .': *Inferno* 3.63: "a Dio spiacenti e a' nemici sui" (displeasing to God and to his enemies). In September 1835 Carlyle was reading about "that class of Damned Souls in Dante, *infesti a Dio ed a i suin Nemici*, precisely 'the respectable people' of this present generation of the world!" (*Letters* 8:212).

81.25-26. '*Non ragionam di lor*, . . .': *Inferno* 3.51: "Non ragioniam di lor." "These . . . were a kind of trimmers; men that had not even the merit to join with the devil. He adds: '*Non ragioniam di lor, ma guarda e passa!*'—'Let us say nothing of them, but look and pass!'" (*History of Literature*, 91). The "trimmers," as Carlyle calls them, are the neutrals, neither rebellious nor faithful, who are rejected by both Heaven and Hell. Their retribution takes the form of the *contrapasso* in which their previous passivity is replaced by posthumous frenzy. Compare "Mirabeau" ([1837], *Essays* 3:410), quoted in the note at 81.29-30 below.

81.26-27. '. . . *Non han speranza di morte*': *Inferno* 3.46: "Questi non hanno speranza di morte" (these have no hope of death). "That is a fine thing which he says of those in a state of despair, 'They have

not the Hope to die'—'*Non hanno speranza di morte!*' What an idea
that is in Dante's mind there of death" (*History of Literature*, 90).
See Revelation 9:6, and the following note.

81.29–30. **'that Destiny itself could not doom him not to die'**:
Attributed to Teufelsdröckh in *Sartor*, 2.7.134. In "Mirabeau" (1837),
Carlyle described the fate of those "plausible persons, who, in the
Dantean Hell, are found doomed to this frightful penalty, that 'they
have not the hope to die'" (*Essays* 3:410). Carlyle considered "it to
be the most dreadful doom not to be suffered to die," even if granted
eternal youth (*History of Literature*, 90). Dante shared this belief:
"Death I so prize / that I am envious of whoever dies" (*Odes*, ode
27, lines 12–13, page 71).

81.34. **I do not agree**: "The 'Inferno' has become of late times
mainly the favorite of the three. . . . It is no doubt a great thing; but
to my mind the 'Purgatorio' is excellent also, and I question even
whether it is not a better and a greater thing on the whole" (*History
of Literature*, 98). Carlyle preferred the "cantica of penitence . . . at
a time when popular taste strongly favoured the *Inferno*" (Brand,
Thomas Carlyle and Dante, 6).

81.36. **Byronism of taste**: "So bounteous was Nature to us [i.e., by
giving us Scott and William Cobbett]; in the sickliest of recorded
ages, when British Literature lay all puking and sprawling in Werter-
ism, Byronism, and other Sentimentalism tearful or spasmodic (fruit
of internal *wind*)" ("Sir Walter Scott" [1838], *Essays* 4:39). See "The
Hero as Man of Letters" at 141.8 below and note.

82.4. ***tremolar dell' onde***: Actually "tremolar de la marina" (*Purgatorio* 1.117). Carlyle also quoted the line in his 1838 lecture (*History
of Literature*, 99).

82.11–12. **"Tell my Giovanna . . ."**: *Purgatorio* 8.71–73. Compare
History of Literature, 99: "One man says: 'Tell my Giovanna that I
think her mother does not love me now'—that she has laid aside her
weeds!" Giovanna was the daughter of Nino Visconti of Pisa. Her
mother, Beatrice, took a second husband, Galeazzo Visconti of Milan, after Nino's death in 1296.

82.13. 'bent down like corbels': Carlyle's rather loose version of *Purgatorio* 10.130–37: "Come per sostentar solaio o tetto, / per mensola talvolta una figura / si vede giugner le ginocchia al petto, / . . . / Vero è che più e meno eran contratti / secondo ch'avien più e meno a dosso" (As for corbel to support a ceiling or a roof, sometimes a figure is seen to join the knees to the breast. . . . They were truly more or less contracted according as they had more and less upon their backs).

82.16. **Heaven's gate**: Compare Shakespeare, Sonnet 29; *Paradise Lost*, 3.541. See also *Sartor*, 2.5.115.

82.17–18. **Mountain shakes . . . a psalm of praise rises**: *Purgatorio* 20.124–51. Compare Psalms 46:3, 114:4, and 148:9.

83.11. **Gehenna**: A name for Hell, from the Vulgate. See note to "The Hero as Prophet" at 62.37 above.

83.14. **as I urged the other day**: In his comments on allegory in "The Hero as Divinity" above, 7.16–7.38.

83.36. **as we said**: At 74.18 and 75.17 above.

84.23–24. **yesterday, today and forever**: Hebrews 13:8: "Jesus Christ the same yesterday, and to day, and for ever."

84.27–28. **Napoleon in Saint-Helena**: "The Emperor greatly admired the Iliad. 'It was,' he said, 'like the Books of Moses, the token and the pledge of the age in which it was produced'" (Las Cases, *Memoirs* 2:137). On St. Helena, Napoleon frequently read aloud from the *Iliad* (3:289) and the *Odyssey* (3:315, 332, 359). For Carlyle's comparison of the exiled Napoleon and Burns see "Burns" (1828), *Essays* 1:264.

84.28–29. **oldest Hebrew Prophet**: Probably a reference to Moses, as the author of the Hebrew Bible. "And there arose not a prophet since in Israel like unto Moses, whom the Lord knew face to face" (Deuteronomy 34:10).

85.8. **the dust of King Agamemnon**: In Greek mythology, the son of Atreus, king of Mycenae, and leader of the Greek army in the

Trojan War. In literature he figures in both the title and action of the first segment of the *Oresteia* by Aeschylus; in Homer's *Iliad;* and in the *Agamemnon*, a tragedy by Seneca. Compare "The Hero as Man of Letters" at 138.13 below.

85.10. The uses of this Dante?: A jibe at utilitarianism. Carlyle frequently made this implicit contrast between value and utility, for example: "Art is to be loved, not because of its effects, but because of itself; not because it is useful for spiritual pleasure, or even for moral culture, but because it is Art. ... To inquire after its *utility*, would be like inquiring after the *utility* of a God" ("State of German Literature" [1827], *Essays* 1:56). But compare the title of the first chapter of Emerson's essay *Representative Men* (1850): "Uses of Great Men."

85.19. Arabians at Grenada and at Delhi: Less than a hundred years after Muḥammad's death, Arab armies of the first Caliphate swept over the Middle East and North Africa. Spain was invaded in 711. The golden age of Islam in India, however, was during the Mogul empire (1525–1857). See "The Hero as Prophet" at 66.18 above and note.

85.35–36. Let a man *do* his work; the fruit of it is the care of Another than he: Perhaps a version of Bhagavad Gītā 2.47: "karmaṇy evā 'dhikāras te / mā phaleṣu kadācana" (On action alone be thy interest, / Never on its fruits) (trans. Edgerton, 24–25). Emerson was an enthusiastic reader of the Bhagavad Gītā, and alluded to it in an 1850 letter to Carlyle that presupposes Carlyle's familiarity with the book (*Emerson and Carlyle*, 261), but whether Carlyle knew this passage in 1840 is uncertain. See, however, the claim of T. R. Sharma (*Carlyle, "The Hero as Poet,"* 92).

85.38. 'fills all Morning and Evening Newspapers': Compare "Varnhagen von Ense's Memoirs" (1838), *Essays* 4:116. Compare also below, "The Hero as King," 192.25–26: "whom no Morning Newspaper makes mention of!"

86.34. Warwickshire Squire: The story of Shakespeare poaching game on the Charlecote estate of Sir Thomas Lucy was initially recorded by Nicholas Rowe ("Some Account," v). The punishments alluded to by Carlyle are not in Rowe but in a later memorandum by Richard Davies. Though several aspects of the story are questionable, the legend has persisted and won the allegiance of several noted Elizabethan scholars. For a survey of the evidence, see Schoenbaum, *William Shakespeare*, 78–80.

87.1. 'Tree Igdrasil': The world tree of Scandinavian mythology. See "The Hero as Divinity" above at 19.9 and note.

87.4. Sir Thomas Lucy: See note at 86.34 above.

87.6. not a leaf rotting: A reference to *Sartor*, 1.11.56. See "The Hero as Divinity" at 9.23–24 above and note.

87.29. St. Stephen's: St. Stephen's chapel, Westminster, was used for meetings of the House of Commons until 1834 when it was destroyed by fire. By a figure of speech, the House of Commons was sometimes called St. Stephen's even after 1834. See also *Sartor*, 1.9.49; *Life of Schiller*, 113.

87.31. Freemasons' Tavern: The meeting place of the debating society established by John Stuart Mill between 1825 and 1830 as a London counterpart to the Speculative Society at Edinburgh (Mill, *Autobiography and Literary Essays*, 129–31). Six weeks after this lecture, on June 24, 1840, Carlyle's efforts to establish the London Library brought together a group of influential men who met at the Freemasons' Tavern and agreed to the founding of the library (Froude, *Life in London* 1:188–89). Compare "Signs of the Times" (1829), *Essays* 2:71.

88.10–13. It has been said ... Bacon's *Novum Organum*: See "Burns" ([1828], *Essays* 1:278): "Shakspeare, it has been well observed, in the planning and completing of his tragedies, has shown an Understanding ... which might have governed states, or indited a *Novum Organum*." The *Novum Organum* by Francis Bacon, Lord Verulam (1561–1626), published in 1620, revolutionized the methods of science.

88.35–36. *Fiat Lux*, Let there be light: Genesis 1:3.

89.13. convex-concave mirror: The image is found in the first chapter of Richter's *Siebenkäs*, which Carlyle translates in his second essay on that writer: "Is this beside me yet a Man? Unhappy one! Your little life is the sigh of Nature, or only its echo; a convex-mirror throws its rays into that dust-cloud of dead men's ashes down on the Earth; and thus you cloud-formed wavering phantasms, arise" ("Jean Paul Friedrich Richter" [1830], *Essays* 2:158). Compare Carlyle's use of the image in his earlier essay on Richter ("Jean Paul Friedrich Richter" [1827], *Essays* 1:2).

89.25–27. 'His characters are like watches . . .': A rather free rendering by Carlyle of a passage in Goethe's *Wilhelm Meister's Apprenticeship* (*Wilhelm Meister* 1:3.11.226): Shakespeare's characters "appear like natural men, and yet they are not. These, the most mysterious and complex productions of creation, here act before us as if they were watches, whose dial-plates and cases were of crystal; which pointed out, according to their use, the course of the hours and minutes; while, at the same time, you could discern the combination of wheels and springs that turned them." The passage echoes a famous comment of Samuel Johnson distinguishing between Fielding and Richardson (Boswell, *Life of Johnson*, 389), which is paralleled by a phrase of Sir Walter Scott's (see Allott, *Novelists on the Novel*, 202–3).

90.14–16. crabbed old Schoolmaster: In a letter to Emerson in December 1838, Carlyle recalled "an old blind schoolmaster in Annan" who "used to ask with endless anxiety when a new scholar was offered him, 'But are ye sure *he's not a Dunce?*' It is really the one thing needful in a man" (*Letters* 10:231). See 28.12 above and note. ·

90.23. We talk of faculties: "I know that there have been distinctions drawn between intellect, imagination, fancy, and so on, . . . but at the same time we must keep this fact in view, that the mind is *one*, and consists not of bundles of faculties at all, showing ever the same features however it exhibits itself—whether in painting, singing, fighting, ever with the same physiognomy" (*History of Literature*, 156). Carlyle's rejection of "faculty psychology," which regarded "will," "reason," "imagination," etc., to be separate powers composing the mind, parallels the thinking of Johann Friedrich Herbart (1776–1841). Coleridge also used the term "faculties" while rejecting the concept of a divided intelligence. See *Table Talk* ([July 29, 1830], 106–7), and Shawcross's introduction to *Biographia Literaria* (1:lxxxvi).

91.20. The human Reynard: Reynard the Fox, legendary hero of numerous satirical "bestiaries" collected during the Middle Ages in

France under the general title *Roman de Renart*. The fox represents a man who artfully preys on society and, through cunning, escapes punishment.

91.33. greatest of Intellects: Compare *History of Literature*, 155–56: "In a word, if I were bound to describe him, I should be inclined to say that his intellect was far greater than that of any other man who has given an account of himself by writing books."

91.35. unconscious intellect: That Shakespeare was unconscious of his genius is a point Carlyle repeats here from "Characteristics" ([1831], *Essays* 3:5; compare "The Hero as Man of Letters" at 155.37 below and note). The importance of the unconscious is a major idea in Carlyle's writing and in Romantic theory generally. This aspect of Carlyle's teaching was identified by John Stuart Mill as being similar to conclusions he reached as a major consequence of his secular conversion (Mill, *Autobiography*, 145). Although Gottfried Leibniz (1646–1716) had earlier asserted the existence of perceptions of which the mind was unconscious, the unconscious was largely the discovery of the nineteenth century. See Barfield, *What Coleridge Thought*; Coleridge, *Biographia Literaria* 1:12.164, 174, 2:250.

91.36–92.8. Novalis beautifully remarks . . . 'new harmonies . . . with the higher powers and senses of man': On Novalis, see the note to "The Hero as Divinity" at 11.3 above. The quotation is among the selections from Novalis that Carlyle translated in his 1829 essay on that author: "When we speak of the aim and Art observable in Shakspeare's works, we must not forget that Art belongs to Nature; that it is, so to speak, self-viewing, self-imitating, self-fashioning Nature. . . . Shakspeare was no calculator, no learned thinker; he was a mighty, many-gifted soul, whose feelings and works, like products of Nature, bear the stamp of the same spirit; and in which the last and deepest of observers will still find new harmonies with the infinite structure of the Universe; concurrences with later ideas, affinities with the higher powers and senses of man" ("Novalis," *Essays* 2:41).

92.13. as the oak-tree grows: "This all-producing earth knows not the symmetry of the oak which springs from it. It is all beautiful, not a branch is out of its place, all is symmetry there; but the earth has itself no conception of it, and produced it solely by the virtue that was in itself" (*History of Literature*, 157).

92.18. Speech is great: Compare Goethe's *Wilhelm Meister's Apprenticeship* (*Wilhelm Meister* 2:7.9.76): "Words are good, but they are not the best. The best is not to be explained by words." See also Froude, *First Forty Years* 2:91.

92.38. 'good hater': According to Mrs. Hester Thrale, afterwards Mrs. Piozzi (1741–1821), Johnson said of Dr. Richard Bathurst (1620–1704?), "Bathurst was a man to my very heart's content: he hated a fool, and he hated a rogue, and he hated a Whig; he was a very good hater" (Piozzi, "Anecdotes," 31). The "Anecdotes of Dr. Johnson, by Mrs. Piozzi" were included in J. W. Croker's 1831 edition of Boswell's *Life*, which Carlyle reviewed in *Fraser's Magazine* ("Boswell's Life of Johnson" [1832], *Essays* 3:62–135).

93.9. 'the crackling of thorns under the pot': Ecclesiastes 7:6.

93.11. Dogberry and Verges: The two constables in *Much Ado About Nothing*, 3.3ff.

93.18–19. *Hamlet*, in *Wilhelm Meister*: In *Wilhelm Meister's Apprenticeship* (*Wilhelm Meister* 1:4.3.251–53 and 1:5.11.358–12.366). In his earlier lecture series, Carlyle said: "One of the finest things of the kind ever produced is Goethe's criticism on Hamlet. . . . I may call it the reproduction of Hamlet in a shape addressed to the intellect, as Hamlet is already addressed to the imagination" (*History of Literature*, 154–55).

93.19–20. August Wilhelm Schlegel: Schlegel (1767–1845) began his translations of Shakespeare into German at Jena in 1796. By 1801 he had published sixteen of the plays, one of the great achievements of German Romanticism. In Vienna in 1808 Schlegel delivered a series of lectures, later published as *Über dramatische Kunst und Literatur* (1809–11), in which he describes Shakespeare's history plays as a national epic.

93.22–23. Marlborough . . . learned from Shakspeare: "I can well understand how the Duke of Marlborough once declared that all his acquaintance with the history of England was owing to Shakespeare" (*History of Literature*, 156). Also "On History" (1830), *Essays* 2:85.

93.29. Agincourt: The battle fought on October 25, 1415, between the English under King Henry V and the French under Charles d'Albret, Constable of France; it is described in the fourth act of *Henry V.*

93.32–33. "Ye good yeomen, . . .": *Henry V,* 3.1.25: "And you, good yeomen, . . ." The quotation is from Henry's speech at Harfleur rather than at Agincourt.

94.13. Globe Playhouse: The new Globe theater, in which Shakespeare had a vested interest, was built in 1598 or 1599. The cylindrical, thatched building was destroyed by fire during a performance of *Henry VIII* on June 29, 1613. It was rebuilt within a year.

94.18. *Disjecta membra*: Literally, "scattered limbs." Horace, *Satires* 1.4.62: "Invenias etiam disiecti membra poetae" (even when he is dismembered you would find the limbs of a poet). Carlyle said of himself: "I am a 'dismembered limb,' and feel it again too deeply" (Froude, *First Forty Years* 2:80).

94.23. deep as Tophet: Isaiah 30:33.

94.24. 'We are such stuff as Dreams are made of!' That scroll: A variant quotation of *The Tempest,* 4.1.156–57. See "The Hero as Divinity" at 32.33 above and note. The lines are inscribed on a scroll held in the left hand of the statue of Shakespeare in Westminster Abbey.

95.28. Æschylus: The earliest of the Greek tragic poets (525–456 B.C.). Carlyle's point had been made by Jonson in lines 31–34 of the poem to Shakespeare's memory published in the First Folio: "And though thou hadst small Latine and lesse Greeke, / From thence to honor thee, I would not seeke / For names; but call forth thund'ring Æschilus, / Euripides, and Sophocles to us."

96.1. prolix absurdity: See "The Hero as Prophet" above, 56.11–14.

96.8. Earl of Southampton: Henry Wriothesley (1573–1624), to whom Shakespeare dedicated *Venus and Adonis* in 1593 and *The Rape of Lucrece* in 1594. Carlyle's allusion to Southampton's patronage is derived from Nicholas Rowe ("Some Account," x), who passed on a story handed down by Sir William D'Avenant that the Earl had given Shakespeare a thousand pounds.

96.8–9. Sir Thomas Lucy: See note at 86.34 above.

96.9. sending to the Treadmill: The treadmill, an instrument for the punishment of prisoners sentenced to hard labor, was invented by William Cubitt in 1822. Its use was ended by the Prison Act of 1898.

96.25–26. Indian Empire will go, at any rate, some day: Carlyle's prophecy was fulfilled in 1947 with the granting of Indian independence. He makes a similar contrast in "Goethe's Portrait" ([1832], *Essays* 2:373): "Napoleon, with his Austerlitzes, Waterloos and Borodinos, is quite gone. . . . While this other!—*he* still shines with his direct radiance." Also in "Death of Goethe" (1832), *Essays* 2:378–79.

96.31. New Holland: The Dutch colony in the northwest of Australia, and by extension an early name for the entire continent.

97.9. Paramatta: City in New South Wales, Australia.

97.17. Italy lies dismembered: Partitioned by various foreign powers, especially Austria and France, following Napoleon's invasion of 1796. In the decade during which Carlyle prepared his lectures on heroes, insurrections in the Papal States provided early signs of the *risorgimento*, the movement that led to the reunification of Italy in 1870.

97.20. The Czar of all the Russias: The czar in 1840 was Nicolai Pavlovich, Nicholas I (1796–1855). The Russian Empire included Russia proper, the Caucasus, Siberia, the Steppes, and Turkestan.

NOTES TO LECTURE IV. THE HERO AS PRIEST.

Sources: The German reformer Luther had been of keen interest to Carlyle for many years. In 1829 he wrote that Luther's character was "the most worth discussing of all modern men's" (Froude, *First Forty Years* 2:75). He thought of spending the winter of 1831 in Weimar to prepare a life of "the great German lion" (Froude, *First Forty Years* 2:101), and in September 1831 he offered the idea of an article on Luther to the *Edinburgh Review*. Since neither book nor article came to fruition, the lecture on the hero as priest gave Carlyle a long-awaited opportunity to deal in some depth with the subject of Luther, which he had briefly touched on in his earlier lectures on the history of literature.

It was Luther's *Tischredin* or *Table Talk* that gave Carlyle the most revealing insights into Luther's nature, and he cites a number of details from that work at 120.29–121.3 of *On Heroes*. However, six months after the lecture Carlyle asked Karl August Varnhagen von Ense, "Is there anywhere a legible Life of Luther; so much as an attainable edition of his *Tischredin*? I fear the answer is, No" (*Letters* 12:316; see note at 120.29 below). Carlyle's comment makes it clear that his knowledge of the *Table Talk* in 1840 was indirect. In fact it was probably derived from the large excerpts contained in *Mémoirs de Luther, écrits par lui même*, translated and edited by Jules Michelet (1835), to which Carlyle referred in a letter of October 1842 (*Letters* 15:145).

Knox had also for some time been a subject of interest to Carlyle. In March 1833 he was impressed by Thomas M'Crie's *Life of John Knox* (1811), a copy of which he had obtained the previous year, and he felt a growing inclination to write a book about "Scotch worthies and martyrs" (Froude, *First Forty Years* 2:340). He relied heavily on M'Crie's *Life* for his lecture, but he also drew on Knox's *The History of the Reformation in Scotland* (1587), which was soon (1846) to be superbly edited by Carlyle's correspondent David Laing. In January 1837, Carlyle had planned an essay on Knox (*Letters* 7:71), but the section in his fourth lecture was his only published account of the Scottish cleric until the "Portraits of John Knox" ([1875], *Essays* 5:313–67).

99.17. 'open secret of the Universe': See "The Hero as Poet" above at 69.7 and note.

100.1. Luther: Martin Luther (1483–1546), founder of the Protestant Reformation and translator of the Bible into German. Luther was Carlyle's mother's "chief Saint in the Christian calendar" (Froude, *Life in London* 2:108) and no praise pleased her son more than her response to his fourth lecture on Luther and Knox (*Letters* 13:93–94). During his 1852 visit to Germany to research his life of Frederick the Great, Carlyle detoured to Marburg, Eisenach, and other locations associated with Luther (see notes at 119.26, 119.28, and 119.32 below).

100.1. Knox: John Knox (1514 or 1515–1572). Knox's birthdate was given as 1505 in David Buchanan's 1644 edition of Knox's *History of the Reformation in Scotland* and remained unchallenged until 1904, when Hay Fleming produced evidence in support of the later date of 1514 or 1515. This is now generally accepted. See Ridley, *John Knox*,

531-34. Carlyle claimed that his wife was a "lineal descendant of John Knox himself," but this genealogy is "exceedingly doubtful" (*Mill, Sterling and Browning*, 27 and note). For Carlyle's view of Knox's life and significance see pp. 123-31 below and notes.

100.12. **warfaring and battling Priest**: Perhaps a Carlylean echo of Milton's "true warfaring Christian" (*Areopagitica* [1644], *Complete Prose* 2:515).

100.34. **wild Saint Dominics**: The Dominican Order founded in France in 1214 by Saint Dominic, born Domingo de Guzman (1170-1221). It is not immediately clear what Dominican "wildness" Carlyle had in mind. The order was marked by extreme ascetic austerity and was entrusted with the conduct of the Inquisition. It was founded mainly to counteract the Albigensian heresy and had the right to enforce its doctrines by fire and sword.

100.34. **Thebaid Eremites**: Thebes in Egypt was a popular haunt for hermits in the third and fourth centuries. "They often usurped the den of some wild beast whom they affected to resemble; they buried themselves in some gloomy cavern which art or nature had scooped out of the rock; and the marble quarries of Thebais are still inscribed with the monuments of their penance" (Gibbon, *Decline and Fall* 4:37.79). The reference was popular with Carlyle; see, for example, *Letters* 15:193 and *New Letters* 2:335.

100.36. **Walter Raleigh**: Walter Raleigh (1552?-1618), English explorer, courtier, and author.

100.36. **Ulfila**: Bishop of the Goths in the fourth century. See "The Hero as Divinity" above at 19.26-27 and note.

100.37. **Cranmer**: Thomas Cranmer (1489-1556), first Anglican Archbishop of Canterbury. Among his "practical Endeavours" was seeking the annulment of the marriage of Henry VIII to Catherine of Aragon and legitimizing the king's later marriage to Anne Boleyn. He was also a powerful agent in separating the new Church of England from Rome, and he drew up the doctrinal statements of the new church that later became the Thirty-nine Articles. Having incurred the anger of Mary Tudor over the succession, Cranmer was condemned for treason and later tried for heresy. Under severe examination he recanted his earlier beliefs and declared in favor of the articles of the Roman Catholic Church. However, during his execution by burning at the stake he repudiated his recantations and plunged into the flames the hand that had signed them.

101.6. Orpheus: The mythological Greek musician who was able with his lyre to enchant trees and rocks, tame wild beasts, turn rivers in their course, and drown out the song of the Sirens.

101.14–15. Theorem or spiritual Representation: An unusual rendering of *theorem*, from the Greek θεώρημα, meaning "a spectacle" or "subject for contemplation."

102.18. eye-servant: A servant who works only when supervised, i.e., under the eye of his master.

103.11. Schweidnitz Fort: An episode in the capture of the fort from Frederick on October 1, 1761, by Gideon Ernest von Laudon (1717–1790), the Austrian field marshal. See also 125.9 below and textual apparatus. The probably apocryphal story of Russian Grenadiers being marched into a chasm between two ramparts to make a roadway for those behind is recounted by Carlyle in *Frederick* 7:20.8.394.

103.28. Arab turban: More likely a slip for *tulwar*, the Pathan curved sword. However, "turban" appears in all editions of *On Heroes* published in Carlyle's lifetime. At the time of Carlyle's lecture, Anglo-Indian forces were making their first encounter with the Afghan tulwar during the first Afghan war (1838–42). Crossed tulwars were the emblem of the Pathan Queen's Own Guides, an elite corps operating on the Northwest Frontier whose exploits were widely reported by the English press at the time.

103.28–29. Thor's strong hammer smiting down *Jötuns*: In various mythic adventures Thor used Mjöllnir, his magic hammer, to destroy giants, but principally in Hymir's hall, in the Kingdom of Geirröð, and in the realm of Útgarðaloki. See "The Hero as Divinity" above, especially 33.19–28.

104.2. cannot away with: Isaiah 1:13: "Bring no more vain oblations; incense is an abomination unto me; the new moons and sabbaths, the calling of assemblies, I cannot away with."

104.4. done under the sun: Ecclesiastes 1:14: "I have seen all the works that are done under the sun; and, behold, all *is* vanity and vexation of spirit."

104.6. Idol is *Eidolon*: εἴδωλον, literally "phantom" in Greek, from εἶδος, "that which is seen," used in the Septuagint (e.g., 2 Kings 17:12) and the New Testament (e.g., 1 Corinthians 12.2) to mean "image of a god, idol."

104.17. Confession of Faith: Doctrines proposed by the Westminster Assembly and adopted by the English Parliament in 1647 as the creed of the English church. The thirty-three chapters of the Confession reflect a revamping in the spirit of Calvinism of the Thirty-nine Articles of the Anglican church. Compare below at 124.25–26.

104.31. Canopus: See "The Hero as Divinity" at 10.6 above and note.

104.31. Caabah Black-stone: See "The Hero as Prophet" at 43.22–23 above and note.

105.12. Ark of the Covenant: The ark, about two feet in height and made of acacia wood, fashioned according to God's instructions to Moses. See Exodus 25:10.

105.15–16. "You do not believe," said Coleridge; ". . . believe": Quoted again, but not attributed to Coleridge, in *Life of Sterling*, 1.7.51. See also 107.19 below.

105.23. magnetic sleep: Hypnotic trance induced by "animal magnetism," a practice popularized by F. A. Mesmer (1734–1815), German physician and hypnotist.

105.30. Koreish: See "The Hero as Prophet" above at 44.24 and note.

105.30. timber and bees'-wax: *Korân*, Chapter 22. See "The Hero as Prophet" above at 54.37–38 and note.

105.31. Tetzel's Pardons of Sin: Indulgences granted by Leo X in 1513 and sold near Wittenberg by the Dominican monk Johann Tetzel (1450?–1519). In the letter sent to the Archbishop of Mainz (October 31, 1517), Luther said he was sickened by what popular imaginations were making of claims like Tetzel's. On the same day, according to tradition, he nailed his Ninety-five Theses to the door of the Schlosskirche at Wittenberg. See Michelet, *Life of Luther*, 127 (references to Michelet are to the Smith translation unless otherwise noted).

106.9-10. 'private judgment': The right, claimed by sixteenth-century religious reformers, of each man, aided by the guidance of the Holy Spirit, to form his own judgment of the meaning of the Bible. This right, a cornerstone of Protestantism, was directly opposed by the Catholic view decreed by the Council of Trent (on which see "The Hero as Divinity" above at 21.11 and note).

106.25. Electoral suffrages: The decade in which Carlyle delivered his lectures on heroes saw the peak of the Chartist agitation for universal adult male suffrage in Britain. See "Chartism" (1839), *Essays* 4:118-204; and "The Hero as Man of Letters" at 151.7-8 below and note.

107.5. Dante had not put out his eyes: Whereas in the nineteenth century even the most orthodox mortal could only believe after the essentially impious effort "to put-out the eyes of his mind" (*Life of Sterling*, 1.7.51).

107.7. Hogstraten, Tetzel and Dr. Eck: Luther's quarrel with Tetzel led to attacks on him by Jacobus van Hogstraten (1454-1527), a Dominican monk and inquisitor; Johann Eck (1486-1543), Professor of Divinity and Vice-Chancellor of the University of Ingolstadt (not to be confused with Johann Eck, secretary of the Archbishop of Trier, who was Luther's interrogator at the Diet of Worms); and Sylvester Mazzolini of Prierio, known as Sylvester Prierias (1446-1523), a Dominican theologian, Master of the Sacred Palace, advisor to Leo X, grand inquisitor, and censor of books. All three were rigidly conservative and were fierce opponents of free enquiry. Luther's written responses to the attacks made on him are collected in volumes 31-32 of *Luther's Works*.

107.12. sophistical Bellarmine: Saint Roberto Francesco Bellarmino (1542-1621), noted Jesuit theologian, who defended the Catholic position against the claims of the Reformation, both in lectures at Louvain where he taught theology and in his three-volume *Disputa-*

tion on Heresy. Bellarmine played a prominent part in the examination of Galileo's writings, suggesting that the Copernican system be presented as a hypothesis until it gained scientific proof. There is little evidence to support Carlyle's prejudice against Bellarmine, many of whose contemporaries saw him as an enlightened theologian noted for impartiality even when dealing with Protestant works.

108.30-31. Serpent-queller: Carlyle's reference to the "black monster, Falsehood" suggests that he was thinking of the Redcrosse Knight in Spenser's *The Faerie Queene* (1596), who meets and quells the snake-like monster Errour (Book 1, 13) and the "old Dragon" (Book 1, xi).

108.35. Sansculottism: From *sansculotte*, literally "without breeches," an aristocratic term of contempt for the poor garb of the French revolutionary army who often wore pantaloons instead of knee breeches.

109.6-7. Liberty and Equality, Electoral Suffrages, Independence and so forth: Carlyle conflates a number of revolutionary aims, echoing the slogans of the first French Revolution ("Liberté, Egalité, Fraternité") and the Chartist agitation for universal adult male suffrage (see note at 106.25 above) and probably alluding to the American War of Independence.

109.16. plummet and level: A plummet or plumb line is used to determine accurate vertical measurement. A level is used to determine whether a surface is horizontal.

109.27. Luther's birthplace: Eisleben in the county of Manfeld on the southern edge of the Harz mountains. The humble origin of great men was a popular subject with Carlyle, who also noted the disadvantageous beginnings of Knox (see 125.37-126.1 below) and of Johnson and Burns (see "The Hero as Man of Letters" at 153.21-22 and 161.37-38 below). See also "another Birth-hour" at 110.5 below.

110.8-9. The Age of Miracles is forever here!: Compare: "Remarkable it is, truly, how everywhere the eternal fact begins again to be recognised, that there is a Godlike in human affairs; that God not only made us and beholds us, but is in us and around us; that the Age of Miracles, as it ever was, now is" ("Characteristics" [1831], *Essays* 3:42). Compare "The Hero as Man of Letters" at 147.11 below.

110.13. He had to beg: Luther was forced by his parents' poverty to leave the Magdeburg school at thirteen and to "beg his bread for support" (Chalmers, "Memoir," xxv–xxvi). Later Luther said: "Let no one speak contemptuously before me of the poor ... who go about singing and crying at every door, *Panem propter Deum!* (bread for God's sake!) ... I, myself, was once a poor mendicant, begging my bread from door to door" (Chalmers, "Memoir," xxvi). Also Michelet, *Life of Luther*, 123; *History of Literature*, 132.

110.29. death of his friend Alexis: "In 1505 ... a friend ... was struck dead by lightning at his side. He uttered a cry; and that cry was a vow to St. Anne to turn monk. The danger over, he made no' attempt to elude a vow into which he had been surprised by terror" (Michelet, *Life of Luther*, 124). Luther alludes to the incident in his preface to *De Votis Monasticis* (November 21, 1521), cited by Michelet (124). Chalmers also recounts the story ("Memoir," xxvi–xxvii), and Carlyle in *History of Literature* (132–33) offers a slightly different version from the one given here.

111.7. Augustine Convent: Luther entered the Augustinian monastery at Erfurt on July 17, 1505. He was ordained there two years later. In 1852, Carlyle visited in Erfurt, "the very room ... where Martin Luther lived when a monk" (Froude, *Life in London* 2:110).

111.11. pious monk: "He became, as he tells us, 'a strict and painful monk'" (*History of Literature*, 133). The source of the remark is Luther's *Tischreden* (*Luther's Works* 54:95).

111.20. he was doomed: "He was very miserable in that life, imagining himself doomed to everlasting perdition" (*History of Literature*, 133).

111.27–28. old Latin Bible: At the Erfurt monastery, Luther, as one of the learned monks, was given the complete Bible in the prescribed Latin translation of St. Jerome. "I was twenty years of age," says Luther, "before I had ever seen the Bible. ... At last, I found a Bible in the library of Erfurth" (Michelet, *Life of Luther*, 209; see also Chalmers, "Memoir," xxvii; *History of Literature*, 133). Use of the Scriptures was strictly controlled and sometimes, as Luther notes, viewed with suspicion. The Archbishop of Mainz, for example, on being asked what the Bible meant to him, replied: "I know not what to make of it, save that all I find in it is against us." Luther also recalled his preceptor at Erfurt, Dr. Usingen, who used to say when he found Luther reading the Bible with evident devotion: "Ah! brother Martin, what is there in the Bible? It is better to read the ancient doctors, who have sucked the honey of the truth. The Bible is the cause of all troubles" (Michelet, *Life of Luther*, 209).

112.9. Friedrich, named the Wise: Frederick III (1463–1525), Elector of Saxony, "that ever-memorable *Kurfürst* [Elector] who saved Luther from the Diet of Worms," by abducting him and conveying him to the safe seclusion of the castle of Wartburg in 1521, where he remained for ten months ("The Prinzenraub" [1855], *Essays* 4:428).

112.10–11. Professor in his new University of Wittenberg: Luther gained his Doctor of Divinity degree in October 1512, and shortly after succeeded his mentor, Johann von Staupitz, to the chair in biblical theology at Wittenberg, the university founded by Frederick the Wise in 1502.

112.15. first saw Rome: In 1512 Luther was sent to Rome to mediate a dispute among seven convents of his order and the vicar-general. When he first arrived he fell on his knees and exclaimed: "Hail, holy Rome, sanctified by holy martyrs and the blood which they have shed here!" He hastened to "every sacred spot, saw all, believed all. But he soon discovered that he was the only believer." The pomp and luxury of the Italy of the Borgias also adversely impressed Luther. "The candid German was somewhat surprised at the magnificence in which humility arrayed herself, at the regal splendour that accompanied penitence" (Michelet, *Life of Luther*, 125–26; see also *History of Literature*, 133–34).

112.16–17. Julius the Second: The ambitious pope, Giulliano della Rovere (1445–1513), under whose direction Michelangelo painted the Sistine Chapel ceiling and Raphael the frescoes in the Stanza della Segnatura, which was to be the Pope's private library.

113.11–12. sorrowfulest of theories: That Luther's opposition to Tetzel sprang from his envy at the sale of indulgences that had once been within the control of the Augustinians. Leo X attributed Luther's opposition to the sale of indulgences to a "mere monkish quarrel" between the Augustinian Eremites, to which Luther belonged, and the Dominican order, to which Tetzel belonged (Harold J. Grimm,

Introduction, *Luther's Works* 31:xvi). Carlyle condemned the appearance of the canard in Taylor's *Historic Survey of German Poetry* where Taylor "repeats that old and indeed quite foolish story of the Augustine Monk's having a merely commercial grudge against the Dominican" ("Historic Survey of German Poetry" [1831], *Essays* 2:359).

113.19-20. Leo Tenth: Giovanni de Medici (1475-1521), who succeeded Julius II on the papal throne in 1513. A "worldly-minded . . . man of both pleasure and business" (Michelet, *Life of Luther*, 126), he managed to squander through his profligacy the resources of three papacies. His costly plans for finishing the great cathedral of St. Peter in Rome led to raising funds through the widespread sale of indulgences. Luther in his Ninety-five Theses questioned why the pope, who was wealthier than "the richest Crassus," should not "build this one basilica of St. Peter with his own money rather than with the money of poor believers" (*Luther's Works* 31:33). See also Chalmers, "Memoir," xxxv, and Macaulay, "Ranke's History of the Popes" (1840), *Essays* 2:49.

113.22. arrived at Wittenberg: The indulgences were not actually offered in Luther's parish, because Frederick the Wise, as civil authority, refused permission in his lands. The vendors did not, therefore, enter electoral Saxony, but came close enough for Luther's parishioners to go over the border into nearby Brandenberg.

113.28. against Indulgences: It was not indulgences as such but the exaggerated claims by Tetzel that drove Luther to attack them. In his Theses, Luther insisted on the traditional view that the indulgence was a remission of ecclesiastical penalties, not a forgiveness of sins, thus confuting Tetzel's claim to be able to give pardon "not only . . . for sins past, but for sins to come" (Chalmers, "Memoir," xxxi). See also *History of Literature*, 134.

114.2-3. He dooms the Monk's writings to be burnt: Known by its opening words "Exsurge Domine" (Arise, O Lord), the papal bull of June 15, 1520, demanded that Luther retract his heresies on pain of excommunication, and warned all Christians to burn his books.

114.5. with Huss, with Jerome: The Czech religious leader Jan Hus (1372?-1415), a follower of the doctrines of Wycliffe, denounced the sale of indulgences, was excommunicated in 1413, and burned at the

stake two years later as a heretic. On Hus, see "Early German Literature" ([1831], *Essays* 2:318). Jerome of Prague (1365?–1416) shared
the opinions of Hus and also his fate.

114.6. Constance Council: Met 1414–18. Its main business was to
settle the question of papal succession and to heal the schism between
the popes of Rome and Avignon. It also examined and condemned
the teachings of the Bohemian reformers Hus and Jerome, who were
declared obstinate heretics and delivered to the secular authorities to
be burned at the stake.

114.7. safe-conducts: Guaranteed to Hus by King Sigismund, who
betrayed him. In December 1536, Luther read in Ulrich von
Richenthal's book on the Council of Constance, *Das Concilium, so
zu Constantz gehalten ist worden* (1536), of the Council's decree that
a safe conduct given to a heretic was not to be observed (*Luther's
Works* 54:215).

114.8. stone dungeon: During his eight-month imprisonment during the Council of Constance, Hus was first placed under house
arrest. Between December 1414 and March 1415 he was held in
the Dominican convent, at first in a dungeon close to the latrines.
In January 1415 he was transferred to a less rigorous detention site.
In March he was removed to the castle of Gottlieben where his legs
were fettered and at night his manacled hands were chained to a wall.
He spent the last four weeks of his life in the Grayfriars prison from
where he sent letters to friends "'written in chains in expectation of
the flames'" (Schaff, *John Huss*, 230).

114.8–9. 'three feet wide, six feet high, seven feet long': Untraced.

114.15. words of truth: Acts 26:25.

114.23–24. 'with a great concourse of people': Untraced.

114.24–25. burning the Pope's fire-decree: On December 10, 1520,
outside the Wittenberg town gate, Luther responded to the Papal
bull by burning it. More significant was his burning of the decretals,
the canon law, which were the foundation of the papacy. "His contemporaries rightly regarded this as his most daring action; the burning of the bull was secondary, and is not even mentioned in the

reports" (Friedenthal, *Luther*, 249). For an identical interpretation see Brecht, *Martin Luther*, 424. To publicly justify his action, Luther wrote *Why the Books of the Pope and His Disciples were Burned by Doctor Martin Luther* ([1520], *Luther's Works* 31:383–95), which ended with a quotation from Judges 15:11, "As they did to me, so have I done to them."

114.25. 'at the Elster-Gate of Wittenberg': Carlyle substituted this specific reference in the second edition of *On Heroes*, replacing the more general "market place of Wittenberg." See textual apparatus.

114.26. 'with shoutings': The ceremony itself was actually a quiet one. Only invited members of the University took part. It was, however, followed by a noisy student demonstration. See Friedenthal, *Luther*, 251–52; Brecht, *Martin Luther*, 424.

114.34. as was said above: At 105.28–29.

114.36. Mahomet said: See "The Hero as Prophet" above at 48.9–10 and 54.37–38 and notes.

115.9. triple-hats: The pope's tiara, a tall cap circled by three crowns.

115.11. Diet of Worms: Appointed by the newly crowned Emperor Charles V, the Diet met on January 6, 1521. Luther appeared before it on April 17, 1521, refusing to retract any of his writings unless he was convinced by scriptural texts of their error. Before its dissolution, the Diet issued an edict denouncing Luther as a convicted heretic and, after the expiry of a twenty-one-day period, forbidding anyone to harbor or protect him.

115.15–16. Charles Fifth: One year after Luther's death, Charles stopped his troops, who were quartered in Wittenberg, from despoiling Luther's effigy and attempting to dig up his bones. "I have nothing further to do with Luther; he has henceforth another judge, whose jurisdiction it is not lawful for me to usurp" (Chalmers, "Memoir," xc).

115.23–24. "Were there as many Devils . . .": Though his books had been burned, and amid general fears that a similar fate awaited his person, Luther announced his intention of attending the Diet at Worms, saying: "I will go, though there should be there as many devils as tiles on the roofs!" (Michelet, *Life of Luther*, 135). Compare *History of Literature*, 135-36.

115.27. "Whosoever denieth me before men!": "Next morning, as he passed through the streets, the people were all on their housetops, calling on him not to deny the truth, and saying, 'Whoso denieth Me before men, him will I deny before My Father.' And there were other voices of that sort which spoke to his heart, but he passed on without a word" (*History of Literature*, 136). Matthew 10:33; Luke 12:9.

115.35-36. His writings . . . partly his own, partly . . . the Word of God: Frederick suggested a ploy to stave off the imminent execution of the papal bull against Luther by arguing, "that it was not evident that the propositions objected to were his; that his adversaries might attribute them to him falsely; that the books . . . might be forged" (Chalmers, "Memoir," lxii). Luther's reaction to this advice is what Carlyle refers to. See also *History of Literature*, 136.

116.2-6. "Confute me . . . God assist me!": "'Till such time as, either by proofs from Holy Scripture, or by fair reason or argument, I have been confuted and convicted, I cannot and will not recant, *weil weder sicher noch gerathen ist, etwas wider Gewissen zu thun. Hier stehe ich, ich kann nicht anders. Gott helfe mir. Amen!*'" ("Luther's Psalm" [1831], *Essays* 2:162n), Carlyle's translation of the words Luther is said to have spoken before the Diet of Worms. Most modern scholars question the wording but not the general sense or the spirit of Luther's response. See also *Letters* 8:307 and *History of Literature*, 136-37.

116.8. French Revolution: The view of the Reformation as the inauguration of modern history and the forerunner of the French Revolution is often presented by Carlyle; see, for example, *Latter-Day Pamphlets*, 8.306. Carlyle's view is shared by modern scholars such as Richard Friedenthal: "The history of Luther's influence . . . is the political, spiritual, intellectual and linguistic history of the succeeding centuries" (*Luther*, 528). See "The Hero as King" at 172.19-21 below and note.

116.20-21. King Augeas's stables: One of the twelve labors of Hercules. To clear the stables of their accumulated filth in a single day, Hercules turned the rivers Alpheus and Peneus through them.

117.14. **The cry of 'No Popery'**: The Oxford Movement, an Anglo-Catholic revival, was at its peak when Carlyle offered his lectures on heroes. Anti-Catholic sentiment was most intense in 1838 and 1839 following the publication of the *Literary Remains* of Richard Hurrell Froude, edited by John Henry Newman and John Keble. The book alarmed the Anglican establishment by its sympathetic attitude to Rome and its hostility to various leaders of the Protestant Reformation. However, the cry of "No Popery," which was the response of some to the Oxford Movement, was a pale shadow of the violence associated with the same slogan during the anti-Catholic Gordon riots of 1780.

117.26. **galvanic**: Referring to the experiments performed by Luigi Galvani (1737-1798) in which electrical charges stimulated the muscles of dissected frogs' legs.

118.32-34. **'will not preach without a cassock'** ... **'three cassocks ... !'**: Luther advised a Berlin cleric, George Duchholzer, to comply with any ceremonial required by his prince as long as he was permitted to preach the gospel in its purity. If the prince is not "satisfied with one cope or chasuble, put on three" (Michelet, *Life of Luther* [trans. William Hazlitt], 456).

118.35. **Karlstadt's wild image-breaking**: During Luther's ten-month seclusion in Wartburg, Andreas Bodenstein von Karlstadt (1480-1541) attempted radical reforms, abolishing the mass and confession and removing images out of Wittenberg churches. Luther condemned the rashness of Karlstadt's iconoclasm and broke with him from this time (Michelet, *Life of Luther*, 142, 150).

118.36. **Anabaptists**: Extreme evangelical sect opposed to infant baptism, which it regarded as a pagan rite. The movement arose in Munster, where a journeyman tailor, John of Leyden, was proclaimed king, and later spread into Westphalia, Brabant, Guelders, Holland, Frisia, and the whole littoral of the Baltic as far as Livonia (Michelet, *Life of Luther*, 172).

118.36. **Peasants' war**: A popular uprising in Germany that was finally put down with considerable brutality. Luther's attitude to the peasants was uncompromisingly harsh. "One cannot but be surprised at the severity with which Luther speaks of their defeat. He could not pardon them, for having compromised the name of the Reformation" (Michelet, *Life of Luther*, 159). Ironically, Catholic princes at the time held Luther responsible for the uprisings that he violently repudiated.

119.6-7. his dialect became the language of all writing: The dialect was the court tongue of electoral Saxony enhanced by several other dialects with which Luther had become familiar on his travels. Luther's use of this mixed but predominantly Saxon dialect helped to develop *Hoch-Deutsch*. See *German Literature*, 31. Carlyle's account of the development of German follows Coleridge: "In Luther's own German writings, and eminently in his translation of the Bible, the *German* language commenced. I mean ... that which is called the HIGH-GERMAN, as contra-distinguished from the PLATT-TEUTSCH ... and from the OBER-TEUTSCH. ... The High German is indeed a *lingua communis*, not actually the native language of any province, but the choice and fragrancy of all the dialects" (*Biographia Literaria* 1:10.140-41).

119.17. 'his words are half-battles': "Luther's prose is a half-battle; few deeds are equal to his words" ("Jean Paul Friedrich Richter" [1830], *Essays* 2:148). See also "Luther's Psalm" ([1831], *Essays* 2:161) and *History of Literature*, 138, and compare "The Hero as Poet" at 68.9 above.

119.22. 'Devils' in Worms: See 115.23-24 above and note.

119.26. Wartburg: Where Luther was taken in secret after leaving the Diet at Worms on April 26, 1521. He dressed as a knight, abandoned his habit, grew hair over his tonsure, and was introduced at the castle as Junker Jorg, a guest of the castle's captain. There is a painting and a woodcut of him as Junker Jorg by Lucas Cranach. "Wartburg, built by fabulous Ludwig the Springer, ... grandly overhangs the town of Eisenach." As Martin Luther lived there, it is "the most interesting *Residenz*, ... now to be found in Germany, or perhaps readily in the world" ("The Prinzenraub" [1835], *Essays* 4:427-28). In 1852 Carlyle visited Wartburg, "where Luther lay concealed translating the Bible; ... to me the most venerable of all rooms I ever entered" (Froude, *Life in London* 2:108-9).

119.28. Luther sat: Visiting Luther's room in Wartburg, Carlyle "kissed his old oak table," and thought, "'Here once lived for a time one of God's soldiers. Be honour given him!'" (Froude, *Life in London* 2:109).

119.32. flung his inkstand: In Wartburg, according to tradition, Luther struggled with the devil and threw his inkpot at him. During his 1852 visit Carlyle saw "the place on the plaster where [Luther] threw his inkstand" and the "outer staircase . . . where he speaks of often hearing the Devil make noises" (Froude, *Life in London* 2:110).

120.3. Duke George: Duke of Saxony (1500–1539). Rigidly conservative and a lifelong foe to Luther, he was cousin to Luther's patron Frederick the Wise. George presided over the theologically conservative university in Leipzig, just as Frederick created and supported the new rival university at Wittenberg. Said Luther: "Did God summon me to Leipsic . . . I would thither . . . though it should rain Duke Georges nine days on end" (Michelet, *Life of Luther*, 143).

120.24. Poet Cowper: William Cowper (1731–1800). He suffered periodic attacks of madness and lived in constant terror of becoming totally insane; despair forced him into seclusion. Many of his poems are marked by a gentle piety. He was, as Carlyle wrote to Goethe in 1829, "a man of pure genius, but limited and ineffectual" (*Letters* 5:49).

120.29. Luther's *Table-Talk*: Luther's mealtime conversations, recorded by numerous students and friends. The first edition, *Tischreden oder Colloquia Doct. Mart. Luthers*, was published by John Aurifaber, Luther's secretary from 1545 to 1546, in Eisleben in 1566. For the reliability of Aurifaber's edition see Tappert, Introduction, *Luther's Works* 54:xiii–xxii. *Dr. Martin Luther's Divine Discourses at his Table*, an abridged English version of Aurifaber's German text, was produced by Captain Henry Bell in 1652. This was reprinted several times in the nineteenth century. William Hazlitt offered a new translation, *The Table-Talk or Familiar Discourses of Martin Luther*, in 1846. By the end of the nineteenth and the beginning of the twentieth century, a number of manuscripts of Luther's conversation were discovered in remote archives or in libraries where they had been overlooked. Some, separately edited and published, contained notes taken by Anthony Lauterbach, Conrad Cordatus, John Schlaginhaufen, John Mathesius, Veit Dietrich, and other recorders unacknowledged by Aurifaber.

120.33. the deathbed of his little Daughter: Luther's thirteen-year-old daughter Magdalen died on September 20, 1542. Looking at her in her coffin, he said: "To think that you must be raised up and will shine like the stars, yes, like the sun! . . . I am joyful in spirit but I am sad according to the flesh" (*Luther's Works* 54:432). See also Michelet, *Life of Luther*, 189. Hazlitt (Luther, *Table Talk*, 369) gives Luther's epitaph for Magdalen. The daughter's name was given as Margaret in the first edition; see textual apparatus.

121.4-5. **his solitary Patmos, the Castle of Coburg**: Luther signed letters from Wartburg "From the Isle of Patmos" (*Luther's Works* 48:256; see also 48:247, 6:138), after the place to which John the Evangelist was, according to tradition, banished by the Romans and where he composed the book of Revelation (Revelation 1:9). Also see Michelet, *Life of Luther*, 139, and *German Literature*, 82. Carlyle sometimes identified Craigenputtoch with Patmos (*Letters* 5:141-42). In the second edition of *On Heroes*, Carlyle, perhaps absent-mindedly, changed Wartburg to Coburg, the castle where Luther stayed in 1530 during the Diet of Augsburg. See textual apparatus.

121.10. **harvest-fields**: "Walking on the Leipsig road and seeing the plain covered with the finest wheat, Luther exclaimed: 'O God of goodness, this fruitful year is thy gift! Not for our piety is this, but to glorify thy holy name'" (Michelet, *Life of Luther*, 180).

121.15. **That little bird**: "One evening, noticing a little bird perched . . . as if to take up its roost for the night he said: 'This little thing has chosen its shelter . . . it does not disturb itself with thoughts of where it shall rest to-morrow, but composes itself tranquilly on its little branch, and leaves God to think for it'" (Michelet, *Life of Luther*, 180).

121.21. **love of Music**: As a boy Luther sang in the *Kurrende*, the door-to-door choir. Later he played the lute and the harp, and as a university student he mastered the theoretical work of Johannes de Muris, which provided training in church modes and musical proportion. He said after one musical evening: "If our Lord grants us such noble gifts in this life, which is but filth and misery, what will it be in the life everlasting? This is a foretaste" (Michelet, *Life of Luther*, 186). Carlyle himself repeats the common view that "the great Reformer's love of music . . . is one of the most significant features in his character" ("Luther's Psalm" [1831], *Essays* 2:160). Compare Froude, *First Forty Years* 2:75-76.

121.24. Devils fled: "Music is the art of the prophets; the only one which, like theology, can calm the troubles of the soul, and put the devil to flight" (Michelet, *Life of Luther*, 124). "The devil is a melancholy spirit, and cheerful music soon puts him to flight" (Michelet, 198).

121.28-29. in Kranach's best portraits I find the true Luther: See Plate 6. In his earlier lecture series, Carlyle noted that the "wild kind of force" in Luther "appears in the physiognomy of the portrait by Luke Chranak, his painter and friend, the rough plebeian countenance, with all sorts of noble thoughts shining out through it. That was precisely Luther as he appears through his whole history" (*History of Literature*, 138).

121.37. weary of living: To James Propst, Luther wrote on December 5, 1544: "I have finished my race; it remains only that the Lord call me to my fathers" (*Luther's Works* 50:245; see also 50:284-85 and 54:343). Carlyle had noted in his earlier lectures: "In Luther we often see an overshadowing of despair, and especially towards the end of his life, when he describes himself as 'heartily sick of existence, and most desirous that his Master would call him to his rest.' Another time he laments the hopelessness of Protestantism, and says that all sects will rise up at last in the day of judgment" (*History of Literature*, 162).

122.2. Day of Judgment is not far: "Now is the time which was predicted to come after the fall of Antichrist" (*Luther's Works* 50:243). "I think the last day is not far away" (54:427).

122.22. Gustavus-Adolphus: (1594-1632), king of Sweden who championed the Protestant cause during the Thirty Years' War.

123.4. Mayflower: Though Carlyle asserts that the Mayflower sailed from Delft Haven (see his similar comment in "Chartism" [1839], *Essays* 4:179), in fact the vessel sailed from Southampton on August 15, 1620, with the Speedwell, which had brought pilgrims from Holland. The ships were twice forced back to port, first to Dartmouth and then to Plymouth, because of serious leaking in the Speedwell, which was finally abandoned. The Mayflower sailed alone on September 16 from Plymouth.

123.13. Star-chamber hangmen: The Court of Star Chamber was created in 1487 and derived its name from the star-painted ceiling in the room in the royal palace of Westminster where it orginally met. It had extensive powers to try noblemen who were beyond the jurisdiction of other courts. Under the Tudors the court's proceedings were open to the public, but under the Stuart sovereigns it was indiscriminately used to suppress political opponents, met in secret, and dealt out draconian punishments.

123.19. *Neal's History of the Puritans*: *History of the Puritans* (1732–38), by Daniel Neal (1678–1743). Carlyle read the 1755 edition (see Carlyle's footnote at 123.37 below) and found the episode he alludes to at 1:490: "On the 1st of *July* the adventurers went from *Leyden* to *Delfthaven*, whither Mr. *Robinson* and the ancients of his congregation accompanied them; they continued together all night, and next morning, after mutual embraces, Mr. *Robinson* kneeled down on the sea-shore, and with a fervent prayer committed them to the protection and blessing of heaven." The minister was the Rev. John Robinson of Leyden. Carlyle also quotes from Neal in *Cromwell* (3:253). To Sterling he wrote on January 6, 1840, "Neal's *Puritans* I have from Maurice; a very considerably stupider book" than J. G. Eichhorn's *Einleitung ins Alte Testament* (1787), which he was also reading (*Letters* 12:7).

124.4. **Columbian Republics:** The new Republic of Gran Colombia, comprising modern Venezuela, Colombia, Panama, and Ecuador, lasted from 1821 to 1830. These regions, together with Paraguay, Peru, and almost all of Spain's South American colonies, were racked by continuous revolts and civil wars in the search for independence during the early nineteenth century. In 1843 Carlyle contemplated the "confused South-American Revolution, and set of revolutions" when he reviewed seven books on Paraguay, Chile, and Peru for the *Foreign Quarterly Review* ("Dr. Francia," *Essays* 4:261).

124.12–13. **under the ribs of this outward material death:** "I was all ear, / And took in strains that might create a soul / Under the ribs of Death" (Milton, *Comus*, lines 560–62). See also *Letters* 12:206.

124.25–26. **Westminster Confession of Faith:** A confession of faith drawn up by an Assembly of Divines under the auspices of the Long Parliament between 1643 and 1647. The Confession is the authoritative exposition of Presbyterianism. Compare 104.17 above.

124.35. James Watt: Watt (1736-1819) began his career as a mathematical-instrument maker. In 1769 he patented his steam engine, which he continued to improve while a partner in the Soho Engineering Works in Birmingham.

125.3. tumult in the High Church: A riot over attempts to introduce the Laudian liturgy at St. Giles' Church, Edinburgh, on July 23, 1637. According to legend, Jenny Geddes, a greengrocer of High Street, initiated the "tumult" by hurling her stool at the bishop's head in protest. In *Cromwell* Carlyle cites, as the first printed record of the incident, the *Continuation of Baker's Chronicle* (1660) by Milton's nephew, Edward Phillips, which quotes her as saying: "Out, thou false thief! doest thou say the mass at my lug?" Geddes, who kept a cabbage stall at the Tron Kirk, was, according to Carlyle, a traditional heroine still in Scotland. During his Highland tour, Burns named his mare Jenny Geddes. Helen of Troy, "for practical importance in Human History, is but a small Heroine to Jenny:—but she has been luckier in the recording!" (*Cromwell* 1:96-97n). See also "Baillie the Covenanter" ([1841], *Essays* 4:226-27). "To me," Carlyle wrote, "she stands as a most memorable monumental Figure, this poor Jenny" (*Letters* 12:300). Between February 1839 and December 1840 Carlyle eagerly sought information about Geddes from John Forster, J. G. Lockhart, and David Aitken (*Letters* 11:36; 12:300, 352; see note on Sources of "The Hero as King," p. 361 below). Matthew Arnold refers to Jenny Geddes in "The Function of Criticism" (1864): "The old woman who threw her stool at the head of the surpliced minister . . . obeyed an impulse to which millions of the human race may be permitted to remain strangers" (*Lectures and Essays*, 264).

125.6. 'Glorious Revolution': Of 1688, which rejected the Catholic James II in favor of his daughter, the Protestant Mary Stuart, and her husband, William of Orange. Invited by both Tories and Whigs to help thwart a Catholic dynasty, William landed in England in November 1688 with an army of nearly fifteen thousand. After the flight of James, Parliament recognized William and Mary as joint sovereigns.

125.6. *Habeas-Corpus* Act: The writ of habeas corpus was first used in the late sixteenth century as a protection against arbitrary imprisonment. It requires a detained person to be produced in a court to determine the legality of the detention. The Habeas Corpus Act, passed by Parliament in 1679, imposed severe penalties on judges who, without good cause, failed to issue the writ. See "The Hero as King" at 178.30 below and note.

125.7. **what we said**: At 103.10–12 above. See note at 103.11.

125.9. **Schweidnitz**: See note at 103.11 above.

125.13–14. **Revolution of Eighty-eight**: The "Glorious Revolution." See note at 125.6 above.

125.14–15. **official pumps and silk-stockings**: Sometimes adopted as court and diplomatic dress. Pumps are lightweight shoes, usually made of black patent leather. Silk stockings are worn with knee breeches.

125.15. **universal three-times-three**: The three cheers, as in "hip-hip-hurrah." On special occasions, the three cheers were repeated three times. Possibly also a reference to the court ceremony of kowtowing to the emperor in Manchu and Ming China, which required a bending of the head "three times three times" (Elegant, *Manchu*, 217), that is "nine inclinations of the head to the ground" (Cotterell and Cotterell, *Chinese Civilization*, 92). See Carlyle's reference to the Mandarin system in "The Hero as Man of Letters" at 145.21 below and note.

125.19–20. **Half-and-half**: A compromiser, half one thing and half another. For a similar usage see John Anthony's comment, in Act III of Galsworthy's play *Strife*, on the "half-and-half manners" of the younger generation.

125.26. **row in French galleys**: On July 31, 1547, the castle at St. Andrews surrendered to a besieging French force. Prisoners were taken to Rouen where some were jailed and others, including Knox, were left in the galleys where they were miserably treated. "Knox sat nineteen months, chained, as a galley slave" ("The Portraits of John Knox" [1875], *Essays* 5:346). The galleys were "the labour camps of the sixteenth century" and conditions in them severe enough to make sentence to the galleys "the heaviest punishment after capital punishment" (Ridley, *John Knox*, 68, 67). See also *History of Literature*, 162.

125.37–126.1. **the son of poor parents**: See note at 109.27 above.

126.1. college-education: At the University of Glasgow.

126.9. standing siege in St. Andrew's Castle: See note at 125.26 above.

126.18-19. burst into a flood of tears: Knox himself records his reaction to the demand that he preach publicly: "Whairat the said Johnne abashed, byrst furth in moist abundand tearis, and withdrew him self to his chalmer" (*Works of John Knox* 1:188). Compare *History of Literature*, 162.

126.21-22. baptism he was called to be baptized: "It was a fiery kind of baptism that initiated him" (*History of Literature*, 162).

126.34-35. "a *pented bredd*": I.e., a painted board or panel. Knox describes how aboard the galleys prisoners were "compelled to kyss a paynted brod, (which thei called 'Nostre Dame')." When the icon of the Virgin Mary was presented to one of the men he said: "Truble me nott; such ane idole is accurssed; and tharefoir I will not tuich it." When forced to handle the idol, he threw it into the river saying: "'Lett our Lady now saif hir self: sche is lycht aneuch; lett hir learne to swyme.' After that was no Scotish man urged with that idolatrie" (*Works of John Knox* 1:227). Carlyle recalls the episode in "Portraits of John Knox" (1875), and assumes that Knox himself is "the hero of the scene" (*Essays* 5:344). Compare *History of Literature*, 162-63.

127.3. He told his fellow-prisoners: Asked if he thought they would be delivered, Knox's answer was: "ever, fra the day that thei entered in the galayis, 'That God wald deliver thame from that bondage, to his glorie, evin in this lyef'" (*Works of John Knox* 1:228).

127.15-16. "He lies there" ... "who never feared the face of man": The newly elected Regent Morton pronounced the eulogy for Knox: "There lies he, who never feared the face of man" (M'Crie, *Life of Knox*, 340; see also *History of Literature*, 164). Ridley (*John Knox*, 518, citing *The Autobiography and Diary of Mr. James Melville* [1600], 60), and William Croft Dickinson ("Introduction," *John Knox's History* 1:lxviii) both give a slightly different wording, that Knox "neither feared nor flattered any flesh."

127.22. Queen Mary: Mary Stuart, "Queen of Scots" (1542-1587).

127.25. actual narrative: The narrative account of Knox's exchanges with the queen are given in his *History of the Reformation in Scotland* (*Works of John Knox* 2:277–393). Carlyle provides an account of these in "Portraits of John Knox" ([1875], *Essays* 5:356–59) and *History of Literature*, 164. His vindication of Knox on this score closely follows the argument of Thomas M'Crie (1772–1835), whose *Life of Knox* (see especially 229–30) Carlyle had read by 1822 (*Letters* 2:93; *Two Notebooks*, 5). M'Crie's effort to refute Hume as one who had "excited prejudices" against Knox "on the score of cruelty to Mary" (259n) found a favorable response with Carlyle.

127.35. ambitious Guises: Mary of Guise, wife of James V of Scotland and herself Regent of Scotland and mother of Mary, Queen of Scots, and her brothers Francis of Lorraine, second Duke of Guise, and the Cardinal of Lorraine. Compare *History of Literature*, 164. In 1855 Carlyle wrote an unfinished account of the Guises that has been recovered and edited by Rodger L. Tarr, "'The Guises': Thomas Carlyle's Lost Renaissance History."

128.1–2. "Better that women weep," said Morton, "than that bearded men be forced to weep": Carlyle would seem to have erred in attributing this statement to James Douglas, fourth Earl of Morton. The phrase "Better bairns greet than bearded men" was addressed by the Master of Glamis to the youthful King James VI during the Ruthven Riot of 1582, several years after Morton had been executed at the Market Cross of Edinburgh (Brown, *Short History of Scotland*, 210–11).

128.6. Mary herself: Knox's own version is: "'What have ye to do,' said sche, 'with my mariage? Or what ar ye within this Commounwealth?' 'A subject borne within the same,' said he, 'Madam. And albeit I neather be Erle, Lord, nor Barroun within it, yitt hes God maid me, (how abject that ever I be in your eyes,) a profitable member within the same'" (*Works of John Knox* 2:388).

128.17. we are not altogether here to tolerate: The argument that there are proper limits to toleration appears elsewhere in Carlyle's writings, for instance in *Latter-Day Pamphlets* where he asks "Does the Christian or any religion prescribe love of scoundrels then? I hope it prescribes a healthy hatred of scoundrels. . . . Just hatred of scoundrels, I say; fixed, irreconcilable, inexorable enmity to the enemies of God" (2.70).

129.12. His *History*: *The History of the Reformation in Scotland* (1597).

129.13. two Prelates: The fight between the Archbishop of Glasgow and Cardinal Beaton at the choir door of Glasgow Kirk on June 4, 1545. The story is given in detail by Knox in his *Reformation in Scotland* (*Works of John Knox* 1:145–47), from which Carlyle quotes in "The Portraits of John Knox" ([1875], *Essays* 5:339–41) and *History of Literature*, 163.

129.22. pipe of Bordeaux: Refers to a measure of wine, not a smoking pipe. Three weeks before his death, Knox broached a new hogshead of wine and urged some visitors to drink freely, "as he himself would not live long enough to finish the wine in that cask" (Ridley, *John Knox*, 515).

129.23–24. They go far wrong: This estimate of amiable features in Knox's character closely corresponds to the one Carlyle gives in "Portraits of John Knox" ([1875], *Essays* 5:356) and in *History of Literature*: "There was a great deal of humor in Knox, as bright a humor as in Chaucer, expressed in his own quaint Scotch" (163).

130.1. "Have you hope?": "Asked to give a parting sign that he was at peace, he lifted his hand, and apparently without pain passed quietly away" (Brown, *John Knox* 2:288). According to another account, "he asked his wife to read aloud the fifteenth chapter of the First Epistle to the Corinthians, and said that he commended his soul, spirit, and body to God, ticking off his soul, spirit, and body on three of his fingers." His physician later asked him if he heard the prayers that were being said in his sick room. Knox replied: "'I would to God that ye and all men heard them as I have heard them; and I praise God of that Heavenly sound'" (Ridley, *John Knox*, 517). A full account of Knox's last illness and death is given in Bannatyne, *Memorials of Transactions in Scotland*, 281–89.

130.21. Regent Murray: Lord James Stewart (1533–1570), Earl of Murray or Moray, bastard son of James V, and appointed Regent by James VI. Despite differences between them, his stern rule was praised by Knox.

130.22–23. **"It is a devout imagination!"**: Knox's efforts to introduce ecclesiastical discipline into Scotland were at first disregarded,
and his plans for Church polity were "derided as a 'devout imagination,' by some of the professors of the reformed doctrine" (M'Crie,
Life of Knox, 209).

130.30. **Hildebrand**: Pope Gregory VII (1020?–1085). Emperor
Henry IV did penance before him at Canossa in 1077. Hildebrand
"reasoned that if Christ was higher than the Emperor the Emperor
ought to subject himself to the Church's power as all Europe was
obliged to do" (*History of Literature*, 75).

NOTES TO LECTURE V. THE HERO AS MAN OF LETTERS.

Sources: As a writer himself, Carlyle's interest in the role of the man of
letters was a natural and long-standing one: he had already given a series
of lectures on the history of literature, he had published articles on two of
his three principal figures, and his reading in the works of the German
Transcendentalists had furnished him with his seminal ideas on the subject
of the literary hero. It was from Kant, Fichte, Goethe, and Richter in
particular that he derived his specific notions on the nature of the artist.

For his account of Samuel Johnson, Carlyle relied on Boswell's *Life
of Samuel Johnson* (1791), a new edition of which, by John Wilson Croker,
he had reviewed for *Fraser's Magazine* in 1832 (*Essays* 3:62–135). He
was undoubtedly familiar with Macaulay's review of the same work, which
had appeared the year before in the *Edinburgh Review*. Carlyle had himself reviewed John Lockhart's *Life of Robert Burns* (1828) for the
Edinburgh Review (*Essays* 1:258–318). In September 1840, he recommended the book to the German writer Heinrich Heintze along with
Allan Cunningham's biography in his eight-volume edition of *The Works
of Robert Burns* (1834), James Currie's biography in his four-volume
edition of the same (1800), and *The Letters of Robert Burns* (Glasgow,
1828) (*Letters* 12:258). Carlyle had not written a separate article on
Rousseau, but he had read the French writer as early as 1819, and his
references in the fifth lecture indicate a familiarity with *Emile* (1762), *Le
Contrat social* (1762), and the *Discours sur l'origine de l'inégalité des
hommes* (1755). He had also read the *Mémoires inédits* of the Comtesse
de Genlis (1825), which contained some information on Rousseau.

133.4. **The Hero as *Man of Letters***: Carlyle shared Fichte's view that
"Literary Men are the appointed interpreters of this Divine Idea; a

perpetual priesthood" ("State of German Literature" [1827], *Essays* 1:58). "The only Sovereigns of the world in these days are the Literary men (were there any such in Britain), the Prophets" (*Two Notebooks*, 184). Though critical of popular hack writing, Carlyle hoped that in time "Men of Letters too may become a 'Chivalry,' an actual instead of a virtual Priesthood" (*Past and Present*, 4.7.293).

133.10. He is new: A product of new social conditions that followed the ending of literary patronage. In Johnson's time, "Literature, in many senses, was in a transitional state; chiefly . . . as respects the pecuniary subsistence of its cultivators. It was in the very act of passing from the protection of Patrons into that of the Public; no longer to supply its necessities by laudatory Dedications to the Great, but by judicious Bargains with the Booksellers" ("Boswell's Life of Johnson" [1832], *Essays* 3:100). Carlyle echoes Fichte's view that as reading replaced other amusements that had gone out of fashion in the eighteenth century, the "new want gave birth to a new trade, striving to nourish and enrich itself by purveying the wares now in demand,— namely, *Bookselling*" (Fichte, *Nature of the Scholar*, 310).

133.17–18. copy-rights and copy-wrongs: A topical subject of the day, the occasion of a parliamentary bill in 1840. See *Letters* 11:34, 43; 12:85, 159; also Carlyle's comments on writing as a profession, *Letters* 14:14–17.

133.18. squalid garret . . . rusty coat: The scholar in the "rusty coat" is Johnson. See "Boswell's Life of Johnson" ([1832], *Essays* 3:72, 114). It was in the garret of his house in Gough Street that Johnson began work on the *Dictionary*. Carlyle made a pilgrimage there, "not without labour and risk" (*Essays* 3:114n). Johnson's first version of "The Vanity of Human Wishes" included the couplet "mark what ills the scholar's life assail, / Toil, envy, want, the garret, and the jail" (lines 159–60). The image of the starving artist in his garret was, by 1840, a Romantic stereotype. With the poverty of Burns, Johnson, and Rousseau, Carlyle would also have associated the image of Thomas Chatterton, the most celebrated of Romantic suicides, who died impoverished in a Bristol garret at the age of seventeen.

134.5. Johnson, . . . Burns, . . . Rousseau: In his essays Carlyle dwelt on the neglect and financial suffering endured by Johnson, Burns, and Rousseau. Of Rousseau he noted: "Society contrived to pay Philippe d'Orléans ... three hundred thousand a-year ... for driving cabriolets through the streets of Paris ... but in cash, encouragement, arrangement, recompense or recognition of any kind, it had nothing to give ... Rousseau" ("Chartism" [1839], *Essays* 4:169). In 1837, as he contemplated his lectures on German literature, Carlyle thought of "Rousseau's case" and prayed to be kept from "the madness of Popularity!" (*Letters* 9:176).

134.20-21. discharging a function: Carlyle's conception of this function is expressed in his essay on "Sir Walter Scott" ([1838], *Essays* 4:76), whose novels he found "not profitable for doctrine, for reproof, for edification, for building up or elevating, in any shape! The sick heart will find no healing here, ... the Heroic that is in all men no divine awakening voice." Literature "*has* other aims than that of harmlessly amusing indolent languid men." In his journal for July 22, 1832, he wrote: "Authors are martyrs—witnesses for the truth—or else nothing" (Froude, *First Forty Years* 2:284; see note at 144.9-10 below).

134.24. I say *inspired*: Carlyle resists the theological conception restricting inspiration to those sacred books assumed to be directly inspired by God, and extends inspiration to all literary works of genius.

135.1. Fichte: Johann Gottlieb Fichte (1762-1814), German Transcendental philosopher and a disciple of Kant. His series of lectures, *Über das Wesen des Gelehrten und seine Erscheinungen im Gebiete der Freiheit* [*On the Nature of the Scholar and its Manifestations*], was delivered in 1805 at Erlangen. He had delivered an earlier series of lectures on the same subject at Jena in 1794. The first and second editions of *On Heroes* (1841 and 1842) give the place of the lectures as Jena, which was revised to Erlangen in the 1846 third British edition, though not in the American edition of the same year. See textual apparatus at 135.2.

135.4. Transcendental Philosophy: Referring specifically to Kant's *Critik der reinen Vernunft* (*Critique of Pure Reason*) (1781), Carlyle says: "The reader would err widely who supposed that this Transcendental system of Metaphysics was a mere intellectual card-castle, or logical hocus-pocus. ... On the contrary, ... it is the most serious in its purport of all Philosophies propounded in these latter centuries" ("Novalis" [1829], *Essays* 2:26). Carlyle was often dismissive of German transcendentalism, but he claimed that it "*neutralised*" the atheism and materialism inherent in French and Scottish philosophy (*Letters* 12:120–21). Although Carlyle probably did more than any other person to make England receptive to "the type of mind expressed in German idealism," he tended to see it "as one body of doctrine without distinguishing between the teachings of Kant, Fichte and Schelling" (Wellek, *Immanuel Kant in England*, 183, 189).

135.6–7. **we ourselves . . . are as a kind of vesture**: An idea originating with the German philosophers and frequently expressed by Carlyle, for instance in "Novalis" ([1829], *Essays* 2:1–55) and *Sartor* (1.8.43): "So that this so solid-seeming World, after all, were but an air-image, our ME the only reality: and Nature, with its thousandfold production and destruction, but the reflex of our own inward Force, the 'phantasy of our Dream'; or what the Earth-Spirit in *Faust* names it, *the living visible Garment of God*." See also Carlyle's journal, September 1830: "What am I but a sort of ghost? Men rise as apparitions from the bosom of the night, and after grinning, squeaking, gibbering some space, return thither. The earth they stand on is bottomless; the vault of their sky is infinitude; the life-*time* is encompassed with eternity" (Froude, *First Forty Years* 2:86).

135.8–10. **'Divine idea . . . at the bottom of all Appearance'**: In *Nature of the Scholar*, Fichte writes: "The whole material world, . . . and in particular the life of man in this world, are by no means . . . that which they seem to be to the uncultivated and natural sense of man; but there is something higher, which lies concealed behind all natural appearance. This concealed foundation of all appearance may, in its greatest universality, be aptly named *the Divine Idea*" (210). Carlyle frequently adopted this idea, as, for instance, in *Essays* 1:58 (see following note). Compare "The Hero as Poet" at 69.10–11.

135.26. **perpetual Priesthood**: A concept derived from Fichte, as Carlyle acknowledged in the "State of German Literature" (1827), *Essays* 1:58: "Literary Men are the appointed interpreters of this Divine Idea; a perpetual priesthood."

135.31. **light of the world**: Matthew 5:14; John 8:12.

135.32. **Pillar of Fire**: Exodus 13:21. Compare "Schiller" ([1831], *Essays* 2:166): "Great men are the Fire-pillars in this dark pilgrimage of mankind." Also "Boswell's Life of Johnson" (1832), *Essays* 3:111. Compare "The Hero as King" at 188.14 below.

136.2. '**Bungler,** *Stümper*': "He who with his Learned Culture has not attained a knowledge of the [Divine] Idea, or does not at least struggle to attain it, is, properly speaking, *nothing;*—and farther on, we have said he is a *bungler*" (Fichte, *Nature of the Scholar*, 218; see also "State of German Literature" [1827], *Essays* 1:59).

136.3. '**Hodman**': A mason's assistant who carries bricks and mortar in a hod, a tray or trough with a pole handle, borne on the shoulder. "State of German Literature" (1827) contains an earlier reference to the same point: If the teacher or scholar who neither possesses nor strives after the Divine Idea "abide diligently by some material practical department of knowledge, he may indeed still be (says Fichte, in his rugged way) a 'useful hodman'; but should he attempt to deal with the Whole, and to become an architect, he is, in strictness of language, 'Nothing';—'he is an ambiguous mongrel between the possessor of the Idea, and the man who feels himself solidly supported . . . by the common Reality of things'" (*Essays* 1:59; compare Fichte, *Nature of the Scholar*, 213). In his journal for August 5, 1829, Carlyle described political philosophers as "the hodmen of the intellectual edifice" (Froude, *First Forty Years* 2:79).

136.9. **Goethe**: Johann Wolfgang von Goethe (1749–1832) was perhaps the most potent and positive influence in Carlyle's life. Carlyle was relatively unknown when, in June 1824, he wrote to Goethe enclosing his translations of *Wilhelm Meister's Apprenticeship*. From then on he corresponded regularly with Goethe until the latter's death (see *Goethe and Carlyle*). Goethe was for Carlyle a revered teacher who formed part of his vision of the hero. It was Goethe who rescued Carlyle from doubt and despair, the "physician of the iron age" as Arnold named him in "Memorial Verses" (1850, line 17). Carlyle's secular "conversion" in Leith Walk in 1821 (see Froude, *First Forty Years* 1:101), symbolically re-enacted in book 2, chapter 7, "The Everlasting No," of *Sartor Resartus*, was partly due to Goethe's healthy influence. "I then felt," he recalled, "and still feel, endlessly indebted to *Goethe* in the business." Goethe "had travelled the steep rocky road before me,—the first of the moderns" (*Reminiscences*, 282). Carlyle said Goethe had driven out his skepticism and "taught me that the true things in Christianity survived and were eternally true" (Allingham, *Diary*, 253). "And knowest thou no Prophet, even in the vesture, environment, and dialect of this age? None to whom the Godlike had revealed itself . . . ? Knowest thou none such? I know him, and name him—Goethe" (*Sartor*, 3.7.202). It was Goethe who "first convincingly proclaimed to me . . . : Behold, even in this scandalous Sceptico-Epicurean generation, when all is gone but Hunger and Cant, it is still possible that Man be a Man!" (*Letters* 8:39). Reading him was a "revelation . . . like the rising of a light in the darkness which lay around and threatened to swallow me up. . . . The appearance of such a man at any given era is . . . the greatest thing that can happen in it—a man who has the soul to think, and be the moral guide of his own nation and of the whole world. . . . There has been no such man as himself since Shakespeare" (*History of Literature*, 211, 214–15). Carlyle recognized that Goethe's "unexampled reputation and influence" ("Goethe" [1828], *Essays* 1:205) did not extend to England. Deploring Goethe's lack of recognition "in the general mind of England, even of intelligent England" ("Goethe's Works" [1832], *Essays* 2:399), Carlyle labored to introduce Goethe to English readers through his essays and translations. In "Goethe" ([1828], *Essays* 1:209) Carlyle anticipated the main reason for his decision to exclude Goethe from his heroic roster in *On Heroes*: "We cannot aim to make Goethe known, but only to prove that he is worthy of being known." See Introduction, pp. xlviii–l.

136.20. **what he did not say**: A reflection of Carlyle's doctrine of silence as expressed, for example, in *Sartor* (3.3.174): "Silence is the element in which great things fashion themselves together; that at length they may emerge, full-formed and majestic, into the daylight of Life." In his journal for September 1830 he wrote: "There is a deep significance in SILENCE. Were a man forced for a length of time but to *hold his peace*, it were in most cases an incalculable benefit to his insight. Thought works in silence, so does virtue. . . . Beware of speaking. Speech is human, silence is divine, yet also brutish and dead: therefore we must learn both arts; they are both difficult. Flower roots *hidden* under soil. Bees working in darkness, &c." (Froude, *First Forty Years* 2:91). See also *Letters* 9:360.

138.3. **Ishmaelite**: See "The Hero as Divinity" at 10.9 above and note.

138.7. **Odin's *Runes***: Odin was also the god of runic magic. See "The Hero as Divinity" at 24.32 above and note.

138.13. Agamemnon: In Greek mythology the King of Mycenae and leader of the Greek host in the Trojan War. En route to Troy he sacrificed his daughter Iphigenia at Aulis, the cause of his later murder by his wife Clytemnestra. His Trojan exploits are described in the *Iliad;* the saga of the house of Atreus is the subject of the *Oresteia* by Aeschylus. Compare "The Hero as Poet" at 85.8 above and note.

138.14. Pericleses: Pericles (495?–429 B.C.), the Athenian statesman and orator, was elected *strategos* almost continuously from 443 to 429, and even though Athens was nominally a democracy, it was, according to Thucydides, ruled by Pericles as its chief citizen. The period of his authority is known as the Age of Pericles.

138.22–23. circulating-library novel, which foolish girls thumb and con: Commercial circulating libraries grew rapidly in the second half of the eighteenth century and are one indication of the spread of literacy. Some of the most popular circulating libraries were located at fashionable resorts. Lydia Melford in Smollett's *The Expedition of Humphry Clinker* (1771), Lydia Languish in Sheridan's *The Rivals* (1775), and Catherine Morland in Jane Austen's *Northanger Abbey* (1818) all patronize the lending library at Bath. Popular sentiment against the circulating libraries often echoed Mrs. Malaprop's estimate of them as "vile places, indeed!" (*The Rivals,* 1.2). The low reputation of the circulating libraries tainted attitudes to the popular novel. See Jane Austen's protest in chapter 5 of *Northanger Abbey* against those who spent their time on what was "only a novel." In fact, scenes of circulating libraries with ignorant booksellers, "avid girl readers and empty-witted fine ladies" became "a commonplace of satire" (Tompkins, *Popular Novel in England,* 3–4).

138.25. 'Celia' felt . . . 'Clifford' acted: Typical rather than actual names for the heroes and heroines of popular romantic novels, as in *Cecelia* by Fanny Burney (1782) and *Paul Clifford* by Bulwer Lytton (1830). Such fictions were the staples of the circulating libraries, many being supplied by William Lane's Minerva Press.

138.29. What built St. Paul's Cathderal?: A variation of Carlyle's comment to Emerson during a visit to Craigenputtoch in 1833: "Christ died on the tree: that built Dunscore kirk yonder; that brought you and me together. Time has only a relative existence" (Froude, *First Forty Years* 2:358).

138.31–32. Midianitish herds: Exodus 2:15–3:1. Fleeing the court of Pharaoh, Moses sheltered in the land of Midian where he tended the flocks of Jethro.

139.4. Teaching: Caroline Fox (1819–1871), a friend of the Mills and Sterlings, attended this and the following lecture and recorded what she recalled of them in her journal. She gives this account of the passage: "He spoke of education, and resolved it into the simple elements of teaching to read and write; in its highest, or university sense, it is but the teaching to read and write on all subjects and in many languages. Of all the teaching the sublimest is to teach a man that he has a soul; the absolute appropriation of this fact gives life and light to what was before a dull, cold, senseless mass. Some philosophers of a sceptical age seemed to hold that the object of the soul's creation was to prevent the decay and putrefaction of the body; in fact, a rather superior sort of salt" (Fox, *Memories*, 106).

139.11. Abelard: Peter Abelard (1079–1144?), medieval philosopher. "Abelard and other thinkers had arisen with doctrines in them which people wished to hear of, and students flocked towards them from all parts of the world. There was no getting the thing recorded in books, as you now may" ("Inaugural Address" [1866], *Essays* 4:453). Abelard was one of the students of William of Champeaux, who early in the twelfth century opened a school for the advanced study of dialectic. The school represented an early stage in the formation of the University of Paris.

139.21. *Universitas*: The medieval sense of *universitas*, "the whole," was not so much a combination of disciplines, a "school of all sciences," but a community of scholars.

139.22. University of Paris: Italy rather than France was the site of the first modern European universities. The great *studium* at Salerno was known in the ninth century as a medical school. The University of Paris formally came into being between 1150 and 1170.

140.8. learn to *read*: Carlyle repeated this advice twenty years later to the students of Edinburgh: "What the Universities can mainly do for you,—what I have found the University did for me, is, That it taught me to read, in various languages, in various sciences; so that I could go into the books which treated of these things, and gradually penetrate into any department I wanted to make myself master of, as I found it suit me" ("Inaugural Address" [1866], *Essays* 4:454–55).

140.12–13. **true University:** "You may have heard it said . . . that 'the true University of our days is a Collection of Books'" ("Inaugural Address" [1866], *Essays* 4:453).

140.14. **to the Church . . . all is changed:** In "Signs of the Times" ([1829], *Essays* 2:77), Carlyle said: "The true Church of England, at this moment, lies in the Editors of its Newspapers. These preach to the people daily, weekly; admonishing kings themselves; advising peace or war, with an authority which only the first Reformers, and a long-past class of Popes, were possessed of; inflicting moral censure; imparting moral encouragement, consolation, edification; in all ways diligently 'administering the Discipline of the Church.'"

140.21–22. **Bishop and Archbishop, the Primate of England and of all England:** The Archbishop of York is the Primate of England; the Archbishop of Canterbury is Archbishop of All England. Compare Carlyle's earlier statement in "Boswell's Life of Johnson" ([1832], *Essays* 3:119): "Who were the Primates of England . . . during Johnson's days? No man has remembered." However, "the true Spiritual Edifier and Soul's-Father of all England was, and till very lately continued to be, the man named Samuel Johnson."

140.31. **a lily of the fields:** Matthew 6:28.

140.32. *handwriting:* The view of nature as the handwriting or text of the Divine was a popular theme in the works of Novalis, Schelling, and Schiller. See also "For in this masse of nature there is a set of things that carry in their front, though not in capitall letters, yet in stenography, and short Characters, something of Divinitie" in Sir Thomas Browne, *Religio Medici*, 1.12.12. Compare *Sartor* (3.8.205): "We speak of the Volume of Nature . . . whose Author and Writer is God"; also *Sartor*, 2.8.142; and "On History" (1830), *Essays* 2:91.

140.38. **a live coal:** Isaiah 6:6.

141.1–2. **'apocalypse of Nature'** . . . **'open secret':** A conflation of Goethe's phrase "the open secret" from *Wilhelm Meister's Travels* (*Wilhelm Meister* 2:13.305; see "The Hero as Poet" at 69.7 above and note) and Carlyle's own reference to the "Apocalypse of Nature" in *Sartor* (2.5.116) and in an 1837 letter to Emerson: "It is the true Apocalypse this when the 'Open Secret' becomes revealed to a man" (*Letters* 9:139). The phrase was popular with Carlyle and recurs in his essays on Richter and Goethe.

141.3. 'continuous revelation': For Carlyle's debt to Fichte in this passage, see Harrold, *Carlyle and German Thought*, 191–92.

141.8. Byron: Carlyle's response to Byron was ambivalent. He resisted Byron's romantic melancholy, describing him in an adaptation of Isaiah 53:3 as "a dandy of sorrows and acquainted with grief" (Froude, *First Forty Years* 2:93), and found the "stormful agonies, . . . volcanic heroism, superhuman contempt and moody desperation" of his early work to be melodramatic ("Burns" [1828], *Essays* 1:269). Carlyle's renunciation of the *sturm-und-drang* phase of Romanticism led to his famous declaration "Close thy *Byron*; open thy *Goethe*" (*Sartor*, 2.9.153). In spite of Byron's failure to make the most of his talents, Carlyle judged him to be one who "loved truth in his inmost heart" ("State of German Literature" [1827], *Essays* 1:69), and who "really had much substance in him" ("Sir Walter Scott" [1838], *Essays* 4:53). He was a "noble" soul, "richly gifted," who, like Burns, was "ruined to so little purpose" ("Burns" [1828], *Essays* 1:316). Compare "The Hero as Poet" at 81.36 above and note, and see the note at 144.3 below. Carlyle anticipated the preference of modern Byron criticism for *Don Juan* ("Burns" [1828], *Essays* 1:269).

141.9. withered . . . sceptic: An allusion to Voltaire, whose skepticism helped to destroy shams but who, in Carlyle's view, lacked constructive genius: "Wilt thou help us to embody the divine Spirit of that Religion in a new Mythus . . . ? What! thou hast no faculty in that kind? Only a torch for burning, no hammer for building? Take our thanks, then, and——thyself away" (*Sartor*, 2.9.154–55). See "The Hero as Divinity" at 14.24 above and note.

141.10–11. sphere-harmony: Through art, "the *whole soul* must be illuminated, made harmonious" (Froude, *First Forty Years* 2:209). The "sphere-melody" of "our highest Orpheus," Jesus, "took captive the ravished souls of men" (*Sartor*, 3.8.210). A reference also to the Pythagorean notion of the music of the spheres. See "The Hero as Poet" at 72.1 above and note.

141.17. Fragments of a real 'Church Liturgy': Echoing *Sartor* (3.7.201–2): "'But is there no Religion?' reiterates the Professor. 'Fool! I tell thee, there is. Hast thou well considered all that lies in this immeasurable froth-ocean we name LITERATURE? Fragments of a genuine Church-*Homiletic* lie scattered there . . . : nay fractions even of a *Liturgy* could I point out."

141.21. Witenagemote: The *witena-gemot*, "assembly of wise men," was the Anglo-Saxon Council of King and Nobles, which was summoned only in emergencies. Anglo-Saxon kings were elected by this body. It became the *Magnum Concilium* of the Norman kings.

141.26. Burke said: The *Oxford English Dictionary* under "fourth estate" notes: "We have failed to discover confirmation of Carlyle's statement . . . attributing to Burke the use of this phrase. . . . A correspondent of *Notes and Queries*, 1st ser. xi, 452 states that he heard Brougham use it in the House of Commons in 1823 and 1824, and that it was at that time treated as original." In 1828 Macaulay said: "The gallery in which the reporters sit has become a fourth estate of the realm" (Macaulay, "Hallam's Constitutional History" [1828], *Essays* 1:71). Carlyle himself titled chapter 5 of book 6, volume 1 of *The French Revolution* "The Fourth Estate." He claimed that Dr. Johnson's "small project" of the "Senate of Lilliput Debates" for Cave's magazine, an early attempt to report the proceedings of Parliament, was the origin of the "stupendous FOURTH ESTATE" ("Boswell's Life of Johnson" [1832], *Essays* 3:113; Boswell, *Life of Johnson*, 84).

141.32. Democracy is inevitable: With the French Revolution, democracy began its "world-thrilling birth- and battle-song," converting "old dead Feudal Europe" into "a new Industrial one" ("Count Cagliostro" [1833], *Essays* 3:270; see also "The Diamond Necklace" [1837], *Essays* 3:337). For all its "rapid progress," Carlyle saw European democracy as "a self-cancelling business; . . . a swift transition towards something other and farther" ("Chartism" [1839], *Essays* 4:158). After the 1848 revolutions throughout Europe, he considered "universal *Democracy*, whatever we may think of it," as an "inevitable fact of the days in which we live. . . . Democracy is the grand, alarming, imminent and indisputable Reality" (*Pamphlets* [1850], 1.8–9). By 1867 he conceded that "no power now extant" could prevent or retard it ("Shooting Niagara: and After?" [1867], *Essays* 5:1).

141.37. garnitures: Here signifying medals, military or civil decorations, or insignia of office.

142.15. thaumaturgic virtue: Wonderworking, the virtue by which miracles are wrought. See *Sartor*, 2.4.95, where Carlyle describes the "grand thaumaturgic art of Thought!"

142.22. Katherine Docks: The St. Katherine docks near the Tower of London, which were opened to traffic in 1828.

143.5. Organisation of the Literary Guild: A method of supporting literature that Carlyle hoped would succeed the bookseller system, which had in its turn replaced the system of patronage. See "Boswell's Life of Johnson" ([1832], *Essays* 3:100–101), and the *Examiner's* report of Carlyle's speech at the founding of the London Library (*Letters* 12:174–75n), in which he insisted that reading and writing are what is most fundmental, comparing a library to a church: "Every devout soul that ever lived spoke out of it."

143.15. Chaos should sit umpire: "*Chaos* Umpire sits, / And by decision more imbroils the fray / By which he Reigns" (Milton, *Paradise Lost* 2.907–9).

143.21. omnipotence of money: Johnson himself said: "No man but a blockhead ever wrote, except for money" (Boswell, *Life of Johnson*, 731). See "The Hero as King" at 192.38 below. In "Boswell's Life of Johnson" ([1832], *Essays* 3:97), Carlyle noted: "The career of Literature could not, in Johnson's day, any more than now, be said to lie along the shores of a Pactolus: whatever else might be gathered there, gold-dust was nowise the chief produce." It was in the river Pactolus that Midas was allowed to wash off the golden touch, turning the river sands to gold.

143.23. Mendicant Orders: Dominican, Franciscan, Carmelite, and Augustinian.

143.35. who will say: Echoing "Boswell's Life of Johnson" ([1832], *Essays* 3:95): "Destiny, in all ways, means to prove . . . Samuel, and see what stuff is in him. He must leave these butteries of Oxford,

Want like an armed man compelling him. . . . In all ways he too must 'become perfect through *suffering*.' . . . The fever-fire of ambition is too painfully extinguished (but not cured) in the frost-bath of Poverty."

144.3. Byron, born rich and noble: Carlyle virtually repeats his comment in "Burns" ([1828], *Essays* 1:315–16): "Byron, a man of an endowment considerably less ethereal than that of Burns, is born in the rank not of a Scottish ploughman, but of an English peer. . . . And what does all this avail him? . . . Byron, like Burns, is not happy; nay, he is the most wretched of all men. His life is falsely arranged: the fire that is in him is not a strong, still, central fire . . . ; but it is the mad fire of a volcano; and now—we look sadly into the ashes of a crater." See also Froude, *First Forty Years* 2:227.

144.7. 'involuntary monastic order': "The first Writers, being Monks, were sworn to a vow of Poverty; the modern Authors had no need to swear to it" ("Boswell's Life of Johnson" [1832], *Essays* 3:98). The idea was derived from Jean Paul Richter's *Life of Quintus Fixlein* (*German Romance* [1827] 2:260–61), which Carlyle translated: "Our schools are now cloisters, and consequently we endeavour to maintain in our teachers at least an imitation of the Three Monastic Vows. The vow of Obedience might perhaps be sufficiently enforced by School-Inspectors; but the second vow, that of Celibacy, would be more hard of attainment, were it not that, by one of the best political arrangements, the third vow, I mean a beautiful equality in Poverty, is so admirably attended to, that no man who has made it needs any farther *testimonium paupertatis*."

144.9–10. Money . . . can do much, but it cannot do all: In his journal for July 22, 1832, Carlyle noted: "Authors are martyrs—witnesses for the truth—or else nothing. Money cannot make or unmake them. They are made or unmade, commanded and held back by God Almighty alone, whose inspiration it is that giveth them understanding; yet for the world whom they address, for the fitness of their language towards it, their clearness of insight into its interests, and the ear *it* shall give them—for all in short that respects their revelation *of* themselves (not their existence *in* themselves)—money, as the epitome and magic talisman of all mechanical endeavour whatsoever, is of incalculable importance. Money cannot hire the writing of a book, but it can the printing of it" (Froude, *First Forty Years* 2:284–85).

144.27. Printer Cave: Edward Cave (1691–1754), London printer and publisher, the original editor of the *Gentleman's Magazine* to which Johnson contributed. Cave's magazine was Johnson's principal source of employment for many years. Cave was "a penurious paymaster" but "a good man" according to Johnson (Boswell, *Life of Johnson*, 1386). Carlyle called him "a dull oily Printer who called himself *Sylvanus Urban*" ("Boswell's Life of Johnson" [1832], *Essays* 3:95). In 1738 Johnson published a Latin ode to Cave entitled *Ad Urbanem*.

144.28. Gauger: As part of his duties as an exciseman or tax official in 1789, Burns was required to gauge or measure the capacity of ale casks. "Certain of his admirers have felt scandalised at his ever resolving to *gauge*; and would have had him lie at the pool, till the spirit of Patronage stirred the waters, that so, with one friendly plunge, all his sorrows might be healed. . . . It reflects credit on the manliness and sound sense of Burns, that he felt so early on what ground he was standing; and preferred self-help, on the humblest scale, to dependence and inaction, though with hope of far more splendid possibilities" ("Burns" [1828], *Essays* 1:301–2).

144.28–29. Rousseau . . . kindling French Revolutions by his paradoxes: "Society in France . . . had nothing to give this same half-mad Rousseau for his work done; whose brain in consequence . . . uttered hasty sparks, *Contrat Social* and the like, which proved not so quenchable again!" ("Chartism" [1839], *Essays* 4:169). See also the chapter "Contrat Social" in *French Revolution* (1:2.7.52–55). Rousseau's "paradoxes" may have been derived from Dr. Johnson (Boswell, *Life of Johnson*, 311).

145.2–3. Pitt . . . Southey: Carlyle repeats this story in "Downing Street" (*Pamphlets*, 3.119), but its source remains uncertain. Lockhart, who was Carlyle's main source, does not mention the incident in his *Life of Robert Burns*, nor do later biographers. Pitt's neglect of Burns and the arts is often recorded. During Pitt's "long administration he did nothing, or next to nothing, to encourage Literature or the Fine Arts. . . . Even that scanty pittance which, under the most inappropriate form of an exciseman's place, was bestowed on Burns, appears to have been the gift, not of Pitt, but of Dundas" (Stanhope, *Life of Pitt* 4:408). Though sharing the fashionable taste for Burns, when "a proposal was made to place the poet in a position where he could give most of his time to poetry, he [Pitt] preferred to resent the democrat's politics, pushed the bottle to Dundas, and did nothing" (Lockhart, *Life of Burns* [ed. Robert Chambers] 4:440).

145.15-16. *punctum saliens*: Latin, a "salient point."

145.17. **in France, in Prussia**: The establishment of academies for the regulation of literature and science. The Berlin Academy of Science was founded by Frederick I; the French Academy was established by Cardinal Richelieu in 1634. In "The Literary Influence of Academies" (1864), Matthew Arnold reflected on the effects of the absence of such institutions in England (*Lectures and Essays*, 232-57).

145.21. **Chinese**: Carlyle makes even more confident claims for the Mandarin system in *Past and Present* (3.15.235-36), where he sees the Emperor as the "one Chief Potentate or Priest in this Earth who has made a distinct systematic attempt at what we call the ultimate result of all religion, '*Practical* Hero-worship': he does incessantly, with true anxiety, in such way as he can, search and sift (it would appear) his whole enormous population for the Wisest born among them; by which Wisest, as by born Kings, these three hundred million men are governed."

146.2-3. **'it is a *hand* which can handle any tool'**: "Intellect is not a *tool*, but a *hand* that can handle any tool" ("Diderot" [1833], *Essays* 3:227).

146.11. **plentiful as blackberries**: *1 Henry IV*, 2.4.239.

146.14. **But we are fallen into strange times**: In "Signs of the Times" ([1829], *Essays* 2:81-82), Carlyle declared: "The time is sick and out of joint. Many things have reached their height; and it is a wise adage that tells us, 'the darkest hour is nearest the dawn.' . . . There is a deep-lying struggle in the whole fabric of society; a boundless grinding collision of the New with the Old. The French Revolution . . . was not the parent of this mighty movement, but its offspring." In 1850, in "The Present Time," the first of the *Latter-Day Pamphlets*, his view though darker in complexion was substantially the same.

146.23-24. **'the third man . . . potatoes'**: In *French Revolution* 3:7.6.312, Carlyle described Ireland as "a Nation, the third soul of whom had not, for thirty weeks each year, as many third-rate potatoes as would sustain him." In a footnote to this passage, Carlyle gives his source as the *"Report of the Irish Poor-Law Commission*, 1836." Compare "Chartism" (1839), *Essays* 4:136.

147.1. *spiritual paralysis*: Conversely, in "Boswell's Life of Johnson" ([1832], *Essays* 3:90), Carlyle rejects as "melancholy stuff" attempts to account for human achievement by "force of circumstances" and "balancing of motives" that picture man, as in a nightmare, "paralysed." Man, he says, "is heaven-born; not the thrall of Circumstances, of Necessity, but the victorious subduer thereof."

147.3. *Sceptical* Century: While Carlyle considered the eighteenth century the age of skepticism, he hoped its influence would "burn itself out" in the nineteenth ("Characteristics" [1831], *Essays* 3:40. Compare *Letters* 12:121, 339–40).

147.11. 'age of miracles': In Protestant theology, the age of miracles is confined to the Biblical period. Carlyle may also have had in mind Hume's argument that miracles violated the laws of nature and that "no testimony for any kind of miracle has ever amounted to a probability" (Hume, *Enquiries*, 10.127). Carlyle was no more susceptible to superstition than Hume, but he viewed all things as inherently miraculous, since all appearance was the outer garment of a secret reality, transcending the world of sense. Hence, for Carlyle, "the Age of Miracles, as it ever was, now is" ("Characteristics" [1831], *Essays* 3:42). Compare "The Hero as Priest" at 110.8–9 above.

147.17. Pagan Skalds: *Skáld*, an Old Norse word signifying a "bard" or "court singer." See "The Hero as Divinity" at 29.22 above and note.

147.18–20. Tree Igdrasil . . . World-Machine: The contrast between organic and mechanical principles was a central one in the nineteenth century and was extensively applied to philosophy, as in Coleridge's *Biographia Literaria* (1:6.74), to art (*Biographia Literaria* 2:18.65), and to society, as in Dickens's *Hard Times*. The metaphorical translation of the attributes of a growing thing into the categories of intellectual activity was a central Hegelian formulation: "Only what is living and spiritual moves, bestirs itself within, and develops. Consequently the Idea, concrete in itself and developing, is an organic system, a totality including in itself a wealth of stages and features"

(Hegel, *Introduction*, 20). For the world-tree Yggdrasill, see the note to "The Hero as Divinity" at 19.9 above.

147.19. **Hela**: See note to "The Hero as Divinity" at 19.11 above.

147.22. **wheel-and-pinion 'motives,' . . . checks, balances**: A descriptive synthesis of various mechanical systems including utilitarian ethics, Newtonian physics, laissez-faire economics, and early democratic politics. In "Signs of the Times" ([1829], *Essays* 2:56–82), Carlyle sums up his age in the epithet "mechanical" and traces the spread of mechanical tendencies from the factories of the Industrial Revolution into almost every branch of human activity, including religion and philosophy.

148.9. **black malady**: Possibly a reference to the Black Death that decimated Europe in the fourteenth century.

148.19–20. **The other day speaking . . . of Bentham's theory**: The "other day" refers to May 8, 1840, the date of Carlyle's second lecture, during which he antagonized J. S. Mill by calling Bentham's philosophy a "beggarlier view" of humanity than Muḥammad's (see "The Hero as Prophet" at 65.22–23 above and note). The recollection of this episode led to the semi-apologetic reference Carlyle makes to Bentham here. See Garnett, *Life of Carlyle*, 171.

148.28. **steamengine Utilitarianism**: An epithet commonly adopted by Carlyle for mechanical philosophies. In the eighteenth century, he claimed, "all was brought down to a system of cause and effect; of one thing pushing another thing on by certain laws of physics, gravitation, a visible, material thing of shoving. A dim, huge, immeasurable steam engine they had made of this world" (*History of Literature*, 191). "He who traces nothing of God in his own soul, will never find God in the world of matter—mere circlings of *force* there. . . . Nothing but a dead steam-engine there" (Froude, *Life in London* 2:386–87). Carlyle also applied the term to John Stuart Mill's *Autobiography*: "It is wholly the life of a logic-chopping engine, little more of human in it than if it had been done by a thing of mechanized iron. Autobiography of a steam-engine, perhaps" (Froude, *Life in London* 2:420).

149.2. Samson grinding in the Philistine Mill: See Judges 16:21ff. The capitalized "Mill" suggests a pun on James Mill, leading spokesman for Bentham's ideas.

149.16. not even a Devil!: Echoing *Sartor*: "But in our age of Downpulling and Disbelief, the very Devil has been pulled down, you cannot so much as believe in a Devil" (2.7.133).

149.18. *caput-mortuum*: In alchemy, the residuum of chemicals after their volatile properties have escaped. Literally, a "dead head" or corpse. Carlyle applied the term to himself: "Either I am degenerating into a *caput mortuum*, and shall never think another reasonable thought; or some new and deeper view of the world is about to rise in me" (Froude, *First Forty Years* 2:79).

149.19. 'Doctrine of Motives': A reference to Bentham. "A motive is substantially nothing more than pleasure or pain, operating in a certain manner" (Bentham, *Works* 1:48). Compare *Letters* 12:200: "this singular moral hypochondria of a Bentham, and his 'motives,' his 'pains and pleasures' &c &c."

149.27. Phalaris'-bull: A brazen bull invented by Perillus, which was used by Phalaris (d. 554? B.C.), tyrant of Agrigentum in Sicily, to enclose his victims and burn them alive. The bull's first victim was Perillus, its last Phalaris. "'The Golden Calf of self-love,' says Jean Paul, 'has grown into a burning Phalaris' Bull, to consume its owner and worshipper'" ("Sir Walter Scott" [1838], *Essays* 4:53).

149.36. σκέψις: *Skepsis*, literally "viewing, examination, speculation, inquiry," but also "hesitation, doubt" as in the Skeptic or Pyrrhonic philosophers.

150.27-28. sentimental vapouring about virtue, benevolence: Referring to the ethical views of the Third Earl of Shaftesbury (1671–1713), who believed that man had an innate sense of benevolence, a "sentimental" doctrine widespread in the eighteenth century.

150.28. Cagliostro: Giuseppe Balsamo (1743–1795), the shopkeeper's son, who, posing as the Count Cagliostro, deceived a fashionable and credulous European society. See "The Hero as Prophet" at 39.24 above and note.

150.31. Chatham ... bandaged: William Pitt the Elder (1708–1778), first Earl of Chatham, known as the "great commoner" for his parliamentary career in which he displayed great oratorical gifts in opposing various policies of Sir Robert Walpole, then prime minister, and in criticizing George III. Carlyle's allusion is to the preliminary debate on the Peace of Paris in 1762, when Chatham was so ill he had to be carried to the House. Macaulay describes his entry in the arms of attendants: "His face was thin and ghastly, his limbs swathed in flannel, his crutch in his hand" (Macaulay, "The Earl of Chatham" [1844], *Essays* 1:436). See also Harrison, *Chatham*, 236–37, and Carlyle's earlier account of Pitt's career in his essay for Brewster's *Edinburgh Encyclopaedia*, reprinted in *Montaigne*, 247–66.

150.32. "has crawled out in great bodily suffering": Untraced.

150.33. Walpole: Horace Walpole (1717–1797), fourth Earl of Orford, inaugurated the craze for the Gothic novel with his publication in 1764 of the *Castle of Otranto*. Also an art critic, decorator of Strawberry Hill, and a Whig parliamentarian, in his *Memoirs of the Reign of George the Third* (1845), Walpole describes how Pitt "crawled" to his seat in parliament on crutches, his legs "wrapped in flannel" to relieve the gout (1:176–78). See note at 150.31 above.

151.7-8. Chartisms: The popular movement that Carlyle wrote about in 1839, calling attention to its violent element, which seemed to threaten revolution ("Chartism," *Essays* 4:118–204). At its peak in 1848 there was a massive demonstration on Kennington Common. The six-point charter of the movement sought universal adult male suffrage, annual parliaments, equal electoral districts, abolition of property qualification for parliamentarians, voting by ballot, and the payment of members of the Commons. Compare "The Hero as Priest" at 106.25 above.

151.11. Here and there: Tennyson for one. "Alfred is one of the few British or Foreign Figures (a not increasing Number, I think!) who are and remain beautiful to me;—a true human soul, . . . to whom your own soul can say, Brother!" (*Emerson and Carlyle*, 363).

151.35-36. not as fools: Adaptation of Ephesians 5:15.

151.38. 'duty of staying at home': "As a great moralist proposed preaching to the men of this century, so would we fain preach to the poets, 'a sermon on the duty of staying at home'" ("Burns" [1828], *Essays* 1:271). Carlyle argues that fiction is valuable for its truthfulness rather than for its exotic, romantic, or escapist features. The "great moralist" is Richter who says in his 1795 preface to the *Life of Quintus Fixlein:* "The most essential sermon one could preach to our century, were a sermon on the duty of staying at home" (translated by Carlyle in *German Romance* 2:195).

152.19. 'wood waxed and oiled': The waxing of wooden idols in medieval Arabia. See "The Hero as Prophet," 54.37–38 above.

152.21–22. *work*, which means difficulty, pain: As he told the students of Edinburgh, if "you are going to write a book,—you cannot manage it (at least, I never could) without getting decidedly made ill by it: and really one nevertheless must; if it is your business, you are obliged to follow out what you are at, and to do it, if even at the expense of health" ("Inaugural Address" [1866], *Essays* 4:480).

152.25. Bookseller Osborne: Boswell offers an account of Johnson knocking down Osborne in his shop with a folio. He also gives Johnson's response: "'Sir, he was impertinent to me, and I beat him. But it was not in his shop: it was in my own chamber'" (*Life of Johnson*, 112; see also "Boswell's Life of Johnson" [1832], *Essays* 3:102). Johnson knew both patronage and the bookseller system. Of the former, note his letter to Lord Chesterfield (Boswell, *Life of Johnson*, 184–85) and his definition of a patron: "Commonly a wretch who supports with insolence, and is paid with flattery" (*Dictionary*, under "Patron"). For Carlyle also, patronage was corrupted by sycophancy, the bookseller system by greed.

152.25. Fourpence-halfpenny a day: For living expenses. See Hibbert, *Personal History of Johnson*, 40. Some comparative idea of how wretched a pittance this was can be gauged by the price of printed materials at the same time. A pamphlet of some fifty pages is estimated to have cost twelve to eighteen pence, Boswell's *Account of Corsica* sold for seventy-two pence, and Johnson's five-volume *Shakespeare* cost two guineas (504 pence) in 1765. The cost of Johnson's *Dictionary* presented to Becky Sharp in *Vanity Fair* (1847) was two shillings and ninepence, that is thirty-three pence. See also "Chartism"

([1839], *Essays* 4:169): "Of your Samuel Johnson, furnished with 'fourpence-halfpenny a-day,' and solid lodging at nights on the paved streets, as his payment, we do not speak;—not in the way of complaint." Nor did Johnson, though he noted that poverty destroyed liberty and made "some virtues impracticable, and others extremely difficult" (Boswell, *Life of Johnson*, 1190). In "Diderot" ([1833], *Essays* 3:202), Carlyle catalogs the financial calamities of authors including Heyne "dining on boiled peascods," Richter "on water," and Johnson "bedded and boarded on fourpence-halfpenny a-day."

152.27. **loadstar:** Properly *lodestar.* A way star that guides and leads, from Anglo-Saxon *lád* (Skeat, *Concise Etymological Dictionary*, under "lodestar"). Compare *Sartor*, 2.6.126.

152.36. **I have already written:** The essay on Johnson appeared in *Fraser's Magazine*, May 1832 (*Essays* 3:62–135), and that on Burns in the *Edinburgh Review* in 1828 (*Essays* 1:258–318). He had not written "expressly" on Rousseau, but refers to him frequently in the essays on both Voltaire and Diderot and in *The French Revolution*.

153.30. **hypochondria . . . pain:** According to Boswell, Johnson also suffered from convulsions, palsy, gout, dropsy, and flatulence.

153.31. **Nessus'-shirt:** The shirt stained with the centaur Nessus's blood that Deianira gave to her husband Hercules in the mistaken belief it would act as a charm against infidelity, but which burned and clung to his flesh as it was torn off. Carlyle often applied this image to his own personal tribulations. Just after completing the lectures on heroes, he complained that none of his companions could "unwrap the baleful Nessus shirt of perpetual pain and isolation in which I am lamed, embated, and swathed as in enchantment till I quit this earth" (Froude, *Life in London* 1:185).

153.34. **scrofulous diseases:** "Young Johnson had the misfortune to be much afflicted with the scrophula, or king's evil, which disfigured a countenance naturally well formed, and hurt his visual nerves so much, that he did not see at all with one of his eyes." Johnson's mother took him to London where he was "actually touched by Queen Anne" in superstitious hopes of cure for the king's evil (Boswell, *Life of Johnson*, 31–32). Nature, says Carlyle, had given Johnson "a high, keen-visioned, almost poetic soul; yet withal imprisoned it in an inert, unsightly body. . . . Ariel finds himself encased in the coarse hulls of a Caliban" ("Boswell's Life of Johnson" [1832], *Essays* 3:91). Modern medical research has suggested that many of Johnson's eccentric behavior patterns were the classic symptoms of Tourette's syndrome (Murray, "Dr Samuel Johnson's movement disorder").

154.1-2. shoes at Oxford: See Boswell, *Life of Johnson*, 55-56. Carlyle also records the incident in "Boswell's Life of Johnson" ([1832], *Essays* 3:94), which cites Sir John Hawkins's *Life of Samuel Johnson* (6-7), "though in a cruelly curtailed form" according to Swinburne (*Swinburne Letters* 4:69). Johnson's anonymous benefactor may have been the Rev. William Vyse (Hawkins, *Life of Johnson*, 279n).

154.2. College Servitor: Oxford undergraduates who could perform menial tasks in order to lower their fees. Johnson once urged the scholar Thomas Warton to get a "Servitour" to transcribe quotations in order to speed up his production of a book on Spenser (Boswell, *Life of Johnson*, 195). Carlyle errs in describing Johnson as a servitor. He was a commoner at Pembroke College (see next note). See Boswell, *Life of Johnson*, 45.

154.4. Gentleman Commoner: Undergraduates at Oxford were either *scholars*, whose expenses were wholly or partially paid by the College; *commoners*, who paid their own way; *gentleman commoners*, who paid double fees and enjoyed certain privileges including dining at High Table; *battelers*, who paid lower fees and did their own chores; or *servitors*, who lowered their fees by performing various tasks including waiting on table.

154.16-17. was there ever soul more tenderly affectionate: "Few men on record have had a more merciful, tenderly affectionate nature than old Samuel. He was called the Bear; and did indeed too often look, and roar, like one; . . . but where, in all England, could there have been found another soul so full of Pity, a hand so heavenlike bounteous as his?" ("Boswell's Life of Johnson" [1832], *Essays* 3:127-28).

154.20. what I said the other day: In "The Hero as Priest" at 108.10 above: "The merit of *originality* is not novelty; it is sincerity."

154.28-38. He stood by the old formulas . . . a venerable place: Johnson kept his faith despite attempts to discredit the literal truth of the Bible. "How Samuel Johnson, in the era of Voltaire, can purify and fortify his soul, and hold real communion with the Highest, 'in the Church of St. Clement Danes': this too stands unfolded in his Biography, and is among the most touching and memorable things there; a thing to be looked at with pity, admiration, awe" ("Boswell's Life of Johnson" [1832], *Essays* 3:111).

154.36–37. St. Clement Danes: A church near Gough Square, where Johnson lived, built under the supervision of Sir Christopher Wren.

155.28. Idols, as we said, are not idolatrous: "Condemnable Idolatry is *insincere* Idolatry" at "The Hero as Priest," 105.10–11 above.

155.35–36. 'scholar' as he calls himself: In the famous letter to Lord Chesterfield: "When I had once addressed your Lordship in publick, I had exhausted all the art of pleasing which a retired and uncourtly scholar can possess" (Boswell, *Life of Johnson*, 184–85). Carlyle observes, "What soul-subduing magic, for the very clown or craftsman of our England, lies in the word 'Scholar'!" ("Boswell's Life of Johnson" [1832], *Essays* 3:113n).

155.37. A noble unconsciousness: "But on the whole, 'genius is ever a secret to itself'; . . . Shakspeare takes no airs for writing *Hamlet* and the *Tempest*. . . . Does the boxer hit better for knowing that he has a *flexor longus* and a *flexor brevis*?" ("Characteristics" [1831], *Essays* 3:5). Compare "The Hero as Poet" at 91.35 above and note.

155.38. 'engrave *Truth* on his watch-seal': "Socinian Preachers proclaim 'Benevolence' to all the four winds, and have TRUTH engraved on their watch-seals: unhappily with little or no effect" ("Characteristics" [1831], *Essays* 3:9). By way of contrast, Carlyle recalls Boswell's anecdote about Dr. Johnson's watch-dial, which had engraved in Greek "Νυξ γαρ ερχεται, being the first words of our SAVIOUR's solemn admonition to the improvement of that time which is allowed us to prepare for eternity: 'the night cometh, when no man can work.' He sometime afterwards laid aside this dial-plate; and when I asked him the reason, he said, 'It might do very well upon a clock which a man keeps in his closet; but to have it upon his watch which he carries about with him, and which is often looked at by others, might be censured as ostentatious" (Boswell, *Life of Johnson*, 395).

156.10. **Mirabeau**: Honoré Gabriel Riquetti Comte de Mirabeau (1749–1791), Carlyle's hero of French revolutionary history. Emerson records a conversation with Carlyle at Craigenputtoch in 1833: "We talked of books. Plato he does not read, and he disparaged Socrates; and, when pressed, persisted in making Mirabeau a hero" (*English Traits*, 9). In 1837 Carlyle wrote an essay on Mirabeau for the *Westminster Review* (*Essays* 3:403–80). See "The Hero as Prophet" at 39.33 above and note.

156.24–25. **Gospel ... of Moral Prudence**: Echoing his earlier statements about Johnson in "Goethe" ([1828], *Essays* 1:214), "His instruction is for men of business. . . . Prudence is the highest Virtue he can inculcate," and in "Boswell's Life of Johnson" ([1832], *Essays* 3:120), "Higher light than that immediately *practical* one; higher virtue than an honest PRUDENCE, he could not then communicate."

156.25–26. **'in a world where ... little is to be known'**: From Johnson's prayer of August 12, 1784, "Against inquisitive and perplexing thoughts," which reads in part: "And while it shall please thee to continue me in this world where much is to be done and little to be known, teach me . . . to withdraw my Mind from unprofitable and dangerous enquiries, from difficulties vainly curious, and doubts impossible to be solved" (Johnson, *Diaries, Prayers, and Annals*, 383–84). See also *Letters* 12:339 and "Boswell's Life of Johnson" ([1832], *Essays* 3:121): Despite vain scruples and ruined faith, how to go "forward . . . 'in a world where there is much to be done, and little to be known': this is what Samuel Johnson, by act and word, taught his Nation."

156.32–33. **'Clear your mind of Cant!'**: From a conversation in 1783 in which Johnson said to Boswell, "My dear friend, clear your *mind* of cant. You may *talk* as other people do: you may say to a man, 'Sir, I am your most humble servant.' You are *not* his most humble servant. . . . You tell a man, 'I am sorry you had such bad weather the last day of your journey, and were so much wet.' You don't care six-pence whether he was wet or dry. You may *talk* in this manner; it is a mode of talking in Society: but don't *think* foolishly" (Boswell, *Life of Johnson*, 1235). Compare *Essays* 3:125–26, and *Emerson and Carlyle*, 428.

157.8. **buckram style**: Buckram is a coarse linen stiffened with glue to give shape to garments. Rogues in "buckrom suits" attacked Falstaff (*1 Henry IV*, 2.4.193). Here "buckram" suggests the stiffness and rigidity of Johnson's style.

157.15. **his *Dictionary***: Though English dictionaries in some form existed in the Middle Ages, one of the first serious attempts at a comprehensive inventory of the English language was Nathan Bailey's *Universal Etymological English Dictionary* (1721), followed by his *Dictionarium Britannicum* (1730), both of which Johnson's *Dictionary* replaced to become the model of English lexicography for a hundred years after its publication in 1755. As Johnson noted in his Preface, when he began his work he found the English language "copious without order, and energetick without rules." He set out to remedy this by doing single-handedly for the English language what the Academies of France and Italy had done for their own languages. Despite this triumph, Johnson modestly defined *lexicographer* as "a writer of dictionaries; a harmless drudge, that busies himself in tracing the original, and detailing the signification of words" (*Dictionary*, under "Lexicographer").

157.22. **poor Bozzy**: To Carlyle, Boswell was a "wine-bibber and gross liver; . . . he was vain, heedless, a babbler" as well as a "sycophant" and a "coxcomb" ("Boswell's Life of Johnson" [1832], *Essays* 3:69). Such estimates were shared by Macaulay (see Macaulay, "Samuel Johnson" [1856], *Miscellaneous Works* 7:98), and more recently by Lytton Strachey: "An idler, a lecher, a drunkard, and a snob. . . . If Boswell had been capable of retiring to the country and economizing we should never have heard of him" (*Portraits in Miniature*, 86, 95).

157.25. **foolish conceited Scotch Laird**: Boswell was the son of Alexander Boswell, the Laird of Auchinleck, an estate near Glasgow. *Laird*, the Scottish equivalent of *squire*, is defined by Carlyle in "Boswell's Life of Johnson" ([1832], *Essays* 3:70) as "the hungriest and vainest of all bipeds."

157.27–28. **genuine reverence for Excellence**: In spite of his obvious faults, Boswell was for Carlyle a "practical witness, or real *martyr*" to the everlasting truth of hero-worship. He attached himself to the impoverished Johnson when he could instead have courted many more prominent and wealthy individuals, and been the "envy of surrounding lickspittles" ("Boswell's Life of Johnson" [1832], *Essays* 3:74, 72).

157.31–32. **no man is a Hero to his valet-de-chambre**: The quotation is attributed to a variety of authors from Antigonus I, king of Sparta, to Montaigne and Goethe, and to two witty Frenchwomen, Mme. Cornuel and Mme. de Sévigné. Carlyle rejected the "mean doctrine" as having no application to the true hero; thus, "Milton was still a hero to the good Elwood" ("Schiller" [1831], *Essays* 2:168). Curiously, Thackeray, reviewing *The French Revolution* in the *Times*, August 3, 1837, contrasted Carlyle's work with that of Thiers whom he called "the *valet de chambre* of this history; he is too familiar with its dishabille . . . it can never be a hero to him."

157.36. *Grand-Monarque*: In 1680 the Council of Paris conferred "the title of *Great*" upon Louis XIV and decreed that it "should be used in all public records" (Voltaire, *Age of Louis XIV*, 126). Carlyle may have recalled, and certainly parallels, the point made by Macaulay in his 1832 review of Etienne Dumont's *Souvenir sur Mirabeau*, a book that Carlyle also read (*Letters* 9:14). Macaulay wrote: "No man is a hero to his valet; and all the world saw as much of Louis the Fourteenth as his valet could see." Yet Louis produced the powerful illusion of being "grand and august" (Macaulay, "Mirabeau" [1832], *Miscellaneous Works* 3:131, 132–33).

158.1. **forked radish**: "When 'a was naked, he was for all the world like a fork'd redish, with a head fantastically carv'd upon it with a knife" (*2 Henry IV*, 3.2.310–12). Compare *Sartor*, 1.9.49.

158.9–10. **waste chaos of Authorship by Trade**: "And thus must the rebellious 'Sam. Johnson' turn him to the Bookselling guild, and the wondrous chaos of 'Author by trade'" ("Boswell's Life of Johnson" [1832], *Essays* 3:103).

158.16–17. **'To the Spirit of Lies . . . he would in no wise strike his flag'**: Untraced.

158.17. **Brave old Samuel**: "Glory to our brave Samuel!" ("Boswell's Life of Johnson" [1832], *Essays* 3:110). "We have no Men of Letters now, but only Literary Gentlemen. Samuel Johnson was the last that ventured to appear in that former character, and support himself on his own legs, without any crutches . . . : rough old Samuel, the last of all the Romans!" ("Jean Paul Friedrich Richter" [1830], *Essays* 2:130).

158.17–18. *ultimus Romanorum*: "Last of the Romans." On the authority of Plutarch, Brutus' words over the corpse of Cassius at Philippi (*Lives*, 1213) that are recalled in *Julius Caesar*, 5.3.99–101: "The last of all the Romans, fare thee well! / It is impossible that ever Rome / Should breed thy fellow." In A.D. 25 Cremutius Cordus was arraigned on "the novel and till then unheard-of charge of publishing a history, eulogizing Brutus, and styling Cassius the last of the Romans" (Tacitus, *Annals*, 4.34). Carlyle also applied the tag to his father James, who was "among Scottish peasants what Samuel Johnson was among English authors" (*Reminiscences* 1:15).

158.22. 'the talent of Silence': Frequently attributed to Napoleon: "Ces Anglais ont un grand talent pour le silence." However, according to Leigh Hunt the phrase was applied by Mme. de Staël to the Earl of Liverpool (*Autobiography*, 210). Carlyle described Shelley as "one of those unfortunates . . . to whom 'the talent of *silence*' . . . has been denied" (*Mill, Sterling and Browning*, 292). Mazzini, reviewing *On Heroes* and *Sartor* in the *British and Foreign Quarterly Review* in 1844, noted that Carlyle preached "the merit of 'holding one's tongue'" to others but that he himself lacked the "'talent of silence'" (cited in Seigel, *Critical Heritage*, 252).

158.24–25. 'to consume his own smoke': "To consume your own choler, as some chimneys consume their own smoke . . . is a negative yet no slight virtue, nor one of the commonest in these times" (*Sartor*, 2.6.120). Perhaps an adaptation of Psalm 102:3, the phrase was popular with Carlyle: see also *Letters* 9:374, 12:49. The source may have been the advertisements for a patent stove invented by his friend Dr. Neil Arnott, to which he refers in *Reminiscences*, 133.

158.33. *hold his peace*: Exodus 14:14: "and ye shall hold your peace." See also "Boswell's Life of Johnson" ([1832], *Essays* 3:85): "*hold thy tongue* . . . till *some* meaning lie behind, to set it wagging."

159.6. French Philosophes: The eighteenth-century connotation being "free-thinker" rather than "philosopher." The name was applied to a group of French intellectuals in the late eighteenth century including the encyclopedists Denis Diderot (1713–1784), Jean d'Alembert (1717–1783), Claude Helvétius (1715–1771), Condorcet (1743–1794), and the Baron d'Holbach (1723–1789). They were characterized by skepticism in religion and a materialist outlook in philosophy.

159.17. Genlis: Comtesse Stéphanie Félicité de Genlis (1746–1830). Her *Mémoires inédits* (2:13–16) contain a full account of the incident Carlyle alludes to. She recalls that despite Rousseau's claimed aversion to publicity, he was piqued at the Théâtre Français, when having made sure he was noticed he was not applauded by the audience. Rousseau's vanity was widely recognized. Burke said of him, "He entertained no principle, either to influence his heart, or guide his undertanding, but vanity" (cited in Russell, *History of Western Philosophy*, 690). Coleridge described "the crazy ROUSSEAU" as "the Dreamer of lovesick Tales, and the Spinner of speculative Cobwebs; shy of light as the Mole, but as quick-eared too for every whisper of the public opinion; the Teacher of stoic *Pride* in his principles, yet the victim of morbid *Vanity* in his feelings and conduct!" (Coleridge, *The Friend* 1:1.132).

159.26–27. A man of some rank: The man was probably Jean Dusaulx (1728–1799), a dinner guest who was taken into Rousseau's kitchen by his host and invited to inspect the soup and stew. "Nothing but carrots, greens, and meat—no poison anywhere" (Josephson, *Jean-Jacques Rousseau*, 503). In 1798 Dusaulx published *De mes rapports avec J. J. Rousseau et de nôtre correspondance*, which contains numerous examples of odd behavior by the Swiss writer.

160.3–4. appeals to Mothers: In *Emile* (1762), Rousseau appeals to mothers to suckle their own children rather than supply them with wet nurses, and deplores the "denatured practice" that avoids it. "Since mothers, despising their first duty, have no longer wanted to feed their children, it has been necessary to confide them to mercenary women. . . . She who nurses another's child in place of her own is a bad mother. How will she be a good nurse?" (*Emile*, 44–45).

160.4. *Contrat-social*: In *Le Contrat social* (1762), Rousseau argues that natural society is based on a contract in which the individual surrenders his freedom for the restricted liberty of citizenship. Caroline Fox recalled Carlyle's lack of sympathy for Rousseau's work: "The Confessions are the only writings of his which I have read with any interest . . . though I can't say that it is a duty to lay open the Bluebeard chambers of the heart" (*Memories*, 107).

160.4. celebrations of Nature: In his *Discours sur l'origine de l'inégalité des hommes* (1755), Rousseau extols the state of nature as a golden age and advances the idea that savage life is natural and innocent, civilized existence artificial and corrupt. Before the *Contrat social*, "he wrote 'Essays on the Savage State'—that it was better to live there than in that state of society around him" (*History of Literature*, 200). While these views excited the derision of Voltaire, they had a profound effect on late eighteenth-century thought, on the Romantic movement, and on such explorers as Bougainville and Captain Cook. Compare 161.12–13 below and note.

160.11. **Persiflage**: Light raillery or banter. See "The Hero as Divinity" at 14.4 above and note.

160.17. **stealings of ribbons**: Rousseau stole "a little pink and silver ribbon" belonging to Mlle. Pontal and, when discovered, he falsely accused the young cook Marion of having given it to him. Rousseau describes the incident and his remorse over this "terrible deed." The desire to unburden his conscience "greatly contributed to my resolution of writing these *Confessions*" (*Confessions*, 2.86–88).

160.30. **Madame de Staël**: Anne Louise Germaine, Baronne de Staël-Holstein (1766–1817), the author of *Lettres sur les écrits et le caractère de J. J. Rousseau* (1788). She was the daughter of Jacques Necker, the French finance minister, and the former Suzanne Curchod, with whom Gibbon had once been in love (see note to "The Hero as King" below at 193.33–34). "A new young Demoiselle, one day to be famed as a Madame and De Staël, was romping about the knees of the Decline and Fall" (*French Revolution* 1:2.5.47).

160.31. **St. Pierre**: Jacques Henri Bernardin de St. Pierre (1737–1814), a follower of Rousseau and author of *Études de la Nature* (1784), *Paul et Virginie* (1788), and *La Chaumière Indienne* (1791). In *Paul et Virginie*, Carlyle wrote, "there rises melodiously, as it were, the wail of a moribund world: everywhere wholesome Nature in unequal conflict with diseased perfidious Art; cannot escape from it in the lowest hut, in the remotest island of the sea. Ruin and death must strike down the loved one; and, what is most significant of all, death even here not by necessity but by etiquette. What a world of prurient corruption lies visible in that super-sublime of modesty! Yet, on the whole, our good Saint-Pierre is musical, poetical though most morbid: we will call his Book the swan-song of old dying France" (*French Revolution* 1:2.8.60). Carlyle recommended the novel to David

Richardson in 1837 (*Letters* 9:374). His brother John had translated the book into English in 1824 (*Letters* 2:348).

160.32. 'Literature of Desperation': The phrase itself is from Goethe. On August 2, 1833, John Stuart Mill wrote to Carlyle promising discussion of various topics including Paris: "my notion of it is chiefly taken from its recent literature, which *is* exactly what Goethe called it, the literature of despair, 'die Litteratur der Verzweiflung'" (*Letters of Mill* 1:62). Carlyle also used the phrase to epitomize tendencies in French literature, especially in the work of George Sand. Of Geraldine Jewsbury, he wrote that she was seeking "some Paradise to be gained by battle; fancying George Sand and the 'literature of desperation' can help her thitherward" (Froude, *Life in London* 1:208). Carlyle associated Sand with the phenomenon he called "Phallus worship," the subject of an unpublished manuscript in the Beinecke Library at Yale University. In it he describes the "New Sand religion" as "an Egg of Eros . . . still albuminous, requiring to be *hatched*" (Kaplan, "'Phallus Worship,'" 22).

160.33-34. Look . . . even at a Walter Scott!: The qualification "even" signifies Carlyle's reservations about Scott, which are fully detailed in "Sir Walter Scott" ([1832], *Essays* 4:22-87). Carlyle dubbed Scott "the great *Restaurateur* of Europe," whose novels were like "a bout of champagne, claret, port or even ale drinking" that left readers neither wiser, holier, or stronger, merely amused (*Two Notebooks*, 71).

161.6-7. the world was not his friend: "The world is not thy friend, nor the world's law" (*Romeo and Juliet*, 5.1.72).

161.12-13. speculations on the miseries of civilised life: In his *Discours sur l'origine de l'inégalité des hommes* (1755), Rousseau holds that man is naturally good, and only made evil by institutions. The primitive state is superior to civilization, which through the institution of property has bred inequalities and also corrupted natural inclinations. Compare 160.4 above and note.

161.25. Vauxhall: Pleasure gardens and a place of fashionable entertainment. See "The Hero as Poet" at 70.18-19 above and note.

161.37-38. Ayrshire hut: Burns was born on January 25, 1759, in a clay-built cottage about two miles to the south of Ayr. "About a week afterwards, part of the frail dwelling, which his father had constructed with his own hands, gave way at midnight; and the infant poet and his mother were carried through the storm, to the shelter of a neighbouring hovel" (Lockhart, *Life of Burns*, 1-2).

162.4-5. **'which threw us all into tears'**: "We lived very poorly; I was a dextrous Ploughman for my years. . . . A Novel-Writer might perhaps have viewed these scenes with some satisfaction, but so did not I: my indignation yet boils at the recollection of the scoundrel tyrant's insolent, threatening epistles, which used to set us all in tears" (*Letters of Burns* 1:137). The scoundrel is the factor described in Burns's *The Twa Dogs: A Tale* (*Poems and Songs* 1:137-45, lines 93-100), and mentioned in Lockhart's *Life of Burns* (6) and "Varnhagen von Ense's Memoirs" ([1838], *Essays* 4:116). Burns's brother Gilbert said, "I doubt not but the hard labour and sorrow of this period of his life, was in a great measure the cause of that depression of spirits with which Robert was so often afflicted through his whole life afterwards" (Lockhart, *Life of Burns*, 17).

162.10. **Burns's Schoolmaster**: John Murdoch, who said in a letter dated February 22, 1799, "In this mean cottage, of which I myself was at times an inhabitant, I really believe there dwelt a larger portion of content than in any place in Europe" (Lockhart, *Life of Burns*, 14).

162.13. **'seven acres of nursery-ground'**: A farm called Mount Oliphant, two miles from the Brig o' Doon in Ayrshire, rented by Burns's father. Carlyle speculates, "Had this William Burns's small seven acres of nursery-ground anywise prospered, the boy Robert had been sent to school; had struggled forward, as so many weaker men do, to some university; come forth not as a rustic wonder, but as a regular well-trained intellectual workman, and changed the whole course of British Literature,—for it lay in him to have done this!" ("Burns" [1828], *Essays* 1:293; see also "Varnhagen von Ense's Memoirs" [1838], *Essays* 4:116).

162.24. **rustic special dialect**: Burns's native dialect was that of Ayrshire, but there are "few, if any, traces of this in his writings" (Craigie, *Primer of Burns*, 159). The language of Burns's writing is the general dialect of southern Scotland, and many of his best poems are often in "English sprinkled with Scots" (Daiches, *Robert Burns*, 37). Furthermore, the Scots of Burns's poems was not the exclusive language of Scottish rustics but was that spoken by "most eighteenth-century Scottish gentlefolk as well" (*Norton Anthology of English Literature* 2:90). The diction and other formal elements of Burns's Scots verse, especially in the Kilmarnock edition of 1786, were drawn from a native tradition established by Robert Henryson (1430–1506), William Dunbar (1465–1530), and Gavin Douglas (1474–1522), which had been preserved and revived by Burns's predecessors, especially Allan Ramsay (1686–1758) and Robert Fergusson (1750–1774). For Carlyle's earlier opinion that Burns's songs were "part of the mother-tongue, not of Scotland only but of Britain," see "Burns" (1828), *Essays* 1:287.

162.36. **Harz-rock**: The Harz mountains range between the Elbe and Weser rivers. Pagan tradition associates the mountains with many romantic legends that have been incorporated into German literature, for example the Walpurgis Night story that centers on Brocken, the highest peak in the Harz mountains, and is featured in Goethe's *Faust*. Carlyle described the myths of the creation of the Teutons in his 1838 lecture series, how the Saxons were formed "out of the Saxa or rock of the Hartz Mountains" (*History of Literature*, 148).

162.37. **wells of living softness**: "While the Shakspeares and Miltons roll on like mighty rivers through the country of Thought, . . . this little Valclusa Fountain will also arrest our eye: for this also is of Nature's own and most cunning workmanship, bursts from the depths of the earth, with a full gushing current, into the light of day; and often will the traveller turn aside to drink of its clear waters, and muse among its rocks and pines!" ("Burns" [1832], *Essays* 1:318).

163.3–4. **Norse Thor, the Peasant-god**: Next to Odin, the greatest god in the Teutonic pantheon (see note to "The Hero as Divinity" at 17.15 above). Carlyle also compares Burns to Thor in *Latter-Day Pamphlets*: "And so, like Apollo taken for a Neatherd, . . . this new Norse Thor had to put-up with what was going; to gauge ale, and be thankful; pouring *his* celestial sunlight through Scottish Song-writing,— the narrowest chink ever offered to a Thundergod before!" (3.119), and in *Frederick*: "Robert Burns, remarkable modern Thor, a Peasant-god of these sunk ages, with a touch of melodious *runes* in him . . . , was raised on frugal oatmeal" (1:4.8.395). See also the note at 163.31 below, and see "The Hero as Priest" at 110.25 above, where Luther is pictured as "a Christian Odin,—a right Thor."

163.5. Burns's Brother Gilbert: Carlyle met Gilbert Burns in May 1821 at Haddington (*Letters* 1:363), and had many other connections with the family. His father knew Burns as a neighbor, and Carlyle knew Burns's sons.

163.7. a fellow of infinite frolic: Perhaps an echo of Hamlet's remark about Yorick: "a fellow of infinite jest" (*Hamlet*, 5.1.184–85).

163.10. 'fond gaillard': Used by the Marquis de Mirabeau in describing his son. "Gabriel Honoré has acquitted himself so well in Paris, turning the great people round his thumb, with that *'fond gaillard,* basis of gaiety,' with that *'terrible don de la familiarité'*; with those ways he has" ("Mirabeau" [1837], *Essays* 3:447). Compare 164.13 below.

163.16. 'dew-drops from his mane': "And like [a] dewdrop from the lion's mane, / Be shook to air" (*Troilus and Cressida*, 3.3.223–24).

163.16–17. laughs at the shaking of the spear: Job 41:29: "Darts are counted as stubble; he laugheth at the shaking of a spear." The reference in Job is to Leviathan, not, as Carlyle has it, to the "swift-bounding horse." See "The Hero as Prophet" at 43.14–16 above and note.

163.20–21. most gifted British soul: In "Boswell's Life of Johnson" ([1832], *Essays* 3:92), Carlyle describes Burns as the "noblest and ablest Man in all the British lands," who instead of "swaying the royal sceptre" was "gauging ale-tubs in the little burgh of Dumfries!" See also "Varnhagen von Ense's Memoirs" (1838), *Essays* 4:116–17. For Tennyson's recollection of this opinion of Carlyle's, see Hallam Tennyson, *Memoir* 1:279.

163.24. Professor Stewart: Dugald Stewart (1753–1828), Professor of Moral Philosophy at Edinburgh University from 1785 to 1820. He was one of the first to recognize Burns's genius and to seek his acquaintance. "From his conversation," wrote Stewart, "I should have pronounced him to be fitted to excel in whatever walk of ambition he had chosen to exert his abilities" (quoted in "Burns" [1828], *Essays* 1:277).

163.31. Witty duchesses: The Duchess of Gordon was the leader of Edinburgh society at the time of Burns's visit. Another duchess who took note of Burns was the Duchess of Atholl. "No 'politer' man was to be found in Britain than the rustic Robert Burns: high duchesses were captivated with the chivalrous ways of the man; recognised that here was the true chivalry, and divine nobleness of bearing,—as indeed they well might, now when the Peasant God and Norse Thor had come down among them again!" (*Pamphlets*, 5.197). Compare "The Hero as Poet" at 72.36–37 above.

163.33. Mr. Lockhart: John Gibson Lockhart (1794–1854), son-in-law of Sir Walter Scott, biographer, and editor of the *Quarterly Review* from 1825 to 1853. His *Life of Robert Burns* was reviewed in 1828 by Carlyle for the *Edinburgh Review* (*Essays* 1:258–318).

163.38. last year: 1839. In the summer of that year, Carlyle took his holiday in Scotland where his encounter with the old gentleman may have taken place. In a letter from Ayr, written August 18, Carlyle describes a visit to "Burns monument birthplace &c" and records his intention to return, "if it were only to get a little more speech with the ploughman who shows the monument.—who is a great philosoph[er] and deals in figurative language—" (*Letters* 11:170).

164.13. what the old Marquis calls a *fond gaillard*: See 163.10 above.

164.16. power of true *insight*: "Alone of all men there [in the National Assembly], Mirabeau may begin to discern clearly whither all this is tending" (*French Revolution* 2:1.2.6).

164.23. National Assemblies: The States General, summoned in 1789 by Louis XVI, assumed the name of "National Assembly." Mirabeau soon became one of its leading figures.

164.24. smuggling schooners: A brig, suspected of smuggling, got into shallow water in the Solway in 1792. Gaugers reinforced by dragoons waded out to the ship. Burns, sword in hand, was the first to board her (Lockhart, *Life of Burns*, 309–11).

164.27. Ushers de Brézé: Marquis de Brézé, Grand Master of Ceremonies, was sent by Louis XVI to dissolve the National Assembly in June 1789. He was confronted by Mirabeau, who told him, "'Go, Monsieur, tell those who sent you that we are here by the will of the People, and that nothing but the force of bayonets shall send us hence!' And poor De Brézé shivers forth" (*French Revolution* 1:5.2.165).

164.30. 'You are to work, not think': Burns's sympathies with the French Revolution drew the notice of his official superiors and he was cautioned "that it was his business to act, not to think" (Lockhart, *Life of Burns*, 321).

165.3-4. Strength is mournfully denied its arena: A quotation from the "Letter to My Friends: Instead of Preface" of Richter's *Life of Quintus Fixlein*, which Carlyle translated in 1827. Man "has not always the force, like Rugendas, in the midst of the Battle to compose Battle-pieces. . . . Still oftener is Strength denied its Arena" (*German Romance* 2:195).

165.25-26. sits at the tables of grandees: After the publication of his *Discourses* had brought him fame, Rousseau was entertained everywhere but could hardly make a living and was forced to copy music. In the *Confessions*, Rousseau complains that wealthy patrons "by trying to spare my purse, . . . succeeded in ruining me." They did not realize, he said, that during his visits, "I was not working also; that my housekeeping and rent, my washing and clothes were no less expensive, that I had to spend twice as much on my barber, and that it cost me rather more to live" with these well meaning patrons "than at home" (10.477).

166.11. visit to Edinburgh: "By much the most striking incident in Burns's Life is his journey to Edinburgh." By the great he was "treated in the customary fashion; entertained at their tables and dismissed." Despite some improvements derived from his visit, Carlyle considers Burns to have been poorer after visiting Edinburgh, "for his heart is now maddened . . . with the fever of worldly Ambition; and through long years the disease will rack him with unprofitable sufferings, and weaken his strength for all true and nobler aims" ("Burns" [1828], *Essays* 1:293, 301).

166.17. Regiment La Fère: The regiment in which Napoleon was appointed sub-lieutenant in 1785. See *French Revolution* 2:2.2.77-78. Compare "The Hero as King" at 206.21 below and note.

166.22. cynosure of all eyes: "The Cynosure of neighbouring eyes" (Milton, *L'Allegro*, line 80). "Luther himself, in order that he might become the cynosure of all eyes, played on the harp like another Orpheus" (Michelet, *Life of Luther*, 135, citing Johannes Cochlaeus, the Catholic biographer, on Luther's journey to Worms).

166.29. 'rank is but the guinea-stamp': "The rank is but the guinea's stamp, / The Man's the gowd [gold] for a' that" (Burns's *Song—For a' that and a' that, Poems and Songs* 2:762-63, lines 7-8).

166.36-37. as I have observed elsewhere, these Lion-hunters were the ruin and death of Burns: "These men . . . were proximately the means of his ruin. Not that they meant him any ill. . . . But they wasted his precious time and his precious talent; they disturbed his composure, broke down his returning habits of temperance and assiduous contented exertion. Their pampering was baneful to him; their cruelty, which soon followed, was equally baneful" ("Burns" [1828], *Essays* 1:303). According to Caroline Fox, Carlyle told his audience that Burns "could not long stand this perpetual lionizing unblighted; it broke him up in every sense, and he died" (*Memories*, 108).

167.6-7. nor no hatred to him: Joseph Neuberg queried Carlyle regarding this passage in his letter of March 20, 1852 (see Note on the Text, pp. xcviii–xcix, and notes to "The Hero as Divinity" at 8.17, 19.1–2, 30.26, 31.18, and 32.12 above): "*page 315.* 'it was out of no sympathy with him, *nor no hatred* to him.'—I don't quite apprehend the drift of that *double negative.* . . . I suppose the aim is to indicate a feeling of *mere indifference* towards him?" Carlyle replied on May 31, "p. 315 (sympathy-hatred). 'nor no hatred' should be 'nor any hatred';—meaning complete indifference or impartiality." However Carlyle made no revision here in the 1852 Fourth Edition or later editions.

167.9. Richter says, in the Island of Sumatra: Carlyle misquotes his own translation of Richter's review of Mme. de Staël's *Allemagne* in *Fraser's Magazine* in 1830: "From of old our learned lights have been by the French, not adored like light-stars, but stuck into like light-chafers, as people carry those of Surinam, spitted through, for lighting of roads" (*Essays* 1:481). Describing his lecturing experience in May 1840, Carlyle used the same image: "Four times spitted on the spear's point like a Surinam *fire-fly* to give light to the fashionable classes: this is enough of times!" (*Letters* 12:141). Caroline Fox recalled the words Carlyle used in his lecture as: "Amusement they [the great] must have, it seems, at any expense, though one would have thought they were sufficiently amused in the common way; but no, they were like the Indians we read of whose grandees ride in their palanquins at night, and are not content with torches carried before them, but must have instead fireflies stuck at the end of spears" (*Memories*, 108).

NOTES TO LECTURE VI. THE HERO AS KING.

Sources: Carlyle's literary interest in the Puritans began as early as 1822 when he planned a study of the principal figures of the civil war, which he did not carry out. His interest in the subject quickened at the time of his lecture series, culminating in the publication in 1845 of his edition of *Oliver Cromwell's Letters and Speeches*. His letters and journals during this period reveal his preoccupation with the subject matter of his final lecture; he is in constant pursuit of books and information.

For example, on February 27, 1839, he asked John Forster if among his books he had "a Narrative of Jenny Geddes's 'Flinging of the Stool' at Edin*r* on the 23*d* of July 1637" (*Letters* 11:36). In May 1840 Carlyle referred to her obliquely in his fourth lecture on heroes (see note to "The Hero as Priest" at 125.3 above). In October 1840 he wrote to John Lockhart, "Perhaps you can tell me something about *Jenny Geddes!*" (*Letters* 12:300). By then Carlyle had derived some details from James Kirkton's *The Secret and True History of the Church of Scotland . . . to the Year 1678* (1817), but was still seeking "to no purpose for any glimmering of light about Jenny" (*Letters* 12:300). In December 1840 he inquired of David Aitken what was "known about Jenny Geddes and her performance in St. Giles's that summer Sunday of 1637?" (*Letters* 12:352). Under such persistent coaxing, the picture of Jenny Geddes finally emerged in *Cromwell* 1:96, where Carlyle acknowledged the bibliographical help of David Laing. See also K. J. Fielding, "Carlyle and Cromwell," 56–58, and the note to "The Hero as Priest" at 125.3.

Among Carlyle's earliest sources of information about the period was Clarendon's *History of the Rebellion and Civil War in England . . .* (1702), which he had read in the 1820s. Other early source materials included: Mark Napier's *Montrose and the Covenanters* (1838), William Sime's *History of the Covenanters in Scotland* (1830), and Daniel Neal's *History of the Puritans or Protestant Non-Conformists . . .* (1732–38), which he borrowed from F. D. Maurice (*Letters* 12:7). By February 1839 he had read James Heath's *A Brief Chronicle of the late intestine wars in the Three*

Kingdoms . . . (1663), Gilbert Burnet's *History of His Own Time* (1724), and Bulstrode Whitelocke's *Memorials of the English affairs; . . . Charles the First to Charles the Second* (1732) (*Letters* 11:36).

His main aim in the final lecture of 1840 was to produce a fair portrait of Cromwell. But by September of that year he told Emerson he was still "head and ears in *Cromwellean* Books; studying, for perhaps the fourth time in my life, to see if it be possible to get any credible face-to-face acquaintance with our English Puritan period" (*Letters* 12:267). By December "Poor Oliver" still lay "like grains of gold dust scattered under continents of cinders and rubbish" (*Letters* 12:345). The image persisted in Carlyle's 1845 description of the thousands of "unread Pamphlets of the Civil War in the British Museum alone. . . . Under such waste lumber-mountains, the wreck and dead ashes of some six unbelieving genera-tions, does the Age of Cromwell and his Puritans lie hidden from us" (*Cromwell* 1:2–3). Nevertheless he persevered, groping "in the dark vacuity of Baxters, Neales; thankful for here a glimpse and the[re] a glimpse" of Cromwell and his background (*Letters* 12:267). In Septem-ber 1840 he wrote John Forster that he planned to "break in upon you soon; and bring away a new great stock of Puritan books" including Mark Noble's *Memoirs of the Protectorate—House of Cromwell* (1784) and Robert Baillie's *Letters and Journals* (1775) (*Letters* 12:261). A week later he received a "magnificent Hamper of books" from Forster, but Carlyle still sought, from the private libraries of his friends, John Rushworth's *Historical Collections* (1659–1701), *A Collection of the State Papers of John Thurloe* (1742), and volumes 11–13 of *The Parliamentary or Constitutional History of England* (1753), among others (*Letters* 12:269–70). Such books were available to him in the British Museum, but he found it disagreeable to be confined to reading them there.

For the picture of Napoleon, Carlyle was put to less trouble. His earlier studies for *The French Revolution* stood him in good stead, and to these he added, at least, Louis Antoine Fauvelet de Bourrienne's *Mémoires sur Napoleon* (1831), the Count de Las Cases's *Mémorial de Sainte-Hélène* (1823), and Mme. de Staël's *Considérations sur les Principaux Événemens de la Révolution Françoise* (1820).

169.9–10. **Rex, Regulator:** Both *rex* and *regulator* are related to the Latin verb *rego*, "to mark out, direct, guide, rule, govern."

169.10. *Könning:* The derivation, though a favorite of Carlyle's, is false. See "The Hero as Divinity" at 12.13 above and note.

169.15. **As Burke said**: Burke made a number of speeches in Parliament on the jury system and said that "trial by Jury" was "one of the greatest excellencies our constitution produced" (Burke, *Writings and Speeches* 2:473). It was probably Burke whom Lord Brougham had in mind in stating "he was guilty of no error . . . who once said, that . . . the whole machinery of the State, . . . and its varied workings, ended in simply bringing twelve good men into a box" (Hansard, *Parliamentary Debates* 18 [Jan. 29–Apr. 22, 1828]: 131). Carlyle makes the same allusion in "Model Prisons," *Pamphlets*, 2.79–80.

169.24. **Reform Bills**: Carlyle is referring to the two bills of 1831 that failed to win parliamentary approval but whose provisions were largely incorporated into the successful Reform Bill of 1832. Its general effect was to provide greater representative government, the destruction of "rotten boroughs," and the enlargement of the franchise in favor of the middle class.

170.17. **'measure by a scale of perfection . . .'**: Carlyle is quoting Schiller's *Über die Aesthetische Erziehung des Menschen (On the Aesthetic Education of Man)*, which argues that artists should be free "from the querulous spirit of enthusiasm that measures by the scale of perfection the meagre product of reality" (Carlyle's translation, "State of German Literature" [1827], *Essays* 1:58).

170.21–30. **No bricklayer . . . welter of ruin!**: Carlyle used this image in his review of W. Taylor's *Historic Survey of German Poetry* (1830). Taylor's work in its present state, he said, "nothing but a continued suspension of the laws of gravity can keep from rushing ere long into a chaos of stone and dust" ("Historic Survey of German Poetry" [1831], *Essays* 2:369).

170.26. **plummet and level**: See "The Hero as Priest" at 109.16 above and note.

170.28. **Law of Gravitation**: A favorite Carlylean image for immutable laws in contrast to changing human fashions.

171.8. **'Divine right of Kings'**: The doctrine that sovereigns are the representatives of God on earth and derive their authority directly from Him. The motto "Christo auspice regno" (I rule by Christ's authority), on a coin minted in 1641 and 1642, reflects Charles I's reliance on this belief. The doctrine was dealt a staggering blow by the execution of Charles I and was finally put to rest by the execution of Louis XVI by the revolutionary guillotine. For Carlyle's view of divine right, see *Two Notebooks*, 185, and Fox, *Memories*, 110.

171.8-9. moulders . . . in the Public Libraries: During his researches for his edition of *Oliver Cromwell's Letters and Speeches*, Carlyle noted between 20,000 and 50,000 "unread Pamphlets of the Civil War in the British Museum alone," huge "piles of mouldering wreck" under which Cromwell and his Puritans lay buried (*Cromwell* 1:2). See note on Sources above, p. 362.

171.25. steamengine: A popular epithet with Carlyle for mechanical tendencies in thought and society. See "The Hero as Man of Letters" at 148.28 above and note.

172.9-10. the *King* is head of the *Church*: The Act of Supremacy passed by Parliament in 1535, following Henry VIII's break with the Papacy over the question of divorce, formally separated the Church of England from the Roman Catholic Church and made the English sovereign its supreme head.

172.18-21. the beginning of it was . . . the Reformation of Luther: That the Reformation paved the way for the French Revolution is a point frequently made by Carlyle, for example in *Pamphlets*, 8.306: "For Luther and Protestantism Proper having, so to speak, withdrawn from the battlefield, as entities whose work was done, there then appeared on it Jean Jacques and French Sansculottism." See "The Hero as Priest" at 116.8 above and note.

172.33. Chimera: A monster in Greek mythology with a lion's head, a goat's body, and a dragon's tail. Chimera was the offspring of Typhon and Echidna.

172.35. Camille Desmoulins: (1760-1794). Onetime secretary general to the Ministry of Justice under Danton, Desmoulins's pamphlets, such as "La Philosophie du peuple français" (1788) and "La France libre" (1789), heralded the Revolution. After factional disputes, he perished alongside Danton on the guillotine on April 5, 1794. "But see Camille Desmoulins, from the Café de Foy, rushing out, sibylline in face; his hair streaming, in each hand a pistol! He

springs to a table: the Police satellites are eyeing him. . . . To arms!—
'To arms!' yell responsive the innumerable voices" (*French Revolution*
1:5.4.175). Desmoulins, said Carlyle, "has a place of his own in the
history of the Revolution; there are not many notabler persons in it
than he. . . . 'A man born to write verses'; but whom Destiny directed
to overthrow Bastilles, and go to the guillotine for doing that" ("History of the French Revolution" [1837], *Essays* 4:12).

173.14. **Bedlam:** Popular name of the first asylum for the insane in
England. Built in 1247 as a priory, it first took in mental patients in
1463. *Bedlam* is a corruption of *Bethlehem* in the hospital's original
name, St. Mary of Bethlehem, which was later changed to Bethlem
Royal Hospital.

173.17. **Three Days of July, 1830:** The almost bloodless revolution
that substituted Louis Philippe for Charles X on the French throne.

173.24. **Poor Niebuhr:** Barthold Georg Niebuhr (1776–1831), German historian and Prussian ambassador to the Vatican from 1816 to
1823. The fact alluded to is recorded in Bunsen's *Life and Letters of
Niebuhr*, 486–87. Carlyle read Niebuhr's *Römische Geschichte* (1811–
12) in preparation for his 1838 lecture series, but confessed, "*Niebuhr*
. . . altogether disappoints me: vain jargon of *cognoscente* scholarcraft . . .
and for result, darkness visible" (*Letters* 10:57–58).

173.28. **Racine's:** Jean Baptiste Racine (1639–1699), French writer
of classical tragedies in the reign of Louis XIV. After losing the king's
favor in 1698, Racine tried, through the good offices of Mme. de
Maintenon, to clear himself of charges of Jansenism, but his appeals
were totally ignored. The royal snub is said to have hastened his
death. "The melodious, too soft-strung Racine, when his King turned
his back on him, emitted one meek wail, and submissively—died"
("The Diamond Necklace" [1837], *Essays* 3:345).

174.25. **pole-star:** Polaris, the North Star.

174.34–35. **wise great men being impossible, . . . foolish small
men would suffice:** Perhaps Carlyle's recollection of J. S. Mill's 1832
essay "On Genius" in the *Monthly Repository*, in which Mill wondered
whether modernity might be "supplying our deficiency of giants by

the united efforts of a constantly increasing multitude of dwarfs" (*Autobiography and Literary Essays*, 330).

175.10–14. **'Bending before men'** . . . **a 'revelation in the Flesh':** "There is but one Temple in the World; and that is the Body of Man. . . . Bending before men is a reverence done to this Revelation in the Flesh" (Novalis, *Schriften* 2:126, also quoted by Carlyle in "Novalis" ([1829], *Essays* 2:39). See note to "The Hero as Divinity" at 11.2–6 above.

176.13–14. **wars of Red and White Roses:** The dynastic struggle between the rival houses of York and Lancaster, 1455–85. Its name is derived from the rose emblems of the two houses, red for Lancaster, white for York. The conflict began with Lancastrian King Henry VI's contention against Richard Plantagenet and ended on Bosworth field with the death of the Yorkist Richard III at the hands of Henry Tudor, the Earl of Richmond.

176.14. **Simon de Montfort:** (1200?–1265), Earl of Leicester. After King Henry III rejected the Provisions of Oxford, which had given the medieval barons a share of government, Simon de Montfort took to the battlefield and captured the king in 1264. The consequence was the establishment of an assembly, a forerunner of Parliament, to assist the King's Council.

176.15. **war of the Puritans:** Collectively the encounters between Cavaliers and Roundheads during the Great Rebellion (1642–49), which opened with the militarily indecisive battle at Edge Hill. This was followed by major victories by Cromwell's Ironsides at Marston Moor (July 2, 1644) and Naseby (June 14, 1645).

176.24. **Poor Laud:** See note at 177.34 below.

177.3. **frightfully avenged on him:** Laud was executed by Parliament in 1645. "Rebellion's vengeful talons seize on Laud" (Samuel Johnson's "The Vanity of Human Wishes," line 168).

177.29. **Funeral Games:** Of the four great Panhellenic festivals, both the Isthmian and the Nemean were said to have originated in funeral games. The games included athletic contests, horse races, and competitions in music and poetry.

177.34. Laud dedicating that St. Catherine Creed's Church: William Laud (1573–1645), Archbishop of Canterbury, a strong supporter of Charles I and the High Church party. The character of the services held by Laud as Bishop of London in St. Catherine Creed's Church in Leadenhall Street, at its consecration in 1631, later formed one of the charges against him at his trial. A strong believer in the "'external worship of God,'" Laud used the Court of High Commission to enforce such practices as the wearing of surplices, bowing at the name of Jesus, and kneeling to receive the sacraments (Williams, *Documentary History of England*, 55). Carlyle mocks Laud's ceremonial preferences in *Cromwell* 1:43.

In his letter to Carlyle on March 20, 1852 (see Note on the Text, pp. xcviii–xcix, and notes to "The Hero as Divinity" at 8.17, 19.1–2, 30.26, 31.18, and 32.12 above), Joseph Neuberg asked: *"page 333. 'St Catherine Creed's Church' Creed*, I suppose, is here used as a *name*: *Mrs* Cath. Creed her Church; *not* the Church of Catherine's *faith*?" Carlyle replied in his letter of May 31: "p. 333. St Catherine Creed (oftener now written *Crea*) Church, the very walls that Laud dedicated in 1630, still stands in Leadenhall Street: the Catherine is undoubtedly the Egyptian Phantasm *Saint*; as to *Creed* or *Crea* (Neal uses the former word) opinions are at variance, and equal only to a guess. The Church, before Laud's time, had been built on an extinct Priory of Saint *Saviour*: 'Crea,' says one is the old French pronounciation of *Christ* (which I do not the least believe with confidence); I *cd* rather guess some unusually conspicuous *Creed* had been painted on Priory or Church; and so had been taken to distinguish it from St Catherine Coleman (Coleman *Street*) which is another Church.—An account of Laud's ceremony at Creed Church one of the strangest ever seen out of Drury Lane is in Neal's *Histy of the Puritans* (4 *vo* London 1754) i. 549;—and has been duly laughed at by [*indecipherable*] in his *History*."

178.23. Rochesters: John Wilmot (1647–1680), Earl of Rochester, courtier and poet. Author of the lines written on the bedchamber door of Charles II: "We have a pritty witty King / Whose word no man relies on, / Who never said a foolish thing / Nor ever did a wise one" (see Fraser, *King Charles II*, 340; Farley-Hills, *Rochester: The Critical Heritage*, 256). Compare Macaulay ("Milton" [1825], *Essays* 1:172), who makes the same point.

178.27. hung on gibbets: A reference to events such as those of January 30, 1661, when, twelve years after the execution of Charles I, the coffin reputedly containing the embalmed carcass of Cromwell was exhumed and taken to Tyburn. There the remains were decapitated and the body publicly hanged and later buried beneath the gallows. The head was mounted on a pole and displayed above Westminster Hall to be execrated by a jeering mob. Other Puritan leaders were treated in the same way. Carlyle's reference is also to the injustices done to Cromwell's reputation (see *Letters* 12:264).

178.30. *Habeas-Corpus*: A writ or court order requiring the prompt production of a person detained in custody, to ascertain the legality of the arrest. Its original intent was to liberate those illegally detained and to act as a protection against arbitary imprisonment. The earliest use of the writ as a constitutional remedy against the tyranny of the crown was in the sixteenth century. In 1641 when the Long Parliament abolished the Star Chamber (see note to "The Hero as Priest" at 123.13 above), it strengthened the writ of habeas corpus. The Habeas Corpus Act was passed by Parliament in 1679. It was, according to Dr. Johnson, "the single advantage which our government has over that of other countries" (Boswell, *Life of Johnson*, 404). See "The Hero as Priest" at 125.6 above and note.

178.39. Eliot: Sir John Eliot (1592–1632). For his part in drawing up the Remonstrance and Petition of Right, he was arrested in 1629 for conspiracy against the king. He died in the Tower of London in 1632.

178.39. Hampden: John Hampden (1592–1643), a member of the anti-Royalist faction in the House of Commons where he consistently opposed the king's efforts to usurp the prerogatives of Parliament. Hampden was brought to trial in 1637 for refusing to pay ship money, and he was one of the five Parliamentary leaders the king tried to arrest and imprison in January 1642, an act that precipitated the civil war. Hampden was mortally wounded at the battle of Chalgrove Field near Oxford, ending, according to Macaulay, Parliament's hopes of "a victory as spotless as their cause" (Macaulay, "Hallam's Constitutional History" [1828], *Essays* 1:44). Hampden's name is commonly associated with resistance to oppression, as in Gray's *Elegy:* "Some village-Hampden, that with dauntless breast / The little Tyrant of his fields withstood" (lines 57–58).

179.1. Pym: John Pym (1584–1643) played a prominent role in the Petition of Right, the impeachment of Strafford, and other events in the struggle between king and Parliament. Pym, with Hampden, was one of the five members of the Commons impeached for treason by Charles I in 1642. Charles himself at the head of 500 men attempted to arrest Pym and his colleagues, only to find that all his "birds" had flown. An unpublished manuscript portrait of Pym by Carlyle is in the Forster Collection of the Victoria and Albert Museum. See Trela, "Carlyle's Pen Portrait of John Pym."

179.1. Ludlow: Edmund Ludlow (1617–1692), Puritan general and regicide. In April 1822, Carlyle was reading "the third volume of Clarendon" and "the whole of Ludlow's Memoirs," first published 1698–99 (*Two Notebooks*, 19).

179.1. Hutchinson: John Hutchinson (1615–1664), a fiercely independent member of the Republican party in the Long Parliament. In religion he was sympathetic to the Independents, in politics he sided with the Army. He was one of those who signed the death warrant for Charles I. The first two British editions of *On Heroes* gave the name as "Hutcheson" here and at 202.27 below. See textual apparatus.

179.1. Vane: Sir Henry Vane (1613–1662), one of the Republican trio who came into later conflict with Cromwell. At the dismissal of the Rump Parliament, Cromwell is reported to have said: "'Oh, Sir Harry Vane,' thou with thy subtle casuistries and abstruse hair-splittings, thou art other than a good one, I think! 'The Lord deliver me from thee, Sir Harry Vane!'" (*Cromwell* 3:36). By way of contrast, Macaulay says, "the King would scarce have been content with praying that the Lord would deliver him from Vane" (Macaulay, "Hallam's Constitutional History" [1828], *Essays* 1:44).

179.2. Conscript Fathers: The Roman Senate were called *patres conscripti*, "enlisted fathers." The phrase may originally have been *patres et conscripti*, referring to a conjunction of patrician members and other members "enrolled" from the plebeians or outside communities.

179.8. no hearty apologist: By the time Carlyle gave this lecture, he had already determined to become Cromwell's "hearty apologist" himself (but see note at 203.8–9 below). In January 1839 he wrote: "I have my face turned partly towards Oliver Cromwell and the

Covenant time in England and Scotland" (*Letters* 11:4), and five months after the lecture, in October 1840, he was busy with "Puritanisms and Cromwelleana" (*Letters* 12:287). The outcome was his publication in 1845 of *Oliver Cromwell's Letters and Speeches*. His interest in Cromwell, however, goes back to 1821–22, when he had proposed writing an essay on the civil wars.

179.11. *Tartufe*: A celebrated literary hypocrite in Moliere's *Le Tartuffe, ou l'Imposteur* (1669). In the British Third Edition of *On Heroes* (1846), as well as in the American edition of the same date, Moliere's spelling was changed to *Tartufe*, apparently by Carlyle. See Discussion of Editorial Decisions and textual apparatus.

179.14. **contrasts with Washington**: George Washington (1732–1799), first president of the United States. An exception to the general rule offered here by Carlyle is Macaulay's 1825 "Essay on Milton" in which he says Cromwell "will not lose by comparison with Washington" (Macaulay, *Essays* 1:182).

179.17–18. **view of Cromwell . . . a century like the Eighteenth**: With a few exceptions, such as Bulstrode Whitelocke and Paul de Rapin de Thoyras, popular historians of the eighteenth century "followed the Royalist party line, whether the fabrications of James Heath's *Flagellum* (1663) or the rolling periods of the first Earl of Clarendon's *History of the Rebellion* (1702)" (Ashley, *Greatness of Cromwell*, 12). Clarendon called Cromwell "the greatest dissembler living" (Clarendon, *History of the Rebellion* 4:305). No man ever "brought to pass what he desired more wickedly" (*History of the Rebellion* 6:91), and posterity would judge him as a "brave bad man" (*History of the Rebellion* 6:97). See also David Hume, *History of England*, chapter 61.

179.38. **euphuisms**: Euphuism is an ornate style, frequently alliterative, antithetical, and characterized by the use of elaborate tropes. The term is derived from John Lyly's *Euphues, the anatomy of wyt* (1578) and *Euphues and his England* (1580). Carlyle alludes to euphuism in "Signs of the Times" ([1829], *Essays* 2:75). In the Library Edition (1870), the word was changed to "euphemism" here and at 180.12, 180.14, and 187.1 below. See textual apparatus.

179.39. **Ship-monies**: A traditional tax levied on seaports and trading towns to maintain the fleet, it was extended by Charles I to all counties in 1634 and 1635, which were thus taxed without parliamentary consent. The new tax was resisted by many leading figures in the Parliamentary party (see *Cromwell* 1:74–75).

179.39. *Monarchies of Man*: A treatise written by Sir John Eliot during his incarceration in the Tower. It suggests that monarchy is the best form of government.

180.6. 'seventhly and lastly': Compare Carlyle's journal entry from the winter of 1840 (Froude, *Life in London* 1:199), where he employs the phrase to convey the tedium of working through documents and tracts of the Puritan Commonwealth: "One dreadful circumstance is that the books . . . one has to read, are of a dulness to threaten locked jaw. I never read such jumbling, drowsy, endless stupidities. Seventhly and lastly!"

180.11. *Baresark*: I.e., berserker. Carlyle also calls Cromwell "a great amorphous semi-articulate *Baresark*" in an 1840 letter to Emerson (*Letters* 12:267). Carlyle's unusual spelling implies the etymological assumption he follows in *History of Literature* (126), that "Berserker" means "bare spirit." The Icelandic term *ber-serkur* actually means "bear-shirted" or "clad in a bear skin" and was applied to warriors clad in "bear-sarks or shirts" (*Njal's Saga*, 222n; *Larousse World Mythology*, 371). In some Germanic tribes berserkers formed a special warrior class whose powers, which made them ecstatic in battle, were supposedly bestowed by Odin and may have involved the use of hallucinatory mushrooms. Their reputed ability to assume animal shape probably derived from their custom of wearing animal skins.

180.27. **Westminster Confessions**: The Confession of Faith proposed by the Westminster Assembly and adopted by Parliament in 1647. See "The Hero as Priest" at 104.17 above and note.

180.29. Liberty to *tax* themselves: An implied reference to the tax issue that, in contrast to the Puritan and French Revolutions, provoked the American War of Independence.

181.19. Not *Hunger* alone . . . French Revolution: "The French Revolution itself had something higher in it than cheap bread and a Habeas-corpus act. Here too was an Idea; a Dynamic, not a Mechanic force. It was a struggle . . . for the infinite, divine nature of Right, of Freedom, of Country" ("Signs of the Times" [1829], *Essays* 2:71).

181.36–37. From of old . . . incredible to me: In 1822, however, Carlyle had thought differently. See *Two Notebooks*, 17, and the Introduction, p. xlv above.

182.15. Pococke asking Grotius: The allegation that Muḥammad trained pigeons to fly to his ear, pretending they were forms of the Holy Ghost, is made by Grotius and refuted by Pococke. See "The Hero as Prophet" at 38.35–39.1 above and note.

182.17. They are not portraits of the man: Carlyle equally objected to pictorial misrepresentations of Cromwell; see for instance "Scottish Portraits" (1854), *Essays* 4:410.

182.24. stories of 'Spectres': "Oliver's Biographers . . . introduce various tales . . . of his seeing prophetic spectres" (*Cromwell* 1:35). According to Carlyle, these fabrications were mostly derived from James Heath's *Flagellum, or Life and Death of O. Cromwell, the late Usurper* (1663), and followed by later writers. The prediction of the "white Spectre" is in Sir Philip Warwick, *Memoirs of the Reign of King Charles I with a continuation to the Happy Restoration of King Charles II* (1702), 249. See Fraser, *Cromwell*, 37. The episode of the "black Spectre" is in Laurence Echard, *History of England* (1700), and also in *A True and faithful narrative of Oliver Cromwell's compact with the Devil . . . as it was related by Colonel Lindsey . . .* (1720). Compare Fraser, *Cromwell*, 387.

182.28. Worcester Fight: Twelve months after his victory at Dunbar (see 183.37 below and note), Cromwell overcame a Scottish army at Worcester on September 3, 1651. The battle marked the end of armed resistance to the Commonwealth. See *Cromwell* 2:325–32.

182.30. Sir Philip Warwick: In his *Memoirs* (1701), Sir Philip reports being told by Dr. Simcott, the Huntingdon physician who treated Cromwell's "hypochondriac maladies," that Cromwell "often thought he was just about to die, and also 'had fancies about the Town Cross'" (cited in *Cromwell* 1:50).

183.3. **gambling:** The stories of Cromwell's "wild living while in Town, of his gambling and so forth, rest . . . exclusively on Carrion Heath; and solicit oblivion and Christian burial from all men" (*Cromwell* 1:45; on James "Carrion" Heath, see note at 182.24 above). Though prominent, Heath was not the sole source of stories of Cromwell's youthful debauchery. Hume (*History of England* 7:61.215) describes Cromwell's "dissolute and disorderly" youth which he "consumed in gaming, drinking, debauchery, and country riots." Other sources include Henry Fletcher, *The Perfect Politician or a full view of the Life and Actions (Military and Civil) of O. Cromwell* (1660); Sir Philip Warwick's *Memoirs* (1701); and *Reliquiae Baxterianae, or Mr Richard Baxter's Narrative of the Most Memorable Passages of his Life and Times* (1696); all cited by Fraser, *Cromwell*, 23–24.

183.15–16. **In all this, what . . . 'ambition':** Perhaps a recollection of Mark Antony's speech in *Julius Caesar*, which follows the same rhetorical strategy. For example, "I thrice presented him a kingly crown, / Which he did thrice refuse: Was this ambition?" (*Julius Caesar*, 3.2.96–97).

183.19–20. **'Ever in . . . eye':** "As ever in my great task-maisters eye" (Milton, Sonnet 7, line 14).

183.22. **Bedford Fens:** Cromwell's opposition to a scheme for fen drainage, proposed by the king in council, earned him great popularity in East Anglia and the ironic nickname "Lord of the Fens," first applied to him by the Royalist newspaper *Mercurius Aulicus*. This was in 1638, when "that operation of going in the teeth of the royal will was somewhat more perilous than it would be now!" (*Cromwell* 1:99).

183.37. **envelopments at Dunbar:** A great Cromwellian victory on September 2, 1650. As Cromwell reported to Parliament: "The best of the Enemy's horse being broken through and through in less than an hour's dispute, their whole Army being put into confusion, it became a total rout" (*Cromwell* 2:214). Among the Scots, Cromwell reported heavy losses: 3,000 killed, 10,000 taken prisoner, and some 15,000 weapons left to be picked from the battlefield. The Covenant forces were "made by the Lord of Hosts as stubble to our swords" (Ashley, *Greatness of Cromwell*, 251).

183.38. 'crowning mercy': Cromwell, writing to Lenthall immediately after the battle of Worcester, said: "The dimensions of this mercy are above my thoughts. It is, for aught I know, a crowning mercy" (*Cromwell* 2:331). Carlyle ironically applied Cromwell's phrase to the utilitarians who were, he said, the "'crowning mercy'" of the nineteenth century (Froude, *First Forty Years* 2:79).

184.3. 'love-locks': Many seventeenth-century Cavalier poets were followers of Charles I, and Thomas Carew, Sir John Suckling, and Richard Lovelace were attached to the court. They often affected lovelocks, tresses of long curled or waved hair that hung over the front of the shoulder (Cox, *Illustrated Dictionary of Hairdressing*, 99).

184.4. living *without* God in the world: Ephesians 2:12: "having no hope, and without God in the world."

184.16. Hampton-Court negotiations: The negotiations took place early in November 1647. "The immeasurable Negotiations with the King" led to the conclusion that "there could be no bargain with the King" (*Cromwell* 1:290). By Monday, November 15, the king had surrendered himself to Colonel Robert Hammond (*Cromwell* 1:293).

184.30-31. "For all our fighting . . . a little bit of paper?": From Cromwell's speech of July 4, 1653, to the Little Parliament. Those advocating the Treaty of the Isle of Wight with the king "would have put into his hands all that we had engaged for, and all our security should have been a little piece of paper!" (*Cromwell* 3:45).

184.38. city-tapsters: Bar employees who draw and serve liquor. When Cromwell began to form his fighting men into Ironsides he weeded out undesirables and imposed a strict discipline that prohibited plundering, swearing, drinking, and impiety.

185.3. *Ironsides*: Following the breakdown of peace negotiations in March 1643, Cromwell recruited a regiment in Cambridge, a troop later known as "Ironsides," a name sometimes extended to all the forces he commanded throughout the civil war.

185.8-9. ". . . I would kill the King": "But the most appalling report that now circulates in the world is this, of his saying once, 'If he met the King in battle, he would fire his pistol at the King as at another'" (*Cromwell* 1:197). Macaulay also defends Cromwell, arguing that "to discharge cannon against an army in which a king is known to be posted is to approach pretty near to regicide" (Macaulay, "Milton" [1825], *Essays* 1:180). Later historians have questioned whether this statement can be safely attributed to Cromwell.

185.30. *vulpine* intellect: See Carlyle's discussion of the vulpine morality and insight in "The Hero as Poet" at 91.18-29 above and the note at 91.20.

185.37. *pie-powder* court: A court set up at fairs and markets to administer justice to itinerant dealers and peddlers. See Ben Jonson's *Bartholomew Fair*, 2.1: "Many are the yearly enormities of this Fair, in whose courts of Piepowders I have had the honour . . . to sit as judge" (*Complete Plays of Jonson* 4:33). The name is probably derived from *pied puldreux*, i.e., "dusty of foot," thus a wayfaring man or itinerant.

186.5. common guinea: Certainly not common in Carlyle's time, the guinea coin had been discontinued in 1816 and replaced by the gold sovereign. Officially a "pound," though increased to a pound and a shilling in 1717, the guinea was named after the Guinea coast, the source of the Africa Company's gold supply. The coin was decorated with the company's badge, an elephant or elephant with castellated howdah, but the term *guinea* became popularly applied to all gold pounds whether they were supplied by the Africa Company or not.

186.8-9. know withal the men that are to be trusted!: From Goethe's *Wilhelm Meister's Apprenticeship:* "Learn to know the men who may be trusted!" (*Wilhelm Meister* 2:7.9.74).

187.1. dainty little Falklands: Lucius Cary, Viscount Falkland (1610-1643), a leading Royalist, close associate of William Chillingworth (see following note), and a central figure of the learned circle that met at his house at Great Tey near Oxford. John Aubrey describes him as a "little man and of no great strength of body" (*Brief Lives*, 57).

187.2. didactic Chillingworths: William Chillingworth (1602-1644), Fellow of Trinity College, Oxford, who was, according to Aubrey, the "readiest and nimblest Disputant of his time in the university" (*Brief Lives*, 64). Chillingworth converted to Catholicism in 1630 but reverted to the Church of England four years later and published his

The Religion of the Protestants, a safe way to Salvation in 1638. The "learned & eminent Mr. Chillingworth" was captured at Arundel, "and *so* ill-treated that he died within a few days" (*Two Notebooks*, 9).

187.2. diplomatic Clarendons: Edward Hyde (1608–1674), first Earl of Clarendon. Advisor to Charles I and Lord Chancellor and Chief Minister to Charles II from 1658 to 1667 when he was impeached for "unconstitutional conduct" and fled to France. His *History of the Rebellion and Civil Wars in England* was published 1702–4. Clarendon was Chancellor of Oxford University from 1660 until his fall in 1667. Profits from the publication of the *History* led to the establishment of a new printing house, the Clarendon Press.

187.27. *Vir-tus*: "*Virtus* (properly *man*liness, the chief duty of man) meant, in old Rome, *power of fighting*; means, in modern Rome, *connoisseurship*; in Scotland, *thrift*" ("Diderot" [1833], *Essays* 3:219n).

187.29–30. *Tugend* (*Taugend, dow*-ing or *Dough*tiness): Carlyle correctly derives the German noun *Tugend*, "virtue," from *taugend*, the present participle of the verb *taugen*, "to be useful, good for." The English *doughty* is also related to *taugen*. Scottish *dow* is a variant of *dae* and *doo*, meaning "do."

188.2–3. 'door of hope': Hosea 2:15. "And I will give her vineyards from thence, and the Valley of Achor for a door of hope." For the meeting of Puritan army officers, see the prayer meeting at Windsor in 1648 that Carlyle records in *Cromwell* 1:313–18. The phrase "door of hope" occurs several times in Cromwell's speech to the first Protectorate Parliament on September 4, 1654. See *Cromwell* 3:106, 124.

188.14. Pillar of Fire by night: Exodus 13:21. Compare "The Hero as Man of Letters" at 135.32 above.

189.12–13. wearing his heart upon his sleeve: *Othello*, 1.1.64–65: "But I will wear my heart upon my sleeve / For daws to peck at."

189.14. a house built of glass: "Those who live in glass houses shouldn't throw stones." The earliest references to the proverb are in Chaucer's *Troilus and Criseyde* (1385?) and George Herbert's *Outlandish Proverbs* (1640). See *Oxford Dictionary of English Proverbs*, 360.

190.2-3. Fontenelle: Bernard Le Bovier de Fontenelle (1657–1757), French philosopher, poet, advocate, and the nephew of the dramatist Corneille. His aphorism is also quoted by Carlyle in "Historic Survey of German Poetry" ([1831], *Essays* 2:368).

190.27-28. Ὑποκριτής or Play-actor: In his journal for November 11, 1869, Carlyle wrote, "If ὑπόκρισις, 'hypocrisy' be the first, second, and third thing in eloquence, as I think it is, why have *it* at all? Why not insist, as a first and inexorable condition, that all speech be a reality; that every speaker be verily what he pretends or play-acts to be?" (Froude, *Life in London* 2:385). *Hypocritēs* means literally "one who answers" and can mean, in addition to "one who plays a part on the stage," an "interpreter or expounder," an "orator," "declaimer," "rhapsodist." In the Septuagint (Job 34:30, 36:13) and the New Testament (Matthew 23:13) it means "pretender, dissembler, hypocrite."

192.17. 'Corsica Boswell': An epithet attached to Boswell for his support of Corsican liberty, which he expressed by pleading the Corsican cause with William Pitt and Voltaire, by raising money for arms, by a newspaper campaign, and by publishing *An Account of Corsica: The Journal of a Tour to That Island, and Memoirs of Pascal Paoli* (1768). He referred to himself as *"Corsican Boswell"* in a letter of 1769 (*Boswell in Search of a Wife*, 202). Despite Boswell's efforts to convert him, Johnson expostulated, "I wish you would empty your head of Corsica, which I think has filled it rather too long." Boswell responded, "Empty my head of Corsica! Empty it of honour, empty it of humanity. . . . No! while I live, Corsica and the cause of the brave islanders shall ever employ much of my attention" (Boswell, *Life of Johnson*, 395–96).

192.18. ribbons round his hat; but . . . Samuel staid at home: The event that Johnson did not attend was the Shakespeare Jubilee held at Stratford-upon-Avon in September 1769. In "Boswell's Life of Johnson" ([1832], *Essays* 3:69), Carlyle had written that Boswell "appeared at the Shakspeare Jubilee with a riband, imprinted 'CORSICA BOSWELL,' round his hat." Boswell did attend in "Corsican dress," making, he claimed, "a fine, striking appearance," but it was not ribbons, but the hat itself—a "bonnet or kind of short grenadier cap, black"—that had the words *"Viva la Libertà . . .* embroidered upon its front in letters of gold" (*Boswell in Search of a Wife*, 278). Boswell wrote an account of the Shakespeare Jubilee for the *London Magazine* (September 1769), which was accompanied by an engraving of him in his Corsican costume. See Plate 8.

192.26. **the salt of the earth**: Matthew 5:13.

192.32–33. *grand talent pour le silence*: See "The Hero as Man of Letters" at 158.22 above and note.

192.35–36. **Solomon says, There is a time to speak; . . . to keep silence**: Rather, "a time to keep silence, and a time to speak" (Ecclesiastes 3:7).

192.38. *want of money*: Johnson "uniformly adhered to that strange opinion, which his indolent disposition made him utter: 'No man but a blockhead ever wrote, except for money'" (Boswell, *Life of Johnson*, 731).

193.6–7. **as Cato said**: Marcus Porcius Cato (234–149 B.C.). To those who wondered that while many persons of little note had their statues, Cato had none, he said that he had much rather it should be asked, why he had not a statue, than why he had one (Plutarch, *Lives*, 425).

193.13–14. **'Seekest thou great things, . . .'**: Jeremiah 45:5: "And seekest thou great things for thyself? seek *them* not."

193.22. **Coleridge beautifully remarks**: Untraced.

193.29–30. **'the only man in France . . .'**: Recalling *French Revolution* 2:3.7.146: "They say that he was ambitious, that he wanted to be Minister. It is most true. And was he not simply the one man in France who could have done any good as Minister?" Compare Carlyle's estimate that Mirabeau was the "one Herculean man" (*French Revolution* 2:116), the "Sovereign man" (2:120).

193.31. **poor Necker**: Jacques Necker (1732–1804), Swiss-born banker appointed to succeed Turgot as controller-general of finance in France in 1776. His insistence on fiscal restraint balked certain extravagances of Marie Antoinette, and her enmity led to his first dismissal by Louis XVI. After his reappointment in 1788, Necker urged the reconvening of the Estates General, but some of that body's radical proposals led to his second dismissal, an event that touched off the storming of the Bastille. Though he was once again recalled by the king, Necker finally resigned in 1790 and retired to live on his estate at Coppet in Switzerland until his death. Carlyle's account of these events in Necker's life are given in Book 2 of his *French Revolution*.

193.33–34. Gibbon mourn over him: After Gibbon visited Necker in 1791, he wrote to Lord Sheffield on February 5 that he "could have wished to have shewn him [Necker] as a warning to any aspiring youth possessed with the Daemon of ambition. With all the means of private happiness in his power he is the most miserable of human beings: the past the present and the future are equally odious to him. When I suggested some domestic amusements of books, building &c he answered with a deep tone of despair 'Dans l'état où je suis, je ne puis sentir que le coup de vent qui m'a abbatû'" (In my present state, I can feel nothing but the blast that has overcome me; *Letters of Gibbon* 3:215). Gibbon mourned perhaps more for Mme. Necker, the former Suzanne Curchod, with whom he had once been in love. "My father," he wrote in his *Memoirs* (85–86), "would not hear of this strange alliance. . . . After a painful struggle I yielded to my fate: I sighed as a lover: I obeyed as a son." Nevertheless he continued to watch over her progress as the wife of M. Necker, observing that "in every change of prosperity and disgrace he [Necker] has reclined on the bosom of a faithful friend."

194.13. ears cropt off: On June 30, 1637, the barrister William Prynne, Dr. John Bastwick, and the Rev. Henry Barton were pilloried in Old Palaceyard and "then had their ears cut off,—bare knives, hot branding-irons,—and their cheeks stamped 'S. L.,' Seditious Libeller; . . . poor Prynne, who had got into new trouble, and here lost his ears a *second* and final time, having had them 'sewed on again' before" (*Cromwell* 1:95–96). When the Long Parliament met in November 1640, "all London turned out to watch its ear-cropped martyr, Prynne, ride in from Westminster. . . . It was the herald of revolution" (Bryant, *Samuel Pepys*, 12). Barton was punished for describing bishops as "(cater)pillars of the Church" and "anti-Christian mushrumps" (Abbott, *Writings and Speeches of Cromwell* 1:153). See Carlyle's further account of this incident in *Historical Sketches*, 271–74.

194.32. 'devout imagination': See "The Hero as Priest" at 130.22–23 above and note.

195.7. 'Faith in the Bible': A slogan of the Reformation.

195.22–23. Chancery Law-Courts: See note at 199.32–33 below.

195.27. Hume: David Hume (1711–1776), Scottish philosopher and historian. Hume's analysis of Cromwell's character confronts but does not resolve the problem of contradictory passions. Thus he finds Cromwell's fanaticism co-existing with a concern for justice and humanity. Hume's evaluation of Cromwell in chapter 61 of his *History of England* drew Carlyle's ire and, later, Lytton Strachey's praise as being "a corrective to the *O, altitudo!* sentimentalities of Carlyle" (*Portraits in Miniature*, 147). Macaulay said Hume "pleaded the cause of tyranny with the dexterity of an advocate, while affecting the impartiality of a judge" (Macaulay, "Milton" [1825], *Essays* 1:172). According to Maurice Ashley, Hume's view of Cromwell is of little value since he "was content to follow the accounts of Cromwell's enemies" (*Greatness of Cromwell*, 21).

195.31. applied since: As for example, in Hallam's *Constitutional History*, which depicts a Cromwell who "sucked only the dregs of a besotted fanaticism" in contrast to Napoleon to whom "the stores of reason and philosophy were open" (cited in Macaulay, "Hallam's Constitutional History" [1828], *Essays* 1:51).

196.1. Antæus-like: Antaeus, the son of Poseidon and Gē (Earth), was a giant who wrestled Heracles. Whenever he was thrown to the ground he rose more powerful from his contact with his mother Earth.

196.6. Orson: From the French romance that appeared in English in the mid-sixteenth century as the *History of Two Valentyne Brethren, Valentyne and Orson* by Henry Watson. It concerns two brothers: Orson, who is carried off by a bear and reared as a wild man, and Valentyne, who is brought up as a knight. A ballad in Thomas Percy's *Reliques of Ancient English Poetry* (1765), "Valentine and Ursine," deals with the story.

196.11. Cromwell's last words: "'Truly God is good; indeed He is; He will not'——Then his speech failed him." On being offered something to drink he answered, "It is not my design to drink or sleep; but my design is, to make what haste I can to be gone." Towards morning "he used divers holy expressions. . . . And truly it was observed, that a public spirit to God's Cause did breathe in him,— as in his lifetime, so now to his very last" (*Cromwell* 4:205–6). For these words, and Cromwell's prayer, Carlyle drew on Charles Harvey, *A Collection of several Passages concerning his late Highness Oliver Cromwell, in the Time of his Sickness. . . . Written by one that was then Groom to his Bedchamber* (1659), a pamphlet in which modern scholars "have only limited confidence" (Ashley, *Greatness of Cromwell*, 360).

196.24. Diocletian prefers . . . cabbages: Diocletian (A.D. 245?– 313?), proclaimed Emperor of Rome in 284, abdicated eleven years later to cultivate his garden. Maximian's efforts urging him to reassume government drew the response that "if he could show Maximian the cabbages which he had planted with his own hands . . . , he should no longer be urged to relinquish the enjoyment of happiness for the pursuit of power" (Gibbon, *Decline and Fall* 1:13.418).

196.34–35. diplomatic Argyles: Archibald Campbell (1607–1661), eighth Earl of Argyll, was leader of the Covenanters who opposed the imposition of the Laudian liturgy on Scotland in 1637. Carlyle's ironic adjective alludes to Argyll's reputation for deviousness and his numerous shifts of allegiance. During the civil war, the Covenanters sided with Parliament, but in 1651 Argyll himself placed the crown on the head of Charles II at his coronation at Scone.

196.37. Montrose: James Graham (1612–1650), first Marquis and fifth Earl of Montrose, initially joined the Scottish forces against Charles I in 1637 and fought with the Covenanters. After twice changing sides he permanently joined the Royalist party in 1641. During the Great Rebellion (1642–49), the king appointed him lieutenant-general of Scotland, and after some initial success against rebel forces he was defeated at Philiphaugh in 1645. Montrose fled to the Continent, but returned after the execution of Charles I, only to be defeated in 1650 at Invercarron. He was soon after betrayed to Parliament and hanged. In 1839, Carlyle judged that "there are but two very remarkable men in the Period visible as yet: Cromwell and Montrose" (*Letters* 11:15). After reading Mark Napier's *Montrose and the Covenanters; their characters and conduct* (1838), Carlyle wrote a brief manuscript, "Gropings about Montrose," part of which has been published. See Parsons, "Carlyle's *Gropings about Montrose.*"

197.17. lies the rub: *Hamlet*, 3.1.64: "ay, there's the rub."

197.19. **Rump Parliament:** The remnant of the Long Parliament (see next note) after Pride's purge (see note at 198.16 below). The Rump Parliament ordered the trial of Charles I and, after his death, governed England through an executive council until 1653.

197.28. **Long Parliament:** The Parliament that met on November 3, 1640. "The *Rump* or Fag-end of it did not finally vanish till 16th March 1659–60" (*Cromwell* 1:107). In Carlyle's view it was "the Acme of Parliaments" and "set a flaming pattern to all the world, which now after centuries all the world is fruitlessly bent to emulate." The Long Parliament and the National Assembly in Paris were the "only two Parliaments . . . that did the work of sovereignty with some effect" (*Pamphlets*, 6.218, 6.228).

197.37. **"for all our fighting . . . piece of paper":** *Cromwell* 3:45. See 184.30–31 above and note.

198.10–11. **Rump Parliament, *you* cannot continue:** Cromwell dissolved the Rump and its Council of State on April 20, 1653. "How can you be a Parliament for God's People? Depart, I say; and let us have done with you. In the name of God,—go!" (*Cromwell* 3:35. See also Milton, *Complete Prose* 4:215–16).

198.16. **Pride's Purges:** The purge of the Presbyterian majority in Parliament on December 6, 1648, when Colonel Thomas Pride forcibly excluded pro-Royalist members from Parliament. Forty-one members on the first day were taken to the nearby Queen's Court and "kept there in a state bordering on rabidity, asking, By what Law?" (*Cromwell* 1:409). Pride's purge continued until the remnant of sixty-seven members formed the so-called Rump Parliament. See "An Election to the Long Parliament" (1844), *Essays* 4:344–45. Defending the purge, Milton wrote there was "No question but it is as good and necessary to expel rott'n Members out of the House, as to banish Delinquents out of the Land" (*Observations Upon the Articles of Peace* [1649], *Complete Prose* 3:328). Milton also supported Pride's purge in *A Defence of the People of England* ([1651], *Complete Prose* 4:457), his rebuttal of Salmasius' *Defensio Regia*.

198.21. **diligent Godwin . . . cannot make it out:** William Godwin (1756–1836), freethinker and revolutionary writer, whose four-volume *History of the Commonwealth* (1824–28) Carlyle had begun reading

by April 1839 (*Letters* 11:72) and finished by December 1840, finding it "faithful, but dead as iron" (*Letters* 12:361). Concerning the
dissolution of the Long Parliament in 1653, Godwin writes, "It cannot be too deeply regretted that we have no account of these transactions from the pens of the republicans. It is beyond measure to be
wondered at, that Vane . . . never committed to writing his own
memoirs, or even any explanation or vindication of his conduct in so
important a crisis. . . . We are reduced therefore to the consulting the
statements of his adversaries only" (3:451). Of the bill that parliament was considering when dissolved by Cromwell (see next note),
Godwin says, "It is beyond measure extraordinary that no copy of the
bill itself for putting an end to the present parliament and calling
another, which had been three years before the house, which had
gone through all the forms, . . . and which was now upon the very
point of passing into a law, is any where to be found: at least it has
escaped my most diligent enquiries and researches. . . . The simplest
and most manly defence that the parliamentary leaders could have
made, was to render this act, in the best way they could have devised,
an imperishable record. If it could not bear the light, if it could not
stand the investigation and dissection of all profound and impartial
enquirers, then indeed the cause of the parliamentary statesmen was
a dishonourable one" (3:458-60).

198.33. **Reform Bill**: Which would have perpetuated the member-
ship of the Rump in a new parliament by controlling the selection of
new members. No copy of the bill survives. "Cromwell's last act
before leaving the House . . . was to snatch the actual bill from the
hand of the clerk and put it under his cloak" (Wolfe, Introduction,
Complete Prose Works of Milton 4:214n).

199.11-12. **Milton . . . looked on it all near at hand**: Milton "looked
on" from his vantage point as Secretary for Foreign Languages from
1649 to 1652. In this capacity, especially as Latin translator, Milton
was closely involved in diplomatic business between the Council of
State and foreign governments.

199.12. **could applaud him**: The lecture audience would have known
Milton's sonnets "Cromwell, our chief of men" and "Because you
have thrown off your Prelate Lord." Milton's applause was not so
unequivocal as Carlyle suggests here. Milton had "mixed feelings"
and he was "too closely identified with the Rump Parliament as an

official of the Council of State to have been wholly sympathetic with Cromwell's abrupt and contemptuous dismissal" of that body (Wolfe, Introduction, *Complete Prose Works of Milton* 4:220; see also Parker, *Milton* 1:429). However, Milton's loyalty to Cromwell was unshaken by these events; see his comment on Cromwell's "rare and all-but-divine excellence" in *A Second Defence of the English People* ([1654], *Complete Prose* 4:668). He also continued to work for the Council of State and to support specific actions of the Parliamentary side. In various pamphlets he defended Pride's purge (see note at 198.16 above) and the regicide, seeking to prove it "Lawfull . . . to call to account a Tyrant, or wicked KING, and after due conviction, to depose, and put him to death" (*The Tenure of Kings and Magistrates* [1649], *Complete Prose* 3:189; see also the conclusion to *Eikonoklastes* [1649], *Complete Prose* 3:582–601).

199.20. **Barebones's Parliament**: The Parliament of 1653, "a real Assembly of the Notables in Puritan England" (*Cromwell* 3:41). The nickname for the Little Parliament was derived from one of its members, Mr. Praise-God Barbon, a Fleet Street leather merchant, Anabaptist preacher, and politician. "Their witty name survives; but their history is gone all dark" (*Cromwell* 3:41).

199.21. *Convocation of the Notables*: Several "convocations of notables" (*assemblées de notables*) were called in France from 1470 on, but Carlyle probably has in mind the one called by Minister Calonne on December 29, 1786, on the eve of the Revolution. See *French Revolution* 1:3.3.70–71. Compare "On History" ([1830], *Essays* 2:87): "At first . . . there is only vague wonder, and fear or hope, and the noise of Rumour's thousand tongues; till, after a season, the conflict of testimonies has subsided into some general issue; and then it is settled, by majority of votes, that such and such a 'Crossing of the Rubicon,' an 'Impeachment of Strafford,' a 'Convocation of the Notables,' are epochs in the world's history, cardinal points on which grand world-revolutions have hinged."

199.32–33. **endeavouring to reform the Court of Chancery!**: The Court of Chancery was established in the fifteenth century. The "Barebones Parliament" attempted to abolish it on December 2, 1653, prompted by the "'Twenty-three thousand Causes of from five to thirty years' continuance' lying undetermined in Chancery" (*Cromwell* 3:79). Though the Little Parliament's attack on Chancery failed, Cromwell reformed the court in 1654 and 1655 (*Cromwell* 3:93). See also "Inaugural Address at Edinburgh" (1866), *Essays* 4:460-62. By 1840 Chancery was again notorious for the tardiness of its decisions. The law's delays in Chancery are central to the social satire in Dickens's *Bleak House* (1852-53).

199.33-200.17. **dissolved themselves, as incompetent; . . . what to say to it:** This passage was included for the first time in the third British edition of 1846, the year after Carlyle had finished his edition of *Oliver Cromwell's Letters and Speeches.* See textual appartus.

199.36-37. **'Commander-in-chief . . .':** "On *Wednesday 26th June* 1650, the Act appointing 'That Oliver Cromwell, Esquire, be constituted Captain-General and Commander-in-Chief of all the Forces raised or to be raised by authority of Parliament . . . was passed" (*Cromwell* 2:176).

200.6. **Instrument of Government:** The constitution framed by the Army Council on December 16, 1653, that gave Cromwell the title of Protector without hereditary succession, and established a triennial Parliament permanently excluding Catholics and temporarily banning Royalists. See *Cromwell* 3:181.

200.18. *first* **regular Parliament:** It met on September 3, 1654. Cromwell dismissed it on January 22, 1655, saying: "It is not for the profit of these Nations, nor for common and public good, for you to continue here any longer. And therefore I do declare unto you, That I do dissolve this Parliament" (*Cromwell* 3:194).

200.25. **rude, chaotic . . . Speeches:** For Carlyle, Cromwell's incoherence was a sign of integrity. See *Cromwell* 3:167-68, 169, and the Introduction, p. lv above.

200.29. **'births of Providence':** "If this be of human structure and invention, . . . and that they are not the Births of Providence,—then they will tumble" (*Cromwell* 3:188).

200.38. **God's finger guided us on:** Compare Exodus 8:19: "This is the finger of God."

201.4–5. **"You have had such an opportunity . . ."**: Cromwell deplored "the loss of those golden opportunities which God had put into your hands for Settlement. . . . You might have had opportunity to have settled peace and quietness amongst all professing Godliness" (*Cromwell* 3:179–80).

201.13–14. **"God be judge . . ."**: The concluding words of Cromwell's speech to Parliament on February 4, 1658: "I think it high time that an end be put to your sitting. And I DO DISSOLVE THIS PARLIAMENT! And let God be judge between you and me!" (*Cromwell* 4:179).

201.38. ***ultra vires***: Literally, "beyond its powers." Exercise of power beyond legitimate limits.

202.19. **Pitt**: William Pitt the Younger (1759–1806), British Prime Minister who organized opposition to Napoleon, strengthened British sea power, and subsidized coalitions on the Continent. Among the essays Carlyle contributed to Brewster's *Edinburgh Encyclopaedia* between 1820 and 1823 were essays on Pitt and his father.

202.19. **Pombal**: Jose di Carvalho (1699–1782), Marquis de Pombal, Portuguese premier who ruled by terror and expelled the Jesuits from Portugal.

202.19. **Choiseul**: Duc Étienne François de Choiseul (1719–1785), favorite of Mme. de Pompadour, author of the agreement of 1761 aligning French and Spanish Bourbons, and noted for his suppression of the Jesuits. He was dismissed from the court of Louis XV through the efforts of the pro-Jesuit Mme. du Barry who succeeded Mme. de Pompadour as the king's mistress.

202.27–28. **Hutchinson, as his wife relates it**: John Hutchinson (1615–1664). See note at 179.1 above. Hutchinson fell out with Cromwell, and, though wooed by the Protector, their differences remained irreconcilable. Thus he held no office under the Protectorate. Caroline Fox reports Carlyle as saying that Cromwell's appeal "was all in vain; a narrow confined mind like Hutchinson's could not take in anything so grand, and he too left him" (*Memories*, 111). The anecdote is reported in *Memoirs of Colonel Hutchinson* (297–98), written by his widow Lucy.

202.36. **his poor Mother**: Cromwell's mother Elizabeth died on November 16, 1654, at the age of ninety-four. Throughout her life she feared for her son's safety and "at the sound of a musket she would often be afraid her Son was shot; and could not be satisfied unless she saw him once a day at least" (*Cromwell* 3:160, quoting Edmund Ludlow's *Memoirs* [1698–99] 2:488). Her dying blessing to Cromwell was: "'The Lord cause His face to shine upon you; and comfort you in all your adversities; and enable you to do great things for the glory of your Most High God, and to be a relief unto His People. My dear Son, I leave my heart with thee. A good night!'" (*Cromwell* 3:159).

203.8–9. **rash in me to be among the first . . . honest man!**: In fact Macaulay preceded Carlyle in defending Cromwell. In his review of Henry Hallam's *Constitutional History of England* in 1828, he wrote of Cromwell's reputation: "Though every device has been used to blacken it, though to praise him would long have been a punishable crime, truth and merit at last prevail" (Macaulay, *Essays* 1:54).

203.12. **sunk in the ditch**: See "The Hero as Priest" at 103.11 above and note.

203.34–35. **Napoleon . . . Cromwell**: Macaulay, in his review of Hallam's *Constitutional History of England* for the *Edinburgh Review* in 1828, noted Hallam's pairing of Napoleon and Cromwell, though Hallam reversed Carlyle's order of preference (Macaulay, *Essays* 1:49).

204.2. **'walking with God'**: Genesis 5:22, 24: "And Enoch walked with God."

204.7–8. **Sceptical *Encyclopédies***: The *Encyclopédie ou Dictionnaire Universal des Arts et Sciences*, begun in 1743 by John Mills and finished by Diderot and D'Alembert, was published between 1751 and 1756, "first 'with approbation and *Privilége du Roi*'; next, it was stopped by Authority: next, the public murmuring, suffered to proceed; then again, positively for the last time, stopped,—and, no whit the less, printed, . . . and circulated, under thin disguises. . . . Finally, to crown the whole matter, a copy of the prohibited Book lies in the King's private library: and owes favour, and a withdrawal of the prohibition, to the foolishest accident" ("Diderot" [1833], *Essays* 3:215).

204.18. **'False as a bulletin'**: "Bonaparte preceded his entry into the capital of Egypt by one of those lying bulletins which only imposed on fools." Every one of these "official words" was "an imposition" (Bourrienne, *Memoirs* 1:220). "The historian . . . ought to put no faith in the bulletins, despatches, notes, and proclamations which have emanated from Bonaparte. . . . The proverb 'As great a liar as a bulletin,' has as much truth in it as the axiom, two and two make four. The bulletins always announced what Bonaparte wished to be believed true. . . . A writer, if he took his materials from the bulletins . . . , would compose a romance rather than a true history" (Bourrienne, *Memoirs* 2:112–13). Napoleon claimed his bulletins were correct except where enemy proximity compelled disguise. Otherwise "all the remainder was very exact. . . . If it was a common saying, *as false as a bulletin*, it was personal rivalships, party spirit," and the "wounded self-love of those who were not mentioned" that were responsible (Las Cases, *Memoirs* 2:39).

204.36. **His *savans***: "I remember that, being upon deck one beautiful night, surrounded by several persons who were arguing in favour of this afflicting dogma materialism, Bonaparte, raising his hand towards the heavens, and pointing to the stars—'Tell me, gentlemen,' said he, 'who has made all these?'" (Bourrienne, *Memoirs* [ed. Sanderson], 119). A similar discussion is reported by Las Cases (*Memoirs* 2:253–56).

204.36. **Bourrienne**: Louis-Antoine Fauvelet de Bourrienne (1769–1834), private secretary to Napoleon in Egypt and during the Consulate.

205.10–11. **gold tassels**: Compare Caroline Fox's report of this passage in Carlyle's lecture: "When he went to see the Tuileries, which was being very splendidly fitted up for him, he quietly cut off one of the gold tassels and put it in his pocket. The workmen were astonished. . . . A week afterwards he came again, took the tassel out of his pocket, gave it to the contractor, and said, 'I have examined the tassel and find it is not gold; you will have this mistake rectified.' Such a man could not be taken in" (Fox, *Memories*, 127).

205.14. **Saint Helena**: Island in the South Atlantic; the place of Napoleon's second exile after his defeat at Waterloo on June 18, 1815, and the place of his death six years later.

205.26. 'La carrière ouverte aux talens . . .': On St. Helena, March 3, 1817, Napoleon told his personal surgeon, the Royal Navy officer Barry O'Meara, "I have always been of opinion, that the sovereignty lay in the people. In fact, the imperial government was a kind of republic. Called to the head of it by the voice of the nation, my maxim was, *la carrière est ouverte aux talens*, (the career is open to talents) without distinction of birth or fortune, and this system of equality is the reason that your oligarchy hate me so much" (O'Meara, *Napoleon in Exile* 1:249). Carlyle was much taken with this saying of Napoleon's and frequently quoted "that great doctrine" ("Mirabeau" [1837], *Essays* 3:409–10). See also *Sartor*, 2.8.143; *History of Literature*, 204; "Sir Walter Scott" (1838), *Essays* 4:37.

205.33. Twentieth of June (1792): The insurrection of June 20, on the anniversary of the Tennis Court Oath, in protest against a Royal veto. A mob invaded the Tuileries and encountered Louis face to face. During the surprise encounter, the king was given and donned a red cap of liberty. The episode is described in *French Revolution* 2:5.12.257–63. Napoleon and Bourrienne were among the spectators who had followed the mob. At the sight of the king in his red cap, Napoleon could not contain himself: "'*Che coglione!*' he loudly exclaimed. 'Why have they let in all that rabble! They should sweep off four or five hundred of them with the cannon; the rest would then set off fast enough'" (Bourrienne, *Memoires* 1:18). He retained an aversion to the red cap even in painting (Bourrienne, *Memoires* 1:375).

205.36. Tenth of August: The date of the massacre of the Swiss guard by a French mob at the Tuileries in 1792. This scene was also witnessed by Napoleon, and is described by Carlyle in *French Revolution* 2:6.7.295–302. Las Cases quotes Napoleon: "Never since has any of my fields of battle given me the idea of so many dead bodies. . . . I saw well dressed women commit the grossest indecencies on the dead bodies of the Swiss" (*Memoirs* 3:91).

206.2-3. Italian Campaigns . . . Peace of Leoben: Preliminary peace negotiations took place at Leoben on October 17, 1797, at the close of Napoleon's Italian campaign (April 1796–October 1797). Terms agreed at Leoben were incorporated into the Treaty of Campoformia, which ceded Austrian Netherlands (present-day Belgium) to France along with the extension of French influence into other territories.

206.13. Wagrams: The battle at the Austrian villiage of Wagram, fought on July 6, 1809. Carlyle's review of "Varnhagen Von Ense's Memoirs" ([1838], *Essays* 4:98–105) contains a detailed description of the battle, in which forces of the Austrian emperor were decisively beaten by Napoleon.

206.13. Austerlitzes: In 1805 Napoleon transferred the army he had mustered for the invasion of Britain to the Rhine to counter the threat posed by an allied force from England, Austria, and Russia. On December 2 a day-long battle was fought to the west of the Moravian town of Austerlitz, which ended in an allied disaster. More than 12,000 soldiers perished and more than that number were taken prisoner. The disaster at Austerlitz is frequently said to have been a major factor in hastening the death of the British prime minister, Pitt.

206.17. babbling *Avocats*: Compare Napoleon's words: "France will be lost through these fine talkers, these babblers: now is the time to save her!" (Las Cases, *Memoirs* 1:144).

206.21. *La Fère*: The artillery regiment in which Napoleon gained a sub-lieutenancy in 1785 at the age of sixteen. Carlyle describes this period of Napoleon's life in *French Revolution* 2:2.2.77–78. Compare "The Hero as Man of Letters" at 166.17 above and note.

206.29. 'given up to strong delusion . . .': 2 Thessalonians 2:11: "And for this cause God shall send them strong delusion, that they should believe a lie."

206.36. Pope's-*Concordat*: Napoleon negotiated an agreement with Pope Pius VII in 1801 for the restoration of the Catholic Church to an official position in France, not as the state religion but as the religion of "the great majority of French citizens."

206.37. pretending to be a re-establishment of Catholicism: "In every country," said Napoleon, "religion is useful to the Government, and those who govern ought to avail themselves of it. . . . I was a Mahometan in Egypt; I am a Catholic in France" (Bourrienne, *Memoirs* 2:76).

207.1. *"la vaccine de la religion"*: Mme. de Staël attributes the phrase to Napoleon. "Il dit à Cabanis: *Savez-vous ce que c'est que le concordat* *que je viens de signer? C'est le vaccine de la religion: dans cinquante ans il n'y en aura plus en France*" (He said to Cabanis: Do you know what the concordat I have just signed is? It is the vaccine against religion: in fifty years there will be none in France; *Considérations* 2:272).

207.4. **Augereau**: Pierre-François-Charles Augereau (1757–1816), Duc de Castiglione. The Concordat became law in April 1802. "A solemn *Te Deum* was chanted at the cathedral of Notre Dame on Sunday, the 11th of April. . . . The next day Bonaparte asked Augereau what he thought of the ceremony. 'Oh! it was all very fine, . . . there was nothing wanting, except the million of men who have perished in the pulling down of what you are setting up'" (Bourrienne, *Memoirs* 2:75–76). The remark has also been attributed to General Delmas.

207.5. **Cromwell's Inauguration**: June 26, 1657. "A throne was erected with a pavilion, and a chair of estate under it, to which Cromwell was conducted. . . . The speaker, with the earl of Warwick and Whitlock, vested him with a rich purple velvet robe lined with ermines, the Speaker enlarging upon the majesty and the integrity of that robe. Then the Speaker presented him with a fair Bible . . . ; then he, in the name of all the people, girded a sword about him; and, lastly, presented him a sceptre of gold, which he put into his hand, and made him a large discourse of those emblems of government and authority" (Clarendon, *History of the Rebellion* 6:32).

207.15–16. **'Lead us not into temptation!'**: From the Lord's Prayer, Matthew 6:13 and Luke 11:4.

207.24. **Duke of Weimar**: Karl August (1775–1828), patron of Goethe and Schiller, who in Carlyle's view "did more for the Culture of his Nation than all the English Dukes . . . since Henry the Eighth gave them the Church Lands to eat, have done for theirs!" (*Past and Present*, 4.6.285).

207.31. **Palm**: Johann Philipp Palm of Nuremberg (1768–1806) was court-marshalled on Napoleon's orders for selling a pamphlet critical of the French. He refused to name the author of the pamphlet, *Deutschland in seiner tiefsten Erniedrigung* (*Germany in its Deepest Humiliation*), and was accordingly shot at Braunau on August 26, 1806.

207.32. paint an inch thick: *Hamlet*, 5.1.192–4: "Now get you to my lady's [chamber], and tell her, let her paint an inch thick, to this favor she must come."

208.4. rude-draught: Rough draft.

208.11. 'another Isle of Oleron to France': "England . . . would in course of time have become a mere appendage to France, had the latter continued under my dominion. England was by nature intended to be one of our Islands, as well as Oleron or Corsica. . . . If, instead of entering upon the Egyptian expedition, I had invaded Ireland; . . . what would England have been to-day?" Napoleon's speculations on St. Helena, reported by Las Cases (*Memoirs* 2:204–5).

WORKS CITED

(The following list identifies all works referred to by page number in this volume. Citations of the Bible are to the King James Version, of classical authors to the Loeb Classical Library, and of Shakespeare to The Riverside Shakespeare, *ed. G. Blakemore Evans, Boston: Houghton, 1974.)*

WORKS BY CARLYLE

References to the following works of Thomas Carlyle are given to the pagination of the Centenary Edition, edited by H. D. Traill (London: Chapman and Hall, 1896–99), the most widely available edition, unless otherwise indicated. Future volumes of the Strouse Edition will contain tables giving the correspondence between their pagination and that of the Centenary Edition.

Cromwell	*Oliver Cromwell's Letters and Speeches with Elucidations.* 4 vols.
Emerson and Carlyle	*The Correspondence of Emerson and Carlyle.* Ed. Joseph Slater. New York: Columbia University Press, 1964.
Essays	*Critical and Miscellaneous Essays.* 5 vols.
Frederick	*History of Friedrich II. of Prussia Called Frederick the Great.* 8 vols.
French Revolution	*The French Revolution: A History.* 3 vols.
German Literature	*Carlyle's Unfinished History of German Literature.* Ed. Hill Shine. Lexington: University of Kentucky Press, 1951.
German Romance	*German Romance.* 2 vols.
Goethe and Carlyle	*Correspondence Between Goethe and Carlyle.* Ed. Charles Eliot Norton. London: Macmillan, 1887.
Historical Sketches	*Historical Sketches of Notable Persons and Events in the Reigns of James I and Charles I.* Ed. Alexander Carlyle. London: Chapman and Hall, 1898.

History of Literature	*Lectures on the History of Literature.* Ed. J. Reay Greene. New York: Scribner, 1892.
Letters	*The Collected Letters of Thomas and Jane Welsh Carlyle.* Ed. C. R. Sanders, K. J. Fielding, C. de L. Ryals, Ian Campbell, Aileen Christianson, Hilary J. Smith, et al. 19 vols. to date. Durham, N.C.: Duke University Press, 1970– .
Life of Schiller	*The Life of Friedrich Schiller.*
Life of Sterling	*The Life of John Sterling.*
Mill, Sterling and Browning	*Letters of Thomas Carlyle to John Stuart Mill, John Sterling and Robert Browning.* Ed. Alexander Carlyle. London: Unwin; New York: Stokes, 1923.
Montaigne	*Montaigne and Other Essays, Chiefly Biographical.* London: Gowans; Philadelphia, Lippincott, 1897.
New Letters	*New Letters of Thomas Carlyle.* Ed. Alexander Carlyle. 2 vols. New York: Lane, 1904.
On Heroes	*On Heroes, Hero-Worship, and the Heroic in History.* All references are to the present volume.
Pamphlets	*Latter-Day Pamphlets.*
Past and Present	*Past and Present.*
Reminiscences	*Reminiscences by Thomas Carlyle.* (1881, ed. J. A. Froude.) Ed. Charles Eliot Norton. London: Dent, 1972.
Sartor	*Sartor Resartus.*
Two Notebooks	*Two Notebooks of Thomas Carlyle, from 23d March 1822 to 16th May 1832.* Ed. Charles Eliot Norton. New York: Grolier, 1898.
Wilhelm Meister	*Wilhelm Meister's Apprenticeship and Travels.* 2 vols.

WORKS BY OTHER AUTHORS

Abbott, Wilbur Cortez. *The Writings and Speeches of Oliver Cromwell.* 4 vols. Cambridge, Mass.: Harvard University Press, 1937–45.

Abrams, M. H. "The Correspondent Breeze: A Romantic Metaphor." *The Kenyon Review* 19 (1957): 113–30. Revised version in *English Romantic Poets: Modern Essays in Criticism.* New York: Oxford University Press, 1960. 37–54.

Acton, John Emerich Edward Dalberg-Acton, First Baron. *The History of Freedom and Other Essays.* London: Macmillan, 1907.

——. *Letters of Lord Acton to Mary, Daughter of the Right Hon. W. E. Gladstone.* Ed. Herbert Paul. London: Allen, 1904.

Ali, Syed Ameer. *A Critical Examination of the Life and Teachings of Mohammed.* 1873. Karachi: Mir, 1978.

Allingham, William. *A Diary.* Ed. H. Allingham and D. Radford. London: Macmillan, 1907.

Allott, Miriam. *Novelists on the Novel.* London: Routledge; New York: Columbia University Press, 1962.

The Anglo-Saxon Chronicle. Trans. Dorothy Whitelock, David C. Douglas, and Susie I. Tucker. New Brunswick, N.J.: Rutgers University Press, 1961.

apRoberts, Ruth. *The Ancient Dialect: Thomas Carlyle and Comparative Religion.* Berkeley: University of California Press, 1988.

Armstrong, T. Percy. "Carlyle and Uhland: Parallel Passages." *Notes and Queries* 169 (1935): 221.

Arnold, Matthew. *God and the Bible.* Ann Arbor: University of Michigan Press, 1970. Vol. 7 of *Complete Prose Works of Matthew Arnold.* Ed. R. H. Super. 11 vols. 1960–77.

——. *Lectures and Essays in Criticism.* Ann Arbor: University of Michigan Press, 1962. Vol. 3 of *Complete Prose Works of Matthew Arnold.* Ed. R. H. Super. 11 vols. 1960–77.

——. *The Letters of Matthew Arnold to Arthur Hugh Clough.* Ed. Howard Foster Lowry. London: Oxford University Press, 1932.

———. *Philistinism in England and America.* Ann Arbor: University of Michigan Press, 1974. Vol. 10 of *Complete Prose Works of Matthew Arnold.* Ed. R. H. Super. 11 vols. 1960–77.

Ashley, Maurice. *The Greatness of Oliver Cromwell.* New York: Macmillan, 1958.

Aubrey, John. *Aubrey's Brief Lives.* Ed. Oliver Lawson Dick. London: Secker, 1958.

Bannatyne, Richard. *Memorials of Transactions in Scotland, A.D. MDLXIX – A.D. MDLXXIII.* Edinburgh, 1836.

Barfield, Owen. *What Coleridge Thought.* Middletown, Conn.: Wesleyan University Press, 1971.

Bartlett, John. *Familiar Quotations: A Collection of Passages, Phrases, and Proverbs Traced to Their Sources in Ancient and Modern Literature.* 14th ed. Ed. Emily Morison Beck. Boston: Little, [1968].

Battisti, Eugenio. *Giotto.* Lausanne: Skira; Cleveland: World, 1960.

Baumgarten, Alexander Gottlieb. *Reflections on Poetry: Alexander Gottlieb Baumgarten's Meditationes philosophicae de nonnullis ad poema pertinentibus.* 1735. Trans. Karl Aschenbrenner and William B. Holther. Berkeley: University of California Press, 1954.

Baumgarten, Murray. "The Mind is a Muscle: Carlyle, Literary Revolution, and Linguistic Nationalism." In *Literarischer Nationalismus: Literature, Language, and National Identity.* Proceedings of the Third International Scottish Studies Symposium. Ed. H. W. Drescher and Hermann Voelker. Frankfurt am Main: Lang, 1989. 43–105.

———. "Revolution as Context: Carlyle and the Example of Cagliostro." *Studies in Scottish Fiction.* Ed. H. W. Drescher and Joachim Schwend. Frankfurt am Main: Lang, 1985. 177–98.

Bell, Sir Charles. *Tibet Past and Present.* 1924. London: Oxford University Press, 1927.

Bentham, Jeremy. *The Works of Jeremy Bentham.* Ed. John Bowring. 1838–43. 11 vols. New York: Russell, 1962.

The Bhagavad Gītā. Trans. Franklin Edgerton. Harvard Oriental Studies 38. Cambridge, Mass.: Harvard University Press, 1944.

Blackwell, I. A., ed. *Northern Antiquities.* By Paul Henri Mallet. London, 1847. *See* Mallet.

Blake, William. *The Letters of William Blake.* Ed. Archibald G. B. Russell. London: Methuen, 1906.

Boccaccio, Giovanni. *Esposizioni sopra la Comedia di Dante.* Ed. Giorgio Padoan. Milan: Mondadori, 1965. Vol. 6 of *Tutte le opere di Giovanni Boccaccio.* Ed. Vittore Branca. 12 vols. 1964–83.

———. *Trattatello in laude di Dante.* Ed. Pier Giorgio Ricci. Milan: Mondadori, 1974. *Tutte le opere di Giovanni Boccaccio.* Ed. Vittore Branca. 12 vols. 1964–83. 3:423–538.

Boswell, James. *Boswell in Search of a Wife, 1766–1769.* Ed. Frank Brady and Frederick A. Pottle. The Yale Editions of the Private Papers of James Boswell. New York: McGraw-Hill, 1956.

———. *Boswell's Life of Johnson.* 1791. London: Oxford University Press, 1960.

Bosworth, Joseph. *A Compendious Anglo-Saxon and English Dictionary.* London, 1848.

Bourrienne, Louis-Antoine Fauvelet de. *Memoirs of Napoleon Bonaparte.* Ed. R. W. Phipps. 4 vols. New York, 1891.

———. *Memoirs of Napoleon Bonaparte.* Ed. Edgar Sanderson. London: Hutchinson, 1904.

Brand, C. P. *Thomas Carlyle and Dante.* Occasional Papers 11. Edinburgh: Carlyle Society, 1985.

Brecht, Martin. *Martin Luther: His Road to Reformation, 1483–1521.* Trans. James L. Schaaf. Philadelphia: Fortress, 1985.

Brown, P. Hume. *John Knox, A Biography.* 2 vols. London, 1895.

———. *A Short History of Scotland.* 1908. Ed. Henry W. Meikle. Edinburgh: Oliver, 1961.

Browne, Sir Thomas. *Religio Medici and Other Works*. Ed. L. C. Martin. Oxford: Clarendon, 1964.

Browning, Elizabeth Barrett. *The Letters of Elizabeth Barrett Browning to Mary Russell Mitford, 1836–1854*. Ed. Meredith B. Raymond and Mary Rose Sullivan. 3 vols. [Waco, Tex.]: Armstrong Browning Library of Baylor University, 1983.

Bryant, Arthur. *Samuel Pepys: The Man in the Making*. 1933. London: Collins, 1959.

Bunsen, [Karl Josias, freiherr von], [Johannes] Brandis, and [Johann Wilhelm] Loebell. *The Life and Letters of Barthold George Niebuhr, and Selections from His Minor Writings*. [Trans. Susanna Winkworth.] New York, 1852.

Burke, Edmund. *The Writings and Speeches of Edmund Burke*. Ed. Paul Langford. 3 vols. to date. Oxford: Clarendon, 1981– .

Burns, Robert. *The Letters of Robert Burns*. Ed. J. De Lancey Ferguson. 2nd ed. Ed. G. Ross Roy. 2 vols. Oxford: Clarendon, 1985.

———. *The Poems and Songs of Robert Burns*. Ed. James Kinsley. 3 vols. Oxford: Clarendon, 1968.

Burton, Sir Richard. *Love, War and Fancy*. 1885. Ed. Kenneth Walker. London: Kimber, 1964.

Butler, Samuel. *The Way of All Flesh*. New York: Modern Library, 1950.

Calder, Grace J. *The Writing of* Past and Present: *A Study of Carlyle's Manuscripts*. New Haven: Yale University Press, 1949.

Campbell, Joseph. *The Masks of God*. 4 vols. New York: Viking, 1959–68.

Carlyle, John, trans. *Dante's Divine Comedy: The Inferno*. New York, 1849.

Carlyle's House, Chelsea: Illustrated Catalogue with a history of the house by Alexander Carlyle and additional notes by Thea Holme. London: Country Life Limited for the National Trust, 1966.

Cary, Henry Francis, trans. *The Vision or Hell, Purgatory and Paradise of Dante Alighieri*. New York, 1844.

Cassirer, Ernst. *The Myth of the State*. New Haven: Yale University Press, 1946.

Chalmers, Alexander. "Memoir." In *The Table Talk of Martin Luther*. Trans. and ed. William Hazlitt. London: Bell, 1911. xxv–xcvi.

Chambers, Robert, ed. *Popular Rhymes of Scotland*. 1826. Edinburgh, [1870].

———. *The Scottish Ballads*. Edinburgh, 1829.

Chesterton, G. K. *Twelve Types*. London: Humphreys, 1906.

Chrysostom, Saint John. *Collected Works*. 4 vols. Frankfurt, 1723.

Clarendon, Edward, Earl of. *The History of the Rebellion and Civil Wars in England*. Ed. W. Dunn Macray. 6 vols. Oxford: Clarendon, 1958.

Clive, John. *Not by Fact Alone: Essays On the Writing and Reading of History*. New York: Knopf, 1989.

Clubbe, John. Introduction. In *Froude's Life of Carlyle*. Columbus: Ohio State University Press, 1979. 1–60. *See* Froude.

———, ed. *Two Reminiscences of Thomas Carlyle*. Durham, N.C.: Duke University Press, 1974.

Coleridge, Samuel Taylor. *Biographia Literaria*. Ed. J. Shawcross. 1907. 2 vols. London: Oxford University Press, 1958.

———. *The Friend*. Ed. Barbara E. Rooke. 2 vols. Princeton: Princeton University Press, 1969. Number 4 of *The Collected Works of Samuel Taylor Coleridge*. Bollingen Series 75. 1969– .

———. *Specimens of the Table Talk of Samuel Taylor Coleridge*. 3rd ed. London, 1851.

Collingwood, R. G. *The Idea of History*. London: Oxford University Press, 1956.

The Concise Scots Dictionary. Ed. Mairi Robinson. Aberdeen: Aberdeen University Press, 1985.

Condorcet, Marie Jean Antoine Nicolas de Caritat, Marquis de. *Oeuvres de Condorcet*. Ed. A. Condorcet O'Connor and M. F. Arago. 12 vols. Paris, 1847–49.

Cotterell, Yong Yap, and Arthur Cotterell. *Chinese Civilization*. London: Weidenfeld, 1977.

Cox, J. Stevens. *An Illustrated Dictionary of Hairdressing & Wigmaking*. London: Batsford, 1984.

Craigie, William A. *A Primer of Burns*. London, 1896.

Culler, A. Dwight. *The Victorian Mirror of History*. New Haven: Yale University Press, 1985.

Daiches, David. *Robert Burns*. London: Deutsch, 1966.

——. "Carlyle: The Paradox Reconsidered." *Scottish Studies* 1 (1983): 365–83.

Dante Alighieri. *Dantis Alagherii Epistolae*. Ed. Paget Toynbee. Oxford: Clarendon, 1920.

——. *The Divine Comedy*. Trans. Charles S. Singleton. Bollingen Series 80. 3 volumes of text with 3 volumes of commentary. Princeton: Princeton University Press, 1970–75.

——. *The Odes of Dante*. Trans. H. S. Vere-Hodge. Oxford: Clarendon, 1963.

Davidson, John. *The Theatocrat: A Tragic Play of Church and Stage*. London: Richards, 1905.

DeLaura, David J. "Arnold and Carlyle." *PMLA* 79 (1964): 104–29.

De Quincey, Thomas. *The Collected Writings of Thomas De Quincey*. Ed. David Masson. 14 vols. London, 1896–97.

Dickens, Charles. *Sketches by Boz Illustrative of Every-day Life and Every-day People*. 1836–37. The New Oxford Illustrated Dickens. London: Oxford University Press, 1957.

Dickinson, William Croft. Introduction. *John Knox's History of the Reformation in Scotland*. 2 vols. London: Nelson, 1949. *See* Knox.

Dyer, Isaac W. *A Bibliography of Thomas Carlyle's Writings and Ana.* 1928. New York: Octagon Books, 1968.

Edda: Die Lieder des Codex regius nebst verwandten Denkmälern. Ed. Gustav Neckel and Hans Kuhn. 2 vols. Heidelberg: Winter, 1962.

Elegant, Robert. *Manchu.* New York: McGraw-Hill, 1980.

Emerson, Ralph Waldo. *English Traits.* Ed. Howard Mumford Jones. Cambridge, Mass.: Belknap, 1966.

——. *The Essays of Ralph Waldo Emerson.* Ed. Alfred R. Ferguson and Jean Ferguson Carr. Cambridge, Mass.: Belknap, 1979.

——. *The Journals and Miscellaneous Notebooks of Ralph Waldo Emerson.* Vol. 16 (1866–1882). Ed. Ronald A. Bosco and Glen. M. Johnson. Cambridge, Mass.: Belknap, 1982.

——. *Representative Men.* Ed. Wallace E. Williams and Douglas Emory Wilson. Vol. 4 of *The Collected Works of Ralph Waldo Emerson.* Cambridge, Mass.: Belknap, 1971– .

Engels, [Friedrich]. *The Condition of the Working Class in England.* Trans. W. O. Henderson and W. H. Chaloner. Oxford: Blackwell, 1958.

Farley-Hills, David. *Rochester: The Critical Heritage.* London: Routledge, 1972.

Fichte, Johann Gottlieb. *On the Nature of the Scholar and its Manifestations* [*Über das Wesen des Gelehrten und seine Erscheinungen im Gebiete der Freiheit*]. In *The Popular Works of Johann Gottlieb Fichte.* Trans. William Smith. 4th ed. 2 vols. London, 1889. 1:207–317.

Field, Carol. *The Italian Baker.* New York: Harper, 1985.

Fielding, Henry. *Joseph Andrews.* Ed. Martin C. Battestin. Middletown, Conn.: Wesleyan University Press, 1967.

Fielding, K. J. "Benthamite Utilitarianism and *Oliver Twist:* A Novel of Ideas." *Dickens Quarterly* 4 (June 1987): 49–65.

———. "Carlyle and Cromwell: The Writing of History and 'DRYAS-DUST.'" *The Norman and Charlotte Strouse Lectures on Carlyle & His Era.* Ed. Jerry D. James and Rita B. Bottoms. 3 vols. to date. Santa Cruz, Calif.: The University Library, 1982– . 2:45–67.

———. "Carlyle and Esaias Tegnér: An Unpublished MS." *Carlyle Newsletter* 5 (Spring 1984): 3–10.

———. "Vernon Lushington: Carlyle's Friend and Editor." *Carlyle Newsletter* 8 (Spring 1987): 7–18.

FitzGerald, Edward. *The Letters of Edward FitzGerald.* Ed. Alfred McKinley Terhune and Annabelle Burdick Terhune. 4 vols. Princeton: Princeton University Press, 1980.

Fox, Caroline. *Memories of Old Friends; Being Extracts from the Journals and Letters of Caroline Fox, of Penjerrick, Cornwall, from 1835 to 1871.* Ed. Horace N. Pym. 2nd ed. Philadelphia, 1882.

Fraser, Antonia. *Cromwell: Our Chief of Men.* London: Weidenfeld, 1973.

———. *King Charles II.* London: Weidenfeld, 1979.

Friedenthal, Richard. *Luther.* Trans. John Nowell. London: Weidenfeld, 1970.

Froude, J. A. *Thomas Carlyle: A History of the First Forty Years of His Life, 1795–1835.* 2 vols. London, 1882.

———. *Thomas Carlyle: A History of His Life in London, 1834–1881.* 2 vols. London, 1884.

Garnett, Richard. *Life of Thomas Carlyle.* London, 1887.

Gaury, Gerald de. *Rulers of Mecca.* London: Harrap, 1951.

Genlis, Stéphanie Félicité, Comtesse de. *Mémoires inédits de Madame La Comtesse de Genlis, sur le dix-huitième siècle et la révolution Française, depuis 1756 jusqu'a nos jours.* 10 vols. Paris, 1825.

Gibbon, Edward. *The History of the Decline and Fall of the Roman Empire.* 1776–88. Ed. J. B. Bury. 7 vols. London: Methuen, 1909–14.

——. *The Letters of Edward Gibbon*. Ed. J. E. Norton. 3 vols. London: Cassell, 1956.

——. *Memoirs of My Life*. 1796. Ed. Georges A. Bonnard. London: Nelson, 1966.

Gilbert, Martin. *Winston Churchill: The Wilderness Years*. London: Heinemann, 1981.

Godwin, William. *History of the Commonwealth of England. From Its Commencement to the Restoration of Charles the Second*. 4 vols. London, 1824–28.

Goethe, Johann Wolfgang von. *Goethes Werke*. Ed. Erich Trunz. 14 vols. Hamburg: Wegner, 1960–63.

Goldberg, Michael K. "From Bentham to Carlyle: Dickens' Political Development." *Journal of the History of Ideas* 33 (1972):61–76.

Goldberg, Michael K. and Jules P. Seigel, eds. *Carlyle's Latter-Day Pamphlets*. [Ottawa]: Canadian Federation for the Humanities, 1983.

Gosse, Edmund. "The Agony of the Victorian Age." *Edinburgh Review* 228 (1918): 276–295.

Gray, Thomas. *The Complete Poems of Thomas Gray*. Ed. H. W. Starr and J. R. Hendrickson. Oxford: Clarendon, 1966.

——. *Correspondence of Thomas Gray*. Ed. Paget Toynbee and Leonard Whibley. 3 vols. Oxford: Clarendon, 1935.

Greg, W. W. "The Rationale of Copy-Text." *Studies in Bibliography* 3 (1950–51): 19–36.

Grierson, H. J. C. *Carlyle and Hitler*. Cambridge: Cambridge University Press, 1933.

——. "The Hero and the Führer." *Aberdeen University Review* 27 (March 1940): 99–105.

Grimm, Harold J. Introduction to Volume 31. *Luther's Works*. Ed. Jaroslav Pelikan and Helmut T. Lehmann. 55 vols. St. Louis, Concordia; Philadelphia: Fortress, 1958–86. 31:xv–xxii.

Grimm, Jacob. *Teutonic Mythology*. 1835. Trans. James Steven Stallybrass. 4 vols. 1883–88. New York: Dover, 1966.

Grimm, Jacob, and Wilhelm Grimm. *Deutsches Wörterbuch.* Leipzig, 1873.

Grotius, Hugo. *De Veritate Religionis Christianæ.* 1627. New ed. Amsterdam, 1662.

Hansard, T. C. *The Parliamentary Debates: Forming a Continuation of the Work Entitled "The Parliamentary History of England, from the Earliest Period to the Year 1803."* New Series. 25 vols. London, 1820–30.

Hardy, Thomas. *Jude the Obscure: An Authoritative Text, Backgrounds and Sources, Criticism.* Ed. Norman Page. New York: Norton, 1978.

Harrison, Frederic. *Chatham.* London: Macmillan, 1905.

———. *Memories and Thoughts: Men—Books—Cities—Art.* London: Macmillan, 1906.

———. *Studies in Early Victorian Literature.* London, 1895.

Harrold, Charles Frederick. *Carlyle and German Thought: 1819–1834.* 1934. Yale Studies in English, vol. 82. Hamden: Archon Books, 1963.

Hawkins, Sir John. *The Life of Samuel Johnson, LL.D. by Sir John Hawkins, Knt.* 1787. Ed. Bertram H. Davis. New York: Macmillan, 1961.

Hazlitt, William. *Life of Napoleon.* 1830. Ed. P. P. Howe. London: Dent, 1931. Vol. 14 of *The Complete Works of William Hazlitt.* 21 vols. 1930–34.

Hegel, G. W. F. *Introduction to the Lectures on the History of Philosophy.* Trans. T. M. Knox and A. V. Miller. Oxford: Clarendon, 1985.

Hibbert, Christopher. *The Personal History of Samuel Johnson.* London: Longmans, 1971.

Holbrook, Richard Thayer. *Portraits of Dante from Giotto to Raffael.* London: Warner; Boston: Houghton, 1911.

Hollander, Lee M., trans. *The Poetic Edda*. 2nd ed. Austin: University of Texas Press, 1962.

Holthausen, F. *Altenglisches Etymologisches Wörterbuch*. Heidelberg: Carl Winters Universitätsbuchhandlung, 1934.

Houghton, Walter E. *The Victorian Frame of Mind*. New Haven: Yale University Press, 1957.

Hughes, Thomas. *Tom Brown at Oxford*. London: Macmillan, 1889.

Hume, David. *Enquiries Concerning Human Understanding and Concerning the Principles of Morals*. Ed. L. A. Selby-Bigge. 3rd ed. Ed. P. H. Nidditch. Oxford: Clarendon, 1975.

——. *The History of England from the Invasion of Julius Cæsar to the Revolution in 1688*. 13 vols. London: Cowie, 1825.

——. *The Natural History of Religion*. 1757. Ed. H. E. Root. Stanford: Stanford University Press, 1957.

Hunt, Leigh. *The Autobiography of Leigh Hunt*. Ed. J. E. Morpurgo. London: Cresset, 1949.

Hutchinson, Lucy. *Memoirs of Colonel Hutchinson*. Ed. Julius Hutchinson. 1806. London: Dent; New York: Dutton, 1965.

Huxley, Thomas Henry. *Life and Letters of Thomas Henry Huxley, by His Son, Leonard Huxley*. 2 vols. New York: Appleton, 1913.

Irving, Washington. *Mahomet and His Successors*. New York, 1850. Ed. H. A. Pochmann and E. N. Feltskog. Madison: University of Wisconsin Press, 1970.

Jamieson, Robert. *Popular Ballads and Songs from Traditions, Manuscripts, and Scarce Editions, with Translations of Similar Pieces from the Ancient Danish Language, and a Few Originals by the Editor*. 2 vols. Edinburgh, 1806.

Jaspers, Karl. *Nietzsche and Christianity*. Trans. E. B. Ashton. [Chicago]: Regnery Gateway, 1961.

[Jeffrey, Francis]. Review of *Wilhelm Meister's Apprenticeship, a Novel*, trans. Thomas Carlyle. *Edinburgh Review* 42 (1825): 409–49.

Johnson, Samuel. *A Dictionary of the English Language: In Which the Words Are Deduced from Their Originals, and Illustrated in Their Different Significations by Examples from the Best Writers. To Which Are Prefixed, a History of the Language, and an English Grammar.* 2 vols. London, 1755.

———. *Diaries, Prayers, and Annals.* Ed. E. L. McAdam, Jr., Donald Hyde, and Mary Hyde. New Haven: Yale University Press, 1958.

Jonson, Ben. *The Complete Plays of Ben Jonson.* Ed. G. A. Wilkes. 4 vols. Oxford: Clarendon, 1981–82.

Josephson, Matthew. *Jean-Jacques Rousseau.* New York: Harcourt, 1931.

Kaplan, Fred. "'Phallus Worship' (1848): Unpublished Manuscripts III—A Response to the Revolution of 1848." *Carlyle Newsletter* 2 (March 1980): 19–23.

———. *Thomas Carlyle: A Biography.* Ithaca, N.Y.: Cornell University Press, 1983.

Karkaria, R. P., ed. *Lectures on the History of Literature.* By Thomas Carlyle. London and Bombay: Curwen, 1892.

Kassis, Hanna E. *A Concordance of the Qur'an.* Berkeley: University of California Press, 1983.

Kaufmann, Walter. Introduction. *The Portable Nietzsche.* New York: Viking, 1968.

Klaeber, Friedrich, ed. *Beowulf and The Fight at Finnsburg.* London: Heath, 1922.

Knox, John. *John Knox's History of the Reformation in Scotland.* Ed. William Croft Dickinson. 2 vols. London: Nelson, 1949.

———. *The Works of John Knox.* Ed. David Laing. 6 vols. Edinburgh, 1895.

The Korân. Trans. George Sale. London, 1734.

Kusch, Robert W. "Pattern and Paradox in *Heroes and Hero-Worship.*" *Studies in Scottish Literature* 6 (1969): 146–55.

Landor, W. S. Letter. *The Examiner* [London], August 16, 1840: 518.

Lane, Edward William. *The Thousand and One Nights, Commonly Called, in England, The Arabian Nights' Entertainments: A new translation from the Arabic, with copious notes.* 3 vols. London, 1839–41.

Larousse World Mythology. Ed. Pierre Grimal. London: Hamlyn, 1973.

Las Cases, [Emmanuel,] comte de. *Memoirs of the Life, Exile, and Conversations of the Emperor Napoleon.* 1818. 4 vols. New York, 1894.

Review of *Latter-Day Pamphlets*, by Thomas Carlyle. *Southern Literary Messenger* 16.6 (June 1850): 330–42.

LaValley, Albert J. *Carlyle and the Idea of the Modern: Studies in Carlyle's Prophetic Literature and Its Relation to Blake, Nietzsche, Marx, and Others.* New Haven: Yale University Press, 1968.

Lehman, B. H. *Carlyle's Theory of the Hero: Its Sources, Development, History, and Influence on Carlyle's Work: A Study of a Nineteenth Century Idea.* Durham, N.C.: Duke University Press, 1928.

Lewes, George Henry. *The Life of Goethe.* 1855. Ed. Victor Lange. New York: Ungar, 1965.

"The Literary Work of Thomas Carlyle." *Scribner's Monthly* 22 (1881): 92–106.

Lloyd-Jones, Hugh. *Blood for the Ghosts: Classical Influences in the Nineteenth and Twentieth Centuries.* London: Duckworth, 1982.

Lockhart, J. G. *Life of Robert Burns.* Edinburgh, 1828.

——. *Life of Robert Burns.* Ed. Robert Chambers and William Wallace. 4 vols. Edinburgh and London, 1896.

Luther, Martin. *Luther's Works.* Ed. Jaroslav Pelikan and Helmut T. Lehmann. 55 vols. St. Louis: Concordia; Philadelphia: Fortress, 1958–86.

——. *The Table Talk of Martin Luther.* Trans. and ed. William Hazlitt. 1846. London: Bell, 1911.

Macaulay, Thomas. *Critical and Historical Essays.* Ed. A. J. Grieve. 2 vols. London: Dent, 1961.

——. *The Letters of Thomas Babington Macaulay.* Ed. Thomas Pinney. 6 vols. Cambridge: Cambridge University Press, 1974–81.

——. *The Miscellaneous Works of Lord Macaulay.* Ed. Lady Trevelyan. 10 vols. New York: Putnam's, [1898].

MacMechan, Archibald, ed. *On Heroes, Hero-Worship, and the Heroic in History.* By Thomas Carlyle. Boston: Athenæum-Ginn, 1901.

Mallet, Paul Henri. *Northern Antiquities: or, A Description of the Manners, Customs, Religion and Laws of the Ancient Danes: Including Those of Our Own Saxon Ancestors, with a Translation of the Edda, or System of Runic Mythology, and Other Pieces, from the Ancient Icelandic Tongue, Translated from "L'Introduction à l'Histoire de Dannemarc, &c. par Mallet."* [Trans. Bishop Thomas Percy]. 2 vols. Edinburgh, 1809.

Marcus, Steven. *Engels, Manchester, and the Working Class.* New York: Vintage, 1974.

Martineau, Harriet. *Harriet Martineau's Autobiography.* Ed. Maria Weston Chapman. 2 vols. Boston, 1877.

Marx, Karl, and Friedrich Engels. *Werke.* 47 vols. Berlin: Dietz Verlag, 1954–89.

Masson, David. *Carlyle Personally and in His Writings.* London, 1885.

Maurice, Frederick Denison. *The Life of Frederick Denison Maurice.* Ed. Frederick Maurice. 2 vols. New York, 1884.

Mazzini, [Giuseppe]. *Essays: Selected from the Writings, Literary, Political, and Religious, of Joseph Mazzini.* Ed. William Clarke. London, [1887].

M'Crie, Thomas. *Life of John Knox.* 1811. Philadelphia, 1831.

Meredith, George. *The Letters of George Meredith.* Ed. C. L. Cline. 3 vols. Oxford: Clarendon, 1970.

Michelet, Jules. *The Life of Luther Gathered from His Own Writings.* Trans. G. H. Smith. London, [1846].

——. *The Life of Luther, Written by Himself.* Trans. William Hazlitt. London, 1846.

Mikhail, E. H., ed. *Oscar Wilde: Interviews and Recollections.* 2 vols. London: Macmillan, 1979.

Mill, John Stuart. *Autobiography and Literary Essays.* Ed. John M. Robson and Jack Stillinger. Toronto: University of Toronto Press, 1981.

——. *The Letters of John Stuart Mill.* Ed. Hugh S. R. Elliot. 2 vols. London: Longmans, 1910.

——. "On Liberty." *Essays on Politics and Society.* Ed. J. M. Robson and Alexander Brady. Toronto: University of Toronto Press, 1977.

Milton, John. *Complete Prose Works of John Milton.* 8 vols. New Haven; Yale University Press; London: Oxford University Press, 1959.

Morley, John. *Critical Miscellanies.* 4 vols. London: Macmillan, 1886.

Muggeridge, Malcolm. *A Third Testament.* Boston: Little, 1976.

Muir, Sir William. *The Life of Moḥammad from Original Sources.* 1861. Edinburgh: Grant, 1923.

Murray, T. J. "Dr Samuel Johnson's movement disorder." *British Medical Journal* 6178 (16 June 1979): 1610–14.

Nabokov, Vladimir. *Transparent Things.* New York: McGraw, 1972.

Nash, Geoffrey. "Thomas Carlyle and Islam." *World Order* 19 (1985): 9–22.

Neal, Daniel. *The History of the Puritans or Protestant Non-Conformists, from the Reformation to the Death of Queen Elizabeth: With an Account of Their Principles; Their Attempts for a Further Reformation in the Church; Their Sufferings; and the Lives and Characters of Their Principal Divines.* 2nd ed. 2 vols. London, 1755.

Nichol, John. *Thomas Carlyle.* New York, London, 1892.

Nietzsche, Friedrich. *The Dawn of Day*. Trans. J. M. Kennedy. Vol. 9 in *The Complete Works of Friedrich Nietzsche*. Ed. Oscar Levy. 18 vols. London: Russell, 1909–11.

——. *Ecce Homo*. Trans. Walter Kaufmann. In *On the Genealogy of Morals* and *Ecce Homo*. Ed. Walter Kaufmann. New York: Random, 1967. 199–367.

——. *Twilight of the Idols, or, How One Philosophizes With a Hammer.* In *The Portable Nietzsche*. Ed. Walter Kaufmann. New York: Viking, 1968. 463–563.

Njal's Saga. Trans. Magnus Magnusson and Hermann Pálsson. Middlesex: Penguin, 1960.

The Norton Anthology of English Literature. Ed. M. H. Abrams. 5th ed. 2 vols. New York: Norton, 1986.

Novalis [Friedrich Leopold von Hardenberg]. *Novalis Schriften*. Ed. Ludwig Tieck and Fr[iedrich von] Schlegel. 2 vols. Berlin, 1826.

Noyes, Alfred. *Voltaire*. 1936. New York: Stokes, 1939.

O'Meara, Barry E. *Napoleon in Exile; or, A Voice from St. Helena: The Opinions and Reflections of Napoleon on the Most Important Events in His Life and Government, in His Own Words*. 2 vols. New York, [1822?].

Orage, A. R. *Readers and Writers (1917–1921)*. New York: Knopf, 1922.

Orwell, George. *The Collected Essays, Journalism and Letters of George Orwell*. Ed. Sonia Orwell and Ian Angus. 4 vols. New York: Harcourt, 1968.

The Oxford Dictionary of English Proverbs. 3rd ed. Oxford: Clarendon, 1970.

Parker, William Riley. *Milton: A Biography*. 2 vols. Oxford: Clarendon, 1968.

Parsons, C. O. "Carlyle's *Gropings about Montrose*." *Englische Studien* 71 (1937): 360–71.

Pater, Walter. *Greek Studies: A Series of Essays.* London: Macmillan, 1910.

Petrarca, Francesco. *Rerum Memorandarum Libri.* Ed. Giuseppe Billanovich. Florence: Sansoni, 1943.

Piozzi, Hester. "Anecdotes of Dr. Johnson, by Mrs. Piozzi." 1785. In *The Life of Samuel Johnson, L.L.D.* Ed. John Wilson Croker. 10 vols. 1831. London, 1839. 9:1–127.

Plutarch. *The Lives of the Noble Grecians and Romans.* Trans. John Dryden. Revised Arthur Hugh Clough. 1864. New York: Modern Library, [1932].

Pocockio, Edvardo [Edward Pococke]. *Specimen Historiæ Arabum.* 1650. Ed. Josephus White. Oxford, 1806.

The Poetic Edda. Trans. Lee M. Hollander. 2nd ed. Austin: University of Texas Press, 1962.

Pope, Alexander. *The Iliad of Homer.* Ed. Maynard Mack. 2 vols. London: Methuen; New Haven: Yale University Press, 1967.

Prideaux, Humphrey. *The True Nature of Imposture Fully Display'd in the Life of Mahomet: With a Discourse Annex'd for the Vindicating of Christianity from This Charge. Offered to the Consideration of the Deists of the Present Age.* 1678. 6th ed. London, 1716.

The Prose Edda of Snorri Sturluson: Tales from Norse Mythology. Trans. Jean I. Young. Berkeley: University of California Press, 1964.

Putnam, George Haven. *A Memoir of George Palmer Putnam, Together with a Record of the Publishing House Founded by Him.* 2 vols. New York: Putnam, 1903.

Reade, Charles. *"It Is Never Too Late to Mend." A Matter of Fact Romance.* 2 vols. Boston, 1856.

Reid, T. Wemyss. *The Life, Letters, and Friendships of Richard Monckton Milnes, First Lord Houghton.* 2 vols. London, 1890.

Ridley, Jasper. *John Knox.* Oxford: Clarendon, 1968.

Robertson, William. *The History of America.* 4 vols. London, 1803.

Robinson, Henry Crabb. *Diary, Reminiscences, and Correspondence of Henry Crabb Robinson, Barrister-at-Law, F. S. A.* Ed. Thomas Sadler. 2 vols. Boston, 1871.

Rosenberg, John D. *Carlyle and the Burden of History.* Cambridge, Mass.: Harvard University Press, 1985.

Rosenberg, Philip. *The Seventh Hero: Thomas Carlyle and the Theory of Radical Activism.* Cambridge, Mass.: Harvard University Press, 1974.

Ross, Sir Edward Denison. Introduction. *The Korân.* Trans. George Sale. London: Warne, 1927.

Rousseau, Jean-Jacques. *The Confessions of Jean-Jacques Rousseau.* Trans. J. M. Cohen. Middlesex: Penguin, 1970.

———. *Emile: or On Education.* Trans. Allan Bloom. New York: Basic, 1979.

Rowe, Nicholas. "Some Account of the Life, &c. of Mr. William Shakespear." In *The Works of Mr. William Shakespear.* Ed. Nicholas Rowe. 6 vols. London, 1709. 1: i–xl.

Ruskin, John. *The Works of John Ruskin.* Ed. E. T. Cook and Alexander Wedderburn. 39 vols. London: Allen; New York: Longmans, 1903–12.

Russell, Bertrand. *A History of Western Philosophy.* New York: Simon, 1945.

The Saga of King Olaf Tryggwason Who Ruled Over Norway A.D. *995 to* A.D. *1000.* Trans. J. Sephton. London, 1895.

Sale, George. "Preliminary Discourse." In *The Korân.* London, 1734.

Schaff, David S. *John Huss: His Life, Teachings and Death, After Five Hundred Years.* New York: Scribner, 1915.

Schapiro, J. Salwyn. "Thomas Carlyle, Prophet of Fascism." *The Journal of Modern History* 17 (1945): 97–115.

Schoenbaum, Samuel. *William Shakespeare: A Documentary Life.* New York: Oxford University Press; Ilkley, Yorks.: Scolar Press, 1975.

Scholem, Gershom G. *Major Trends in Jewish Mysticism*. New York: Schocken, 1971.

Schopenhauer, Arthur. *The World as Will and Representation*. Trans. E. F. J. Payne. 2 vols. [Indian Hills, Colorado]: Falcon's Wing Press, 1958.

Scott, F. N. Letter. *The Nation* [New York], December 24, 1903: 502–3.

Scott, Sir Walter. *Redgauntlet*. Ed. Kathryn Sutherland. Oxford: Oxford University Press, 1985.

Seigel, Jules Paul, ed. *Thomas Carlyle: The Critical Heritage*. New York: Barnes, 1971.

Shakespeare, William. *The Riverside Shakespeare*. Boston: Houghton Mifflin, 1974.

Sharma, T. R. *Carlyle: "The Hero as Poet" and "The Everlasting Yea."* Ghaziabad: Vimal Prakashan, 1987.

Shaw, [George] Bernard. *Three Plays for Puritans: The Devil's Disciple, Caesar and Cleopatra, and Captain Brassbound's Conversion*. London: Constable, 1931.

———. "First Aid to Critics." In *John Bull's Other Island and Major Barbara*. New York: Brentano, 1907. 157–200.

Shelley, Percy Bysshe. *A Defence of Poetry*. Ed. John E. Jordan. Indianapolis: Bobbs, Library of Liberal Arts, 1965.

Shepherd, Richard Herne, ed. *Memoirs of the Life and Writings of Thomas Carlyle*. 2 vols. London, 1881.

Shillingsburg, Peter L. *Scholarly Editing in the Computer Age*. Athens, Georgia: University of Georgia Press, 1986.

Shine, Hill. *Carlyle and the Saint-Simonians: The Concept of Historical Periodicity*. Baltimore: Johns Hopkins Press, 1941.

———. *Carlyle's Early Reading, to 1834, with an Introductory Essay on His Intellectual Development*. Lexington: University of Kentucky Libraries, 1953.

Shirer, William L. *The Rise and Fall of the Third Reich.* New York: Simon, 1960.

Singleton, Charles S., trans. *The Divine Comedy.* By Dante Alighieri. Bollingen Series 80. 3 volumes of text with 3 volumes of commentary. Princeton: Princeton University Press, 1970–75.

Skeat, Walter W. *A Concise Etymological Dictionary of the English Language.* 4th ed. New York, 1894.

Smith, Adam. *The Early Writings of Adam Smith.* Ed. J. Ralph Lindgren. [New York]: Kelley, 1967.

Smith, James Robinson. *The Earliest Lives of Dante: Translated from the Italian of Giovanni Boccaccio and Lionardo Bruni Aretino.* 1901. New York: Russell, 1968.

Smith, Jane I. *An Historical and Semantic Study of the Term 'Islām' As Seen in a Sequence of Qūr'ān Commentaries.* Missoula, Montana: Scholars Press for Harvard Theological Review, 1975.

Smith, R. Bosworth. *Mohammed and Mohammedanism: Lectures Delivered at the Royal Institution of Great Britain in February and March, 1874.* New York, 1875.

Speer, Albert. *Inside the Third Reich.* Trans. Richard and Clara Winston. New York: Macmillan, 1970.

Spencer, Herbert. *The Study of Sociology.* 1873. Ann Arbor: University of Michigan Press, 1961.

Staël, Madame la Baronne de. *Considérations sur les Principaux Événemens de la Révolution Françoise.* 3 vols. Paris, 1820.

Stanhope, Philip Henry Stanhope, 5th Earl. *Life of the Right Honourable William Pitt.* 4 vols. London, 1861.

Stephen, Leslie. *Hours in a Library.* 4 vols. 1904. Grosse Pointe, Mich.: Scholarly Press, 1968.

Sterne, Laurence. *Tristram Shandy.* Ed. Howard Anderson. New York: Norton, 1980.

Strachey, Lytton. *Portraits in Miniature and Other Essays.* New York: Harcourt, 1931.

Strich, Fritz. *Goethe and World Literature*. 1945. Trans. C. A. M. Sym. New York: Hafner, 1949.

Sturluson, Snorri. *Heimskringla: History of the Kings of Norway*. Trans. Lee M. Hollander. Austin: University of Texas Press, 1964.

Sweet's Anglo-Saxon Reader in Prose and Verse. Revised Dorothy Whitelock. Oxford: Clarendon, 1967.

Swinburne, Algernon Charles. *The Swinburne Letters*. Ed. Cecil Y. Lang. 6 vols. New Haven: Yale University Press, 1959–62.

Symonds, John Addington. *The Letters of John Addington Symonds*. Ed. Herbert M. Schueller and Robert L. Peters. 3 vols. Detroit: Wayne State University Press, 1967–69.

Tanselle, G. Thomas. "Greg's Theory of Copy-Text and the Editing of American Literature." *Studies in Bibliography* 28 (1975): 167–229. Rpt. in *Selected Studies in Bibliography*. Charlottesville: University Press of Virginia, 1979. 245–307.

Tappert, Theodore G. Introduction to Volume 54. *Luther's Works*. Ed. Jaroslav Pelikan and Helmut T. Lehmann. 55 vols. St. Louis: Concordia; Philadelphia: Fortress, 1958–86. 54:ix–xxvi.

Tarr, Rodger L. "'The Guises': Thomas Carlyle's Lost Renaissance History." *Victorian Studies* 25 (1981): 7–80.

———. *Thomas Carlyle: A Bibliography of English-Language Criticism, 1824–1974*. Charlottesville: University Press of Virginia, 1976.

———. *Thomas Carlyle: A Descriptive Bibliography*. Pittsburgh: University of Pittsburgh Press, 1989.

Taylor, A. J. P. *Englishmen and Others*. London: Hamilton, 1956.

Tennyson, G. B. "The Carlyles." In *Victorian Prose: A Guide to Research*. Ed. David J. DeLaura. New York: Modern Language Association, 1973. 31–111.

[Tennyson, Hallam]. *Alfred Lord Tennyson: A Memoir by His Son*. 2 vols. New York, 1897.

Thackeray, William M. Review of *The French Revolution*, by Thomas Carlyle. *The Times* [London], August 3, 1837.

Thatcher, David S. *Nietzsche in England 1890–1914.* Toronto: University of Toronto Press, 1970.

Thoreau, Henry D. "Resistance to Civil Government." In *Reform Papers.* Ed. Wendell Glick. Princeton: Princeton University Press, 1973. 63–90.

——. "Thomas Carlyle and His Works." In *Early Essays and Miscellanies.* Ed. Joseph J. Moldenhauer, Edwin Moser, and Alexander C. Kern. Princeton: Princeton University Press, 1975. 219–67.

Tillotson, Kathleen. "Matthew Arnold and Carlyle." In *Mid-Victorian Studies* by Geoffrey and Kathleen Tillotson. London: Athlone, 1965. 216–38.

——. *Novels of the Eighteen-Forties.* Oxford: Clarendon, 1956.

Tompkins, J. M. S. *The Popular Novel in England, 1770–1800.* 1932. Lincoln: University of Nebraska Press, 1961.

Toynbee, Paget. *Dante Alighieri.* 1900. New York: Harper, 1965.

——. *Dante in English Literature.* 2 vols. New York: Macmillan, 1909.

Trela, D. J. "Carlyle's Pen Portrait of John Pym." *Carlyle Newsletter* 4 (Spring 1983): 12–15.

Trench, Richard Chenevix. *Letters and Memorials.* 2 vols. London, 1888.

Trevelyan, G. M. *An Autobiography and Other Essays.* London: Longmans, 1949.

——. *Carlyle: An Anthology.* London: Longmans, 1953.

Turner, Captain Samuel. *An Account of an Embassy to the Court of the Teshoo Lama, in Tibet; Containing a Narrative of a Journey Through Bootan, and Part of Tibet.* London, 1800.

Tylor, Edward B. *Researches into the Early History of Mankind and the Development of Civilization.* 1865. Ed. Paul Bohannan. Chicago: University of Chicago Press, 1964.

van Gogh, Vincent. *The Letters of Vincent van Gogh to His Brother, 1872–1886*. Trans. J. van Gogh-Bonger. 2 vols. London: Constable; Boston: Houghton, 1927.

———. *Letters to an Artist: From Vincent van Gogh to Anton Ridder van Rappard, 1881–1885*. Trans. Rela van Messel. New York: Viking, 1936.

Voltaire. *The Age of Louis XIV*. Trans. Martyn P. Pollack. London: Dent; New York: Dutton, 1961.

Walpole, Horace. *Memoirs of the Reign of King George the Third*. Ed. G. F. Russell Barker. 4 vols. London, 1894.

Warwick, Sir Philip. *Memoirs of the Reign of King Charles I with a Continuation to the Happy Restoration of King Charles II*. London, 1702.

Watt, W. Montgomery. "Carlyle on Muhammad." *The Hibbert Journal* 53 (1954–55): 247–54.

———. *Muhammad at Mecca*. Oxford: Clarendon, 1953.

———. *Muhammad at Medina*. Oxford: Clarendon, 1956.

Wellek, René. *Confrontations: Studies in the Intellectual and Literary Relations between Germany, England, and the United States during the Nineteenth Century*. Princeton: Princeton University Press, 1965.

———. "Carlyle and the Philosophy of History." *Philological Quarterly* 23 (1944): 55–76.

———. *Immanuel Kant in England, 1793–1838*. Princeton: Princeton University Press, 1931.

Weygand, Max. *Turenne: Marshal of France*. Trans. George B. Ives. Boston: Houghton, 1930.

Whitman, Walt. *Prose Works 1892*. Ed. Floyd Stovall. 2 vols. New York: New York University Press, 1963–64.

Wilde, Oscar. "Mr. Pater's Last Volume." 1890. Rpt. in *The Artist as Critic: Critical Writings of Oscar Wilde*. Ed. Richard Ellmann. Chicago: University of Chicago Press, 1982. 229–34.

Willey, Basil. *Nineteenth Century Studies: Coleridge to Matthew Arnold.* New York: Columbia University Press, 1949.

Williams, E. N. *A Documentary History of England, 1559–1931.* Vol. 2 of *A Documentary History of England.* 2 vols. Middlesex: Penguin, 1965.

Williams, Raymond. *Culture and Society, 1780–1950.* New York: Columbia University Press, 1960.

Wilson, David Alec. *Carlyle on Cromwell and Others (1837–48).* London: Kegan Paul, 1925.

Wolfe, Don M. Introduction. *Complete Prose Works of John Milton.* 8 vols. New Haven; Yale University Press; London: Oxford University Press, 1959. 4:1–283.

Woolf, Leonard. *Quack, Quack!* New York: Harcourt, 1935.

Wylie, Wm. Howie. *Thomas Carlyle: The Man and his Books.* London, 1881.

Yeats, W[illiam] B[utler]. *Autobiographies: Reveries over Childhood and Youth and The Trembling of the Veil.* New York: Macmillan, 1927.

Young, Jean I., trans. *The Prose Edda of Snorri Sturluson: Tales from Norse Mythology.* Berkeley: University of California Press, 1964.

Young, Louise Merwin. *Thomas Carlyle and the Art of History.* Philadelphia: University of Pennsylvania Press, 1939.

TEXTUAL APPARATUS

EMENDATIONS OF THE COPY-TEXT

ALL departures of the present edition from the copy-text are listed below. The copy-text for this edition is composite: the 1841 first edition is the earliest extant form of the text, except for the two proof pages corresponding to pages 25 and 26 of the first edition, 15.13–16.14 of the present text.

All variant readings found in the collated versions of the text are reported in the Historical Collation beginning on page 445 below. Because the two lists serve distinct purposes, the variants reported below in the list of emendations are repeated in the Historical Collation.

In both lists, each item is keyed to the text by the number of the page and line on which the variant begins (lecture titles are not counted as lines, but the blank lines that separate some paragraphs are counted). The top line of each item gives the copy-text reading, followed by the symbol of the version serving as copy-text at that point. In the list of emendations, the second line in each item gives the variant reading adopted in the present edition, followed by the symbol of the version in which that reading first appeared. (It has not been found necessary to make any emendations not sanctioned by one or more authoritative editions.) Because variants that first appeared simultaneously in both the 1846 British Third Edition and the 1846 American edition have been accorded increased authority for that reason (see the Note on the Text, pp. xcvi–xcviii), such variants are marked in this list "46 & Am." Variants marked simply "46" did not occur in the American edition. In the Historical Collation, the other lines of each item give the complete record of variant readings in chronological order. In both lists, variant readings adopted in the present edition are printed in boldface, and items treated in the Discussion of Editorial Decisions (pp. 431–39) are marked with an asterisk. The symbol "¶" indicates that a new paragraph begins at that point.

Symbol	Version
U	Unrevised proof sheets for the first edition (15.13–16.14 only).
R	Revisions in Carlyle's hand on proof sheets for the first edition (15.13–16.14 only).
41	First edition. London: James Fraser, 1841.
42	Second Edition. London: Chapman and Hall, 1842.
46	Third Edition. London: Chapman and Hall, 1846.
Am	First authorized American edition. New York: Wiley and Putnam, 1846.
52	Fourth Edition. London: Chapman and Hall, 1852.
58	Volume 6 (1858) of the Uniform Edition. 16 vol. London: Chapman and Hall, 1857–58.
70	Volume 12 (1870) of the Library Edition. 30 vol. London: Chapman and Hall, 1869–71.
72	Volume 13 (1872) of the People's Edition. 37 vol. London: Chapman and Hall, 1871–74.

Lecture I. The Hero as Divinity.

5.9	unseen	41
	unseen and	46 & Am
5.21	life there.	41
	Life!	46 & Am
6.12	all.	41
	all things.	46 & Am
6.19	Hamilton's *Travels* into	41
	Turner's *Account of his Embassy* to	42
7.20	Symbols	41
	symbols	46 & Am
8.17	Aristotle's,	41
	Plato's,	52
8.18	were	41
	was	52
8.19	be, says the Philosopher,	41
	be,	52
8.26	the	41
	this	52
8.26	Aristotle.	41
	Plato's.	52
8.31	unveiled	41
	not veiled	46 & Am
10.6	then there	41
	there then	70
10.25	infinitude	41
	Infinitude	46 & Am
14.38	things,	41
	things	46 & Am
15.14*	Paganism	U
	Paganism,	41
15.14*	here	U
	here,	41
15.19	ways,—strange:	U
	ways. Strange:	R
15.28	geyrers,	U
	geysers,	R
15.29	sulphur pools	U
	sulphur-pools	46 & Am

15.33	and what	U
	and of what	R
16.1	Saemund,	U
	Sæmund,	R
16.4	this	U
	that	58
16.8	Saemund's	U
	Sæmund's	R
16.8	afterwards	U
	afterwards,	R
17.3	lived there	41
	that lived	46 & Am
18.36*	winds'	41
	winds,'	Am
18.37	work	41
	work,	46 & Am
21.22	"Wednesday,"	41
	"*Wednes*day,"	70
25.27	howsoever	41
	however	52
25.33	light	41
	kind of lights	46 & Am
25.36*	Type-Northman;	41
	Type-Norseman;	Am
26.2	day?	41
	Day?	46 & Am
26.5	Norseman, in	41
	Norseman;—in	46 & Am
26.6	Northman;	41
	Norseman;	46 & Am
28.34	Powers; and	41
	Powers; and,	46 & Am
28.34	whole	41
	whole,	46 & Am
30.26	*Havamal*	41
	Völuspa	52
30.29	their	41
	their	46 & Am
31.9	Hermode	41
	Hermoder	46 & Am
31.13	Hermode	41
	Hermoder	46 & Am

32.12	*Childe Etin*	41
	Hynde Etin, and still more decisively *Red Etin of Ireland,*	52
32.13	Ballads is a Norse mythus; *Etin* was	41
	Ballads, these are both derived from Norseland; *Etin* is evidently	52
33.23	merely	41
	only	42
34.26	eartnestness	41
	earnestness	42
34.32	*Havamal*	41
	Völuspa	52
34.32	song;	41
	Song;	46 & Am

Lecture II. The Hero as Prophet.

38.14	call	41
	call very	46 & Am
39.5	Mahomet's word	41
	Mahomet's word,	46 & Am
39.6	hour	41
	hour,	46 & Am
39.14	Scepticism;	41
	Scepticism; they	42
42.13	them:	41
	these:	42
43.30	these	41
	those	46 & Am
45.23*	years	41
	years'	42
46.35	business	41
	business, again	58
48.7	this is	41
	these are	46 & Am
48.7	or is	41
	or are	46 & Am
56.27	original.	41
	original. This may be a great point; much perhaps has been lost in the Translation here.	42

58.3	Ah, no!	41
	No, no!	46 & Am
58.29	study	41
	con over	42
59.17	make	41
	change	42
59.18	creatures;	41
	creatures; they come ranking home at evening time,	42
59.19	'and they are	41
	'and are	42
59.19	Ships,	41
	Ships also,	46 & Am
59.24	you,	41
	you,	46 & Am
61.31	kind of man	41
	kind of a man	52

Lecture III. The Hero as Poet.

67.1	Prophet	41
	Prophet,	46 & Am
68.16	that!	41
	these!	46 & Am
71.23	be	41
	be,	46 & Am
73.38	Blank	41
	Lonely	42
73.38	painted	41
	painted as	42
74.15	equable, implacable,	41
	equable,	46 & Am
74.35	state,	41
	State,	46 & Am
75.16	Florence	41
	Florence would have	46 & Am
76.13	strange now	41
	strange, now,	46 & Am
76.14	do so much to amuse us,	41
	make himself so entertaining;	46 & Am

76.16	it is not strange, if you think of	41
	not strange; your Highness is to recollect	46 & Am
77.8	*segui la*	41
	segui	46 & Am
77.10	"Follow	41
	"Follow thou	42
79.31	Sordello,	41
	Brunetto Latini,	52
80.34	too: she speaks of '*questa forma;*'—so innocent;	41
	too: *della bella persona, che mi fu tolta;*	42
80.36*	he 'will	41
	he will	42
80.36*	her.'	41
	her!	42
80.37	again,	41
	again, to wail	42
81.15	far: ah, one	41
	far:—one	46 & Am
82.13	corbels'	41
	corbels	46 & Am
82.13	building,	41
	building,'	46 & Am
82.15	top,	41
	top, which is	46 & Am
82.16	Mercy	41
	Mercy shall have	46 & Am
84.36	arrangement,	41
	arrangement	46 & Am
86.9	more! Ah yes, the	41
	more! The	46 & Am
86.10	men.	41
	men!	46 & Am
87.27*	King Henrys,	41
	King-Henrys,	42
87.27*	Queen Elizabeths	41
	Queen-Elizabeths	42
88.7	vision,	41
	vision, such a	46 & Am

88.8	depth,	41
	depth;	46 & Am
88.16	fit, every way	41
	fit,—every-way	46 & Am
88.18	things; we	41
	things,—we	46 & Am
88.34	like; the	41
	like; does the	46 & Am
88.35	*lux,*	41
	lux, Let there be light;	42
90.28	indeed require us so to speak;	41
	perhaps prescribe such forms of utterance;	46 & Am
91.9	it, without	41
	it,—without	46 & Am
91.9	him, he	41
	him; a thoroughly immoral *man*	46 & Am
91.16	bad, the	41
	bad, to the	46 & Am
91.34	about	41
	concerning	46 & Am
92.26	had not	41
	failed to have	46 & Am
93.2	butt,	41
	butt he is bantering,	46 & Am
93.3	roars and	41
	with his whole heart	70
93.13	hope that they	41
	hope they	46 & Am
94.36	unison!	41
	harmony!	58
95.15	God:' I ask, was	41
	God:' and was	46 & Am
96.12	repeat,	41
	repeat:	46 & Am
96.24	Empire, no	41
	Empire, or no	42

Lecture IV. The Hero as Priest.

100.14	service, a	41
	service, and a	70
100.20	things, a *seer*,	41
	things; a *seer*,	46 & Am
101.32	desires	41
	devises	42
102.32	only the	41
	merely the	42
102.34	too,	41
	too	46 & Am
104.2	must	41
	have to	46 & Am
106.25*	Kings,	41
	Kings,	70
107.28	isolation,	41
	isolation;	46 & Am
108.3	believe in	41
	believe in, and	42
108.4	sincerely.	41
	sincerely to believe in.	42
110.37	hand.	41
	feet.	46 & Am
113.34	heart's desire	41
	heart's-desire	46 & Am
113.35	from	41
	other than that of	46 & Am
113.37	Christendom. The	41
	Christendom.—The	46 & Am
114.9	voice	41
	voice of him	46 & Am
114.20	*another's,*	41
	another's than his,	46 & Am
114.25	in the market-place of Wittenberg.	41
	'at the Elster-Gate of Wittenberg.'	42
115.8	one man, on	41
	but on	46 & Am

115.20	man, Hans Luther the poor miner's Son.	41
	man, the poor miner Hans Luther's Son.	42
118.30	go as	41
	go very much as	46 & Am
118.31	comes that	41
	comes to him that	42
119.1	man	41
	man, he	46 & Am
119.2	written works	41
	Written Works	46 & Am
119.7	four-and-twenty quartos	41
	Four-and-twenty Quartos	46 & Am
120.1	They spoke once about his not being at Leipzig, as if 'Duke George had hindered him,'	41
	'The Devil is aware,' writes he on one occasion, 'that this does not proceed out of fear in me. I have seen and defied innumerable Devils. Duke George,' of Leipzig,	42
120.4	his. It was not for Duke George, answered he: No; "if	41
	his, 'Duke George is not equal to one Devil,'—far short of a Devil! 'If	42
120.6	go,	41
	ride into Leipzig,	42
120.6*	Duke Georges	41
	Duke-Georges	42
120.7	running."	41
	running.' What a reservoir of Dukes to ride into!—	42
120.35	Margaret	41
	Magdalene	42

121.2	Margaret	41
	Magdalene	42
121.4*	'Patmos,' the Wartburg,	41
	Patmos, the Castle of Coburg,	42
121.6	huge,—who	41
	huge:—who	46 & Am
123.19*	*Neale's*	41
	Neal's	46 & Am
123.19	*Puritans*	41
	Puritans[1]	46
123.23	prayer (the Prayer too is given),	41
	prayer,	46 & Am
123.38	[*no footnote*]	41
	* Neal (London, 1755), i. 490.	46 & Am
123.38*	* Neal	46
	[1] Neal	52
125.9	Schwiednitz,	41
	Schweidnitz,	72
128.17	tolerate! We do	41
	tolerate! We are here to resist, to control and vanquish, withal. We do	42
128.18	vanquish,	42
	vanquish	46 & Am
128.18	tolerate Falsehoods,	41
	'tolerate' Falsehoods, Thieveries,	42
128.20	false and unjust!	41
	false, thou art not tolerable!	42
128.20	*extinguish* Falsehoods	41
	extinguish Falsehoods, and put an end to them,	42

Lecture V. The Hero as Man of Letters.

| 134.31 | it not, | 41 |
| | not the fact, and are untrue to it, | 42 |

135.2	Jena,	41
	Erlangen,	46
136.38	clearness,	41
	clearness, or	46 & Am
137.2	These	41
	There	42
141.12	Milton; the humble	41
	Milton! They are something, too, those humble	42
141.14	there! Fragments	41
	there! For all true singing is of the nature of worship; as indeed all true *working* may be said to be,—whereof such *singing* is but the record, and fit melodious representation, to us. Fragments	42
141.28	figure of a speech,	41
	figure of speech,	42
144.7*	order;	41
	order;'	42
145.3	answers	41
	adds	42
145.12	it will	41
	the world will	42
147.10	Formalism	41
	Formulism	42
147.21	Machine; it	41
	machine: I say that it	42
147.22*	not go	41
	not go	42
147.22	wheels and pinions at all! The	41
	wheel-and-pinion 'motives,' self-interests, checks, balances; that there is something far other in it than the clank of spinning-jennies, and parliamentary majorities; and, on the whole, that it is not a machine at all!—The	42

150.7	thought, belief	41
	thought, your belief	46 & Am
151.14	and the	41
	and that the	70
153.39	'fourpence halfpenny	41
	'fourpence-halfpenny	46 & Am
155.18	improvements, changes	41
	improvements, with changes	42
156.35	this, call	41
	this, I call	42
162.13	nursery-ground,' nor	41
	nursery-ground,'—not that, nor	42
162.38	whirlwind in	41
	whirlwind of	46 & Am
164.22	men were not	41
	men are not	42
165.3	Why	41
	"Why	46 & Am
165.3	this?	41
	this?"	46 & Am
165.3	Strength	41
	"Strength	46 & Am
165.4	old.	41
	old."	46 & Am
165.5	say I!	41
	answer I!	42
165.10	Poetry, in	41
	Poetry, so in	42
165.38	it not, by	41
	it is not alterable by	46 & Am
166.10*	history his	41
	history,—his	42
166.32	*burst*	41
	burst,	46 & Am

Lecture VI. The Hero as King.

| 169.5 | *summary* | 41 |
| | summary | 46 & Am |

169.8	us, furnish	41
	us, to furnish	46 & Am
169.8	teaching, tell	41
	teaching, to tell	46 & Am
172.33*	are a Chimera,	41
	are—a Chimera,	42
172.35	Palais Royal,	41
	Palais-Royal,	46 & Am
173.23	madness-quietus,	41
	'madness' quietus,	46 & Am
173.34	Fact, and the	41
	Fact, and that the	46 & Am
179.1	Hutcheson,	41
	Hutchinson,	46 & Am
179.4	wicked.	41
	wicked now.	42
179.11*	*Tartuffe;*	41
	Tartufe;	46 & Am
181.12	The cash is	41
	The purse is	42
182.22	earnest, hearty, sincere	41
	earnest, affectionate, sincere	46 & Am
182.24	You remember that story of his having a vision	41
	Of those stories of 'Spectres;'	46 & Am
182.24	Evil Spirit,	41
	white Spectre in broad daylight,	46 & Am
182.25	would be Sovereign	41
	should be King	46 & Am
182.25	England, and so forth. In broad daylight, some huge white Spectre, which he took to be the Devil, with preternatural monitions of some sort, shews itself to him: the Royalists made immense babble about it; but apart from their	

speculations, we can suppose this story of the Spectre to be true. Then there are afterwards those hypochondriacal visions: the Doctor sent for; Oliver imagining that 'the steeple of Huntingdon was about to tumble on him.'   41 England, we are not bound to believe much;—probably no more than of the other black Spectre, or Devil in person, to whom the Officer *saw* him sell himself before Worcester Fight! But the mournful, over-sensitive, hypochondriac humour of Oliver, in his young years, is otherwise indisputably known. The Huntingdon Physician told Sir Philip Warwick himself, He had often been sent for at midnight; Mr. Cromwell was full of hypochondria, thought himself near dying, and "had fancies about the Town-cross." The things are significant.   46

182.33   Town-cross." The   46
Town-cross." These Am

182.34   bulk of his; in other words, a soul of such *intensity*, such sensibility, with all its strength!   41 strength of his, is not the symptom of falsehood; it is the symptom and promise of quite other than falsehood!   42

182.37   law; falls,   41
Law; falls, or is said to have fallen, 46 & Am

182.38   but speedily   41
but if so, speedily 46 & Am

183.2   He   41
'He 46 & Am

183.3   gambling;—he   41
gambling,' says the story;—he 46 & Am

183.9   at Ely as   41
at St. Ives and Ely, as 42

183.10   true devout   41
true and devout 46 & Am

186.9   shall we so   41
shall we even so 46 & Am

186.10   The vulpine   41
For the vulpine 46 & Am

186.31   One   41
In brief, one 42

192.15   *much life*   41
much of life 46 & Am

192.20   paradings   41
paradings, 46 & Am

192.20   hat do   41
hat, do 46 & Am

193.3   I happily   41
happily I 46 & Am

193.8   statue? than say, There it is!"——   41
statue?"— — 46 & Am

195.19   him,—England   41
him,—why, then, England 42

195.21   joint   41
united 42

196.13   him, He   41
him and this Cause, He 46 & Am

196.29   war,   41
          War,   46 & Am

199.33   They appointed Cromwell Protector, and went their ways. The second Parliament,   41
They dissolved themselves, as incompetent; delivered up their power again into the hands of the Lord General Cromwell, to do with it what he liked and could. What *will* he do with it! The Lord General Cromwell, 'Commander-in-chief of all the Forces raised and to be raised;' he hereby sees himself, at this unexampled juncture, as it were the one available Authority left in England, nothing between England and utter Anarchy but him alone. Such is the undeniable Fact of his position and England's, there and then. What will he do with it! After deliberation, he decides that he will *accept* it; will formally, with public solemnity, say and vow before God and men, "Yes, the Fact is so, and I will do the best I can with it!" Protectorship, Instrument of Government,—these are the external forms of the thing; worked out and sanctioned as they could in the circumstances be, by the Judges, by the leading Official people, 'Council of Officers and Persons of interest in the Nation:' and as for the thing itself, undeniably enough, at the pass matters had now come to, there *was* no alternative but Anarchy or that. Puritan England might accept it or not; but Puritan England was, in real truth, saved from suicide thereby!—I believe the Puritan People did, in an inarticulate, grumbling, yet on the whole grateful and real way, accept this anomalous act of Oliver's; at least, he and they together made it good, and always better to the last. But in their Parliamentary *articulate* way, they had their difficulties, and never knew fully what to say to it!— ¶Oliver's second Parliament, properly his *first* regular Parliament,   46 & Am

200.19   rule these Notables had fixed upon,   41
rule laid down in the Instrument of Government,   46 & Am

200.23   one. Most   41
one. So likewise to his third Parliament, in similar rebuke for their pedantries and obstinacies. Most   46 & Am

200.25   chaotic, as all his   41
chaotic, all these   46 & Am

200.35	all, played	41	203.23	then	41
	all, and played	46 & Am		then,	46 & Am
201.18	things these	41	204.21	these are	41
	things the	46 & Am		there are	46 & Am
202.21	wanted	41	204.21	has any liberty	41
	waited	42		has liberty	42
202.27	Hutcheson,	41	205.16	*resultat*	41
	Hutchinson,	46 & Am		*result*	46 & Am
202.28	Hutcheson	41	206.3	Lœben,	41
	Hutchinson	46 & Am		Leoben,	42
202.33	Hutcheson,	41	207.3	Notre-Dame there,	41
	Hutchinson,	46 & Am		Notre-Dame,	46 & Am
202.34	Presbyterian	41	208.4	rude-draught;	41
	Republican	46 & Am		a rude-draught never	
203.1	twice	41		completed;	46 & Am
	at least once	46 & Am	208.5	not?	41
				other?	46 & Am

DISCUSSION OF EDITORIAL DECISIONS

FOLLOWING are discussions of the editorial decisions made with respect to problematic variants. These are for the most part either cases in which a change of wording found in an authoritative edition was *not* accepted as an emendation of the copy-text or cases in which a change of punctuation *was* so accepted. As elsewhere in the apparatus, emendations are set in boldface. For an explanation of the symbols used, see the Historical Collation below, p. 445.

7.17	Allegory-theorists	41
	Allegory theorists	46 → 72

We accept as authorial revisions all new variants that appear in both the 1846 British and American editions (see the Note on the Text, pp. xcvi–xcviii), except where the coincidence can be plausibly explained as the result of the independent action of typesetters on both sides of the Atlantic. The loss of this hyphen, as of the ones at 8.4, 8.10, and 86.24 below, could easily have been a regularization, deliberate or inadvertent, made by both typesetters independently.

8.4	firm-land	41
	firm land	46 → 72

See 7.17 above.

8.10	quack-theory	41
	quack theory	46 → 72

See 7.17 above.

12.19	even:	41
	even;	46 → 72

Although this change is found in both of the 1846 editions, there are nine other instances of the same change from colon to semi-colon that occur in the British but not in the American edition, and twenty-eight instances of the same change in the American but not in the British edition. Those in the American edition are clearly the work of the American typesetter, those in the British probably the work of the British typesetter. This instance is therefore most probably a coincidental intersection of the two sets.

13.27	paralysis;	41
	paralysis:	46 → 72

As with the change from colon to semi-colon discussed at 12.19 above, there are four other instances of this change, from semi-colon to colon, that occur in the 1846 British edition but not in the American, and thirteen instances in the American but not the British. The same argument applies.

15.14	Paganism	U
	Paganism,	41 → 72
15.14	here	U
	here,	41 → 72

See Note on the Text, p. lxxxvii.

18.36	winds'	41
	wind,'	46 52 → 72
	winds,'	Am

The plural is more correct (see note at 18.35), and the change was apparently not made at the same time as most of the other changes of wording that appear in the 1846 British Third Edition, since the plural is still found in the 1846 American edition (see 83.5 below). The change to the singular, therefore, does not appear to be authorial. On the other hand, the addition of the comma in both 1846 editions has been accepted.

19.3	Hyper-Brobdignagian	41
	Hyper-Brobdingnagian	Centenary Edition

The spelling *Brobdignag* rather than *Brobdingnag*, the correct Swiftian form, is consistent throughout all lifetime editions, here and at 32.5 and 34.25. The *Oxford English Dictionary* gives three citations under "Brobdingnag" for the currency of the alternative spelling *Brobdignag*: from Pope, Southey, and the instance at 32.5 of the present work.

21.22	"Wednesday,"	41
	"*Wednes*day,"	70 72

The change from roman to italic type or the reverse, while not amounting to a change of wording, is nevertheless a change that is likely to represent the preference of the author, except in those cases, such as 43.4 and 123.19 below, in which such a change might be thought to be called for by some rule of style, and can therefore be explained as a regularization. In the present instance, the italicization of *part* of a word is typically Carlylean.

25.36	Type-Northman;	41
	Type Norseman;	46 52 → 72
	Type-Norseman;	Am

The change of wording from "Northman" to "Norseman" must have been ordered by Carlyle in both printer's copies for the two 1846 editions, but the loss of the hyphen in the British edition is more likely to have occurred during the setting of that edition, inadvertently or as a regularization by the typesetter.

35.37	one: it	41
	one? it	42
	one? It	46 → 72

The change from colon to question mark in 1842 is a regularization that does not commend itself as probably authorial. The capitalization of the following word, though occurring in both of the 1846 editions, is a necessary correction, given the question mark, that could well have been made by both typesetters independently.

39.2	one hundred and eighty millions	41
	one-hundred-and-eighty-millions	58
	a hundred-and-eighty millions	70 72

Although this is a change of wording, we see it as a response, not necessarily by the author, to the excessive 1858 hyphens (see Note on the Text, p. c).

| 43.4 | Book of Job | 41 |
| | *Book of Job* | Am → 72 |

This italicization of a *title* can be seen as a regularization. That it first occurred in the 1846 American edition but not in the 1846 British edition suggests that it was not indicated on the common printer's copy. That it occurred again independently in the 1852 British edition is merely evidence that the force of the rule was felt on both sides of the Atlantic.

| 45.23 | years | 41 |
| | years' | 42 → 72 |

We regard the addition of the needed apostrophe as a correction expressive of Carlyle's intention.

| 57.4 | *bonâ-fide* | 41 |
| | *bona-fide* | 42 → 72 |

We are indebted to Ian Campbell for the observation that the circumflex here is Carlyle's usual device for indicating a long vowel to distinguish the ablative from the nominative in first-declension Latin nouns and adjectives. Compare *"invitâ Minervâ"* in *Letters* 1:188.

| 80.36 | he 'will | 41 |
| | *he* will | 42 → 72 |

| 80.36 | her.' | 41 |
| | her! | 42 → 72 |

The four changes of punctuation and italicization encompassed in these linked revisions are clearly a part of the simultaneous revision of this passage, 80.34–37, in the Second Edition, and have therefore been accepted.

| 83.5 | our | 41 |
| | or | 46 52 → 72 |

Although the later reading is plausible, we judge it to be more probably the result of a typographical error. That the change is not found in the 1846 American edition suggests that it was not indicated in the printer's copy for that edition, unlike most of the changes of wording that appear in the 1846 British Third Edition. See the Note on the Text, pp. xcvi–xcviii, and further examples at 193.38 and 201.20 below.

| 86.24 | chivalry-way | 41 |
| | chivalry way | 46 → 72 |

See 7.17 above.

| 87.27 | King Henrys, | 41 |
| | King-Henrys, | 42 → 72 |

| 87.27 | Queen Elizabeths | 41 |
| | Queen-Elizabeths | 42 46 52 → 72 |

See below at 120.6.

| 87.29 | Stephen's, | 41 |
| | Stephens, | 46 52 58 |

Although the change in spelling of a proper name would ordinarily be taken as authorial, the fact that the change did not occur in both 1846 editions counts against it, as does the fact that the copy-text spelling was restored in 1870.

| 91.24 | reflexions | 41 |
| | reflections | 46 → 72 |

This modernization of spelling, though it occurs in both 1846 editions, is far more likely to be the coincidental activity of both typesetters than to represent Carlyle's altered preference, especially since the same change occurs at 153.2 in the British but not in the American edition.

| 95.25 | be still | 41 |
| | still be | 46 52 → 72 |

Although technically a change of wording, this transposition, which does not occur in the American 1846 edition, is most likely a typesetter's error.

| 100.34 | Thebaid | 41 |
| | Thebaïd | 46 52 → 72 |

This situation is similar to that of 87.29 above, except that whereas that change could be considered an error (and was so considered in 1870), this one could be considered a regularization.

| 102.20 | downfal. | 41 |
| | downfall. | 46 → 72 |

As in the variant at 91.24, it is easier to imagine that typesetters on both sides of the Atlantic saw the earlier spelling (incidentally the spelling in Johnson's *Dictionary*) as unacceptably obsolete than that Carlyle changed his orthographic preference.

104.16	Godhood;	41
	Godhead;	46 52 → 72
	God;	Am

Whether the revision in the 1846 British Third Edition represents a change in Carlyle's choice of words or a typographer's emendation from a less familiar to a more familiar usage is impossible to say, and the evidently erroneous reading in the 1846 American edition gives no guidance. "Godhood" is elsewhere attested in Carlyle's writings.

| 106.25 | Kings, | 41 |
| | *Kings,* | 70 72 |

Italicization here is certainly a clarification of the passage, but not a necessary regularization. The author's preference is therefore the most probable explanation.

| 107.14 | adviseablest | 41 |
| | advisablest | 46 → 72 |

The arguments of 91.24 and 102.20 above apply here as well, with the additional observation that there are twelve analogous instances of the change from an *-eabl-* form to *-abl-* that occur in the 1846 British edition but not in the 1846 American. (The latest citation of the spelling *adviseable* in the *Oxford English Dictionary* is 1790.)

| 107.30 | makes it | 41 |
| | make it | 70 72 |

Like the analogous instances at 145.13 and 198.10 below, this change from the singular to the plural verb could have been regarded, by someone other than the author, as a necessary correction of Carlyle's grammar.

| 120.6 | Duke Georges | 41 |
| | Duke-Georges | 42 → 72 |

This occurs within an extensive revision of the passage, 120.1–7, and is typically Carlylean. We have therefore accepted it, and also the two analogous added hyphens in the same edition at 87.27.

| 121.4 | 'Patmos,' the Wartburg | 41 |
| | Patmos, the Castle of Coburg, | 42 → 72 |

Although this revision changes a correct allusion to an apparently incorrect one (see note at 121.4–5), there can be little doubt that Carlyle himself intended it.

123.19	*Neale's*	41
	Neal's	46 → 58
	Neal's	70 72

The correction of the spelling of Neal's name, contemporary with the addition of the footnote in 1846, is clearly Carlyle's revision. The change from italic to roman in 1870, on the other hand, is likely a regularization.

| 123.38 | * Neal | 46 |
| | ¹ Neal | 52 → 72 |

In the 1846 British Third Edition, in which this footnote first appeared, the reference symbol in the text is a superscript numeral *1*, while the reference symbol leading the footnote itself is an asterisk. The asterisk was changed to a superscript *1* in the 1852 Fourth Edition. Since the inconsistency in the Third Edition cannot have been intended, we have followed the correction as it was made in the Fourth Edition.

| 135.2 | Jena, | 41 |
| | **Erlangen,** | 46 52 → 72 |

This is the only unambiguously authorial revision that occurs in the 1846 British but not the 1846 American edition. It is impossible to say when Carlyle made the revision, or whether it represents a divergence between the "precisely identical" printer's copies, but that it is Carlyle's revision cannot be doubted. For the explanation of the revision itself, see note at 135.1.

| 144.7 | order; | 41 |
| | order;' | 42 → 72 |

An opening quotation mark without a closing quotation mark is clearly an error. We follow the Second Edition in supplying the missing punctuation at this point.

| 145.13 | called | 41 |
| | call | 72 |

In fact, Carlyle *had* made this point earlier in the lecture, at 137.10–16. It is therefore likely that this change was made by the typographer, under the impression that he was correcting a grammatical error. See 107.30 and 198.10.

| 147.22 | not go | 41 |
| | *not* go | 42 → 72 |

This instance of italicization, like that at 80.36 above, appears to be part of the simultaneous authorial revision of the passage in which it occurs, in this case 147.21–25, and has therefore been accepted as such.

159.37	and contorsions	41
	and contortions	46 → 72
159.38	The contorsions	41
	The contortions	46 → 72

As with the similar cases at 91.24, 102.20, and 107.14 discussed above, in which spellings that were rare or obsolete in the nineteenth century were modernized in both 1846 editions, we believe it more probable that both typesetters would have made the changes independently than that Carlyle would have changed his preferred spelling. (The latest citation of the spelling *contorsion* in the *Oxford English Dictionary* is 1773.)

166.10	history his	41
	history,—his	42 46 52 → 72
	history—his	Am

The absence of punctuation at this point in the first edition is unlikely to have been a typesetter's error, as the line is very widely spaced and the typesetter would not have overlooked any punctuation present in his copy that might have tightened it. But the sense requires some punctuation here, and the characteristic comma-dash combination is typically Carlylean. We therefore take this to be an authorial revision.

| 171.3 | *it* | 41 |
| | it | 42 → 72 |

The loss of italics here seems at least as likely to have been inadvertent as deliberate.

| 172.33 | are a Chimera, | 41 |
| | are—a Chimera, | 42 → 72 |

In contrast to the case of 166.10 above, it is precisely because the sense does *not* require any punctuation here that we conclude that this dash must also have been added by the author.

| 179.11 | *Tartuffe;* | 41 |
| | *Tartufe;* | 46 → 72 |

Although the modern French word for "hypocrite," *tartufe*, is spelled with one *f*, it is derived from the eponymous character in Moliere's *Le Tartuffe, ou l'Imposteur* (1669), where the spelling, like the commonest spelling in both Britain and America in all centuries, is with two. Why Carlyle would have indicated this change in the printer's copies of both 1846 editions is a mystery, but the fact of the change in both editions is more easily explained by his having done so than by both compositors independently changing from a more to a less familiar spelling.

179.38	euphuisms,	41
	euphemisms,	70 72
180.12	no euphuistic	41
	no euphemistic	70 72
180.14	in euphuistic	41
	in euphemistic	70 72
187.1	Euphuisms;	41
	Euphuisms,	42 46 52 58
	Euphuism,	Am
	Euphemisms,	70 72

Beyond doubt, the word that Carlyle intended here was *euphuism*, not *euphemism* (see note at 179.38). The typesetter of the Library Edition must have made the change from a word he did not recognize to one he knew, under the impression that he was only modernizing the spelling.

193.38	do a priceless	41
	do priceless	46 52 → 72

The dropping of the somewhat unidiomatic article here seems at least as likely to have been unintended as deliberate. (See 83.5 above.)

197.6	hand,	41
	hands,	46 52 → 72

Although technically changes of wording, this and the variant at 201.19 below, which do not occur in the 1846 American edition, are judged to be more probably regularizations by the London printers, who we know read their own proofs in 1846, than authorial revisions.

198.10	call	41
	calls	70 72

This is likely to be a regularization of Carlyle's grammar, like the similar changes at 107.30 and 145.13.

201.9	into Chaos	41
	in Chaos	72

We judge this alteration a typographical error, not an authorial revision.

201.19	Cromwell's	41
	Cromwell	46 52 → 72

See 197.6 above.

201.20	Jesuistic	41
	Jesuitic	46 52 → 72

The *Oxford English Dictionary* cites the later version of this passage, dating the citation "1840," in establishing the form *Jesuitic* as a "now *rare*" equivalent of *Jesuitical*. There is no citation for the copy-text form *Jesuistic; Jesuist* is called both obsolete and rare, with no citation later than 1645. Nevertheless, we do not feel that the copy-text form is so impossible that we can conclude that it was unintended. Also, we see that here again the 1846 American edition follows the copy-text form, reducing the probability that the change was a deliberate revision. We therefore do not feel entitled to emend in favor of the later form, though only by doing so could we have preserved the accuracy of the *OED* citation.

LINE-END HYPHENS IN THE COPY-TEXT

THE following are the editorially established forms of possible compounds that were hyphenated at the ends of lines in the 1841 first edition. A slash (/) indicates the position of the line-break in the copy-text where this is not obvious.

6.30	eldest-born	108.25	*dis*believe
7.12	life-guidance	108.30	Serpent-queller
8.34	rock-built	108.37	everlasting
12.13	*Kön-ning*	114.19	God's-message
12.26	Hero-worship	114.31	God's-world
14.17	tavern-waiters	115.30	Nightmare
14.36	Hero-worship	117.18	dull-droning
16.20	Northland	117.34	Popehood
16.27	Summer-heat	120.37	Awestruck
17.12	*Ice-bergs*	123.13	Star-chamber
19.4	giantlike	124.24	Hero-worship
23.2	overflowed	125.19	Scotchmen
23.35	camera-obscura	127.18	narrow-looking
24.23	everlasting	128.28	much-enduring
25.36	Type-North/man	131.7	Regent-Murrays
27.24	childlike	143.38	ill-conditioned
29.11	Sea-kings	146.11	blackberries
29.25	forest-feller	148.2	death-/in-life
32.19	world-tree	148.36	half-and-/half
34.9	*Midgard-snake*	149.35	straightway
34.35	world-embracing	150.28	Quack-squadron
37.8	Hero-worship	150.35	half-hero
38.20	Hero-worship	151.22	great-looking
38.34	well-meaning	152.25	Fourpence-half/penny
39.2	life-guidance	153.37	school-languages
42.8	swift-handed	154.32	glared-in
47.10	good-opinion	155.15	footsteps
50.8	god-announcing	156.19	everlasting
56.20	shoulder-blades	156.22	seed-field
57.18	pellmell	157.36	valet-de-/chambre
61.27	manhood	160.4	*Contrat-social*
62.5	well-beloved	162.1	hard-handed
62.10	gray-haired	162.14	clay-farm
63.14	life-death	162.36	Harz-rock
65.4	three-score	165.29	Hero-worship
74.23	school-divinity	165.30	well-being
77.17	broken-hearted	166.18	ploughman
81.12	sore-saddened	167.13	Fire-flies
84.27	Saint-Helena	169.19	*Able-man*
93.11	Dogberry	170.4	ballot-box
94.13	Playhouse	170.27	bricklayer
106.12	Hero-captain	171.25	steamengine

171.36	self-interest		196.1	lion-hearted
172.24	everlasting		197.2	Hero-Cavalier
173.2	death-sleep		197.30	constitution-builders
173.15	nonentity		198.37	Englishmen
173.23	life-system		199.20	Barebones's
176.29	College-rules		200.30	forethoughts
185.37	*pie-powder*		200.34	*foreseen*
186.22	Ballot-boxes		202.23	no-whither
186.28	ballot-boxes		202.28	battle-mate
186.29	Valet-World		204.13	Fanatic-Hypocrite
187.27	*hero*hood,		206.2	onwards
190.22	starting-point		206.23	charlatan-element
193.32	broken-hearted		206.33	*self*-deception
195.3	Statesman		207.3	Notre-Dame

NOTES

17.12. The only other instance of "iceberg" in the copy-text is at 32.4 where it reads "Ice-bergs" (in-line hyphen). All other editions print it as a single unhyphenated word unless at line ends. Following the copy-text, the hyphen has been retained.

25.36. "Type-North-/man" in the copy-text at 25.36 was revised to "Type Norse-/man" in the 1846 British edition, "Type-Norseman" in the American. The present text follows the latter reading.

77.17. "Broken-hearted" occurs four times in the copy-text. Besides these two instances (here and at 193.32) where the hyphen is at a line end, one of the others is hyphenated in-line (at 173.25) and the other (at 144.27) is unhyphenated. Clearly the hyphenated form is normal, and the hyphens will therefore be retained in the ambiguous cases. However there seems to be no reason to impose a hyphen at 144.27 for the sake of mere consistency.

120.37. "Awestruck" occurs four times in the copy-text. It is hyphenated (in-line) at 83.24, but unhyphenated at 120.36 and at 157.26. Because the word is unhyphenated on the line above the line-end hyphen, the hyphen has been dropped.

123.13. This is the only instance of "Star-chamber" in the text. The *OED* gives many variations of spelling, but only two instances (from 1560 and 1596) of an unhyphenated compound. The *OED*'s preferred spelling is with a hyphen. The hyphen has therefore been retained.

154.32. "Glared in" occurs twice in the text. Besides this case, it is printed at 47.24 as two words. The Uniform Edition adds the hyphen at 47.24 in keeping with its pattern, and this added hyphen is kept through subsequent editions. But the hyphen at 154.32 is not kept by the Library Edition or subsequent editions, a distinct departure from the pattern (see "Note on the Text" above, p. c).

171.25. "Steam-engine" occurs with an in-line hyphen at 65.24; "steamengine" occurs unhyphenated at 148.28 and 149.25. Following both the more common and the more proximate form, the hyphen is dropped here.

193.32. See 77.17 above.

LINE-END HYPHENS IN THE PRESENT TEXT

In quotations from the present edition, no line-end hyphens are to be retained except the following:

3.21	light-fountain		85.17	Hero-Poet
8.10	quack-theory		86.27	long-enduring
9.26	never-resting		88.16	every-way
11.36	Hero-worship		107.37	long-run
12.9	Hero-worship		108.30	Serpent-queller
16.26	Sea-tempest		110.13	school-children
16.27	Summer-heat		114.31	God's-world
19.3	Hyper-Brobdignagian		119.7	Four-and-twenty
23.35	camera-obscura		121.29	crag-like
25.15	lion-heart		125.14	silk-stockings
30.35	square-built		125.19	Half-and-half
31.25	Summer-heat		129.25	cautious-hopeful
32.19	world-tree		134.3	god-inspired
32.37	Giant-land		137.13	Book-writers
34.23	Mimer-stithy		141.10	sphere-harmony
35.15	under-zeal		147.23	spinning-jennies
42.4	sand-sea		148.2	death-in-life
43.37	festoon-rows		155.13	dim-struggling
46.30	true-meaning		156.19	heart-*sincerity*
56.15	State-Paper		157.36	valet-de-chambre
60.4	rock-mountains		166.29	candle-light
61.20	ill-provided		167.9	Light-chafers
62.30	mealy-mouthed		173.2	God's-world
63.8	amateur-search		173.18	death-struggle
65.4	three-score		182.33	deep-feeling
68.16	song-writer		187.13	Sorrow-stricken
68.27	spindle-shanks		190.27	Play-actor
83.6	world-wide		195.22	Law-Courts
84.27	Saint-Helena		195.33	hero-hearts
84.37	heart-song			

HISTORICAL COLLATION

FOLLOWING is a complete historical collation of *On Heroes, Hero-Worship, and the Heroic in History*. All variant readings found in the collated versions of the text are reported. The standard of collation (the copy-text of the present edition) is composite: the 1841 first edition is the earliest extant form of the text, except for the two proof pages corresponding to pages 25 and 26 of the first edition, 15.13–16.14 of the present text.

Each item is keyed to the present edition by the number of the page and line on which the variant begins (lecture titles are not counted as lines, but the blank lines that separate some paragraphs are counted). For each item, the top line gives the copy-text reading—which for most items will be the same as the reading in the present text—followed by the symbol of the version serving as copy-text at that point. The other lines of each item report all variant readings in chronological order. Where a variant has been accepted as an emendation, the emended reading that will be found in the present edition is printed in boldface. Items treated in the Discussion of Editorial Decisions (pp. 431–39) are marked with an asterisk.

Each variant reading is followed by the symbols of all versions in which that reading occurred, as given in the table below. An arrow between two such symbols (e.g., 46 → 72) signifies that the reading in question is found in all intervening versions. (For this purpose, the 1846 American edition is considered as intervening between the 1846 British Third Edition and the 1852 Fourth Edition.) Any version not accounted for in this way agrees with the copy-text reading. For example, from the second line of the item at 8.38, where the symbols "46 52 → 72" appear, one can conclude that "42" and "Am" agree with the copy-text reading, while "46," "52," "58," "70," and "72" agree with the variant reading.

Double brackets ([]) signify that one character or punctuation mark is absent at that point in the indicated version, but that extra blank space is found at that point, suggesting broken type. The symbol "¶" indicates that a new paragraph begins at that point. The symbol "/" indicates the end of a line when relevant.

Symbol	Version
U	Unrevised proof sheets for the first edition (15.13–16.14 only).
R	Revisions in Carlyle's hand on proof sheets for the first edition (15.13–16.14 only).
41	First edition. London: James Fraser, 1841.
42	Second Edition. London: Chapman and Hall, 1842.
46	Third Edition. London: Chapman and Hall, 1846.
Am	First authorized American edition. New York: Wiley and Putnam, 1846.
52	Fourth Edition. London: Chapman and Hall, 1852.
58	Volume 6 (1858) of the Uniform Edition. 16 vol. London: Chapman and Hall, 1857–58.
70	Volume 12 (1870) of the Library Edition. 30 vol. London: Chapman and Hall, 1869–71.
72	Volume 13 (1872) of the People's Edition. 37 vol. London: Chapman and Hall, 1871–74.

Lecture I. The Hero as Divinity.

3.15	embodiment,	41
	embodyment,	Am
3.23	world:	41
	world;	42 → 72
4.5	widely distant	41
	widely-distant	58 → 72
4.9	but,	41
	but	Am
4.33	No-world;	41
	No-World;	70 72
5.9	unseen	41
	unseen and	46 → 72
5.16	look,	41
	look	70 72
5.16	little,	41
	little	70 72
5.20	falsehoods,	41
	falsehoods	72
5.21	life there.	41
	Life!	46 → 72
5.24	worshipped	41
	worshiped	58
6.12	savage	41
	sovage	Am
6.12	all.	41
	all things.	46 → 72
6.14	at	41
	into	Am
6.19	Hamilton's *Travels* into	41
	Turner's *Account of his Embassy* to	42 → 72
6.27	Priests	41
	priests	70 72
6.27	Man	41
	man	Am
7.1	shadowing forth,	41
	shadowing-forth,	58 → 72
7.1	personification,	41
	personification	58 → 72

7.5	speak out	41
	speak-out	58 → 72
7.13	should	41
	would	Am
7.16	I	41
	¶I	70 72
7.17*	Allegory-theorists	41
	Allegory theorists	46 → 72
7.20	Symbols	41
	symbols	46 → 72
7.29	symbolizes!	41
	symbolises!	58 → 72
7.33	certainty,	41
	certainty	70 72
7.38	what was	41
	what is	Am
8.3	cloudfield,	41
	cloudfield	70 72
8.4*	firm-land	41
	firm land	46 → 72
8.8	men,	41
	men	70 72
8.10*	quack-theory	41
	quack theory	46 → 72
8.17	Aristotle's,	41
	Plato's,	52 → 72
8.18	were	41
	was	52 → 72
8.19	be, says the Philosopher,	41
	be,	52 → 72
8.26	the	41
	this	52 → 72
8.26	Aristotle.	41
	Plato's.	52 → 72
8.31	unveiled	41
	not veiled	46 → 72
8.32	flashing in	41
	flashing-in	58 → 72
8.38	rain:	41
	rain;	46 52 → 72

9.19	me!—what	41
	me—what	70 72
9.22	*us.*	41
	us.	Am
9.26	envelopes	41
	envelops	58 → 72
9.28	Creation,	41
	creation,	72
9.29	of	41
	at	Am
9.30	what not,	41
	what-not,	58 → 72
9.31	bottled up	41
	bottled-up	58 → 72
9.31	jars,	41
	jars	70 72
9.38	stripping off	41
	stripping-off	58 → 72
10.3	eye	41
	eyes	Am
10.6	then there	41
	there then	70 72
10.6	shining down	41
	shining-down	58 → 72
10.11	glancing out	41
	glancing-out	58 → 72
10.13	*worshipped*	41
	worshiped	58
10.14	worshipping	41
	worshiping	58
10.25	infinitude	41
	Infinitude	46 → 72
10.25	itself?'	41
	itself'?	70 72
10.26	loveable.	41
	lovable.	58 → 72
10.29	did,—namely,	41
	did, namely	Am
10.34	saying,	41
	saying	70 72
10.36	Man!"	41
	man!"	Am

11.1	Being	41
	being	Am
11.3	temple	41
	Temple	70 72
11.8	turn out	41
	turn-out	58
11.16	finished off	41
	finished-off	58 → 72
12.19*	even:	41
	even;	46 → 72
12.27	gone out,	41
	gone-out,	58
12.28	some time	41
	sometime	Am
12.30	Shew	41
	Show	58 → 72
13.2	For	41
	¶For	70 72
13.8	crumbling down	41
	crumbling-down	58 → 72
13.27*	paralysis;	41
	paralysis:	46 → 72
13.35	burst out	41
	burst-out	58 → 72
13.37	life,	41
	life	58 → 72
14.1	Voltairism	41
	Voltaireism	70 72
14.6	comes up	41
	comes-up	58
14.12	realized	41
	realised	58 → 72
14.17	Maitre	41
	Maître	52 → 72
14.18	Postilion:	41
	Postillion:	Am
	Postillion,	70 72
14.21	beautifullest,	41
	beautifulest,	70 72
14.22	beautifuller,	41
	beautifuler,	70 72
14.25	worshipped.	41
	worshiped.	58

14.26	bow down	41	16.1	Saemund,	U	
	bow-down	58		**Sæmund,**	R → 72	
14.27	nay	41	16.3	Chaunts	U	
	nay,	Am		Chants	58 → 72	
14.27	bow down	41	16.4	this	U	
	bow-down	58		**that**	58 → 72	
14.38	things,	41	16.6	Sturleson,	U	
	things	46 → 72		Sterleson,	58	
15.5	rushings down	41	16.8	Saemund's	U	
	rushings-down	58 → 72		**Sæmund's**	R → 72	
15.12	incipient	41	16.8	afterwards	U	
	recipient	Am		**afterwards,**	R → 72	
15.13	set forth.	U	16.13	still:	U	
	set-forth.	58		still;	Am	
15.14*	Paganism	U	16.21	be	41	
	Paganism,	41 → 72		be the	Am	
15.14*	here	U	16.24	before,	41	
	here,	41 → 72		before	Am	
15.16	century;	U	16.26	demonic	41	
	century:	42 → 72		demoniac	Am	
15.16	eight hundred	U	16.26	Frost,	41	
	eight-hundred	58 → 72		Forest,	Am	
15.17	worshippers	U	16.30	Asen	41	
	worshipers	58		Asen,	70 72	
15.19	ways,—strange:	U	16.31	Home	41	
	ways. Strange:	R → 72		home	52 → 72	
15.24	burst up,	U	17.2	god,	41	
	burst-up,	58 → 72		God,	Am	
15.28	snow-jokuls,	U	17.3	lived there	41	
	snow jokuls,	70 72		**that lived**	46 → 72	
15.28	geyrers,	U	17.3	too,	41	
	geysers,	R → 72		too	58 → 72	
15.29	sulphur pools	U	17.5	Norse	41	
	sulphur-pools	46 → 72		North	Am	
15.32	seabord	U	17.5	Hoary	41	
	seaboard	72		hoary	52 → 72	
15.33	and what	U	17.10	or fleet	41	
	and of what			or	Am	
		R → 46　52 → 72	17.11	*Frost-winds.*	41	
15.36	lost	U		*Frost-Winds.*	52 → 72	
	lost,	70 72	17.12	*Ice-bergs:*	41	
15.36	burst up	U		*Icebergs:*	42 → 72	
	burst-up	58 → 72				

17.17	drawing down drawing-down	41 58 → 72	
17.20	peal: peal;	41 58 → 72	
17.20	beard;' that beard,'—that	41 58 → 72	
17.23	beautifullest beautifulest	41 70 72	
17.25	hear tell of hear tell-of	41 58 → 72	
17.29	shews shows	41 58 → 72	
18.9	speech Speech	41 46 52 → 72	
18.13	Scandinavian Scandinavianism	41 Am	
18.27	come down come-down	41 58	
18.28	sending out sending-out	41 58	
18.29	cauldron caldron	41 70 72	
18.31	walking off walking-off	41 58	
18.36*	winds' wind,' winds,'	41 46 52 → 72 Am	
18.37	work work,	41 46 → 72	
19.2	scull skull	41 46 52 → 72	
19.4	enormous;—to enormous; to	41 Am	
19.10	Ash-tree Ashtree	41 Am	
19.11	deep down deep-down	41 58 → 72	
19.37	First first	41 Am	
20.18	Man man	41 Am	
20.24	Sphinx-enigma sphinx-enigma	41 42 → 72	

20.25	there. there?	41 46 52 → 72	
20.28	this Odin this Odin,	41 58 → 72	
20.28	origin of origin of the	41 Am	
20.29	First first	41 Am	
20.29	was a man was	41 Am	
21.1	flung out flung-out	41 58 → 72	
21.2	Picture picture	41 42 → 72	
21.3	canvass, canvas,	41 58 → 72	
21.6	ever new ever-new	41 58 → 72	
21.14	thought of thought-of	41 58 → 72	
21.20	we; we:	41 46 52 → 72	
21.22*	"Wednesday," "*Wednes*day,"	41 70 72	
21.23	history: history;	41 42 → 72	
21.30	forth,—and forth, and	41 Am	
21.31	worshipped worshiped	41 58	
21.34	find out find-out	41 58	
22.3	environment, environment	41 70 72	
22.10	such like, suchlike,	41 70 72	
22.18	adjectives, adjectives	41 Am	
22.19	it,—did it, did	41 Am	
22.21	were was	41 Am	

22.23	Indeed	41		25.6	Phenician	41
	Indeed,	70 72			Phœnician	70 72
22.24	whatsoever	41		25.25	noblest;	41
	whatsover	58			noblest:	Am
22.27	tree,—as	41		25.27	howsoever	41
	tree, as	Am			**however**	52 → 72
22.36	god?—that	41		25.33	light	41
	god? that	Am			**kind of lights**	46 → 72
23.3	Odin,—since	41		25.36*	Type-Northman;	41
	Odin, since	Am			Type Norseman;	
23.6	himself,—should	41				46 52 → 72
	himself, should	Am			**Type-Norseman;**	Am
23.20	"Wuotan?"	41		25.37	burst up	41
	"Woutan?"	Am			burst-up	58 → 72
23.20	"Wuotan!"—	41		26.2	day?	41
	"Woutan!"—	Am			**Day?**	46 → 72
23.29	contemporaries,	41		26.5	Peoples:	41
	contemporaries	52 → 72			Peoples;	58 → 72
23.30	three hundred	41		26.5	Norseman, in	41
	three-hundred	58 → 72			**Norseman;—in**	46 → 72
23.31	three thousand	41		26.6	Northman;	41
	three-thousand	58 → 72			Norseman;	46 → 72
23.38	Mind,	41		26.13	develope	41
	mind,	72			develop	58 → 72
23.39	light:	41		26.15	Teutonic	41
	light;	46 52 → 72			Neutonic	Am
24.1	shine out,	41		26.30	shew	41
	shine-out,	58			show	58 → 72
24.5	through.—Curious	41		27.3	to! It	41
	through. Curious	Am			to!—It	58 → 72
24.12	Fantasy	41		27.25	greathearted	41
	Phantasy	72			great-hearted	70 72
24.20	building up	41		28.11	*Destiny,*	41
	building-up	58 → 72			*Destiny;*	42 → 72
24.20	'Allegories!'	41		28.13	Slain;	41
	'Allegories'!	70 72			Slain:	58 → 72
24.26	Criticism!'— —On	41		28.14	slain:	41
	Criticism'!— —On	70 72			slain;	58 → 72
24.36	marking down	41		28.15	believer;—as	41
	marking-down	58 → 72			believer; as	Am
25.6	Norsemen;	41		28.24	out,	41
	Norsemen:	42 → 72			out	Am

28.33	man,—trusting	41
	man, trusting	Am
28.34	Powers; and	41
	Powers; and,	46 → 72
28.34	whole	41
	whole,	46 → 72
29.1	coming on,	41
	coming-on,	58
29.3	a ship;	41
	a ship,	Am
29.4	sent forth,	41
	sent-forth,	58
29.5	blaze up	41
	blaze-up	58 → 72
29.7	say,	41
	say	Am
29.11	Nelsons.	41
	Nelsons!	58 → 72
29.12	audacity,	41
	audacity	Am
29.13	them;—to	41
	them; to	Am
29.22	latter,—misleading	41
	latter, misleading	Am
29.25	forest-feller,—the	41
	forest-feller—the	Am
29.28	shewing	41
	showing	58 → 72
30.9	so,	41
	so	Am
30.11	'the	41
	"the	Am
30.12	likeness?'	41
	likeness'?	70 72
30.13	such like,	41
	suchlike,	70 72
30.20	nay	41
	nay,	46 52 → 72
30.26	*Havamal*	41
	Völuspa	52 → 72
30.29	their	41
	their	46 → 72

30.30	symbolizing,	41
	symbolising,	58 → 72
30.34	fragments	41
	fragment's	72
31.1	goodhumour	41
	good humour	
		Am 70 72
31.4	'draws down	41
	'draws-down	58
31.9	Hermode	41
	Hermoder	46 → 72
31.9	rides,	41
	rides	52 → 72
31.13	Hermode	41
	Hermoder	46 → 72
31.18	remembrance.—Ah	41
	remembrance—Ah	72
31.24	Thunder-god?	41
	Thunger-god?	72
31.36	Jötun-land,	41
	Jötun land,	Am
31.37	Cauldron,	41
	Caldron,	70 72
31.38	grey	41
	gray	58 → 72
32.4	Ice-bergs.	41
	Icebergs.	42 → 72
32.5	tamed down;	41
	tamed-down;	58 → 72
32.7	Thundergod	41
	Thunder-god	Am 72
	Thunder-/god	70
32.10	Belief,	41
	Belief	42 → 72
32.12	*Childe Etin*	41
	Hynde Etin, **and still** **more decisively** *Red Etin* *of Ireland,*	52 → 72
32.13	Ballads is a Norse mythus; *Etin* was	41
	Ballads, these are both **derived from Norseland;** *Etin* **is evidently**	52 → 72

32.29	shew,	41
	show,	52 → 72
32.32	Thinker	41
	Thinker,	52 → 72
33.5	staid	41
	stayed	46 52 → 72
33.10	turned out	41
	turned-out	58 → 72
33.23	merely	41
	only	42 → 72
33.28	high,	41
	high	46 52 → 72
33.36	bent up	41
	bent-up	58 → 72
34.4	now	41
	now,	70 72
34.9	*Midgard-snake,*	41
	Midgardsnake,	Am
34.10	keeps up	41
	keeps-up	58 → 72
34.11	ruin.	41
	ruin!	70 72
34.22	mythus,	41
	mythus	70 72
34.24	mythus	41
	Mythus	42 → 72
34.26	eartnestness	41
	earnestness	42 → 72
34.32	*Havamal*	41
	Völuspa	52 → 72
34.32	song;	41
	Song;	46 → 72
35.3	Curious:	41
	Curious'	72
35.6	Phœnix	41
	phœnix	70 72
35.33	drawing down	41
	drawing-down	58 → 72
35.37*	one: it	41
	one? it	42
	one? It	46 → 72
35.38	thus	41
	thus,	42 → 72

36.2	'seen!'	41
	'seen'!	70 72
36.3	me,	41
	me	70 72
36.5	that,	41
	that	72

Lecture II. The Hero as Prophet.

37.12	god,	41
	god	Am
37.14	this, any more,	41
	this any more	70 72
37.17	he is,	41
	he is	Am
38.14	call	41
	call very	46 → 72
38.19	irrational,	41
	irrational	70 72
38.20	Hero-worship;	41
	Hero worship;	Am
	Hero-worship:	58 → 72
38.21	Indeed	41
	Indeed,	70 72
38.22	well. [extra leading between paragraphs] ¶We	41
	well. ¶We	70 72
39.2	life-guidance	41
	life guidance	Am
39.2*	one hundred and eighty millions	41
	one-hundred-and-eighty-millions	58
	a hundred-and-eighty millions	70 72
39.3	twelve hundred	41
	twelve-hundred	58 → 72
39.4	hundred and eighty millions	41
	hundred-and-eighty-millions	58
	hundred-and-eighty millions	70 72

39.5	Mahomet's word	41	
	Mahomet's word,	46 → 58	
39.6	hour	41	
	hour,	46 → 70	
39.14	Scepticism;	41	
	Scepticism; they	42 → 72	
39.15	paralysis,	41	
	paralysis	Am	
39.21	hundred and eighty millions;	41	
	hundred-and-eighty-millions;	58	
	hundred-and-eighty millions;	70 72	
39.27	bursts up	41	
	bursts-up	58 → 72	
39.28	such like,	41	
	suchlike,	70 72	
39.33	any thing,	41	
	anything,	42 → 72	
40.12	glares in	41	
	glares-in	58 → 72	
40.17	first hand.	41	
	first-hand.	70 72	
40.23	glares in	41	
	glares-in	58 → 72	
40.35	below:	41	
	below;	46 52 → 72	
40.36	cast up	41	
	cast-up	58 → 72	
41.7	heart?'	41	
	heart'?	70 72	
41.14	acts	41	
	acts,	42 → 72	
41.23	wreck;	41	
	wreck,	Am	
41.25	falls?'	41	
	falls'?	70 72	
41.30	put up	41	
	put-up	58 → 72	
41.32	mis-estimate	41	
	misestimate	42 → 72	

41.35	candidly,	41	
	candidly	58 → 72	
42.13	them:	41	
	these:	42 → 72	
42.29	They worshipped	41	
	They worshiped	58	
42.30	Sabeans; worshipped	41	
	Sabeans; worshiped	58	
42.35	beauty,'	41	
	beauty'	42 → 72	
42.37	Prophets	41	
	Prophets,	70 72	
43.2	devoutness	41	
	devotedness	Am	
43.2	noble-mindedness	41	
	noblemindedness	42 → 72	
43.4*	Book of Job	41	
	Book of Job	Am → 72	
43.9	destiny	41	
	destiny,	70 72	
43.13	*true,*	41	
	true	58 → 72	
43.13	every way;	41	
	everyway;	58 → 72	
43.14	Horse,—'hast	41	
	Horse, 'hast	Am	
43.23	Caabah, at	41	
	Caabah at	72	
43.25	half-century	41	
	half century	52	
43.29	gushing out	41	
	gushing-out	58	
43.30	these	41	
	those	46 → 72	
43.32	*zem-zem;*	41	
	zem zem;	58	
43.34	them,	41	
	them	Am	
43.35	object	41	
	object,	70 72	
44.26	cut asunder	41	
	cut-asunder	58 → 72	

44.28	war, war	41 70 72
45.1	world, world.	41 72
45.19	brought up brought-up	41 58 → 72
45.21	such like; suchlike;	41 70 72
45.23*	years years'	41 42 → 72
45.33	taken in, taken-in,	41 58 → 72
46.4	take in, take-in,	41 58
46.24	untrue un true	41 46
46.27	swelled up swelled-up	41 58 → 72
46.27	black, black	41 42 → 72
46.32	working out working-out	41 58
46.35	business business, again	41 58 → 72
46.37	grew: grew;	41 Am
47.4	impostor-theory, impostor theory, 	41 46 52 → 72
47.10	good-opinion good opinion 	41 Am 70 72
47.12	burnt out, burnt-out,	41 58
47.14	set up set-up	41 58 → 72
47.18	eyes, eyes	41 70 72
47.24	glared in glared-in	41 58 → 72
47.24	him; him,	41 58 → 72

47.32	Death! Death?	41 Am 58 → 72
48.6	shews shows	41 58 → 72
48.7	this is these are	41 46 → 72
48.7	or is or are	41 46 → 72
48.10	God:' God;'	41 42 → 72
48.11	waited on waited-on	41 58
48.21	Shiek Sheik	41 Am 58 → 72
48.23	impostor-hypothesis, impostor hypothesis, 	41 46 52 → 72
49.24	cooperates coöperates	41 58 → 72
49.25	otherwise;—and otherwise:—and	41 42 → 72
49.25	cooperating coöperating	41 58 → 72
49.28	Christianity,—for Christianity;—for 	41 46 52 → 72
49.31	flesh and blood; flesh-and-blood;	41 58 → 72
49.33	cruellest cruelest	41 Am 70 72
49.34	befals befalls	41 70 72
50.17	doubt; doubt:	41 42 → 72
50.30	friend, friend	41 Am
50.34	indifference: indifference;	41 58 → 72
51.2	stood up stood-up	41 58 → 72
51.6	started up, started-up,	41 58 → 72

51.9	there, there	41 Am	
51.11	broke up broke-up	41 58 → 72	
51.14	shews shows	41 58 → 72	
51.18	said, If said, if	41 Am	
51.20	two too	41 Am	
51.27	we all; we all:	41 Am	
51.27	worshippers worshipers	41 58	
52.4	went on went-on	41 58	
52.9	quit quite	41 46	
52.13	dismallest. dismalest.	41 70 72	
52.16	all over all-over	41 58 → 72	
52.21	tribe tribe,	41 46 52 → 72	
52.29	our era, our Era,	41 42 → 72	
52.29	fifty-third fifty third	41 Am	
53.25	long-run, longrun,	41 58	
53.34	dust dust,	41 Am	
53.36	wheat,—the wheat—the	41 Am	
54.2	Nature. Nature!	41 70 72	
54.3	motherly, motherly	41 Am 58 → 72	
55.3	"Allah 'Allah	41 58 → 72	
55.3	akbar, abkar,	41 42 → Am	

55.3	great." great.'	41 58 → 72	
55.5	flesh and blood, flesh-and-blood,	41 58 → 72	
55.7	do!—And do! And do! ¶And	41 Am 70 72	
55.8	lay hold lay-hold	41 58	
55.13	cooperating co-operating coöperating	41 Am 58 → 72	
55.15	cooperating co-operating coöperating	41 Am 58 → 72	
55.28	fire. [extra leading between paragraphs] ¶It fire. ¶It	41 Am	
55.33	Work Work,	41 Am	
55.37	gone upon gone-upon	41 58 → 72	
56.4	twelve hundred twelve-hundred	41 58 → 72	
56.7	seventy thousand seventy-thousand	41 58 → 72	
56.13	longwindedness, long-windedness,	41 72	
56.19	written down written-down	41 58 → 72	
56.24	end; end:	41 42 → 72	
56.27	chaunting chanting	41 58 → 72	
56.27	original. original. This may be a great point; much perhaps has been lost in the Translation here.	41 42 → 72	
57.4*	bonâ-fide bona-fide	41 42 → 72	

57.6	got up	41
	got-up	58 → 72
57.18	pell-mell;	41
	pellmell;	Am
	pellmell:	58 → 72
57.18	say	41
	say,	58 → 72
57.21	flung out	41
	flung-out	58 → 72
57.29	meaning	41
	meaning,	58 → 72
57.32	worse:	41
	worse.	58
58.1	making up	41
	making-up	58 → 72
58.3	Ah, no!	41
	No, no!	46 → 72
58.5	Life	41
	life	72
58.19	made up	41
	made-up	58 → 72
58.29	study	41
	con over	42 → 52
	con-over	58 → 72
59.3	Mahomet	41
	¶Mahomet	70 72
59.6	see,	41
	see	Am
59.13	pour down	41
	pour-down	58 → 72
59.15	palm-trees	41
	palm trees	Am
59.15	date-clusters	41
	date clusters	Am
59.16	them:	41
	them;	46 52 → 72
59.17	make	41
	change	42 → 72
59.18	creatures;	41
	creatures; they come ranking home at evening time,	42 → 72

59.18	evening time,	42
	evening-time,	58 → 72
59.19	'and they are	41
	'and are	42 → 72
59.19	Ships,	41
	Ships also,	46 → 72
59.20	spread out	41
	spread-out	58 → 72
59.23	cries he:	41
	cries he.	Am
59.24	you,	41
	you,	46 → 72
59.25	Ye were	41
	You were	Am
59.27	comes on	41
	comes-on	58 → 72
59.27	grey	41
	gray	Am 58 → 72
59.33	eyesight,	41
	eye-sight,	70
60.3	hung out	41
	hung-out	58 → 72
60.8	Day,	41
	Day	70 72
60.12	Splendour,	41
	Splendour	Am
60.15	talks of	41
	talks-of	58 → 72
60.24	timber among	41
	timber, among	46 52 → 72
60.32	one; with	41
	one: with	42 46 52 → 72
61.3	things, and	41
	things and	Am
61.5	Shew	41
	Show	58 → 72
61.9	burns up	41
	burns-up	58 → 72
61.17	frugalest;	41
	frugallest;	46 52 58
61.23	three and twenty	41
	three-and-twenty	42 → 72

61.31	of man	41		63.29	marks down	41
	of a man	52 → 72			marks-down	58 → 72
61.33	three and twenty	41		63.37	Mahomet,	41
	three-and-twenty	42 → 72			Mahomet	Am
61.36	struggling up,	41		64.7	long for,	41
	struggling-up,	58 → 72			long-for,	58
62.1	him:	41		64.8	seats,	41
	him;	Am			seats	Am
62.2	every way	41		64.18	comes upon	41
	everyway	58 → 72			comes-upon	58 → 72
62.10	gray-haired	41		64.27	shewn:	41
	grey-haired	46 52 72			shown:	58 → 72
62.18	shew	41		64.30	certain	41
	show	58 → 72			sudden	Am
62.21	rough	41		65.3	man,	41
	rough,	Am			man	Am
62.28	generosity,	41		65.4	three-score	41
	generosity	42 → 72			threescore	Am 58 → 72
62.30	called for,	41		65.18	No:	41
	called-for,	58 → 72			No;	42 → 72
62.36	Eternity?	41		65.26	beggarlier	41
	eternity?	Am			beggalier	Am
62.37	but 'Hell	41		65.28	Mahomet!— — ¶On	41
	'but Hell	42 → 72			Mahomet!— ¶On	Am
62.37	turns up:	41		66.7	cries,	41
	turns-up:	58 → 72			cries	Am
63.1	weighed out	41		66.9	*akbar,*	41
	weighed-out	58 → 72			*abkar,*	42 → Am
63.4	written down	41		66.11	Idolators;	41
	written-down	58 → 72			Idolaters;	Am 58 → 72
63.11	Truth;—'living	41		66.17	see,	41
	Truth:—'living	Am			see	Am
63.17	*cleanly,*—just	41		66.21	life-giving.	41
	cleanly—just	Am			live-giving.	72
63.24	over much,	41		66.26	said,	41
	overmuch,	58 → 72			said	Am
63.26	equalizer	41				
	equaliser	58 → 72				

Lecture III. The Hero as Poet.

63.27	kingships;	41		67.1	Prophet	41
	kingships:	Am			**Prophet,**	46 → 72
63.27	men,	41		67.6	fellow man	41
	men	Am			fellow-man	58 → 72

67.8	questionable, questionable	41 Am	
67.17	names, names	41 Am	
68.15	well: well;	41 Am	
68.16	that! these!	41 46 → 72	
68.28	Samson, Samson	41 42 → 72	
68.37	world.— ¶Poet world.— [extra leading between paragraphs] ¶Poet	41 46 52 → 72	
69.7	secret!' secret.'	41 42 → 72	
69.21	pity;—a pity:—a	41 Am	
69.31	shows shews	41 42 → 52	
69.33	man, once man once	41 70 72	
70.7	Earth earth	41 52 → 72	
70.11	springing up springing-up	41 58 → 72	
70.12	looking out looking-out	41 58 → 72	
70.14	Beauty?—In Beauty? In	41 58 → 72	
70.18	*false,* *false*	41 70 72	
70.20	periods, periods	41 70 72	
71.2	forgotten: forgotten;	41 Am	
71.10	'infinitude' 'infinitude,'	41 70 72	
71.23	be be,	41 46 → 72	
71.28	that! that.	41 Am	

71.32	chaunting; chanting;	41 58 → 72	
71.36	chaunt, chant,	41 58 → 72	
72.17	such like! suchlike!	41 70 72	
72.21	was. I was. ¶I	41 70 72	
72.30	comes out comes-out	41 58 70	
72.31	shows shews	41 42 → 52	
72.32	fatalest fatallest	41 46 52 58	
72.35	show shew	41 42 → 52	
72.35	*him:* *him;*	41 Am	
72.35	*worshipped* *worshiped*	41 58	
72.37	duchesses, Duchesses,	41 58 → 72	
73.1	that that,	41 46 52 → 72	
73.1	whole whole,	41 46 52 → 72	
73.7	cast out cast-out	41 58 → 72	
73.8	shows shews	41 42 → 52	
73.9	swept out, swept-out,	41 58 → 72	
73.10	non-extant, non-extant;	41 46 52 → 72	
73.14	*canonized,* *canonised,*	41 58 → 72	
73.17	Shakspeare Skakspeare	41 58	
73.18	them: them;	41 Am	
73.20	canonized, canonised,	41 58 → 72	

73.25	Poet, will		41
	Poet will	42 → 72	
73.26	fashion. [extra leading between paragraphs]		
	¶Many		41
	fashion. ¶Many		58
73.38	Blank		41
	Lonely	42 → 72	
73.38	painted		41
	painted as		
		42 46 52 → 72	
	paint-/ted as		Am
74.3	mournfulest		41
	mournfullest	46 52 58	
74.8	looking out		41
	looking-out	58 → 72	
74.11	eating out		41
	eating-out	58 → 72	
74.13	life-long		41
	lifelong	46 52 → 70	
	life-/long		72
74.15	equable, implacable,		41
	equable,	46 → 72	
74.16	looks out		41
	looks-out	58 → 72	
74.28	realize		41
	realise	58 → 72	
74.29	but,		41
	but		Am
74.35	state,		41
	State,	46 → 72	
75.1	grown up		41
	grown-up	58 → 72	
75.16	Florence		41
	Florence would have		
		46 → 72	
75.22	knew not		41
	knew not,	42 → 72	
75.22	do		41
	do,	42 → 72	
76.1	apologizing		41
	apologising	58 → 72	
76.2	pride,		41
	pride:	42 → 72	

76.13	strange now		41
	strange, now,	46 → 72	
76.14	do so much to amuse us,		41
	make himself so entertaining;	46 → 72	
76.16	it is not strange, if you think of		41
	it is not strange; you are to recollect		42
	not strange; your Highness is to recollect		
		46 → 72	
76.20	resting place,		41
	resting-place,	58 → 72	
76.21	to wander, wander;		41
	to wander;		Am
77.1	bursts forth		41
	bursts-forth		58
77.3	It		41
	¶It	70 72	
77.5	times, that		41
	times, That	42 → 72	
77.8	*segui la*		41
	segui	46 → 72	
77.8	*stella'*—so		41
	stella,'—so	58 → 72	
77.10	"Follow		41
	"Follow thou	42 → 72	
77.11	haven!"		41
	heaven!"		46
77.12	This Book		41
	This Book,	70 72	
77.16	history		41
	history,	70 72	
77.19	*oris.*		41
	orris.		Am
77.21	shut out		41
	shut-out	58 → 72	
77.21	shores." [extra leading between paragraphs] ¶I		41
	shores." ¶I	70 72	

77.28	together,	41
	together	42 → 72
78.15	chaunt.	41
	chant.	58 → 72
78.23	look out	41
	look-out	58 → 72
78.24	piled up	41
	piled-up	58 → 72
78.31	Ah,	41
	Ah	70 72
78.33	come out	41
	come-out	58 → 72
78.33	*divine,*	41
	divine	46 52 → 72
79.3	worked out,	41
	worked-out,	58 → 72
79.13	greatness	41
	greatness,	Am
79.22	gloom;—so	41
	gloom; so	Am
79.29	a matter;	41
	a matter:	70 72
79.29	cuts into	41
	cuts-into	58
79.31	Sordello,	41
	Brunetto Latini,	
		52 → 72
79.38	*'fue!'*	41
	'fue'!	70 72
80.11	*sympathized*	41
	sympathised	58 → 72
80.17	come out	41
	come-out	58
80.19	surplusage:	41
	surplusage;	Am
80.24	of seeing!'	41
	of seeing'!	70 72
80.28	take away	41
	take-away	58 → 72
80.34	too; she speaks of *'questa*	
	forma;'—so innocent; 41	
	too: *della bella persona,*	
	che mi fu tolta; 42 → 72	

80.36*	he 'will	41
	be will	42 → 72
80.36*	her.'	41
	her!	42 → 72
80.37	again,	41
	again, to wail	42 → 72
81.5	avenged upon	41
	avenged-upon	58 → 72
81.15	far: ah, one	41
	far:—one	46 → 72
81.19	insight,	41
	insight	70 72
81.23	*spiacenti,*	41
	spiacenti	58 → 72
81.25	aversion:	41
	aversion;	58 → 72
81.26	this:	41
	this;	58 → 72
82.8	under foot;	41
	underfoot;	58 → 72
82.13	'bent down	41
	'bent-down	58 → 72
82.13	corbels'	41
	corbels	46 → 72
82.13	building,	41
	building,'	46 → 72
82.14	crushed together	41
	crushed-together	58 → 72
82.15	top,	41
	top, which is	46 → 72
82.16	Mercy	41
	Mercy shall have	
		46 → 72
82.18	repentance,	41
	repentance	58 → 72
82.24	make up	41
	make-up	58 → 72
83.5*	our	41
	or	46 52 → 72
83.6	world-wide	41
	worldwide	72
83.18	facts;	41
	facts,	58

83.21	an Allegory.	41
	in Allegory.	Am
83.22	got up	41
	got-up	58 → 72
83.29	world:	41
	world;	58 → 72
83.30	nature;	41
	nature:	42 → 72
84.15	Desert,	41
	Desert	72
84.15	seven hundred	41
	seven-hundred	58 → 72
84.17	emblemed forth	41
	emblemed-forth	58 → 72
84.27	Saint-Helena	41
	Saint Helena	Am
84.36	arrangement,	41
	arrangement	46 → 72
85.3	bodies	41
	bo dies	46
85.4	practice:	41
	practice;	Am
85.12	sung forth	41
	sung-forth	58 → 72
86.6	piastres	41
	piasters	42 → 72
86.9	more! Ah yes, the	41
	more! The	46 → 72
86.10	count up	41
	count-up	58
86.10	men.	41
	men!	46 → 72
86.11	usefulest	41
	usefullest	46 52 58
86.11	times.— —	41
	times.——	Am
86.17	thinking,	41
	thing,	Am
86.20	Modern	41
	modern	58 → 72
86.24*	chivalry-way	41
	chivalry way	46 → 72

86.24	on	41
	no	52
87.5	every thing	41
	everything Am	58 → 72
87.5	cooperate	41
	coöperate	58 → 72
87.27*	King Henrys,	41
	King-Henrys,	42 → 72
87.27*	Queen Elizabeths	41
	Queen-Elizabeths	
		42 46 52 → 72
87.29*	Stephen's,	41
	Stephens,	46 52 58
87.31	Freemasons'	41
	Freemason's	Am 70
88.7	vision,	41
	vision, such a	46 → 72
88.8	depth,	41
	depth;	46 → 72
88.16	fit, every way	41
	fit,—every-way	46 → 52
	fit,—everyway	58 → 72
88.18	things; we	41
	things,—we	46 → 72
88.34	like; the	41
	like; does the	46 → 72
88.35	*lux,*	41
	lux, **Let there be light;**	
		42 → 72
89.6	heart	41
	heart,	52 → 72
89.9	thing follows, of itself,	41
	thing, follows of itself	
		42 → 72
89.12	triumph over	41
	triumph-over	58
89.17	takes in	41
	takes-in	58 → 72
89.21	quite	41
	qnite [*u* in *quite* set upside down]	42
89.26	crystal;	41
	chrystal;	Am

89.26	shew	41	
	show	58 → 72	
89.29	wrapped up	41	
	wrapped-up	58 → 72	
90.20	a man	41	
	a man,	Am	
90.25	feet	41	
	feet,	Am	
90.28	indeed require us so to speak;	41	
	perhaps prescribe such forms of utterance;	46 → 72	
91.4	him. You	41	
	him. you	Am	
91.9	it, without	41	
	it,—without	46 → 72	
91.9	him, he	41	
	him; a thoroughly immoral *man*	46 → 72	
91.12	sympathize	41	
	sympathise	58 → 72	
91.15	Nature with	41	
	Nature, with	46 52 → 72	
91.16	truth	41	
	truth,	46 52 → 72	
91.16	bad, the	41	
	bad, to the	46 → 72	
91.16	pusillanimous,	41	
	pusillanimous	46 52 → 72	
91.18	merely.—But	41	
	merely. But	Am	
91.24*	reflexions	41	
	reflections	46 → 72	
91.29	dimensions;	41	
	dimensions,	Am	
91.30	stating,	41	
	stating;	46 52 → 72	
91.34	about	41	
	concerning	46 → 72	
92.3	precontrivance.	41	
	pre-contrivance.	Am	

92.3	grows up	41	
	grows-up	58 → 72	
92.13	him;—as	41	
	him:—as	Am	
92.18	under ground!	41	
	underground!	58 → 72	
92.23	truly,	41	
	truly	Am	
92.26	had not	41	
	failed to have	46 → 72	
92.28	offhand,	41	
	off hand,	Am	
92.31	fall in	41	
	fall-in	58 → 72	
92.37	Shakspeare:	41	
	Shakspeare;	42 → 72	
93.2	butt,	41	
	butt he is bantering,	46 → 72	
93.3	roars and	41	
	with his whole heart	70 72	
93.13	hope that they	41	
	hope they	46 → 72	
93.14	City-watch.—Such	41	
	City-watch. Such	70 72	
93.15	me. ¶We	41	
	me. [extra leading between paragraphs] ¶We	70 72	
93.18	Plays	41	
	plays	70 72	
93.25	coherence:	41	
	coherence;	46 52 → 72	
94.26	Seer.	41	
	seer.	58 → 72	
94.36	unison!	41	
	harmony!	58 → 72	
95.2	nor sceptic,	41	
	no sceptic,	46 52	
95.12	every way	41	
	every-way	58	
	everyway	70 72	

95.15	God:' I ask, was	41
	God:' and was	46 → 72
95.23	simulacrum,	41
	simulacrum;	70 72
95.25*	be still	41
	still be	46 52 → 72
95.28	Compared	41
	¶Compared	70 72
95.35	speak out	41
	speak-out	58 → 72
96.3	Nature;	41
	Nature:	46 52 → 72
96.3	springs up	41
	springs-up	58 → 72
96.10	us;—on	41
	us; on	Am
96.12	repeat,	41
	repeat:	46 → 72
96.15	give up	41
	give-up	58 → 72
96.20	give up	41
	give-up	58 → 72
96.24	Empire, no	41
	Empire, or no	42 → 72
96.27	give up	41
	give-up	58 → 72
96.28	him	41
	him,	Am
96.29	tangibly useful	41
	tangibly-useful	58 → 72
96.34	fall out	41
	fall-out	58 → 72
97.7	view,	41
	view	70 72
97.13	politician	41
	politician,	58 → 72
97.16	speak forth	41
	speak-forth	58 → 72
97.23	greatness. He	41
	greatness He	Am

Lecture IV. The Hero as Priest.

99.17	Universe,' which	41
	Universe,'—which	58 → 72
100.10	Captain	41
	Captain,	70 72
100.14	service, a	41
	service, and a	70 72
100.20	things, a *seer*,	41
	things; a *seer*,	46 → 72
100.21	shows	41
	shews	42 46 52
100.21	worshipper,	41
	worshiper,	58
100.22	things: a Priest,	41
	things; a Priest,	58 → 72
100.25	building up	41
	building-up	58 → 72
100.28	carried on	41
	carried-on	58 → 72
100.34*	Thebaid	41
	Thebaïd	46 52 → 72
101.13	shaken off,	41
	shaken-off,	58 → 72
101.17	highly discursive	41
	highly-discursive	58 → 72
101.29	trace out	41
	trace-out	58 → 72
101.32	desires	41
	devises	42 → 72
102.5	summed up	41
	summed-up	58 → 72
102.6	epochs.	41
	epochs,	Am
102.12	fact	41
	fact,	70 72
102.16	suffrage; if	41
	suffrage, if	Am
102.20*	downfal.	41
	downfall.	46 → 72
102.23	cleared off	41
	cleared-off	58

102.27	beautiful	41	104.34	Poets:	41
	beau-/ful	42		Poets;	Am
102.32	only the	41	104.37	worshipping	41
	merely the	42 → 72		worshiping	58
102.34	too,	41	105.3	word,	41
	too	46 → 72		word	Am
103.6	Pagans,	41	105.8	Idol,	41
	pagans,	Am		Idol	52 → 72
103.11	fill up	41	105.11	eaten out	41
	fill-up	58 → 72		eaten-out	58 → 72
103.12	march over	41	105.13	balefulest	41
	march-over	58 → 72		balefullest	46 52 58
103.17	too,	41	105.22	paralyzed	41
	too	Am		paralysed	46 52 → 72
103.23	army;	41	105.26	Blameable	41
	army,	58 → 72		Blamable	46 52 → 72
104.1	Prophets:	41	105.28	phasis.—I	41
	Prophets;	Am		phasis. ¶I	70 72
104.1	worshipping	41	105.30	bees'-wax,	41
	worshiping	58		bees-wax,	46 52 → 72
104.2	away with,	41	105.33	stand	41
	away-with,	58 → 72		stands	Am
104.2	must	41	105.34	not shows	41
	have to	46 → 72		not shews	42 → 52
104.6	Idol	41	105.36	hollow shows	41
	Idle	Am		hollow shews	42 → 52
104.16*	Godhood;	41	106.17	of it;	41
	Godhead;	46 52 → 72		of it:	Am
	God;	Am	106.21	branches out.	41
104.21	say,	41		branches-out.	58
	say	Am	106.25*	Kings,	41
104.24	Where then	41		*Kings*,	70 72
	Where, then,	70 72	106.29	is, that	41
104.31	worshipped Canopus,	41		is that	Am
	worshiped Canopus,	58	106.31	hatefulest	41
104.31	Caabah	41		hatefullest	46 52 58
	Cabaah	Am	107.4	we	41
104.31	Black-stone,	41		he	Am
	Black-Stone,		107.5	put out	41
		42 46 52 → 72		put-out	58 → 72
	Black Stone,	Am	107.7	Tetzel	41
104.32	worshipped nothing	41		Tetzel,	Am
	worshiped nothing	58			

107.11	reign,	41
	reign	Am
107.11	there,	41
	there	Am
107.14*	adviseablest	41
	advisablest	46 → 72
107.21	bottom,	41
	bottom	Am
107.28	isolation,	41
	isolation;	46 → 72
107.30	half-belief,	41
	half-belief	46 52 → 72
107.30*	makes it	41
	make it	70 72
107.37	long-run,	41
	longrun,	58 → 72
108.2	of in	41
	of, in	58 → 72
108.3	believe in	41
	believe in, and	42 → 72
108.4	sincerely.	41
	sincerely to believe in.	
		42 → 72
108.11	believes he	41
	believes, he	42 → 72
108.14	original,—all	41
	original; all	70 72
108.21	Hero-worship?	41
	¶Hero-worship?	70 72
108.30	Hero,	41
	Hero	70 72
108.32	valour;	41
	valour:	Am
109.6	Suffrages,	41
	suffrages,	42 → 72
109.7	take,	41
	take	Am
109.13	believers	41
	Believers	42 → 72
109.19	World	41
	world	Am
109.23	Worshippers	41
	Worshipers	58

109.28	November,	41
	November	58 → 72
109.37	household:	41
	household;	58 → 72
109.38	unimportant-looking	41
	unimportant looking	Am
110.12	brought up	41
	brought-up	58 → 72
110.17	shows	41
	shews	42 → 52
110.23	nursed up	41
	nursed-up	58 → 72
110.24	step forth	41
	step-forth	58 → 72
110.30	struggled up	41
	struggled-up	58 → 72
110.30	displaying	41
	displaying,	46 52 → 72
110.31	hindrances	41
	hindrances,	46 52 → 72
110.34	consented:	41
	consented	58
110.37	hand.	41
	feet.	46 → 72
111.1	ours;—gone	41
	ours?—gone	42 → 72
111.1	burnt up	41
	burnt-up	58 → 72
111.5	God,	41
	God	70 72
111.8	Luther,	41
	Luther[]	72
111.12	work out	41
	work-out	58 → 72
112.1	This then	41
	This, then,	70 72
112.15	Rome;	41
	Rome,	58
112.17	going on	41
	going-on	58 → 72
113.3	struck at,	41
	struck-at,	58 → 72

113.4	attending to, attending to 52 → 72	41
113.11	sorrowfulest sorrowfullest 46 52 58	41
113.15	now, now: 42 → 72	41
113.27	step forth step-forth 58 → 72	41
113.34	heart's desire heart's-desire 46 → 72	41
113.35	from other than that of 46 → 72	41
113.37	Christendom. The Christendom.—The 46 → 72	41
114.4	Rome—probably Rome,—probably 58 → 72	41
114.6	Constance Constant	41 42
114.8	'three feet 'three-feet 58 → 72	41
114.9	six feet six-feet 58 → 72	41
114.9	seven feet seven-feet 58 → 72	41
114.9	voice voice of him 46 → 72	41
114.20	*another's,* another's, another's than his, 46 → 72	41 42
114.22	next; next: 42 → 72	41
114.22	tenth 10th 58 → 72	41
114.23	Luther Luther, 70 72	41
114.25	in the market-place of Wittenberg. 'at the Elster-Gate of Wittenberg.' 42 → 72	41
114.25	looked on looked-on	41 58
114.26	looking on. looking-on.	41 58
114.27	'shout!' 'shout'! 70 72	41
114.29	Popism, Popeism, 70 72	41
114.35	bringer back bringer-back 58 → 72	41
115.8	friendless, friendless	41 Am
115.8	one man, on but on 46 → 72	41
115.14	civilization civilisation 46 52 → 72	41
115.18	himself, himself	41 Am
115.19	stands up stands-up 58 → 72	41
115.20	man, Hans Luther the poor miner's Son. 41 man, the poor miner Hans Luther's Son. 42 → 72	
115.22	rode out rode-out 58 → 72	41
115.32	Luther ¶Luther 70 72	41
115.38	doubtless doubtless,	41 Am
116.15	contentions, contentions 58 → 72	41
116.21	Augeas's Augea's	41 Am
116.29	walk by walk-by 58 → 72	41
116.33	of it: of it;	41 Am
116.36	the right, a right,	41 Am
117.1	me?—No! me?—/—No!	41 Am

117.14	Popery,'	41
	Popery'	70 72
117.16	chapels, and	41
	chapels and	Am 70 72
117.17	count up	41
	count-up	58 → 72
117.19	See,	41
	See	Am
117.20	Popism	41
	Popeism	70 72
117.32	going:	41
	going;	46 52 → 72
118.16	stirred up	41
	stirred-up	58 → 72
118.17	swept away	41
	swept-away	58 → 72
118.17	it. Such	41
	it! Such	42 → 72
118.29	tolerance: he	41
	tolerance; he	Am
118.30	go as	41
	go very much as	
		46 → 72
118.31	comes that	41
	comes to him that	
		42 → 72
118.36	shews	41
	shows	58 → 72
119.1	man	41
	man, he	46 → 72
119.1	speaks forth	41
	speaks-forth	58 → 72
119.2	written works	41
	Written Works	46 → 72
119.6	greatest:	41
	greatest;	72
119.7	four-and-twenty quartos	
		41
	Four-and-twenty Quartos	46 → 72
119.11	flashes out	41
	flashes-out	58 → 72

119.18	was that	41
	was, that	42 → 72
119.19	human	41
	Human	Am
119.25	turns up;	41
	turns-up;	58 → 72
119.27	shew	41
	show	58 → 72
119.29	worn down	41
	worn-down	58 → 72
119.32	started up,	41
	started-up,	58 → 72
119.32	fiend-defiance;	41
	fiend defiance;	Am
119.37	before,	41
	before	70 72
120.1	Earth	41
	earth	Am
120.1	They spoke once about his not being at Leipzig, as if 'Duke George had hindered him,'	41
	'The Devil is aware,' writes he on one occasion, 'that this does not proceed out of fear in me. I have seen and defied innumerable Devils. Duke George,' of Leipzig,	42 → 72
120.4	his. It was not for Duke George, answered he: No; "if	41
	his, 'Duke George is not equal to one Devil,'—far short of a Devil! 'If	42 → 72
120.6	go,	41
	ride into Leipzig,	
		42 → 72
120.6	Leipzig,	42
	Leipzig	Am
120.6*	Duke Georges	41
	Duke-Georges	42 → 72

120.7	running."	41	
	running.' What a reservoir of Dukes to ride into!—	42 → 72	
120.23	preeminent	41	
	preëminent	58 70	
	pre-/eminent	72	
120.25	Luther,	41	
	Luther	58 → 72	
120.25	observer,	41	
	observer	70 72	
120.28	stirred up	41	
	stirred-up	58 → 72	
120.28	defiance;	41	
	defiance,	52 → 72	
120.29	*Table-talk,*	41	
	Table-Talk,	58 → 72	
120.35	Margaret	41	
	Magdalene	42 → 72	
121.2	Margaret	41	
	Magdalene	42 → 72	
121.4	looks out	41	
	looks-out	58 → 72	
121.4*	'Patmos,' the Wartburg	41	
	Patmos, the Castle of Coburg,	42 → 72	
121.4	Coburg,	42	
	Coburg	Am	
121.6	huge,—who	41	
	huge:—who	46 → 72	
121.17	home!— —Neither	41	
	home!——Neither	Am	
121.23	spoke forth	41	
	spoke-forth	58 → 72	
121.25	other:	41	
	other;	58 → 72	
121.29	rude,	41	
	rude	70 72	
121.32	unnameable	41	
	unnamable	46 52 → 72	
121.35	him;	41	
	him:	Am	
122.6	loveable	41	
	lovable	46 52 → 72	
122.8	setting up	41	
	setting-up	58 → 72	
122.10	Heavens;—yet	41	
	Heavens; yet	58 → 72	
122.14	Heaven. [extra leading between paragraphs] ¶The	41	
	Heaven. ¶The	72	
122.18	country,	41	
	country	70 72	
122.22	Voltairism	41	
	Voltaireism	70 72	
123.1	wager of battle	41	
	wager-of-battle	58 → 72	
123.4	two hundred	41	
	two-hundred	58 → 72	
123.10	driven out	41	
	driven-out	58 → 72	
123.13	Star-chamber	41	
	Starchamber	58 → 72	
123.14	Heaven	41	
	heaven	58 → 72	
123.16	worshipping	41	
	worshiping	58	
123.19	In	41	
	¶In	70 72	
123.19*	*Neale's*	41	
	Neal's	46 → 58	
	Neal's	70 72	
123.19	*Puritans*	41	
	Puritans [1]	46 52 → 72	
123.20	departure:	41	
	departure:*	Am	
123.22	brethren	41	
	brethern	Am	
123.23	prayer (the Prayer too is given),	41	
	prayer,	46 52 → 72	
	prayer	Am	
123.30	arm:	41	
	arm;	46 52 → 72	

123.33	Scotland	41		
	Scotland,	70 72		
123.38	[no footnote]	41		
	* Neal (London, 1755),			
	i. 490.	46 → 72		
123.38*	* Neal	46		
	¹ Neal	52 → 72		
124.10	dwelling on!	41		
	dwelling-on!	58		
124.10	soul;	41		
	soul:	42 → 72		
125.5	came out,	41		
	came-out,	58		
125.5	fifty years	41		
	fifty-years '	46 52 → 72		
125.9	Schwiednitz,	41		
	Schweidnitz,	72		
125.10	pass over	41		
	pass-over	58 → 72		
125.14	step over	41		
	step-over	58 → 72		
125.17	three hundred	41		
	three-hundred	58 → 72		
125.24	'unblameable'	41		
	'unblamable'	46 52 → 72		
125.25	to the battle	41		
	to battle	Am		
125.27	shot at	41		
	shot-at	58 → 72		
125.29	apologize	41		
	apologise	46 52 → 72		
	apolgize	Am		
125.30	two hundred and fifty	41		
	two-hundred-and-fifty			
		58 → 72		
125.32	we for	41		
	we, for	46 52 → 72		
125.33	sake	41		
	sake,	46 52 → 72		
125.33	ought	41		
	ougth	Am		

126.1	college-education;	41		
	college education;			
		52 → 72		
126.5	doctrine:	41		
	doctrine;	Am		
126.15	What	41		
	what	70 72		
126.17	stand up;	41		
	stand-up;	58 → 72		
126.19	tears,	41		
	tears	Am		
126.22	baptized	41		
	baptised	46 52 → 72		
126.34	God: this	41		
	God; this	Am		
126.34	"a	41		
	'a	42 → 72		
126.35	bredd,"	41		
	bredd,'	42 46 52 → 72		
	bredd,	Am		
126.36	worshipped,	41		
	worshiped,	58		
126.36	Knox:	41		
	Knox;	42 → 72		
127.3	He	41		
	¶He	70 72		
127.7	worshipped!	41		
	worshiped!	58		
127.18	narrow-looking	41		
	narrow looking	Am		
127.36	under foot	41		
	underfoot	58 → 72		
128.16	just	41		
	just,	42 Am		
128.17	tolerate! We do	41		
	tolerate! We are here to			
	resist, to control and			
	vanquish, withal. We do			
		42 → 72		
128.18	vanquish,	42		
	vanquish	46 → 72		
128.18	tolerate Falsehoods,	41		
	'tolerate' Falsehoods,			
	Thieveries,	42 → 72		

128.20	false and unjust!		41
	false, thou art not tolerable!	42 →	72
128.20	*extinguish* Falsehoods		41
	extinguish Falsehoods, and put an end to them,	42 →	72
128.23	sense, Knox was,		41
	sense Knox was,	46 52 →	72
	sense, Knox, was		Am
128.24	such like,		41
	suchlike,	70	72
128.24	teaching		41
	teacing		Am
128.34	heart,		41
	heart	46 52 →	72
128.34	healthful, strong,		41
	healthful strong		Am
128.36	pulling down		41
	pulling-down	58 →	72
129.2	pulling down		41
	pulling-down	58 →	72
129.8	subsist		41
	exist		Am
129.17	every way!		41
	everyway!	58 →	72
129.18	mounts up		41
	mounts-up	58 →	72
129.20	honesthearted,		41
	honest-hearted,	58 →	72
129.28	present:		41
	present;		Am
130.4	him.		41
	him!	70	72
130.6	unforgiveable		41
	unforgivable	46 52 →	72
130.7	set up		41
	set-up	58 →	72
130.9	offences;		41
	offences,	46 52 →	72
130.10	sin,		41
	sin;	42 →	72
130.18	clutch hold		41
	clutch-hold		58

130.25	true;		41
	true,	46 52 →	72
130.26	remained,		41
	remained	70	72
130.34	(well-named		41
	(well named	52 →	72
130.35	nameable		41
	namable	46 52 →	72
130.35	God'),		41
	God')	46 52 →	72
131.8	Hero-Priest		41
	Hero-priest	42 →	72
131.9	wears out,		41
	wears-out,	58 →	72

Lecture V. The Hero as Man of Letters.

133.4	shew		41
	show	58 →	72
133.5	today,		41
	to-day,		Am
133.13	speak forth		41
	speak-forth	58 →	72
134.1	us		41
	us,	42 →	72
134.1	men,		41
	men		Am
134.15	glance		41
	glance,	42 →	72
134.15	us		41
	us,	42 →	72
134.22	uttering forth,		41
	uttering-forth,	58 →	72
134.27	Divine		41
	Divine,		Am
134.31	it not,		41
	not the fact, and are untrue to it,	42 →	72
135.2*	Jena,		41
	Erlangen,	46 52 →	72
135.5	first,		41
	first:	42 →	72

135.7	Appearance; Appearance:	41 42 → 72
135.12	shews shows	41 58 → 72
135.24	Fichte ¶Fichte	41 70 72
136.16	them! them.	41 42 → 72
136.18	here, here	41 42 → 72
136.24	hundred and fifty hundred-and-fifty	41 58 → 72
136.25	But ¶But	41 70 72
136.38	clearness, clearness, or	41 46 → 72
137.1	shew show	41 58 → 72
137.2	These There	41 42 → 72
137.7	society: society;	41 Am
137.12	disorganization; disorganisation;	41 42 → 72
137.12	from which from which,	41 70 72
137.12	to which to which,	41 70 72
137.16	shew. show.	41 58 → 72
137.17	give give an	41 Am
137.24	civilised civilized	41 Am
137.31	preaching, preaching	41 58 → 72
138.17	called up called-up	41 58 → 72
138.30	HEBREW Book, Hebrew BOOK,	41 52 → 72
138.32	four thousand four-thousand	41 58 → 72

139.5	existence too existence, too,	41 Am
139.6	Books. Books,	41 Am
139.12	thirty thousand, thirty-thousand,	41 70 72
139.29	teacher Teacher	41 42 → 72
140.1	others. But others But	41 Am
140.3	take in take-in	41 58 → 72
140.18	Easy-writing, Easy-writing	41 72
140.22	all All	41 70 72
140.24	Nay, Nay	41 70 72
140.30	shews shows	41 58 → 72
140.31	shew show	41 58 → 72
141.1	authentic. Literature, authentic. ¶Literature, 	41 70 72
141.9	nay, nay	41 70 72
141.12	Milton; the humble Milton! They are something, too, those humble	41 42 → 72
141.12	something, something	42 46 52 → 72
141.14	there! Fragments there! For all true singing is of the nature of worship; as indeed all true *working* may be said to be,—whereof such *singing* is but the record, and fit melodious representation, to us. Fragments	41 42 → 72

141.17	'body	41
	'Body	42 → 72
141.28	figure of a speech,	41
	figure of speech,	42 → 72
142.2	only	41
	only,	42 → 72
142.3	itself by and by	41
	itself, by and by,	42 → 72
142.4	unincumbered,	41
	unencumbered,	70 72
142.18	steamengines,	41
	steam-engines,	Am
142.22	Katherine	41
	Katharine	Am
142.23	brick.—The	41
	brick. The	Am
142.36	unrecognised	41
	unrecognised,	Am
142.38	cast off	41
	cast-off	58 → 72
142.38	step forth	41
	step-forth	58 → 72
143.2	another:	41
	another;	Am
143.6	incumbered	41
	encumbered	70 72
143.8	arrangement,	41
	arrangement	52 → 72
143.12	bring out	41
	bring-out	58 → 72
143.19	endowments,	41
	endowments	46 52 → 72
143.23	shew	41
	show	58 → 72
143.28	say	41
	say,	70 72
143.34	Begging	41
	¶Begging	70 72
144.1	cast out	41
	cast-out	58 → 72
144.2	torn out	41
	torn-out	58 → 72

144.2	cast forth	41
	cast-forth	58 → 72
144.3	made out	41
	made-out	58 → 72
144.6	setting up	41
	setting-up	58 → 72
144.7	are,	41
	are	Am
144.7*	order;	41
	order;'	42 → 72
144.9	make it too do	41
	make it to do	52 58
144.12	money-furtherances,	41
	money-futherances,	58
144.25	nine hundred and ninety-nine	41
	nine-hundred-and-ninety-nine	58 → 72
144.27	Cave,	41
	Cave;	46 52 → 72
144.27	brokenhearted	41
	broken-hearted	70 72
144.28	Gauger,	41
	Gauger;	46 52 → 72
145.2	applied to	41
	applied-to	58 → 72
145.3	answers	41
	adds	42 → 72
145.12	it will	41
	the world will	42 → 72
145.12	its	41
	it[ ]	52
145.13*	called	41
	call	72
145.36	hope;	41
	hope:	46 52 → 72
145.37	shewn	41
	shown	Am 58 → 72
145.37	them,	41
	them:	42 → 72
146.1	some understanding,	41
	some Understanding,	70 72

146.2	are too apt	41
	are apt	Am
146.9	noblehearted	41
	noble-hearted	Am
146.10	humane	41
	humane,	52
146.16	These,	41
	These	Am
146.36	put up	41
	put-up	58 → 72
147.1	age	41
	Age	Am → 72
147.5	moral Doubt;	41
	moral doubt;	Am
147.10	Formalism	41
	Formulism	
		42 46 52 → 72
147.17	men.	41
	men!	42 → 72
147.19	died out	41
	died-out	58 → 72
147.20	and 'machine:'	41
	and 'Machine:'	42 → 72
147.21	no Machine;	41
	no machine:	42 Am
	no machine!	46 52 → 72
147.21	it	41
	I say that it	42 → 72
147.22*	not go	41
	not go	42 → 72
147.22	wheels and pinions at all!	
	The	41
	wheel-and-pinion	
	'motives,' self-interests,	
	checks, balances; that	
	there is something far	
	other in it than the clank	
	of spinning-jennies, and	
	parliamentary majorities;	
	and, on the whole, that	
	it is not a machine at	
	all!—The	42 → 72
148.22	one would	41
	one word would	Am

148.28	steamengine	41
	steam-engine	Am
148.29	laying down	41
	laying-down	58 → 72
148.36	half-and-half	41
	half-and half	Am
149.6	Universe, has	41
	Universe has	58 → 72
149.7	fatalest	41
	fatallest	46 52 58
149.15	worshipped	41
	worshiped	58
149.25	Steamengine,	41
	steamengine,	
		42 46 52 → 72
	steam-engine,	Am
149.28	dying!—	41
	dying!	46 52 → 72
149.29	the healthy	41
	a healthy	Am
149.30	process	41
	process,	42 → 72
149.35	clutch up	41
	clutch-up	58 → 72
150.5	speak of	41
	speak-of	58 → 72
150.7	thought, belief	41
	thought, your belief	
		46 → 72
150.10	shew	41
	show	58 → 72
150.11	turned up	41
	turned-up	58 → 72
150.12	going on!	41
	going-on!	58 → 72
150.19	mournfulest,	41
	mournfullest,	46 52 58
150.22	dexterous	41
	dextrous	58 → 72
150.23	gone out;	41
	gone-out;	58 → 72
150.24	come in.	41
	come-in.	58 → 72

150.32	"has	41
	'has	42 → 72
150.32	crawled out	41
	crawled-out	58
150.32	suffering,"	41
	suffering,'	42 → 72
151.14	and the	41
	and that the	70 72
151.24	semblant;	41
	semblant,	Am
151.29	Heroic World!	41
	Heroic World.	Am
	heroic world!	52 → 72
151.38	home!'	41
	home'!	70 72
152.1	'worlds'	41
	'world's'	70
152.6	world's	41
	world's'	70
152.8	gone. ¶Now	41
	gone.— ¶Now	
		46 52 → 72
152.11	Truths	41
	truths	58 → 72
152.13	intimation in	41
	intimation, in	
		46 52 → 72
152.17	Johnson's girt	41
	Johnson's, girt	42 → 72
152.22	make out	41
	make-out	58 → 72
152.29	truly,	41
	truly	46 52 → 72
153.2	reflexions	41
	reflections	46 52 → 72
153.3	struggling	41
	struggling,	42 → 72
153.10	gave way	41
	gave-way	58 → 72
153.12	got not	41
	got no	Am
153.14	more, Original	41
	more Original	Am

153.31	shoots in	41
	shoots-in	58 → 72
153.32	misery:	41
	misery;	Am
153.32	stript off,	41
	stript-off,	58 → 72
153.33	manner,	41
	manner	70 72
153.39	'fourpence halfpenny	41
	'fourpence-halfpenny	
		46 → 72
154.2	seamy-faced,	41
	seamed-faced,	Am
154.3	worn out;	41
	worn-out;	58 → 72
154.6	of window!	41
	of the window!	Am
154.7	beggary: we	41
	beggary; we	Am
154.10	pitching away	41
	pitching-away	58 → 72
154.25	manner,	41
	manner	42 → 72
154.32	glared-in	41
	glared in,	70 72
154.32	forever,	41
	forever	70 → 72
154.37	*worshipped*	41
	worshiped	58
155.3	'artificial?'	41
	'artificial'?	70 72
155.11	finds out	41
	finds-out	58 → 72
155.11	somewhat,—were	41
	somewhat—were	Am
155.18	improvements, changes	41
	improvements, with	
	changes	42 → 72
155.29	worshipper's	41
	worshiper's	58
155.34	sincere,—of	41
	sincere, of	Am

155.35	hard-struggling,	41
	hard struggling,	Am
156.8	*him,*—fearful	41
	him—fearful	Am
156.11	heard of	41
	heard-of	58 → 72
156.14	second-hand:	41
	secondhand:	42 → 72
156.20	pleasure	41
	pleasure,	Am
156.24	them,—as	41
	them—as	Am
156.26	done	41
	done,	70 72
156.27	done	41
	done,	70 72
156.29	godforgetting	41
	god-forgetting	70 72
156.31	coupled,	41
	coupled	Am
156.35	this, call	41
	this, I call	42 → 72
157.2	now	41
	now,	72
157.2	were	41
	were,	72
157.8	style,—the	41
	style—the	Am
157.12	put up with.	41
	put-up-with.	58
	put-up with.	70 72
157.13	styles,	41
	styles	70 72
157.20	finished,	41
	finished	Am
157.31	Frenchman, That	41
	Frenchman, that	70 72
158.1	radish	41
	raddish	70 72
158.5	whole,	41
	whole	Am
158.9	right valiant	41
	right-valiant	70 72
158.10	Trade;	41
	trade;	70 72
158.35	high,	41
	high	70 72
159.6	Philosophes	41
	Philosophers	Am
159.19	"*He*	41
	'*He*	42 72
159.19	world!"	41
	world!'	42 72
159.33	onions;	41
	onions:	Am
159.37*	and contorsions	41
	and contortions	46 → 72
159.38*	The contorsions	41
	The contortions	46 → 72
160.1	looks on	41
	looks-on	58 → 72
160.10	Scepticism,	41
	Scepticism	70 72
160.30	Madame	41
	Madam	Am
161.7	any way	41
	anyway	58 → 72
161.10	wild beast	41
	wild-beast	58 → 72
161.14	such like,	41
	suchlike,	70 72
161.22	Century,	41
	Century	42
161.22	up,	41
	up	Am
161.34	acting-figures,	41
	acting figures,	Am
162.1	Peasant.—His	41
	Peasant. ¶His	70 72
162.5	brave	41
	brave,	70 72
162.13	nursery-ground,' nor	41
	nursery-ground,'—not	
	that, nor	42 → 72
162.16	swallowing down	41
	swallowing-down	72

162.18	newspaper-paragraphs	41	
	newspaper paragraphs	52 → 72	
162.27	recognised	41	
	recognized	52	
162.37	world;—rock,	41	
	world; rock,	Am	
162.38	whirlwind in	41	
	whirlwind of	46 → 72	
163.7	sense,	41	
	sense	58 → 72	
163.9	such like,	41	
	suchlike,	70 72	
163.10	This basis	41	
	The basis	Am	
163.28	gracefulest	41	
	gracefullest	46 52 58	
163.31	insight:	41	
	insight;	58 → 72	
163.35	bed,	41	
	bed	Am	
163.38	with him, That	41	
	with him. That	58 → 72	
164.6	every way,	41	
	everyway,	58 → 72	
164.8	better gifted	41	
	better-gifted	42 → 72	
164.12	thicknecked	41	
	thick-necked	72	
164.22	men were not	41	
	men are not	42 → 72	
164.36	*un*thinking	41	
	*un*thinkg	Am	
164.38	it, as	41	
	it as	58 → 72	
165.3	Why	41	
	"Why	46 → 72	
165.3	this?	41	
	this?"	46 → 72	
165.3	some.	41	
	some:	42 → 72	
165.3	Strength	41	
	"Strength	46 → 72	

165.4	old.	41	
	old."	46 → 72	
165.5	say I!	41	
	answer I!	42 → 72	
165.9	here	41	
	here,	70 72	
165.10	Poetry, in	41	
	Poetry, so in	42 → 72	
165.11	fantasticalities;	41	
	fantasticalities:	58	
165.22	for worshipper.	41	
	for worshiper.	58	
165.22	had worshippers	41	
	had worshipers	58	
165.28	his worshippers	41	
	his worshipers	58	
165.30	well-being	41	
	wellbeing	Am 58 → 72	
165.36	summer-sunshine,	41	
	summer sunshine,	70 72	
165.38	it not, by	41	
	it is not alterable by	46 52 → 72	
	it is not alterable, by	Am	
166.3	priest	41	
	priest,	52 → 72	
166.9	obeyed.— —	41	
	obeyed.——	Am	
	obeyed.—	52 → 72	
166.10*	history his	41	
	history,—his	42 46 52 → 72	
	history—his	Am	
166.19	jail.	41	
	Jail.	52 58	
166.30	shew	41	
	show	58 → 72	
166.32	*burst*	41	
	burst,	46 → 72	
166.33	whom,	41	
	whom	52 58	
166.34	body:'	41	
	body;'	58 → 72	

| 167.8 | amusement;—and | 41 |
| | amusement:—and | Am |

Lecture VI. The Hero as King.

169.5	*summary*	41
	summary	46 → 72
169.8	us, furnish	41
	us, to furnish	46 → 72
169.8	teaching, tell	41
	teaching, to tell	46 → 72
169.11	Able-man.	41
	Ableman.	58
169.17	order 'to	41
	'order to	52 → 72
169.19	*Able-man,*	41
	Ableman,	58
	Ableman	70 72
170.12	regulated;	41
	regulated:	Am
170.29	rush down	41
	rush-down	58 → 72
171.2	stretch out	41
	stretch-out	58 → 72
171.3*	*it*	41
	it	42 → 72
171.5	burst forth	41
	burst-forth	58 → 72
171.12	behind,—I	41
	behind—I	70 72
171.21	Divine-right men	41
	Divine right men	Am
171.25	steamengine.	41
	steam-engine.	Am
171.27	look out	41
	look-out	58 → 72
171.29	Wo	41
	Woe	42 → 72
171.30	wo	41
	woe	42 → 72
171.37	that in short	41
	that, in short,	46 52 → 72

172.11	book-shelves.	41
	bookshelves.	42 → 72
172.33*	are a Chimera,	41
	are—a Chimera,	42 → 72
172.35	Palais Royal,	41
	Palais-Royal,	46 → 72
172.36	burst up	41
	burst-up	58 → 72
173.17	July, 1830,	41
	July 1830	58 → 72
173.18	Nation	41
	nation	Am
173.23	made up	41
	made-up	58 → 72
173.23	madness-quietus,	41
	'madness' quietus,	46 → 72
173.29	shocks	41
	shocks,	42 → 72
173.34	Fact, and the	41
	Fact, and that the	46 → 72
174.3	*preter*natural,	41
	*preter*natural;	46 52 → 72
174.4	take fire	41
	take-fire	58 → 72
174.25	pole-star	41
	polestar	70 72
174.28	Men; not	41
	men; not	Am
174.29	hope,	41
	hope	58 → 72
174.32	give up	41
	give-up	58 → 72
174.38	it!	41
	it.	Am
175.1	in	41
	into	Am
175.3	gold!"—I	41
	gold!" I	42 → 72

175.12	Hero-worship; a	41
	Hero-worship[ ] a	52
	Hero-worship,—a	
		58 → 72
175.24	whose whole soul	41
	whose soul	Am
176.2	come out	41
	come-out	58 → 72
176.8	step forth	41
	step-forth	58 → 72
176.12	Two. ¶We	41
	Two. [extra leading	
	between paragraphs] ¶We	
		42 → 72
176.18	makes up	41
	makes-up	58 → 72
176.19	World,	41
	world,	Am
176.27	loveable	41
	lovable	46 52 → 72
176.37	College-rules	41
	College rules	Am
177.24	utterance at all	41
	utterance all	Am
177.30	is not only	41
	is only	Am
177.30	accepted; it	41
	accepted,—it	58 → 72
177.32	worshipping	41
	worshiping	58
177.32	*shows;*	41
	shews;	42 46 52
	shews:	Am
177.36	*Pedant,*	41
	Pedant	Am
177.37	'College-rules,'	41
	'College rules,'	Am
178.5	men:	41
	men;	Am
178.10	him;	41
	him:	46 52
178.11	man—! We	41
	man—!—We	70 72

178.12	three hundred thousand	
		41
	three-hundred-thousand	
		58 → 72
178.18	fought out	41
	fought-out	58 → 72
178.26	ushered in,	41
	ushered-in,	58 → 72
178.38	nay	41
	nay,	Am
178.39	canonized.	41
	canonised.	46 52 → 72
179.1	nay	41
	nay,	Am
179.1	Hutcheson,	41
	Hutchinson,	46 → 72
179.4	anybody	41
	any body	Am
179.4	wicked.	41
	wicked now.	42 → 72
179.10	forth:	41
	forth;	Am
179.10	Cause!	41
	Cause.	52 → 72
179.11*	*Tartuffe;*	41
	Tartufe;	46 → 72
179.20	bodyguards	41
	bodyguards,	Am
179.34	love,	41
	love	46 52 → 72
179.37	men	41
	men,	70 72
179.38*	euphuisms,	41
	euphemisms,	70 72
179.39	Ship-monies,	41
	Ship-moneys,	
		46 52 → 72
179.39	unblameable,	41
	unblamable,	46 52 → 72
180.2	get up	41
	get-up	58 → 72
180.3	break forth	41
	break-forth	58 → 72

180.4	breaks down	41
	breaks-down	58 → 72
180.7	brick clay;	41
	brick-clay;	70 72
180.10	all,	41
	all	52 → 72
180.12*	no euphuistic	41
	no euphemistic	70 72
180.14*	in euphuistic	41
	in euphemistic	70 72
180.24	Scepticism	41
	Scepticism,	
		42 46 52 → 72
180.28	demanding,	41
	demanding	Am
180.32	pay out	41
	pay-out	58 → 72
180.33	shewn?	41
	shown?	58 → 72
181.3	him,	41
	him	Am
181.9	worshipping	41
	worshiping	58
181.11	help, No!	41
	help, no!	42 → 72
181.12	The cash is	41
	The purse is	42 → 72
181.15	you, and on	41
	you, and, on	70 72
181.15	whole	41
	whole,	70 72
181.17	revolting,	41
	revolting	Am
181.26	soul,	41
	soul	58
181.34	'Madness,' 'Hypocrisy,'	41
	'madness,' 'hypocrisy,'	
		58 → 72
181.37	Nay,	41
	Nay	58 → 72
182.2	shadows:	41
	shadows;	Am 58 → 72

182.22	earnest, hearty, sincere	41
	earnest, affectionate,	
	sincere	46 → 72
182.24	You remember that story	
	of his having a vision	41
	Of those stories of	
	'Spectres;'	46 → 72
182.24	Evil Spirit,	41
	white Spectre in broad	
	daylight,	46 → 72
182.25	would be Sovereign	41
	should be King	46 → 72
182.25	England, and so forth. In	
	broad	41
	England. In broad	42
182.25	England, and so forth. In broad daylight, some huge white Spectre, which he took to be the Devil, with preternatural monitions of some sort, shews itself to him: the Royalists made immense babble about it; but apart from their speculations, we can suppose this story of the Spectre to be true. Then there are afterwards those hypochondriacal visions: the Doctor sent for; Oliver imagining that 'the steeple of Huntingdon was about to tumble on him.' 41 England, we are not bound to believe much;—probably no more than of the other black Spectre, or Devil in person, to whom the Officer *saw* him sell himself before Worcester Fight! But the mournful, over-sensitive, hypochondriac humour of Oliver, in his young	

years, is otherwise indisputably known. The Huntingdon Physician told Sir Philip Warwick himself, He had often been sent for at midnight; Mr. Cromwell was full of hypochondria, thought himself near dying, and "had fancies about the Town-cross." The things are significant. 46 → 72

182.31   sent for   46
          sent-for   58

182.33   Town-cross." The 46
          Town-cross." These
                        Am → 72

(182.25) the Royalists made immense babble about it; but   41
          it is a universal story of those times; and,   42

(182.25) their speculations,   41
          all Royalist and other speculations on it,   42

(182.25) can   41
          can well   42

(182.25) those   41
          those other   42

(182.25) imagining that 'the steeple of Huntingdon was about to tumble on him.' 41
          'has fancies about the town-cross of Huntingdon.' These things are significant. 42

182.34   bulk of his; in other words, a soul of such *intensity*, such sensibility, with all its strength! 41
          strength of his, is not the symptom of falsehood; it is the symptom and promise of quite other than falsehood! 42 → 72

182.37   law; falls,   41
          Law; falls, or is said to have fallen,   46 → 72

182.38   but speedily   41
          but if so, speedily
                        46 → 72

183.2   He   41
          'He   46 → 72

183.2   pays back   41
          pays-back   58 → 72

183.3   gambling;—he   41
          gambling,' says the story;—he   46 → 72

183.7   shows   41
          shews   42 → Am

183.9   at Ely as   41
          at St. Ives and Ely, as
                        42 → 72

183.10   true devout   41
          true and devout 46 → 72

183.14   nay,   41
          nay   70 72

183.15   this,   41
          this   70 72

183.18   *thither*   41
          thither,   42 → 72

183.20   eye.'—It   41
          eye.' ¶It   42 → 72

183.20   comes out   41
          comes-out   58 → 72

183.25   influence?'   41
          influence'?   70 72

183.28   Eternity;—it   41
          Eternity; it   58 → 72

183.29   'ambitious!'   41
          'ambitious'!   70 72

183.33   men. His   41
          men His   58

184.1   deephearted   41
          deep-hearted   42 → 72

184.2   worshipping   41
          worshiping   58

184.9	him: it is		41
	him; it is		Am
184.10	or, far		41
	or far		Am
184.16	shews		41
	shows		58 → 72
184.20	nay,		41
	nay	46 52 → 72	
184.24	play off		41
	play-off		58 → 72
184.35	shows,		41
	shews,		42 → 52
184.36	expediencies:		41
	expediences:		70 72
185.12	King:' but		41
	King;' but		58 → 72
185.14	calling forth		41
	calling-forth		58 → 72
186.7	quacks?'		41
	quacks'?		70 72
186.9	shall we so		41
	shall we even so	46 → 72	
186.10	'detect?'		41
	'detect'?		70 72
186.10	The vulpine		41
	For the vulpine	46 → 72	
186.24	hundred and fifty		41
	hundred-and-fifty		58 → 72
186.27	Quacks and Quackeries!		41
	quacks and quackeries!		42 → 72
186.31	One		41
	In brief, one	42 → 72	
186.33	go on		41
	go-on		58
187.1*	Euphuisms;		41
	Euphuisms, 42 46 52 58		
	Euphuism,		Am
	Euphemisms,		70 72
187.9	affections;		41
	affections:		58 → 72

187.16	*seeing*		41
	seeing,		70 72
187.23	withal,		41
	withal		Am
187.26	logicizing;		41
	logicising;	46 52 → 72	
187.28	fairspoken		41
	fair-/spoken		70
	fair-spoken		72
187.29	*Dough*tiness),		41
	Dough-tiness),		72
188.10	them,—how		41
	them, how		Am
188.20	'Hypocrisy?'		41
	'Hypocrisy'?		70 72
188.34	days,		41
	days		58 → 72
189.8	turns out		41
	turns-out		58 → 72
189.14	taking up		41
	taking-up		58 → 72
189.16	shew		41
	show		58 → 72
189.26	history,		41
	history		70 72
190.1	incredible:		41
	incredible;		Am
190.5	practice.		41
	practice!		52 → 72
190.6	practise		41
	practice		Am
190.12	through		41
	though		52
190.18	But, in fact,		41
	But in fact		58 → 72
190.20	such like.		41
	such-/like.		70
	suchlike.		72
190.25	mapped out;		41
	mapped-out:		58 → 72
190.27	Play-actor		41
	Play-actor,		Am

190.30	does	41
	does does	72
190.36	fall away	41
	fall-away	58 → 72
191.3	duly,	41
	duly	70 72
191.11	thrown down	41
	thrown-down	58 → 72
191.23	keep out	41
	keep-out	58 → 72
191.34	grey;	41
	gray;	58 → 72
192.6	man,	41
	man	58 → 72
192.14	businesses.	41
	business.	Am
192.15	*much life*	41
	much of life	46 → 72
192.17	shows	41
	shews	42 → 52
192.18	staid	41
	stayed	46 52 → 72
192.19	wrapt up	41
	wrapt-up	58 → 72
192.20	paradings	41
	paradings,	46 → 72
192.20	hat do	41
	hat, do	46 → 72
192.29	Wo	41
	Woe	42 → 72
192.30	*shew,*	41
	show,	58 → 72
193.2	sect?"—"Truly,"	41
	sect?" "Truly,"	58 → 72
193.3	I happily	41
	happily I	46 → 72
193.6	'honour?'	41
	'honour'?	70 72
193.8	statue? than say, There it is!"——	41
	statue? than say, There it is!"— —	42
	statue?"— —	46 → 72

193.10	blameable,	41
	blamable,	46 52 → 72
193.15	develope	41
	develop	58 → 72
193.16	speak out,	41
	speak-out,	58 → 72
193.17	act out,	41
	act-out,	58 → 72
193.23	therefore,	41
	therefore:	42 → 72
193.30	there?'	41
	there'?	70 72
193.30	Hopefuler	41
	Hopefuller	52 58
193.38*	do a priceless	41
	do priceless	46 52 → 72
194.1	Earth,	41
	Earth;	42 → 72
194.5	flamed up	41
	flamed-up	58 → 72
194.13	cropt off,	41
	cropt-off,	58 → 72
194.20	for itself:	41
	for itself;	Am
194.22	thither. He	41
	thither. ¶He	70 72
195.2	purpose:	41
	purpose;	42 → 72
195.5	shews	41
	shows	58 → 72
195.16	fifteen hundred	41
	fifteen-hundred	58 → 72
195.18	ten;	41
	ten:	52
195.19	him,—England	41.
	him,—why, then, England	42 → 72
195.21	joint	41
	united	42 → 72
195.22	problem	41
	problem,	46 52 → 72
195.33	hero-hearts	41
	hero hearts	70 72

195.34	flings forth	41
	flings-forth	58 → 72
195.37	befel	41
	befell	46 52 70 72
196.12	God, that He	41
	God, that he	Am
196.13	him, He	41
	him and this Cause, He	
		46 → 72
196.14	breathed out	41
	breathed-out	58 → 72
196.20	grey;	41
	gray;	58 → 72
196.29	shewn,	41
	shown,	58 → 72
196.29	war,	41
	War,	46 → 72
196.32	it,	41
	it	58
196.35	such like:	41
	suchlike:	70
	suchlike;	72
196.37	one:	41
	one;	Am
197.2	it:	41
	it;	46 52 → 72
197.6*	hand,	41
	hands,	46 52 → 72
197.21	England, Chief	41
	England; Chief	42 → 72
197.21	England: but	41
	England; but	Am
197.27	given up	41
	given-up	58 → 72
197.37	"for	41
	"For	70 72
198.2	itself, in	41
	itself in	52 58
198.10*	call	41
	calls	70 72
198.19	do;	41
	do:	46

198.27	According	41
	¶According	70 72
198.32	keep out	41
	keep-out	58 → 72
199.13	Realities	41
	realities	52 → 72
199.24	shape out	41
	shape-out	58 → 72
199.32	broke down,	41
	broke-down,	58 → 72

199.33 They appointed Cromwell Protector, and went their ways. The second Parliament,   41 They dissolved themselves, as incompetent; delivered up their power again into the hands of the Lord General Cromwell, to do with it what he liked and could. What *will* he do with it! The Lord General Cromwell, 'Commander-in-chief of all the Forces raised and to be raised;' he hereby sees himself, at this unexampled juncture, as it were the one available Authority left in England, nothing between England and utter Anarchy but him alone. Such is the undeniable Fact of his position and England's, there and then. What will he do with it! After deliberation, he decides that he will *accept* it; will formally, with public solemnity, say and vow before God and men, "Yes, the Fact is so, and I will do the best I can with it!" Protectorship,

Instrument of Government,—these are the external forms of the thing; worked out and sanctioned as they could in the circumstances be, by the Judges, by the leading Official people, 'Council of Officers and Persons of interest in the Nation:' and as for the thing itself, undeniably enough, at the pass matters had now come to, there *was* no alternative but Anarchy or that. Puritan England might accept it or not; but Puritan England was, in real truth, saved from suicide thereby!—I believe the Puritan People did, in an inarticulate, grumbling, yet on the whole grateful and real way, accept this anomalous act of Oliver's; at least, he and they together made it good, and always better to the last. But in their Parliamentary *articulate* way, they had their difficulties, and never knew fully what to say to it!— ¶Oliver's second Parliament, properly his *first* regular Parliament,   46 → 72

199.33	delivered up			46
	delivered-up		58 → 72	
199.35	it!			46
	it?		58 → 72	
200.3	it!			46
	it?		58 → 72	
200.7	worked out			46
	worked-out			58

200.7	in the				46
	in these				Am
200.8	Judges,				46
	judges,				Am
200.19	rule these Notables had fixed upon,				41
	rule laid down in the Instrument of Government,		46 → 72		
200.19	laid down				46
	laid-down		58 → 72		
200.23	one. Most				41
	one. So likewise to his third Parliament, in similar rebuke for their pedantries and obstinacies. Most			46 → 72	
200.25	chaotic, as all his				41
	chaotic, all these			46 → 72	
200.33	might!				41
	might.			42 → 72	
200.35	all, played				41
	all, and played			46 → 72	
200.35	puppetshow				41
	puppetshew			42 → 52	
201.9*	into Chaos				41
	in Chaos				72
201.13	Christ's Law				41
	Christ's Law,		58 → 72		
201.18	things these				41
	things the			46 → 72	
201.19*	Cromwell's				41
	Cromwell		46 52 → 72		
201.20*	Jesuistic				41
	Jesuitic		46 52 → 72		
201.33	theories,				41
	theories		58 → 72		
201.35	lay down				41
	lay-down				58
201.38	laying down				41
	laying-down		58 → 72		

202.2	Shew	41	
	Show	58 → 72	
202.19	Choiseul;	41	
	Choiseul,	Am	
202.21	wanted	41	
	waited	42 → 72	
202.23	no-whither	41	
	nowhither	Am	
202.27	Hutcheson,	41	
	Hutchinson,	46 → 72	
202.28	Hutcheson	41	
	Hutchinson	46 → 52	
	Hutchinson,	58 → 72	
202.33	fellow soldiers,	41	
	fellow-soldiers,	70 72	
202.33	Hutcheson,	41	
	Hutchinson,	46 → 72	
202.34	Presbyterian	41	
	Republican	46 → 72	
202.38	go off,	41	
	go-off,	58 → 72	
203.1	twice	41	
	at least once	46 → 72	
203.2	day	41	
	day,	42 → 72	
203.6	History'—place	41	
	History,'—place	70 72	
203.6	forsooth—has	41	
	forsooth!—has	70 72	
203.9	man!	41	
	man?	Am	
203.11	step over	41	
	step-over	58 → 72	
203.17	hushed up	41	
	hushed-up	58 → 72	
203.18	broke out	41	
	broke-out	58 → 72	
203.19	hush up,	41	
	hush-up,	58 → 72	
203.23	then	41	
	then,	46 → 72	
203.30	build up	41	
	build-up	58 → 72	
203.32	shew	41	
	show	58 → 72	
204.2	Awful,	41	
	Awful	58 → 72	
204.2	Unnameable	41	
	Unnamable	46 52 → 72	
204.4	burst out	41	
	burst-out	58	
204.9	every-way	41	
	everyway	58 → 72	
204.13	Fanatic-Hypocrite,	41	
	Fanatic Hypocrite,	Am	
204.14	Napoleon,	41	
	Napoleon	52 → 72	
204.16	blameable	41	
	blamable	46 52 → 72	
204.16	shews	41	
	shows	58 → 72	
204.20	keep up	41	
	keep-up	58 → 72	
204.21	these are	41	
	there are	46 → 72	
204.21	has any liberty	41	
	has liberty	42 → 72	
204.22	been	41	
	been,	42 → 72	
204.22	long-run	41	
	long-run,	42 → 72	
204.25	found out;	41	
	found-out;	58 → 72	
204.32	manœuvrings	41	
	manœuverings	70 72	
204.33	blameable,	41	
	blamable,	46 52 → 72	
204.35	Nature	41	
	nature	Am	
205.3	runs off	41	
	runs-off	58 → 72	
205.5	Practice:	41	
	practice:	Am	
205.9	Napoleon,	41	
	Napoleon	Am	

205.13	functionary:	41
	functionary;	42 → 72
205.16	*resultat*	41
	result	46 → 72
205.18	piece	41
	picture	Am
205.24	down:	41
	down;	46 52 → 72
205.28	Revolution or	41
	Revolution, or	42 → 72
205.29	Revolution could	41
	Revolution, could	
		42 → 72
206.3	Lœben,	41
	Leoben,	42 → 72
206.6	feels,	41
	feels	Am
206.7	bridle in	41
	bridle-in	42 → 72
206.24	apostatised	41
	apostatized	Am
206.29	'given up	41
	'given-up	58 → 72
206.31	fearfulest	41
	fearfullest	46 52 58
206.37	re-establishment	41
	reëstablishment	70
	re-/establishment	72
207.3	Notre-Dame there,	41
	Notre-Dame,	46 → 72
207.5	that!"	41
	that"!	70 72
207.12	cloud:	41
	cloud;	58 → 72

207.15	into temptation!'	41
	into temptation'!	70 72
207.32	make out	41
	make-out	58 → 72
208.4	rude-draught;	41
	a rude-draught never	
	completed;	46 → 72
208.5	not?	41
	other?	46 → 72
208.8	flung out	41
	flung-out	58 → 72
208.11	'another	41
	"another	42 → 72
208.11	France.'	41
	France."	42 → 72
208.17	half dissolved	41
	half-dissolved	58 → 72
208.18	turbid	41
	turpid	Am
208.18	Fanfaronade.	41
	fanfaronade.	70 72
208.19	trodden down	41
	trodden-down	58 → 72
208.27	Man! [double extra	
	leading between	
	paragraphs] ¶*Our*	41
	Man! [extra leading	
	between paragraphs]	
	¶*Our* 42 → 52 70 72	
	Man! ¶*Our*	58
208.36	vitalest	41
	vitallest	46 52 58
208.38	break ground	41
	break-ground	58 → 72
209.3	thrown out	41
	thrown-out	58 → 72

INDEX

INDEX

Printed in the United Kingdom
by Lightning Source UK Ltd.
99796UKS00001B/7